A Lifetime of Communication

Transformations Through Relational Dialogues

LEA's SERIES ON PERSONAL RELATIONSHIPS
Steve Duck, Series Editor

A Lifetime of Communication

Transformations Through Relational Dialogues

Julie Yingling
Humboldt State University

LAWRENCE ERLBAUM ASSOCIATES, PUBLISHERS

2004   Mahwah, New Jersey   London

Lawrence Erlbaum Associates, Inc., Publishers
10 Industrial Avenue
Mahwah, New Jersey 07430

Cover art by Rick Davids
Cover design by Sean Trane Sciarrone

Library of Congress Cataloging-in-Publication Data

Yingling, Julie.
    A lifetime of communication : transformation through relational
    dialogues / Julie Yingling.
        p. cm.
        Includes bibliographical references and index.
    ISBN 0-8058-4092-3 (hard : alk. Paper)
    ISBN 0-8058-4093-1 (pbk. : alk. Paper)
        1. Interpersonal communication—Textbooks. 2. Developmental
    psychology—Textbooks. I. Title.   II. Series.

BF637.C45Y56 2004
153.6—dc22
                                                        2003049452
                                                            CIP

Books published by Lawrence Erlbaum Associates are printed on acid-
free paper, and their bindings are chosen for strength and durability.

Printed in the United States of America
10 9 8 7 6 5 4 3 2 1

Contents

Series Foreword

Since its inception, the Personal Relationships series from Lawrence Erlbaum Associates has sought to review the progress in the academic work on relationships with respect to a broad array of issues, and to do so in an accessible manner that also illustrates its *practical* value. The LEA series already includes books intended to pass on the accumulated scholarship to both the next generation of students and those who deal with relationship issues in the broader world beyond the academy. The series thus not only comprises monographs and other academic resources exemplifying the multidisciplinary nature of this area, but also includes books suitable for use in the growing numbers of courses on relationships and in the growing number of professions that deal with relationship issues.

The series has the goal of providing a comprehensive and current survey of theory and research in personal relationships through the careful analysis of the problems encountered and solved in research, yet it also considers the systematic application of that work in a practical context. These resources not only are intended to be comprehensive assessments of progress on particular "hot" and relevant topics, but also have already shown that they are significant influences on the future directions and development of the study of personal relationships and application of its insights. Although each volume is well centered, all series authors attempt to place the respective topics in the broader context of other research on relationships and within a range of wider disciplinary traditions. The series already offers incisive and forward-looking reviews, and also demonstrates the broader theoretical implications of relationships for the range of disciplines from which the research originates. Collectively, the volumes include original studies, reviews of relevant theory and research, and new theories oriented toward the understanding of personal relationships both in themselves and within the context of broader theories of family process, social psychology, and communication.

Reflecting the diverse composition of personal relationship study, readers in numerous disciplines—social psychology, communication, sociology, family studies, developmental psychology, clinical psychology, personality, counseling, women's studies, gerontology, and others—will find valuable and insightful perspectives in the series.

Apart from the academic scholars who research the dynamics and processes of relationships, there are many other people whose work takes them up against the operation of relationships in the real world. For such people as nurses, police officers, teachers, therapists, lawyers, drug and alcohol counselors, marital counselors, members of the clergy, and caregivers to the elderly, a number of issues routinely arise concerning the ways in which relationships affect those whom these people serve and guide. Examples are the role of loneliness in illness and the ways to circumvent it, the complex impact of family and peer relationships on a drug-dependent person's attempts to give up the drug, the role of playground unpopularity on a child's learning, the issues involved in dealing with the relational side of chronic illness, the management of conflict in marriage, the establishment of a good rapport between physicians and seriously ill patients, the support of the bereaved, the correction of violent styles of behavior in dating or marriage—even the relationships formed between jurors in extended trials, because these may influence the jury's decisions. Each of these examples is a problem that may confront some of the aforementioned professionals as part of their daily concerns, and each demonstrates the far-reaching influences of relationship processes on much else in life that is presently theorized independently of relationship considerations.

The present volume is an extended discussion of the ways in which communication develops across the life cycle, the means in which relationships and social cognition affect that development, and the manner in which these other variables intersect with the growth of self. Clearly, then, this book is about topics of fundamental significance in the understanding of human life. It has relevance to those concerned with ontological development, those interested in language acquisition and elaboration, those concerned with the parent–child (or teenager–parent) relationship, those interested in the ways that self depends on sociality, and all that the army of researchers whose work on relationships ultimately must attend to the building blocks that are laid down in childhood for later social activity. In addition, the book contains a theoretical position on these matters that is in itself of considerable importance. This is especially relevant in view of the fact that there has been almost no systematic attempt to understand the development of communication, let alone an approach that so neatly intertwines the many different elements woven together here.

"Communication" is often taken for granted in other disciplines, for whom the conundrums of "messages," "meaning," "interpretation," "audience reception," and "identity projection" are treated unproblematically. In demonstrating the importance of a more sophisticated understanding of communication for the mixture of disciplines that seek to understand the human being, in this volume Julie Yingling enlarges not only communication theory per se, but also the understanding of the conglomeration of other elements of human development. In short, a better understanding of the development of communication is offered here as that emulsifier in the ontological soup that helps to blend and bind together other elements that are wanting coherence. In demonstrating the value of this integrative approach, this text presents many stunning insights and connections between otherwise disparate literatures. As such, it promises to be a major milestone in the road toward interdisciplinary connectivity.

All this and a practical twist also! In the course of this volume, there are many startling and illuminating insights into the ways in which the maturation of children and teenagers can be handled, coaxed, steered, and improved. From those who seek to be better parents right through to those who must deal with the later results of unsuccessful early development, this book provides both wisdom and suggestions. Therefore, as the author indicates in the Preface, it is a book with something for both the academic expert and the relatively unsophisticated, the undergraduate and the advanced graduate, the theorist and the practitioner. As such, this book exemplifies the goals of this series perfectly.

—Steve Duck
Series Editor
University of Iowa

Preface

A Lifetime of Communication has been my "baby" through many years spent nourishing the hope that the field of communication might fulfill its promise to close the gaps across the human sciences. In preparation, I have spoken with and observed children, studied many aspects of development, and consulted colleagues about the need for a body of communication literature that explains the origins of our phenomena. And here it is—the child I send forth with high hopes and modest expectations.

My intention was to provide a starting point for developmental study of communication. We have had contributions in the past: introductory texts gone from print, partial treatments of communication at various age levels, models of relationship development. However, there has been no overview of the interdisciplinary developmental literature as it addresses communication. In particular, there has been no coherent theoretical perspective that can frame such a body of literature. My hope is that this text can serve advanced undergraduates, graduate students, and colleagues.

For undergraduates: The text provides a detailed explanation of how communication develops. You might use this to inform your own developmental path, or to prepare for a career involving communication with children, teens, or adults. Yes, it is a scholarly text, and it does cite a broad array of literature. It may be a challenge for you, but I mean that in a good way! Whenever possible, I include examples and illustrations of the findings I report, and have included a glossary of specialized terms. Furthermore, I integrate these reports under the umbrella of a dialectical/dialogical perspective, as set forth in the first chapter, so that you may understand that the various strands of developmental research have common roots in fundamentally human symbolic behavior. My own undergraduate students did complain at the outset about the unfamiliar scholarly style, but have since demonstrated amply that they do understand the perspective, they do use the examples, and they do have a feel for the developmental process. Many thanks to them for their suggestions, tolerance, and enthusiasm!

For graduate students: Whether your primary focus is relational communication, social cognition, identity formation, or human development, an understanding of communication development will inform your thinking. I believe you will find this book readable, accessible, and applicable to human social behavior in general. Specifically, you will find an explanation of the interfaces among interaction, self, and social cognition. Even if you have no developmental background, the glossary and examples will assist your integration of this literature to your primary area. Ultimately, there may be some of you who are grounding yourself in the developmental literature because you have made this your priority. I salute you! This text will make it much easier for you to begin your journey into the complex set of factors involved in human communication development.

For my colleagues: Many of you will have been trained in other social sciences and may have a background in developmental processes. Others of you have been trained in communication, in which case you have been hard-pressed to find developmental research or a coherent developmental theory. To the first, as social scientists, you may be familiar with the foundational developmental theories, and you may find some literature from your area. What may be new is a theoretical explanation grounded in the basic assumption that the way we communicate influences all other human behavior, and also the addition of communication literature to the interdisciplinary mix. To the second, as communication scholars, you may have discovered that to study relational communication, or family communication, or health communication, you need some understanding of developmental processes. In this text you will find some explanations and some informed guesses about the origins of communication variables. I am hopeful that some of you will contribute more tangible evidence for developmental models of communication.

In the final chapter, I summarize the theory and discuss implications of this perspective of development, both for the future of communication study and for personal growth. My dearest wishes are that my "child" will influence both the study of communication development and readers' views of their own developmental pasts and futures. I ask that you bring critical compassion to your interaction with the text. Do not hesitate to send comments and suggestions. This, as everything else, is a work in progress and I anticipate many transformations.

ACKNOWLEDGMENTS

The list of people who have contributed to my development as a scholar, colleague, and communicator is unending, and many will have to be satisfied with the knowledge that whatever I bring to the feast was flavored by their ingredients. Thanks are due to many; I will mention a few.

My first mentor was Frank Dance, who opened my eyes to the need for explaining communication development. The second was Steve Duck, who let me believe I had something to say on the subject. In my visiting year at the University of Iowa, Steve recognized the germ of a perspective and nurtured it until I could see it too. Thanks also for the dialogues with fellow scholars in Steve's seminar. Linda Bathgate, my LEA editor, was a calm and tolerant presence throughout the process, reassuring me in more than one jittery moment. Rebecca Walker, my research assistant, spent hours doing clean-up searches and, more recently, read and commented on drafts of half of the chapters for nothing more than a unit of credit. Tia Newby, one of our top graduates, read and commented on the remaining drafts while using them as course readings.

Many people read portions of the chapters, but a few made outstanding contributions. Aimée Langlois, professor of child development and speech pathology at Humboldt State University, provided detailed feedback for chapter 2. Larry Erbert, University of Texas–El Paso, was one of my seminar fellows at Iowa and provided enlightening suggestions on chapter 1. Jon Nussbaum, of Pennsylvania State University, suggested additional chapters for the adult years along with ideas for coverage. Bob Powell, of California State University at Fresno, encouraged me to use my own voice. Several anonymous reviewers of the original proposal sent me to literature that proved essential in refining my assumptions.

Finally, to Howard and Eileen, thanks for setting me safely on the developmental path. To Pat, Ray, Terry, and Mike, much appreciation for the irreplaceable highs and lows of sibling interactions. To Kurt and Dorothy, for the shared joys, sorrows, and changes of enduring friendship. To Rick, for knowing who I had become and honoring both the identity and the work. And to the friends and lovers, colleagues and students too numerous to mention, who brought me to this transformational task.

Chapter 1

Developmental Processes:
A Brief Theoretical History

"OH, GROW UP!" Such is the common cry of those frustrated with partners' immaturities. Beyond the immediate complaint lies an increasingly acceptable assumption that growth is something we can decide to do. However, this wasn't always the case The awareness we claim for our own capabilities and responsibilities has been shifting for some time. Although that shift manifests in different ways dependent on culture, mobility, educational background, and perhaps even by temperament, it manifests nonetheless. That our bookstores devote entire sections to "self-help" tomes is symptomatic of such increased self-awareness and longing for growth and development or, in other circles, for fulfillment or self-actualization.

I choose to focus on the communicative and developmental processes involved in this phenomenon of becoming a human self. Having developed the scientific capacities of the mind, many of us find that, as spectacular as those capacities are, they are not sufficient. The search is on for the path to full integration of all that makes up our human nature. Broadly considered, human development encompasses processes of physical maturation as well as those processes of individuation that may be more self- and Other-directed. *Other,* in its capitalized form, is not just any other, but the abstracted concept of a general other in relationship with this self. Such an Other is ultimately generalized from all the significant relational others with whom we interact. What is missing from our recent assumption that the individual, in Western cultural parlance, is self-made, is the role that relational interaction plays in development. In fact, it is misleading to talk about "individual development" as though human growth occurred in a vacuum. We know that it does not, from documented cases of isolation and neglect, such as that of Genie, a 12-year-old who was unable to complete social and linguistic development after early neglect.[1] The fully functioning human is physically adept, intellectually resourceful, emotionally expressive, communicatively competent. Although these dimensions unfold together, it is the symbolically communicative capacity that seems particularly suited to optimal integration of peculiarly human capacities.

The critical point to be made is this: *The nature of human communicative development is dialogical and relational.* Our distinctively human mode of communication—spoken, symbolic, and interactive—leads us to perceive contrast, dichotomy, and binary oppositions. The primary binary opposition fostered by our human form of communication is most likely represented as self-other and discovered in the first interactive relationship between child and caregiver. The infant, Peggy, enjoys a sense of union with her caregiver until she recognizes that Ellen, her mother, is a separate being with separate needs, thus casting her from that paradisiacal state of unity. From this original distinction, all the complexities of individuation unfold in the context of a series of relational interactions that demonstrate who one is in the human milieu. However, such a progression is neither smooth nor easy. All binary oppositions are related in their contrast; to know light necessitates a sense of dark.

The gift of contrast in dichotomous perception may also be a curse. Although dialectical reductionist thought (which manifests in such language pairs as "either-or," and "cause-effect") has contributed rigorous method to our search for ways of understanding, it equally has limited our range of creativity and ability to handle the complexities of human relationships. Thus, the pleasure of the intellect begins with the dialectic, but the pain of an individuated self with tenuous links to others ensues. Development beyond dialectic to dialogic perception is a move to relational thinking. This process of development, requiring increasingly deliberate levels of awareness, is the process to be explicated in this book. The underlying premise is that our particular form of communication allows us the capacity to continue developing throughout the life span. Thus, "Oh, grow up!" is a challenge to be more human, more individuated, and at the same time, more humanly related than before. Taken in that light, far from being an insult, it is the best thing you could wish for another.

In this chapter, we take on two problems that we rarely think about until we try to understand human social and cognitive development: Where does a "mind" come from, and how is "mind" related to "body"? In the following paragraphs, we briefly explore some of the key approaches to these questions that span history and culture. Answers range from the claim that there is no such thing as "mind"—that thought is simply a result of brain structure and chemistry—to the claim that human thought and self-awareness emerge from the ability to use spoken symbols interactively—that is, that mind, self, and thought would not exist without social intercourse, and the brain is simply a physiological substrate that matures and expands through the use of symbols, much as muscles develop and strengthen through activity.

Not only is there a vast difference between those two positions, and a lot of room for creative oppositions and variations between them, but the ideas are difficult to ingest all at once. Therefore, I won't expect you to master it now, and I don't want you to expect it either. I sketch the various positions here, and go into them in greater detail later. Some readers, depending on their background, will "get it" right away, but many more will not. You may wish to reread parts of this chapter, particularly after reading subsequent chapters. That's OK. As we shall learn, such initial puzzlement, subsequent reflection, and ultimate integration of new experience is precisely what this book is about. It took over 20 years of that kind of processing for me to write this book. Your own processing of complex new ideas will reflect the very developmental processes we are trying to understand. Earmark difficult ideas, and trust your own ability to internalize them over time and repeated use.

TRADITIONAL EXPLANATIONS OF DEVELOPMENT

As with any corpus of scientific explanations, theories about development have emerged from their cultural/historical contexts. The major schools of thought most often have been labeled as behaviorist, nativist, and interactionist. Although these are convenient terms to describe broad ontological positions, they do not capture the diversity within each position. Each position has merit, particularly as an artifact of a culturally founded philosophy, so next I sort out these schools by their conceptual labels. However, I detail only the various forms of interactionism, because it is the most currently useful and commonly adopted of the positions.

Behaviorists

B. F. Skinner (1957) and his followers held development to be largely a matter of nonknowing organisms soaking up the surrounding reality by means of some form of conditioning to stimuli. Although behaviorism still has its proponents, it is not favored by scholars of development, because it fails to adequately explain how a child acquires language facility. An example of a Skinnerian explanation of verbal development might go something like this: If Peggy at 10 months of age is interested in the smooth, red ball that is rolling away from her and leans toward it while vocalizing, her mother Ellen may say something like, "Oh, do you want the ball? Shall I get the ball for you?" With enough repetitions of the word *ball* along with the stimulus of the ball in sight, Peggy will ultimately link the sound "ball" with the object. That is, Peggy's behavior is conditioned over time by her environment.

Stimulus-response conditioning, although valid to describe some sorts of learning, does not explain how children can be creative with language (e.g., develop a personalized word, *bamu*, for ball), nor does it explain how they learn syntactical structures with which to express ideas that go beyond simple referencing of an object ("Mommy ball blue?"). A superior explanation, claimed the nativists, is that humans are prewired with the capacity for a syntactical, symbolic form of communication.

Nativists

Chomsky, Fodor, Pinker, and more recently the new neuroscientists such as Crick (1994) claim that human behavior may be explained by human physiology. Thus, development is a matter of allowing the genetic endowments to unfold. Again, there are theoretical variants. For example, Chomsky, whose revolutionary linguistic theory (1957) roundly criticized behaviorist explanations for language development, almost certainly would argue against the reductionist assumptions of the neuroscientists that all sensations and thoughts are reducible to simple neuronal properties.

Chomsky argued for a language acquisition device (LAD), which is a genetic endowment bestowing the capacity to order the elements of human language. Keep in mind that when we use the term *language acquisition* we mean the emergence of the capacity to use spoken symbols and grammatical rules for ordering them; we do not mean simply learning words of a particular language such as English, Japanese, or Spanish. For example, the general rule for word order in English is subject-verb-object. If Peggy were born into a different language community, she would as easily acquire some other word order, but Ellen does not need to tell her what the culturally appropriate order is; Peggy figures it out herself by entering data from spoken interaction to her LAD, and then applies it to her own creative sentences. One criticism of Chomsky's nativism is that the notion of genetic transmission of language facility is too limiting and ignores the influence of environment. Lieberman (1991) noted that the principle of genetic variation would mean that "some children would lack one or more of the genetically coded components of the language facility" (p. 131) if it resided in a module such as the LAD. The fact that nearly all human children— even those with cognitive delays or deficits—acquire language argues against a language acquisition device for grammar and, instead, for a flexible brain configuration that allows for construction of complex pathways to support symbolic communication.

Interactionists

To put it simply, interactionists take the middle route by allowing that humans do indeed learn, and probably do so in a particularly human fashion because they are so genetically endowed. However, what we must explain is more complex than a simple download of any old environmental stimuli to a preset brain structure. Humans need interaction with other symbolizing humans to trigger the construction of knowledge systems that can handle symbolic, syntactic communication. If it seems as though this might be a fairly complicated position to fully explicate, then we have begun to do it justice. Additionally, it is a position that may be embraced by scholars who articulate surprisingly different explanations of developmental phenomena. As one group of developmental scholars put it: "It is difficult not to be an interactionist today" (Ignjatovic-Savic, Kovac-Cerovic, Plut, & Pesikan, 1988, p. 89); just about anyone studying human development today can claim the label.

A fruitful first step in sorting out various interpretations of interactionist assumptions is to distinguish a dialectic from a dialogic approach to understanding human behavior. As we specify the theoretical assumptions of each approach, it becomes clear that each is useful for describing certain properties of human behavior. Again, historical/cultural factors in large part determined what sorts of explanations have emerged.

Dialectical approaches to development bring social processes to the fore by focusing on the dialectic as the point of change. This could be a dialectic between self and other, individual and society, ego and id, hand and eye, or any number of other polar forces, but always *involving a relationship between two seemingly opposing positions*. Most, but not all, dialectical approaches derive from Hegelian (e.g., Holden & Ritchie, 1988) or Marxist (e.g., Riegel, 1976) philosophies about opposing forces. But neither focuses sufficiently on the tension created between the two polar forces.[2] Later in this chapter, we examine a few of the specifics of these theories, and why they stop short of explaining developmental processes fully.

Dialogical approaches better capture the nature of the movement created between opposing social forces by the tension between them. That nature is inherently developmental. Although *dialectic* is the umbrella term for approaches that acknowledge change through contrast, the dialectic generally implies *structural stability of the contrasts*, whereas the dialogic *implies oscillation or fairly constant change set in motion by the contrast between opposing poles*. And it is this movement that inevitably brings change. Mao Tse-Tung (1952/1965), for example, acknowledged the nonstatic nature of contradiction: Each contradictory element of a dialectic transforms into its opposite, the result being that "the nature of the thing changes accordingly" (p. 32). Although dialectical scholars such as Mao acknowledge this movement, the first to draw attention to the dialogic approach as a variant of dialectics was Bakhtin (Baxter & Montgomery, 1996). For Bakhtin, dialogue referred not simply to that movement between dialectics, but also to the social and human nature of literal interactive dialogue. Because we engage in dialogue between separate identities, we set up opportunities for change or development in the oscillating dialectics between us. Before we explore his and other dialectical approaches in more detail, we examine the contributions of scholars working in the early decades of this century to the progression of interactionist thought.

BREAKTHROUGHS IN DEVELOPMENTAL THEORY: 1900–1930

Jean Piaget

Piaget, who did much of his foundational work in the 1920s, was undoubtedly the first scholar of development who could be considered a dialectician, and indeed one of the first to systematically study the behavior of children. The field of psychology held sway in the human sciences and fostered his interest in the individual development of logical thought. Considering the psychological traditions of the time, founded in the scientific tradition and focused on mental functioning, his choice to study individual psychological processes makes sense. However, he went beyond his scientific training.

In his recognition that development involves qualitative transformations, he moved away from behaviorism and from the scientific reductionist tradition generally. He was, in Tolman's words (1983), a naive dialectician; that is, he developed a spontaneous dialectical method in order to focus on the study of interrelationship and change (Bidell, 1988). The dialectical approach attempts to "grasp processes in the full complexity of their interrelationship," as opposed to reductionism, which "artificially separates processes into elements for temporary study out of context"

(Bidell, 1988, pp. 331–332). His well-known concepts of assimilation and accommodation were described as oppositional yet interdependent processes, thus describing a dialectic. Despite his immersion in the Western scientific tradition, which was fast becoming dogma, Piaget conveyed the notion of process in his theory. Nonetheless, his is a structural theory.

Piaget's stages of intellectual development constitute the most well-known portion of his work. Each stage is associated with a structure or cluster of concepts (Ginsburg & Opper, 1988). Psychologists and educators, starved for adequate developmental explanations, rushed to employ his stages in their work, often without adequately testing their assumptions. With increasingly sophisticated testing in the last several decades, scholars have found the stages unsatisfactory predictors of further development (Gelman & Baillargeon, 1983).

Piaget articulated a fresh perspective on cognitive development, but he assumed that communication was secondary to cognition. He took the position that the child possesses incipient thought processes that remain egocentric until they are expressed and thus vulnerable to the feedback of others, at which point those processes may become socialized. That is, communication is simply the tool we use to express thought. On Piaget's heels nipped a Soviet psychologist named Vygotsky, who would take issue with this assumption and move the developmental dialectic toward dialogism.

Lev Semyonovich Vygotsky

The new voice in Soviet psychology in the 1920s made his mark at around the same time that Piaget worked in Switzerland. Vygotsky was a more outspoken critic of orthodox behaviorism than was Piaget, and was no fan of subjective introspection as a method either. Neither behavioralist nor rationalist, he was a thorough scientist who carefully tested his ideas, but wisely used theories that had already found acceptance in his academic culture. In order to move his ideas past the dogmatic Marxists who idolized Pavlov, he used Pavlov's notion of the Second Signal System, "the world as processed through language" (Bruner, 1986, p. 70). With that vehicle, he introduced his more controversial ideas about speech, language, and cognition. Vygostky was interested in the dynamics of human activity rather than static representations. One of his basic tenets is that the child uses speech to alter the power of thought. To explicate that process, he undertook a critique of Piaget's "egocentric speech."

Piaget described egocentric speech as characterized by "remarks that are not addressed to anyone ... and that ... evoke no reaction adapted to them on the part of anyone to whom they may chance to be addressed" (1926/1954, p. 55). Furthermore, he concluded that egocentric speech serves no purpose except for the discomfort that spurs the child to a more socialized speech, planned for, and directed to another. (See Fig. 1.1.)

Vygotsky took his observations of children a step further than did Piaget, by varying the difficulty of the tasks set to them. He found that egocentric speech increased with task difficulty and concluded that egocentric speech indeed had a purpose: to serve the child in regulating his/her own behavior. As Vygotsky noted,

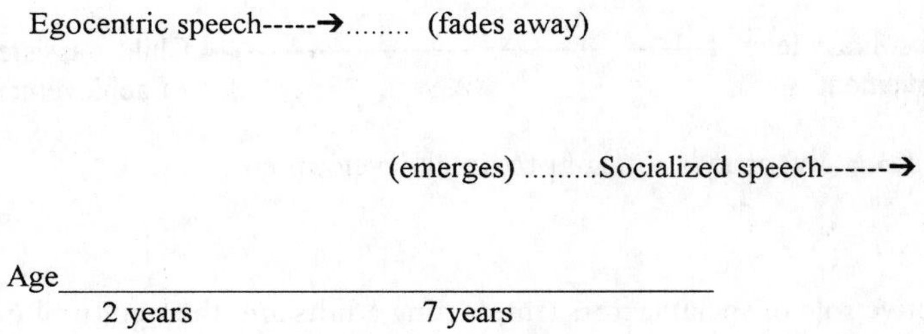

Egocentric speech-----➔........ (fades away)

(emerges) ....Socialized speech------➔

Age_____
            2 years   7 years

FIG. 1.1.   Piaget's view of speech development.

"Egocentric speech is inner speech in its functions; it is speech on its way inward, intimately tied up with the ordering of the child's behavior" (Vygotsky, 1962, p. 46).
Thus, egocentric speech is speech for one's own purposes, spoken externally first,
then internalized to be used silently—mentally—to direct behavior. Once speech
and thought are linked, speech serves thought and thought serves speech; they become enmeshed. (See Fig. 1.2.)

Vygotsky's later work examined the development of word meanings in concept
formation and the process of learning in children that culminated in his notion of
the "zone of proximal development" (1978, p. 86). This conceptualization of a
learning window, in which children learn from more capable thinkers, has become
the most frequently employed of his contributions. (See Fig. 1.3.)

Although many scholars have labeled Vygotsky a dialectician in the Marxist
sense, some have recognized his thoroughly interactionist perspective, and a few
have acknowledged his contributions to a more dialogic view. Yes, he viewed the infant as a social being, in contrast to Piaget's "autistic" infant. Yes, he emphasized the

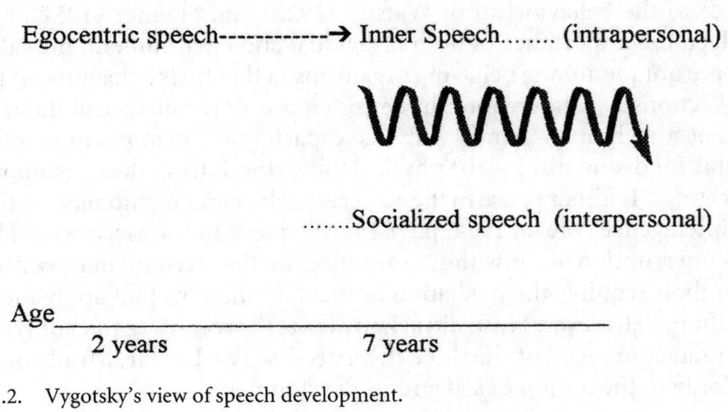

Egocentric speech------------➔ Inner Speech........ (intrapersonal)

〰〰〰〰〰〰

.......Socialized speech (interpersonal)

Age_____
            2 years   7 years

FIG. 1.2.   Vygotsky's view of speech development.

Child's solitary level ▮---▮ Child's assisted level
achievement   of achievement

FIG. 1.3.   Vygotsky's zone of proximal development.

constructive role of social factors (interacting adults and their cultural milieu) in forming the child's psychological functions, in contrast to Piaget's view that intellectual functions are primary and then inform social interaction. But most important, he claimed that consciousness itself is inherently social.

Vygotsky's "general genetic law of cultural development" (Hart, Kohlberg, & Wertsch, 1987, pp. 251–252) may be illustrated by the process by which Ellen and Peggy "remember" where Peggy's shoes are. Ellen and Peggy are preparing to leave the house, but Peggy can't locate her shoes. Ellen asks: "Where were you when you took them off? Do you remember if your feet were hot? Or did your socks itch?" Peggy's memory is stimulated by these questions and she leads Ellen to the shoes in the yard. Neither participant to the dialogue does the remembering—the dyad does the remembering. The remembering is a function of the movement between the mother's problem-solving skills and the child's simple recall. Rather than either mother or child performing the memory function, *both* recall. Intellectual function cannot be assigned to individual properties or to environmental ones; it is "relations among people (that) genetically underlie all higher functions and their relationships" (Vygotsky, 1981, p. 163).

George Herbert Mead

Oddly, or perhaps not so oddly considering the premise that theories are situated historically and culturally, another radically innovative voice from the United States joined those in Switzerland and Russia in the early years of the 20th century. Mead called his brand of psychology "social behaviorism," although it bore little resemblance to the behaviorism of Watson (1925) and Skinner (1957). Mead acknowledged the importance of both individual and environment, but added that humans are unique among behaving organisms in that their behaviors, or more accurately "actions," are interrupted by consideration of various possibilities. He suggested that the human hand, with its capacity for manipulating objects, is responsible for distinguishing the physical thing [food] from the consummation of the act [eating]. It is that pause in the act, created by hand manipulation, that is the basis of intelligence (Mead, 1974, p. 184).[3] My question for Mead would be: How does this interruption occur without the reflection that accompanies symbols? The use of symbols requires the mediation of mental functions that apply meaning to acts and things. However, Mead did acknowledge the role of significant symbols[4] in human interaction. And of the three theorists discussed so far, Mead contributed most directly to the notion of self and its development.

For Mead, the mind—"that part of experience in which the individual becomes an object to himself in the presentation of possible lines of conduct" (1982, p. 177)—arises from a social process in which self as a social object "enters the field of adjustment on the same basis as other objects" (p. 185). That is, a concept of self develops in much the same way as a concept of anything develops. Furthermore, self-consciousness, necessary to an embryonic self-concept, arises from taking the perspective of the other toward self, and that perspective-taking ability is contingent on communicative competence. As Mead states, "The importance of what we term 'communication' lies in the fact that it provides a form of behavior in which the organism or the individual may become an object to himself" (1934/1974, p. 138). That is, "self is a cognitive, communicative, and social achievement" (Hart et al., 1987, p. 241).

What seems apparent from Mead's analysis of the genesis of self-consciousness is that it requires the manipulation of objects, including people, as well as the use of significant symbols to exchange perspectives with another (a more abstract sort of manipulation); "self is a cognitive construct of communicative origin" (Hart et al., p. 242). In this acknowledgment of social origins for the self, Mead agreed with his less well-known predecessor, Baldwin.

James Mark Baldwin

Working at the turn of the century, Baldwin also emphasized the social origins of the developing self and posited that early social receptivity is "the consequence of both evolution and mental development" (Hart et al., 1987, p. 227). His claims about human evolution have been rediscovered recently by biologists interested in the assumption that the ontogenetic development of intelligence is the primary force in controlling evolution. Organic evolution, Baldwin (1896) suggested, has "a sort of intelligent direction after all; for of all the variations tending in the direction of an adaptation, but inadequate to its complete performance, only those will be supplemented and kept alive which the intelligence ratifies and uses" (p. 447). Furthermore human evolution, or phylogenetic development, is not simply a matter of maintaining genetic mutations that allow flexibility in problem solving, but is also affected by social environment.[5] Adaptations can be transmitted from preceding generations in social rather than genetic fashion, and lead the species toward an increasingly social nature.

Baldwin (1902), like Piaget, developed a structural or stage theory of self development, based on the assumption that learning is a consequence of imitation. The four stages in becoming a self are:

1. *Projective*: distinguishing people from objects.
2. *Subjective*: recognizing the difference between own actions and others, and the rise of volition and self-awareness.
3. *Ejective*: acknowledging that others' bodies have experiences such as own body does, others are also "me"s.
4. *Ideal*: incorporating the social rules of the group.

Note that the first two stages are based on contrast, the third on a dialectic, and the last appears more dialogic. The ideal self is not bipolar in the sense that the first three stages are. In observing the parent's obedience to the rules of society, the parent's self is seen as simultaneously ejective (commanding the child) and subjective (obeying the rule). This capacity apparently arises in the kind of thinking that is first imitative of other in the subjective stage, then ejective or assimilative of other's "me." Finally, the child can ride the social oscillations between "right" and "wrong" action.

Baldwin considered self-understanding and understanding of the other to be identical. What a child thinks of "another is—not stands for, or represents, or anything else than *is*—his thought of himself, until he adds to it a further interpretation; the further interpretation is in turn, first himself, then is—again, nothing short of this *is*—his thought of the other" (1902, p. 89). The young child strives toward similarity with other after the initial recognition of difference. Peggy recognizes that she is separate and distinct from Ellen, and subsequently tries on Ellen's distinctive behaviors.

Mead viewed this early similarity of self to significant other as an indirect result of role taking in communication; the child's meanings become like that of other because they respond similarly to symbols they share. Mead stressed *cooperative interaction,* in which roles are different, rather than Baldwin's *imitation,* in which roles must be similar. The difference between the two theorists may have more to do with their failures to specify the point at which these processes occur than with conceptual disagreement. We now know that infants indeed do behave similarly to caregivers very early in life (Meltzoff & Moore, 1997), but later they go beyond behavioral mimicry to thoughtful action in accord with significant others; they assume other's role by use of symbols. This leads to increased perspective-taking abilities (Delia, O'Keefe, & O'Keefe, 1982), by which an understanding of Other as well as of self is constructed.

Clearly Mead and Baldwin agreed that humans are innately social, and that the self is a cognitive construct. Baldwin more clearly articulated the process of self as dialectical. For him, the self was one pole of the self-other dialectic; one cannot have had "a thought of self, unless one had a thought of another" (Hart et al., 1977, p. 243). In another part of the world, Bakhtin was developing this notion further.

Mikhail Bakhtin

Although Bakhtin was not a developmental theorist by any stretch, he contributed to the rise of dialectic and dialogic explanations for human phenomena. Bakhtin wrote about literature, language, culture, and religion in the Soviet Union of the 1920s and 1930s. Reasonable though it might be to assume that Bakhtin and Vygotsky were colleagues, they never met: "Bakhtin knew Vygotsky's early work, but there is no record that Vygotsky was aware of Bakhtin" (Clark & Holquist, 1984, p. 382). The similarities between their approaches to human behavior are striking, however. Bakhtin, although he claimed not to study psychology but rather "translinguistics" (Clark & Holquist, 1984, p. 228), suggested that "the reality of the inner psyche is the same reality as that of the sign" (Volosinov, 1973, p. 26).[6] He further proposed (Clark & Holquist, 1984) that the locus of consciousness lies on the border between the organism and the exterior world, the workings of each being at such variance as to require a means of translation found in the sign[7] (or symbol, in our terms). In other words, the internal workings of a human brain are quite different from the external workings of the world, so the mediating mechanism that evolved to translate internal to external, and external to internal, was the symbol. (The specifics of this mechanism are explained in chap. 4).

Bakhtin was a critic of his many contemporaries who studied human mental capacities because they did not account for the unity of mental functions. For example, Freud's notion of a discontinuity between the conscious and the unconscious made little sense to Bakhtin, who insisted that there were no differences between inner and outer speech, simply degrees of sharedness between the deepest level of language, "where mind borders mere brain," and the highest, "where outer speech converges with the language of the encompassing social system" (Clark & Holquist, 1984, p. 229).

Bakhtin paralleled Vygotsky's thinking about the development of self. Vygotsky acknowledged a rudimentary consciousness before language acquisition, with self-consciousness arising only after the child's entry to the languaging culture. Bakhtin insisted, as Mead and Baldwin did, that the self comes from Other, that it is the result of social forces. The self is not an internal but a "boundary phenomenon"—it is not the result of isolated creation of meaning about self—it is, like all meanings, the result of the dialogue between Other and self.

To Bakhtin, dialogue was not simply a matter of two people conversing, although it is that, but dialogue, more broadly conceived, "means communication between simultaneous differences" (Clark & Holquist, 1984, p. 9). Dialogism was not merely a way of thinking about language, but it was "Bakhtin's attempt to think his way out of ... monologism" (Clark & Holquist, 1984, p. 348). Beliefs in single, absolute truths could not, in Bakhtin's view, account for relations between people, between persons and things, between persons and ideas. And these were the issues that were timeless for him: "The contexts of dialogue are without limit. They extend into the deepest past and the most distant future" (Bakhtin, as cited in Clark & Holquist, 1979, p. 350).

THE LEGACY: CONTEMPORARY THOUGHT
ABOUT HUMAN INTERACTION

For those scholars of development familiar with the theoretical foundations mentioned previously, interaction has become the key concept in the study of humans. Neither nativism nor behaviorism sufficiently explains human development. Many claim the interactionist label, and of those, quite a few use some form of dialectical or dialogical thinking. Far from an exhaustive review, the following material summarizes some of the current interactionist thinking on human social behavior and serves to introduce some of the scholars and concepts to be featured in later chapters.

Dialectic, Dialogic, and Relational Thought About Human Behavior

Sampson's work *Celebrating the Other* (1993) detailed the movement from monologism—the celebration of the individual self—to dialogism—the celebration of other. He argued, citing Mead, Bakhtin, Vygotsky, and Wittgenstein, that "mind and all its attributes, as well as personality and personal identity (i.e. self), are emergents of a dialogic, conversational process and remain socially rooted as an ongoing accomplishment of that process" (p. 107). He considered the context of power and suppression throughout his work and concluded his 1993 text with a chapter entitled "Dialogic Ethics: On Freedom, Responsibility and Justice." Sampson apparently viewed the "dialogic turn" to be inherently political; John Shotter shared this view.

Shotter referred to his sort of interactionism as "social constructionism," and called his sort of dialogic psychology "knowing of the third kind" (1993b). This kind of knowledge is not about facts or theory ("knowing that") nor about practical or technical skill ("knowing how"); it is rather "knowledge which only has its being in our relations to others ... which is prior to both" (p. 7) other kinds of knowing. The crux of the matter, for Shotter, was that this knowledge is of a moral kind, depending on others' judgments "as to whether its expression or its use is ethically proper or not" (p. 7). He also relied on Bakhtin, Vygotsky, and Wittgenstein, as well as Vico, an Enlightenment scholar who generated a theory of sociality in his *New Science* of 1744 (Vico, 1968). Shotter claimed that it is Vico's account, "not Mead's, that provides us with the new understanding of the genesis and development of practical sociality that we need" (Shotter, 1993b, p. 57).

Vico, over 200 years ago, formulated methodological maxims that seem to have predicted some modern criticisms of scientific method. His notion of "sensory topics" are "places" in awareness we have in the living of our lives. The difficulty is that we cannot represent such entities in discourse; at best, we can give them form metaphorically, perhaps in poetry as did the ancient Greeks. Shotter added that we need "not only a poetics but also a rhetoric of relationships, where a rhetoric is concerned with the giving of a first linguistic form to the 'feelings' to be found again in topics" (p. 72). Shotter closed his book *Cultural Politics of Everyday Life* by discussing the "politics of identity and belonging" as a creative endeavor involving the "invention of 'our' form of citizenship," stressing the "formative and relational power of language" to give us the resources to "shape and reshape our lives" (1993b, p. 201). Shotter, in other words, acknowledged the developmental implications of our dialogic natures, both culturally and individually.

Csikszentmihalyi has succeeded in bringing his ideas about human behavior to a broader, nonacademic audience (1990, 1993). In his book *The Evolving Self,* he argued that "becoming an active, conscious part of the evolutionary process is the best way to give meaning to our lives at the present point in time, and to enjoy each moment along the way" (1993, p. 11). However, some of us follow genetic instructions or societal dictates with little consciousness, whereas others develop "autonomous selves with goals that override external instructions" (p. 23). The challenge to develop an autonomous self is complicated by the necessity of establishing values.

One of the most basic of the decision points in choosing values is described by the dialectical tension between differentiation and integration. Csikszentmihalyi described the progressive transition points between turning inward and outward as a lifelong "ascending spiral, where concern for the self becomes steadily qualified by less selfish goals, and concern for others becomes more individualistic and personally meaningful" (p. 235).

His version of the dialectic is apparently Hegelian[8]; he claimed that the transcendent self harmoniously combines opposing tendencies (p. 238). If this sounds like Hegel's synthesis of thesis and antithesis, Csikszentmihalyi left no doubt by specifying that a self must resolve the "apparent antinomy" of the two poles of a dialectic such as individuation/integration in order to participate fully in the "flow of evolution" (p. 238). Although his ideal self may be unrealistic from a dialogic view, his is a useful perspective to add to current conceptualizations of the constructive nature of self.

Of those who study communication and social processes, Irwin Altman, Leslie Baxter, Barbara Montgomery, Steve Duck, and William Rawlins are a few of those who have adopted some form of dialectical or dialogic thought to explain those processes. *Altman*, known best for his early work on interpersonal processes, adopted a transactional perspective (1990) and most recently combined dialectics and transactional values to explore the possibilities for the study of personal relationships (1993). He suggested that we need to examine how dialectical processes apply to individuals, dyads, and between groups, such as the relationship between a married couple and the larger family, or a couple and its religious community. Most of the scholars he acknowledged work from a similar perspective perform communication research.

Montgomery, taking a dialectical approach to relationship development, demonstrated that contrary to previous work on relationship maintenance that focused on stability, change is "at the heart of social processes." Dialectical oppositions, "the simultaneous presence of two relational forces that are interdependent and mutually negating," (1993, p. 207) result in constant change. Even as oppositions are resolved, new forms of oppositions emerge in a dialectic pattern called the "law of the negation" in which "any current tension is situated in a historical chain of past and future tensions, which are linked by transformations" (p. 208). In essence, social activity is developmental in that dialectical dilemmas constantly change. A more concrete application of dialectical theory may be found in Rawlins' work.

Rawlins, in a series of studies examining friendships (1992), described dialectical tensions experienced in voluntary relationships across the life span. He tracked the evolution of dialectical transformations as friends adapt to contingencies in their relationships. Also studying personal relationships, but more often in marriages and romantic relationships, Leslie Baxter (1988, 1990) has been a prolific proponent of dialectical and, more recently, dialogical perspectives of human communicative behavior.

Baxter explained that one sort of dialectical thinking is Bakhtin's dialogism. Not only is social life to be taken metaphorically as dialogue—the quality of simultaneous fusion/distinctiveness of social voices—but social life also is literally constituted in dialogue (1993, p. 140). As a theory, dialogism describes the contradicting process in the "ongoing tension between centripetal (i.e., unifying) and centrifugal (i.e., differentiating) dialectical poles" (p. 141). Bakhtin posited this opposition as the "deep structure" of social experience that "constitutes the essence of dialogue." He, however, did not specify the phenomena constituting these forces for any particular context. This extension to the specifics of personal relationships has been Baxter's focus for the past several years. She has demonstrated the internal and external manifestations of three fundamental dialectics: integration-separation, stability-change, and expression-privacy.

Duck (1994) proposed a move toward considering relationships in terms of dialogic complexity rather than the more traditional "progress" of unidirectional movement, which is more often how relationship phenomena have been described. Where we might have spoken deterministically about contradiction as a cause of change, Duck proposed that we view change as emergent; where we described relational change linearly, Duck proposed cyclic change as well. In the past, scholars of human relationships have often masked the inherent complexity of relationships with the benediction of traditional scientific methods unsuited to studying human behavior, or they have apologized for the indeterminacy of human relationships. Duck's acknowledgment of complexity invites us to consider dynamic change in all of its manifestations: intrinsic and extrinsic, linear and cyclical, quantitative and qualitative.

Thus far, the work in dialectics has begun with considerations of adult human behavior, but in considering dialectical/dialogic processes, these scholars have started to approach questions that sound suspiciously developmental. In later chapters, we explore these implications for adult development. Now, we move to those who are facing developmental questions head on.

Dialectic, Dialogic, and Relational Thought About Human Development

Bruner, a well-respected scholar of human development, created a sophisticated, useful, and elegant theory of development from his several decades of research. Although he has written about modes of thought, the development of self, and much about mother–child transactions, he may be the best known of the interactionists because he clearly explained that human development could not be merely a matter of biological propensity or of behavioral conditioning. He added to Noam Chomsky's LAD, or language acquisition device, his concept of LASS, or language acquisition support system. He considered indispensable the parents' contribution of "scaffolding" for the child's language construction.

In this, as in other of his interactionist notions, Bruner has consistently acknowledged his debt to Vygotsky. He recalled (1986) his attendance at an international conference in 1954, where he heard papers from the Russian delegation that usually started with "a genuflection to Pavlov, followed abruptly by interesting accounts of studies of attention or problem solving that seemed to have little to do with the paleo-Pavlov" he'd read (pp. 70–71). It seems Vygotsky had done at least one politically expedient thing—used Pavlov's notion of the Second Signal System to talk about the role of language in culture. Although his work was officially banned in Russia, scholars still circulated his work and cited the Pavlov link in order that they would continue to be allowed to do so. Vygotsky was regarded with suspicion by the officials in power, although he was devoted to Marxism and proposed that humans are "subject to the dialectical play between nature and history, between ... biology and ... human culture" (Bruner, 1986, p. 71). Of Bruner, more later, but he is by no means the only interactionist with a debt to Vygotsky.

Fogel, in a long-needed contribution to developmental scholarship (1993), formulated the perspective that "individuals develop through their relationships with others" (p. 3), and specified three aspects of development: communication, self, and culture. Contrary to earlier perspectives from psychology, Fogel claimed that "developmental change arises in everyday communication" rather than some "inaccessible area of the brain or the cell" (p. 5). His core concept is "co-regulation," which occurs "whenever individuals' joint actions blend together to achieve a unique and mutually created set of social actions" (p. 6). It is this creative process that is the "fundamental source of developmental change" (p. 6). Influenced by Mead and Bakhtin as well as Vygotsky, he borrowed from contemporaries as well. For example, the notion of dialogic self—as opposed to objective self—is from Hermans, Kempen, and van Loon (1992). Rejecting the "old psychology" that distinguished the *I* as the thinking agent from the *me* as the object of that thinking, Fogel instead considered the self "as a dialogical process between multiple cognitive positions" (p. 140). Indeed, true to the both/and nature of a dialogic view, Fogel claimed that "we are the dialogue and not one voice or another" (p. 144).

Riegel, in agreement with the notion that dialogues best reveal the nature of development, formally presented a "dialectics of human development" (1976) in the tradition of Marx, Hegel, and Heraclitos' notion of "ceaseless flux" (p. 696) rather than stability and "the tranquility of balance" (p. 690). He emphasized the temporal order of "events brought about by conflicts and contradictions" (p. 689), and suggested that asynchronies in developmental progressions generate crises that then generate change.

His discussion of balance and imbalance sounds nearly dialogic in that the relationship of the two changes continuously—that is, we must consider balance simultaneously with imbalance. However, his suggestions for future work indicate an interest in the identification of dialectical structures; in fact, his "dimensions of developmental progressions" sound very much like structural stages. Still, his dialectical ideas are sound as well as integrative and creative. One we pursue in this text is that new levels of consciousness are created in interactively stimulated dialectics "until the individual becomes aware of dialectics itself" (1976, p. 697). The case is made in later chapters that beyond dialectical tension lies dialogical awareness.

Erikson's stage theory (1950) broke ground for the consideration of self-concept as the core issue of individual development. Although stage models are not as popular as they once were, Erikson is acknowledged for developing a structural foundation that incorporated the influence of dialectical tensions on the process of self growth. He postulated eight stages, each with a specific task, the completion of which was required for transition to the next stage. The task, or challenge, characterizing each stage was described dialectically by opposing forces such as "trust versus mistrust." The very term separating the two words indicates the either/or nature of this conceptualization of the choices a self must make. Levinson (1978) continued the description of the dialectic of self into adulthood by proposing four polarities to be integrated in later years (e.g., attachment and separation, an often stated and seemingly fundamental dialectic).

More current conceptualizations (Hattie, 1992) of identity view self as a process of "parallel developments" (p. 119) rather than ordered stages. There may be "loose associations" between self-concept development and age, and the sets of distinctions one must make to become individuated. Hattie suggested a series of early recognitions concerning self, including personal causation, distinctions between self and other, self and environment, and related cognitive capacities such as reflexivity.

Nudler (1986) brought social adaptation to the conceptualization of individual development. Indeed, he specified that the two are dialectically related. He proposed a human need to develop that goes beyond the biological forces of growth, and requires an information environment. However, he emphasized that a human "cannot be reduced to ... biological heritage or sociocultural influence or to the sum of both"; each person has some "irreducible originality" (p. 127). It is what becomes of that originality in the dialectic between the two forces (biological and social) that concerned Nudler.

The consequences of the development-adaptation dialectic are either overadaptation or underadaptation. For the overly adapted individual, who adjusts only too well to "average expectations" (p. 128), the question is: What has been repressed? For Freud, the answer would be sexual impulses; for Nudler, in our post-Victorian society, it is simply the impulse to grow. That is, in moving toward the adaptation pole of the dialectic, one has moved away from the developmental pole. In the underadapted individual, the lack of adaptation may result from either a failure in early socialization (e.g., the physical effects of extreme poverty or the psychological effects of lack of nurturance), or a later destruction of the adaptive niche the person had found (e.g., forced retirement, loss of family).

In true dialectical fashion, Nudler suggested transcendence over adaptation as an option to the shifting between poles. Rather than merely adapting, "personalizing" the cultural heritage makes for integration or "a deep dialogue with oneself" (1986, p. 134). A dialogic view could germinate from his discussion of the nature of this transcendence: "Instead of denying [the] uncertainty" found in the movement between the oppositions, the transcendent person actively searches for "new development patterns with its associated increase of uncertainty" (p. 135). That is, the transcending individual embraces the uncertainty found in the oscillation between the poles of personal development and sociocultural adaptation. Nudler added that this healthy individual accomplishes development with others, that individual "development is at the same time *co-development*" (p. 135). He further suggested that, rather than trying to eliminate the paradox posed by the development-adaptation dialectic, we accept its paradoxical nature and explore its "mechanisms and consequences" (p. 137). In sum, the perfect balance of individual development and social order may not be possible; new and more creative contradictions would appear with attempts to be rid of them.

Having ended our march through the literature with a salute to the inevitability of contradictions in development, a nod to my own scheme of developmental principles is in order. What follows is a preview of the assumptions that will serve to support the developmental perspective to be constructed throughout remainder of the book. Because these foundational statements have yet to be fully explained, we allow Peggy to exemplify each assumption.

ASSUMPTIONS OF A RELATIONAL-DIALOGICAL PERSPECTIVE OF DEVELOPMENT

1. Human communicative development, although it begins with and continues for some time to be influenced by physiological maturation, is characterized by a series of progressive internalizations of symbolic interactions or "boundary experiences" that result in the unfolding of individuality.   Peggy, a normally developing little girl, by the age of 4 has a fairly large vocabulary of useful words, although they are not as abstract in their meanings as her mother Ellen's meanings. One day, Peggy experiences an interaction with a police officer, which is atypical for her. Ellen is stopped for speeding on the freeway and, in the course of writing the ticket, the officer engages Peggy on the topic of driving and safety, telling her that "police are here to protect and serve; we just want to slow people down so that everyone is safe." The "boundary experience" between Peggy and the officer is something Peggy continues to talk about repeatedly in the ensuing days and weeks. Ultimately, this experience, internalized in her thinking aloud about it, becomes not only a part of her sense making about police and safety, it comes to influence her beliefs about herself as a citizen.

2. These boundary experiences, or dialogues between self and others, are internalized in a process that creates the mind. (Yingling, 1994a).   All of Peggy's interactions inform her sense-making system in a series of progressive internalizations that build what we call a "mind." Loosely speaking, the mind is the system of meanings and accompanying feelings we use to process experience. That collection of processes is active in relationship with others and malleable in relation to others' meaning systems.

3. Mind is a mediating process between a material brain, subject to physiological maturation, and an energetic consciousness that is active at the boundary between self and other. The active mind, then, is materially aware of itself in relationship to another mind.   Peggy has a functioning brain with all of its capacity for constructing neural networks. The brain's networks, however, would not increase in complexity in the absence of interaction and a set of related meanings created in interaction. In relationship to her mother, Peggy's consciousness meets Ellen's at the boundary between the two. That boundary marks the current limits of Peggy's meaning system, or mind, meeting the current limits of Ellen's. The brain, the physical foundation or holding place of this system, supports this functioning just as a hard drive "holds" the materials formerly created and organized at the boundary between a person at a keyboard and a word processor. When Peggy encounters an unfamiliar word used by her mother (e.g., *justice*), she may increase activity at the boundary to create meaning, and possibly search the core of her system as well for links to existent meaning. If Ellen, as a savvy mother, suggests to Peggy that "justice" is linked to her experience with the police and the speeding ticket, she has assisted Peggy in consciously negotiating new meaning.

4. *Mind, mediating between internal perception and external activity, processes experience in terms of a symbolic self, or identity.*   Aware that Ellen already has meaning for *justice*, Peggy searches for insight by reflecting on the difference between her own meager system and Ellen's rich system. Concurrently, the distinction crystallizes the sense of separate selves (one knows *justice*, the other does not), but at the same time creates the opportunity for Peggy's identity to grow into a more knowledgeable self (and thus more like Ellen).

5. *Identity is the ongoing process of being "objectively aware of self" (West, 1995) as a result of the constructed mind. Identity arises from cumulative internalizations of external experiences at the boundary between self and other. The self is that for which one is accountable to others; self is presented rhetorically for the Other, and the cumulative result, mediated by memory, is identity.*   As Peggy is confronted with many similar instances in her early years, she becomes more and more self reflexive. Over time, she internally loads a great many of these boundary experiences onto the word *justice*. Fortunately, *justice* is one of those user-friendly terms that invites multiple layers of abstraction. With time, she is held accountable for her actions as they related to *justice:* "Peggy, it just isn't right that you lied to your friend. Do you think it's fair and just for her to be left wondering what happened?"

6. *The development of personal identity is described by a series of cycles wherein external social experience is internalized. Identity is processual and multiple, more or less fluctuating, in that it is reflective of current self-in-interaction as well as expressive of the cumulative self-perceptions constructed rhetorically in a series of boundary experiences.*   By the time Peggy is a young adult, she has internalized these sorts of interactions to form an identity that is fairly stable; Peggy knows how she must behave to experience a comfortable fit between her sense of identity and her actions. She may indeed experience discomfort when she lies to a friend, but if her sorority sisters typically tell and tolerate "white lies," those experiences will come to influence her identity as well.

7. *The nature of human communication—spoken symbolic interaction between identities in various states of transformation—allows increasing sophistication in processing interactive experience.*   The first distinction is generalized by our abstracting symbolic capacity, which assumes the perception of contrast as well as

similarity. The process may be characterized roughly as a sequence (not necessarily linear or stagelike) in ways of experiencing interaction:

- Unity with other (newborn as one with caregiver).
- Contrast with other (infant as contrast perceiver).
- Rules for difference (child: toward dualism).
- Skills for synthesis (youth: toward dialectics).
- Playing the tensions (adult: toward dialogics).

Because we communicate symbolically, we have the capacity to develop from the experience of organic unity to the perception to contrast (based on proto-symbols) to dichotomous percepts (based on symbolic rules for communication) to dialectical concepts (abstractions, logics, rule exceptions) to dialogic frames (sets of contextual logics).

For example, at Peggy's birth, she and Ellen experienced a holistic intimacy that is difficult to replicate. For Peggy, Ellen was her entire milieu; breathing, feeding, and sleeping are all experienced in the "surround" of Ellen and there is no sense of separateness. After several months, Peggy begins to play with speech sounds and use some of them preferentially, probably to refer to favored feelings or events. Around the same time, Peggy begins to show a "will" for certain toys more than others. In general, Peggy is developing volition that only a being who knows she has some power can do. Invariably, that sense of power and control comes up against the will of the other.

By the age of 2, Peggy uses the word *no* in a gamelike way. She is delighted by her power to shift what is to what is not. By the age of 7, she is learning that rules can help her when personal power is equal. Rather than giving up the game to the larger or more powerful Roy who can run her down in hide-and-seek, she can use the rules ("He peeked!") to win.

By the age of 25, Peggy may still use rules but they are not as magical as they once were, because she is finding that relationships don't always work according to rules. It seems that no matter how many rules she and her new husband negotiate ("We each are entitled to one night out a week"), she always seems to be the one who wishes for more time together. After many long talks with friends and professional counseling, she begins to recognize that she and her husband occupy different positions on the "togetherness/separateness" dialectic. Although the distance between them comes and goes, the marriage continues.

In her 40s, she recognizes that she can shift her place on that dialectic and often does; indeed, it is not necessarily a "gender issue," but a human issue. As she approaches retirement age, Peggy has a broader understanding of this particular dialectic as well as others. She experiences the diverse range of desire, from separateness to togetherness, and revels in her capacity to enjoy it all. She finds herself having to stifle a smile when her granddaughter brings her complaints about her boyfriend's desire for freedom. Peggy has integrated in a highly successful fashion.

I used the phrase "capacity to develop" to indicate that this set of steps is neither inevitable nor smoothly progressive. Although the nature of symbolic interaction is such that we *may* experience this sequence, the varied nature of experience at the boundaries ensures a wide range of achievement.

Certainly, if a child's interactive experience is limited, if his or her perceptions are unchallenged, and if he or she is rarely challenged to account for self, then dualistic rules for understanding boundary behavior may continue to suffice. What is described is a series of ways to handle the perceptions of differences, ending with a return to some sense of unity—but this time by way of difference.

8. Variations in the rate of physiological maturation, in the nature of interaction experienced with others, and in sociocultural habits affect the speed and regularity of these cycles of internalization. That is, it is possible to describe threshold points in the way individuals perceive self and other. Some are stably related to physiological changes; but others, such as the nature and timing of life "crises," vary from culture to culture, between genders, even among individuals. That is, the further we develop past physiological "maturity," the more variety we observe in such thresholds. In fact, we may find that the individual can predict his or her own thresholds—based on current and past interactive experience—more successfully than a social scientist can find a "norm" for such adult changes. Peggy could have neglected to take Ellen's offer of funding for therapy, and married five more times. She never might have come to a comfort point in playing the tensions of dialogics. But she did; and it is likely that she will be better able to predict her granddaughter's major life thresholds than a book that tracks "standard" life passages.

SUMMARY

The trend in the developmental literature has been away from physiology as an explanatory concept for human behavior. Lieberman (1991), speaking of evolutionary trends, claimed that human communicative (speech) capacities allow us to "transcend the constraints of biological evolution" (p. 9). Later in this text we examine the evidence that the same is true in ontogenesis, or individual development, as apparently is true in phylogenesis, or species evolution. Maturation is not merely biological, but also constructive. We do not simply grow, we construct our minds and thus identities. And we don't do it simply in a brain; indeed, co-construction occurs between people in relational discourse and then is internalized selectively. We oscillate between working the boundary (negotiating meaning with the relational other) and working the core (further developing our meaning systems).

This book is about dialectical oscillations between the distinctions we perceive: between self and Other, then between contrasting poles of all sorts constructed in relationships and stored in personal constructs. The remaining chapters flesh out the premise of development as a series of relational and dialogical processes. The story of "Peggy" will lead the reader through developmental transformations: the discoveries of difference in infancy, the cocreations of self and mind in interaction, the development of communication skills in early relationships, the tensions of adolescent egocentrism and conceptual thought, the confrontations of personal values in the college years, and the myriad relational challenges of adulthood. We conclude with a view toward the future of communication and relationships.

NOTES

1. See Rymer (1993) for documentation of Genie's case.
2. Mao Tse-Tung, however, interpreted Marx and Lenin a bit more dialogically. He pointed out (1952/1965) that in contradiction, one aspect is principal and the other nonprincipal, but their roles are never static: "When the principal aspect which has gained predominance changes, the nature of a thing changes accordingly" (p. 33).
3. Ivan Pavlov's famous experiment with dogs demonstrated that a natural impulse to salivate upon presentation of food may be conditioned to an artificial stimulus, in this case a bell, which will trigger the same response, once learned. What Mead suggested is that the introduction of the hand into the sequence of food-eat accounts for the possibility of our interrupting the natural impulse. Vygotsky and Luria would argue that symbols have this effect and that they are more critically mediated by speech than by hand manipulation.
4. Significant symbols are those symbolic creations that are meaningful to two (or more) people in the same way.
5. Note that Baldwin's idea foreshadowed biologist Richard Dawkins' (1976) notion of "meme." Csikszentmihalyi (1993) summarized the concept: "a unit of cultural information comparable in its effects on society to those of the chemically coded instructions contained in the gene on the human organism" (p. 120).
6. Although Volosinov's name appears on this work, his friend Bakhtin is widely considered to be the author. There remains controversy about a number of works that appeared from members of Bakhtin's circle (see Clark & Holquist, 1984, chap. 6).
7. *Sign* may be defined as an umbrella term for the sorts of communication tools that include symptoms and symbols. Cronkite (1986) provided a useful taxonomy of these terms.
8. Hegel proposed the opposing tendencies of thesis and antithesis, but added the notion of synthesis as a way of integrating the two oppositions. A nice idea, but perhaps not entirely realistic.

Pressure, movement, pressure, pressure …
Light … blinding, painful. Noise … ringing, reverberating.
Space … to fling into, to cry out to.
But wait, more … recognition of a voice, a familiar heartbeat.
Comfort …
The Voice … motion breaks up the light … concentrate … dark
Comfort … the feel of soft to mouth.

She who is to be Peggy enters the world from dark, cramped space. The light in the delivery room is like nothing she has experienced and she winces. There is the motion of Ellen, Roger, the doctors and nurses, hands, faces, voices. It's all too much to try to take in. She manages to bring her fist to her mouth, sucks, closes her eyes. Rests. Later, she hears that familiar Voice of Ellen's, cranes her neck, opens her mouth and eyes, searches. And Ellen leans over her so that Peggy can see the face, the dark shadows cast by eyebrows, nose, lower lip, cheekbones, chin. She follows the face when it moves, attending to the motion. Ellen speaks softly, in musical tones that lift and fall, and Peggy stops the cry she had begun. Ellen puts Peggy to her breast. Peggy suckles. She has arrived.

Chapter 2

Infant Development:
Biological Endowments and Beyond

Think how it is to have a conversation with an embryo.
You might say, "The world outside is vast and intricate.
There are wheatfields and mountain passes,
And orchards in bloom ..."
You ask the embryo why he, or she, stays cooped up
In the dark with eyes closed.
            Listen to the answer.

There is no "other world."
I only know what I've experienced.
You must be hallucinating.

(Rumi, quoted in Barks, 1995, p. 71)

THE NATURE OF BECOMING HUMAN: ONTOGENY

For a very long time, our Western cultural traditions were dominated by a focus on the individual alone on the path of self-discovery—the hero who overcomes all odds—and that focus on self-celebration has kept us from recognizing that the individual cannot become a person without others. Sampson's (1993) phrase "celebrating the Other" represents a shift in thinking from human power embodied in individual monologue to the shared ownership of this power in dialogue. But where does it all begin? Does not the infant come into life alone?

We can only imagine the nature of earliest perception, because infants cannot describe what they know. The defining characteristic of infancy as a human state is lack of communicative capacity. Indeed, "the very word *infant* is derived from 'in,' meaning *without*, and 'fari,' meaning *speech*" (Dance & Larson, 1972, p. 67). Still, infants perceive and experience. Sometimes our creative powers have failed us and we have assumed the infant to be *tabula rasa* or a blank slate on which experience writes. At other times, we have imagined the infant as one who arrives in a state of

23

perfect unity with all things and then must learn the pain of embodiment and differentiation. More recently, we have found reason to believe that even the newest of humans have the capacity for making simple distinctions. So, do we begin life in a blissful state of undifferentiation, or is individuation a hallmark of human embodiment from the start? And what has either one to do with communication?

The Bliss of Unity

Gunter Grass's (1959/1961) precocious narrator, Oskar, relates early in *The Tin Drum* that the first sight he could recall was the light of two 60-watt bulbs, blinding in their brilliance after the dark of his journey down the birth canal. Although it is unlikely that Oskar, unusual as he was, could decide to remember what his parents said about the future on his first day,[9] Oskar might well have experienced the contrast between the bright light of the bulbs and the dark of his former space. That first transformation from physiological unity with mother to independent biological being is likely accompanied by a multitude of new distinctions and responses to them.

In many cultures, the notion of coming into material existence implies the birth of duality. Eastern cultural thinking pairs existence with nonexistence. The yin and yang of being are seen as similar to the "breathing" of the universe itself—inhaling and expanding, exhaling and contracting. This ancient dialectical explanation was captured well by Robert Bly (1979), who summarized a three-stage tale:

> Once we lived in the mouth of the cow. We were the hay and the cow and the stomach and the ears. We enjoyed the mouth cavern, and the saliva and the great grainy tongue, for we were the tongue, and the tongue rang in the bell of the mouth, and we too were the sound of the bell, and the clapper and the bell and the sound were all one, and had no names. And that was lovely and we wanted it to go on forever, but it didn't.

> The cow started to lick a rock—and all of a sudden—it took about eighty thousand years—a woman appeared. The rock became a woman, and when the cow licked a flint nearby, the flint became a man. And the man was determined not to be eaten by the cow, so he—that is, the man and woman together, now both out of the cow's mouth—developed language. The first thing they did was to create two words, one for human beings and one for cow's mouth, so they would not forget the difference. Then for a hundred and ninety thousand years (a time which is just now ending) they thought of nothing but differences: the difference between leaf and root, between black and white, between man and woman, between post and hole, between tongue and book, between sound and silence, between going right and going wrong. During this time silence didn't say much, and we remembered the fragrant noisy silence of the cow's mouth as a Golden Age.

> But an odd thing happened: because the man and woman had invented a word for night, and one for day, they began to experience night and experience day in a different way than they had inside the cow's mouth. (Night and day were fused or confused inside the cow's mouth.) Night led them to experience the moon, and day led them to experience the sun; the word "darkness" led them to experience the smaller darkness on the underside of every leaf, and "the sun" led them to experience the small light on the tip of the lance, and so eventually they became at home on the earth; they estab-

lished a residencia en tierra. They were free of the Great Unity, which was too high up anyway, and their feet felt firmly placed on the earth.

Once they felt firmly at home on the earth, they began to long for the third thing that was neither light nor dark. It is strange: the same power, language, that leads us to divide human being and cow's mouth leads us to this longing.

The danger that language will trap us in opposites, of right and wrong, man and woman, is tremendous, but language when loved and entered contains also the healing of opposites. (pp. ix–x)*

Although the story describes a metaphor for the phylogenesis of humans, it also gives us a lyrical explanation of the effect of language[10] on perception and experience. From this point on, the reader may assume that "the cow's mouth" refers to the state of undifferentiation and the bliss we associate with it.

In many of the original, traditional views of development—including those proposed by James (1890), Piaget (1926), and Freud (1905/1962)—development is a process that begins in *adualistic confusion*, or total absence of differentiation. William James, the father of modern psychology, described this adualistic state, as a feeling that all is "one great blooming buzzing confusion ..." (1890, p. 488). Thus, explanations of infant perception have ranged from confusion (James) to narcissism (self-absorption; Freud) to solipsism (perception limited to one's own position; Piaget).[11] Others have also described the newborn as undifferentiated (Mahler, Pine, & Bergman, 1975), but these views have been undermined in the last few decades.

The Pain of Individuation

It is as natural to die as to be born; and to a little infant, perhaps, the one is as painful as the other.

Francis Bacon, 1625
(quoted in *The Oxford Dictionary of Quotations*, 1980, p. 26)

Without doubt, the process of becoming a distinctive human is accompanied by the pain of feeling separate and alone. Otto Rank (1929/1952) introduced the notion of birth anxiety as an anxious feeling about one's own existence as one emerges into an experience of self. Feeling anxious about existence (existential angst) is certainly something that adults do but, as has been pointed out by Freud and many others since, it cannot be something that newborns do. At birth, there is no objective self-awareness, no cognitive conception of existence. It is not possible, when emerging into life, to think about one's own existence, much less to imagine one's nonexistence. Thus, James' state of confusion is much closer to the mark than Rank's anxiety.

---

*"The Story in Three Stages" by Robert Bly, from UNITING HEAVEN AND EARTH by Sukie Colgrave. Used by permission of Jeremy P. Tarcher, an imprint of Penguin Group (USA) Inc.

But what sort of early experience *did* Peggy have in her first days? Likely, she began to sort out some of the blooming and buzzing into light and dark, Mom and not-Mom, speech and not-speech. Still, she had no sense of a "me" making these distinctions. Although it is difficult for us to imagine such a state, it may be something like what we experience when we are completely present and engrossed in some very involving activity, like finishing a race or playing a piano concerto, or writing an emotion-laden letter to an intimate friend. It may be much like the concept of "flow."[12] According to Csikszentmihalyi, flow activities merge action and awareness (1990), rather than separating out a "me" who is aware and apart from the action "I" perform. Flow activities are never done in self-consciousness but always in consciousness; furthermore, they order that consciousness in some fashion. For a newborn, this ordering can be as simple as noting the difference between Mom's voice and Dad's voice. Infants act, they are aware, and they are capable of merging the two, as we shall see further on in this chapter.

Note that "flow" is not the same as "the cow's mouth." In the mouth of the cow, no distinctions are possible. Whereas flow is voluntarily *experienced* as pleasurable, the mouth of the cow simply and involuntarily *is*. What is pleasure in the first case is bliss in the second. Flow experiences are often described as involving a sense of control, or more precisely, a feeling of effectiveness that lacks "the sense of worry about losing control that is typical" of many daily situations in which adults find themselves (Csikszentmihalyi, 1990, p. 59). What Csikszentmihalyi called "the paradox of control" for adult humans[13] is not so paradoxical for infants. That is, they do not know yet what control is, or what expectations and responsibility are. They do not want to control, or fail to control, or fear a lack of control. They experience feeling good and feeling bad. They can order their experiences on a very basic level. Thus, when they succeed in making distinctions, they are effective in ordering experience. Keep in mind, however, that ordering an experience is not necessarily the same as knowing that one is doing so. Self-awareness is a later development.

When Peggy hears her mother's voice and responds differently to it than to the rhythmic sounds of monitors or the murmurs of other infants in the nursery, she has effectively made a distinction and one that is likely to bring her external rewards as she uses it. For now, the distinction itself is inherently pleasurable and rewarding. But if this state cannot be defined as adualistic confusion, what is it?

An alternative explanation to the adualistic confusion proposed by early psychologists has been available for some time. The philosopher Thomas Reid (1764/1990) proposed "natural dualism" as a given capacity of mind to make differentiations. Reid's natural dualism influenced modern scholars, including Gibson, Neisser, and Butterworth.

Gibson's version of dualism concerns the information infants perceive about objects in their environment by preserving the energy patterns they can sense (Butterworth, 1995, p. 38). Central to Gibson's theory of perception is proprioception as the capacity to sense one's own body position in relation to the environment. Rather than simply a kinesthetic sense of one's own movement, Gibson extended the meaning of proprioception to include "external feedback arising as a normal correlate of the exploratory activity of perceptual systems.... Proprioceptive information is given by the fact that we are embodied and in the world" (Butterworth, 1995, p. 38). And, infants apparently do make rudimentary differentiations between self and other-than-self. Even on her first day, Peggy could manage to orient toward that interesting voice. Recent research demonstrates that "perception in very young babies is adequate to put them into a naturally dualist contact with reality" (Butterworth, 1995, p. 38).

Distinctions and Contrast: Humans as Binary Sense Makers

The idea that humans are natural contrast perceivers and pattern seekers is fairly common throughout philosophy, psychology, and most of the social sciences. We reviewed a number of those perspectives in chapter 1; now we turn to those researchers who share the dialogic turn but focus on its roots in infancy.

Gibson (1995) noted that babies discover their own agency—capacity to act—and that this process begins in early abilities to hear, see, and feel their own movements and postures. She suggested that infants detect a difference between two kinds of events: movements of things in the world *around* me, and movements perpetrated *by* me. Furthermore, two kinds of information are available to detect this difference: flow patterns in the visual field caused by movement of my head or body, and multimodal perception produced by my activity. Even neonates may perceive multimodal information as specifying the same object (Gibson & Walker, 1984). As Gibson noted, "Information for the *same* event perceived simultaneously via two separate receptor systems is an unassailable argument for the existence of something external to one's own organism" (1995, p. 6). In this case, reaching toward Ellen's face as Ellen picks her up, Peggy is presented with the visual pattern of movement as she is brought to Ellen, and at the same time, Peggy sees her own arm reaching while she feels the arm moving (vision plus kinesthesia). Thus far, we have an explanation for why many mammals can make distinctions early in life.

Butterworth (1995) concurred with evidence that babies too young to even crawl can compensate appropriately to shifts in their visual field created by a "moving room" around their suspended seat. Even before they can cause the shifts in their visual field, babies make the distinction between a change of place of the body and a change of state of the environment. Again, these are fairly impressive capacities, not yet distinctly human, but definitely beyond adualistic confusion.

These rudimentary differentiations between self and environment, present at birth, are "fragile, very limited, and linked to basic, probably prewired functional propensities to respond in particular ways to specific stimulus configurations" (Rochat, 1995, p. 11). The point Rochat made is that these early differentiations are linked to "a general attunement infants bring with them" not just to the environment, but particularly to people. Undoubtedly, the Other at this point is an unspecified but nonetheless inherently interesting part of the environment. Rochat would say that infants are on their way to becoming objects to themselves by way of exploring objects in the environment. He suggested the example of an infant systematically kicking a mobile hanging above the crib: "By exploring the results of her own action, the infant detects ... a perfect contingency" (p. 61), or causal sequence of action-response. Peggy, interested by the shifting patterns of the mobile, increases her kicking movements. But is this merely a conditioned response, or is it recognized by her as a means to an end? Babies do not understand consequences much before 9 months of age, but this early pattern detection is one step on a fairly steep path toward such understanding.

The introduction of people into the equation contributes to resolution. Melzoff and Moore (1995) assisted us with attention to the role of imitation early in life. They claimed that "neonates recognize the equivalence between self and other because they imitate, but that imitation is not solely confined to pure body perception. Rather it appears to be mediated by a representation of themselves and other people" (p. 74). Certainly, simple imitation of, say, tongue protrusion changes and transforms in the first 2 years, but begins in the imitative responses of infants to interacting adults.

Here, we have a recognition of the importance of the interacting Other to development. Poking out their own tongues in response to adults who have just done so is not only supportive of infants' capacity for proprioception, but to their innate responsiveness to other humans who can share recognition of similar body schema (Meltzoff & Moore, 1995). The fact that neonate imitation of facial and manual gestures has been demonstrated across cultures in independent laboratories is fairly compelling evidence of this sort of matching behavior as universal. Meltzoff and Moore did not believe that it is mere reflex, but instead a process of "active intermodal mapping," or a matching-to-target process. In their study, when an adult added difficulty by pushing out the tongue to the side, infants—whose tongues take up more of their limited mouth space and thus are less maneuverable than adults'—poked out their tongues and simultaneously turned their heads to the side. That is, it was a novel act not found in the stimulus: "a creative act in which infants extracted the 'goal' of the act and tried to get their bodies to duplicate it" (p. 78). Here, we find a behavior that appears to be more than a conditioned reflex. It would appear that it is very important for infants to demonstrate some willingness to play the interaction game even in their first hours.

This very early sense of one's own being is apparently multidimensional. Neisser (1995) specified five aspects of self of which two, ecological and interpersonal, are available from earliest infancy. The ecological self "is the individual situated in and acting upon the immediate physical environment ... specified by visual/acoustic/kinesthetic/vestibular information" (p. 18). The interpersonal self "is the individual engaged in social interaction with another person ... [which is] specified by typically human signals of communication and emotional rapport: voice, eye contact, body contact, etc." (p. 18). If they are available from birth, these two sorts of defining distinctions must rest on some genetic inheritance. We proceed now to attempt to tease out the innate physiological capacities that mature on a predictable biological timetable from the more variable interactive processes that result in individuation.

NATURE AND NURTURE: THE RECIPE FOR A HUMAN

For decades, the community of scholars interested in human development maintained a dichotomous orientation often labeled "the nature versus nurture controversy." In recent years, interactionists have refused to claim such a controversy and instead revealed the false dichotomy on which it depends. For interactionists, human development depends in part on the maturation of genetically inherited capacities and in part on the interactive acquisition of spoken symbolic communication. We next examine both, acknowledging that they begin to blend at birth—physiology serves interaction and interaction boosts maturation.

The Nature of Embodiment: Specialized Human Capacities

At least since Descartes, and probably before, Western thinkers have tended to consider human perception in dualistic terms: mind/body, subjective/objective, phenomenal/material. However, scholars like Karl Pribram (1971, 1986) have revolutionized thinking about human perception based on discoveries in neurology as well as physics. Pribram's position is neutral monism. From this perspective, mind and body are not separate, but rather "transform back and forth in structure via a matter-energy transform" (Ricillo, 1994, p. 39). Mentality is not something separate from the body, but is instead developed by way of brain processes. The kind of mentality necessary for human thought and social interaction may be the result of selective evolution for distinctive neural networks and specialized anatomical features for audition and vocalization.

Basing her philosophy on scientific findings about behavioral variations among species, Suzanne Langer (1972) suggested that, at some point in our evolution, we left the realm of *communion* and entered into *communication*. Among other animals, relationship is "almost a physiological condition, a felt communion of action and emotion and desire; in man that communion is progressively weakened by the growing tendency to individuation" (p. 312) that accompanies the increase in mental functions consequent to changes in vocal tract formation, audition, and brain size and specialization.

The Vocal Tract

Mature human vocal tracts, in comparison to those found in nonhuman primates *and* in human infants, are very specialized "bent two tube" systems (Lieberman, 1977). Although most mammals use two tubes—one for ingesting food and the other for breathing—in mature humans these tubes overlap, which results in a capacity for articulate speech but leaves us at risk for choking. Note that chimpanzees do not use the Heimlich maneuver; there's a reason for that. Chimps (as well as human infants and most mammals) cannot inhale what they ingest, because the two pathways do not overlap; therefore, they can breathe and drink at the same time (See Fig. 2.1).

As humans mature, the larynx migrates down below the sharp angle formed at the back of the oral cavity and thus below the point at which it can be contiguous with the nasal cavity. At this point, the airway and food passage share space; the larynx can no longer form "a watertight seal with the entrance to the nose" (Lieberman, 1991, p. 54). Additionally, the lower jaw shortened, causing crowding of the teeth and, frequently, impaction and infection. Why, you might reasonably

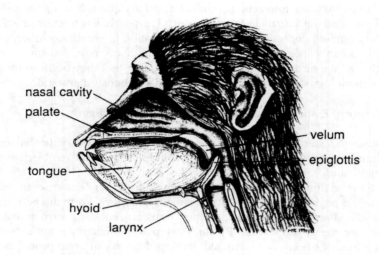

Air passage of chimpanzee

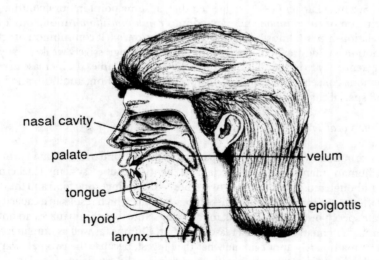

Air passage of human

FIG. 2.1   Comparison of air passages and laryngeal positions.
Note. Sketches reprinted by permission of the publisher from *Uniquely Human: The evolution of speech, thought, and selfless behavior* (p. 55), by Philip Lieberman, Cambridge, Mass.: Harvard University Press, Copyright 1991 by the President and Fellows of Harvard College.

ask, would we evolve in such an apparently nonadaptive manner? The only positive result accompanying this change was the capacity to form more distinctive speech sounds, which made for a huge difference in communicative capacity.

To be specific, adult humans can produce nonnasal and quantal sounds, resulting in the capacity for very rapid speech production. Nasalized sounds are "misidentified by human listeners 30 to 50 percent more often than are nonnasalized sounds" (Lieberman, 1991, p. 57). Nasalized sounds occur when we do not, or cannot, seal off the nasal cavity.[14] Human languages tend to avoid nasalized phonemes because they induce more errors in perception.

Quantal sounds are exceptionally crisp or easily distinguishable speech sounds. They are acoustically salient—their formant frequency patterns form spectral peaks. Such sounds are produced by creating "an abrupt change in the cross-sectional area of the supralaryngeal vocal tract" (Lieberman, 1991, p. 58). Some of these crisp sounds may be produced by other mammals (dental consonants) and by primates (labial consonants), but only humans can change the configuration of the tongue in the right-angle space at the back of the oral cavity and the top of the spinal column to produce the vowels /i/, /u/, and /a/ and velar consonants /k/ and /g/. These sounds are also acoustically stable, meaning that we can be fairly sloppy in positioning our tongues and still produce distinct signals. The advantage of these acoustically salient and stable sounds for human communication is that the identification error rate is very low (Lieberman, 1991).

Finally, given the peculiarities of the human vocal tract, speech production is 3 to 10 times faster than the vocal transmission rate of other primates. Lieberman suggested that we consider the survival value of being able to say "There are two lions, one behind the rock and the other in the ravine" in the same time it takes to produce "lliiooonn rooockkk" (1991, p. 59). Suffice it to say that if your hunting partner said the latter, you would not have the leisure to consider the value of knowing where the second lion was.

In terms of the vocal tract, the newborn is equipped for survival (breathing and eating) but not yet for speech. It is functional for the infant to be able to drink without choking, so survival is optimized if the larynx is undescended until the child can coordinate swallowing and breathing. The effective result is that the more distinctive speech sounds are impossible for the newborn. Although infants produce cry sounds and cooing (vowel-like sounds) in the first months, the addition of consonant-like sounds to vowel-like sounds typically does not occur much before the sixth month. However, neonates are fully equipped to attend to speech stimuli and to begin to engage in making some sense of them. For that, they need a specialized brain.

The Brain

Distinctive sounds alone would not give you much help in the absence of a brain that evolved to handle those sounds. Indeed, by some accounts, speech capacity evolved to handle increased brain capacity. In any case, the human brain is unique, both in the unusually large capacity of its frontal lobes and in the functional asymmetry of its hemispheres. Both peculiarities are to be found in the neocortex, a layer of gray matter (nerve cells, dendrites, and nerve fibers) atop the more fundamental structures. This newer layer, found in some mammals, has been crammed into the skull around a core of subcortical tissue controlling largely reflexive activity. Because a large volume of gray matter has been folded into a limited space, the neocortex appears on its surface—most particularly in human and dolphin brains—to have many deep fissures or convolutions.

One index of relative intelligence of a species is size of the brain in proportion to body surface (Jerison, 1976). By Jerison's calculation of encephalization quotient (EQ; brain weight to body weight), human EQ is highest, with dolphins just behind. The brain size of higher mammals is in large part due to the increased size of the neocortex. The frontal regions of the neocortex are much larger in humans than in other primates, and it is the voluntary control of speech that apparently involves much of the human neocortex.

The neocortex, particularly the left hemisphere, is specialized in humans for communicative functions. Throughout the discussion of left hemisphere specialization, keep in mind that the circuitry for speech is more complex than the follow-

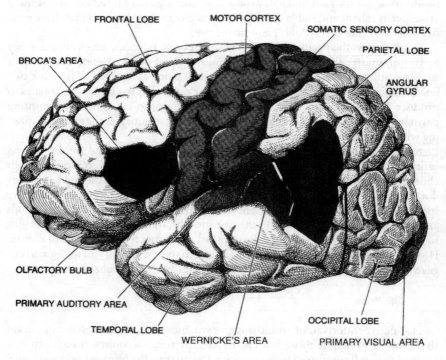

FIG. 2.2.   Human left brain specialization.
Note. Reprinted by permission of the artist, C. Donner, from *The Brain* (p. 111), A Scientific American Book, 1979, Copyright by W. H. Freeman and Company.

ing summary implies, additionally involving the basal ganglia and other subcortical areas (Lieberman, 1991).

Broca's area is located in the left frontal cortex, near the bottom of the motor strip of the brain, and is largely responsible for the motor programming of speech and language expression (Ricillo, 1994). Damage to Broca's area can result in permanent language deficits in humans that impair sentence formulation, leaving comprehension intact. There is no functional equivalent to Broca's area in nonhumans, but damage to the prefrontal cortex in all primates, including humans, results in "a loss of 'vigilance,' ... as well as in other deficits in learning and performing complex tasks" (Lieberman, 1991, p. 24).

Wernicke's area is in the left temporal lobe, adjacent to sensory areas of the brain and just behind the ear. As Ricillo stated, "Wernicke's area is responsible for auditory reception and language comprehension" (1994, p. 49). Damage to this area can result in reception aphasia and impaired comprehension.

Different sorts of language deficits derive from interrupted circuits. Lieberman explained, "For example, lesions in the connection between Broca's and Wernicke's areas, the *arcuate fasciculus*, result in ... sharp differences in speech comprehension and production" (1991, p. 27). In this case, if a person with such lesions were presented with a peach, that person would insist that he or she knew the name and understood what it was, but would be unable to produce the word.

The upshot of all this specialization is that humans are equipped to communicate in a very specialized way. However, infants do not come into life with all systems fully functioning. Although the brain at birth is approximately 25% the size it will be in maturity, it has most of the neurons it will ever have. What increases in development are the connections between those neurons. In part, learning involves making links among neurons to form associational pathways. Another contribution to increased brain weight is the development of myelin, which is a fatty sheath that accumulates along most connecting nerve fibers to enhance the transmission of neural impulses (Ramsberger, 1994).

Myelin increases the rapidity of impulse transmission by 50%; that is, it makes for rapid and in some cases automatic responses. This automatization of everyday tasks makes for quick, effortless completion of routine behaviors and as such is highly useful. Myelination of nerve fibers peaks around birth, but continues throughout childhood, and lasts into one's 40s, particularly if interrupted by ill health or poor nutrition (Leviton & Gilles, 1983). It has been linked to milestones such as babbling and word use (Lecours, 1975); peaks in myelination correspond roughly to critical periods for language acquisition. The earliest myelination occurs in the prethalamic acoustic pathway as early as the 20th fetal week and myelination of the postthalamic acoustic pathway has begun by birth (Lecours, 1975). This information will ring a bell when we examine infant auditory abilities.

After birth, peaks of myelination occur at 3 months, 1 year, 5 years, and 15 years, when babbling, word use, syntax, and abstract thought are, respectively, in rapid development. Critical periods for language acquisition—age limits within which one may successfully learn a syntactic language system—have been proposed variously for 5 years of age (Krashen, 1973; Molfese, 1972) and for approximately 13 years or puberty (Lenneberg, 1967). Quite possibly, there are several critical stages for various aspects of language acquisition. In any case, the brain must be used to process interactive language early in life in order to set it up efficiently for the optimal use of symbols. Just what can we expect of this specialized brain in terms of human cognition?

Ivan Pavlov (1928–41) ventured a theory about human brain function long before advanced medical technology allowed observation of the brain at work. Instead, Pavlov used the conditioned reflex to study the psychological processes unique to humans. He defined three "signal systems" involved in human cognition.

The simplest is the "subcortical signal system," which controls largely reflexive activity, such as regurgitating to clear the digestive tract of an intrusive object (say, a hairball). The "first cortical signal system" goes beyond simple reflexes and, for more complicated animals, serves to alert the being to environmental stimuli (e.g., the lion in the ravine) by means of distance reception by sight and hearing (seeing and identifying the lion, hearing it roar). Finally, the "second cortical signal system," available to humans, "links multiple stimuli together by a unitary verbal signal" (Dance, 1967, p. 15).

The newest system provides us with "a signal of signals ... the capacity to use a single *symbol* to represent multitudinous sensory signals" (Dance, 1967, pp. 16–17). This capacity—to arbitrarily link sound to a complex of meanings—is central to the link between thought and speech, and thus to the kinds of thought processes we associate with humans. (To illustrate: The word *lion* produced by my hunting partner may be linked for me to "dangerous, hairball-producing creature," which in turn is linked for me to "unfortunate, painful outcomes" and simultaneously to "I should fight or flee"—and all of this may occur in the absence of concrete, perceptual experience of the ostensible referent: *lion*.) Of course, the unitary verbal signals have to be heard to be useful.

Audition

Although the hearing of newborns is not quite as sensitive as that of adults, it is far more mature than the other distance receptor, vision. Recall the prebirth myelination of acoustic pathways. Indeed, audition is the only capacity useful before birth for gaining information about the world outside the womb. It is likely that this early auditory attunement predisposes infants to find the human voice very interesting (Aslin, 1987). Moon and Fifer (2000) concluded from the research on prenatal learning that prenatal auditory experience does affect postnatal responses to speaking voices. The prosodic features of speech (rhythm, stress, pitch) are perceivable in the womb, but the individual segments or syllables of speech are not. Prenatal auditory learning may not explain all of what the neonate seems to know, but it does account for a newborn's preference for the "music" of mother's voice.

Infants prefer higher-pitched to lower-pitched sounds, which may be linked to the vagaries of auditory maturation. In any case, it has the effect of training adults to speak in "motherese," which exaggerates the "music" of speech. This adult-to-infant talk is typically higher pitched than adult-to-adult speech and has other special characteristics that we take up later in this chapter and in the next. The newborn's attunement to the rhythm of speech may be a result of fetal exposure, but there are other competencies neonates have that appear to be biological adaptations.

One interesting piece of research that supports the evolution of specialized reception for speech sounds demonstrates that 1-month-old infants can distinguish similar quantal speech sounds (Eimas, Siqueland, Jusczyk, & Vigorito, 1971). Infants were presented a pacifier connected to machinery set to count the frequency of the infants' sucking. Then, by way of earphones, the infants heard a particular speech sound ("ba") repeated monotonously. As repetitions continued, infant sucking decreased and leveled out. As a new yet similar sound was presented ("pa"), infant sucking increased, demonstrating more interest and thus recognition of "pa" as distinct from "ba." Interestingly, the ability to make distinctions among sounds is later lost unless the distinctions continue to be used in the language to which the child is exposed (Lasky, Syrdal-Lasky, & Klein, 1975; Streeter, 1976).

Ricillo (1994) observed that newborns stop their own vocalizations when they hear other infants cry or vocalize. He noted that babies must ultimately develop the ability to voluntarily control their speech and that these initial interactive capacities prepare them for that control. He proposed that neonatal "suppression of vocalization in the presence of acoustic stimuli is the first voluntary attempt to listen" (p. 51) and, as such, is the infant's first attempt to interact with the environment. In a series of studies (Ricillo & Watterson, 1984; Watterson & Ricillo, 1983, 1985), infants suppressed their own cry behavior in the presence of a variety of acoustic stimuli. Apparently, there is a capacity for auditory attention that is fully functional at birth.

Human Physiology and Meaning Making

Creating Meaning

These very early capacities to attend to speech sounds are astounding, but how do they serve the neonate? Clearly, the interest of the infant may make interaction with an adult more likely, and we examine that next. But how is the infant using the information? Dance (1979) ventured the hypothesis that speech provides an "acoustic trigger" to conceptualization. This explanation rests on the assumption that infants not only distinguish one sound from another, but with the gradual maturation of speech articulators, recognize which sounds are their own and which are others'. The value of this exercise rests in the contrast provided by perceiving internally that one has acted to produce the sound, and at the same time perceiving externally that the sound has returned to one's ear. Meanwhile, one's sound has also been made public and thus possibly interactive.

The sort of sound production we can assume Dance had in mind is clearly present in babbling, which begins around 6 months of age. Before that time, infants certainly make sounds, but not the kinds of maximally distinct sounds we identify as speech. Profoundly deaf infants produce sounds in the first half-year of life, and then decrease their production often to the point of cessation at about 6 months, when babbling usually begins its explosive development in hearing infants

(Mavilya, 1969). Well-formed syllables are produced within the first 10 months of life by hearing infants, but not by deaf infants (Oller & Eilers, 1988). Based on this evidence, babies need to hear their own sound production in order to improve their articulation. Furthermore, they need to "own" their sounds to be motivated to continue producing them. Six-month-olds clearly enjoy sound making and will engage themselves with this play, whether alone or with others.

Elbers (1982) noted that repetitive babbling appears to have the effect of allowing the child to grasp the advantage of articulatory contrasts. The 6-month-old who can produce "bababa" will be the 7-month-old who tries out "babamamadada." Elbers suggested that neither sheer maturation nor reinforcement account for this kind of development. Repetitive babbling is a "self-directed process of exploration, during which the infant uses certain operating principles for constructing his[her] own springboard to speech" (1982, p. 61).

The types of contrast available in consonantlike and vowel-like sounds lend themselves to use by the infant for developing speech capacity, and perhaps for using that capacity in a meaningful way. Although there appears to be a gap between the children's babbling (6–8 months) and their first recognizable words (10–12 months), it is interpreted as a gap by adults already immersed in language. But what is the 9-month-old doing?

Based on his careful observations of infants' preferred vocables, Ferguson (1978) posited that these early sounds are meaningful to the child: "The child plays a highly active, creative role in the acquisition process. [S]He 'gets the idea' of having particular sound sequences 'mean,' i.e., that they should have appropriate occasions of use" (p. 281). The important point here is that infants are using sounds of their own creation; that is, they are discovering the meaning-sound link rather than having it imposed.

If Peggy, while eating pureed peaches, produces a sound like "didi" after Ellen asks "Is that good?" *and* if she produces it in each feeding situation when Ellen follows the spoonful with the question, we might surmise that Peggy means something in general. And we might further surmise that the meaning is positive, given her eagerness for the next bite. If Ellen responds "Yes, it's gooood" emphasizing the long /o/ in "good," Peggy may change the sound to "doo doo," then "dood" and finally, months later, "good." That is, word production may describe a sort of morphing process from a sound chosen by the child to comment on a situation or feeling to a sound closer to the one that an interacting other may recognize and repeat. Again, the ability to contrast the fine distinctions in sound between adult and child productions is what gets the child ultimately to a culturally agreed-on word.

Thus, if our capacity for symbolic communication is based in physiology, what becomes of those whose critical capacities for speech are impaired? The most serious impairment to spoken language is profound deafness, of the sort that would preclude hearing even one's own sound making. However, it is very rare; only one of every 1,000 children is born deaf (NIH, 1993). The majority of hearing-impaired individuals acquire the deficit after the first year of life; most of those after the critical periods for development (Poizner, Klima, & Bellugi, 1987; Sacks, 1989). One well-known example of an individual who acquired her impairment just at the critical point when most toddlers discover symbols is Helen Keller.

Helen was 18 months old when illness took her hearing and sight. Eighteen months is typically when we note an explosion in words that we attribute to the discovery of symbols. In Ms. Keller's own words, we can share with her the rediscovery she experienced years later when Annie Sullivan's hard work led 8-year-old Helen back to the symbol. Before this epiphany, Helen had responded like any well-trained animal. She had learned signs to represent the things she wanted, such as cake, and used them to fill her needs, but she did not converse and she did not seem to need or want to signal anything but her basic needs. Miss Sullivan took her for a walk:

> We walked down the path to the well-house, attracted by the fragrance of the honeysuckle with which it was covered. Someone was drawing water and my teacher placed my hand under the spout. As the cool stream gushed over one hand, she spelled into the other the word *water*, first slowly then rapidly. I stood still, my whole attention fixed upon the motion of her fingers. Suddenly I felt a misty consciousness as of something forgotten—a thrill of returning thought; and somehow the mystery of language was revealed to me. I knew then that "w-a-t-e-r" meant the wonderful cool something that was flowing over my hand. That living word awakened my soul, gave it light, hope, joy, set it free! There were barriers still, it is true, but barriers that could in time be swept away.

> I left the well-house eager to learn. Everything had a name, and each name gave birth to a new thought. As we returned to the house every object which I touched seemed to quiver with life. That was because I saw everything with the strange, new sight that had come to me. On entering the door I remembered the doll I had broken [earlier, in a fit of temper]. I felt my way to the hearth and picked up the pieces. I tried vainly to put them together. Then my eyes filled with tears; for I realized what I had done, and for the first time I felt repentance and sorrow.

> (Keller, quoted in Percy, 1954, pp. 34–35)

Note that Ms. Keller not only realized in this experience a new kind of thought, but also a new kind of self—one that feels responsible and in control of her own behavior, and thus feels regret for a past act.

More recently, Grimshaw, Adelstein, Bryden, and MacKinnon (as cited in Green & Vervaeke, 1997) reported a case of a child who was also profoundly deaf, but in this instance from birth. Identified only as "E.M." from Mexico, this congenitally deaf child was not taught sign language in childhood, but at age 15 his hearing was restored. Grimshaw et al. reported that, after 2 years of exposure to his native Spanish, E.M. understood many of the words said to him, but his language production was limited to single words, combined with gesture. He has particular difficulty with pronouns, word order, and verb tense. Note that the difference between E.M. and Helen Keller is that E.M. heard no speech until he was 15 years old, whereas Helen had 18 months of aural stimulation before she was deprived of it. E.M. was past the critical period for setting up the brain to connect speech and meaning in syntactic language.

Deaf individuals today learn alternative methods of communication, often using visual perception rather than audition, and their gestural symbol system (such as American Sign Language, or ASL) apparently uses the same portions of the brain usually devoted to spoken language. However, before the creation of sign language systems, the profoundly deaf—lacking the abilities both to interact with others and subsequently to develop symbolizing brain functions—were often relegated to the ranks of the nonhuman and institutionalized. The genetically prepared mode of acquiring symbolic communication is spoken and heard. However, the brain is set up for the use of symbols and will accept input in alternative modes only if the notion of the symbol—abstract, arbitrary meaning carrier—can be conveyed by other means. But that is apparently difficult to do.

In the past, some audiologists and deaf educators believed that acoustic stimulation was critical to jumpstart the brain's symbolizing capacity. In some cases of deafness, these professionals went to great lengths to introduce some acoustic stimulation by way of bone conduction bypassing the middle ear structures (by means of powerful headphones placed over the temporal lobes). This was believed to have a trigger effect on the brain, stimulating residual hearing (Furth, 1973). Berry (1969) claimed that audition alone can produce this "tonic influence" on the level of spontaneous activity in the brain.

More recently, the refinement of cochlear implants brought a new method to introduce auditory stimulation to the deaf. Cochlear implants bypass the ear and directly stimulate the residual nerve fibers in the cochlea. Recent research supports the conviction that early stimulation is optimal for communication development. A child implanted with the device at 19 months achieved rapid language gains in both phoneme production and later vocabulary size (Ertmer & Mellon, 2001). On the other hand, children older than 8 years when implanted developed speech production skills much more slowly than those receiving implants earlier. Furthermore, their improvement slowed to a plateau at 6 years after implantation (Blamey, Barry, & Jacq, 2001). Clearly, the earlier the better, if the goal is to assist deaf children in making the kinds of contrasts necessary for speech production and perception.

If the infant is indeed a "pattern seeker" who uses the acoustic contrasts found in speech to distinguish sound from silence, intonation from monotone, and consonant from vowel (Studdert-Kennedy, 1979), it is probably because speech was adapted for human communication and, as such, became critical to human social and intellectual development. For whatever reason (i.e., the superiority of aural/oral communication transmission across distances, around visual obstructions, in the dark of night), speech was selected as the primary mode for human communication. There are those who would argue that visual communication systems work just as well and, at least in infancy, vision surely is crucial to making sense of the social environment.

Vision

Infants do use other sensory receptors in addition to audition; hearing just appears to be primary for symbolic communication development. However, vision is an important receptor for nonspoken communication.

Faces are particularly attractive to newborns, who can focus best on objects about 15 to 18 inches from their faces; that is the range that an adult chooses for face-to-face interaction. Infants tend to be interested in movement, three-dimensional rather than two-dimensional stimuli, contrast between light and dark, curved lines rather than straight, and symmetry around a vertical rather than horizontal axis (Messer, 1994). There is some disagreement about the interpretation of these preferences, but obviously faces have all of these characteristics, and infants show a distinct interest in faces. Now, some say that infants simply prefer high-contrast stimuli (Kleiner, 1987) and not necessarily faces. However, it would seem to be more than coincidental that human faces do provide such contrast, and that infants are highly dependent on adult interaction and interest, given their helpless state and inability to fill their own needs.

Johnson and Morton (cited in Rochat & Striano, 1999) proposed the newborn response to faces as an innate subcortical response that does not require the detection of similarities or differences among faces. However, at around 2 months, this function comes under the control of a "cortically mediated mechanism" and infants show preferences for some sorts of facial displays over others.[15] Clearly, infants prefer people over other stimuli and the simple beginnings of that preference appear to be inborn. By 6 weeks infants are able to fixate visually, and by 3 months their focal distance is close to adult range (Stern, 1977). Ahead, we examine the visual mode in interaction.

Other Perceptual Capacities

Gibson's notion of proprioception includes all receptive information about one's own movements, through vision, audition, touch, and certainly, kinesthesia. Butterworth's (1992, 1995) studies of infants' responses to a moving visual field demonstrate that babies perceive visual information in terms of the spatial location of their own body. The infant apparently does "make the distinction between a change of place of her own body and a change of state of the environment" (Butterworth, 1995, p. 39). This, Butterworth claimed, is supportive of Neisser's "ecological self," "primary consciousness," or "natural dualism" as the original basis of experience (p. 40).

Although I agree that "natural dualism" is a reasonable place to start to map human development, I am not convinced that the origins of specifically human experience may be traced to proprioception. Rather, it is the "interpersonal self" when added to the "ecological self" that leads us to our humanity. Let us turn now to the role of the Other in early interaction and add that contribution to the equation of early development.

The Nurture of Interaction: The Inevitable Other

The paradox inherent in the nature/nurture controversy is that nature apparently sets us up to nurture and be nurtured. We are by design interacting beings.

If our sort of communication rests on physiological predispositions but develops in interaction, what becomes of those biologically normal children who are isolated and neglected? Although we certainly could not humanely allow studies of this serious a deprivation given the projected consequences, we do have one well-documented case of neglect serious enough to prevent the acquisition of a fully syntactic human language.

Genie was brought to Children's Hospital of Los Angeles in November 1970. She was 13 years old, but looked to be about half that age. She had been kept in virtual solitary confinement, restrained in a small room of a modest house in a Los Angeles suburb. Her severe neglect and lack of interaction left her unable to talk when she arrived. She was met with a great deal of interest by psychologists and linguists. In retrospect, she was met by perhaps too much academic intrigue and inconsistent personal involvement.

After a year of work, Genie's grammar resembled that of a normal 18- to 20-month-old child, which was a vast improvement. There was great hope among her team of professionals that she would be able to debunk Eric Lenneberg and learn syntactic language despite her age, which put her just at the edge of his critical period for language acquisition. However, the language explosion usually expected after the two-word stage never occurred: "Four years after she was talking in strings she was still speaking in the abbreviated non-grammar of a telegram" (Rymer, 1992, p. 57). The gaps in her knowledge of syntax included pronouns, relative markers, WH-words (e.g., *who, what*), and many of the rules for transforming word order for sentences (Curtiss, 1977). In essence, she could not ask a real question, or express any but the simplest of ideas.

Genie was not only a failed experiment in language acquisition, but a tragic human figure who never really mastered interaction with others of her kind. Some blame the failure on the poverty of her relationships, others on her multiple physical ailments from the neglect, and still others on the late date of her discovery. She lived out her days in an institution, forgotten.

We are a social species. Even before Peggy can converse in words, she forms human relationships *if* she has willing partners in her life. The task for the caregiver is to provide the structure of social activities—to model conversation. The task for the child is to transform communication abilities from simple behavioral responses to rule-negotiated voluntary activities. Sander (1977) described this transformational shift as one from "biosocial to psychosocial" interaction. He summarized his theory about infant–caregiver interaction by reference to the apparent polarities that characterize their exchanges. For example, interaction challenges include: (a) complexity/specificity (complexity of the range of interactive events vs. the precise specificity required for stable regulation of interaction); (b) context/content (a simultaneity shared in fluctuating moments vs particularized initiated action with contingent effects; (c) synchrony/differentiation (background of dyadic equilibrium vs. foreground of self-initiated infant activity; and (d) unconscious/conscious (background of automatized temporal organization vs. foreground of voluntary goal-directed activity). We unpack these dualities in the next few chapters, but for now, how do these apparent paradoxes play out and why are they necessary? We first look to the caregiver's mature capacities for interaction and how they are adapted when in interaction with infants.

Caregivers—parents, grandparents, aunts, uncles, siblings, and paid providers—most often possess wide repertoires of interaction scripts that frame the rules for appropriately using human communication. Most often, they also recognize that infants are just beginners in this dance of interaction, and that the caregiver must lead by modeling the structure of the steps involved. Research on the nature of this interaction burgeoned in the last 25 years or so. What follows is a brief summary of types of caregiver behavior; in the next chapter we unpack more of this literature.

Adult Caregivers' Skills

Caregiver responsiveness is still of great interest to those who study the effects of early interaction. In particular, *attachment theory* has received a great deal of attention. Proponents (Ainsworth, Blehar, Waters, & Wall, 1978) claim that a caregiver's consistent perceptions and accurate interpretations of infant behaviors, accompanied by appropriate responses to the infant's signals, nurture the development of a secure attachment to the caregiver (and secure infants make for well-adjusted adults). If the primary caregiver's responses are inconsistent or negligent, insecure attachment ensues and, in theory, results in a poorly functioning adult.

Isabella and Belsky (1991) examined early interaction for this sort of responsiveness. They observed mother–infant interaction at infants' third and ninth months, and found that mothers who responded smoothly—reciprocally and synchronously—had infants who developed secure attachments. Conversely, mothers who failed to time the structure of interaction well—who were either too aggressively interactive or not responsive enough—had infants who developed one of two insecure attachment styles: insecure-avoidant or insecure-resistant.

The insecure-avoidant infant, who was not distressed when mother left the room, interacted with a mother whose responses were too intense, intrusive, or ill-timed. For example, when Peggy shows signs of tiring of a game of peek-a-boo—shifting her posture and gaze to a toy and away from Ellen—Ellen continues to insist on playing the game until Peggy cries and/or goes to sleep. This is an infant who is thwarted from regulating the interaction and thus shuts down the game.

The insecure-resistant infant, who became highly distressed when mother left the room and did not calm down on mother's return, interacted with a mother who was underinvolved and inconsistent. In this case, as Ellen approaches Peggy to change her diaper, Peggy is alert and ready to interact following Ellen with her gaze and vocalizing. Ellen either fails to respond, or responds briefly at one changing and not at all in another. In either case, the infant is frustrated by her inability to connect and develops angry, ambivalent perceptions of the relationship.

Is insecure attachment the kiss of death for later relationships? Infant attachment apparently is predictive of attachment interactions later in childhood (Bartholomew & Horowitz, 1991; Sroufe, Egeland, & Kreutzer, 1990), but the stability of attachment styles into adulthood has not been demonstrated adequately.

Nevertheless, the first attachment is likely to have long-term effects on social functioning well into childhood.

Thus far, we have examined responsiveness in a very general sense. However, there is reason to believe that caregiver speech is particularly important to the infant's later language and learning skills. Certainly, parents use a special form of language that had been dubbed *motherese.* (I prefer the more inclusive *caregiver* but it doesn't make for a catchy label.) More recently *ACL,* or adult–child language, has become the preferred term. Cross-culturally, although not universally, early ACL employs special prosodic features, including higher pitch, more varied pitch, and exaggerated intonation (Gleason, 1993). Of course, all this is functional. Recall that the infant is more responsive to higher frequencies and prefers contrastive patterns. The more contrast found in intonation, the easier it is to discover the important distinctions.

Apparently, later parental speech input affects vocabulary growth in particular. The more parents name shared objects, the greater the variety of words infants use at 18 months (Smith, Adamson, & Bakeman, 1988). Sheer amount of parental speech is related to the size of the child's vocabulary in the second year (Huttenlocher, Haight, Bryk, Seltzer, & Lyons, 1991). Mothers who ask questions and confirm child responses apparently influence their child's interest in language and syntactic ability (Yoder & Kaiser, 1989). In the next chapter, we explore the variations found in parenting. Now we turn to infants' abilities to enter into the human conversational milieu.

Infant Interactive Capacities

Infants' repertoire for interaction include vocalization, gaze, and smiling—the observable activities with which we are most familiar. Other more subtle abilities include attention to adult speech and gesture, and synchrony of movement with adult behavior.

One of the few instruments we have to assess neonatal interaction responses was developed by T. Berry Brazelton (1973). A pediatrician and activist for universal parental leave, Brazelton's purpose was to better predict neurological health because he suspected that infants' nervous systems were tuned for interaction. And indeed, the BNBAS (Brazelton Neonatal Behavioral Assessment Scale) does perform well as a neurological measure, but it also has been used very successfully as an intervention to demonstrate to new parents the important effects of early interaction. The BNBAS measures newborns' neurological responses, as well as their orientation and behavioral responses to humans. Summarizing his observations, Brazelton (1974) concluded that healthy infants must be able not only to pay attention to their environment—most specifically, mother or significant caregiver-—but must also be able to withdraw their attention.

What he observed was a cycle or pattern: a gradual buildup and gradual decrease of attention. At the peak of the buildup, he noticed a difference in the neonate's behavior with mother as opposed to objects. With a person, the newborn will intersperse excitement with efforts to control that excitement and thus stay alert. These strategies include bringing the hand to the mouth to suck, sucking on the tongue, yawning, or holding onto the hands or another part of the body to decrease the tension buildup (Brazelton, 1974).

Brazelton (1974) hypothesized that the mother provides a "holding" framework (with hands, eyes, voice, smile) in which the infant learns to contain self, control own responses, and attend for longer and longer periods. Apparently, these strategies to control excitement are critical to the infant's neurological health as well as to attachment. An infant who cannot attend to the interaction input provided by the caregiver will quickly extinguish the motivation of the adult to interact. Beyond the need to successfully attend to social interaction, infants must also signal their needs.

One of the first vocalizations the infant produces that is a never-fail attention getter is *cry*. Cry not only calls the adult to the helpless newborn, but it can inform the alert parent to the infant's state (Wolff, 1966). Parents respond to infant cry with intuitive parenting responses such as soothing (contact, rhythmic rocking, singing) and cry-prevention strategies. Infants vocalize beyond the cry, but most early vocalizations are vocalic—mostly cooing, vowel-like sounds—as opposed to the adult-preferred syllabic or speechlike sounds.

One of the more successful ways to regulate interaction early in life is the use of *eye contact* to initiate or terminate contact. The neonate will search for a face when hearing speech, and will withdraw gaze when overwhelmed. The control of gaze allows the infant to regulate social visual contact, which is critical to human interaction. But gaze is an attachment behavior as well and serves a signal function in human interaction (Stern, 1974)—particularly important in the regulation of turn taking. Regularities in mother–infant gaze are similar to those found in adult conversations, which suggests that the patterns first seen in attention-regulating behavior constitute an early property of human interaction that continues throughout life (Jaffe, Stern, & Peery, 1973).

Smiles are powerful social stimuli for humans, and parents will work hard to elicit them. However, the newborn smile seems to bear no relationship to any external cause. From 2 to 3 months, infants will smile to a number of stimuli, including the human face. By 3 months, infants smile more to familiar than to unfamiliar people (Camras, Malatesta, & Izard, 1991). Blind infants start to smile at about the same age as sighted babies (Freedman, 1974), giving support to the notion that smiling is part of normal maturation. At this very early stage (2–3 months), the smile is most probably a response to an internal state rather than a voluntary response to interaction (Fogel, 1982). Now, how do all these capacities serve interaction?

Interactive Behavior and the Beginning of Turn Taking

The newborn brings structured responses to interactions with people, and those interactions begin to influence and change the newborn's innate responses. One of these structures has to do with the uncanny capacity infants demonstrate for imitation and matching behaviors. Meltzoff and Moore (1995) found that 12- to 21-day-old infants imitated four adult gestures: lip protrusion, mouth opening, tongue protrusion, and finger movement. The specificity of the imitation suggested a "generative matching mechanism" (p. 77). Furthermore, when the researchers imposed a temporal gap between adult gesture and baby imitation (by introducing a pacifier during the gesture presentation), the infant was still able to imitate. Meltzoff and Moore claimed that this imitation involves making an internal representation of self and other.

Other researchers found that in the first 4 months of life, babies match or synchronize behaviors with the caregiver quite predictably (Condon & Sander, 1974; Stern, 1974). They move their arms, legs, and heads in synchronized rhythm to adult speech or gesture. Trevarthen (1979) would say that infants are born with a dialogic mind and that the "primary intersubjectivity" he observed is based on a motive to interact. Meltzoff and Moore would agree that the infant makes early distinctions between self and other, and has intentions in interaction. There are those who do not concur.

Barresi and Moore (1996), skeptical of neonatal imitation, claimed that interactive experiences are necessary before the child can "get" that others are similar to self. Children need interaction in which they can observe from their own perspectives and, simultaneously, observe reactions from Others' third-person perspectives. Gergely and Watson (1999) would attribute the effect to "social mirroring," which means that it is the adults who match infant behavior, exaggerating and thus marking it for the infant. Tomasello (1999) would say that infants may understand that their actions produce results but they understand little of how this works. It is likely that infants are predisposed to matching adult behavior, but show no sign of varying the imitations for interaction effect until later in the first year.

What is not in question is the influence a caregiver has on how well the infant capitalizes on these inborn propensities to interact. Although the infant may be sensitive to the structure of protoconversation, it is the adult who must provide the structure. Fogel (1982) examined the structure of gaze, smile, and cry in early interaction and found that, at 2 months, gaze is one of the few behaviors for which infants have some control. Most of the time, the caregiver is responsive to infant changes in a "pseudo-dialogue" (Kaye, 1977; Newson, 1977) in which mothers try to fit their behavior into the infant's ongoing patterns. It is likely that a mother's behavior is shaped by her infant's needs (Gewirtz & Boyd, 1977) in the early months, giving the infant consistent patterns for learning how to converse.

What seems most likely is that infants and adults mutually influence each other. Although they enter the conversation with wildly different skill levels, they do manage to influence each other's behavior. Vocalization and speech-related behaviors have been observed to match consistently across infant–caregiver dyads.

Cappella and Greene (1982) endorsed Stern's (1974) discrepancy-arousal theory to explain the nature of the mutual influence that has been found for "vocal behavior, body motions, facial displays, eye gaze, and generalized involvement" (Cappella & Greene, p. 91). They suggested that "arousal is a function of the discrepancy between the infant's cognitive schema (or expected state) and the mother's behavior (an observed state)" (p. 96). If there is little or no discrepancy between the two, no arousal occurs; moderate discrepancy is moderately arousing and thus pleasurable; and extreme discrepancy is highly arousing and thus unpleasant. When changes in arousal fall within an acceptance region, behaviors should be reciprocated; when changes are excessive, behaviors should be compensated. Because expectations are "set by personal preferences and individual differences" (Cappella & Greene, 1982, p. 97), we must assume that they are set on the basis of previous interaction and that learning these expectations begins immediately in the newborn.

For example, if Peggy is greeted at her first feeding with Ellen's soothing voice and eye contact, which Ellen repeats at each feeding, Peggy may respond with reciprocal eye contact and will form an expectation for eye contact in that situation. If Ellen is distracted on Day 5, and is trying to pay attention to a phone call while nursing, Peggy is likely to respond by crying in compensation to the extreme discrepancy from what she expected. Cappella and Greene (1982) applied this theory not only to infant–adult interaction but to much of the moment-to-moment influence of expressive, largely nonconscious, behaviors between adult partners. However, among adults, there are multiple layers of influence at play, some of them symbolic and highly conscious. When do these additional sources begin to be available to the developing child?

By 9 months, a new understanding emerges for infants; they begin to perceive their own roles as actors capable of achieving ends through means. At this point, infants no longer automatically match behaviors (Thomas & Martin, 1976). Although we begin life predisposed to match interactions (smiling, vocalizing), we then apparently shift to fewer matching behaviors, and later return to reciprocal matching but with the addition of intent. The 9-month revolution has been noted by many, but interpreted in a variety of ways. Rochat and Striano (1999) referenced this as the emergence of secondary subjectivity when infants begin to take an "intentional stance" (p. 5) in their interactions as a partner who can reciprocate as well as cooperate with others.

The 9-month revolution may be the outcome of what Sander described as the shift from biosocial to psychosocial interaction. I find it useful to think that Sander's two levels correspond to Vygotsky's two lines of development, which ultimately merge: natural-psychological and cultural-psychological. That is, the child comes into the world equipped to make sense of it by perceiving distinctions among stimuli, but fairly rapidly becomes a part of the rich, symbolic set of sense-making tools (language and other patterns) already in use in the culture. That immersion, fostered by social and physical needs, becomes the medium for cultural-psychological development that combines with natural-psychological development (nurture plus nature) to result in new forms of thought and action.

All of the innate capacities we have examined must be part of a biological preparedness for interaction, but no single one of them reflects any conscious expectation for interaction. The shift to a cognitive representation requires "the coordination of at least two sensorimotor systems into a higher-order skill" (Fischer & Corrigan, 1981, p. 269). Apparently speech is one system well suited for coordination with others. The two activities of audition (sensory) and vocal production (motor) are naturally coordinated in the speaker. The contrast between two actions in one system fosters self-regulating feedback. This sort of system is not available until around the sixth month, when the infant can begin to produce articulated speech. In chapter 3, we delve further into how the infant uses this system between 6 and 9 months to build representations, and thus participate more fully with the increasingly distinct Other.

SUMMARY

We have examined some of the literature regarding infant capacities and the nature of early human development. Beyond the notion of adualistic confusion lies natural dualism, and much of the recent research on infant behavior supports the idea that human infants make distinctions and perceive contrasts from the start.

Our nature is steeped in nurture and thus we cannot legitimately separate the two. Human interaction and symbolic thought are thoroughly grounded in the physiology of brain and speech. However, without interaction these genetic endowments fall on fallow ground and fail to bloom into mature human communication capacity. We have sorted out some of the predispositions that mature in the first year, and some of the interactive forces that influence individuation. The closing section of this chapter anticipates the content of chapter 3 by providing some groundwork regarding interaction. We examine the basics of interactive behavior—the caregiver's and the infant's capacities and performances that bring them together—in turn taking and the foundations of conversation.

Ideally, it probably does take a village to raise a child. But in a pinch, one solid, responsive, caring adult can provide the necessary interactive structure for one developing child. Next we look to the structural makeup of this interaction, and to the origins of internalization and individuation.

NOTES

9. Voluntary recall is apparently mediated by symbols; semiotic memory is the type that can be called forth purposefully. Certainly other types are less symbolically mediated but are also at the whim of chance association.
10. The term *language,* although often used to refer to human communication, is too limiting to capture the nature of the dynamic at the root of dialogue and dialectics. To be more specific, I use the label *spoken symbolic communication.*
11. Thanks to Kessen, Haith, and Salapatek (1970, p. 287) for the pithy labels for the three foundational theories of early human perception. Freud's narcissism refers to absorption with the self to the exclusion of others. Piaget's solipsism refers to perception that references only the self and one's own position in the world to the exclusion of others' positions.
12. I owe this suggestion, and the link to "flow," to Michael Lewis (1995, p. 113).
13. The paradox of control is that, most of the time, although we are controlling our experience, we are worried about losing control of experience. That is, we fear lack of control, but also dread the constant effort and worry of the act of controlling—except when we are in the state of "flow."
14. The effects of nasalization on vowel sounds are audible in cases of severe cleft palate.
15. The fact that the response to faces is first subcortical, and then cortical, would suggest that the response is first involuntary and then becomes more a matter of voluntary choice.

Around the corner of the house, Ellen suspected she would find Nan tormenting Peggy, because she could hear Peggy's wail announce her displeasure. As Ellen turned into the backyard, she saw Nan walking away from Peggy with the pink rubber ball they'd been vying for all day. "Nan, could you give your sister a turn?" "But she's had it a loooong time." Yeah, a few seconds I'm sure, thought Ellen as she retrieved the ball, tucked it in her pocket, and picked up Peggy.

But oddly, Peggy was wriggling in her arms and slippery from the wading pool to boot. Awkwardly, Ellen started toward the stoop to set her down. As she had almost reached it, Peg slipped from her arms, hitting her head on the side of the porch. Horrified, Ellen reached for the howling Peg, but stopped in mid-motion, frozen by Peg's expression. Peggy's face was still contorted from the pain, but a second emotion was taking over—an odd, distant, dismissive look—a look Ellen had seen before, but not on a 3-year-old. Ellen continued reaching with a softer expression, but Peggy rolled away from her and slowly meandered toward Nan. Trust had been broken, and Peggy had removed herself somehow. As Peggy had fallen into her ability to manage her emotional response, Ellen had fallen from grace as all-powerful Mother.

Chapter 3

Cocreating Self and Other: Influence and Reciprocity in the First 2 Years

> Human beings are discourse. That flowing moves through you whether you say any-
> thing or not. Everything that happens is filled with pleasure and warmth because of
> the delight of the discourse that's always going on.
>
> (Rumi, quoted in Barks, 1995, p. 76)

MUTUAL INFLUENCE

The interaction we have noted in the first months of life does not necessarily constitute
a relationship, but instead more of a discourse. Rumi's discourse refers very generally to
interaction, human commerce. Dialogue is a specialized form of human discourse that
involves not only the coregulation of turns, but the negotiation of meaning. In dialogue, we engage each other in gesture—touch, facial expression, head and limb movement— as well as in speech. A relationship, however, implies a degree of knowing the
unique partner in terms of what distinguishes that person from self and others; this sort
of knowing requires not only time but symbolic capacity.

The infant's social milieu is limited, usually to parents and perhaps grandparents, although the cultural variations on early matrices vary a great deal. For example, Israeli children raised in a kibbutz typically have many more adult as well as
peer interactants, even at the age of 3 months, than do American children (Lewis,
1987). For now, we focus on adult–child interaction; in later chapters, we return to
the effects of peer influence.

To understand the nature of this early dialogue between child and caregiver, we
examine the caregiver's influence on the child, the child's influence on the caregiver, and the nature of reciprocal influence. These early dialogues affect and are affected by all the modalities available to the human child for solving developmental
tasks: action, emotion, goal orientation, and cognition (van Lieshout, Cillessen, &

Haselager, 1999). We conclude with a look at the developmental milestones of the first 18 months.

In the previous chapter on physiological foundations of communication, we did not address on the large body of literature on the physiology of feelings or emotions. Yet, "emotion is an ongoing quality of conversation" (Planalp, 1999, p. 11) and as such is characteristic of all dialogue. In this chapter, we begin to incorporate some of the material on emotion as it pertains to interaction. We explore the entryway of dialogue that culminates in the halls of human relationship.

Hartup (1985) made a useful distinction between interactions and relationships; the former are meaningful encounters and the latter are "aggregations of interactions between individuals that persist over time and that involve distinctive expectations, affects, and configurations" (p. 74). That is, relationships are built on sets of interactions, mostly dialogues, that take on a particular flavor or pattern. To build a relationship would seem to require cognitive capacities that are unavailable to the infant, such as voluntary memory to build those expectations and an understanding of consequences. In this chapter, therefore, we also explore some of the cognitive achievements of the first year—their reliance on dialogue as well as their contributions to creating relationship.

To make the case that individuals are "producers of their own development" (Lerner & Wall, 1999, p. 7) by way of dialogue, Brandstadter (1999) proposed four lines of early development that produce an individual capable of relationship:[16]

1. The capacity to recognize action-outcome contingencies, behavioral consequences, and, ultimately, means-ends relationships or causation.
2. The constitution of a semantically formatted self-concept, or a meaningful name.
3. The ability to regulate self—to evaluate, correct, and control one's own actions.
4. The origins of an identity structure that integrates the previous three processes.

I would add to Brandstadter's developmental markers:

5. The discovery of symbols and their gifts.

The beginnings of all these developmental paths may be found within the first 2 years. In this chapter, we use several terms to refer to the developing person. For our purposes, *child* will be used generally to refer to offspring of any age. However, *infant* and *toddler* specify different developmental stages; infants do not use symbols, whereas toddlers do. The symbol, a communicative and cognitive tool, gains its significance from the arbitrary agreements of users rather than some concrete connection to its referent (see the end of this chapter for details). The ability to apply such significance emerges around 18 months of age; thus, infancy is a time of learning how to signify. To map the labyrinth of the five lines of human development, we begin with the child's first influences.

Caregiver's Influence on the Child

Emotional Modality: Innate Parenting Behavior and Responsiveness

Parents, however terrified they may be of the responsibility for the new, tiny person in their lives, just seem to know what to do. When the infant cries, the caring adult cradles, rocks, walks—in general, provides strong body stimulation to soothe the infant. When the infant coos, parents make eye contact and respond vocally. These parental responses to young infants, up to 4 months, apparently are cross-cultural. Found in West German, Greek, Trobriand Island, and Yanomami parents, intuitive parenting behaviors seem to be natural responses to stable inborn characteristics the very young infant displays (Keller, Scholmerich, & Eibl-Eibesfeldt, 1988). What we do not know as much about is how fathers and mothers influence differently.

Much of the bonding behavior between parent and child has been described in terms of attachment theory (see chap. 2). In short, secure attachments between parent and child are related to interactional synchrony, or the coordination of action between the two. In the attachment studies, these "two" are mother and child; hence, the father's influence is studied only indirectly. Furthermore, the link between interaction and attachment is not necessarily a stable and predictive one. The emotional instability that has been observed over the first year of life has been assumed to be either a result of measurement error (Hubert, Wachs, Peters-Martin, & Gandour, 1982) or a reasonable response to the variety of interactions that infants experience.

One source of emotional variation could be the existing family system into which the child is born. Belsky, Fish, and Isabella (1991) studied relationships between attachment and three factors affecting mother and father: mental health, marital satisfaction, and harmonious interactions with the infant. From their observations of mother–infant interactions, Belsky et al. concluded that maternal factors account for infant stability, or a gradual decrease in negative infant emotionality. Paternal factors apparently are responsible for increases in negative infant emotionality. The authors suggested that it is the family system that affects the factors they assessed: psychological health, satisfying marriage, and smooth maternal interactions with the infant. For example, the father who is uninvolved, insensitive, and dissatisfied with his marriage may effect a system dynamic in which the mother is overinvolved and intrusive with her infant. (Note the assumption that the mother is the parent involved with the infant.) And, of course, multiple factors affect the family system: marriage relationship prior to the birth, individual characteristics and motivations for parenting, external stressors, and probably more. The child, then, enters and affects an existing system and in turn is affected by it. Mother–infant interaction is undoubtedly important and constitutive of their bond. Nevertheless, that interaction does not occur in a vacuum, but instead in a larger system of dialogue.

More recently, one of the basic premises of attachment theory has been questioned (Atkinson et al., 2000). In their extensive meta-analysis, the authors assessed 41 studies of the attachment/sensitivity link with 2,243 mother–infant dyads. They questioned the "internal working model" explanation for attachment, which hypothesizes the existence of innate cognitive structures that allow the child to form stable expectations for mother's behavior. They observed that infant expectations of mother's behavior, rather than being stable, do change over time. Specifically, Atkinson et al.'s data indicated that the greater the time between measuring maternal sensitivity and measuring infant attachment, the poorer the prediction. They concluded that the environmental change that occurs between the two measurements plays a larger role in attachment security than the supposed stability contributed by internal working models. Thus, the very young infant may be responding more to the immediate interaction than to an internal model that presupposes innate cognitive structures.

Attachment theory, then, would appear to provide a useful but incomplete explanation for the security of the child's bond to primary caregivers. What we can glean from the results of attachment research is that the very young infant (in the first 6 months) may not actually use an internal working model. In terms of parental influence, we can assume that healthy parents who are able to follow their innate parenting intuition, in the absence of interfering systemic factors (e.g., relational strife, job stressors, extended family expectations, postpartum depression), do want to guide their babies rather than train or ignore them. Although systems are not always optimally functioning to support healthy parenting, optimal parent–child interaction patterns may be learned from external systems such as health care teams and parent training programs.

Cognitive/Verbal Modality: Adult–Child Speech

Adults typically speak differently to children than to other adults. Speech to infants and toddlers—motherese or Adult–Child Language (ACL)—contains fewer words, is slower, is more repetitious, is higher pitched, and uses more exaggerated intonation. These same characteristics even appear in mothers' signs to deaf children (Masataka, 1992). The verbal content also is specialized. Most ACL is in present tense, concerning here-and-now events (Snow, 1977), and more often uses proper names rather than pronouns (Conti-Ramsden, 1989). According to Ferguson (1964), a variety of languages, from Arabic to Syrian, contain special words for use with children: kin names, nicknames, body parts, body functions, animals, games, and taboo subjects (as cited in Messer, 1994). Most of these terms simplify sounds ("Tummy" for stomach) or reduplicate parts of words ("Dada"). Further ahead in this chapter, we see that later in their first year, infants reduplicate their babbled sounds and thus the spoken input suits their early capabilities for speech production.

Thus, parents adapt their speech to the phonetic features that infants are genetically equipped to easily perceive and subsequently produce. But the meaningful dimension of sound—semantics—is entirely dependent on learning rather than innate preparedness. Adults must provide the words that will prove to be significant to interacting others. The more mothers refer to objects that they share with their infants, the greater variety of words their infants use at 18 months (Smith et al., 1988). Sheer amount of parental speech and child vocabulary size are related. In a study of parental effects on vocabulary growth from 14 to 26 months, Huttenlocher et al. (1991) found that the frequency of *specific* adult words is related to the emergence of those very words in the child's speech. Their data also confirm that girls generally have a speech advantage until about 2 years,[17] which then dissipates as language exposure becomes more significant.

Beyond semantic flexibility, syntactic sophistication is also affected by caregiver input. Yoder and Kaiser (1989) observed mothers' language style and changes in toddlers' language use between two time periods. The first observation was late in the second year (18 to 26 months), the second was 5 months later. Mothers who, at Observation One, used confirming responses and many requests for unknown information had children who were syntactically advanced and interested in conversation at Observation Two. The 2-year-old who has maintained an interest in conversation has undoubtedly acquired the basics of turn taking.

Action/Interaction Modality: Structuring Conversation

One of the most important contributions of the interactionists has been the recognition of scaffolding: the adult structuring of a communicative event to assist the child in learning about the rules and routines of the languaged culture. Lev Vygotsky (1962) coined the phrase "Zone of Proximal Development" (ZPD) to refer to the performance gap between what children can do without assistance and what they can do with the guidance of a more sophisticated interactional partner. For Vygotsky, the space between individual and assisted achievement is where learning occurs.

Bruner (1983) then extended that concept of the ZPD to his idea of LASS, or "language acquisition support system."[18] For Bruner (1975), these structures for meaning are first accomplished in contingency games, or "standard action frames" such as peekaboo and the like. In arranging these early speech interactions in routinized ways, parents give infants a dialogic format for early conversation that allows them, after many routine repetitions, to anticipate their contributions to conversation.

For example, at age 6 months, Peggy knows the peekaboo game. Ellen approaches Peggy, who has started to fuss and vocalize. She calls out Peggy's name in exaggerated intonation, drawn-out syllables, higher pitch on the first, lower on the second. She repeats this until Peggy establishes eye contact. Ellen then covers her eyes with her hands. At that point, attentive Peggy maintains eye contact and makes her body tense, almost quivering with anticipation. As Ellen releases her hands from her eyes and crows "Peekaboo!" drawing out the first and third syllables, Peggy's body tension releases, her eyes and mouth open, and then she smiles. Clearly, Peggy recognizes the structure, predicts the exciting ending, and performs her part in the game.

Turn taking can be considered a subset of the standard action frames that serve to structure interaction. Specifically, turn taking is a skill set peculiar to spoken conversation and yet predating language (Ervin-Tripp, 1979). Ervin-Tripp contended that the child's intrinsic interest in speech is sufficient to derive the rules of turn taking from the language environment. On the other hand, Snow (1977) claimed that parental influence is necessary for the child to learn appropriate turn-taking responses. We know that the child is predisposed to spoken communication, but how early are the rules for structuring that communication learned?

Bloom (1988) compared adult turn taking to more random adult behavior with 3-month-old infants. When the adult responded only after each infant vocalization (turn response), infants produced a greater proportion of syllabic sounds (compared to simpler vocalic sounds) and paused longer between vocalizations. The child gave the impression of more sophisticated speech (i.e., syllabic) in more clearly marked turns (by pauses). According to Bloom, adult turn taking stimulates the subcortical activity necessary to elicit infants' mimicry of adult speech; that is, turn taking stimulates early speech production. But what of the fact that specific rules for turn taking vary across cultures? These culture-specific rules for turns are learned much later than 3 months, but culture-bound speech practices exert some effects even in the first few months.

Cultural Variations

We know that some aspects of parenting are universal, such as intuitive responses to infant distress, and the vocal behaviors of ACL. Another universal feature of maternal behavior is engaging the infant in play with an object, a toy of some sort. Although the play itself is observed across cultures, the talk about the play varies. For example, French mothers carefully frame their nonverbal play with verbal formulations—talk describing the play—whereas African mothers do not (Rabain-Jamain, 1989). European mothers are more likely to stress the object of play and its properties, whereas African mothers tend to emphasize the relationships between people and social events.

Maternal responsiveness to infant attention-getting behavior also differs by culture. Richman, Miller, and LeVine (1992) observed that Kenyan mothers respond with physical behaviors, such as holding. Mexican and U.S. mothers responded to the same sort of infant behaviors (vocalizations, cry, or gaze) with more talking and looking to the infant. Richman et al. concluded that Kenyan mothers take on a calming, protective role, whereas U.S. and Mexican mothers assume a more educational role. It is useful to note that the authors found that education affected their results, particularly among the Mexican participants who achieved a wider range of educational levels than the other populations studied. The higher the educational level, the more talking was used as compared with simple eye contact.

Although maternal speech input demonstrates distinct cultural variations, semantically and syntactically, one feature seems similar across cultures. The most prominent feature of early ACL is exaggerated prosody: the music of speech. Prosody includes variations in pitch, tempo, and intonation; it is used not only to mark the meaningful aspects of syntax but also to suggest turn endings and express emotion. Grieser and Kuhl (1988) observed maternal use of prosody in three languages: German, English, and Mandarin Chinese. A tonal language, Mandarin exhibits more prosodic variation in any context. Nevertheless, Mandarin mothers adjusted the tempo, pitch, and duration of speech to their infants. Among the three languages, "motherese" was very similar despite differences in language forms; increased pitch, lengthened intonation contours, longer pauses, and shorter phrases all characterize the prosody of ACL. When I described Ellen playing with Peggy, you undoubtedly heard in "Peekaboo" the lengthened intonation, highest pitch on the first syllable, dropping pitch on the second to signal the ending, and the pause to allow Peggy to perform her part. Evidently, mothers all over the world use this same sort of exaggeration with their infants.

Beyond the vocal signals we use to mark speech, mothers use particular speech sounds and words to convey what is culturally valued. Toda, Fogel, and Kawai (1990) compared maternal speech input to 3-month-olds in the United States and Japan. The U.S. mothers most often vocalized in response to their infants, whereas the Japanese mothers used more physical contact and less vocalization. Specifically, U.S. mothers used more imperatives and yes-no questions; Japanese mothers' speech used combinations and variations of nonsense sounds. Toda et al. concluded that the goals of Japanese mothers are to empathize with their infants and to acknowledge their distinctive babylike qualities. The goals of U.S. mothers, on the other hand, are to express their authority and to encourage individual expression and independence for the infant.

Some of the types of sentences, or syntactic forms, used by mothers seem universal; others are not. Bornstein, Tal, and Rahn (1992) observed mother–infant speech in several language cultures from infant's fifth month to the start of toddlerhood at 13 months. In that time span, mothers increased their use of direct statements and questions; their speech became more informative and less affective. According to these authors, one reason for that shift is that all infants become more interested in objects in the second half of their first year; thus, mother's information-salient speech meets that interest while fulfilling her goal of socialization. Nevertheless, there are some cultural variations. Japanese mothers, preferring an empathic style, continued to use more affect-salient speech than did the others. Argentinian mothers, favoring an authoritative style, used more direct statements. Mothers' goal is to enculturate their babies. To some extent, the spoken language skills for introducing the concepts of the culture are universal, but the way in which it is done can vary by both cultural mores and individual style.

Individual Variations

Caregivers' speech style is likely to affect variations in the child's focus, responsiveness, and, ultimately, on their early preferences for language use. Bayer and Cegala (1992) proposed that adults bring communicative predispositions to parenting. Although their research was with older children, I suspect these parenting tendencies begin to have their influence much earlier. Bayer and Cegala based their style variables on Infante's concepts of verbal aggressiveness and argumentativeness (Infante & Rancer, 1982; Infante & Wigley, 1986). They found verbal aggressiveness to be related to an authoritarian parenting style—demanding, unresponsive to child's needs, using unilateral messages. This style is negatively related to child's positive self-concept development. Argumentativeness was found to be related to an authoritative parenting style—encouraging, child centered, using reason and verbal give and take. Authoritative parents include the child's self as an issue for evaluation, but not necessarily in a negating fashion. Because communication style is believed to be relatively enduring, these predispositions could be identified in parenting programs before they become stable characteristics of parental style.

Socioeconomic Class Variations

Basil Bernstein (1971, 1973, 1977) hypothesized speech code differences among social classes that could affect the child's capacity for code use and code switching. A British sociolinguist, Bernstein defined two speech codes: elaborated and restricted. Elaborated codes are syntactically complex and semantically abstract; they allow explicit and contextually adaptive messages. Restrictive codes are syntactically simple, semantically condensed, and may rely more on nonverbal expression; they allow shortcuts to shared social meanings. For example, elaborated code between two friends engaged in a video game might sound like this: "But didn't we promise Liz we'd pick her up after her class?" "Well, yes, but I propose that we continue with this game and not interrupt it to fetch her. She won't think it's important." On the other hand, restricted code use for the same message might sound like this: "What about Liz?" "Ah, blow it off, no biggie." Bernstein (1977) asserted that members of the lower class would use restricted code exclusively, whereas members of the middle class could and would employ both types of codes, thus affording them more flexibility in expression.

There is support for Bernstein's theory. Although the tests were done with older children, we can surmise that the influence would begin early in the parent–child relationship. Middle-class mothers use elaborated, personalized code to control their children (Cook-Gumperz, 1973), and their children tend to base their own communication strategies on obligations of role and status (Turner, 1973). For example, Ellen would focus on Peggy's needs to guide her: "Peggy, I see you're interested in playing with your doll now, but we could come back to that after we shop." Peggy, trying to get what she wants, might reply: "I'm not done yet; I'm her mom and I have to dress her!" On the other hand, lower-class mothers use restricted, positional code, and their children prefer imperative strategies. In this case, Ellen would rely on her status to exert authority: "Peggy, put the doll away, you're going shopping with me." "Mom, you go by yourself; I don't want to." "I'm your mother; do what I tell you."

One criticism of Bernstein's work is that code use may be more a function of educational level than socioeconomic class. Recall that Bernstein performed his research in England, where class determines educational level to a greater degree than in the United States. However, it is possible that education could be a confounding factor in less limiting circumstances. For example, if Ellen were to be divorced or widowed, she could quickly become part of the lower socioeconomic class, despite her college degree. Would Peggy use restricted or elaborated code? My guess is that she would become fluent in both, as she moved to a neighborhood in which restricted code is in common use and yet maintained a close and consistent relationship with Ellen by way of elaborated code.

The obvious fact is that middle-class mothers are likely to have more time for interaction with their children than lower-class mothers do. That interaction may take the form of informal conversation or more formal reading sessions. Reading seems to minimize social class differences in mother–child interaction (Hoff-Ginsberg, 1991). In general, parents who have the time to converse and read with their children tend to adapt their speech for the needs of the child and to suit a variety of contexts. Parents who feel pressures of time and money tend to interact in very concretely defined roles and situations that allow them to use the language shortcuts available in restricted code.

Gender Variations: Mothers and Fathers

Most of the research on parent effects has been conducted with mother–child pairs, and thus we know quite a bit about mother's influence. *Mothers'* frequent verbal stimulation is related to toddlers' vocabulary growth at 13 and 24 months (Olsen, Bayles, & Bates, 1986). Of course, mothers vary in their speech styles. If a mother's interaction focuses on the referential (words for objects and events), her child is likely to specialize in word forms. If mother's style features the expressive (prosodic variation), her child is likely to emphasize intonation (Dore, 1974). Even so, most mothers are sensitive to their children's needs and capacities for communication and adapt to them. As children mature, mothers first model appropriate turn taking, then use questions to cue the expected response until children can create their own messages (Moerk, 1974). Mothers simplify their speech, structure learning opportunities, and shape possible responses. They also use the zone of proximal development by posing tasks that are just slightly out of reach given the child's current abilities (Heckhausen, 1987).

The question remains: Do *fathers* behave as mothers do with infants? Unfortunately, fathers suffer the limitations of cultural myths about their parenting skills (Parke & Sawain, 1981). For example, they are assumed to be less interested and involved, less nurturing, less caretaking, and thus less capable of meeting infants' needs. But Park and Sawain found fathers to be highly involved with their newborns—touching, kissing, and vocalizing as frequently as mothers did. The one difference they did find was in caretaking. Left alone, fathers fed their infants less than mothers did. Are fathers less active caretakers by preference, or are they at the mercy of the cultural myths? Lamb (1977a, 1977b, 1978, 1987) found that fathers and mothers are equally competent caretakers with newborns. Lamb suggested that as mothers spend more time in child care and become more attuned with their unique infant, fathers come to feel less competent to surmise their child's needs, and thus decrease their attentiveness and involvement.

Regardless of the source of the differences, fathers' characteristic interaction behaviors are distinctive. Mothers hold their babies to take care of them (feed, bathe, burp), whereas fathers hold their infants to play with them. Fathers are more physically playful with their infants, whereas mothers engage in more verbal play. Seemingly, mothers and fathers specialize somewhat differently[19] and thus provide another source of contrast for the child.

In terms of later verbal interaction, mothers tend to pose problems to be solved, while fathers prefer to give directions (Bellinger & Gleason, 1982; Masur, 1982). Fathers also seem more concerned with appropriate gender-role behavior in their children (Henshell & McGuire, 1986). Fathers encourage gender-stereotyped behaviors (Snow, Jacklin, & Maccoby, 1983), and in particular, are more consistent in reinforcing boys' use of gender-typed toys and behaviors (Sigel, 1987). As early as 1 year, but commonly by 18 months, fathers are concerned about appropriate gender-typed behavior. In later chapters, we look at some of the effects on identity.

Both parents are providing the scaffolding conversation for their children so as to encourage appropriate, socialized interaction—each parent seems to take on a specialized role. In general, fathers model physical play, authoritative guidance, and gender-role behavior appropriate to the culture. Mothers model verbal play, problem solving, and flexibility in response to individual needs.

Many infants will be born into a family system that already includes other children. The effects of *siblings* is covered in greater depth in later chapters, but we touch here on their early influence. Inevitably, when siblings greet a new arrival, they do so with some trepidation. Here is another needy child to draw on limited parental resources. Mothers of multiple children use less metalinguistic speech with them than do mothers of only children (Jones & Adamson, 1987), and will be more likely to interact with their infant in the presence of other siblings rather than one on one. Infants who are exposed to both siblings and peers spend more time interacting with their mother than with the other children. Furthermore, interactions with older siblings are brief, and siblings do not respond contingently as mothers do (Vandell & Wilson, 1987). Sensibly, the infant prefers the responsiveness mother can provide and will capitalize on these episodes. Even though younger siblings receive less maternal focus and language input, they may have the edge in acquiring turn-taking skills.

In triads consisting of mother–infant–sibling, infants take more turns than during one-to-one interaction with either mother or sibling alone (Barton & Tomasello, 1991). By 19 months, toddlers contribute their own turns in triadic episodes involving joint attention (Woollett, 1986). Siblings offer richness and variety to the young child's interactive environment. In contrast to the careful scaffolding that parents provide, older siblings will be less likely to meet the needs of "the baby" and will demand that the younger sibling adapt to them. Siblings begin to tease the toddler as early as 18 months, and the teasing increases and becomes more verbal and detailed in the second year (Dunn & Munn, 1985). Older siblings provide challenging situations to the young child; the toddler with siblings first learns to receive and respond to the "slings and arrows" of life in a protected environment.

Child's Influence on Caregiver

The other side of mutual influence in these early dialogues is the less communica-tively skilled but richly endowed child. We have examined the biological bases of in-teraction in terms of the infant's readiness for attending to the adult communication environment. Now we turn to the infant's and toddler's abilities for expressivity.

We have long assumed that the infant was at the mercy of adult influence. Lewis and Rosenblum (1974) were among the first to argue that the infant is also influen-tial. Most interactionists now acknowledge the reciprocal nature of mutual influ-ence. Does this mean that the infant intends to influence, or does so purposively? No, not at first. In the remainder of this chapter, we chart the trajectory of influence from nonstrategic behavior to voluntary, motivated action.

One point to keep in mind is that despite the fact that the studies reported here often conclude in generalities about infants and toddlers, each child is different and brings his or her own needs and tendencies to interaction. Some of these sources of difference have to do with demographics: sex, birth order, parent's marriage status, and sibling group characteristics. Other sources include the child's idiosyncracies: physical health, appearance, temperament, and neurochemical setup.[20] Although we acknowledge and occasionally comment on these factors, the main purpose of the book is to sketch the "average" developmental course. From that foundation, we can make more informed guesses about variations from the normative popula-tions that are usually the target of research.

Feeling States: Expressivity and Recognition

What does the infant feel? We assume that the newborn feels distress (pain, hun-ger) and perhaps interest (attention), but do these feelings arise from affect, emo-tion, mood, or temperament? We look first to definitions, then to theories about infant expressivity. *Affect* is a general term used variously to refer to a range of feel-ing states from simple arousal to symbolic emotion. Emotion is a specific mental state referencing an affective experience, usually with symbols ("I feel uneasy"). *Mood* is a less specific but enduring affective tendency across experiences ("My mood has been pretty low for months"). And *temperament* refers to an enduring in-dividual affective bias ("She has an outgoing temperament").

Temperament is probably the broadest category of the feeling taxonomy, and re-fers to the most enduring quality. In his opus on the topic, *Galen's Prophecy*, Kagan (1994) defined temperamental constructs by "inherited coherences of physiological and psychological processes that emerge early in development" (p. 35). Some defin-ing behaviors reflective of temperament require maturation of the brain and its cir-cuitry, and thus not all are present at birth. However, in Kagan's view, we are born with predispositions or biases that favor certain affects. The two enduring tempera-ments he identified are inhibited (about 2 of every 10 infants), and uninhibited (about 4 of 10). Inhibited infants are both aroused and distressed by stimulation in the first year, and avoid unfamiliarity in the second year. Uninhibited infants are re-laxed at 4 months and relatively fearless later on. Kagan did not imply that shy infants are doomed to an isolated life, but he did suggest that "initial emotional reactions to new knowledge are influenced by temperamental processes" (p. 11).

Support for Kagan's theory comes from a longitudinal study in which the child's temperament in the second year of life was predicted by feeling state measures early in the first year (Izard, Lawler, Haynes, Simons, & Porges, 1999–2000). Izard and his colleagues concluded that measures of feeling states in the first few months of life provide clues to the child's later personality. I would add that reliable measures of affective functioning may also provide clues to the quality of child–caregiver interaction, and possibly forestall failures in attachment formation.

Consider the effect of the child's temperament on caregiver. "Difficult" infants (easily distressed) do not respond to parents' intuitive strategies for calming their distress, thus straining initial social interaction and inhibiting the natural support the parent wants to offer (Papousek & Papousek, 1990). Such a crushing effect on parenting increases the likelihood of interaction failures and, eventually, syndromes of neglect and abuse. Papousek and Papousek suggested intervention programs, such as the parent training based on Brazelton's measure of neonatal social responses (1973), to restore the intuitive resources of the parents and initiate the cycle of parent–infant communication.

Although infants do display individual differences in their reactions to novelty and frustration, those early predispositions are then subject to social influences. Calkins and Fox (1992, 1994) studied children from birth to 2 years and found that early reactivity interacted with attachment processes. Infants who were most likely to cry when presented with novel stimuli were also those more likely to be classified as insecure-resistant at 14 months *and* were more the most inhibited 2-year-olds in their study. Calkins and Fox concluded that caregivers are faced with choices when a child has a low threshold for novelty; they may reinforce, ignore, or intervene. Each response pattern may produce a different outcome for the child. (Calkins & Fox, 1994).

We expect children to have temperaments that may bias them toward attending to some feeling states over others. But then, beyond that predisposition to either meet the social world head on or to shrink from it, what do infants express? Much of the research on expressivity uses the term *emotion* to refer to the states expressed, but this is an inaccurate term for what the infant expresses. For clarity, we will distinguish affect from emotion.

Affect is considered the more general term. Frijda (cited in Anderson & Guerrero, 1998) described "affect as 'the irreducible aspect' of emotion" (p. 5). Central to much of later emotional experience, affect consists generally of feeling either pleasant or unpleasant, positive or negative. As well, early responses are generally approach or withdraw, interest or fear.

On the other hand, *emotion* refers to specific "internal mental states that are focused primarily on affect" (Ortony, Clore, & Foss, 1987, p. 325). If emotions are internal mental states, then some development is necessary for their use. Affect, however, is present from the start; it is more "phylogenetically and ontogenetically primitive than emotion " (Batson, Shaw, & Oleson, cited in Anderson & Guerrero, 1998, p. 5). Planalp (1999) summarized process theories of emotion and finds five common components to all conceptualizations of emotion: "(1) objects, causes, precipitating events, (2) appraisal, (3) physiological changes, (4) action tendencies/action/expression, and (5) regulation" (p. 11). The distinctive features for our purposes are appraisal and regulation.

Newborns, although they certainly feel, just as certainly do not appraise events or choose emotions, much less regulate them to any degree. Thus, it would be safer to say that the infant expresses affect in response to feeling states, whereas the experience of emotion requires the capacity to appraise a situation symbolically and to make distinctions among named feeling states that take on different shades of meaning.

At birth, pain elicits distress expressions, novelty elicits interest expressions, and offensive odors elicit disgust expressions. There is a "natural concordance" (Izard & Malatesta, 1987, p. 508) between feeling and expression in these early affective behaviors; a congruence between the internal feelings and the external affect signs. Izard and Malatesta asserted that this concordance is an innate preadaptation that serves to gain attention to the infant's needs. However, there are other theoretical explanations.

Haslett and Samter(1997) provided a summary of the theoretical positions regarding emotional development. The first could be labeled innate affect, and suggests that innate feeling states are signaled by specific facial displays that reflect feeling states until children learn to mask or control them (Izard & Malatesta, 1987). The second is attachment theory, which claims that affective signals are activated by a biological capacity for motivated, goal-directed bonding behaviors (Bowlby, 1973, 1980). The third is cognitive constructivism, which maintains that early feeling states are limited to distress or nondistress, and that distinctive expressions rely on some minimal cognitive development (Sroufe, 1979a, 1988, 1989). The fourth and final is a relational systems approach, which proposes that change in affect expression occurs as a result of interactions among aspects of the infant's system states: physiology, cognition, behavior, and social environment (Fogel & Thelen, 1987).

All of these theories are supported by research, and they are not necessarily in contradiction. It is likely that infants' earliest expressions are reliable indicators of their internal states, that their interactive expressions do serve to bond them to their caregivers, and that some relational learning is necessary for the development of distinctive, emotional expressions. The relational approach is the most integrative in terms of taking into account all sources of change in the infants' expressive system.

Prior to the development of speech, infants most often display indicators of their internal states by facial expression. Whether these indicators are reliable reflections of discrete emotions is a matter of controversy (Camras, Sullivan, & Michel, 1993). However, adults do draw conclusions from infant expressions. It is important to keep in mind that what the infant is feeling may not be the same state the adults identify. According to Abe and Izard (1999), adult-interpreted interest, joy, sadness, and anger account for 95% of infants' expressions, and each functions adaptively. Joy invites social interaction and attachment, interests in change and movement guide exploration and foster cognitive development, sadness elicits empathy and support, and anger empowers the infant to create change and develop voluntary behavior.

Abe and Izard also sketched the role of affect in developmental milestones, including reciprocal interaction and attachment formation. In the development of synchronized interaction, the infant's expressions signal the caregiver to either sustain the current interaction or to alter the dynamic; likewise, caregivers' emotion expressions initially demonstrate the appropriate exchange. A number of studies note that depressed mothers display a restricted range of expressions and appear less attuned to their infants' expressions. In turn, their infants are generally listless and socially withdrawn.

As caregivers and infants repeat these interactions, the result is the formation of an attachment bond. According to Abe and Izard, the single most important expression to attachment formation is the social smile—the smile we employ to respond to another person. In the first few months, the smile is indiscriminately produced to any pleasing stimulus, but the infant becomes more selective in the first year and, increasingly, the attachment figure is the recipient of the approachable social smile. According to Bowlby's theory, the smile is not the only expression that stimulates parental responses. Fear elicits protection, anger deters abandonment, and sadness invites comfort: "Infant affect serves to keep the caregiver ever present, an important evolutionary feat since infants cannot survive otherwise" (Faude, Jones, & Robins, 1996, p. 233). Again, note that the infant does come to signal discrete feelings within the first year, but most are not innate. In contrast to Abe and Izard's conclusions, Camras et al. (1993) found that adult judges could not reliably discriminate discomfort, anger, or sadness in 7- to 9-week-old infants, so it seems likely that these, like the social smile, either require maturation or are learned expressions, rather than being innate and discrete as Izard (1994) would claim.

Sroufe (1979a) also argued against the notion that newborns have discrete feelings. He proposed that three very general feeling states are present from birth: wariness-fear, rage-anger, and pleasure-joy (as cited in Lazarus, 1991). According to Sroufe, we enter the world with some basic reactions, but emotional life becomes much more complex in early development as the child copes by avoiding or approaching sources of distress or pleasure.

Although young infants use similar facial expressions to those we label surprise, disgust, and fear, we cannot be certain that their experiences are the same as the ones that we link with those labels. However, there is evidence of a set of facial expressions that are universally recognized in adults by a significant proportion of subjects. Although controversy exists about the list (Izard, 1994), it may include interest, joy, surprise, sadness, anger, disgust, fear, and possibly shame or shyness. Perhaps we are equipped to respond to the vicissitudes of life in ways well adapted to the types of bodies we share. Until we encounter all of these various obstacles and shocks, we may need only a few responses to the relatively cushioned life of an infant. Although controversy remains about exactly when and how children acquire discrete emotions, few would argue with the principle that "biological and social forces gradually change full-face instinct-like expression to more restricted and controlled emotion signals" (Izard & Malatesta, 1987, p. 512).

Even if we do not know precisely what infants feel, we can reasonably expect that very young infants, attuned as they are to interaction, will be susceptible to contagion of affect. Planalp described "emotional contagion" in terms of "catching" the emotions of others from their expressions (1999, p. 62). This is similar to Langer's concept of empathy as "an involuntary breach of individual separateness" (1972, p. 129), or feeling a physical reaction in perceiving another's experience, such as feeling nauseous at the sight or sound of vomiting. As she pointed out, in animals empathy is unchallenged and always operative, but in humans it is often replaced by sympathy or some other response mediated by symbolic thought. Unfortunately, the distinction between perspective taking (seeing a situation from another's point of view) and empathy (feeling what another is feeling) is often muddled. Taking another's perspective is a cognitive process requiring socialized symbolic thought; empathy is an affective process involving physiological responses. And although mature humans are capable of both, they can get muddled in operation. Infant Peggy may cry from sheer empathy when her mother cries, feeling what Ellen feels. However, 10-year-old Peggy may know that Ellen is disappointed in the loss of a career opportunity, understand and sympathize with her, and then empathize when Ellen shows the disappointment in her face.

As we unpack the developmental milestones of the first 2 years, we see how affective behavior develops along with interaction and cognitive developments; that is, how the system functions as a whole.

Vocal Behavior: From Cry to Speech

We already know that infants orient to adults' speech, but what sounds are they making, and with what effect? Newborns surely cry, but they also vocalize. Most vocables in the first 6 months are vocalic (vowel sounds) but include nasals and bilabials (closed mouth sounds). A wider variety of consonants are available once the infant attains seated posture (Langlois, Baken, & Wilder, 1980; Yingling, 1981) around 6 months, and those new syllabic sounds (consonants plus vowels) are reduplicated in practice sessions. Much of this activity is for the child's own pleasure, but meanwhile the caregiver is listening and responding.

Early research on the infant's effects on parents (Gewirtz & Boyd, 1977) described the child's influence as "conditioning" the mother. Specifically, vocalizations of 2- to 3-month-old infants "reinforced" the verbal responses of mothers. The fact that mothers spoke to and smiled at their infants may as well be explained as the normal response of a socialized human to a new player who is giving all the signs of learning to speak and interact appropriately. Not surprisingly, mothers respond more enthusiastically when their infants begin to vocalize socially.

When asked to rate infants engaged in social vocalization, adults generally preferred infants who produced syllabic rather than vocalic sounds (Bloom & Lo, 1990). Syllabic vocalizations sound like spoken language and thus "frame the infant as a potential conversational partner" (p. 218). Exchanges in which infants use syllables that approximate adult speech are likely to be those in which the adult partner adjusts to the child as the child adjusts to the adult. That is, they are mutually influential and thus require coordination.

Timing and Expectations: Turn-Taking Routines

The structure of social interaction may be a part of our biological preparedness for communication. Within an hour or two of birth, infants coordinate their movements with adult speech, which Condon and Sander (1974) would call "entrainment" of infant body activity to the rhythms of speech. However, by the ninth month of life, this response has diminished, and infants match caregivers' behaviors only minimally (Thomas & Martin, 1976). Later in life, interactional synchrony is often a sign of healthy, enjoyable relationships. The early predisposition to synchronize social behaviors may be one of our instinctive behaviors, such as the walking reflex observed in the early days of life that then disappears until true walking is learned about a year later. Social interaction is an adaptive behavior for us, so we inherit early instinctive patterns to ensure our survival that then dissipate as our social behavior becomes more voluntary and self-regulated.

Trevarthen (1977, 1982) maintained that humans possess an innate ability for intersubjectivity; furthermore, he attributed motives to our earliest interactive behaviors. Such motives, he claimed, are internal processes through which infants may anticipate and interpret consequences. Although Trevarthen charted the growth of intersubjectivity in a clear, useful fashion,[21] his reference to such early intentions relies on a view of infant cognition that is unlikely, given the kinds of developments in cognition and self-regulation we observe later in the first year. A further test of the theory of innate motivations for reciprocity was undertaken by Murray and Trevarthen (1985). They concluded that 2-month-old infants can discriminate between television screens of mother interacting with them via live TV and a videotape of mother performing one-way interaction. This suggests that infants are interactive agents and behave as differentiated selves at 2 months. However, Rochat, Neisser, and Marian (1998) replicated that research and found no evidence of discrimination between live and taped interaction. These authors did not rule out the possibility of early interpersonal contingency, but instead suggested further research. Clearly, infants are sensitive to interaction, and simple intentions may be in use by 2 months, but we have yet to explain the underlying cognitive process.

We do know that young infants cannot retrieve a cognitive standard (say, an expectation) for comparison with a present stimulus (Kagan, Kearsely, & Zelazo, 1978). Hence, the first synchrony established in infant–caregiver interaction is more likely based on subcortical neural processes than anticipation of an established pattern. However, the shift to more strategic behavior does begin in the first year.

Goals: Successes and Failures

After the sixth month, infants begin to exert more control in conversations (Yingling, 1985). They begin with simple escape methods such as gaze avoidance, and build increasingly complex combinations of strategies, such as direct gaze plus loud vocalization plus increased proximity to caregiver (Yingling, 1990/1991). Caregivers' conversational strategies also changed between 6 and 9 months. Parents increasingly yielded to infants' resistance with apologies, requests for repairs, accounts, and reformulations in order to give expression to what they perceived to be the infants' agenda.

In one example (1990/1991, pp. 95–96), a mother had been trying to gain her 9-month-old infant's compliance to play the give-and-take game. In order to do so, she had to take away the rattle with which her child had been playing because it had been distracting the child from interacting. Let's call them by the names we know. Ellen had been trying to get Peggy to rock back and forth to her by chanting "Rock, rock, rock," but Peggy clearly was more interested in the rattle she'd picked up earlier. Holding out her hand, palm up, Ellen repeated the request, "Can I have the rattle?" five times in a row, with varied intonation. Peggy responded by pulling the rattle away from her mother and producing a loud, intense vocalic sound, "Aaaaah!" ending on raised intonation and direct eye contact. Ellen requested a repair to this obvious departure from good-interactant expectations: "Does that mean no?" Peggy quickly glanced to Ellen and as quickly away, simultaneously hitting Ellen on the arm with her rattle. Ellen acknowledged Peggy's complaint with "Peggy, you little stinker" and a hug.

Conversation analysts have labeled a sequence like this a "misapprehension sequence" consisting of a request for repair, clarification, and acknowledgment (Jefferson, 1972; McLaughlin, 1984). Mother and infant are negotiating relational realities in this early type of conversation, or protoconversation, by playing the boundary between the adult's established interpretive procedures for interaction and the infant's increasing need for effectiveness. It is in the failures that learning to negotiate occurs. In this case, the failure had to be either Ellen's will to structure the interaction, or Peggy's will to keep the rattle. Ellen persisted for a time, but like many a good mother, she allowed Peggy to take control of coregulating the interaction. We turn now to a few explanations of reciprocal influence.

RECIPROCITY IN PROTOCONVERSATION

The infant is particularly well equipped to deal with the temporal order of events, to make sense of sequential patterns. Sander (1977) viewed this ability as crucial to developing an understanding of the human social world. In his words:

> It is the domain of time and the temporal organization of events that provides the framework for the resolution of the paradoxes and the polarities which confront the developing organism in the biological system.... [T]ime in a properly organized system allows for a meaningful co-occurrence of paradoxical elements ... setting the stage for considerations of an ongoing context-content relationship. (p. 137)

What this implies is that the child must figure out not only the distinctions among discrete events, but also how they may be connected. The child can only produce one act at any one time (*content* of the dialogue), but must take into account other actions as *context* for that act. Thus, shared interaction frames, such as in the peekaboo turn-taking game, grow into reciprocal interactions in which meaning is negotiated and co-constructed. We next examine some of the early frames that lend themselves to the development of reciprocity.

Scaffolding and Scripts

The introduction of this concept by Bruner (1975) helped us to move beyond earlier explanations of infant learning as conditioned behavior to explanations that describe the framework for acquisition that is built in joint activity. Infants perceive patterned information that allows them to form scripts of how action, especially social action, works in their environment. In Schank's (1982) terms, the infant makes a "first discrimination" (p. 130) in setting up an indexing method for information input. In any set of items, one must come first (e.g., mother verbalizes child's name), the next is indexed in terms of the first (mother repeats the sound), and so forth (mother covers eyes). In infancy, these first scripts (e.g., Peekaboo) are initially introduced in highly structured contexts directed by adults (Nelson, 1986).

Gradually, infants adapt scripts over time, to correct them when they fail to predict, or to adjust them to features of new situations. When infants notice a discrepancy between the script they know from repeated patterns and the current event they experience, and they can adjust their behavior accordingly (say, hit mother on the arm rather than play the rocking game), then true expectation may begin. Nonvoluntary scripts, formed in subcortical neural rhythms, change to voluntary expectations, formed in higher cortical processes. Bever (1982) found evidence of such a neurological discontinuity from subcortical reflex control to more voluntary cortical control; it is this switch that is reflected in the developing infant's increasing control.

By way of scaffolding, satisfying social interaction also provides the raw material for the child's sense-making system. The child learns to interpret interaction from experience, but the usefulness of the experience will depend on the flexibility of the sense-making system. If scripts never failed, no flexibility would accrue. The wise caregiver provides opportunities for both success and failure; for motivation as well as challenge.

Joint Referencing

Reference is often thought of as one of the hallmarks of early symbolic behavior. However, referencing occurs before symbol use; gestures (nonvocal communicative expressions) and sounds stand for things even before the child can produce mutually significant words. This early referencing is a dialogue task; a problem of developing "procedures for constructing and using a limited taxonomy for distinguishing among limited arrays" of objects to which the child and cooperative caregiver relate in their interactive play (Bruner, 1977, p. 275). This sort of scaffolding provides the dyad with ways to differentiate among possible present items.

Bruner (1977) identified three aspects of early referencing: (a) *indicating*, which refers to "gestural, postural and idiosyncratic vocal procedures" to bring the partner's attention to something; (b) *deixis*, which refers to the use of "spatial, temporal and interpersonal contextual features of situations as aids in joint reference"; and (c) *predication*, which involves using spoken symbols to name events or things (pp. 275–276). These forms are presented in order of their complexity and degree of dependence on cognitive and linguistic achievements.

Indicating, being the simplest to accomplish, is practiced in the infant–caregiver pair. An early form takes advantage of the mother's almost constant eye contact when interacting with her infant. Mother typically tracks where her infant is looking to infer the focus of his or her attention (Collis & Schaffer, 1975). As early as 4 months, the infant can follow adult's line of regard when it is directed to an object removed from the child (Scaife & Bruner, 1975). *Deixis* is the ability of both caregiver and the older infant to "mark" for each other the object to which they wish to attend, by pointing, touching, and so forth. Thus, they are developing procedures for establishing joint attention, for having a common "topic" about which to interact.

Of course, this early sort of referencing has its limitations. Butterworth and Cochran (1980) found that infants, when following the mother's line of gaze when she is looking behind the infant, will search through about 40 degrees in their own visual field looking for the object, then give up. Beginning at 18 months, the toddler will succeed in searching the space behind him- or herself when the caregiver looks there, thereby showing recognition that contextual features are stable and may be perceived differently by two viewers. Butterworth and Cochran suggested that the infant assumes that his or her own visual field is shared with the partner, whereas the toddler does not. Later in this chapter we note that 18 months typically marks the start of symbolizing, and thus the beginning of *predication.*

Patterns of Interaction: Coacting and Turns

By 3 or 4 months, caregivers and infants use two patterns of interaction: a coaction pattern in which vocalizations are simultaneous, and a turnlike pattern in which vocalizations alternate between the two (Stern, Jaffe, Beebe, & Bennett, 1975). At this age, the coaction pattern occurs almost twice as frequently as the turn pattern, but all dyads observed were capable of both. In any play session, the pair produced several short "runs" of turn vocalizations, and several "runs" of coaction vocalizations. Stern et al. concluded that the coaction pattern is used mostly during the highest levels of arousal (positive or negative), whereas the turn pattern is more evident at midrange levels. Coacting, then, occurs at the extremes; either the infant is fretting while the parent murmurs in soothing tones, or infant and parent are laughing together.

Simultaneous vocal behavior is observed among many primates, including humans. When our feelings are aroused negatively, we all wail, moan, or shout together ("bad call!"); when they are aroused positively, we cheer, hoot, and howl together ("We're number one!"). On the other hand, when we wish to really hear others, know who they are, learn from their wisdom, or gain from their experience, we give up the conversational floor and listen. Turn patterns require self-regulation and a motivation to know; that is, they require us to quell strong feeling responses in favor of more cognitive activity. Turn-taking patterns increase over the course of the first year. I found that as infants increase the length of their vocal turns from 6 to 9 months, their caregivers decrease the length of their turns (Yingling, 1984). What I suspect is that caregivers scaffold their average turn length by producing sentencelike turns while the young infant listens; as the infant gains in both articulatory maturity and speech experience, he or she uses preferred sounds in longer repetitive runs, and the cooperative caregiver waits for an available turn-switching opportunity. Indeed, I found that infants often interrupted if their caregivers' turns continued longer than the infants' turns. Not only is the child gaining control of his or her own vocalizations, but increasingly regulating the flow of interaction as well.

Coregulation and Constituting Relationship

Fogel (1993) described the structuring role of the adult as participation "in the co-creation of consensual *frames* making the environment informative for the infant" (p. 109). These frames or structures carry themes of information. Frames should become relatively stable so as to allow the discovery of subthemes, or combinations of themes in different frames. Fogel proposed two types of frames necessary for cocreating such themes: consensual frames for rigidity and dissolution, and consensual frames for creativity and innovation.

The frame for rigidity may be the first to be useful for infant and caregiver; the peekaboo game is one example. Characteristic of frames for rigidity is a sameness, a motivation to avoid creativity. Although this serves early structuring of interaction and allows the infant to anticipate the rules of interaction, it can quickly lead to boredom or lack of pleasure. In the case of the young infant, when tiring of the peekaboo game, he or she will simply cease to respond. Later in development, the infant or parent may try a variation to this theme, but it continues to be rigid in terms of the expectations each party holds. These themes serve relationships by their very capacity for prediction—it is much easier to begin the creative portion of conversation after an initial, rigid greeting ritual such as "Hey, how ya doin'?" Only after the response "Not bad" can we add the information that could lead to a more creative exchange.

The frame for creativity, on the other hand, is "maintained by continued co-regulation" (Fogel, 1993, p. 114); that is, it is mutually negotiated and dynamic. This is where true reciprocity begins, and the work of constituting a unique *relationship* occurs, but this sort of coregulation cannot be sustained indefinitely. Relationships need the relief of rigid frames to break the intensity of creative frames; a balance of both is necessary for relationship maintenance. Innovation is jointly constructed on the fly, but we can choose particular frames for this innovation.

For example, if one of 6-month-old Peggy's favorite objects is a red rubber ball, she may spend a lot of time exploring its characteristics. When she is occupied with the ball, she may not want to engage with Ellen. Ellen can respect this wish, or she can intrude, take the ball, and substitute another toy. If she intrudes, Peggy probably will protest and fuss; the decision will affect their relationship. If Ellen waits until Peggy offers the ball, or drops it from the rim of her playpen, she affords Ellen the opportunity to enter the "red ball" frame. At this point, Ellen also has choices: She can simply hand it back (a give-and-take theme), she can roll it to Peggy (creating another play theme if Peggy rolls it back), she can bounce it (demonstrating another feature), or she can hide it and find it (displaying the object's permanence). And, of course, Peggy can respond in a number of ways, creating new paths for play. Let's say Ellen hands it back. Peggy might drop it from a higher position to see it bounce and, in turn, Ellen could take the cue and bounce it even higher. After a few variations, Peggy may grab the ball as it rolls near to her and roll it away again. Clearly, when the frame is not rigid, and both participants are willing to respond dynamically, the variations are theoretically infinite.

Negotiations, Narratives, and Self

The concept of coregulation is related to that of negotiation. In a reciprocal interaction, both parties negotiate what their contribution to the interaction will be; the negotiation is enacted and constituted by coregulation. Fogel (1993) described the continuously changing nature of such reciprocity in a simple example of a mother reaching to help her 4-month-old to a seated position: "The child is on his back on the floor and the mother takes hold of his hands, gently. She pauses expectantly and the child strenuously pulls himself upward against the hands, using his arms and legs to effect this. The mother then completes the infant's actions and pulls him to a sitting position"[22] (p. 256). Fogel described this episode in terms of the force exerted by both a mother and infant son as a continuously changing function of time. Neither partner knows in advance what the outcome will be or how it will be accomplished; it is determined in the communicative process. Gradually, the infant becomes aware of his own exertion as distinct from his mother's. As his exertion either exceeds or falls below hers, he experiences a heightened awareness of his control, or lack of it. In such dialogues, both self- and other contributions are clarified, and relationship becomes possible.

Based on the dialogical processes he observed in joint activity, Fogel (1995) proposed further that the prelinguistic self is constituted in relational narratives. *Narratives* are coherent stories that "unfold as part of the interpersonal process of telling the story" (Fogel, 1995, p. 120). There is an established body of literature concerning dialogic narrative (Bochner & Ellis, 1992; Gergen & Gergen, 1983; Goffman, 1974; Harre, 1988), but few, save Fogel, have examined the role of narrative in early development. Through dialogical processes we establish stable patterns called *frames*. Frames, as we know (see page 68), are "rituals, plots, or routines, regularities in the social process to which participants return, keeping the same overall pattern of coaction against a background of variability" (Fogel, 1995, p. 120). The self-identity is derived from its set of self-frames and the links among them (p. 121). These self-frames may be narratives or "stories"—including nonverbal patterns—one uses to recognize and maintain the sense of self.

Fogel (1995) argued that explanations of a coherent infant self, such as Neisser's (1991) concept of an ecological self, do not jibe with the reality of a later flexible and questioning self. The notion of an infant sense of core self rests on some innate cognitive representation of self that magically leaps from a unitary concept of self to a multiplicity of self sets. I would agree that although Neisser and others have given us useful conceptualizations of some developmental milestones, their idea of infant selfhood presumes the primacy of a private self, which conflicts with current conceptualizations of self as a discursive construction. If the infant self is also dynamic and relational, and able to construct narrative frames (nonverbally, at first) across encounters, then dialogue partners clearly contribute to the infant's developing. According to Fogel (1995), self–other dialogues have the same characteristics of verbal narratives. As young as several months, infants show very different patterns of action with different partners, and will repeat similar patterns with the same partner on repeated occasions. Each pattern of action "reflects a different dialogically constructed narrative of self-in-relation" (p. 132). We create a unique "story" for each particular relationship. Later, in the second year, a sense of self-identity emerges from comparisons among relational narratives. That is, the sense of self very much rests on relational dialogues, the narratives formed from those dialogues, and the capacity to contrast and compare pluralistic narratives. And this process continues throughout life, resulting in a dynamic and flexible self.

We turn now to some of the highlights of the first 2 years. We feature the kinds of discoveries that infants and toddlers make on the road to becoming a fully functioning relational self.

DEVELOPMENTAL MILESTONES OF THE FIRST 2 YEARS

At the beginning of this chapter, we set out five markers of early development that serve to ready the child for relationships, social cognition, and human society. We have examined the early stages of contingency behaviors and the possibility of self-regulation. As we chart the major achievements of the first 2 years, we take them in more or less chronological order, but note particularly the accomplishments leading to: recognizing causation, self-labeling, self-regulation, identity formation, and symbol use.

The Two-Month Revolution[23]

As we now know, newborns are especially sensitive to social stimuli and they are particularly attuned to people—what Rochat and Striano (1999) called an "*attentional*" *stance* (p. 4). Many of newborns' behaviors appear to have the goal of attending to people: self-calming in hand-to-mouth coordination, imitation, and exploring activity. At this early stage, infants are not explicitly aware of goals; their perception and action are basically the same. They perceive their actions; they act their perceptions.

Between 6 weeks and 8 weeks, a new position emerges: the "*contemplative*" *stance* (Rochat & Striano, p. 12). Now the infant truly smiles in response to social interaction; it is no longer simply reflexive. Rather than sitting in the corner and observing the party, the baby is now ready to participate. Crying and fussing peak at 6 weeks (Brazelton, 1962; St. James-Roberts & Halil, 1991), but the time spent in alert and awake states also dramatically increases (Wolff, 1987). Infants begin to attend to the world differently, through a more deliberate cognitive lens.

The first sense of shared experience, or *primary intersubjectivity*, develops in a dyadic context. One sign of this change is that infants' interest in faces transforms, from newborns tracking a facelike visual display to 2-month-olds systematically exploring facial features (Maurer & Salapatek, 1976). At this point, infants have shifted from noting changes in the larger overall shape (face vs. not face) to noting changes in the internal features (smile vs. nonsmile).

Rochat and Striano (1999) surmised that the 2-month-olds were beginning to uncouple the earlier link between action and perception. To test this, they presented 2-month-olds with a pacifier and seated them between two speakers that produced discrete synthesized sounds when the infants sucked the pacifier. A computer recorded the sucking pressure exerted and, when it went above a set threshold, the computer generated sounds varying in pitch. Infants who heard sound levels commensurate with the pressure they applied sucked more frequently just at threshold level, compared to infants who heard the same sound level regardless of pressure applied. Newborns subject to both conditions showed no difference in sucking pattern regardless of contingency. Rochat and Striano concluded that 2-month-olds explore the consequences of their own actions, whereas newborns do not.

By *4 months,* infants are developing a sensitivity to protoconversation, or interaction that is predictably structured so that both parties can participate. In a study comparing 2-, 4-, and 6-month-olds, 2-month-olds smiled and gazed equally whether engaged in structured or unstructured games (Rochat, Querido, & Striano, 1999). In contrast, by 4 months they smiled significantly more and gazed significantly less in the structured game than in the unstructured game. Recall that parents often scaffold the peekaboo game for infants, and that the game must have a predictable sequence of actions. When Rochat et al. mixed up the sequence, the 2-month-olds didn't really care as long as they were interacting. However, the 4-month-olds did notice: They smiled less, and increased their monitoring of the stranger, perhaps gathering information about this new game with new and unknown expectations for timing and structure. That is, they became sensitive to the structural demands for *protoconversation.*

At this stage, feeling states are also becoming more distinct in the service of interaction, and the infant is gradually becoming capable of effective expression. When a 4-month-old is restrained by the arm, he or she displays anger and looks at the experimenter's restraining hand (Sternberg & Campos, 1990). But a few months later, the 7-month-old looks with anger at the face of the experimenter. What happens in the meantime that leads the infant to look at another's face as a person capable of agency, rather than at the hand as an offensive object? Lazarus (1991) proposed that the older infant who reacts in anger to a person must also differentiate that person from self. When and how does this differentiation occur? It does so probably in the control of voluntary actions (as opposed to reactions), and speech play may be the suitable type of chosen action.

Achievements at 6 Months

Once infants have prepared for the structure of conversation, they develop speech, an instrument of reference, to serve the development of symbols. Throughout the first 6 months, the articulators are maturing, the larynx is descending, but speech will still be limited until the child can sit up without assistance (Langlois et al., 1980;

Yingling, 1981). Once the child sits erect, the respiratory system is in a speech-friendly position, such that the infant can begin to control subglottal pressure and thus prolong speech sounds toward conversational utterance lengths in the practice of babbling—speech play.

Vocalic speech (vowel-like) increases in variety from 4 to 6 months, then there occurs a shift to *reduplicated speech syllables,* including consonants. From 6 to 10 months, the infant practices using syllables in long strings of repetitions, at first of one type, then combinations of several syllabic types (Oller, 1980). For example, Peggy at 6 months might become enamored of the syllable /da/ and repeat it over and over in long strings with some pitch and duration variations: "Dadadadadada-dadaaaaadaaadada." This kind of practice assists the child's control of respiration and articulation. Just as Ellen is about to stuff a sock in the babbler's mouth, she may start to combine some of the syllables she has been practicing ad nauseam: "dadamumumudadadi." A shift in the nervous system occurs when infants make the change to syllables. Bever (1961, 1982) claimed that the shift from vocalic to consonantal sounds matches a shift from subcortical reflex control to more voluntary cortical control of speech. One explanation is that once the child can produce syllables, to elaborate those syllables requires analyzing differences among phonemes, and that demands cortical activity (Bever, 1982).

Further evidence of the link being formed between brain and speech comes from Elbers (1982), who suggested that infants cognitively grasp articulatory contrasts among phonemes and vary them with purpose; in other words, babbling is functional. I found that when infants babble alone, as they often do, they decrease the length of the repetitive strings of sounds and stabilize to a preferred mean length of utterance, or MLU (Yingling, 1984). Ferguson (1978) suggested that infants come to prefer particular speech sounds as well, and that they are used by the infant to link meaning with sound. According to his observations, infants use particular sounds in particular experiential contexts. What becomes of these preferred sounds in later months?

The 9-Month Revolution

The new features of the ninth month include *secondary intersubjectivity* and a triadic context (Rochat & Striano, 1999). Now, the infant and caregiver begin to engage *about* something and the third party to the triad is usually some object of play, a topic about which to dialog. The *intentional stance* is a position of understanding self and others as intentional agents. This is a rich and busy time for infants, characterized by triadic skills involving joint attention: pointing, gaze following, and social referencing. The social cognitive processes underlying these skills include understanding protosymbols, object permanence, and means-ends relations.

A general term often used to reference a set of triadic social skills, *joint attention* (Moore & Dunham, 1995) includes gaze following, pointing/following, communicative gestures, and social referencing. Tomasello (1999) found a consistent ordering of such tasks across children. First, they shared and checked adult attention (looking to adult during joint engagement), then they followed adult gaze (following adult attention to distal objects), and, finally, pointed (directing adult attention to distal objects). In Tomasello's view, the special way that human infants identify themselves with other persons is in the recognition that the other is "like me" (p. 307). Furthermore, it is the "infants' understanding of their own intentional actions" (p. 310) that stimulates a new understanding of others as intentional agents.

As early as 6 months, babies follow a change in the attention of their partner to find an interesting sight (Butterworth, 1995). By 9 months, infants can follow mother's pointing gesture to an "away" position (away from baby and to the opposite side of mother), but not reliably to "forward" (ahead of both) or "across" (to baby's side opposite mother) positions until 14 months (Murphy & Messer, 1977). At 9 months, the infant may associate pointing with an interesting sight to search for, but may not understand its directive nature. It is interesting to note that 14-month-olds produce pointing gestures themselves, a reflection of their new understanding of directional positions. Butterworth (1995) reminded us that pointing is a species-specific gesture that bridges nonverbal and verbal communication. Not only do these babies point to their object of interest, but they check visually to be certain that the adult has followed the gesture. Even when 14-month-olds are placed in pairs, they point for each other and check for attention (Franco, Perrucchini, & Butterworth, 1992, as cited in Butterworth, 1995).

In Vygotsky's (1978) view, pointing is one example of the social foundations of mind. The child originally makes grasping movements toward the desired object beyond reach. The caregiver, observing this, senses the desire and provides the object. From an object-oriented movement, it becomes a person-oriented movement: "It becomes a true gesture only after it objectively manifests all the functions of pointing for others and is understood by others as such a gesture" (Vygotsky, 1978, p. 56). The way that Vygotsky used the term *gesture* here implies something akin to a symbol, or what we will call a *protosymbol*. In their use, these gestures and/or sounds function as symbols to the adult, although the child does not yet recognize their full power.

By 9 months, infants are quite competent at communicating their desires with gestures, vocalizations, eye contact, and combinations of these. Scholars often have assumed that we treat the child as intentional, and thus pull intentionality from the infant by interpreting the infant's goals from observed actions (Newson, 1978). But about half the time mothers initially fail to understand their infant's signals (Golinkoff, 1986). So, how does *intention* emerge?

For Vygotsky, the answer rested in the internalization of external social activity, or his "general genetic law of cultural development" (1981). He explained that "any function in the child's cultural development appears twice, or on two planes. First it appears on the social plane, and then on the psychological plane" (p. 163). As in the case of pointing, first the behavior appears between mother and child, and then, according to Vygotsky, it is internalized by the child so that he or she can intend to point in order to obtain things. Vygotsky argued even more strongly that speech grows out of social foundations and is internalized to the sphere of the child's mental processes. Let's look at how this might happen.

Preverbal children can indicate *that* they prefer or do not prefer—that is, express positive or negative disposition in a situation—but will have some difficulty expressing *what* "it" is that they prefer. When a parent immediately understands what the child wants, it is usually because the child looked at an object, pointed to it, and/or vocalized (Golinkoff & Gordon, 1988). When parents fail to understand, they will ask questions to negotiate the episode.

For example, when Peggy makes eye contact with Ellen, vocalizes loudly, and then looks in the direction of the kitchen table, Ellen knows Peggy wants something but doesn't know if it's a grape, a banana, a spoon, a set of keys, or any of the other items on the table. Ellen then makes a guess and offers a grape while asking, "Do you want a grape?" In her turn, Peggy can either accept the grape (succeed) or push it away and continue to signal with vocalizations, gestures, and eye contact until Ellen offers the keys with, "Oh, do you want the keys?" Golinkoff and Gordon (1988) observed that infants increase their chances of success by using communicative chains—consecutive episodes in which the infant's signals refer to the same object or event. By chaining discourse, even preverbally, the infant prepares to acquire the shared meanings, or significant symbols, necessary to human dialog. The child needs the *deictic function* of words. In their persistence in signaling their desires, infants also increase their opportunities to hear the names of things.

Recall that Bruner introduced three aspects of early reference: indicating, deixis, and predication. We have examined indicating procedures, and the early felt need for deixis. Thus, now the child can call the attention of the partner, and can begin to point, by gesture or sound approximations, to the specific object to which he or she would like attention directed. *Predication* goes one step further, and specifies what it is one wishes to say *about* the object. In any complete sentence, or complete idea for that matter, the minimal requirements are *topic* and *comment*. Topic is the "what" of the idea and may be conveyed interpersonally by deixis. Comment is the "why" of the idea—as in, "Why bring it up?"—and is conveyed socially by predication. Making a comment may seem to be quite beyond the capabilities of a 9-month-old, and technically, it is. The infant does not have the use of symbols yet, and thus cannot yet produce subjects and predicates of sentences. However, Bruner (1977) made the case that a sort of confirming comment is used by 9-month-olds. He called this vocalization the "proclamative" (p. 280), and it is used at two points: when the infant is about to take part in jointly attended action, and when the action is complete. The first, Bruner suggested, seems an accompaniment to intention; the second to completion. Hence, the baby is learning the rudiments of predicating even before his or her first words.

Problem Solving at 12 Months

With all of the cognitive activity attendant to internalizing the joint attention dialogues between caregiver and child, we might expect infants to be figuring out quite a lot about their world as well as about people—and they are. Two of the capacities that Piaget observed late in the first year were what he labeled *object permanence* and *means-ends relations*. Piaget identified multiple stages in the acquisition of these abilities (1926/1954), but here we assume late-stage achievement as evidence of the ability to use these cognitive abilities to solve problems.[24] Although Piaget maintained that these abilities were simply the result of cognitive maturation, others have since linked them to protoconversational skills as well.

As children approach their 1-year mark, they begin to use sounds that match conventional words used in their language environment. Soon after, they begin to figure out that objects and people continue to exist even if the children can't see them anymore. In the classic Piagetian task for *object permanence,* an item of interest to the child is shown, then is hidden under a succession of three pieces of cloth by the experimenter, who leaves the item under one of the cloths. If the hand with the item goes under Cloth A, then B, then C, and the item is left under C, the child is likely to first try to find it where the saw it last: under A. The successful first search under Cloth C, where the hand is last seen, demonstrates that children understand that the item has an existence independent of their visual observation of it.

The *means-ends* task is meant to measure how well the infant understands the connection between his or her own actions and the outcomes of those actions. One test[25] using the same materials, an interesting item and cloth, involves placing the item at the far end of the flattened cloth, with only the near end of the cloth within the infant's reach. He or she will first reach for the item and be frustrated with not grasping it; but later, when the infant pulls the cloth *in order to* get the item within reach, he or she demonstrates an understanding of the relationship between means and ends, and truly purposive action begins.

Gopnik and Meltzoff (1986) ventured the guess that these two lines of development—linguistic and cognitive—are related. They found strong correlations between the ability to solve the object permanence task and the emergence of disappearance words, such as "A' gone" (all gone), as well as the ability to solve a means-ends task and the emergence of success/failure words, such as "Uh oh." Just as infants are figuring out a difficult problem about the physical world, they are using words that reference that problem. In Vygotsky's terms, they are internalizing the word to use as a tool to figure out the problem. Of course, Piaget would claim that they have already figured out the problem because the necessary cognitive process has matured, and that the word is just a way to express it. Gopnik and Melzoff (1988) believed that their results do not allow them to say which comes first, thought or word. They interpreted their results as evidence that conceptual and semantic developments are closely intertwined by 1 year, and that they influence and facilitate each other.

Further evidence from a study of language-delayed children (Snyder, 1975) demonstrates that they perform significantly poorer on means-ends tasks than do children acquiring language on an earlier schedule. Remember that intention—"the capacity to perform an action on purpose" (Mascolo, Fischer, & Neimeyer, 1999, p. 147)—requires one to control both the means (action) and the end (the desired outcome). Mascolo and colleagues pointed out that one doesn't have to be aware that one has a goal, only that there is a relation between action and outcome. When we act intentionally, we act in order to obtain a desired state. Simple means-ends connections are available at around 8 months (grasping a toy in order to look at it), but, by 1 year, true intentional exploration using multiple means-ends relations begins. Language acquisition is apparently intimately connected with certain cognitive developments. How, then, are self-identity and emotions affected by this link?

The infant's *sense of self* is changing at the end of Year 1, and the start of Year 2. Lewis and Michalson (as cited in Lazarus, 1991) identified the emergence of self-permanence between 9 and 12 months. Infants can then differentiate self from others, and maintain that distinction regardless of context. But early in the second year, the sense of self continues to consolidate; and in the months leading up to symbolizing, the child's emerging sense of self could be described as self-recognition or self-awareness (Lewis, 1987). Self-identification will continue to be a gradual process of differentiation. Because the child increasingly understands social rules as they pertain to self and other, emotions are becoming more complex as well.

One of the unique emotional developments of the first year is *stranger anxiety,* which may start around 8 months and continue long into the second year. Rheingold and Eckerman (cited in Lewis & Brooks-Gunn, 1981) noted that not all infants are fearful of strangers, but most display some signs of wariness to unfamiliar people. Ainsworth and Wittig (1969) developed a procedure to study infant response to mother's absence versus presence. In the Strange Situation, the baby is given a chance to explore toys in mother's presence, then a stranger enters and sits quietly in a chair, then speaks with the mother, then invites the child to play. The test sequence for anxiety goes like this: Mother leaves the baby with the stranger, returns, both mother and stranger leave the baby completely alone, the stranger returns, and finally the mother returns.

It was the infant's response to mother's returns that the attachment theorists found interesting (Bretherton, 1987). Some infants cried on separation and then asked to be held when she returned; others did not cry, but did seek her proximity when she returned. Both response types came from securely attached infants who had experienced harmonious interaction with mother. The groups Ainsworth defined as avoidant and resistant were most interesting in terms of the insecure attachment they displayed. The avoidant group did not cry on separation and snubbed mother on return. The resistant group showed intense distress on separation, but were angry even as they wanted to be held at mother's return (Ainsworth & Wittig, 1969).

Although the attachment theorists explain these responses by way of attachment history with the primary caregiver, Kagan (1987) added several other factors: the child's temperamental tendency to become uncertain in unfamiliar contexts, and parental practices that teach the infant to control the signs of anxiety. For example, irritable newborns are likely to become resistant infants, and uninhibited newborns are more likely to respond securely. Kagan suggested that the child's temperament, as observed in either inhibited or uninhibited behavior with mother in the lab room at the outset of the test, is a better predictor of resistant response to mother's return than even maltreatment at home.

So, is stranger anxiety simply a manifestation of a particular level of temperament, or a learned response based on the bond with the primary caregiver? It may be a bit of both. In any case, it does not seem to manifest at all until the child reaches the point of having some rather clear sense of a self distinct from the caregiver. One possibility is that the child, especially the securely attached child, knows what to expect from mother but, knowing that the stranger could be quite different from mother, cannot predict what the stranger might do. This precludes ease of interaction. If mother is somewhat unpredictable anyway, and the child's attachment is insecure, the child may already have formed an angry response to unexpected and unwanted interactional events, and a stranger popping up is just another one of those uncomfortable situations mother is likely to allow. To give Kagan his due, the child's inhibited or uninhibited temperament may have a lot to do with the ease or difficulty with which the parent is able to scaffold interaction, and thus with the outcome of smooth or problematic dynamics. In any case, children at 1 year have a sense of who they are, what they want, and how to reach their goals. And gradually, they are moving toward another huge shift in their way of relating to the world.

Achievements at 18 Months

Something quite incredible happens between 18 and 24 months—the child discovers that there is a name for everything, and we can talk about it all and more. We can talk about what is not present to be pointed out, and we can talk about things that we've never seen. We can talk about self and we can talk about other. All this bestows us with incredible potential for creative intelligence. Vygotsky put it this way: "The most significant moment in the course of intellectual development, which gives birth to the purely human forms of practical and abstract intelligence, occurs when speech and practical activity, two previously completely independent lines of development, converge" (1978, p. 24).

Symbols and their developmental link with human cognition are examined in detail in the next chapter. The short story of symbols is that they are a mode of communication that shapes human nature in such a unique way that we stand out as peculiar animals among species. Leslie White (1949) defined a symbol as "a thing the value or meaning of which is bestowed upon it by those who use it" (p. 25). Even earlier, John Locke proposed that symbols "have their signification from the arbitrary imposition of men" (cited in White, 1949, p. 25). Dance (1982) integrated much of the classic literature on symbols in his definition: "A stimulus whose relationship with that with which it is associated is a result of the decision or arbitrary agreement of human user(s). Symbols are learned, abstract, contextually flexible, and anthroposemiotic" (p. 126). This final list deserves unpacking; for now, we'll use an example.

Let's say that Peggy's first real word is "goggie," an approximation of "doggie." Although she may have made a sound in the presence of dogs that meant something to her (e.g., "dededaah"), it was not significant for anyone else and referred only to the dog next door. Thus, it was neither communicative nor symbolic. In the absence of routines for adding meaning to that sound, usually by way of others' input in addition to one's own use and reuse, it would never have become a true concept with all the cognitive benefits of one. Thus, "goggie" was learned from mother's use of "goggie" to identify that intriguing, four-legged creature. Once Peggy realizes that there is a name for everything and that "goggie" is one of those, she will show her capacity for abstraction. Not only will the dog next door be called "goggie," but the cat down the block, the sheep in the meadow, and perhaps Dad on his knees looking for his glasses. Although her naming system will become more specific, for now the abstraction serves her well—she can talk about a great many things that are brought to her mind by "goggie." Clearly, she can also use the word in a number of different contexts. At 18 months, she doesn't just repeat a word when the referent is right there in front of her; she can retrieve the word *in order to* talk about the animal that is not physically present. That is, she is using words in a purposeful, goal-oriented way. Finally, her word is part of the human community alone; symbols are anthroposemiotic. Suffice it to say, for now, that Spot does not know what "goggie" means. Spot may respond to his name, and even respond to his human's name (Ellen), but he will never ask where Ellen is. Peggy will. At 18 months, when Peggy says, "Goggie?" with questioning intonation, she is commenting on her four-legged topic.

Holophrastic utterances are protosentences; they mark the beginning of very simple syntax. One-word sentences are used occasionally by adults (e.g., "No"), but they *are* the language of 18-month-olds. Although holophrases are not as specific, complex, or understandable as truly syntactic sentences, they are the first step in that direction. They are, in other words, the prototype for later syntactically complete sentences consisting, minimally, of topic and comment, or subject and verb. How do they accomplish both in one word? Intonation.

When Peggy says "Goggie?" with raised pitch at the end, she is posing something like a question, or protoquestion, and usually expects a response, preferably the dog's presence. Most often these are asked in the absence of the topic. What Peggy is doing is filling in the predication by intonation; supplying the comment about the topic (i.e., "Where is the doglike thing?"). On the other hand, if the dog (or perhaps Dad on all fours) is present, she might say when first seeing it, "Goggie!" with emphasis on the first syllable, lowered pitch at the end (i.e., "Wow, there's a doglike thing!"). In this case, something like a declarative, or a protodeclarative, is produced. Alternatively, when seeing the dog in the next yard, she may point through the window, look to Ellen, and say "GOGGIEEE" with increased volume, intensity, and emphasis overall (i.e., "Get me that doglike thing"). Here, the intonation functions as an imperative, or protoimperative, a demand.

In this one-word stage, the child can encode either topic or comment, but not both. Here, our example has been a topic word, but a comment word is just as probable. The word *more* may be used to make a request or a command ("More?" vs. "More!"), but now the topic is missing. "More of what?" a parent might wonder. Usually, the child will encode the element that gives the most information. In the case of a physically present object of desire, such as grapes, Peggy could point and say "More?" to indicate both topic and comment. In the case of the absent four-legged interest, she can say "Goggie?" and if Ellen is attuned to her child's current infatuation, she will know what Peggy wants.

Self/Other Transformations

Before we move on to examine the incredible expansion of human behavior that occurs once speech and thought merge, we will take a quick look at the sort of self that the child is constituting in the second year. At this point, we use the term *toddler*, in light of the fact that the child is no longer an infant. *Infant*, from the Latin *in fari*, literally means without speech. More accurately, the child is no longer an infant when he or she can use that speech symbolically.

Lewis and Michalson (in Lazarus, 1991) acknowledged the role of symbols in the 18-month-old's new ability to articulate an *elaborate categorical self* as distinct from others. The child who can reference self in symbols ("me," "mine") is the child who can start to build the idea of a self conceptually. Lewis (1987) considered this symbolic knowledge as a way of knowing in which classification—having worded categories—becomes important. Furthermore, symbolizers will shortly be able to experience complicated emotions such as empathy, guilt, shame, pride, and embarrassment, which all depend on the ability to recognize, although in a rudimentary way, the interpersonal and intrapersonal significance of dialogic events. Note that the toddler now has the potential for an internal life as well as an external one. When 20-month-old Peggy is found sitting on the floor among the shards of the cookie jar and the tablecloth she pulled to get it, she may display either pride or shame, depending on Ellen's reaction (or prior reactions to similar situations), but she probably will demonstrate some emotion expressive of her recognition that she caused that event.

Recall that *empathy* is a "feeling in with" another. It should be noted here that many scholars of emotion use the term *empathy* in such a way that it overlaps with perspective taking. Stern (1985) distinguished empathy from attunement. In his view, attunement is automatic and out of awareness, whereas empathy "involves the mediation of cognitive processes" (p. 145). In view of the widespread use of this definition, and in the interests of clarification, we view this use of empathy as something a step beyond attunement, but on the road to a link with perspective taking. Stern claimed that empathy consists of four processes: "the resonance of feeling state," "the abstraction of empathic knowledge from the experience of emotional resonance," "the integration of abstracted empathic knowledge into an empathic response," and "a transient role identification" (p.145). He distinguished *perspective taking* as an entirely intellectual exercise on the order of imagining what it must be like to be so-and-so. In my view, once thought and speech merge, emotions also become intertwined with thought and language, and it may not be possible to make any crisp, dichotomous distinctions between emotion and thought any longer. Clearly the child can "feel in" by attunement, but that attunement also becomes something that can be spoken of and thought about. Not only can it be, but emotion is likely to be meshed with symbolic behavior. But what does the toddler understand of their emotional experiences so early in this process?

Toddlers can use words like "happy," "afraid," "mad," and "sad" at around 2 years (Smiley & Huttenlocher, 1989), and they use them for self first, then for others. Smiley and Huttenlocher noted that observations from Bretherton's research as well as their own include a child who climbed into a box, started to cry, and said "I afraid." But none of the children studied used the words for others until 26 months, at which age one child watched her mother cry and said "Mommy's sad." Furthermore, these authors interviewed children about their understanding of these terms, and found that when the toddlers had to infer others' internal states, about half of the 2- to 3-year-olds can accurately apply "happy," and about a quarter use "sad," and "mad" appropriately. Smiley and Huttenlocher concluded that by about 2 years, at least half the children use at least one word for their own emotional state. By 2½ years, they are beginning to be able to infer others' internal states.

Given that toddlers begin to recognize emotional distinctions between self and other, what we may infer is that they are learning about boundaries, about the invisible separation point between "you" and "me." The child will continue to sort out these invisible and created distinctions throughout life. In view of the fact that the child has learned about distinctions in relationship with another, and that self/other is one of those distinctions, then what is the self but a set of impressions gained in relational dialogues? In toddlers, it is a symbolic construct ("I" or "me") that they have developed on the basis of all the dialogues they have experienced. In Fogel's (1993) terms, "the self is the individual's participatory and imaginative cognition of co-regulated relationships" (p. 146). That is, *it is in the negotiation of relationships that we constitute a sense of self.* And once we can use symbols to represent aspects of self, we can bring that sense to awareness purposefully, and add meaning to it by means of all the dialogues we create.

SUMMARY

Congratulations on finishing a long and winding chapter about the dialogic origins of self, relationship and communication. It is a complex process, but on the basis of what you know now, you will better understand the nature of being human and all that follows these early dialogues.

By the age of 2, toddlers know that objects have permanency, that actions have consequences, and that everything can be named and commented on. They have a sense of who they are, and of their own powers in the coregulation of discourse. They came to these abilities, in part because they were biologically prepared to seek dialogue, in part because their caregivers are motivated to demonstrate how dialogue works, but also because of the dynamic of dialogue itself. To hear another requires turn taking; to add meaning to words requires internalizing the spoken dialogue and its effects; to specify particular emotions requires words that have become linked to identifiable affective states. The toddler has moved beyond proto-conversation to truly human conversation; beyond affect to emotion; beyond response to volition; beyond and through dialogue to relationship.

In chapter 4, we examine the process of developing speech/thought/emotion. In that exploration, we have opportunities to reconsider the shift to symbolization, and probable changes in self-concept in the movement between external and internal, boundary and core.

NOTES

16. These are my adaptations of Brandstadter's 1999 (p. 51) list. See hers for specifics.
17. This advantage apparently is genetic; see Kimura (1999).

18. Bruner's LASS acronym was in response to Chomsky's LAD, or "language acquisition device." Recall that Chomksy believed that there was an innate language acquisition structure. In contrast, Bruner believed that we need not only the innate predispositions, but also the interactional environment to acquire language (or LAD plus LASS equals language acquisition).

19. For more information on gender differences, see Kimura (1999), particularly chapter 5 on spatial abilities and chapter 8 on verbal abilities.

20. The list of child characteristics was adapted from Ambert (2001, pp. 32–33).

21. See Haslett and Samter (1997, p. 102) for a useful summary of Trevarthen's stages of intersubjectivity.

22. Fogel is basing his description on an example from Clark (1978, p. 246).

23. The terms *2-month revolution* and *9-month revolution* are from the work of Rochat and Striano (1999) on social cognitive development.

24. For some of the difficulties with attaching age references to these achievements, see Hattie (1992, p. 123).

25. For a more complete list of means-ends measures, see Gopnik and Meltzoff (1986, p. 1043).

She sat on the ground in back of the large house on Norman Avenue. She was 4 years old and the sinking feeling was one she'd never had before. She felt disconnected; no, worse, she felt there was no one who knew her. That she was alone in the world and would have to fend for herself. It was not just terrifying—that part was dissipating—it was very, very sad. Yes, that was the word she decided on: *sad*.

The house was huge but they only occupied part of it, the first floor. Ellen was inside, cleaning up the mess the baby had just made of his cereal. She had already managed to get Nan, her oldest, off to her first day of second grade in a new school. Nan had not wanted to go; she knew no one here and missed her friends back in Madison. Milwaukee might be a fine place, but Nan was not ready for it and Ellen was exhausted from trying to convince her. "I don't want to stay here, I don't like it." "But you will like it, there are lots of nice kids here. And Mrs. Wintograd has a desk set up for you next to Charlene, who will help you get to know everyone else." "I don't want to. Don't make me." "Well, I am making you. You have to go to school. So sit down. I'll be back to get you for lunch." Then the tears silently streaked Nan's cheeks as she followed Ellen's retreating figure, a baby in one arm, a toddler hanging onto her other. Ellen felt the push and pull of her conflicting feelings. She hated the effects of this move on her children, but the job was so much better for Roger and the money … well, they couldn't do without it.

Now, back in this large space, surrounded by moving boxes still unpacked, cleaning cereal off the wall, highchair, and floor, she had yet another reason to feel like a horrible witch of a mother. When Ned had begun to demand her attention, she had banished the whining Peggy to the back yard. Peggy had been difficult during the move. She had not wanted to get on the train when Roger had seen them off—he would drive the car later, after he'd completed training his replacement in Madison. This small child seemed unduly disturbed with fears of being left behind, or losing track of her parents. Once she was on the train, she was fine and settled down to play with the new toys bought for the trip. But then, the past few days, she had become whiney and demanding. Ellen just could not bear another scene and had sent her to play in the yard. She glanced out occasionally and noted with considerable guilt that Peggy was not playing, or really doing anything. She was just sitting there on the ground, head lowered. Well, Ellen couldn't worry about it. She had Ned to clean up so that "Madame" (as she thought about Roger's mother, Anna, to herself) would not make some cutting remark about her mothering skills. Anna meant well, she supposed, but she had the leisure to be critical—she who had not married until she was 30 and who had raised only one child. Well, "Madame" wasn't up yet and so she had some time to get the baby smelling of talc rather than his breakfast and resulting diaper. And continue to unpack. And get Nan back for lunch. And plan dinner. And listen to Roger's concerns about this new administrative position with its attendant headaches and responsibilities. Poor Peggy. Well, she couldn't worry about it now.

Creating A Mind: Dialogue in Symbols

When you're with children, talk about toys.
From playthings, little by little, they reach
into deeper wisdom and clarity. Gradually,
they lose interest in their toys.

(Rumi, quoted in Barks, 1995, p. 76)

Far from implying that we become grim with development, the mystic's own playfulness comes through in his writing. (He added: "If they were completely demented, they wouldn't play at all.") What he does imply is that children are on the path toward interests beyond the concrete and material. It is this path that we follow in chapter 4, looking at what is unique about human communication, and what are the characteristics and capabilities of that form. Then, we follow the process of constituting a mind, from brain plus dialogue, to symbols plus relationship. Finally, we explore the development of meaning from heaps to concepts, and further, to a special sort of concept: the self.

THE PECULIARITIES OF HUMAN COMMUNICATION

Many before me have noted that human communication is unique; some have written volumes on the topic (e.g., Adler, 1967; Langer, 1972). The effects of human communication are largely agreed on; the characteristics that make it unique have remained somewhat controversial. Few would disagree, for example, that humans display unique abilities to think about what is *not* as well as what is, to consider a future and voluntarily reflect on a past, thus allowing us to build a sense of historical culture. Furthermore, our mental processes are syntactical: We can specify distinct categories for things and put them in some sort of sequential order. One of the types of sequences we have found most useful is the cause-effect sequence, and its counterpart, a serial sense of time. This last hints at what may be most peculiar about our form of communication: syntax. We order our words, our thoughts, our meanings. We not only refer to "things" (objects, events, people, ideas), we also comment on those topics.

But what is it that makes for these unique capacities? Some would say it is the use of the symbol; others claim that it is the ordering of those symbols. Among those who study the communication of other intelligent mammals (chimpanzees, gorillas, dolphins), different scholars make different claims for their capacities. We need some clear definitions of those capacities in order to examine their claims.

Signs and Symbols

Sign

The most widely used communicative stimulus across species is the *sign*. A sign is "a stimulus announcing that of which it is a part, concrete, and fixed regardless of context" (Dance, 1982, p. 124). Any particular sign will always signify the same thing. For instance, when Peggy cries in hunger, Ellen, who is nursing, will invariably respond by letting down her milk. This is an automatic, fixed response to her baby's hunger cry; it is not a decision. Nevertheless, it is communicative; Ellen's body has acted on the information provided by the hunger cry. The cry stimulus, announcing that of which it is a part (hungry baby), calls forth a predictable response in the nursing mother.

Signal

A subset of signs are *signals* that acquire "their sign characteristics through the process of pair-wise conditioning" (Dance, 1982, p. 125). The signification is still concrete and fixed, but in this case, rather than being tied to a physiological response, it is conditioned. Ellen bathes Peggy every night at the same time, and at the end of each bathing time, Ellen sings the same lullaby and Peggy falls asleep. The sleep response to the relaxation of bathing has become linked as well to the lullaby. Thus, under the same conditions of end-of-the-day fatigue, if the lullaby is sung alone, without the bath, Peggy's sleep response will be the same.

Symbol

As you may recall, *symbols* are quite different sorts of stimuli indeed. A symbol is "a stimulus whose relationship with that with which it is associated is a result of the decision or arbitrary agreement of human user(s)" (Dance, 1982, p. 125). Contrary to signs, their meanings are learned, abstract, arbitrary, and contextually flexible; symbols are the constituents of human language.

Suzanne Langer (1972), in her discussion of "the great shift" to symbols, noted that "speech is a process which has created an instrument, language" (p. 298). That instrument is made up of organized symbols. To ask when we as a species began to speak is, as Langer stated it, "a bootless question" (p. 297). The process of speaking has gone through many long phases in its evolution, from "a system of vocal signals influencing the behavior of other members of one's own kind" to true symbols "which would keep a fundamental conceptual meaning" across contexts (p. 298).

For example, at one time, simple calls (e.g, warning hoots) sufficed for our survival, but then an "overgrowth of mental functions" led to protosymbolic behavior in which a particular vocalization could generate common imagery among its users (Langer, 1972). Langer's guess is that the sounds sung during ritual dance movement may, when produced again at a later date, evoke the entire feeling—the gestalt of the ritual. This should bring to mind what Peggy did in using a preferred sound (protosymbol) to recall certain preferred interactions, such as the play that accompanies bathing. However it may have happened, the fact is that we do speak, and it is this vocal mode of communication that has evolved along with the brain to produce symbols.

The Triangle of Meaning Versus the Arrow of Signification

You may be familiar with the ideas concerning behavioral conditioning and its reliance on reactions to signs. Pavlov originated the research paradigm to study behavior, and B. F. Skinner became the primary proponent for explaining human behavior as a series of conditioned responses. This model presupposes a direct reaction between the sign stimulus and the behavioral response.

$$\text{(sign as Stimulus) } S ===> R \text{ (behavior as Response)}$$

When this sign formula ultimately failed to explain all of human behavior, especially developmental patterns, scholars looked for a new model.

Vygotsky (1978), Ogden and Richards (1953), and Kelly (1955/1963, 1969/1979) used triangulation to explain the manner in which humans signify. Walker Percy called it the "Delta Factor" (1954), in that there are three elements involved in every symbolic act: something signified, a signifier/symbol, and a person doing the signifying, as shown in Fig. 4.1.

In the natural order of things, the actual creature we call a dog has no real relationship with the word we've chosen to represent it. Indeed, the word only represents that furry reality when we decide it does (e.g., we could just as well name it "fleppenduff"). What becomes possible with this new kind of meaning is the uncoupling of automatic response to direct stimulus; instead, as Vygotsky (1978) put it, "an auxiliary stimulus that facilitates the completion of the operation by indirect means is incorporated" (p. 40). Symbols have the characteristic of "reverse action" (Vygotsky, 1978, p.39), meaning that they operate on the individual, not the environment. That is, the use of the symbol cannot make a dog appear materially, but it *can* stimulate the thought of a dog in the individual (and each individual will probably conjure up a different dog concept). Furthermore, this mental operation on the individual permits humans to control their own behavior.

Let's say that 7-month-old Peggy likes the furry active creature next door, and enjoys pulling his hair. As she hears "doggie" and sees the dog at the same time, she

Person   (cognition)

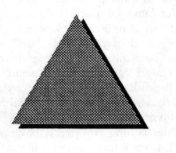

(thing signified)   "DOG"
                                     (signifier/symbol)

FIG. 4.1.   A triangle of meaning.

may come to associate the two, such that when she hears the word she will look for this source of delight, expecting to be able to torment him. If the dog is not present along with the word, the association will be extinguished. Thus far, we explain this response in simple behavioral terms. However, once the word is applied by 18-month-old Peggy, knowing that it is a means to get things done—one symbol among all that may be used to get things done—the word itself has an effect on her. This time, when she hears the word, she may reply "Goggie here!" to attempt to effect his appearance. Alternatively, she may also use the word herself to demand his presence, or to comment about her desire of him: "Goggie mine!" Let's examine more closely how this process works.

The Process of Symbolizing

Reference and Representation

The referencing function of symbols might seem, at first blush, to be their primary and distinguishing function. It is certainly one function, but if it were the only one, then many other animals would also be found capable. True, we may use sounds to refer to things (e.g., dog, ball, bottle), but this we could do by means of simple associations created in a conditioned fashion between the sound and the thing, much in the same way that Rover links the sound "frisbee" with the retrieval of his toy. And indeed, that has been the claim of many of the primatologists; that chimpanzees, gorillas, and orangutans are capable of reference, and thus of language (Gardner & Gardner, 1969; Premack, 1971). What they fail to note is that simple representation is not the only function of symbolic language. Herbert Terrace (1979), in a carefully controlled study, tested the assumption that chimpanzees like Washoe learned American Sign Language.[26] He found that a chimp, Nim, produced approximations of signs that had been linked to rewards but were consistently cued by trainers.

Categorization: Groupings of Qualities—Thesis

As you know, the "naming explosion" occurs around 18 months of age. This sudden capacity to recognize that everything can be named is manifest in categorization. Children in their second year begin to sort objects into piles that represent categories to them. For example, a child who has succeeded in using the word "doggie" to talk about the neighbor's pet may then lump all furry, four-legged animals into that category, thus enabling him- or herself to talk about a whole set of animals with one symbol. Beyond this ability to group qualities, we distinguish differences among categories, and generalize these categories to large and tenuously connected groupings.

Differentiation: Contrast of Qualities—Antithesis

Once toddlers recognize that words can refer to sets of things, they also have the means to distinguish one grouping from another. Indeed, the birth of the dialectic is what we can observe with the beginning of symbolizing. The child now has the means to contrast two poles—"x" versus "not-x"—and thus, the means to build concepts and constructs. One of the primary differentiations we explore here is the one between "me" and "not-me."

Sensible to a dialogical approach, symbols are often conceptualized in terms of opposition. Wundt's "antithetical concept formation" involves the creation of a pair of oppositions as well as a tension between the pair (cited in Josephs, Valsiner, & Surgan, 1999, p. 261). Because it is in the nature of human meaning making to discover that meaning in opposition, our kind of thinking is founded in dualities, in dichotomies, in contrast: "When humans construct meaning to relate with their world, the field of opposites is automatically implied at every moment" (Josephs et al., 1999, p. 261). In essence, without the notion of nondog qualities against which to compare dog qualities, we could have no concept of dog. However, contrast alone does not capture the nature of symbol use. Kelly (1969/1979) noted that human sense making is based on construing both "similarity and difference simultaneously" (p. 103). Again, it is triangulation that characterizes symbolic capacity. From Kelly's perspective, we can perceive of introversion/extroversion as a construct with which to figure out people while at the same time knowing that neither pole of the construct is applicable to a shoe. In similar fashion, we may have a construct for dog/not-dog (e.g., furry and four-legged vs. finny and scaled) in the knowledge that the construct poles are similar in their applicability to living, moving things and yet qualitatively different in their behavior and appearance.

Along with this capacity to differentiate categories comes the possibility for the construction of analytic thought, which requires that one be able to consider and compare several distinctive categories of thought at once. What is also required is some way of organizing those categories; that method is syntax, which we consider just after generalization.

Generalization: Abstraction of Qualities—Synthesis

With the discrimination of features into categories of similar objects, and the differentiation of one category from another, we have the basic requirements for abstraction—or generalizing a word or idea from one context to another. "Goggie" at first may literally represent the collie next door, but very soon, "goggie" stands for a four-legged, furry, interesting thing, which is distinct from "baba," which stands for the bottle and the drink within. Because the child has few words, abstraction serves very well as it allows the child to use and overuse the word. As the toddler wants to comment on everything of interest, "goggie" is soon used to refer to dogs, cats, roosters, horses … just about any living, moving creature for which the child has no serviceable word. Gradually, differentiations become finer as vocabulary grows, but the capacity for abstraction then begins to serve mental functions.

Syntax: Organization and Why It's Necessary

All of the previously discussed elements of symbols serve us well, but we are still really looking at refinements of representation. Without syntax, or a method of organizing these categories, we would not be able to build complex meanings consisting minimally of both topic and comment, and a means to link the two. But why syntax?

For those who consider the evolution of the human brain and speech mechanisms (Lieberman 1973, 1991), as well as theoretical claims about the nature of syntax (Chomsky, 1965), the answer is not simple, but it is obvious. Given the limitations of the human vocal tract and the enormous associative capacity of the human brain, syntax evolved as a solution to match these two unlikely partners in language.

The vocal tract allows us to create a variety of sounds, but certainly not an infinite number; therefore, we would run out of sounds before we ran out of things to talk about. Chomsky coined the term "surface structure" to refer to the phonetic representation of the utterance, or the sound used to represent the experience, object, or idea. He also coined the term "deep structure" to refer to an hypothesized semantic representation of the utterance—a form suitable for long-term memory storage. In theory, this deep structure evolved to link the demands of the brain to the limitations of sound.

If we can order sounds in sequences, we can build meaning beyond just the number of meanings that may be linked to the limited number of sounds we can produce. If we can combine meaningful sounds (phonemes) into strings of sounds—longer words and sentences—the capacity for carrying meaning in long-term memory becomes infinite. We can make up a sound set for just about anything, and for any idea.

Before we proceed, a note on the structure of sentences is in order. We know something about the peculiarities of human language: Our vocabularies are large, even theoretically infinite; we are prone to contrast, or duality of patterning; and we tend to subject-predicate combinations.[27] We apparently—through the combination of our speech capacities, brain functions, and social natures—deal with experience in terms of object/action, topic/comment, foreground/background, new information/given information. Although in this text we continue to explore these sorts of patterns, consider for now how these patterns show up in symbols, language, thought, and interaction.

In combination, the elements of human symbol use endow us with incredible capacities.[28] Let's look at a few of the gifts (and dilemmas) that symbolic communication bestows.

The Endowments of Symbols

The Negative: Primary Contrastive

"No!" is one the first symbols to be acquired, and is a reliable indicator that the toddler has become a symbol user. How useful is the negative? Consider: With one word, the child can now refuse whatever is proposed, and typically does so with glee. It marks the first language game, and with it comes a sense of personal power to regulate external influences. Parents may not be thrilled with the negative but children are, and with good reason.

Burke (1966) described humans, in part, as inventors of the negative. In one of his early contributions to the communication literature, Burke (1952, 1953) elucidated the nature of the negative. First, there are no negative conditions in nature; everything is simply what it is. As Burke noted, "We may say that something 'is not' in such and such a place. But so far as nature is concerned, whatever 'is not' here is positively somewhere else; or, if it does not exist, then other things actually occupy all places where it 'is not.'" (p. 251). The negative is a "distinctive marvel" to human language. It is this quirk of human communication that starts us down the linguistic road to human functions that serve us both well and ill.

Consider the ramifications of the ability to make a distinction between what "is" and what "is not." If we can entertain the notion of what "is not," we can further entertain the concept of what "is not yet," and from there a notion of time, future, and past. We can also label these contrasting notions of "x" and "not x" in terms of good and bad, positive and negative. If what I do is "good" and what you do is "bad," I have given myself a reason to be superior to you and thus created the notion of hierarchy: Some people/ideas/behaviors are better than others and should be accorded more authority. You see how the notion of dualities and dichotomies starts with the negative. Let us look at some of the more influential of the effects of contrasting dualities.

Time: Future and Past

In the recognition that we can speak about what may not now exist, we open up the possibility for something that may happen in future. And, given that words hold concepts in mind for voluntary recall, we can consider our past as well. Or, as Mead would have it, "Minds arise in breaking out of the present"

(Miller, 1982, p. 20). In that new ability to think beyond present events, we situate ourselves cognitively in time:

> Through verbal formulations of past situations and activities, the child frees himself from the limitations of direct recall; he succeeds in synthesizing the past and present to suit his purposes. The change that occur in the child's perceptual field ... not only makes fragments of the past available, but also results in a new method of uniting the elements of past experience with the present. (Vygotsky, 1978, p. 36)

Roger Brown (1973) called this capacity *displacement* and considered it a property of language. This capacity to talk about things that are not present seems to appear around the age of 2, when the child can copy another's action after a time lapse—when the model is no longer present (Golinkoff, 1983).

Being timebound may seem like an achievement; we can learn from the past and plan for a future. However, it also brings the possibility for negative emotional responses to an imagined fate. Anxiety is fear of ... we know not what. It is a fear without a discernable stimulus, and arises from the ability to imagine what *might* happen. No one enjoys anxiety—it can make us cautious, paranoid—but it can also make us safe. The joyful flipside of future-oriented fear is future-oriented imagination.

Creativity: What May Be if I Make It So

If I can imagine a future, then a reasonable extension of that is to imagine our own part in that future, especially concerning the regulative function of human communication. This sense of one's own ability to create what does not now exist is often considered one of our greatest gifts. To imagine what may be has produced not only works of art, dance, and music, but also cultural, scientific, and technological achievements as well as personal joy and fulfillment.

Individuation: Self in Contrast to Other

When a toddler begins to recognize the communicative power that he or she can control, and attaches self to that power with self-labels, individuation takes off in leaps and bounds. The move away from the kind of pure empathy we share with other animals—"felt communion of action and emotion and desire" (Langer, 1972., p. 313)—commences with the possibility for individuation—the ability to think about our own distinctiveness. Kelly (1969) pointed out that the words one uses not only hold the structure of thought, but that the "names by which he calls himself give and hold the structure of his personality" (p. 56).

Decentration is the flipside of egocentrism. It is "the ability to see activities and relationships from other than a purely selfish point of view" (Dance & Larson, 1976, p. 68). We can decenter only when we recognize that there are points of view different from our own; that recognition is possible only after the awareness of self as distinct from other. As Dance and Larson noted, as the child moves from egocentric to nonegocentric communication, the role of other becomes more and more distinct from the role of self, and the child realizes that self can take on the role of other to adapt messages effectively. This role-taking ability is something we pursue in greater detail in chapter 6.

The capacity for *self-reflexiveness* is the hallmark of human consciousness. The "leap from the sensory to the rational world" (Luria, 1982, p. 41) is made possible by "the word's function as a mediating factor between the stimuli of the environment and the response of the individual, thereby permitting human choice" (Vocate, 1994, p. 23). The ability to step back and view one's self and one's behavior objectively allows one to interrupt strings of instinctual or conditioned behavior and thus consider one's responses.

As Vygotsky (1934/1986) put it, "individual consciousness is built from outside through relations with others. The mechanism of social behavior and of consciousness are the same" (p. xxiv). It is this sense of *consciousness* that Volosinov (1929/1986) linked closely to verbal symbols (i.e., words): "Consciousness becomes consciousness only once it has been filled with ideological (semiotic) content, consequently, only in the process of social interaction" (p. 10).

Internalization: Thinking from the Outside in

Internalization is a process of bringing external experience within, where it may be stored in symbols and structured in new ways. In that process, a new kind of thought is formed with the raw material of symbols. For Langer, human cognition is the outcome of the process of symbolizing: "A genuine symbol is, above all, an instrument of conception, and cannot be said to exist short of meeting that requirement" (Langer, 1972, p. 289). And it is in this thorough transformation from speech used for simple reference to spoken symbols that our capacities to plan, dream, and create emerge, but not alone. We not only share our constructions, but construct them together by means of significant symbols. Mead (1934/1974) would say of these multiple outcomes: "the same procedure responsible for the genesis and existence of mind or consciousness—taking the attitude of the other towards self, or toward one's own behavior—also necessarily involves the genesis and existence at the same time of significant symbols" (pp. 47–48).

For Vygotsky, human mental functions are "products of *mediated* activity" of the "*psychological tools*" provided by spoken symbolic interaction (Kozulin, in Vygotsky, 1934/1986, p. XXIV). Leont'ev explained the outcome for cognition: "The process of internalization is not the transferral of an external activity to a pre-existing, internal 'plane of consciousness': it is the process in which this plane is formed" (Leont'ev, cited in Wertsch & Stone, 1985, p. 163). That process is detailed next as the creation of a new way of thinking.

HUMAN THINKING: CONSTITUTING A MIND

The mind is not so much a physical entity as it is a way of talking about the capacities for thought/emotion/spirit that cannot be explained by the brain alone. The odd thing about individual human thinking is that it can benefit from "the cognitive labors of the others in a way that gives it unprecedented powers" (Dennett, 1994, p. 3). Our kind of thinking is social and dialogical.

The mind emerges from the activity of the brain, but is not the same as the brain. My view is that, as I stated in chapter 1, "mind is a mediating process between a material brain, subject to physiological maturation, and an energetic consciousness that is active at the boundary between self and other." After writing that, I found Siegel's (1999) work in which the psychiatrist presents principles that are compatible to my concept of mind:

1. The human mind emerges from patterns in the flow of energy and information within the brain and between brains.
2. The mind is created within the interaction of internal neurophysiological processes and interpersonal experiences.
3. The structure and function of the developing brain are determined by how experiences, especially within interpersonal relationships, shape the genetically programmed maturation of the nervous system. (p.2)[29]

We are accustomed to believing that our notions of reality occur within the boundaries of our bodies; in our brains and sensations. But, "the germ of the child's higher mental functions appear *somewhere between* the adult and child" (Ignatovic-Savic et al., 1988, p. 93). That *somewhere between* is the field wherein energy and information flow between brains. The creation of a mind begins at the boundaries between child and adult and then is internalized, not the reverse.

Social to Individual Thought

You may recall from chapter 1 that Piaget's studies of children led him to believe that the toddler's thought was egocentric and that speech reflected such egocentrism. Egocentric speech is different from communicative speech in that it is not addressed to another person, but may be—and often is—uttered in the presence of other people. Piaget proposed that egocentric speech served no purpose other than a phase on the way to socialized speech. He (1962) later softened his position that egocentric speech was a functionless stage after he read Vygotsky's critique of his work on egocentrism.

Vygotsky believed that egocentric speech is used as a tool by the child to solve problems, and that as it is gradually internalized to serve thought, a more socialized speech is possible at the surface level. In this way, the child comes to think out the problem internally, and to adjust surface structures to suit the social situation. For example, if 4-year-old Peggy wants a cookie at 4:00 and presents her request directly, she is denied on the basis that she will ruin her 5:00 dinner. If 7-year-old Peggy wants a cookie at 4:00, and has internalized the unsuccessful requests, she may remind herself internally and adjust her external speech accordingly: "If I can have a cookie now, I'll eat all my broccoli at dinner." In Vygotsky's scheme of development, speech is first social and interactional, then egocentric and self-serving, and finally egocentric speech is internalized—and from that internal (mental) position, inner speech can be used to adjust external speech in consideration of the other's needs (Vygotsky, 1934/1986).

As we consider how he came up with this notion, it is worthwhile to note that the primary written explication of Vygotsky's theory is found in his *Myshlenie i Rech*, a literal translation of which is *Thinking and Speech* (**not** *Thought and Language*, which has become the well-known English title). I mention this because the difference would have been important to him, had he lived to see the translation. Wertsch (1979a) explained that Vygotsky was "mainly concerned with emphasizing the social activity of speech or speaking rather than the structure of the language system" (p. 4).

Furthermore, the Russians used a broader interpretation of speech than scholars from the United States typically have. They considered speech to involve social interaction, rather than simply being the mechanism for producing spoken messages. It is this more general conception of speech that Vygotsky observed to serve the development of human thought processes: "The internalization of socially rooted and historically developed activities is the distinguishing feature of human psychology" (Vygtosky, 1978, p. 57). And, I would add, it is also a necessary explanatory feature of human communication. If peculiarly human communication is what leads us to certain sorts of thought processes, then the field of communication is positioned to explain some of those processes from the primary variable—spoken symbolic interaction.

The children first use egocentric speech to regulate their own behavior, then to direct their thought; speech does not merely accompany action, it transforms action. As Vygotsky posited, "Egocentric speech is inner speech in its functions; it is speech on its way inward, intimately tied up with the ordering of the child's behavior" (Vygostky, 1934/1986, p. 86). Consider Vygotsky's observation of this process in his 5½-year-old subject:

> He was drawing a streetcar when the point of his pencil broke. He tried, nevertheless, to finish the circle of the wheel, pressing down on the pencil very hard, but nothing showed on the paper except a deep colorless line. The child muttered to himself, "It's broken," put aside the pencil, took watercolors instead, and began drawing a *broken* streetcar after an accident, continuing to talk to himself from time to time about the change in his picture. The child's accidentally provoked egocentric utterance so manifestly affected his activity that it is impossible to mistake it for a mere by-product, an accompaniment not interfering with the melody…. What happens here is similar to the well-known developmental sequence in the naming of drawings. A small child draws first, then decides what it is he has drawn; at a slightly older age, he names his drawing when it is half-done; and finally he decides beforehand what he will draw. (Vygotsky, 1934/1986, p. 31)

If speech goes underground to serve thought, it does so originally in the form the child first uses—fully formed speech for oneself. However, as internalization proceeds, it does become transformed for the purposes of thought.

Speech for oneself certainly continues to be used throughout life—to daydream, to solve problems, to rehearse, to imagine—but it takes various forms. Let's say you're faced with a difficult task that you have not performed often, or at all. For example, you've been hired as a lifeguard at the local beach. You've been trained in water rescue techniques but you've never had to use them. When you see a flailing figure and hear shouts for help, you stand up on your chair and you start talking out loud, but to yourself: "Grab the float; whistle for assistance; where's the boat?" You are running through the procedures you've been taught, but need the structure of the words to regulate your action. This is observable, audible thought. Such vocalized speech for the purpose of regulating one's own behavior is what we called egocentric speech in Peggy; it is the only method she has for "thinking" about difficult problems alone. At later stages in development, when we already have developed a thinking mind, we still use speech for self, or *private speech*, to solve problems that have not yet become internalized.

Let's clarify the terms we use to follow the development of mind. *Private speech* (first arising in the child as egocentric speech) is voluntary, conscious, and vocalized; *inner speech* is also consciously directed, but covert, silent. In this definitional framework, private speech demonstrates overtly the process of working out a new problem, calling for immediate action, which has not been yet internalized. Inner speech is done with awareness and purpose; it is often strategic.

As for inner speech, Kuczaj (1982) and Fodor (1975) maintained that it is innate (akin to Chomsky's language acquisition device); that it is a representational system available before birth that serves to translate information from the senses to a brain. Their argument is not compelling, and would be difficult to support. I favor Wertsch's (as cited in Kuczaj, 1982) explanation that inner speech is first expressed in private speech that has a specialized structure: it "shows a tendency toward ... abbreviation ... namely omitting the subject of a sentence and all words connecting with it while preserving the predicate. This tendency toward predication appears in all our experiments with such regularity that one must assume it to be the basic syntactic form of inner speech" (pp. 287–288). Bruner (1985) and Wertsch (1979b) further explained Vygotsky's notion of predication as a very broad one; that *predicate* does not refer so much to grammatical verb (as compared to subject), but instead to foreground compared to background, or new compared to old information.

As with the case of the child's first holophrastic utterances, in inner speech we choose the symbolic element that gives us the most information. As Wertsch noted, "In the case of private speech, given information is that knowledge that is in the speaker's consciousness at the time of the utterance. So-called new information is what is being introduced into the speaker's consciousness as a result of the action he is carrying out" (Wertsch, 1979b, p. 95). Take the case of walking through a park where a group of people are playing with a frisbee. If the frisbee comes flying toward your head, it isn't likely you'll stop and say to yourself: *Gosh, the trajectory of that frisbee is such that if I don't take evasive action, I'll get beaned.* More likely is that you'll note the general similarity of the event to others with unfortunate results (background information) and choose the inner speech that gives you the most direction (foreground information): *Duck!* I conclude that inner speech is the result of many cycles of internalization of private speech. Ultimately, private speech goes underground to form inner speech, which is at first consciously directed, but may become more automatic with multiple occasions for internalization and use. Thus, speech is thoroughly transformed to serve conceptual thought.

To explain the development of speech-for-thought, several scholars (Kuczaj, 1982; Thomas, 1979) have adapted Vygotsky's work into a set of loosely structured stages:

1. Primitive stage: Speech is nonconceptual; thought is in unorganized "heaps."
2. Naive psychology stage: Words become symbolic in function; speech and thought begin to merge.
3. Egocentric speech stage: Private speech is used to solve problems; thought and speech merge to produce verbal thinking.
4. Ingrowth in speech stage: Inner speech emerges and makes possible true conceptual thought (adapted from Kuczaj, 1982, pp. 280–281).

This last point is the crux of the intellectual matter; the process of internalizing speech makes us the kinds of thinkers we are. Does this mean that inner speech is the same as thinking? No. Thinking, in a concrete fashion, oriented in the present, is certainly possible without speech. But once speech comes to serve thought, one can think in "pure meanings" (Vygotsky, 1934/1986, p. 249), not necessarily just in words, but semantic meanings. Nor is inner speech synonymous with thinking in words only (Vocate, 1994). Inner speech is a mental function originally created from external words, but transformed into a plane of thought that consists of complex, condensed meanings. As Vygotsky (1934/1986) put it, "in external speech thought is embodied in words, in inner speech words die as they bring forth thought.... It [inner speech] is a dynamic, shifting, unstable thing, fluttering between word and thought ... every thought creates a connection, fulfills a function, solves a problem" (p. 249). How do these meanings become complex, condensed, and rich enough for human thought?

Creating Concepts: Heaps, Complexes, Pseudoconcepts

Peggy and Ellen are happy to believe that they share meaning for the word *love* as they take delight in their bedtime ritual in which they confirm their mutual delight and depth of feeling in the phrases "I love Peggy" or "I wuv Mommie." However, Peggy's meaning is just beginning to develop, whereas Ellen has the use of an already constructed and complex concept (love) to apply to the situation. Their meanings do not coincide, because their opportunities to internalize experience vastly differ. Just how does Peggy develop meaning for the word she has learned to use in interaction with important others? Vygotsky suggested a progression of concept formation from "unorganized heaps" to several kinds of "complexes" and finally to "concepts." Throughout, I refer to Vygotsky's (1934/1986) experiments to demonstrate: Children were provided an array of blocks in various shapes, colors, and sizes. The researcher presented one block and asked the child to create a grouping of similar blocks. Children's responses to "Make a pile of

'Tuesday' blocks like this one" will vary, depending on what phase of concept development each one is processing.

Heaps

Heaps emerge when the child lumps together a number of referents on the basis of chance impressions alone. Peggy is shown a small, yellow, triangular block among a full set of blocks of various shapes and sizes and colors. When asked to create a pile of "Tuesday" blocks like this one, she makes of pile of blocks, willy-nilly; a set of disparate objects linked by no common theme. *Complexes* are of several progressive types and pave the way to concepts. With complexes, toddlers forge concrete links between referents and words.

Complexes

An associative complex may be based on a similarity the child happens to notice. Given a small, yellow, triangular block, Peggy may throw a yellow, round block onto the pile, then a blue, triangular block, then a small, red, square block. That is, any bond between the nucleus block given and any other block suffices to designate the grouping as "Tuesday" blocks. Indeed, the bond may not have to do with size, color, or shape, it could just as well rely on proximity; a block resting next to the original block may be added. The word in this case *(Tuesday)* is a "family name for a group of objects related to one another in many different ways," (p. 114); it is the way toddlers form categories of things.

A collection is a set of things grouped together on the "basis of some one trait in which they differ and consequently complement one other" (Vygotsky, 1934/1986, p. 114). In this case, starting with the small, yellow, triangular block, Peggy would choose "Tuesday" blocks on the basis of contrast; she might end up with a pile of blocks, each of a different color. Here, she is using association by contrast rather than similarity. Thus, first the child heaps things by chance subjective links, then associates things based on concrete similarities, then collects them based on complementary differences. What must be next, if the child can now categorize and contrast? A mode of synthesizing the general and the particular is on its way.

A chain complex has no stable nucleus of meaning, but is based on consecutive links between one referent and the next. If Peggy is ready to make chain complexes, she may pick out a few triangular blocks until her attention is captured by the blue color of the block she just threw on the pile. Hence, she switches to blue blocks of any shape until a round block catches her fancy and she's now off in pursuit of rounded blocks. The attribute that links these "Tuesday" blocks keeps changing during the process of creating the meaning for the grouping. The original block may have no significance by the end of the chain formation; each link in the chain is as important to meaning as the last. This type of thinking that fuses the general and the particular is "distinctive of all complex thinking" (Vygotsky, 1934/1986, p. 117). It is in the active synthesis of categorization and differentiation that the groundwork for conceptual thought is performed. In genuine concept formation, it is equally important to unite and to separate: Synthesis must be combined with analysis.

Pseudoconcepts

A *pseudoconcept* is the "bridge" between complexes and concepts. As Vygotsky asserted, "What we confront here is the appearance of a concept that conceals the inner structure of a complex" (1934/1986, p. 119). Now, given the yellow, triangular block, Peggy may create a grouping of all triangular blocks, or she may choose all yellow blocks. It would appear that the set has been assembled on the basis of an abstract concept of what a triangle is, or what the color yellow is. But Peggy is guided by concrete similarities and distinctions. Indeed, Ellen may think that when Peggy enters preschool, they are sharing meaning for "I love you" as they leave each other in the morning, but there is a time lag between the appearance of mature use and actual conceptual thought. In that lag, internalization occurs.

As Vygotsky (1934/1986) noted, it is difficult to find the borderline between pseudoconcept and true concept, because in appearance they seem the same to a concept user. But the child does not freely construct pseudoconcepts at will, but instead "receives all the elements of his complexes in ready-made form, from the speech of others" (p. 122), whereas the adult freely constructs concepts.

Peggy begins to practice conceptual thinking, with the tools given her, before she is aware of really how to construct it herself. Vygotsky (1934/1986) stated, "The concept-in-itself and the concept-for-others are developed in the child earlier than the concept-for-myself" (p. 124). As Peggy uses "love" as a pseudoconcept, it serves to link her with Ellen's by means of conceptual meaning, and the preconditions exist for Peggy to begin to use conceptual operations. Vygotsky elaborated, "But the advanced concept presupposed more than unification … it is also necessary to abstract, to single out elements, and to view the abstracted elements apart from the totality of the concrete experience in which they are embedded" (p. 135).

Concepts

Potential concepts are the next step in the development of abstraction, and occur when a grouping is formed on the basis of a single attribute. Although the same basis of a core attribute is true for concepts, potential concepts are products of habit, not truly created. They are based on a rule "that situations having some features in common will produce similar impressions" (Vygotsky, 1934/1986, p. 137). However, potential concepts further the potential for abstraction. Note that associative complexes presuppose "abstraction" of one trait, but that trait is unstable, "has no privileged position" (Vygotsky, 1934/1986, p. 139). In potential concepts, "a trait once abstracted is not easily lost again among the other traits. The concrete totality of traits has been destroyed through its abstraction, and the possibility of unifying the traits on a different basis opens up" (Vygotsky, 1934/1986, p. 139).

A *concept* is formed by two lines of development. First, the child combines diverse objects under a common "family name," (categorizes) and then singles out certain common attributes (differentiates). As Vygotsky maintained, "In both the use of the word is an integral part of the developing processes, and the word maintains its guiding function in the formation of genuine concepts" (1934/1986, p. 145). He also asserted, "Learning to direct one's own mental processes with the aid of words ... is an integral part of the process of concept formation" (1934/1986, p. 108) and reaches full potential in adolescence.

Understand that I have taken you through Vygotsky's theory of concept formation in some detail because not only is this process dependent on symbolic behavior, but it also comes to then direct later (transformed) symbolic behavior. I think it unlikely that we can explain communicative development in the absence of such a model for the link between communication and conceptualization.

The use of concepts to build intellectual functions is critical to human functioning, and we take that up in the next section. For now, let's look at how concepts are used in social cognition.

Constructs and Scripts: Concepts in Use

George Kelly (1955/1963) proposed "a psychology of personal constructs" that has widely influenced scholars in communication and social psychology. Kelly considered the term *concept* to have overtones of something too abstracted from human use. For him, the classical notion of concept "as a property attributable to two or more objects which are otherwise distinguished from each other" (Kelly, 1969/1979, p. 9) ignored the fact of their human construction. That is, a concept serves "no human purpose unless the user is immediately concerned with at least one other object in which he intends to negate the property" (p. 9). Note that this idea harkens back to the notions of contrast and negation, both characteristics of symbols.

Constructs

As concepts in use, constructs serve to "differentiate objects as well as associate them" (Kelly, 1969/1979, p. 9). Agreeing in principle with Vygotsky, Kelly maintained that not only do humans devise constructs, but that these "pairs of sharply drawn distinctions" (p. 10) enable us to make choices and engage in distinctively human enterprises. Not a category of events, a *"construct is a reference axis devised by a [hu]man for establishing a personal orientation toward the various events he [or she] encounters"* (p. 10). For example, Peggy at 2½ may develop a fairly simple construct for approachable people that has two poles: "nice" or approachable and the converse "not nice" or unapproachable.

Noting that personal experience leads us to perceive events differently, thus leading to disagreement about reality, Kelly wanted to explain the phenomenon leading to these personal sense-making frames. For symbol users, there is no "objective reality" that we all construe in the same way. Instead, we construct our dimensions of psychological space in terms of reference axes and project experience onto these axes. Kelly noted, "The more independent axes upon which we project an event the greater the psychological depth in which we see it, and the more meaningful it becomes to us" (1969/1979, p. 27). One way to figure out human behavior is to try to understand the relevance of the behavior to the one behaving. That is, we must *infer* the personal constructs—reference axes—used by a person to understand the link between objectives and behavior. Thus, to know something about a person's construct system is to be able to anticipate his or her choices and thus predict his or her behaviors. In Peggy's case, Ellen observes Peggy's talk about "nice" people and her behavior with them, and subsequently will be able to predict the sorts of people to whom Peggy is likely to be drawn.

Although Vygotsky used the term *concept,* I do not think he would disagree with Kelly about the contrastive nature of these "constructions." Whether we call them *concepts* or *constructs,* they are created to serve sense making. However, for Kelly (1955/1963), constructs are primary psychological frameworks for patterning experience that are available to other animals as well as humans. Vygotsky would say that we use symbols, words as the raw material for loading meaning onto these sense-making frames. Kelly would emphasize the nature of constructs as psychologically primary. That is, the basic framework for thinking is about similarity and contrast. Presumably, simple construction is an innate psychological endowment.

Adams-Webber (1982) expanded on Kelly's "dichotomy corollary," which asserts that "a person's construction system is composed of a finite number of dichotomous constructs" (1955/1963, p. 59). He noted our figure versus ground perceptual tendency and, furthermore, the "minimal contrast" that is "the basic principle of linguistic analysis" (Adams-Webber, 1982, p. 101). Adams-Webber asserted, "Minimal contrast occurs whenever two items differ in terms of a single feature that is relevant to a linguistic distinction" and, furthermore, "linguistic marking" occurs when a new feature is added to a basic form to produce a new "marked" version. The two forms, marked and unmarked "lie in a general relationship of minimal contrast" (p. 101). Thus, which comes first, contrastive patterning or symbols to label the contrasts? Clearly, infants can perceive contrasts and similarities before they symbolize, and for Kelly that was a kind of construction. But until we name these contrasts, can they serve us to predict and explain?

Adams-Webber's linguistic analysis implies that we do need words to set up these useful polar distinctions. He categorizes the "nominal pole" as the positive or "unmarked" pole, in that it provides the name of the construct as a whole (e.g., "nice"). The negative or "marked" pole is the "contrast pole" in that it designates the other end (i.e., "not nice").

What seems clear is that these sorts of distinctions are made possible by having symbols to constitute the marked and unmarked poles. Adams-Webber (1982) and others observed that children's construct poles are close together and lopsided; they become more balanced as they mature. He suggested that children's memories for information are encoded in terms of the contrasting poles of their constructs; and that, with age, their recall of distinctions between persons improves until after midadolescence, when their judgments tend to converge. What this means for Peggy is that although her first distinction may be based on the "nice" continuum, with age the construct may be identified more clearly as "people's social predispositions," and she probably will develop as many ways to identify the negative pole as the positive.

Indeed, she will probably develop a number of constructs subsumed by this broad one, such as "upbeat," "friendly," "inquisitive," "generous," and the like; each with their contrast poles ("negative," "antisocial," "self-involved," "stingy," etc.).

If symbols work in this fashion, in terms of sets of contrasts, then this is additional support for the link between communication and cognition. In the field of communication, the *constructivists* have adapted Kelly's basic notion of constructs and built a theory that relies on the notion of "cognitive complexity" as an explanatory variable for communication behavior. Their position aligns them as more sympathetic with Piaget's primary focus on cognition than with Vygotsky's on interaction. Their theoretical stance implies that children do develop more complex cognitive systems for regulating social behavior. However, the explanation for that development has relied more on advancing maturation (age) than on interaction and internalization.

Using a measure of cognitive complexity that counts the number of cognitive constructs—identified by descriptive words—that an individual uses to describe others, they found correlations between complex construct systems and advancing levels of persuasive strategies (Applegate & Delia, 1980; Clark & Delia, 1976; Delia & Clark, 1977; Delia, Kline, & Burleson, 1979). They concluded that the more constructs one has available with which to differentiate people, the more effectively one may take the perspective of others and thus the more successfully one may adjust communication to influence others. In chapter 6, we examine their research more closely. For now, let's assume that their theoretical conclusion is a sensible one: that the more tools one has for describing others and thus for thinking about their uniquenesses, the more capable one might be in adjusting their surface utterances to meet others' needs. On the face of it, this is not so far off from Vygotsky's notion of inner speech in symbols serving the problem-solving needs of the child and later emerging as socialized speech. However, the explanatory mechanisms for the development of socialized speech are quite different (cognition vs. spoken interaction). To predict, as the constructivists have done, from cognitive complexity to communicative behavior may be a case of putting the cart before the horse. Regardless of the direction of causation, spoken interaction and problem-solving capacities are linked.

Assuming that the child has the use of symbolic constructs that are rapidly increasing in number and complexity, and that their number and complexity are linked to interactive experience, let's see how scripts are useful in planning social behavior.

Scripts

A script may be viewed as a sort of scaffold for social behavior. In that sense, interaction games such as "peekaboo" are examples of very early interactive scripts. Nelson (1981) considered a script to be a detailed sequence of acts designed toward a particular goal. With interactive experience, we add script knowledge, and that knowledge becomes more and more generalizable to various activities. For example, Peggy's earliest script may be "peekaboo," but that script is fairly rigid and consists of very specialized actions. Later, she may learn a script for "going to the store with Mom" that has many variations allowing her freedom at specified choice points (e.g., when entering the store, I may ride in the grocery cart or walk along beside it).

Corsaro (1985) acknowledged the contribution of script theory to understanding development, but claimed that it is not enough to say that scripts guide children's interaction. What we need instead are explanations of how children identify script features in interaction and link that with their social knowledge. In his own research, he has examined how peer cultures negotiate meaning in shared routines, pretend play, and conflict. Rizzo and Corsaro (1988) explained the incorporation of both peer and adult routines by means of Vygotsky's notion of internalization as "a series of cyclical movements from the interpersonal to the intrapersonal with the contribution of cognitive reflection ... increasing in importance and complexity with successive cycles (p. 236). In this way, children learn script variations over the course of many cycles of internalizing interaction sequences.

Mental Functions

If speech is indeed becoming internalized such that thought processes are assisted by the tools of symbols, what sorts of mental functions can we expect to be formed and transformed? When speech may be used for one's own purposes; how is it used to recall, to solve problems, and to figure out others; and, ultimately, how does it change the nature of thought from egocentric to socialized, from a spoken monologue to an unspoken dialogue? We look at a few of these functions here, but as we examine the nature of various relationships in the next chapter, keep in mind that the child's relational experiences are critical to cognitive development. Hartup (1985) proposed that "relationships account for both normative change in certain cognitive functions and the generation of individual differences in certain cognitive skills" (p. 75); thus, those who serve as cognitive mediators are very special Others indeed. The quality of these relationships undoubtedly influences the child's process of creating a mind.

Memory: Stretching Meaning

Even in the first year of life, long-term recognition memory matures rapidly. Recognition memory is involuntary and cued; it occurs when a set of associations is triggered by a stimulus. Such memories of scenes or events are imprinted in neural networks, but may not be recalled unless cued. Thus, in the absence of some cuing mechanism under the individual's control, voluntary or "free" recall is not possible. It is worthwhile to note that memory "props" are not limited to rehearsing words to move them beyond short-term memory, nor to writing words down. Cole and Scribner (1977) pointed out that, contrary to Leont'ev's views regarding literacy and memory,[30] some nonliterate cultures use both external memory props such as tying knots in ropes, but also use internalized devices such as epic poems.

Once children can use words or other symbols to hold an idea or an association, their memory performance improves. For Vygotsky, the merging of natural processes (recognition memory) and cultural means (symbols: words, pictures) is a process of internalization. Valsiner and van der Veer (2000) noted, "Subjects originally rely on material, external means but gradually learn to replace them by internal means" (p. 367).

Toward the end of the second year, children begin to be able to "hold two items in memory and to establish relations between the two" (Hartup, 1985, p. 69). Later, young children are likely to use external means of memorizing, such as writing down a number, or relying on other people to help them; and older children are more likely to use internal means such as rehearsing (Meacham, 1977).

A dialectical model of memory emphasizes the interdependence of development in different domains. In Leont'ev's (1959/1964) words: "Changes do not occur independently of one another but [are] intrinsically connected with one another. In other words, they do not represent independent lines of development of the various processes (perception, memory, thinking, etc.)" (cited in Meacham, p. 289). Hence, the young child is first cued for memory, then begins to use internal cues (symbols) to recall aspects of a problem or event, then can combine those recalled cues to think about past experiences and the links among them: "Memory rather than abstract thought is the definitive characteristic of the early stages of cognitive development.... For the young child, to think means to recall; but for the adolescent, to recall means to think" (Vygostky, 1978, pp. 50–51). That is, for the toddler, thinking requires remembering what he or she has experienced by way of the symbols linked to those experiences; for the teenager, remembering occurs in inner speech that is fully conceptual and in individually creative thought.

With the development of voluntary memory in mind, let us turn to problem solving as another mental process assisted by internalizing external cues.

Problem Solving: Working in the Zone

For Hartup (1985), the cognitive functions "most closely linked to social relationships are the 'executive regulators'—the planning, monitoring, and outcome-checking skills involved in problem-solving" (p. 76). The dialogues between cognitive mediators (mothers, tutors, etc.) and children center on problem-solving skills, and in that process the child shifts from other-regulation of his or her behavior to self-regulation.

Because problem-solving thought occurs in the context of social interaction, speech is the mediator of developmental change. And it is spoken interaction, in *the zone of proximal development* (ZPD) that provides the external model for solving problems. The ZPD is "the distance between the actual developmental level as determined by independent problem solving and the level of potential development as determined by problem solving under adult guidance or in collaboration with more capable peers" (Vygotsky, 1978, p. 86). The "actual" developmental level is where the child can function alone; it is defined by mental functions that have already matured. The "potential" level is where the child can function with assistance; it is defined by mental functions that are in the process of internalization but are not quite there. Let's look now at how this potential level is tapped.

A. R. Luria (1979), a colleague to both Leont'ev and Vygotsky, conducted a series of classic experiments to trace the development of behavior regulation by verbal means. He tested children from age 2 through age 6. Each child was given a set of verbal instructions, and the child's ability to follow the directions was observed. The child's task was to learn to press or refrain from pressing a rubber bulb when a set of lights came on.

Between 2 and 2½ years, children cannot follow the simplest verbal directions if they are given prior to the task itself. In this case, as the instructions were given ("When the red light appears, squeeze"), they responded by immediately pressing the bulb rather than waiting for the lights. Often, once the light came on, they stopped responding altogether, as if distracted. Indeed, when hearing the word "squeeze" they produced a whole series of involuntary bulb squeezes. Even when told to "stop" their squeezes continued with even less control.

Between 3 and 4 years, they could follow the instruction "squeeze" with few extra responses. In the course of repeated tests, they learned to listen to the directions, withhold the response until the lights appeared, and then to squeeze. Luria concluded that at this age, the children verbally formulated "a general rule for themselves which served as a barrier against the tendency to respond directly to the verbal instruction" (1979, p.107). It is interesting to note that in other mammals, it is difficult if not impossible to get the animal to interrupt an impulse once it has begun. Clearly, young children develop the ability to mediate their own impulses. However, they are still in the process of organizing those impulses. When the researcher made the task harder by giving them choices ("When you see a green light, do nothing. When you see a red light, squeeze"), the children responded in one of two ways. Either they continued to respond when the green light followed the red light, or they failed to respond when the red light followed the green light. By the way, the problem was not that the children forgot the instructions; they could repeat them at the end of the tests.

By the age of 6, the children had no difficulty performing accurately. Gradually, complex models of verbal regulation had been formed. First, toddlers simply react to the action word "squeeze" in a fairly indiscriminate manner—the word itself has the effect of externally initiating the child's behavior, but once begun it could not be stopped (negated) by words. Then, at 4, they wait for the appropriate stimulus before they respond; that is, they have formed a "functional barrier" against an immediate response to the word. Finally, by age 6, children have internalized the means of regulating their own behaviors.

One note about the upshot of problem-solving development for later thinking: Regardless of our assumptions about how complex and abstract problem solving appears to be, we continue to refer to concrete experience (Hundeide, 1985). That is, even though we internalize and, to some extent, abstract mental operations so they may be used in a variety of contexts, we continue to link certain sequences of solution steps to particular settings. In this way, we internalize particular episodes, add others on, and ultimately have a set of episodes with similar characteristics. Hundeide (1985) offers an example: A fourth grader with a long history of school failure repeatedly insisted he could not solve equations because it was too difficult and he was so stupid that he didn't even know how to read properly. Based on his past experience with classroom tasks, he had drawn a conclusion about this sort of problem solving. A tutor, outside of the classroom, asked the boy if he'd like to play a game. He agreed. Then she asked, "Think of a number, add 2, what do you get?" He answered "6" and the tutor told him he'd been thinking of 4. This clever trick astonished the boy and he wanted to know the secret. After a few trials, they changed roles and he had no trouble solving the equations mentally. The following day, as the boy was trying again to explain equations in the traditional classroom manner, he gave the tutor the old response: He didn't understand. Apparently, problem solving is linked to particular episodes *and* to the self-definitions we form in those episodes. Thus, the success or failure of early episodes, as well as the bond between the learner and the more sophisticated mediator, are critical to later flexibility of mental functions.

Wood and his colleagues (Wood, 1980; Wood, Bruner, & Ross, 1976; Wood, Wood, & Middleton, 1978) explored the importance of the mediator's sensitivity to the learner's cognitive development. In setting the "scaffolding" necessary for learning in "the zone" (ZPD), caregivers should follow a "contingency strategy" in trying to solve a problem with their child. What this strategy implies is that the caregiver's intervention in the process should closely follow the child's successes and failures. When the child errs, the mother should give suggestions just one level lower than she did before; conversely, when the child is doing well, she should increase her demands slightly. In this fashion, the caregiver uses the ZPD to the child's greatest advantage.

The affective bond between caregiver and child may also influence cognitive development. Interested in the influence of attachment on joint problem solving, van der Veer and van Ijzendoorn (1988) conducted sequential analyses of mother–child interactions around problems. In securely attached dyads, mothers responded meaningfully to their children's requests for help; they gave direction or physically assisted. In anxiously attached dyads, requests for assistance were not met with prompt maternal reactions, not even after several time lags. The results of this study suggest that the responsive mother is likely to optimize the use of the zone of proximal development for her child's problem-solving development: "Children from a securely attached dyad ... will feel emotionally secure when coping with difficult cognitive problems" (p. 242); this is likely to affect their success with such tasks.

What other changes in the affective bond are likely to influence developing mental processes? The shift to symbolically mediated emotions along with the possibility of controlling emotion is likely to have multiple effects on relationships and social cognition.

Affect and Symbols: Emotion Regulation

Once the child begins to use symbols, and can use them to label self, it becomes possible to own one's affect—to recognize that this state of being is mine and may not be the same that someone else is experiencing. To say "I sad" means that Peggy knows what she feels and particularizes it to herself. Thus, Peggy now has a subjective experience of her feelings; they have become emotions in that move from an affective expression of an internal state to an emotional experience she can now make the subject of dialogue, to herself or another.

Once it is possible for toddlers to consider their own feeling states, to attach meaning to them, then thought and emotion become intertwined: "Creating artificial ... boundaries between thought and emotion obscures the experiential and neurobiological reality of their inseparable nature ... we can say that emotion and meaning are created by the same processes" (Siegel, 1999, pp. 158–159). Now the child begins to load meaning on all sorts of words and constructs, including those for feelings.

We know that 7-month-olds can express feelings like anger toward persons restraining them; that is, they have learned not only that some of their immediate feelings have identifiable causes, but also that they can express those feelings to influence others. But when they begin using their first words for emotion, they open not only a door to true relationship among equals, but a gateway to controlling as well as expressing their feeling states. By 2½ years, toddlers can talk about feelings (Lewis & Michalson, 1983), discuss past and future emotions, and recognize emotional sequences (Bretherton, Fritz, Zahn-Waxler, & Ridgeway, 1986).

Smiley and Huttenlocher (1989) suggested a developmental sequence in the acquisition of emotion terms. First, the child uses emotion words *(sad, mad)* to refer to current feeling states of their own. Next, the child notices external cues for others' emotional experiences and uses the terms to describe others accordingly. Finally, the child starts to sort out others' emotions in varied contexts and can distinguish emotions (e.g., mad from scared) in novel situations.

Beyond primary emotions (happiness, sadness, anger, fear), more complicated emotions like pride and shame take more sophistication and experience to understand. Because they rely on reference to others' approval or disapproval, they require minimally a sense that another can have opinions that affect one's feelings. Between 6 and 7 years, children have some understanding of pride and shame, but this understanding is used only when the child commits an act in the presence of a significant other, such as a parent (Harter & Whitesell, 1989). Later, the external audience becomes an imagined audience—that is, the experience is internalized—so the child can experience pride or shame even when alone.

What takes even more time is the recognition that people can experience more than one emotion at a time. Harter and Whitesell (1989) found that this sort of advanced understanding develops between the ages of 5 and 12. Originally, children claim that it is impossible to feel two emotions at once. Although some 6-year-olds do admit such a possibility, they do not seem to be able to give an example of that occurring until much later. What seems to happen first is an understanding of successive feelings about a particular target, and only after this accomplishment does the child understand simultaneous mixed feelings.

Empathy and Perspective Taking: A Special Feeling/Cognition Link

In most of the literature on empathy, it is considered an abstracted knowing of the other's feeling that goes beyond mere resonance, yet stops short of the intellectual imagination of the other's options found in perspective taking. By the age of 2, we begin to see the first signs of empathy, which requires the recognition that others' distress is separate from one's own. However, appropriate empathic *response* apparently calls for more sophistication in understanding emotional blends.

Omdahl (1995), who has done the bulk of the work on empathy in the communication field, wrote of this more advanced ability to recognize multiple emotions, "It makes sense to me that the closer the match on all emotions experienced by the sender, the greater the empathy" (p. 17). Children younger than 8 years do not recognize that people can experience two or more emotions at once, especially when the emotions are opposite in their valence (Harter, 1982). For example, Ellen may be both pleasantly relieved and furiously angry when 6-year-old Peggy is found wading in the creek after Ellen's half-hour search. However, Peggy is unlikely to recognize both feelings, or even admit that Ellen could feel possibly feel both. Understanding these complicated emotional blends may require the more intellectual process of perspective taking in addition to empathy.

Scholars still "debate whether people can experience the same emotion as another person without taking that person's perspective" (Omdahl, 1995, p. 17). Omdahl asserted "that empathy can and does occur without perspective taking. However, I also believe that perspective taking abilities are associated with an increased likelihood of empathy, and that claim is supported by several studies" (Borke, 1971; Feshbach & Roe, 1968, as cited in Omdahl, 1995).

Although emotion language is available between 18 and 20 months of age, and by 28 months numerous explicit emotion labels (e.g., happy, scared) are in use, role taking as the last stage in the development of empathy is acquired more gradually.[31] Role taking requires deliberate cognitive effort at imagining oneself in another's place. What must occur is "cognitive restructuring" such that, "what is happening to the other is viewed as happening to the self" (Hoffman, 1982, p. 284). Although Piaget would claim that role taking can only emerge after the stage of egocentrism (approximately 7 years), this claim was challenged by Shatz (1977), who maintained that role-taking skill develops gradually, in line with Vygotsky's internalization. Shatz cited a study in which 2½-year-old girls produced "socially adapted" conversational turns over 75% of the time. When Maratsos (1973) asked 3- to 5-year-olds communicate information to blind or sighted persons, they were more explicit in helping the blind person. Borke (1971) found preschoolers accurate in identifying emotions experienced by children pictured in different situations; 4- to 5-year-olds demonstrated an ability to accurately assess a situation and identify which emotions were most likely to result. The abilities to "role take based on situational cues and to perspective take based on individual and situational cues increase with development ... [demonstrating a] leap at about 6 years of age" (Omdahl, 1995, p. 35). Such a leap would be the likely result of an accumulation of many previous cycles of internalizing interactions with a variety of people.

What is the child's likely empathic response? Just past the origins of empathy, children develop comforting skills, starting with patting or touching, and later use of verbal reassurances, sharing, and assistance (Thompson, 1987). Many of these responses are learned skills for expressing their empathic impulses. To take the negative example, abused children learn from their abusers. At first, they will attempt to console a distressed partner, but, if that fails, they express anger and then physical violence (Klimes-Dougan & Kistner, 1990). It may be that the primary impulse to console is linked to more spontaneous, instinctual communion between like beings; however, if it is thwarted, a learned, scripted strategy acquired from intimates comes into play.

Socialization of adaptive emotional expressions continues to develop as the child becomes more capable of regulating emotion. Even 6-year-olds know they should curb their honest feelings if someone is likely to be hurt if they express those feelings, but they also know that children who don't express their real feelings might be disliked even though they'd avoid getting into hot water (Saarni & Crowley, 1990). Once faced with choices such as emotional expression versus social appropriateness, children make decisions adaptive to the situation. Elementary school children control emotional expression more with peers than with parents, probably because they can anticipate peers to be less forgiving than parents (Zeman & Garber, 1996). Along with developing capacities for thinking about what they feel, children have also been constructing a sense of who they are.

SELF AS A SPECIAL CONCEPT

> My earliest memory is of sitting in a double pram opposite my twin brother. Both hoods were up protecting us from the rain which tapped on the canvas above our heads. Outside was the cold, wet country lane. Inside we were secure in the warm darkness of our private world. I looked across at the person with whom I shared every day and night, with whom I had even shared the months in my mother's womb, and suddenly, out of this moment of complete security and belonging, arose a feeling of utter aloneness. In this instant I met my own individuality for the first time. Although I was only two years old and still intimately bound to my brother, I was now also separate, independent and isolated. (Colegrave, 1979, p. 1)

The Symbols for a Self: Identity Development

In Colegrave's example, the sudden conscious realization of distinctiveness was all the more stunning because her closest "other" was in many ways similar to herself. For most of us who are not twins or are only children, the differentiation between self and other may be easier to dichotomize than it is with an other so like self.

The process of identity formation has often been viewed as dialectical. Berzonsky (1989) called his a "process orientation to identity" in which one constructs a theory of self in a dialectical exchange of assimilative and accommodative processes (p. 365). He relied on Piaget for the contrasting procedures of assimilation (taking in information from the external environment) and accommodation (changing the internal system to adapt to information that doesn't quite fit anywhere),[32] and noted that when assimilation fails, dissonance exists and accommodation follows to modify and revise the dissonant aspects of the self-theory.

Berzonsky (1990) further borrowed Erikson's 1968 definition, noting "the self-identity emerges from experiences in which temporarily confused selves are successfully reintegrated in an ensemble of roles which also secure social recognition" (p. 211). The confusion Erikson mentioned arises from experiences at variance with what has been previously internalized. And, as we know, we internalize those social experiences that we share with others.

Peggy may know by the age of 3 that she is a girl and have already assimilated from her parents a number of beliefs about the roles girls should assume. Then she may be told by a new and significant other, the preschool teacher, that boys can play with dolls too. The accommodation of this new belief will likely be resisted because it does not fit with her current gender schemas; she will continue to view herself as a someone who plays with dolls in contrast with her friend, James, who plays with trucks. However, the sight of her new school chum, Jack, playing with dolls, will stir up some dissonance in her self-theory about being a girl, and that theory will probably shift gradually as she internalizes her experience with Jack and, for that matter, with Jill who plays with trucks!

For Shotter (1993a), selves, relationships, and our understandings of reality are all constituted within dialogical joint transactions. To use Bakhtin's term, we "oscillate" between interaction at the periphery of self with others and subsequent reintegration at the core. In this oscillation lies the movement that leads to growth and change. Thus, for Piaget, the movement is between assimilation and accommodation; for Bakhtin, it is between periphery and core. For Lovlie (1982), the dialectic is between reflection and differentiation: "As I differentiate, I reflect, and as I reflect, I differentiate.... The total self, then, is made up of the 'I'—that aspect of the self that relates to the 'me,' and the 'me'—the funded reservoir of meanings" (pp. 99–100). The "I" is the active knower, the one interacting at the boundary; the "me" is the object that is known, the core set of constructs for self that are the subject of reflection and revision. As the infant becomes an object to self, a relationship *with* self is established.

For Bakhtin, humans do not have an internal territory, inviolate to the individual. Indeed, we become conscious of self while revealing to another (Shotter, 1993b). Stating it another way, "I come to know myself as who and what I am, in terms of how, until now, I have resolved all the 'differences' that have arisen in me—the differences between me (as I have become) and what I experience as 'other than' me" (Shotter, 1993b, p. 124). Within this dialogic construction of a self emerges the possibility for *true relationship* between equally powerful symbolizers. Shotter wrote about the "zone of uncertainty as to who can do what in the construction of a word's significance" (p. 125) as the point of power where two people attempt to shape the social reality in the boundary between them ... "the combat zone of the word" (Holquist, 1983, p. 307).

Self-Tasks and Achievements

Given what we know about the construction of the self, what tasks does the toddler face? Fogel (1995) noted that once a child has a sense of self, then begins the work to establish an identity: "a coherent sense of the self through time" (p. 122). He proposed that a cohesive and unified identity is explained by the same processes that create stable consensual frames in a relationship. That is, the procedures for establishing expectations for a relationship and for establishing expectations for a self are not all that different. "Self-frames" may be narrative forms or self-stories, they may be preferred cognitive-emotional patterns or patterns of value for particular kinds of relationship. For all of these frames, spoken dialogue provides the raw materials for building expectations.

The toddler uses language to represent self, often with appropriate pronouns as the first tools, such as "Look at me" "I'm Peggy," and "Mine." Case (1991) suggested that such verbal skills permit the shift from the "explicit" sensorimotor self (the "I" in interaction) to the "implicit" referential self (the "me" self that is the object of knowing). What also becomes possible now is for toddlers to symbolically represent the rules set by caregivers. In the process of internalizing standards, toddlers are empowered with the ability to regulate their own behavior (Emde, 1988), and from there to construct their own stories about their "goodness" or "badness" in light of those standards.

Recall that a construct is a reference axis between two poles for establishing a personal orientation; in this case, toward the self. Often social constructs, set up for understanding people, are formed in terms of how the self falls on the axis. For example, a child may have a construct featuring friendly and not friendly. Typically, the child will use one pole of the construct more frequently, and probably it will be the one they identify with self ("friendly"); but with age, that tendency to feature one pole decreases (Adams-Webber, 1985). As Adams-Webber suggested, "The average proportion of unlike-self judgments in the [construct] repertory grids of normal children gradually increases with age and eventually stabilizes ... during midadolescence" (1985, p. 63). As this lopsidedness decreases with age (from 8 to 13), the child should be able to structure experiences of self and others with increasing differentiation; that is, to elaborate the self-other distinction (Hayden, 1982). Constructs become more balanced with increased opportunities for using them to refer to both self and others.

One way to describe self is to tell stories. Narratives about self may be a powerful source of constructs for the "me." Eder (1994) reviewed the research on stories told *around* children, stories told *about* children, and children's *own* storytelling. Narratives told in the presence of children can contribute to emotional responses to the world; they learn how others feel about events (e.g., if stories about the world as a dangerous place are consistently heard, children will come to feel fearful about their world). Stories told about a child in his or her presence often provide the child with information about the teller's attitude toward them, and may reinforce their emotionality by replaying particular experiences (e.g., if children hear stories about themselves that include evaluative terms such as "weak" or "cowardly," they will internalize those terms for the "me.") Finally, children's own stories seem to serve two functions. First, they replay and change stories to resolve internal conflict and thus regulate their own feelings about self; and second, they disclose information about the self for others. Personal storytelling is a more advanced behavior, because it requires some sophistication in controlling own expression. Knowing this, we can assume that adult narratives about the child occur first and serve a socializing function as well as providing self-construction materials. However, children's own stories are likely to present features of self that they select to present and thus affirm. Self-presentation is a more advanced ability than self-labeling and necessitates choices among self-labels about what the children wish to reveal. And self-presentation skills continue to change throughout the lifetime.

Hecht (1993) started to construct an identity theory of communication in response to his assumption that "identity is inherently a communicative process and must be understood as a transaction in which messages are exchanged" (p. 78). Eight assumptions ground the theory; some serve to summarize what we have already examined, and others are explored in later chapters:

1. Identities have individual, social, and communal properties.
2. Identities are both enduring and changing.
3. Identities are affective, cognitive, behavioral, and spiritual.
4. Identities have both content and relationship levels of interpretation.
5. Identities involve both subjective and ascribed meanings.
6. Identities are codes that are expressed in conversations and define membership in communities.
7. Identities have semantic properties that are expressed in core symbols, meanings, and labels.
8. Identities prescribe modes of appropriate and effective communication.

A final word before we leave these notes on the early development of identity. Identity is a process that continues throughout life. In Nudler's (1986) view, our need to develop beyond sheer biology can lead us to either underadaptation (resulting from insufficient or damaged socialization) or overadaptation (often resulting in repression), but the acceptance of dialectical paradoxes is what can lead us to transcend our socialization and enculturation. Instead of denying the uncertainty we find, or trying to accommodate constantly to the uncertain nature of conscious existence, the transcendence to which Nudler referred is characterized by "an active search for new development patterns with its associated increase of uncertainty" (p. 135).

We explore these ideas further—by reference to issues of abuse, neglect, attachment, and the like—in future chapters. However, the interested reader may wish to develop a better feel for the concept of transcendence and its relationship to uncertainty by reference to Maslow (1968/1982), Gandhi (1980), or Watts (1951).

SUMMARY

We have examined the raw materials and processes for creating a mind as well as the consequences of those processes, including a sense of self and enduring identity. We are peculiar communicators; we use symbols to communicate, which means that we go beyond representation to process information by categorization, differentiation, and generalization. We organize our meaningful sounds syntactically, stretching memory to both past history and future plans. We internalize our meaningful experiences to create a mind and identity. With the possibility for true relationship with other identities, we turn now to the role of the Other in development.

NOTES

26. Washoe was the chimp first trained by the Gardners to use American Sign Language. Herb Terrace wanted to document their reported results more scientifically than they had done. What Terrace found was that his subject, Nim Chimsky (yes, in "honor" of Noam Chomsky) was typically being cued for appropriate responses; that is, he was imitating his caregivers. For an exceptionally accessible overview of animal communication research, see Pinker (1994; especially chap. 11).
27. Carstairs-McCarthy (1999) provided a detailed but readable linguistic explanation of the evolutionary beginnings of such features for language and how we arrived at the sort of language we have.
28. Dance and Larson (1976) developed theory regarding three functions of human communication: linking, mentation, and regulation. Their text gives detailed treatment of each.
29. Worth noting here is that variations in intelligence have been linked to myelination differences; more intelligent brains show faster nerve conduction and reaction times (Miller, 1994). Furthermore, the brain and the environment are continually in interplay with social factors, and not at all constant in its development (Casaer, 1993). Brain development is affected by our social behavior and is not purely a function of maturation.
30. Leont'ev, Vygotsky's colleague, believed that literate people have superior memory systems because of the assistance of writing systems. Cole and Scribner (1977) argued that the evidence from nonliterate as well as literate cultures demonstrates that various cultures specialize differently in memory methods; some nonliterate cultures are better than literate ones at certain memory tasks, such as memory for narratives, as with the use of epic poems.
31. Role taking requires that one understand the position one fills socially in a particular situation. However, it does not require that one understand the individual. Perspective taking requires that one understand both the social position the other faces in the situation as well as the options the individual faces from his or her unique point of view.
32. Piaget (1926/1954) wrote, "In their initial directions, assimilation and accommodation are obviously opposed to one another, since assimilation is conservative and tends to subordinate the environment to the organism as it is, whereas accommodation is the source of changes and bends the organism to the successive constraints of the environment. But if in their rudiment these two functions are antagonistic, it is precisely the role of mental life in general and of intelligence in particular to intercoordinate them" (p. 352).

Peggy's life had consisted of long days playing in the yard with neighborhood children, visiting the elderly threesome next door—two ancient sisters and a
brother—and trying to do what Ellen did, whatever that flurry of activity was. Until
today. Today, Ellen walked with her up the long block to the three-story brick school.
Peggy was excited until she got to the door of the kindergarten class. Then she was
scared. More children than she'd ever seen at once were spreading out over the room.
She clung to Ellen's skirt as the teacher approached them. Miss Bassington was slender
and blonde and smiling. She looked nice. Just as Peggy considered that here might be
someone who would see and welcome her, Miss Bassington turned to welcome another mother. Ellen was speaking: "Now, I have to leave but I'll be back to get you at
lunchtime." *What? Leave me here with these strangers and no one who knows or cares
about me?* "No, I wanna go home!" "You have to go to school, Peggy. I'll be back
soon." And she turned and walked away. Peggy could feel the tears start.

And then, Miss Bassington was back, kneeling with her face close to Peggy's. "Would
you like to paint? That's what we're going to do first. Why don't you come over to the
easels with Mark and Erin." A broad expanse of paper was set up at her height. *Yes, I
would like to paint.* On her right, Mark looked over. "Who are you?" "I'm Peggy." "I'm
Mark and I'm bigger than you and I'm a good painter." She turned left to Erin who
also had residual tears on her lashes. Their eyes met. *Yes, she feels sad too.* When they
left the easels to learn a song at the pink piano, Erin and Peggy held hands.

Early Relationships: Knowing the Other

And so when I start speaking a powerful right arm
of words sweeping down, I know *him* from what I say,
and how I say it, because there's a window open
between us, mixing the night air of our beings.

(Rumi, quoted in Barks, 1995, p. 32)

RELATIONSHIPPING: CREATING SELF AND SOCIALITY

For most of us, relationships are fulfilling and frustrating, mysterious and mystical. They are the source of great joy and deep despair. For scholars and students of human behavior, they are complex and challenging, mazelike and multifaceted. Simple linear explanations of stepwise relational development and maintenance have failed us, so many of us have moved to dialectical and dialogical descriptions. And, although these models may not be as clean and neat as earlier theories, they better capture the nature of relationships.

Relating as the Humanizing Process

Relationships are not entities or outcomes, but instead are ways of being in a human, social environment. Baxter and Montgomery (1996) described relationship as the gap between two, or the hyphen in "self-hyphen-other" (p. 234). They also noted:

> A relationship begins with the interplay of contradictory voices. A relationship's "end" is marked by dialogic silence—that is, the absence of contradiction. A relationship, thus, is constituted in and through its dialogic complexity. A relationship's dialogic complexity is captured by simultaneous moreness *and* lessness on a variety of contradiction-based characteristics.... (Baxter & Montgomery, 1996, p. 73).

This quote captures the nature of adult relationships well, but does not explain the earliest relationships and how they *acquire* dialogic complexity. That complexity does have its foundations in contradiction; the child's understanding of relationship begins in the contrast between self and other. I suspect that the very young child recognizes when the other's will is different from his or her own, but cannot yet recognize the range of "moreness and lessness" positions possible in that distance between the polar extremes of mine and yours. That takes experience. And that interactional experience, by way of symbolic interaction, is what makes us human.

Fogel (1993) suggested that relational processes give rise to the sense of self and to the rest of human cognition as well. In his view, relationships develop in the process of creating consensual frames and, furthermore, they sustain themselves in this process of creative coregulation. For Fogel, adults are not the agenda setters for relationships with children, but instead are participants who may suggest socially appropriate structures for relating.

Steve Duck (1991) also viewed relationship formation as a continuous process of creation in which intimacy emerges from mutual negotiation. That is, the bond forms in the creation of a set of intimacy frames over time. As Fogel (1993) asserted, relationships are "dynamic systems ... created out of repeated interactions between the same two individuals" (p. 89). But what else is required beyond interaction over time?

Fogel certainly acknowledged that relationships are constrained to some extent by cultural norms and individual preferences and motivations. Miller (1993) took the position that "relationships themselves can be construed as constraints, or limitations that partners place on each other's behavior" (p. 2). She suggested that constraints are necessary for mutual understanding and predictability. You may recall (from chap. 3) that Fogel described two kinds of "consensual frames" that may be considered as sets of constraints. One type is for creativity and innovation, and the other for rigidity and dissolution. He further proposed that both types are needed to maintain relationships. Miller assumed that constraints change as we negotiate new understandings; that learning occurs when prior expectations are "adjusted to accommodate new relationship experience" (p. 3).

Note that contrast—differentiation—is foundational for learning about relationships. For any adaptive change to occur to a conception of relationship, the child must first observe new relationship constraints, and then recognize that these new limits are different from the ones previously affecting the relationship. As we follow relationships over time, we track this learning process to ever richer conceptions of various relationship models.

My position is that very young infants are not capable of relationship as we normally understand the term in reference to adult activity. Infants certainly do interact but, in order to begin to form a model of relationship, they must establish stable frames with a consistent partner and develop methods for storing and retrieving those frames. That is, the capacity for symbolic interaction, for the formation of a "story" about the link between self and particular other, is necessary. Thus, we follow the traces of relationship from its origins in the toddler.

Generalized Other: The Model for Self

Put simply, the self *is* the "imaginative cognition of co-regulated relationships" (Fogel, 1993, p. 146). Thus, others are necessary to the development of a self. Furthermore, the fully developed identity rests on a concept of Other, or what Mead (1925) referred to as the "generalized other." For Mead "the individual comes to adopt the generalized perspective of a group of significant others that shares a particular societal perspective on the self" (Harter, 1999, p. 19). Mead implied that the cumulative judgments of numerous significant others combine to give the individual an overall sense of self in the light of the surrounding community. At first, it is enough for Peggy to know that she is different from Ellen. But with time and a variety of other relational partners, she will form a concept of Other to balance the concept of self. This generalized Other is a model against which the self may be tested. *Other is the social audience for which the self is presented.*

Distinctive Other: The Model for Significant Relationships

A young child's interaction partners provide the scaffolding for relational expectations. We have examined the nature of those early interactions in great detail. For our purposes, we rely here on an overview of developing social knowledge outlined by Haslett and Samter (1997) in three stages over the first 3 years of life. In the first year, Peggy learns that she is distinct from her fellow interactants and begins to acknowledge the independence of others' actions. At 12 months, she begins to recognize some situational constraints and dispositions of others. Then, she begins to acquire knowledge about different social settings as well as knowledge about others as unique individuals. This last stage is marked by rapid growth at around 3 years of age; Peggy has begun to build true relationship models that acknowledge the distinctive characteristics of others while providing contrast to her own idiosyncracies.

Who are these others whom Peggy is likely to know, and how does she view their relationships with her? Bigelow, Tesson, and Lewko (1996) warned against describing any one relational domain in isolation from others. They identified both peer (friendships) and family domains (parents and siblings) as well as nonfamily adult contexts (teacher, extended family, etc.). They also pointed out that this last set of relationships has largely been ignored in the literature on social relationships. Keeping in mind that some relationships have received more attention than others, we examine here both child–adult relationships and child–child relationships as developmental contexts.

BEGINNERS' RELATIONSHIPS: DICHOTOMIES
ON THE WAY TO DIALECTICS

Child–Adult Relationshipping: Contrasts Between Unequals

Adult caregivers carry the burden of socializing young children; their relationships with children are complex and constrained in many ways. Humans are dependent on elders for material sustenance far longer than most species; thus, parents become agents of change and development beyond simple behavioral routines to social and intellectual knowledge, emotional responsiveness, and control.

Parents have expectations for their roles in the parent–child relationship, and they include both the responsibilities of parental duties as well as the rewards of a dominant relational role. Children's first expectations, on the other hand, are built not so much on cultural norms as they are on relational frames and routines—that is, on their relational experiences. A relational model is "a cognitive representation of what relationships are supposed to be like" (Dixson, 1995, p. 49), including the child's standards for judging relationships (Hinde, 1981, p. 000). Because this sort of cognitive ideal is the result of internalizing relational experiences, we would expect the model to change as relationships develop and as exposure to other relationships increases (Duck, 1986). As children develop models for relationships, they can begin to compare actual interactions with the model and may find some interactions lacking. When reality does not conform to expectation, then the relationship may be judged as out of the norm, or breaking the rules. When experiencing such discomfort, the child may reference the original rule ("You're supposed to take care of me!"), but ultimately may have to change the expectation ("Big kids have to learn to take care of themselves"). First we explore children's models for parenting, and then we look at the research on early parent–child relationships for clues as to how those models are constructed.

The Child's View of the Parent–Child Relationship

Dixson (1995) confirmed that children's expectations are important. The more their relationships with parents met their expectations, the more satisfied they were with these relationships. Certain of these expectations were specific to an open style of communication. The more family members encourage honest communication and accept disagreement, the higher the child's reported satisfaction is and the smaller the difference between expectations and experiences is. Dixson concluded that the perception of an open family environment is key to a child's ability to challenge perceived inadequacies in the relationship. Children who feel able to confront differences between expectations and actual interactions are the children who comfortably express the rules for relationship that emerge from their models. In such expression, models are brought into the learning zone (ZPD) with other, clarified, and possibly adjusted models. In other words, the "story" about the relationship that is expressed aloud reflects the model that is being constructed internally. Those models that remain unexpressed, or indeed suppressed, are more likely to be maintained as standards that may not be met and thus result in dissatisfaction with the relationship.

In a follow-up study designed to examine children's models of the parent–child relationship, Dixson and Stein (1997) surveyed 88 children ranging in age from 6 to 12 about their perceptions of what children and parents are *supposed* to feel and how they are *supposed* to behave with each other, and the rules they *should* use in their interaction. Although the study is limited, it is unique in examining the child's model of relationship. We know about children's models for friendship (LaGaipa, 1987), but there is little information about what children expect of their parents. Results of their categorical data give us some direction regarding children's first relational models. For example, girls and boys differed in their expectations: Girls were more likely to hold expectations about going places (social occasions, dining, shopping, vacations) and about communication rules (talk nice, don't interrupt) than boys, who were more likely to respond that children should be emotionally supportive with parents (give hugs and kisses, help them, cheer them up). The girls' emphasis on communication rules confirms earlier research, but boys' emotional supportiveness seems contrary to stereotypes about masculine roles.

Younger children focused on parental child care responsibilities, which is sensible in light of their greater dependence. Older children emphasized going places with parents, and expected emotional support. As the authors pointed out, the developmental trend is away from instrumental needs and toward expecting social support needs to be met in the relationship with parents (Dixson & Stein, 1997).

Although simple behavioral rules receive less attention with age and experience, more sophisticated rules for talk and conflict grow increasingly important, as do expectations for giving and receiving emotional support. Apparently, children's models develop in the direction of the social and emotional aspects of relationships.

Emotions in the Parent–Child Zone

Recall that children increasingly consider emotional support an important part of their relationship with parents. Parents, the primary agents of socialization, in most cases do have the greatest influence on children's interpretations and management of emotions. However, despite the emphasis in the literature on parental effects, keep in mind that relationships with other adults and with peers also affect the child's structuring of emotional response.

Parents influence their children's emotional development profoundly and by multiple methods, from modeling to direct instruction (Anderson & Guerrero, 1998). Regardless of how parents *intend* to influence children, they *model* the mores of the culture in their emotional displays. Modeling, then, is a most powerful influence on young interactants. According to Stearns' (1989) history of emotional suppression, expressions such as anger and jealousy have often been discouraged whereas familial love was socially approved; therefore, children have had few models for the former. Such suppression makes it difficult for the child to recognize or express suppressed emotions, and thus the cycle will continue until cultural norms again shift toward expression.

One example of a shift in cultural norms for emotional expression is found in the reaction of the generation raised in the 1950s, a decade following the trauma of war and characterized by its suppression of negative emotions. As the baby boomers came of age, interest in therapy as well as in mind-altering drugs increased, in part to serve their suppressed interests in expressivity. This generation sought different relational models to learn alternative emotional modes. What they then modeled for their children resulted from a blend of relational models based on their own parental relationships as well as later peer and professional relationships. You might guess that such mixed models give somewhat inconsistent messages with muddled results. The following generations—"X" and "Y"—apparently have little difficulty expressing emotion but may have some problems managing them. What we observe in these cycles is a dialectic between expression and management of emotion. If one manages emotion well, expression may suffer; if one expresses emotion well, management may suffer. It is a variation on the open/closed dialectic and, as such, a tension that each individual experiences to some extent.

Regardless of the modeling parents provide, each individual eventually is presented with both poles of emotional dialectics. In the early years, parents may present modeling slanted to one pole, or each parent may specialize in a particular pole. Parents apparently model a greater range of emotions to girls than to boys (Brody & Hall, 1993), thus giving girls the edge for range of emotional expression. Interestingly, although boys seem to feel they should emotionally support their parents, they also suffer the effects of gender stereotyping that emphasizes management over expression for males. Indeed, these stereotypes are often stated explicitly.

Beyond modeling cultural norms, parents provide *active instruction* to their children regarding the appropriateness of emotional expression. Certain emotional expressions are expressly discouraged, thus becoming the likely candidates for management and control: "Big boys don't cry," "Don't sulk," and "Calm down" are all attempts to diminish the child's expression. For Americans, anger is considered a negative emotion to be suppressed, especially for girls, and its expression is often punished as well as expressly forbidden ("Don't you raise your voice to me!").

Parents' expectations also *shape* the child's expressions. Certain expressions are subtly encouraged or discouraged, often by nonverbal means. For example, a parent may smile at an angry boy, but frown at an angry girl (Lemerise & Dodge, 1993). Adults who believe they are observing an infant girl—regardless of the infant's actual gender—label negative affect as fear; those who believe they are watching an infant boy label negative affect as anger (Condry & Condry, 1976). When parents expect a child to be anxious, the child's behavior over time conforms to that expectation (Jones, 1977).

Parents can choose to reward and punish emotional expression but, from a dialogical view, active instruction and reinforcement are not as powerful influences as are the modeling and shaping that children observe and experience in interaction. Nevertheless, parents do provide *reinforcement* for preferred responses. Rewards include love and attention, gifts, privileges, and the like. Punishments include disapproval and removal of rewards. What is important about reinforcement is the message the child receives about parents' expectations and the effect they have on the child's model for the parent–child relationship. Boys expect their parents to respond negatively to boys' display of sadness, and thus they express less sadness; girls expect their mothers to react negatively if they express anger but positively if they express sadness. Girls, then, express less anger and more sadness than boys do (Fuchs & Thelen, 1988).

All of these types of influence are predicated on the early *attachment* formed between parent and child. As we have seen, the attachment bond is based, in part, on emotional expression. One type of emotion that has only recently been examined from a communication perspective (Pendell, 2002) is *affection*. Affection is a human social emotion that is thought to "facilitate cohesive, psychologically rewarding family relationships and paternal investment in children" (MacDonald, 1992, p. 753). Although affectionate communication may be biologically adaptive, it is a set of learned behaviors that serve our social natures (Pendell, 2002).

Affection has been linked to a range of relational and individual effects, including the exchange of help and support between parent and child (Parrott & Bengtson, 1999); the child's extroversion as a function of father's affection (Kuterovac-Jagodic & Kerestes, 1997); and the child's self-esteem as a function of affective ties to parents (Roberts & Bengtson, 1996). Pendell (2002) concluded from her review of the affection literature that "the types of behavior people perceive as affectionate will be those they associated with secure, caring relationships as infants and at various growth stages" (p. 94). The expression of affection, along with a range of other emotions, is critical in the first relationship as the model for later relational expectations.

Thought in the Parent–Child Zone

In chapter 4, we examined the close connection between symbolic communication and human thought. Rather than repeat that material here, we explore an explanation for the "missing link" between thought and speech that implicates the parent–child relationship. Gupta (1998) pointed out that the actual merging of the separate lines of development—thought and speech—is not clearly explicated in Vygotsky's work. Inner speech is the connection point between external speech and internal thought, but the roots of inner speech in social interaction are merely implied.

Gupta (1998) sought to demonstrate those roots by documenting the various roles that private (egocentric) speech can take for the child when her or she is actively involved in interaction. By coding both social functions as well as self-regulating functions, Gupta demonstrated that the toddler uses various forms of private speech in interaction with an adult, and that those forms serve multiple purposes, some social and others task oriented. An example of combined function is the child who says "This is right?" while frowning, tapping the problematic puzzle, and looking to the adult. Gupta concluded that private speech does not serve merely to solve problems and thus become inner speech directly following internalization. Rather, the development of private speech describes a gradual and systematic progression from birth and through interaction, serving both social and instrumental purposes. Higher mental processes are actively constructed on the basis of this progression as private speech merges with all forms of interactive expression, verbal and nonverbal.

When Ellen asks 4-year-old Peggy to find the picture of the dog, Peggy may look over the pictures in front of her, saying softly "Dog dog dog" which serves to both remind her of what the task is and to confirm with Ellen what she is doing. Then, Peggy picks up a picture with an emphatic gesture, shows it to Ellen, and glances up to her. In the latter sequence, Peggy not only solves the problem with flair for her own edification but demonstrates to Ellen her achievement and checks for her reaction. Thus are parents foils for children's mental construction.

Behavior Between Unequals: Control, Discipline, and Compliance

Schaefer's (1959, 1997) view of parent–child interactions—that they describe a circular order of behaviors—employs several relational dialectics. Schaefer's circle is defined by a vertical axis between autonomy and control, and a horizontal axis between love and hostility. In most conventional adult–child interaction, the bias is for behaviors toward the *control-love* quadrant. Most parent–child relationships are characterized by a degree of nurturance and protectiveness. And, so long as the child is dependent on parents materially and emotionally, this is apparently functional. Referencing Fig. 5.1, we see that parental love can give rise to the urge to protect and control, which the child will ultimately resist, leading to hostility and to parental relinquishing of control, allowing movement again toward love.

Discipline is a specific kind of control that parents exert to structure safety and prosocial behavior. Although control may be gained by a number of means, the specifically communicative strategies used by parents to gain control are most often compliance gaining messages. We now examine both and then look at adult–child relationships gone awry.

Parental beliefs about discipline are created from their own social history, which is situated in the broader social history of a culture. A parent develops a "philosophy" of childrearing from multiple sources, but "primary socialization" (Mechling, 1975) is the result of internalizing experience from childhood. Thus, each parent's values regarding parenting are established individually, yet conform generally to cultural norms. "Secondary socialization" methods such as learning from manuals or workshops, or adapting to parenting situations in unique ways, are not necessarily linked to the primary beliefs handed down from parents' parents.

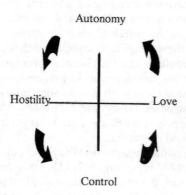

FIG. 5.1.   Parental role dialectics in parent–child relationships.

The result of primary learning processes on parenting practice is that change (like any internalization process) occurs slowly; there is often a lag between observing the trial new behavior and incorporation of the behavior as an idea that may fit in the belief system. Let's say that Ellen grew up with parents who practiced corporal punishment; their belief was that unless children felt physical discomfort the children would continue dangerous or antisocial behavior—"spare the rod and spoil the child." Ellen then felt the need to slap Peggy's hand when she reached for a pan on the stove. Ellen then read Dr. Benjamin Spock (1977), who recommended that parents use corporal punishment sparingly and instead provide limits supported by explanation—that is, talk with their children instead. Although Ellen was skeptical, as her children grew she did try on several occasions to talk about the limits she set. Ellen still used physical punishment much of the time, but Peggy remembered the explanations and incorporated communication into her beliefs about parenting. Peggy's later childrearing practices excluded corporal punishment (see chap. 10).

Societal norms for disciplining children have varied over time and across cultures (Peisner, 1989). In 19th-century America, consistency was the prevailing theme. If the child "turned out badly, it was due to poor training" (Peisner, 1989, p.131), and thus inconsistent parental discipline was blamed. Moreover, mothers became the primary disciplinarians and, as the century wore on, values shifted and mothers were advised to be more permissive, although systematic. As behavioral science came into its own, expert advice grew in value. Parent education was delivered via the Parent–Teacher Association (PTA), emphasizing social and emotional growth. With the 1940s, psychological welfare became a concern. As Peisner commented, "While mothers still were responsible for their children's and society's future, producing well-adjusted and intelligent children now was seen as the best way to fulfill obligations to both" (p. 134). This meant that mothers' duties had expanded greatly to include cognitive, emotional, and social nurturing. Now, the question of discipline was how to use it so that "children learn what is expected of them, and then learn to expect it of themselves" (Peisner, 1989, p.135).

Current expectations differentiate between acceptable versus unacceptable (abusive) techniques of punishing misbehavior and rewarding compliance. Wilson and Whipple (1995) summarized the differences between nonabusive disciplinarians and abusive ones: Nonabusive parents are more likely than abusive ones to vary their strategies, using power-assertive techniques (punishment) when the child breaks social conventions and less coercive strategies when the child fails to comply with parental wishes; nonabusive parents are also more likely to discipline specific misbehaviors consistently; and nonabusive parents are more likely to praise the child's compliant behavior. One way that children learn what is expected of them is in response to parents' *compliance-gaining* attempts.

Abe and Izard (1999) maintained, "By following parental directives, children learn to regulate their behaviors ... and to internalize societal values and norms" (p. 000). Parents apparently use a wide range of strategies to get children to do what they would prefer, and the outcome is not simply parental sanity but also child social competence. Compliance-gaining strategies are communication behaviors designed to influence partners' behaviors. Marwell and Schmitt (1967) developed a set of 16 categories of compliance-gaining messages. Many communication researchers have since used that set to study compliance gaining in adults (Boster & Stiff, 1984; Cody & McLaughlin, 1980; Dillard & Burgoon, 1985; Miller, Boster, Roloff, & Seibold, 1977), and some have examined its use with adolescents (deTurck & Miller, 1983). But how parents communicate specific control attempts with children is largely unknown. McDermott (1986) found this gap in the literature and set out to find what strategies parents use, and with what success.

Observations of 173 parent–child pairs (45 fathers and 128 mothers) interacting in public places yielded intriguing results. McDermott found first that the original category system was inadequate to capture the observations. Although all categories were used, he added categories observed in a pilot study: simple command ("Do it now"), use of a proper name with raised voice ("Ted, get over here!"), physical punishment, and general nonverbal communication (tongue clicks, hand slapping, pointing).

Only 13% of parents gained compliance with one attempt; the average number of attempts to success was three (McDermott, 1986). All parents were successful by the sixth try. On the first try, command and proper name were most often used, followed by nonverbal means, pregiving (offering a treat), threat, and promise. The largest variety of strategies was evidenced in the final attempt before successful compliance. The most frequent final strategy was command, followed with decreasing frequency by physical punishment, nonverbal, threat, proper name, pregiving, promise, moral appeal ("Be a good boy …") and love withdrawal ("… or I won't like you").

What is most interesting about McDermott's study is that the most frequently used compliance-gaining strategies were those not included in the original category system developed with adults; indeed, the additional categories accounted for 60% of successful strategies. Thus, parent–child compliance-gaining trials call for different communication skills than do adult–adult attempts. McDermott concluded that traditional clustering of parental styles into either positive versus aversive, or coercion versus "love withdrawal," is too simplistic a treatment for how parents relate to children. Parents not only have a broad repertoire of strategies, but their strategies with children are specialized for early socialization. However, some parents employ inappropriate, unhealthy control practices, which distort the control/autonomy dialectic and exploit the love/hostility dialectic.

Distortions of Unequal Status: Child Abuse

Cicchetti (1989) identified child maltreatment as a "relational psychopathology" or dysfunction in the parent–child–environment system (cited in Harter, 1999, p. 264). Victims of chronic abuse report not only low self-worth, but also profound inner badness, self-blame, and feelings of responsibility (Harter, 1999). Although sexual abuse receives the most attention, it is most likely that traumatized children are abused in multiple ways, including physical, sexual, psychological, and emotional abuse (Cicchetti, Beeghly, Carlson, & Toth, 1990). Many of the forms of psychological abuse[33] represent extremes of the authoritarian parenting style (Baumrind, 1966, 1971, as cited in Harter, 1999, p. 265).

Victimized children can experience severe psychological outcomes, including dissociative identity disorder (Harter, 1999). However, we focus here less on extreme disorders in favor of the more common effects of abuse on sense of self. Effects on *self-awareness* are likely to include hypervigilance to others' reactions to the point of interference with one's own needs and desires (Briere, 1989). Very young maltreated children (30–36 months) use less internal-state language than do their securely attached peers (Cicchetti, 1989; Cicchetti et al., 1990). Several studies have observed that toddlers as well as older children who have been maltreated use less descriptive speech about their feelings and inner states (cited in Harter, 1999). That is, abuse victims know little of their own needs and wants.

Effects on *self-agency* or authorship of one's own actions and experiences include passive experience of events and depersonalization in which the person observes self from a detached perspective (Putnam, 1993). In general, victims of abuse lack feelings of efficacy, independence, and control (Harter, 1999). *Self-continuity*, a sense that one is the same person over time, also suffers. The loss of significant memories, often induced by trauma, deprives the child of the autobiographical memory on which the sense of self relies (Harter, 1999).

Neither is the abused child able to *integrate the self* successfully. The sense of a coherent, integrated self is a developmental achievement, usually emerging at the end of adolescence (Harter & Monsour, 1992). Young children usually do have a fragmented sense of self, "particularly along attributes that can be categorized as either positive or negative, good or bad" (Harter, 1999, p. 273). That is, children come to their sense of self by way of dichotomous understandings that serve to dissociate poles of personality attributes. However, the maltreated child's capacities for compartmentalization are limited by trauma and frozen by self-protection. When other children are starting to recognize that their personalities are not so simply characterized by one pole or another, abused children will remain fragmented in their self-understanding.

In summary, abuse impairs the development of "I" (the actor or knower or subject self) by the creating the need to maintain separate selves, by preventing awareness of inner states, and by leaving gaps in one's history or self-narrative. Abuse impairs the development of "me" (the known or object self) by fostering impressions of incompetence, low self-worth, blame, guilt, shame, and thus the need for presenting a false self (Harter, 1999).

Let's turn now to the dialectical communication dynamics that may be in play in cases of *sexual abuse*. Recall that most adult–child interactions fall toward the control and love poles of the control/autonomy and love/hostility dialectics. At one time or another, interaction behaviors in parent–child relationships probably fall in all the circle's areas, but one stands out in cases of child *sexual abuse*. Bennell, Alison, Stein, Alison, and Canter (2001) suggested that the "coercive nature of offender–child interactions in child sexual abuse relies on the offender gaining and abusing the trust of the victim by exploiting a range of conventional adult–child relationship patterns" (p. 155). Bennell et al. examined a set of police records gathered in the United Kingdom from victims 5 through 12 years of age. They found that although offensive behaviors fell in all quadrants of the circle de-

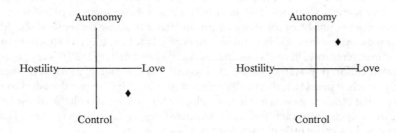

Frequent position in parent-child interaction   Frequent position of abuser-child interaction

FIG. 5.2.   Normal and distorted parent–child dialectics.

scribed by the two sets of dialectics, most of them fell in the *autonomy-love* quadrant. In these cases, abuse involved the use of nonthreatening seduction and minimization of the offensive behaviors—abusers manipulated the children by allowing them the impression of autonomy and the illusion of love. Binnell et al. (2001) commented, "Just as nurturance and protection are major factors throughout childhood in conventional adult–child relationships, granting children a certain degree of control appears to be a major component of offender–child relationships in cases of child sexual abuse" (p.167).

Thus, the control/autonomy dialectic is a critical one in child–parent relationships. The line between allowing a child a degree of autonomy and manipulating the child with the *impression* of autonomy in order to gratify the parent is a fine one. Our most challenging legal issues regarding children arise in this territory between the rights of parents to socialize children and the rights of children to be free of coercion. This issue arises again under the discussion of alternative nurturing. Now, we examine the role relationships of conventional nurturing roles: mothers and fathers.

Mothering

I often hear students express the belief that our culture has changed from one in which women perform most of the childrearing tasks to one in which parenting tasks are shared. Although extreme role specialization may have declined, I think these students overstate the case. Even if you ignore the self-reports from women regarding their "home" work in addition to their salaried work and simply rest your judgment on the number of studies using mother–child participants, mothers apparently remain the more active parents. Even if you believe that these studies do not reflect the actual parity of parenting, our current knowledge of parenting rests largely on data from mothers.

The literature already reported in chapter 3 regarding early parent–child interaction depends heavily on data from mother–infant pairs. With that as a basis, we examine the findings from toddlers and young children regarding their relationship with mother.

We know a great deal about the mother–child attachment bond and effects on emotional adjustment and relationship formation. A more subtle effect that mothers have is in the "emotional work" that they do. The bond between mother and child is not the only link she structures; she also brings the child into the family system.

Women's contributions to the social and emotional life of the family has been called "invisible work" (Daniels, 1987) because it has been unacknowledged and, until recently, rarely studied. Recall that mothers in the 20th century became responsible for nurturing the child's social, emotional, and cognitive development. Women construct a sense of family—feelings of belongingness among the members—by their daily work, such as meal construction (Devault, 1991).

Women also tend to kin relationships—make calls and visits, send letters and presents, and organize gatherings (di Leonardo, 1987). A recent study examined the ways in which "women's work" also includes building and maintaining father–child relationships. Seery and Crowley (2000) observed middle-class women who had at least one child older than 2 years. Of these women, 78% either reported that they deliberately promoted father–child relationships or were observed doing so. According to Seery and Crowley (2000), mothers' strategies for maintenance work included promoting joint involvement (suggesting what they might do or talk about, or managing the household schedule to foster joint activity, praising fathers for the time spent with children, and "not doing" activities so as to allow time); creating positive images of fathers (speaking so as to enhance the father's status to children; and peace keeping (monitoring interactions to intercede, separating fathers and children during disputes, and gathering and relaying information between fathers and children).

Importantly, not all women did this work, and the ones who did varied in their efforts. Apparently, the quality of the father–child relationship influences the mother's choice of strategy; positive relationships brought forth maintenance strategies (joint involvement, positive image work), whereas negative relationships demanded peace-keeping efforts. The "not doing" strategy is particularly interesting and has been echoed in other findings about emotion work. Deliberate acts of "willful nonaction" (Dressel & Clark, 1990) have been observed in women's caring behavior and probably contribute to the "invisible" nature of some of this family work. The fact that women historically assumed the primary parenting role explains to some extent women's need to step back and allow fathers to nurture.

Fathering

Research on male parenting was sparse until the 1970s, when it surged as the baby boomers began to have children and young social scientists were looking for new ways to understand their parenting experience. In a series of studies, Kotelchuck (cited in Lamb, 1978, p. 89) found that toddlers (12–21 months) show no preference for parent, regardless of context. However, his studies used different measures for attachment than most earlier studies, so Lamb repeated the tests and found very similar results—infants showed no consistent preference for either mother or father into the 2nd year (Lamb, 1976, 1977b). Well into the second year, Lamb found that boys showed consistent preferences for their fathers (1977a).

As we know from chapter 4, mothers and fathers do behave differently; fathers engage in physically stimulating play whereas mothers tend to initiate conventionally structured play routines. We also know that fathers are more concerned with gender-appropriate behavior in their children. Thus, parents each serve different functions—and fathers may be more important to gender identity and personality development, whereas mothers may have more to do with socio-emotional development.

Cognitive effects are mixed. In families without fathers, children tend to do less well on standardized intelligence tests and are more likely to rank higher on verbal than on math portions (Biller, 1974; Lynn, 1974). In general, fathers' involvement is related to better school performance for children; but, in particular, boys seem to do better with interactive fathers. Boys perform better in school when they have highly involved fathers (Blanchard & Biller, 1971), and perform less well when their fathers are restrictive (Epstein & Radin, 1975).

The effects of parenting on girls' cognitive development are less consistent. Aldous (1975) asserted that the relationship between parenting and child problem solving is complex. She found that fathers' directions in problem-solving tasks were positively related to their daughters' originality of solutions. Fathers gave fewer directions to low-originality daughters, whereas mothers gave more. Recall that mothers typically provide a good deal of structure in well-recognized games and play situations, whereas fathers use more idiosyncratic, free-form physical play. In later years, these two styles may be internalized as the parent who specializes in normative social structures (Mom) and the parent who specializes in creative activity (Dad). Thus, the child will come to expect to engage with each parent in different frames, and will internalize different capacities from them.

Alternative Nurturing

Not all families consist of mother, father, and their offspring. Family systems may vary by culture, or be created out of necessity, convenience, or preference.[34] In the U.S. legal system, the conventional family consisting of biological parents and their offspring is a legally protected entity. That protection extends to the freedom of parents "to direct the upbringing and education of children" (*Meyer v. State of Nebraska*, 1925, p. 399). Such protection is not afforded to all types of families in the United States.

Single Parenting

Of all children born in the United States in 1997, 32% were to unmarried mothers; this represents a sixfold increase since 1960 (Coley, 2001). Although most unmarried fathers have good intentions of being involved with their children (Johnson, 2000), their actual involvement decreases over time. In the first few years, about half have regular contact with their children, but by school age and adolescence, the rate of contact decreases 20% to 35% (Furstenberg & Harris, 1993; Lerman, 1993). In the case of divorce, one third of fathers have no contact with their children (Nord & Zill, 1996). Given the number of children living with only one parent, the societal expectation of involvement with both biological parents becomes problematic. But is it truly a problem for children?

Research about the effects of single parenting reveals mixed results. By adolescence, there appears to be a connection between living with a single parent and dropping out of high school or becoming pregnant. However, there are multiple factors involved in single parenting. According to McLanahan and Sandefur (1994), father absence is an important factor, but they go on to report that a stepfather in the home does not improve the child's chances of escaping the statistics, nor does the presence of another biological relative. Many single-parent homes have live-in grandmothers, which means the child is left home alone less frequently; however, such children are still susceptible to the same problems.

Children whose fathers were present until the they reached puberty were no better off than those whose fathers left when they were babies. Oddly, the only fatherless children who are better off are those whose fathers died. Children of widows fare nearly as well as those with two living biological parents (McLanahan & Sandefur, 1994). Why are fathers better dead than gone?

Let's look at assumptions about fathers. We assume that fathers will provide financial support, care, emotional support, and establish legal paternity (Doherty, Kouneski, & Erickson, 1996). We further assume that fathers' involvement enhances children's development, but there is little evidence to support a direct relationship between paternal influence and development. We found that fathers influence cognitive development, but that effect may be mediated by other effects of single parenting.

Harris (1998) pointed out that the link between single parenting and child problems is not strong and probably misleading. Most homes headed by *single mothers* are poor; half are below the poverty level. This lack of or loss of (in the case of divorce) income affects children in numerous ways. Money determines, in large part, where children live and where they can go to school. The poorer neighborhoods are likely to be places where there are higher rates of unemployment, school dropout, and teen pregnancy. In Harris' view, one of the important effects of poverty is that it affects children's status with their peers. Not only may poor children have to forgo some of the advantages that others take for granted (e.g., orthodontists, music lessons, sporting equipment), but they may never even consider attending college.

Even though we may explain some of the negative effects of single parenting by simple economics, we cannot dismiss entirely the contributions of a second parent to a child. What may be most important is the child's *expectations* of parenting. Certainly, there are discrepant results from the research on father involvement. For example, Furstenberg and Harris (1993) found that strong father attachment is related to fewer symptoms of teen depression; however, they also found that having a poor father–child relationship or having one that decreased in closeness was more harmful than having no relationship at all. Apparently, it is the *quality* of the relationship that is important. Moreover, that quality is defined by the child's expectations—problem adolescents are probably disappointed in the failure of the model they had once constructed of their relationship with the now-absent parent. Young children are pretty adaptable; they may well be able to adjust their expectations as their frames with parents change after separation. But the child who is close to adolescence and has had many years of framing his or her relationship with a father is likely to be very disillusioned when that parent leaves.

But what of the *single father*? Although there are fewer families headed by single fathers, they are more likely to escape the dangers of poverty. As well, fathers evidently adapt to the role. Hatfield and Abrams (1995) performed a multimethod (self-reports, observations, and observer reports) study of the communication in families headed by single fathers. They found that these family members report greater cohesion and higher adaptability than in traditional families. Furthermore, the interaction in these families displayed less competitive symmetry; that is, these members tend to discuss problems rather than to compete for control. Overall, these fathers communicated more frequently with their children than did traditional fathers. The quality of interaction was not rated differently by members of the two family types.

So, is single parenting detrimental to a child's development? The answer, I believe, is "not necessarily." If single parenting means that the child will live in poverty, yes the poverty may be devastating. If a parent has already established distinctive interaction frames with the child, yes the child's expectations will be disappointed and the parent–child relationship model will be deficient. But there are incredibly successful children emerging from single-parent homes; such a situation is not the clear sentence of continuing poverty, crime, and lack of motivation that has been assumed in the past.[35]

Polygamous Parenting

For fans of the nuclear family, the flipside of having too few parents is having too many, but again, it isn't that simple an equation. In our scientific zeal to define the "normal" family, we often miss the fact that our version is not all that common. According to Valsiner (1989), polygamy has been overwhelmingly dominant all over the world until very recent times. Only 20% of cultures globally have been strictly monogamous (Stephens, 1963) , so around 80% of world cultures allow some version of polygamy. As Valsiner (1989) noted, "It follows from the widespread nature of polygamic marriages that the social environment of many children growing up in different cultures around the world is likely providing them with a unique angle of knowledge of social relationships and experiences that differ from those of their Western counterparts" (p. 67).

There are three variations of polygamy: polygyny (one husband, several wives), polyandry (one wife, several husbands), and polygynandry (group marriage). By far the most frequent is polygyny (Valsiner, 1989). The latter two are only found in specific cultures on or near the Indian subcontinent. Thus, much of the research has been done on polygynic families.

Valsiner (1989), having conducted much of the research comparing family types, reported the contrasts between children's experiences in polygynic and monogamic configurations. One fairly large difference is that children have more opportunities to observe adult–adult interaction between father and several mothers in dyads, triads, and small groups. Another is the opportunity to observe changes in family composition; not only the addition of new wives, but the births and deaths of siblings are more frequently observed than in a monogamic household. Hence, these children experience loss more directly and earlier than do children from monogamic families. Additional social support is also available in the polygynic family; the child continues to be cared for in the event of the birth mother's absence or demise.

What is particularly intriguing for us are the effects on interaction and relationships. The child in a polygynic family has less opportunity to influence husband–wife relations because of the greater distance and lesser dependency between husband and co-wives; whereas in the monogamic family, the child can only influence two people and may play one against the other. There is also a unique effect on children: The relationships among co-wives can affect the framing of siblings' relationships. That is, mothers may promote rivalry (or cooperation) among their children and those of a co-wife. Perhaps most interesting is the fact that in the polygynic family, there is more opportunity for peer relationships to develop. Not only are there simply more siblings, but the odds are much better that a child will have a sibling very close in age (Valsiner, 1989).

Valsiner (1989) also commented, "All forms of marriage ... are adaptations to the need of organizing both everyday life, and the transition from one generation to the next" (p. 83) Despite our reservations about polygamic families in Western cultures, there are advantages, particularly for children. Given that the child remains in the family,[36] the opportunities for observing and participating in a wide range of close relationships are generally greater for the child in a polygynic family than for a child in a monogamic family.

Homosexual Parenting

Estimates of the number of young children with at least one gay parent run into the low millions (Bozett, 1987; Gottman, 1990). Thus, quite a few children are affected both by attitudes arising from the social norm for the husband–wife configuration and by the traditions of the legal system. Although the "best interests of the child" typically have been interpreted as placement with biological parents, that tradition lately has been challenged in the case of homosexual parents. If the court determines that the parents' sexual practices are relevant to the "best interests" of the child, then judges' biases may enter into custody issues.

According to Allen and Burrell (1996), courts may base their decisions on the argument that homosexual parental modeling would create problems for a child's socialization, and in particular for the presumed results of confused sexual identity and ostracization from the community. But are these indeed outcomes?

Green, Mandel, Hotvedt, Gray, and Smith (1986) compared children of single, heterosexual women with those of lesbian mothers and found no significant differences in sexual identification among boys. Although girls of lesbian mothers were less traditionally feminine in dress, play, and activity preferences, none of them suffered a gender identify disorder. Furthermore, no significant differences were found in the parenting skills of gays and lesbians compared to heterosexuals (Clay, 1990).

By means of meta-analysis of existing studies up to 1995, Allen and Burrell (1996) summarized the literature on homosexual parenting culled from both adult sources and child reports. Overall, they found virtually no difference between homosexual and heterosexual parenting in either adult or child reports. Children's reports demonstrated no difference between gay and straight parents regarding sexual orientation and life satisfaction, but a slight advantage for homosexual parents regarding moral and cognitive development. Allen and Burrell concluded that none of the measured variables showed any difference on the basis of parent's sexual orientation. Even though our mores, reflected in our laws, have defined homosexuality as a crime, apparently sexual preference has little bearing on parenting. Indeed, "The best interests of the child lay with a loving parent, not with a heterosexual parent or a homosexual parent" (Basile, 1974, p. 18). Nonetheless, gay parents may experience more stress originating outside their families than heterosexual parents do (West & Turner, 1995).

Grandparenting

This is a different sort of adult–kin relationship. "Grandparent" has been historically an enviable title; it does not carry the kinds of expectations for socialization that primary parenting does. However, one variation is the grandparent who *does* serve as primary caregiver, and that role is becoming more common.

Custodial Grandparenting

Casper and Bryson reported that from 1970 to 1997, the number of children living in grandparent-headed homes rose 76% to 3.9 million (cited in Goodman & Silverstein, 2001, p. 57). Most of these children have one or both parents also sheltering in the grandparents' home (64%), but the remainder—some 1.3 million—are solely under the care of grandparents. Although this type of family arrangement is more common among African Americans (13% of children), it is certainly found among Hispanics (5.7%) and non-Hispanic Whites (3.9%; Saluter, 1996).

There are some benefits to the grandchild placed in a stable grandparental household (Solomon & Marx, 1995); however, the effects on grandparents are less positive. Role conflict affected African American caregivers, who report problems in keeping paid employment and finding time for themselves (Burton, 1992). Grandparents assuming the parental role reported lower sense of well-being and lower satisfaction with their grandparenting role (Shore & Hayslip, 1995).

Goodman and Silverstein (2001) recognized that these grandparents are filling family roles that are not well understood, and I would add that the expectations for

all parties—parent, grandparent, and child—are unclear. From 149 survey responses, Goodman and Silverstein found that "virtually all" of the grandmothers
who responded cared for their grandchildren because of dysfunction in the mid-
dle-generation parents—drug addiction (74.5%), abuse or neglect of the grandchild (33.6%), plus a few cases of parental death, illness, incarceration, or
employment. They concluded that emotional closeness among members of the
family triad have consequences for the grandmother (and undoubtedly for the
grandchild, although we have only grandmothers' reports thus far).

The two most satisfying configurations were connected triads (equal links among
grandparent, parent, and child) and grandmother-linked triads. Connected triads
are apt to characterize families in which there is good parental involvement, and hope
for the parent resuming his or her role. When grandmother is the link between child
and parent, she expresses the highest life satisfaction. When the child was the link between parent and grandparent, grandmother expressed lower life satisfaction; indeed, the power of this mediating position may be unhealthy for the child (Goodman
& Silverstein, 2001). Grandmothers who clearly hold the parenting authority and also
have contact with the parent are those who are most satisfied. Goodman and
Silverstein (2001) noted, "One grandmother said her son helped her with household
repairs almost weekly, although he seldom provided child care. She preferred this arrangement because her grandson knew that she was in charge and she considered it
'less confusing' for him" (p. 572). Thus, if this family triad is linked by the appropriately authoritative party, then the outcomes are more positive. But these arrangements are seemingly born of distressed families. The more typical grandparent–
grandchild relationship is a different one, with fewer responsibilities.

Noncustodial Grandparenting

Most often, grandparents do not serve as sole caregivers and, although their role
is not voluntary, it is less fraught with legal and social obligations than most family
positions are. Grandparenthood has been described "as a social role that functions
to coordinate the familial generations, to maintain family culture" (Boyd, 1969, p.
90). But is grandparenting as glorious and valued as it once was?

Although we may expect grandparents to provide the narratives that link generations, our highly mobile families have come under the influence of "the new social
contract" (Kornhaber & Woodward, 1981) in which "no one is obliged to anyone
else" (p. 97). As a result, in Western cultures, grandparenting styles are greatly diverse, from detached or passive to supportive or influential (Cherlin & Furstenberg,
1985). Typically, grandmothers report higher satisfaction with their roles (Downs,
1988, 1989) than do grandfathers, who are relatively uninvolved (Hagestad, 1985),
but grandparents vary so much that the roles they internalize vary not only with
gender role but also with age, employment status, marital status, and educational
level (Robertson, 1977).

The sex of grandparent and grandchild seems to mediate the closeness and importance of the relationship (Dubas, 2001). In a longitudinal survey examining perceptions of children in sixth, seventh, eighth, and twelfth grades and at 21 years, 206

young adults reported on their family relationships, including grandparental ones. Granddaughters reported their relationship with grandmother was the closest and most important of their grandparental relationships; grandsons identified grandfathers as their closest and most important link to the older generation. Although prior research has suggested that maternal grandparents are most important in grandchildren's lives, this study did not find a significant difference between family lines. Dubas did note that the gender-related findings probably hold only in the absence of mitigating factors, such as divorce, social class, or farming context (in which farm land and work are typically passed down to sons). She further suggested that cultural norms regarding gender relations may play a role in the grandchild–grandparent relation, particularly for young adults.

Although I agree that gender role identity may be one factor in this relationship, the varieties of grandparenting styles and the inconsistency of results in the literature lead me to believe that this is another, among the many nonobligatory relationships in life, that may develop relatively free of cultural restraints. Let's look at possible effects when they do or do not develop.

Because the grandparenting role is relatively undefined in the modern family, and the older generation is often at such a distance that visits are infrequent, grandparents can feel ambiguity or ambivalence about this role (Wood, 1982). *Disconnected grandparents* express regret about their failure to pass on family heritage (Kornhaber & Woodward, 1981). Kornhaber and Woodward also noted that Grandchildren who have "no knowledge of ancestry, no sense of bloodline" (p. 42) and little vision of their own future as elders feel frustration and anger at the separation.

On the other hand, if frequent interaction between grandparent and grandchild is the rule, a "vital connection" marked by feelings of satisfaction and significance is reported (Kornhaber & Woodward, 1981). Three factors may influence the development of such bonds: proximity among the generations; visiting opportunities, particularly in the grandparents' home as a gathering place; and frequency of interaction among generations (Boyd, 1969). Overall, grandparents are seen as the link among generations that binds together the extended family. Although we do not know much about the interaction behavior between grandparents and grandchildren,[37] we do know something of the perceptions of grandchildren and grandparents.

Interaction between grandchildren and grandparents often involves the grandparent sharing experiences and history in stories (Kornhaber & Woodward, 1981). Grandparents report feeling a sense of continuation of family, as well as emotional self-fulfillment and vicarious achievement, through interaction with their grandchildren (Crawford, 1981). Children who have frequent interaction with older, significant adults have fewer age-related prejudices (Hickey, Hickey, & Kalish, 1968), do not consider their grandparents to be out of touch, and feel a responsibility to assist and emotionally support their grandparents when needed (Robertson, 1976). Baranowski (1982) concluded that grandparents provide another source of identity development, improved relationships with parents, and positive attitudes toward aging (cited in Downs, 1989). The grandparent–grandchild role, then, is a special one. It is an established, nonvoluntary kin relationship, yet without the obligations of other kin roles. This relationship allows the child to situate herself or himself within the extended family as well as within his or her own life expectations.

Nonkin Adult–Child Relationships

In loco parentis means, literally, in the position of a parent. In a broad sense, it describes any adult–child relationship in which the adult takes on responsibility for the child's well-being. Legally, teachers assume this role in the classroom. Less formally, babysitters and nannies do the same. Under certain contractual agreements, health care providers assume care provision. Little research has been performed on these relationships; therefore, we use teacher–student as the basic model for nonkin relationships, with a brief look at medical practitioner–patient relationships.

Teacher–Student

Cultural expectations and resource limitations contribute to a teaching model of a relationship in which one person addresses many, and that particular person is "responsible for controlling all the talk that occurs while class is officially in session" (Cazden, 1988, p. 3). Although this is the instructional model for much of the Western world, the teaching role may be seen much more broadly. For Vygotsky, the teaching process "forms the development of the child, creates new mental formations, and develops higher processes of mental life" (Leontiev & Luria, 1968, p. 365). That is, teaching is the type of interaction that stimulates development as it is internalized and, as such, may occur in relationships with parents, caregivers, healthcare providers, classmates, and chums, as well as with teachers. In essence, all of our discourse partners are teachers, but instructors have a special charge to model the specifics of certain intellectual processes.

Much has been written about teaching, but little about the relationship between the teacher and student. When we consider that classroom learning is taking place in the interaction between teacher and students, among students, as well as in teacher–student–student combinations, we realize we know little about the dynamics leading to optimal learning situations. For now, we leave the strategies for directing group instruction to the education specialists. Instead, we will focus on *instructional discourse* and what is instructive about it. Courtney Cazden leads the way.

Cazden, professor of education at Harvard and former primary school teacher, was a student of child linguist Roger Brown. She has spent her career examining the discourse of the classroom, often in the role of teacher/observer (1972, 1986, 1988). She has adopted a social interactionist perspective to her research and has contributed greatly to understanding student–student learning.

In the mid-1970s, Cazden left Cambridge for San Diego and entered an ethnically diverse, public school classroom to teach, observe, and try out collaborative learning ideas. She discovered much about the kinds of talk used in the classroom and about the outcomes of different sorts of interaction. One distinction she made is between the "teacher-talk register" and the "student-talk register" (1988).

Teacher talk is characterized by rank, power and distance. Talk designed to control the classroom includes showing or attracting attention, controlling the amount of speech, checking understanding, summarizing, defining, editing, correcting, and specifying topic (Stubbs & Delamonte, 1976, 1983). What is special about these message behaviors is that they are "radically asymmetrical" (1976, p. 162); that is, students rarely use them. Students expect there to be a "rank of imposition," or an understanding of the situation and the rights and obligations of both students and teacher in that situation (Cazden, 1988), and they expect teachers to use those understandings to keep the classroom structured. Much in the way that parents provide "scaffolding" for infant routines, teachers provide structures for learning more formally. Teachers typically use more questions, requests, and commands in their indirect forms than do parents (e.g., "I wish you could tell me" vs. "Tell me"), thus pointing up a distinction between these two relational roles. Mothers have a clearer authority relationship with their children, and thus do not soften their control statements as teachers do (Hess, Dickson, Price, & Leong, 1979).

As we might expect, teachers express greater social distance than do parents. Although affect is part and parcel of social life, it is nearly absent in U.S. classrooms (Goodlad, 1983). Some part of this lack of affect may be related to an accompanying lack of "comembership" that may be felt by teachers who do not share ethnic background or other group affiliations with their students.

A teacher's knowledge of students' cultures is critical to understanding their communication habits and expectations. Students, on the other hand, must learn the culture of the classroom to succeed. *Student talk* includes specialized timing and syntax as well as decontextualization and explicitness regarding the material. Not only must students contribute at the right time in order to be effective, but they must do so in the preferred language of the teacher. If timed correctly, substandard syntax will be tolerated but corrected in much the same way that parents often do, using expansions—repetition of the child's original utterance but in adult normative syntax. Cazden provided this exchange from a British classroom studying the function of sea animals' shells. The expansion is in italics:

T: What does protection mean? Any idea, Carl?
S: Sir, to stop other things hurting it.
T: Right, stops other things hurting it. Now, if it came out of its shell, and waggled along the seabed, what would happen to it? Yes?
S: It might get ate.
T: *It might get eaten by something else, yeah.*
     (Edwards, 1980, as cited in Cazden, 1988, pp. 188–189)

Students also learn that their classroom contributions must be decontextualized and explicit to the teacher's concerns. Language learners naturally reference their own experiences; that is, they talk about the context in which they internalized an idea or concept. However, teachers encourage their pupils to remove the personalization in favor of a more universal characterization. This example, with deperson-alized answer in italics, comes from a kindergarten discussion of word meanings:

T: What is a lullaby?
S1: It helps you go to sleep at night?
T: But what is it?
S2: *It's a song.*
T: That's right.
(Edwards, 1980, cited in Cazden, 1988, p. 190)

Although the first student's answer was not incorrect, it was not accepted by the teacher who pressed for a more conventional, abstract definition rather than the contextualized function the child offered.

Thus, children are encouraged to speak in a specialized register for formal learn-ing. Conciseness of expression and relevance to the teacher-defined topic are also re-warded, and woe to the child who does not meet these requirements. Certainly, these teacher demands are functional; children learn to reconceptualize phenomena, to see things in new ways. This not only leads them to acquire scientific knowledge, but it contributes to more universalized perspective-taking abilities—to recontextualize experience from a variety of mind sets. However, as Cazden pointed out, "We have to ask not just whose scaffold but whose world view" (p. 188). Children vary in the abili-ties and experiences necessary to participate in the Western culture classroom atmo-sphere. Sources of variance may include learning disabilities, emotional difficulties, family interaction patterns, and cultural norms. Without entering into a lengthy dis-cussion of each, let's briefly take the case of *cultural norms.*

What is relevant in one culture may not be in another; similarly, what is appro-priate interaction practice in one may not be in another. Given the multicultural nature of U.S. classrooms, these variations become a source of disparity in the edu-cational experience. Labov (1982, cited in Cazden, p. 143), who studied urban, Afri-can American adolescents' language and school performance for 20 years, was convinced that one source of reading retardation is the contrast between these stu-dents' home culture and school. Specifically, he pointed to the cultural value for co-operative group interaction on home ground versus the independent achievement demanded in school.

Forman and Cazden (1985) noted that if teaching is conceived as "assistance to the child in the child's zone of proximal development" (1985, p. 324), then teachers will encounter problems when faced with a group of children, each in different zones. But rather than focus on the diversity teachers will face in any group of stu-dents, Forman and Cazden chose to attend to the potential contribution of social interactions among the children. They implied that teachers can begin to address disparity by scaffolding peer–peer interaction in the classroom. We often assume that peers in childhood contribute only to social development; but school peers, in the right circumstances, also contribute to cognitive development. Later, in the dis-cussion of classmates, we examine that contribution.

Medical Practitioner–Patient

In the lives of many children, health care practitioners will play a minor albeit consistent role. Typically, when a child is taken to the pediatrician for some acute, temporary illness, the doctor will invite some explanation of the problem, and by gaze, gesture, and silence the parent and child will negotiate which of them will respond (Stivers, 2001). However, some children will face serious and/or chronic health crises early in life; for those children, participation in the treatment becomes critical, and health providers can become adversaries or confederates.

Among children who must deal with the effects of cancer, doctors can be saviors or demons. Here, a teen in long-term treatment expressed her view:

> I don't want to talk to these doctors anymore. I give them snappy answers. I don't like them. I don't know why, they're nice people.... I had a doctor come in yesterday, and he told me that he was busting his ass for me. What is he doing? He doesn't have any physical contact with me, he's not doing anything to me.... So I don't know where they came up with that. All they probably do is sit back in their offices. (Bearison, 1991, p. 70)

Much of the literature regarding the child–practitioner relationship has examined the adult's effectiveness in explaining illness to children. That literature relies heavily on psychology and has examined message behavior but little (Whaley, 2000). Another line of research has examined the effects of social support on health. In consideration of the fact that children do need explanations of both their illness and their treatment, and that social support is particularly important to those experiencing the stress of illness, I attempted to examine both from the child's point of view (Yingling, 2000). I leave the message specifics for the next chapter, but report here on the child's view of supportive relationships in the condition of health challenges.

I asked children visiting the pediatric oncology unit of a large West Coast hospital to take photos of every person they encountered in the clinic, to wear a voice-activated tape recorder, and to engage in an interview. At the end of the clinic day, children arranged the photos on a grid to display who gave them the most useful information, and who gave the best emotional support.

Health providers were most often identified as informative interactants (nurses, then doctors), and parents were most often identified as supportive interactants. The biggest difference between the two chosen adults in terms of message behavior was that *informative adults* used more interpretation than did supportive adults—they started with the child's message and categorized their understanding of it, often taking it further in detail. Children who had been in treatment for a long time, regardless of their age, expressed their familiarity with the routine by giving their preferred provider more medical advice, and their care providers responded reciprocally. Interestingly, the children who had been in treatment longest expressed understanding of their condition beyond what we might expect for their years. That is, the extent of their experiences in treatment had more of an influence than age on their internal models and expectations about themselves and their health.

In summary, ill children looked to their care providers for interpretations of information, and for acknowledging their concerns; effective care providers listened actively and gave guidance. Health care providers are evidently special sorts of teachers who, at their most effective, engage children in receiving both support and information.

Children learn a great deal from adults, but we often lose sight of what children gain from each other. Without the restraints imposed by power and size, learning may be very different on a level playing field.

Child–Child Relationshipping: Comparisons Among Peers

Siblings

From a relational viewpoint, siblings should affect each other's relational models, cognitive habits, and communication skills. However, much of the literature regarding sibling relationships has concerned the effects of birth order. That is, scholars have assumed that position in the family lineup alone will predict a constellation of outcomes, including intelligence, temperament, and personality. After a long and popular run in the psychology literature, birth order as a developmentally predictive variable is coming under fire. Sibling position *across* families is being replaced by a focus on the relational dynamics *within* families. Although we favor a relational view, an overview of the birth order research may stimulate more relational explanations for sibling effects.

Birth Order. In the past, researchers have reported *personality differences* linked to birth order. For example, firstborns who seek acceptance thus have a greater need to achieve (Phillips, Long, & Bedeian, 1990). Lastborns are more carefree and affectionate, and thus are more popular and socially oriented. And the less studied middleborns (ever ignored!) are noncompetitive and compromising, and thus diplomatic mediators (Kidwell, 1982; Perlin & Grater, 1981).

Parenting style has also been linked with birth order, with mothers reporting higher expectations for firstborns than for laterborns (Baskett, 1984). In a study examining personality and parenting style, more firstborns reported an authoritarian parent and tended more toward introversion and judging than did laterborns (Stansbury & Coll, 1998). Laterborns scored higher on extroversion and perceiving, and reported a combination of parenting styles.

Age spacing has been considered important to *personal adjustment and social skills.* More years between children led to better adjustment, and fewer years between led to greater social skill (Pfouts, 1980). When age spacing is fewer than 4 years, the older sibling tends to introversion; when siblings are spaced more than 4 years apart, the younger sibling reports more introversion (Stansbury & Coll, 1998). Sensibly, the closer siblings are in age, the more the younger one can take for granted the social advantage of his or her constant partner.

Like the ones reported previously, most of the hundreds of studies performed on the relationship between birth order and behavioral outcomes have used comparisons *across* families to support causal links between birth position and development (e.g., *all* secondborns are similar enough to be comparable). However, those studies using *within*-family data have found no correlations between birth order and development (Rodgers, Cleveland, van den Oord, & Rowe, 2000). Therefore, the link between birth order and variables such as intelligence is not well established. One assumption has been that laterborn siblings experience poorer learning environments and, thus, larger families produce low-IQ children. Rodgers and his colleagues (2000) asked the question: Which comes first, large families or low IQ?

In any large cross-sectional data set, a number of other selection factors may influence results, including fertility patterns, changes in intelligence over time, maternal age effects, parental IQ variations, famine, and poverty patterns (Rodgers et al., 2000). Rodgers et al. (2000 asserted:

> Imagine comparing the first-born child in a large middle-class White family in Michigan to the second-born child in a medium-sized affluent Black family in Atlanta to a third-born child in a small low-income Hispanic family in California. If differences between these children's intelligence are observed, it is impossible to tell whether they are due to SES, race, region of the country, birth order, family size or other variables related to these. (p. 602)

To adequately study birth order, we need within-family data. This means that information from all children in each household that contributes to the data set would be collected, thus allowing competing sources of influence to be separated out from the effects. Based on the few studies to adequately partial out competing influences, plus their own analysis of a large national sample, Rodgers and colleagues concluded that although low-IQ parents may make larger families, the assumed correlative—that large families make low-IQ children—does not hold. As they pointed out, family size is a between-family measure, whereas birth order is a within-family measure. When birth order is measured between families, "It acts as a proxy for between-family variables like SES, educational level ... and so forth" and relationships between birth order and IQ appear (p. 611). However, when measured within families, the differences disappear. Rodgers et al. suggested an *admixture hypothesis* forwarded by Page and Grandon (1979) as the best explanation for the earlier results: Birth order and family size do not cause developmental differences, but instead are caused by the statistical distribution of variables (such as IQ) in the population.

Family Dynamics.   We do know that children who grow up in the same family, and who share genetic material, parents, and environment, are likely to be very different people, psychologically and cognitively. Hence, if birth order is not the cause of such variation, what is? Dunn (1991) suggested the variation arises in nonshared experiences within families that go beyond birth position: consistency of parenting behavior to each child at each age (e.g., Ellen structuring Peggy's play at 2 years as she structured Nan's play at 2 years); stability of behavior with each child over time (e.g., responding to Peggy's distress with comfort at age 2, age 8, and age 15); and the attention that even young children give to interaction among other family members. Dunn maintained, "Parents behave differently toward their different children, and the children respond to such differences, and comment on them in no uncertain terms" (p. 118). In other words, children notice differential treatment and respond accordingly.

Children, even from the end of their first year, attend to and respond to their parents' behavior, especially emotional exchanges (Dunn, 1991). Furthermore, children as young as 5 or 6 report that there are differences in their relationships with parents compared with their siblings relationships with parents (Koch, 1960). And it is not just concurrent parental behavior that affects children; evidently, the earlier relationship between mother and her partner affects siblings as well. Where there is low affection and/or high dissatisfaction between parents, children report more conflict with their siblings (Erel, Margolin, & John, 1998; Stocker, Ahmed, & Stall, 1997).

In a study of sibling pairs and their mothers, Dunn, Deater-Deckard, Golding, and Pickering (1999) tracked the path of influence from *marital relationships* to sibling behavior 4 years later. Lack of affection and high hostility between mothers and partners prior to the younger child's birth were related to negativity from older to younger sibling 4 years later. Likewise, there was a path from marital affection to later sibling friendliness. But, in the case of stepfamilies, there was no link between mother–stepfather hostility and sibling hostility. Furthermore, positive marital relations between mother and stepfather seem linked to difficult parent–child relations (Hetherington, 1988). Thus, the dynamic is evidently very different in stepfamilies; children apparently do *not* emulate the relationship between parent and stepparent in forming their sibling relationships.

Disparities in parental treatment have effects on sibling relationships. Specifically, more conflict and hostility is found among siblings whose parents treat them differentially, and the effect holds for preschool children (Dunn, 1988), for middle childhood (Brody, Stoneman, & Burke, 1987), and for children with disabled siblings (McHale & Gamble, 1987).

Especially interesting for communication scholars are the effects of differential treatment on emotional sensitivity and self-esteem. When mothers showed greater affection to a younger, preschool sibling, the older sibling's affective perspective-taking abilities increased. And the greater the difference in affection displayed to the two siblings, the better the older sibling was at judging others' feelings and motives (Dunn & Munn, 1985, 1986, 1987). These findings are based on observations; mothers' perceptions are that they treat their children similarly.

We know that children who have low self-esteem may also have later emotional problems; we know less about how family affects esteem. Dunn (1991) reported from her extensive studies with Munn (1985, 1986, 1987) that there are "marked differences in how the two siblings feel about themselves.... In families in which mothers reported being more affectionate and attentive to the younger than the older sibling, the older siblings had lower self-esteem" (p. 120).

Apparently, one of the more important variables influencing both the sibling relationship and differential outcomes on a variety of affective, cognitive, and communication measures is the relative difference between parental treatment toward the siblings, or the "favoritism" effect. Parents, whether they think so or not, apparently do have favorites, at least at some time during siblings' childhoods, and siblings notice and are affected by that favoritism. The other two factors Dunn (1991) reported as influences to sibling relationships are temperamental match and age difference between them.

To this point, we have considered the effects of parental relationships and favoritism on sibling relationships, but little on *spoken communication effects*. However, given that younger siblings have additional sources for communication within the family, we might expect a different set of relationships to affect the skills of younger siblings. With multiple children in the home, mother's talk time to each child is diluted among siblings, with the effect of fewer opportunities for interaction between mother and the younger siblings. Some claim that this is disadvantageous for laterborns (Wellen, 1985), but others claim that the increased opportunities to overhear conversations among other family members provides beneficial models of communication (Oshima-Takane, 1988; Woollett, 1986; Zukow, 1989).

Caregivers' communication to older siblings is more complex than speech likely to be directed to younger children, and thus does appear to provide ideal input for the young learner. In one study (Oshima-Takane, Goodz, & Derevensky, 1996), pronouns were selected for studying language effects on secondborns, because pronouns are fairly advanced linguistic forms that must be reversed to be used accurately (e.g., *you* becomes *me*), and because children have limited opportunities to observe the use of second-person pronouns in speech directed to themselves (e.g., *my* toy). And indeed, although secondborns did not differ from firstborns in general language development, they were more advanced in personal pronoun production. Thus, secondborns do have some advantages in learning aspects of language that are more easily modeled by third-party conversations.

Despite the manner in which the sibling research has been conducted, I do not mean to imply that sibling effects rely entirely on caregiver influence. Although birth order does seem to affect mothers' language use, differences in mother's language are also affected by the particularities of her child's language to her (McCartney, Robeson, Jordan, & Mouradian, 1991). Parents and children influence each other in the context of their relational interaction, despite the dearth of research to support reciprocal influence beyond infancy. In order to understand family dynamics fully, the multiple variables influencing siblings' relationships must be examined for dialectical outcomes. For example, siblings who are further apart in age may be more likely to prefer the "closed" pole of the open/closed dialectic, and the "autonomy" pole of the autonomy/dependence dialectic.

In contrast to the obligatory nature of sibling relationships, friendships are chosen and must be pursued to be maintained.

Friends

Friendships, even though they most often are founded on sheer proximity early in life, are voluntary relationships among children. Early research on friendships among children focused on whether they were liked and disliked, thus simply examining social attractiveness, but the dynamics of friendships among children have increasingly been scrutinized. Youniss (1978, 1980) collected children's accounts of friendships and found that child–child and child–adult relationships are funda-mentally different in form and outcome. Adult–child relations are unilaterally au-thoritative and lead to self-constructions that reflect societal expectations for interaction; peer relations are co-constructed and lead to mutuality (1978a), and thus allow for more creativity in their negotiation and variation in their forms.

Friendship Models. Based on early peer interactions, children begin to de-velop models for friendships. Toddlers are responsive to peers, and by the age of 2 apparently have some preliminary notion of a "'friend' as a familiar peer from whom one expects particular responses and with whom one engages in a distinctive and enjoyable set of activities" (Rubin, 1980, p. 28). Selman (1981), who has charted changes in conceptions of friendships, described early friendships (3–7 years) as "momentary physicalistic playmates." These relationships are selected from children who live nearby or attend the same school, and are described by physical features or possessions. Yes, these are material girls and boys—their friendships are concrete and very much centered in the present.

Although conflicts are frequent, they typically are brief (Gottman & Parkhurst, 1980). Selman (1981) suggested that these fights are over toys and space, not feel-ings or affection. Children begin using the word *friend* around 3 or 4 years of age, commenting on their current engagement with a child (Mannarino, 1980). At this age, they are also separating peers into those who are included and those who are ex-cluded. Rawlins (1992) explained, "The boundaries drawn through social interac-tion continuously shift by denoting new friends and demoting others" (p. 28). Young children make decisions about who is and who is not a friend, and they do so in a clearly dichotomizing fashion.

As the child enters school (6–9 years), friendships are characterized more by "ac-tivity and opportunity" (Rawlins, 1992). These friends still live close to each other, and they typically have in common their age, sex, size, intelligence level, social class, and physical maturity (Rubin, 1980). Most commonly, they spend much of their time in activity together. Note that children past the age of 7 are probably capable of simple perspective taking and socialized speech. They begin to realize that others may see social events differently than they see them. Nevertheless, one's own view still is used as the standard to which the friend's behavior is held (Selman, 1981). Selman called this "one-way assistance," and Bigelow (1977) labeled it the "re-ward-cost" stage in which friends—typically in second or third grade—compare the costs of their efforts with the gains received.

In middle childhood (8–12 years), equality and reciprocity become more im-portant in friendships (Rawlins, 1992). Increasingly, children pick their friends for their similar attitudes (Gamer, Thomas, & Kendall, 1975), as they become more skilled at inferring those attitudes and dispositions in others. Furthermore, they be-gin to recognize that others can do the same; that is, they not only take the perspec-tive of others, but expect others to as well. Now the concept of friendship is one based on "cooperative reciprocity" in which both parties deliberately conceive of and enact an acknowledged relationship (Youniss, 1980). Reciprocal trust defines the expectations of these friendships. Each assumes that the other will assist with either resources or verbal support; and, conversely, that the partner will accept assistance (Damon, 1977). This "rule" of reciprocity demonstrates Bigelow's (1977) "normative" stage of friendships in which procedures and sanctions evolve. The rules are becoming explicit and are clearly still dichotomous—friends support each other, nonsupporters are not friends.

As children enter preadolescence, they often form an intimate relationship with a person of their age and sex (Sullivan, 1953). Proximity is less important than personal characteristics as older children develop the capacities for intimate relationships. By 9 or 10 years, mutual role taking (Shantz, 1975) begins to emerge with the child's realization that his or her partner can "mutually and simultaneously take the self's view of other into consideration at the same time as the self takes the perspective of other toward the self" (Selman, 1976, p. 172). This grasp of mutual and multiple perspectives may mark the beginning of the possibility for dialectical thinking. This acknowledgment of "the mutual composition of human relationships as ongoing interpersonal experiences that transcend either individual" (Rawlins, 1992, p. 33) is the dawning of a new way of viewing the nature of relatedness. Now disagreements do not end the relationship because multiple perspectives are expected. By the age of 12, friends understand how the community or "generalized other" might view their friendship (Shantz, 1975). Rawlins (1992) stated, "This 'moment' comprises a watershed in the dialectical constitution of self and other through friendship. Basically, the young adolescent simultaneously realizes that self and the friend each comprises integrated personalities and that friendships are ongoing and negotiated bonds" (p. 34). We return to the adolescent friends in chapter 7. Now we turn to the function of talk in constituting friendship.

Discourse variables have been studied, but in the context of peer acceptance or rejection rather than how discourse serves friendship maintenance. For example, children who use more verbal aggression (Coie & Kupersmidt, 1983; Dodge, 1983; Ladd, 1983) and give fewer compliments and verbal praises (Gottman, Gonso, & Rasmussen, 1975; Hartup, Glazer, & Charlesworth, 1967) are often rejected by their peers. Both adults and children suffer from self-focused communication, or a lack of perspective-taking skill. Lonely adults make fewer partner-focused statements and ask fewer questions (Jones, Hobbs, & Hockenbury, 1982). In the next chapter, we look more closely at the sorts of communication skills that contribute to social acceptance. For now, we focus on the dynamics of children's friendships from a relational perspective.

Corsaro (1985) and Rizzo (1989) observed young children in everyday activities. From a constructivist perspective, they assumed that the children must experience friendship and must internalize that experience to develop a model of friendship. Talk, then, is not just a way to express one's relational model, but is also critical to the development of that model. Therefore, to examine how friendships are constituted, we must have data from both parties to the friendship consisting of talk *within* the friendship as well as *about* the friendship. On the basis of the few studies conducted from this approach, including my own (Yinging, 1994b), I propose that children talk friendships into existence, children cocreate friendship rules, and children internalize friendship interactions to form a model of friendship that then structures further interaction.

On the basis of transcripts of "good" or "best" friends' interactions, as well as interviews with each child about the friendship, I found several configurations of expectations (forming the model of friendship) as well as of behavior (constituting the friendship). Although they are not expected to exhaust the possible friendship patterns, these five may be representative of the kinds of patterns likely to be experienced in the age range of 3 through 10 years.

One pattern, found in 9- and 10-year-olds, revealed a well-established set of expectations for the friendship. In these cases, the friends share control (based on their conversation behaviors) but they both share a perception that one partner holds the control, and agree that their interactions do not change the relationship. On the other end of the spectrum, we have a relationship that is neither well established nor particularly important to the parties. This was not considered a "best" friendship and, although both agreed that one partner had more control of the interaction, neither really seemed to care about the changes that control caused.

In the remainder of the patterns, we find important relationships in flux; these are relationships in which models are being built and tested. In these pairs, partners report either little disagreement and lots of change (each partner specialized in perceiving either control or change), lots of disagreement and little change (in which the controlling partner used more other-focus and the controlled used more verbal aggression and interruption), or both disagreement and change (a very young pair, in which they disagreed on just about every aspect of the friendship but apparently were learning a lot). These are relationships in the process of building and changing, and it shows not only in their talk together, but in their talk about the friendship. These children are trying out various strategies to maintain (other-focus skills) and regulate (self-focus skills) relationships. In the next chapter, we look more closely at the strategies they learn and how they function.

Finally, young friendships are often same-sex relationships, and apparently are related to *gender identification*. Children prefer same-sex friends from the age of 2 throughout childhood. Gottman (1986) described gender role as "the most potent psychological determinant of friendship choice in middle childhood" (p. 140). Girls tend to play with one other girl, and their friendship is typically more intimate than those of boys (Buhrmester & Furman, 1987). Boys tend to play in groups and were more expansive, including additional boys more freely (Lever, 1976). The tendency of each sex to interact with same-sex friends may reflect a need to know about and reinforce one's own gender identity. We examine the kind of discourse likely to contribute to gender identification in the next chapter.

Classmates

Fellow students are not the same as friends. Although a child may have a friend who is also a classmate, we can assume that these are two categories of relationship with different expectations. Although the "school chums" category has not been explicitly examined for expectations, often the two relationships are muddled in the friendship literature by asking children to choose their preferred school chum, and using that preference as a guide to friendship formation. However, school chums are relationships of convenience that function in the specialized intellectual realm. Classmates may have a great deal of influence on how a child thinks, but less in other realms. Let's examine the potential cognitive effect of classroom interaction.

On the basis of comparing peer-involved learning tasks, Forman and Cazden (1985) concluded that even though the assimilation of general human experience must be grounded in adult–child interactions, peer relationships function as "intermediate transforming contexts between social and external adult–child interactions and the individual child's inner speech" (p. 345). In collaboration, "each child learns to use speech to guide the actions of her or his partner and, in turn, to be guided by the partner's speech" (p. 343).

The first sort of task involved *giving verbal instructions* to peers, after learning the task from the teacher. In this case, the teacher carefully structured the task by asking questions to direct the student through a sequence of steps. Gradually, the child came to anticipate the step sequence and her verbalizations of the assigned task directions to the teacher became more precise. As the student, in turn, became the teacher and led her peers through the steps, she became clearer in her explanations.

In another type of *peer tutoring*, children held "peer conferences" about their writing as they awaited an individual consultation with the teacher. This type of learning is more reciprocal in that each child takes turns reading his or her story aloud and receiving questions about it from the peer tutor. In this case, the teacher had already modeled how to ask helpful questions about content and the students had had practice in using such questions to adjust their stories. Peer tutoring apparently works best when the teacher "models a kind of interaction in which the children can learn to speak to each other" (Forman & Cazden, 1985, p. 320).

Forman set up another sort of *collaborative task* by structuring 11 problem-solving sessions comparing solitary problem solvers' process and outcomes with those from collaborative partnerships. Middle-school subjects were asked to solve a series of chemical reaction problems, ordered in terms of logical complexity. Each session included two demonstration experiments by the teacher, followed by a standard set of questions about the demonstration. Children were then asked to set up the experiments they wanted to try to solve the problem posed; this portion was observed. Children then performed their experiment and observed the results. Finally, the teacher repeated the original set of questions to assess outcomes. Three levels of interactions were observed: *parallel* (share materials and comments, but engage in little monitoring of each other's work or informing of own actions), *associative* (exchange information about the selections each has made, but make little attempt to coordinate roles), and *cooperative* (both children constantly monitor each other's work and coordinate roles in performing task). Pairs solved the problems faster than singletons, and the one pair who discovered cooperative interaction first and continued to use it solved more problems than other pairs.

Forman and Cazden concluded that collaboration involves two kinds of social interactive processes: in the planning phase, either parallel patterns or cooperative patterns emerge; and in the analysis of data phase, as each child comes to a conclusion, he or she may find that the partner does not agree, in which case an argument ensues. Arguments producing consensus are those that use supporting evidence;

thus, conflicting perspectives can produce better results. In summary, collaborative tasks require common sets of assumptions and procedures, and demand that children integrate conflicting conceptions into a mutual plan. As Forman and Cazden maintained, "More importantly, experience with social forms of regulation can provide children with just the tools they need to master problems on their own" (1985, p. 343).

SUMMARY: IMPLICATIONS FOR RELATIONAL DIALECTICS

Children form a variety of relationships with various family members, friends, caregivers, and schoolmates. From each relationship, the child accumulates interaction frames that are then internalized to form a model for that kind of relationship. Although the early relationships are founded in contrasts between self and other, children quickly learn that there are many ways to conceptualize and frame relationship behavior and expectations. In the next chapter, we examine the rules children develop for various relationships, and the dualistic nature of those rules when they are first formed. The concrete nature of the child's developing models lends itself to understanding dichotomous sets of characteristics. That is, children do not yet understand the nature of dialectics (e.g., love *and* hostility), but rather form their relational models with choices between two opposing poles (e.g., love *or* hostility). They will be well into adolescence before they will consider that the poles may be related and that a related pair of poles may be characteristic of any one relationship.

Aside from Rawlins' (1992) work, there has been little research to support the notion of dialectics in children's relationships. Nevertheless, we suggest that the origins of relational dialectics reside in the dichotomous choices children make about the natures of their relationships, and even the nature of the various aspects of self.

Self-Dialectics

The earliest dichotomous distinction between "I" and "Thou" is the simple recognition of a self separate from other. Based on progressive internalizations of external interactions, the self accumulates schemas for the good me versus the bad me, for boy versus girl. Gradually, those contrasting notions lead to choice points for gender identity, for self-esteem, and more. It is in interactions with significant others that we begin to frame a model of who we are: *introvert/extrovert, open/closed, affectionate/detached.*

Parent–Child Relational Dialectics

Most often parents are the primary significant others for the developing child. This relationship is characterized by the dialectics of *autonomy/control, love/hostility,* and perhaps more subtle ones as well. As children develop increasing independence from parental control, the dialectic may shift slightly to *autonomy/dependence.* If each parent specializes in a particular type of interaction, children may perceive a contrast between socially normative behavior (mom's role) and idiosyncratic behavior (dad's role), or a *social/individual* dialectic. Certainly, parents provide the first models for gender identification: *masculine/feminine*. If children have models for both supportive, affectionate, attentive behavior and neglectful, dismissive, nonresponsive behavior, this may provide another dialectic for relationship: *intimate/distant*.

Grandparent–Grandchild Relational Dialectics

From the existing literature, we derive two models of grandparenting—the custodial and noncustodial grandparent. The custodial version would be likely to provide models for the same dialectics set up in parent–child relationships. The noncustodial or traditional version, however, would be more likely to model comparisons in terms of time: *old versus young, past versus future*. According to grandchildren, grandparents also model gender identity. What we do not know is how the *masculine/feminine* dialectic modeled by grandparents varies from the gender comparisons we learn from parental relationships.

Sibling Relational Dialectics

Siblings are often our first opportunity for equal-status relationships. As such, we learn about status comparisons of all sorts, and much about *cooperation/competition* and *judgment/acceptance*. Furthermore, sibling relationships extend the earlier *autonomy/dependence* dialectic modeled in primary caregiver relationships.

Friendship Dialectics

Friends are voluntary relationships and, as such, provide opportunities to learn about how to maintain relationships as well as begin them. Rawlins (1992) suggested four friendship dialectics and traced their origins in childhood. Conflicts between the freedoms to be both autonomous and dependent on a friend are common throughout childhood, from easily broken early links to more enduring ones as the *autonomy/dependence* dialectic matures. The *affection/instrumentality* dialectic models the difference between a friend as someone who can be a means to a desired end versus a friend for the sake of friendship itself. Clearly, friendships also demonstrate the *judgment/acceptance* dialectic; the choice of a friend is an exercise in judgment, whereas the maintenance of friendship requires more mutual judgment and acceptance. Finally, the *expressiveness/protectiveness* dialectic begins and transforms through childhood friendships. Young children are open to the point of bluntness; the development of tact comes along with the ability to recognize the partner's feelings and perspective.

Teacher/Care Provider Dialectics

Although children will continue to refine the dialectics of autonomy/dependence, social/individual, and cooperativeness/competitiveness in the classroom, teachers introduce some new ways of making distinctions. One is the *personal/impersonal* dialectic arising from the limits of the professional role teachers play. Another may emerge from the emphasis placed on impersonal or decontextualized talk about ideas. *Contextual/decontextual* or *particularized/universal* are the sorts of dialectics that foster abstract thinking and intellectual growth.

Classmate Interaction Dialectics

Finally, classmates in an open classroom may help children extend the dialectics of cooperativeness/competitiveness, acceptance/rejection, and supportive/dismissive. In a school environment that encourages peer learning opportunities, children can become critical evaluators for each other, thus setting up a distinction between intellectually critical and unquestioning, or an *analytical/undiscriminating* dialectic.

These many forms of relationships occur within larger social networks, and inform the internalization of social rules. Chapter 6 begins with a consideration of these larger issues, how relationships fit into social systems, and how communication skills are learned.

NOTES

33. Briere (1992) summarized the major forms of caretaker psychological abuse, including rejection leading to feelings of unworthiness, degradation leading to feelings of inferiority, terrorization, isolation, corruption, deprivation of responsive caregiving that results in neglect, and unreliable parenting involving contradictory demands.
34. See Weston (1991, pp. 38–41) for a discussion of choice versus biology as the basis for family.
35. For an example, see the story of Lauralee Summer, *Learning Joy From Dogs Without Collars* (2003).
36. Valsiner (1989) did clarify that there are variations in polygynic families that he did not observe. One is that families may include distant relatives or grandparents who could alter the structure he described. The other is the practice of child exchange between related families that could remove a child from his or her original family grouping.
37. My gratitude goes to Valerie Downs (1989) for one of the few treatments of the grandparent–grandchild relationship in communication terms. Her summary of the literature and implications for communication research were invaluable in beginning my search.

"Peggy used to be so talkative. When did she get so quiet?" Ellen mused to Roger one evening after the kid were in bed. "Well, she always talked to adults, but other kids seemed too much for her. She'd watch, but eventually play quietly or go to sleep." Peggy was in second grade, and while she had friends—those who pursued her—she was not outgoing. She had deep sympathies and cried easily for others.

I feel sorry for Tommy. He doesn't have many friends. So when he follows me home, I'll play with him awhile…. I like to be invited to play with a group of kids, but they're so noisy and pretty soon I leave and they don't notice. Sometimes I'd rather read….

Peggy had a shy temperament, but loved words. She did best in quieter environments and had to be invited to participate in class. She didn't particularly like attention to be paid to her, but did like to feel she'd learned something, so she contributed when asked.

Chapter 6

Childhood: Negotiating Competence Between Self and Other

And so when I start speaking a powerful right arm
of words sweeping down, I know *him* from what I say,
and how I say it, because there's a window open
between us, mixing the night air of our beings.

(Rumi, quoted in Barks, 1995, p. 32)

COMMUNICATIVE AND RELATIONAL COMPETENCE

We all have experienced times when we felt misunderstood, and longed to be able to open that window between us and the other person. But how do we develop that powerful right arm of words? Communication scholars do not agree about what constitutes communication competence, or even if the construct is a useful one to study. However, if we are to identify the elements necessary for successful communication development, we must have some standards to apply. But whose expectations of competency do we use? Which social rules are peculiar to relational context, which are largely cultural, and which more universal? Which are innate and which acquired? In the next several chapters, we'll frame our examination of specific communication capacities and behaviors with the concept of "competence"—or, more accurately, *(in)competence*, as Spitzberg (1993) labeled the dialectic of competence/incompetence. Our assumptions about identity, internalization, and interaction skill[38] can serve as a basis for discussing how this (in)competence is acquired dialogically.

In the last chapter, we sorted out the various relational others with whom children are likely to interact. In this chapter, we look at what children are learning in these relationships. The youngster who is actively constructing mind and identity is, at the same time, gaining sophistication in interaction by learning the rules and skills necessary to social and relational development. First, we examine some defi-

149

nitions of competence. Then, we sort out the capacities involved in competence to three categories: knowledge, skill, and motivation. Finally, we look at a few child-hood contexts in which competence is acquired.

Historically, the communication discipline examined competence in light of the acquisition of communicative behaviors in children and consequent implications for instruction (Allen & Brown, 1976). One of the outcomes of a 1975 conference on the issue were a set of assumptions about competence. Two are important for our purposes: "Communication educators are primary interested in the pragmatics of communication" and "The communication behaviors of children can be modi-fied" (Allen & Brown, 1976, pp. 246–247).

The first speaks to the various components of language: phonetics, syntax, se-mantics, and pragmatics. Although we acknowledge all four as important to basic language competence, the first assumption holds true: The first three components are largely the purview of linguistics and speech pathology, although they are foun-dational to most communicative behavior. Pragmatics, on the other hand, has to do with what we accomplish with communication rather than the structures and con-ventions of language, and thus that component is more clearly related to what hap-pens socially—between and among people—and thus, to our concerns.

The second assumption rests on another, more primary assumption that com-petence is learned. Recently, that assumption has been questioned by communica-tion scholars; we try to sort out various claims for biological versus acquired aspects of competence.

Definitions of Competence

Of the few scholars to thoroughly review the literature in communication compe-tence, Spitzberg and Cupach (1984) did a creditable job, and went a step further to formulate a model for relational competence. We use their framework to begin the discussion.[39] First, what is human social competence?

Communication competence is "the ability to adapt messages appropriately to the interaction context" (Spitzberg & Cupach, 1984, p. 63). Spitzberg and Cupach pointed out that this is a broader concept than linguistic competence. Although necessary for communication competence, the ability to use language is not enough to ensure its appropriate use in specific contexts. We can know very well which meanings we would like to convey (semantics), how to construct an ade-quate sentence (syntax), how to articulate the necessary sounds (phonetics), but yet be incapable of formulating an appropriate message for the context (pragmatics). If Peggy is unfamiliar with the church context, she may be speaking as she normally would to Ellen, rather than in the abbreviated forms and muted tones we learn to adopt for worship.

Interpersonal competence is "the ability of communicators to accomplish tasks successfully" (Spitzberg & Cupach, 1984, p. 65). In this literature, social effectance is at issue—abilities that enhance successful outcomes in social situations. For ex-ample, at age 7, Peggy knows how to articulate her wishes ("I want that ball"), yet she may not adapt the message appropriately to the situation (the boy playing with the ball is practicing knocking down pins with his friends) and thus fail to achieve her goal. As she gains experience with the context, she may try a variety of strategies, including altercasting ("I know you're practicing, and I'll wait until you all have one more turn"), and thus learn which strategies have a better chance of allowing her to control her social environment. Note that, thus far, these constructs for competence emphasize *either* the functional skills necessary to social success (social rules) *or* the contextual sensitivity for socially appropriate messages (knowledge about flexible scripts). This much will get us through common social situations, but will these guarantee competence in close relationships?

Relational competence focuses on "the perception of competence by the participants in a given conversation and relationship" (Spitzberg & Cupach, 1984, p. 68). This conceptualization avoids normative judgments, which are calculated as the average of social skills across relationships, and instead acknowledges the "reciprocal and interdependent nature of human interaction" (p. 68). Such interdependence led Spitzberg and Cupach (1984) to the premise that "a person can be interpersonally competent *only* in the context of a relationship" (p. 68). That is, the ability to collaborate and negotiate with others is central to competence, and results in relationship. Some of the abilities seen as central to this notion of competence come under the umbrella of "other orientation" or the capacity to support the partner's self-concept. I would add that although supporting self *and* other's self, both parties also must maintain and/or negotiate a definition of the relationship, and acknowledge the goals of both—a tall order indeed. A model of relational competence assists us in sorting out the factors involved.

A Model of Relational Competence

Impressions, Skills, or Relationship?

Where is competence? According to Spitzberg (1994), traditional places to look were in *skills* related to desirable outcomes, in the subjective *impressions* of the interpreter, and in the *social unit*. Although it is tempting to look for sets of individual skills that are identifiable as competent, we are able to do so only if we can be satisfied with statistical averages of what skills generally work in a type of relationship within a particular culture. If we take seriously the assumption that relationship expectations are negotiated by the parties to it, we quickly find that what works in one relationship may not work in another. Expectations and models are negotiated between parties to the relationship; thus, it is the partner's impressions we must consider. In this case, we would have to ask what behaviors lead to impressions of competence as well as how the perceiver typically arrives at that impression. In this case, we would examine both *actor skills* and *partner attributions*, but still we might be missing the connection between the two—the *relational dynamic*.

If the locus of competence is the relationship, then we would have to identify "mutual relational sources of actor and coactor competence and the factors that influence these sources" (Spitzberg, 1994, p. 31). When we are concerned with variables such as conversation management, relational turning points, conflict negotiation, and the like, the task of identifying the sources of competence (and incompetence) becomes very complex indeed. Yet, *if relational communication is a major source of human development, it is in the relationship that competence resides and develops, and it is there we must seek it.*

Now that we've established that relationship is where human development occurs, we're faced with sorting out what it means to become a competent communicator in our relationships. Is it an ability or a quality? If ability, what must we be able to *do*? If quality, what characteristics must we *possess*?

Ability or Quality?

Still a matter of some controversy is whether competence is an individual quality that others generally see in us, or whether it is an ability to perform in response to particular situations. If competence is a *quality* that one possesses, we must ask who assesses the quality. Spitzberg (1993) proposed that it is the relational other's "attribution or judgment made regarding the appropriateness, effectiveness, clarity or goodness of a behavioral performance or a person's capacity for behavioral performance" (p. 138). In the case of a child, an adult may ascribe "competence" to him or her based on the behaviors observed in social situations (e.g., Peggy whispered rather than shouted in church). Although we now have a judgment, we still don't know if the observed behaviors are the result of innate traits or learned skills (is Peggy simply a quiet child, or did she learn the church rule?).

If, on the other hand, competence is an *ability*, it represents capacities the child "possesses or acquires that enable the repeated enaction of goal-directed behavioral routines" (Spitzberg, 1993, pp. 137–138). In this sense, competence is a set of rules, scripts, and skill performances that, although they are flavored by the child's innate qualities, he or she learns in relationships.

What if competence is both a quality and an ability? Then, we would have to take into account *both* the child's developing knowledge (for scripts, rules) and internal motives (emotions, temperament, identity) *as well as* the other's (adult and/or peer) inferences about the child's observable skill. We turn now to a consideration of what portion of competence may be tied to genetic endowments and what portion may be linked to environmental opportunities and constraints. Then we return to a consideration of knowledge, motives, and skill.

The Bases of Competence: Genetics/Environment?

Parenting a second (or third, or fourth …) child is likely to spur some serious consideration of just how much of that child's social behavior is a matter of individual predisposition rather than the effects of significant others. Temperament has been linked to biology as well as to certain simple behavioral responses. Minimally, the tendency to approach or to withdraw from stimuli, as well as one's typical response to novel stimuli, appear to be linked to brain structures (Nelson, 1994). However, even these fundamental responses "are not independent of the child's history and experience in dyadic interactions" (Calkins & Fox, 1994, p. 209). Experience tempers genetics from the start.

In Peggy's case, she may have had a tendency to withdraw from stimuli from the start, but the loss of attention associated with getting a new brother and moving to a new home probably had more to do with her communication apprehension.

Given the possibility of a neurobiological link to competence, Beatty and McCroskey (1998) devised a theory to explain that link (see also Beatty, McCroskey, & Valencic, 2001). In one study (2001) Beatty, Marshall, and Rudd examined the heritability of perhaps the most broadly touted competence trait: communicative adaptability. They claimed that this ability to adjust to social situations is common to a number of constructs such as rhetorical sensitivity, self-monitoring, and listener-adapted messaging. Furthermore, they described communicative adaptability as involving strategy (e.g., wit) and emotional reactivity (e.g. social composure), as well as the individual-specific capacity to adjust to immediate surroundings.

To test for genetic influence on competent (flexible) communication, they compared twins' responses to various dimensions of communicative adaptability.[40] Two factors—wit and social composure—demonstrated high heritability (90% and 88%, respectively), and two others—articulation and disclosure—showed zero heritability. Given that intelligence is apparently one of the most heritable traits, the use of wit to cope with social situations may indeed rest on biological inheritance. As the authors pointed out, social composure is related to social anxiety, and thus is probably related to the basics of temperament. They concluded that the value of the "communibiological" perspective is probably limited to the role of affect and emotion in communication; thus, the genetic component of competence affects inner motivation (composure) to some degree, knowledge (wit) to some degree, and skill indirectly if at all.

Much of competence, then, is a matter of learning from interaction. Each relationship, in the process of developing beyond approved role behavior, gives rise to unique rules that may require violating other, more general social rules. Such creativity and flexibility is particularly difficult for very young children, who view rules for social behavior in dualistic terms—behavior is either right or not right, regardless of the situation.[41]

Four-year-old Peggy may have learned that the appropriate way to answer the telephone is to state the family name and ask who is calling: "Barowsky residence; who may I say is calling?" However, she has an uncle who refuses to follow the rule and is attempting to set a different script for their calls: "C'mon Peggy, you know who this is. What's up?" This may upset her at first, because it interrupts her answering rule; she may even say so directly: "You're supposed to tell me your name and who you want to talk to!" However, with enough variations on the script, by age 6 or 7 Peggy comes to recognize that different rules work with different people, and thus to move beyond the dualistic tendency to treat rules as laws, and toward more dialectical adaptations. Wishing to be both effective and appropriate, she will learn to negotiate the rules with each relational partner.

So, what's the proper ratio of biology to social environment? We might expect that a person's intelligence and temperament would influence capacities like empathy, perspective taking, and self-monitoring; whereas other communication skills, having more to do with language (articulation and conversation management) and rules of social appropriateness (disclosure, conflict, and compliance gaining), rely largely on interactive learning and are thus more easily changed.

Interfacing Motivation, Knowledge, and Skill

The terms we use here to categorize components of competence are borrowed from Spitzberg and Cupach (1984), who used them to sort out internal motivators, knowledge about social processes, and the skilled performances required to bring motives and knowledge to fruition.

Motivation may be the most foundational component of communication competence. At its core, "the most basic reaction to any interpersonal encounter is one of approach-avoidance" (Spitzberg & Cupach, 1984, p. 119). The tendency to approach or avoid apparently has a genetic component that may be altered by experience. These tendencies may then become mediated by learned emotional responses and acquired identity and values. Children are naturally motivated to be effective—to obtain what they need or desire. We can typically assume that very young children are as competent as their behaviors reflect, unlike adults who may have either failed to acquire social norms, or may choose to perform incompetent behavior.

Knowledge, in this model (Spitzberg & Cupach, 1984), "consists of the possession of, or ability creatively to acquire, the requisite cognitive information necessary to implement conversationally competent behaviors" (p. 123). Such knowledge of communication *rules* exists on three levels: linguistic, social, and interpersonal. The linguistic level involves rules for the planning and execution of language, the social includes rules for normative standards of appropriateness, and the interpersonal applies to the idiosyncratic rules negotiated for a specific relationship. The designers of this competence model include the social capacities for person memory and script procedures, cognitive complexity, perspective taking, and self-monitoring.

Skill resides in the actual performance of behavior—the basis of others' inferences—and probably depends on and is mediated by levels of motivation and knowledge. Peggy may know very well how to greet a visitor to her home, but be too frightened or anxious to do so. The significant skill factors involved in creating impressions of competence are other-oriented behaviors, social anxiety, expressiveness, and interaction management (Spitzberg & Cupach, 1984). Behavioral indicators of these factors include interaction management skills, expressiveness (including disclosure), and altercentrism indicators (including empathy, concern, and attention).

Worth noting here is that a great many outcomes of competence have been suggested, including communication satisfaction, interpersonal attraction, relational trust, conflict satisfaction, and intimacy. More recently, negative outcomes have also been examined more closely (Cupach & Spitzberg, 1994), although with adult populations. Popularity and its lack is one of the few negative social outcomes studied in children. Although in this text we continue to consider outcomes in the long run of development, this unit focuses on individual and relational behaviors and impressions. At this point, a note is in order about the dialectical nature of competence.

To be considered competent requires a delicate dance at the boundary between self and other. It is not just a matter of identifying the correct mix of a dollop of disclosure with a handful of verbal involvement and a smidge of empathy. The relationship of many communicative skills is curvilinear to impressions of competence (Cupach & Spitzberg, 1994). That is, too much or too little of a particular behavior often leads to impressions of incompetence. Indeed, children at the extremes often have no friends, and worried parents turn to professionals. "Friend doctors" (Walsh, 2002) pair children who suffer from isolation, because they are either extremely introverted or extremely extroverted—they approach peers too aggressively or not at all. As Walsh noted, "They overpower or they cower" (p. A23).

Thus, it is in the middle range of use that we dance between the dialectical poles. Given that Peggy has acquired the foundational levels of knowledge from socially skilled parents, and her motivation is healthy although moderated by introversion, she then is free to choose how to interact in each moment with her friend, Erin. Given that Erin is similarly equipped, she makes choices in their interaction as well. It is these moment-to-moment choices that ultimately constitute the competence of that relationship. Later in the chapter we take a closer look at specific dialectics of competence/incompetence. Because of the complexity of the factors that make up motivation, knowledge, and skill, Fig. 6.1 is a

A Map of Developing Relational Competence

	Motivation	Knowledge	Skill
Foundational (biological or cultural givens) ⇓ ⇓	Temperament Emotion empathy congruence	Wit Language rules Social scripts	Interaction management turn-taking verbal involvement
Derived (symbolically created)	Identity ----------	Identity self-awareness self-monitoring Perspective-taking Cognitive complexity	Disclosure/deception Role-play Persuasion conflict
	Morality ----------	Morality	Support conversational sensitivity comforting

FIG. 6.1. Capacities involved in relational competence.

map of the various factors we include in our discussion. I know the discussion is complicated. But, although this sketch may not do it justice, I hope that it helps the reader negotiate the maze of competence development. One more hint: If you get bogged down in the text discussion, skim to the end, read about "contexts," and back up as required.

Motivation to Relate Competently

Not only do people vary in their tendencies to approach novel social situations, they also vary in the types of interaction influences available for learning how to encode, decode, and regulate their emotional experience. Furthermore, their capacities for emotional expression and interpretation are likely to produce relational outcomes that in turn feed the development of identity and morality. The motivation to competently relate to others lies in a complex set of individual tendencies and relational processes.

Temperament: Individual Predisposition to Approach or Avoid

Temperament is considered an enduring predisposition to be aroused either positively or negatively. The capacity to regulate one's own emotion appears to influence the valence of social experience as well. Children vary a great deal in how they approach peers, from highly sociable to withdrawn, and this variation is related to brain function. Specifically, highly sociable 4-year-olds show greater activation of the left frontal lobe during visual stimulation, whereas socially withdrawn youngsters exhibit greater right frontal lobe activation (Fox et al., 1995).

Some evidence points to a link between these biologically based orientations and the subsequent interactions children establish (Hart, Olsen, Robinson, & Mandleco, 1997). Withdrawn children observe classmates and discourage interaction, speaking less often and pushing others away (Broberg, Lamb, & Hwang, 1990). Natural internalizers may call forth responses that reinforce their style, or may have a caregiver who was insensitive from the start, leading to the same reinforcement of an internalizing style.

Thomas and Chess (1977) suggested that temperament and environment combine to produce either a "good fit" when the child's responding style and interaction demands are in harmony, or a "poor fit" that produces maladjustment. Children with difficult temperaments are less likely to receive sensitive caregiving (Crockenberg, 1986), and by the child's second year, the parents often rely on authoritarian discipline. The child responds with defiance, which in turn leads to inconsistent parenting—first resisting, then giving in (Lee & Bates, 1985). Temperament, although it may be an important starting point in setting up the motivating influences for interaction, does not determine competence. The parent who can adapt responses to the child's temperament is more likely to assist the child to adapt his or her temperament successfully to social demands. We proceed to learn how to adapt our biological style to the styles of those around us by recognizing and regulating emotions and behavioral responses to them.

Emotion: Encoding, Decoding, and Regulating Affect

Parke and O'Neil (1999) proposed that children learn to encode their own emotions and decode others in the context of parent–child play. In playful interaction, particularly the active sort that fathers often provide, children "learn how to use emotional signals to regulate the social behavior of others" (p. 218). When Dad, signaling his intent with a broad smile, raised eyebrows, and encircling arms, tickles Peggy in the course of their play, she begins to laugh shrilly and squirm as she gasps for air. She has decoded his intention as benign and thus she does not cry, but nevertheless she is feeling physically distressed. If Dad stops tickling, Peggy learns which signals of hers work to encode her emotional state and thus meet her immediate needs.

Emotional interpretation and display capacities, then, serve the child in expressing his or her own emotions and identifying the emotional states of other children, and may contribute to peer acceptance (Buck, 1975). Specifically, peer acceptance among 5- and 6-year-olds is linked to their abilities to identify emotions, acknowledge experiences of emotion, describe causes of emotions, and respond appropriately to emotional displays (Cassidy, Parke, Butkovsky, & Braungart, 1992).

Just as important as encoding and decoding emotion is the ability to regulate emotion effectively. Sroufe (1979b) proposed that learning to manage negative affect is important in the context of social relationships. Parents who comfort the angry or distressed child are more likely to have kids who deal constructively with anger (Eisenberg & Fabes, 1994). Fathers may play a critical role in modeling emotional display and regulation because of the range of intensity that fathers are more likely to show, and the spontaneity of their play with children (Parke, 1996). Parke and O'Neil (1999) concluded from the literature and their own series of studies that "various aspects of emotional development—encoding, decoding, cognitive understanding, and emotional regulation—are important in accounting for variations in peer competence" (p. 221).

Empathy is the most basic way to share emotion. The capacity to share feeling with another may have its foundation in the physiology of emotional contagion (Feschbach & Roe, 1968), or in the egocentric assumption that others will experience the same emotions that we would in a given situation (Allport, 1924). In any case, the empathic response is central to human interaction and appears early in development. Borke (1971) found that children as young as 3 years are aware of others' feelings and what events evoke them, and such sensitivity increases with age. This capacity becomes more linked with cognition, particularly perspective taking, as Omdahl (1995) and others have claimed. Later in this section on "knowledge," we explore the relationship between emotional contagion and perspective taking as well as the outcome for communicative empathy.

Congruence has been used to describe similarity in body posture as well as in messages. Generally, congruence is viewed as a tendency to synchronize our behavior with a partner, and has been observed to occur between interactants during presumably positively valenced interaction (Scheflen, 1964). *Interactional synchrony* refers to a finely timed harmony in communication behaviors, although not always the same behaviors. Rather than simple congruence of body posture (e.g., both partners crossing their legs), interactional synchrony may refer to matching rhythms between one partner's speech and the other's body movements. Even newborns apparently synchronize their changes in body movement to the rhythms of adult speech (Condon & Ogston, 1966; Condon & Sander, 1974). Thus, there may be a biological predisposition to entrain behavior to the rhythms of human communication.

One theory that attempts to explain the relevance of congruence and its dialectical partner, convergence, is *accommodation theory* (Giles, 1980). Giles suggested that a speaker who wishes to gain the favor or approval of a partner will converge aspects of communication behavior (dialect, speech style, etc.). However, if the speaker instead wants to assert independence or distinguish self from partner, his or her communication will diverge from the partner. Wallbott (1995) clarified some distinctions among mutual contingency (partners moving closer to a common mean for their behavior), reactive contingency (movement of one partner toward the other—e.g., to curry favor), and pseudo-contingency (convergence due to certain characteristics of the situation—crossing arms in response to cold). Presumably, mutual contingency is something that occurs over time in the context of a relationship, whereas the other two may occur in specific interactions for a variety of reasons.

The basis for observed convergence/divergence is a tendency to exhibit communication behaviors "that resemble those of our interaction partners, when we evaluate them positively or when we want to be evaluated positively by them" (Wallbott, 1995, p. 93). Although our foundational capacity for empathy seems to be based in the biological similarities of our emotional responses, our tendency to converge to liked or needed partners appears to arise from a desire to appear more behaviorally similar to the partner, and thus involved. That is, empathy is an *affective* response to another's perceived affect; convergence is a *behavioral* response to another's interactional behaviors. As children learn to identify their own and others' affect in relationships, they also are learning who they are, their preferences, and how they appear to others.

Identity: Forming a Sense of What Motivates Self

Children "become active creators of their own emotional experience" (Saarni, 2000) as they learn how to recognize and label their emotions in the terms of their culture. And, to the extent that children create their emotional experience, they also create their sense of who they are. However, the raw materials still are mined from significant others.

Although identity is also a function of knowledge, we examine here the link between motivating emotional experience and the construction and reconstruction of identity. As language emerges (note the involvement of "knowledge"), children become capable not only of labeling self-characteristics (e.g., "I am a nice girl") that then reside in semantic memory, but we also hold experience by means of episodic memory (e.g., "I was angry with my friend yesterday for not sharing"). A special form of episodic memory is *autobiographical* (Harter, 1999) or *personal narrative memory* (Eisenberg, 1985; Nelson, 1986). Although toddlers can construct episodic memories for events, autobiographical memories typically begin in the third year (Pillemer & White, 1989). In early interactions, caregivers first tell stories about the child's past, then co-construct stories with the child that emphasize and reinforce what they think is important (Fivush, Gray, & Fromhoff, 1987). Thus, the first self-narratives are highly influenced by caregivers, and continue to be influenced by the significant others with whom the child shares stories about self.

Typical self-representations in 3- to 4-year-olds are concrete, referring to physical characteristics, activities, social links and psychological states, but they also include possessions and preferences (Harter, 1999). Most self-evaluations are unrealistically positive in that desired and actual abilities are not clearly differentiated. Particularly interesting is young children's inability to perceive that they can possess attributes of opposing value (nice/mean); indeed, most will deny that they even experience negative emotions. Fischer and Ayoub (1994) believed that this *dichotomous* thinking, or "affecting splitting," is a natural form of dissociation that the young child applies to characterizing both self and other. I would say, rather, that it is a natural result of the contrastive nature of symbolically mediated thinking that children are beginning to use. Erikson labeled the challenge of this last part of preschool childhood (ages 3–6) as one of initiative and guilt; children wish to act more independently but may feel guilt in doing so (Socha, 1997).

By the time children are approaching "the age of reason," or 7 years, they are starting to organize self-representations into categories and to "map" these sets of representations, especially as sets of *opposites* (Harter, 1999). Younger children could not conceive of themselves as capable of being bad if they first perceived themselves as good. Now, they can admit that they could possibly be bad even if they are usually good. Thus, the dichotomizing of the earlier stage becomes more dualistic in this stage; children can conceive of themselves as being at either one pole or the other of a dualism.

Juveniles from 7 to 12 years spend more time outside the family and feel the tension between mastery of this larger world and feelings of inferiority as they enter groups whose norms are unfamiliar (Socha, 1997). The urge for mastery leads juveniles to repetitive practice of skills they view as socially rewarding. Thus, peers become important influences on competence, although media may be used as a substitute for relational interaction (see the discussion on media later in this chapter). Representations of self become more abstract and typically more interpersonal as peer relationships become more important (Harter, 1999). Evaluations of self are more global, revealing on overall sense of self-worth, or one's emotions about oneself. Children are better able to integrate positive and negative self-conceptions, and thus to conceive of self more *dialectically* in terms of simultaneous perceptions of smart/dumb, nice/mean.

Morality: Forming a Sense of What Is Right and Wrong

Moral development surely arises from interactions with caregivers and peers. Although moral reasoning is also part of the knowledge component, the judgments we form about what is right and wrong are closely linked with our emotions about others and self. According to nativist theories, babies the world over feel empathy as soon as they notice the existence of others and react negatively to unjust behavior (Damon, 1999). The core moral values observed across cultures are those "necessary for sustaining human relationships" (p. 76). However, the fact that there may be a baseline of human morality linked to human sociality does not preclude a developmental path for moral judgment.

Kohlberg (1969) identified a six-stage sequence that progresses from *self-interest* (based on punishments and rewards) through *social approval* (based on social relations and social order) to *abstract ideals* (founded on the social contract and universal rights). The sequence seems reasonable, but does not stand up to careful observation. Evidently, very few people reach the final stage, in which morality is almost entirely a matter of abstract principles. And, according to Damon, very young children do not appear to be limited to sheer self-interest. Preschoolers back up their beliefs about fairness and equality with rationales founded in empathy, reciprocity, and egalitarianism. Furthermore, they learn the value for fairness in the context of their conflict interactions with peers.[42] Humans learn quickly that in order to meet their own needs, they must acknowledge the sometimes competing needs of others. First, these competing needs are treated as dichotomous choices, but gradually the possibility for win/win resolutions emerge through improved perspective taking and dialogue.

Damon (1999) defined *moral identity* as the "use of moral principles to define the self" (p. 76). In his view, the key to connecting these guiding ideals to one's own identity lies in bridging the gap between recognizing principles of right and wrong, and resolving to behave according to those principles. That is, the morally mature person has internalized moral ideals that then guide action. The many interactions that inform the constitution of a moral identity include negotiations among peers, explicit feedback from parents, observations of interaction outcomes, and the subsequent personal reflections about those interactions.

Moral Inferences. Of course, children are not developing morality in a vacuum. Not only do they look to models for values, but they are also influenced by the impressions others make of their behavior. An authoritative *parenting style* apparently facilitates moral development more effectively than either permissive or authoritarian styles, which tend to foster low social responsibility and poor self-control (Baumrind, 1966, 1989). The authoritative style employs the kind of clear and consistent rules and limits that young children understand and appreciate, but also encourages open discussion and possible revision in rules; this latitude becomes increasingly necessary for internalizing values. It is this combination that promotes integration of self and moral concerns. Damon (1999) further proposed that parents also should encourage the "right kinds of peer relations" (p. 77). *Peer interaction* can spur children to examine the conflict between their current way of seeing a moral dilemma and the social reality of competing views of the same dilemma. However, children's interaction influences do not end with parents and peers; the larger community includes teachers, coaches, and other guides in social groupings.

Ianni (1989) called the set of shared community standards a *youth charter*. A community may share and reinforce moral values, or fail to provide moral guidance. Unfortunately, professionals are not likely to intervene in moral problems in these litigious times. We have come to rely more heavily on legal codification than on our own moral systems, and that is problematic for moral development. Children use consistent messages to integrate their own rule systems, and thus communities lacking confidence in a shared system will fail to contribute to the repeated consistent value messages that children integrate. This may affect the children's competence negatively.

High levels of moral reasoning are associated with popularity (Enright & Sutterfield, 1980) and with participation in social activities (Harris, Mussen, & Rutherford, 1976). All children will develop rules for directing their behavior, whether the rules continue to be based on self-interest or proceed to abstract ideals. However, socially competent children have more opportunities to engage with peers and to negotiate the challenging issues of social morality. We look next to the knowledge foundation for competence with moral standards.

Knowledge at the Core

Given adequate motivational stimuli for sociality, the child develops relationship models as well as the capacity to perceive the motivations and models that others bring to relationship. The cognitive information necessary to relational competence would include *language structures* sufficient to characterize people and their behaviors, the *ability to take the perspective* of a partner, the capacity to *monitor own behavior* in light of a partner's needs, and *adaptability* to a variety of social contexts, including diverse relationships.

Language Structures

We have examined the dimensions of language that must work in concert for effective human communication: phonetics, semantics, syntactics, and pragmatics. Even though the process can go awry, we will assume for now that language acquisition proceeds normally.[43] Virtually all children, by the age of 5, perform equally well on measures of linguistic ability (Burleson, 1986) and are capable of producing syntactically complex sentences. But the types of words children prefer and the extent of their vocabularies do differentiate individual children.

Toddlers vary in their preferences for either referential (context-flexible names, such as *toy*) or expressive (emotive, such as *mad*) words (Shore, 1995). Toddlers who use referential language can clarify the content of their conversation more clearly than those who specialize in expressive language. But does the preferred style early in life remain so throughout development? This remains a controversial question (Shore, 1995), but what is clear is that individual variation increases. By midway into the second year of life, the expressive children are using more names, and the referential children are using more pronouns; that is, the styles appear to converge (Bloom, Lightbown, & Hood, 1975). Although referential children presumably have the edge for vocabulary development, it may be a temporary advantage (Shore, 1995). Vocabulary—all the words known to the communicator—does influence the communicative effectiveness an individual can command, and mediates most tests of intelligence (Hart & Risley, 1995). Social intelligence is probably a foundational capacity for language facility and other aspects of competence, such as social scripts, person expectations, and cognitive complexity.

Scripts, Rules, and Expectations

You may recall that very young children develop scripts for social situations so that they may anticipate appropriate responses to partners' behaviors. The first are very simple scripted responses to interaction games (e.g., peekaboo), which gradually give way to more complicated scripts allowing contextual variation (e.g., greetings on the playground vs. in church), and thence to rules for social behavior (e.g., entering an ongoing conversation). At the relational level, we might call these *interpersonal expectancies* (Jussim & Eccles, 1995), which refer to what others expect of us as well as what we expect of them. Jussim and Eccles were particularly critical of the assumption that we become what others expect us to become. They found the strongest expectancy effects between parents and children, and between teachers and students.[44] As they put it, "When people have unclear self-perceptions [as young children are likely to do], they are more susceptible to all sorts of social influence" (p. 102). However, parental expectations had minimal effects by Grades 9 to 12 (Eccles, 1993). Hence, children become less susceptible *to* authority expectations over time, but how are the children forming expectations *for* others?

Children's descriptions of people generally fall into two categories: *peripheral* (concrete, behavioral, or appearance-based characteristics) and *central* (inner, psychological, or motivational characteristics). Something apparently happens between 7 and 8 years that leads children to use significantly more central descriptors (Livesley & Bromley, 1973), suggesting that "the eighth year is a critical period in the developmental psychology of person perception" (p. 147). Behavior predictions also become more consistent between the ages of 5 and 9; that is, children become increasingly capable of making accurate attributions regarding others' stable motivations or predispositions. We would expect a leap in this sort of thinking as children move away from egocentric thought to more socialized thought after the age of 7. With more constructs available for describing people, children have the raw materials for putting themselves in others' positions. Let's examine both types of social knowledge: cognitive complexity and social perspective taking.

Cognitive Complexity

Recall from chapter 4 that constructs are cognitive structures consisting of sets of contrasting labels. Cognitive complexity, in the constructivist tradition, is a measure of the number of constructs available to the individual as well as the complexity of their organization. Constructivists assume that developmental changes reflect transformations in these underlying cognitive structures (Delia &

Clark, 1977; Delia, O'Keefe, & O'Keefe, 1982).[45] Furthermore, cognitive complexity "provides a crude, general index of developmental differences in social perception" (Delia & Clark, 1977, p. 328). In a study of 6-, 8-, 10-, and 12-year-old males, children were asked to describe a liked and a disliked peer to yield a sum of the "constructs" in use by the child, and also asked to create messages for a set of figures drawn in hypothetical situations. The participants were then assigned scores for listener-adapted communication and for cognitive complexity. They reported significant communication-relevant differences among children as a function of age and cognitive complexity.

Despite criticisms of the methods and measures for cognitive complexity (Hall, Hecht, & Boster, 1985; Johnson, Powell, & Arthur, 1980; Powers, Jordan, & Street, 1979), the findings are suggestive of a knowledge base in constructs. They concluded that "making communication-relevant inferences about listeners' characteristics is a prerequisite to formulating listener-adapted communications" (p. 000), or, in other words, children must have ways of understanding their partners in order to set expectations for their behavior, and thus fulfill those expectations.

What they fail to address is the source of children's construct representations; however, they do point to a lag between the ability to make communication-relevant distinctions among people and the ability to adapt messages on the basis of those distinctions. Six-year-olds perceive differences among people 75% of the time, but not until age 12 do the children adapt over half of their messages to partners' perceived characteristics (Delia & Clark, 1977). From the perspective of relational dialectics, this lag has to do with the time needed to internalize interactional experience for use in directing one's own behavior. Once children use symbols to construct distinctive polar (dichotomous) constructs, they can begin to build their repertoire of distinctions and practice applying them to various interactants. Then begins the internalizing process of testing one's application of these constructs against one's predictions about subsequent behavior. If Peggy decides that her liked peer is pretty and her disliked peer is plain, she may then decide that pretty peers are more likely to share their candy than plain ones. Of course, when testing that theory, she may have to revise her predictions and reconfigure that construct (pretty/plain) in relation to others she regularly applies (generous/stingy).

Children use their people representations to form expectations and to adapt their communicative behavior, and they do so with increasing competence as they approach puberty. The capacity that appears to mediate between person expectations and adaptive communication is perspective taking.

Perspective Taking

The cognitive capacity to adopt the viewpoint of another person is known as *perspective taking* (Mead, 1934/1974; Piaget, 1932). In chapter 3, we distinguished this cognitive capacity from the more affective processes of feeling *what* another feels or feeling *about* what the other feels. As children clearly use all these capacities in their communication behavior, we examine here the relationship between them and the resulting communication responses.

A research team led by Stiff and Dillard (Stiff, Dillard, Somera, Kim, & Sleight, 1988) described three dimensions of empathy: perspective taking, emotional contagion, and empathic concern. *Emotional contagion*, or feeling what the other feels, appears to be part of our biological heritage and is available within days of birth. *Perspective taking* is a cognitive process involving symbols and, more specifically, constructs for characterizing others' traits and tendencies. The final component has been the most difficult to capture. It has variously been called "humanistic orientation," "sympathy," and "altruistic motivation," among others.[46] Stiff and his colleagues pointed out two features of *empathic concern* that distinguish it from emotional contagion and perspective taking: "1) a general concern and regard for the welfare of others and 2) the stipulation that the affect is *not* parallel to that of the target person" (p. 200). Clearly, then, empathic concern is quite different from emotional contagion, but probably does overlap with perspective taking. Does that make it part of motivation, knowledge, or skill? Most scholars (cited in Stiff et al., 1988) agree that perspective taking (knowledge) initiates the empathic process, and as long as we are talking about the response of empathic concern (a motivational stimulus that can lead to a skill, such as comforting), I would probably agree. Emotional contagion, however, is available developmentally before perspective taking is even possible. Therefore, unless consciously controlled, it may be a separate function, available without cognitive mediation. Let's look at two examples.

We all have seen movies that made us cry, or at least gave us the urge to cry. However, we had the advantage of knowing the entire story up to that point and had used some cognitive structures to understand the characters. That is, perspective taking probably occurred prior to empathic concern and communicative response. But does this process work the same way in early development?

Peggy recognizes very early in life the signs of distress, and becomes distressed herself when she sees another baby cry; this is emotional contagion. When Peggy is 4, she can recognize situations that may make other children sad, identify them (Borke, 1971), feel concern, and attempt to comfort the child she observes responding to that situation (Zahn-Waxler, Cole, Welsh, & Fox, 1995); this is empathic concern. Between Peggy's acquisition of symbols (around age 2) and her simple prosocial behaviors, she has begun to take the perspective of others.

According to Piaget, it isn't likely that Peggy is adopting her partner's view, because children under the age of 7 think egocentrically. However, Piaget's claim about the age limit for socialized thought and speech has been discredited (Maratsos, 1973), and the more current view is that perspective-taking ability improves gradually, and with it so does the capacity for empathic concern and increasing sophistication in prosocial behaviors. That is, as Peggy interacts with various partners, and internalizes constructs for understanding their positions, she becomes more capable of altercentrism rather than egocentrism. And as she begins to take into account the perspectives of her partners, the possibility for assessing the effects of her own behavior arises.

We often take for granted that communicators take each other's perspective into account when interacting, but the process of doing so is probably fairly complex. Clark and Marshall (1981) suggested two sources that we may use to establish mutual knowledge: the *physical copresence heuristic* and the *linguistic co-presence heuristic.* In the first case, we assume the environment (including mutual past environments and physical appearance) to be known mutually, and in the second, we assume mutual knowledge of the course of our conversation (including both content and relationship information). As Krauss, Fussell, and Chen (1995) pointed out, we are likely to use our prior beliefs and social knowledge system as well as current interactional feedback in the process of taking a partner's perspective. However, in early development, our beliefs and constructs are still being constructed; indeed, we may have no basis on which to draw for making sense of some communicative situations. Thus, if one part of the process is *intrapersonal*—using cognitive models for kinds of people, built from constructs—and the other is *interpersonal*—using feedback from the current situation to adapt messages—we would expect very young children to rely heavily on the second part in order to build simple models. As those models develop in complexity, the child becomes more capable of assessing how his or her own communication is judged by various interactants.

Self-Awareness and Self-Monitoring

Haslett's (1984) four stages of pragmatic communication development ends with "monitoring communication" as the final stage emerging at approximately 5 years of age. Having recognized the interpersonal, relational basis of human communication, children then learn to create communicative effects intentionally, use communicative strategies to accomplish goals, and finally acquire the ability "to evaluate the adequacy of messages and to make repairs" (p. 199). This last assessment process is a "metacognitive" monitoring of messages that probably develops in middle childhood. However, Haslett offered some precursors of this sort of monitoring from the work of Bates (cited in Haslett, 1984, p. 220), who found that children begin to use polite linguistic forms before the third year, and thereafter have a general sense of politeness and how it works to help them achieve their goals. By age 5, children are beginning to evaluate the effectiveness of their messages, to adapt messages when necessary, to explicitly discuss communication per se (metacommunicate), and to use knowledge of others to construct communication strategies.

To be aware of the effectiveness of one's communicative behavior requires *self-awareness* as well as awareness of others. Duvall and Wicklund (1972) described two mutually exclusive states of self-awareness: objective and subjective. To be objectively self-aware is to focus internally on self; to be subjectively self-aware is to focus attention externally on the environment. In the first case, self is the object of consciousness, concerned with the image he or she presents as an object to others. In the second, self is more concerned with the environment's effect on self than with the self's effect on others in the environment. Spitzberg and Cupach (1984) noted, "Objectively self-aware people strategically control their behavior to create desirable impressions on others" (p. 78). Objectively self-aware people are also likely to be high self-monitors.

Self-monitoring (Snyder, 1974) refers to the tendency of an individual "to monitor the social environment for cues that could inform the appropriate adaptation of interaction to that context" (Spitzberg & Cupach, 1984, p.123). High self-monitors have use of a complex knowledge base about person types, which sounds very much like cognitive complexity. However, the results of research regarding a self-monitoring link to competence have been mixed. It may be that the measure is not a pure knowledge measure or it may be that self-monitoring is "a necessary but not sufficient characteristic of competence" (p. 80). However the characteristic is configured, high self-monitors focus on others' responses to them, and the result is that they are typically attentive, other oriented, and *adaptable* to a range of communication contexts.

In any case, the use of self-constructs is integral to competence, and the likely optimal configuration is a balance between objective and subjective awareness. If objective and subjective orientations describe a dialectic of self-awareness, then undoubtedly each individual uses both types to some extent, but may focus on one pole only at any one time. Thus, we are faced with a dialectical choice in each situation concerning whether our own goals and self-protection or the expectations of the interactional other are more important to current communication goals. The choice of boundary or core depends on situational goals; however, people may develop a preference for one pole over the other as a personal rule.

Skill Development at the Boundaries

Interaction Management

Knowing how to engage in conversation seems to be second nature, until we focus on the mechanics and begin to notice some of the difficulties children have, and some of the discomfort adults can continue to feel in conversation. Not only are we monitoring partners' messages and behaviors, we are monitoring our own in response to the feedback we are receiving. Furthermore, we must know how to take and yield turns in an organized fashion. When smoothly accomplished, turn taking employs multiple nonverbal as well as verbal cues.

Turn taking is a complex skill involving intonation, pausing, pitch, hand gestures, eye gaze, and certain kinds of clauses and syntax (Spitzberg & Cupach, 1984). Snow (1977) maintained that mothers shape their children's turn taking with "motherese"—or exaggerated intonation, tag questions, and the like—in effect training children to take turns. Ervin-Tripp (1979) argued that no such deliberate shaping is needed because children's interest in the interaction process is sufficient for them to acquire the structure of turns. Surely parents notice that their young children are imperfect turn takers, but even 2-year-olds are sufficiently competent to carry on a conversation.

Ervin-Tripp (1979) noted that we expect certain conventions of competent conversationalists, including little or no overlap of turns (Jaffe & Feldstein, 1970), brief gaps between speakers—so brief that cued anticipation is required, overlap at "transition-relevant points" or plausible stopping places (Jefferson,

1973), and remedies to overlaps, including slower speech, repetition, or increased volume to compensate for the loss of audibility (Sacks, Schegloff, & Jefferson, 1974). Young children are not capable of this kind of precision, but nonetheless do converse effectively.

Children's turn-taking difficulties vary with partner and context (Ervin-Tripp, 1979). Even 2-year-olds take non-overlapping turns, although the gaps between turns are longer than adults find acceptable, particularly at topic transitions. They are attentive to partners, but perform best in dyads. When a third party is added, especially if that party is an adult, the children vie for attention although they continue to monitor each other's contributions.

Another problem that young children encounter is entering ongoing interaction among elders. One reason this proves difficult is that they are simply slower to process the available cues for an appropriate turn, given their relative lack of practice with the turn-taking script. But perhaps more importantly, their contributions are often ignored by older partners because the partners' expectations are lower for the younger child. Indeed, the younger the child who tries to enter a conversation, the more likely he or she is to be ignored. However, children quickly learn how to remedy these failures. By the fourth year, they will try several tactics to get turns, including stopping and waiting, repeating, or continuing with increased volume. Finally, children are sensitive to the demands of the situation. They recognize that turns are not necessary or even desired in the relative freedom of fantasy play; indeed, they may overlap with abandon. However, they also know that conversational exchange demands rule-ordered behavior. By the fourth year, some children explicitly state turn-taking rules; for example, "I can't talk to you if you talk to me" in response to interruptions from a peer (Ervin-Tripp, 1979). Children quickly learn and use the conventions for turn taking, because they are motivated to participate. However, they also must have something to say, and manage to make it fit.

Verbal Involvement: Topics and Tactics.   On the face of it, interactants speak because they have something to say. But how do we decide if our content is competent? Grice (1975) described four *conversational maxims*: quality, quantity, relation, and manner. Of the four, he considered quality to be primary, and specified subcategories further defining quality: "be truthful" and "have evidence for what you say." The quantity maxim limits the extent of the contribution, the relation maxim has to do with topic continuity, and the manner maxim has to do with clarity and precision. Do children violate the maxims? Indeed, they do, but so do adults. The difference is that adults are more familiar with appropriate ways to license or repair violations.[47]

Obtaining a *license to violate a maxim* requires negotiation between the speaker and listener such that the listener agrees that the speaker intends to cooperate, but is running the risk of appearing noncooperative. According to Eakins and Eakins (1978; cited in Mura, 1983), one way to initiate a license is to use a qualifier that softens the violation. One type is a *hedge,* such as "Well, I think …"), and another is a *disclaimer,* such as "I'm no expert.…" (pp. 104–105). These are fairly sophisticated techniques that probably take some time to discover and perfect. In the meantime, how do children maintain coherence?

According to Sanders, even very young children who have limited mastery of language can participate "neo-rhetorically" in conversation. Neo-rhetorical participants fashion their turns at speaking to progressively influence the course of interaction (Sanders & Freeman, 1998). This implies that the speaker has a goal, goal attainment depends on the other's cooperation, cooperation cannot be presumed, goal attainment other than by influencing the interaction is unwise or impossible, and speaking turns are designed to constrain the other's participation such as to make goal achievement more likely.

Sanders and his colleagues collected interactions between pairs of 5- and 6-year-olds building a structure of their choosing with Legos. They found that not only did the children use a variety of speech acts, and sustain topical coherence in their task interactions. The children's turns were responsive as well as anticipatory, which allowed them to coordinate their turns in a goal-directed manner. That is, they adjusted to each other's turns and effectively cooperated with each other. However, this does not mean that they were equal in participation. In each dyad, one child took control of the task and the other adapted to the first. Interestingly, in Sanders et al.'s data, the less popular (lower in peer rankings) child was the one to take control of the task. However, it was the more popular child who took the neo-rhetorical lead in fashioning turns to constrain the interaction. If we take peer rankings as one measure of social competence, it is the child capable of negotiating the course of conversation who is perceived as competent, not necessarily the one who controls the course of action.

Role Play

Peggy is with a group of children in a section of a children's museum that is set up as a grocery store. It is her turn to be the cashier, and it has taken some time to convince the earlier "cashiers" to give up the post. As she pulls each item toward her, she names it and calls out the amount: "Bread: $2.50." Her "customer" complains, "Isn't that a lot?" Peggy retorts, "Well, do you want it or don't you?" Peggy is learning not only what cashiers typically say, but why they might say so, and how it would feel to be in that position. She is playing the role she has observed.

Over the course of many interactions, meanings have been attributed to Peggy's actions by her partner's actions as they interpret the behavior between them. Such "framed behaviors constitute roles that are assumed, denied, and recreated by the child in the interactional process" (Oliveira, 1998, p. 104). In pretend play, the child substitutes an everyday meaning for an absent object as she takes on another's role, with its gestures, postures, and talk. In this process, she clarifies who she is as distinct from her various interactional partners and, at the same time, she acquires meanings for the different needs, intentions, and identity characteristics of her partners.

One common form of role play is mother–baby enactment. Garvey (1977) examined "talk-to-baby" and "baby-talk" as 3-year-olds marked these roles. For both roles, third-person pronouns and proper names were used instead of first- and second-person pronouns (e.g., "That's for baby. It's not for mommy") to clearly identify the roles (p. 45). Baby-talk included "whining, crying and imitations of babbling," whereas talk-to-baby consisted of "short, simple clauses, with frequent repetition of phrases, frequent interjection of *Baby* as term of address, and the sentence tag, *Okay?*, and some diminutive forms, e.g., *handsies, shoesies*" (p. 46). That is, they accurately represented how mothers and babies often interact.

Beyond appropriately enacting familiar roles, young children are learning the rules for enacting gender as well. Edelsky (1977) observed that children continue to learn the rules for competent gender talk throughout the grade school years. Indeed, she found that some language forms steadily increased in consistently being judged as either male or female language, reaching peaks in adulthood (e.g., "adorable," "oh dear," "my goodness," and tag questions as female forms). However, other forms are apparently learned early as explicit rules (e.g., men swear but ladies don't), later overgeneralized as lawlike stereotypes, and subsequently softened by noting exceptions.

It is in these shared activities, noted Oliveira (1998), that children learn to perceive their actions as separate from their partners, creating meanings for self and other "through a dialectical movement of fusion with the partners and differentiation from them" (p. 107). The child becomes familiar with alternating roles, trying on various positions and styles of talk, assuming different characters. Two-year-olds use sound, action, and objects to support these roles, whereas 3-year-olds rely less on memory of role activity and more on rules they have learned for how language structures their role play (e.g., "It's a man's thing. Isn't it?"; pp. 108–109). Together, they are creating situations in which they can try on various aspects of identity. One aspect of taking on roles is subordinating self-expression in the interests of self presentation. To play a role successfully may mean that one must control the amount and level of disclosure; indeed, it may mean that one must deceive.

Disclosure and Deception

The process of monitoring one's behavior in the interests of presenting self as appropriately in role may require judicious disclosure or selective distortions. Role play is mutually understood to be removed from the "real" situation in that each party is trying on a role that each does not normally fill. Thereby, the child learns to constitute symbolic reality, to create a truth, and to practice deception.

Learning to consciously alter the truth becomes possible when the child can use symbols beyond simple signification to complex creation and negation. Not only is deception a self-defense against others' symbolic force (Cousinet, 1938), but it is part and parcel of imaginative capacity. The creative person is capable of distorting reality; the competent person is conversant with the dialectical range from truth to untruth.

Disclosure and deception describe "the dialectical contradiction between the need to reveal and the need to conceal" (Dindia, 1998, p. 104). For children, the need to reveal and express is tempered by the growing need to protect their developing identities against judgments of incompetence. Petronio (1991) described this "communication management of privacy" as a process of managing boundaries by regulating tensions between telling and withholding private information. This dialectic ranges from complete openness to complete closedness, such as "secrets" of veiled information that could damage identity.

Deception and disclosure messages in childhood have not been studied extensively—some reports claim that lying skill improves with age (Allen & Atkinson, 1978; Morency & Krauss, 1982), whereas others contradict that conclusion (Feldman, Jenkins, & Popoola, 1979). I suspect that all sorts of skills relative to impression management may improve with practice and experience; thus, the children who need to protect their boundaries most will undoubtedly improve most. Clearly, it does take practice time to integrate the complex of behaviors necessary to manage disclosure.

Grade school children who were asked to dissemble with nongenuine verbal praise used different nonverbal behavior than when their praise was sincere. Specifically, they smiled less, paused more, and were perceived to be less pleased (Feldman, Devin-Sheehan, & Allen, 1978). At least until sixth grade, children who can lie verbally cannot successfully synchronize their nonverbal behavior with the lie. But how do children who are challenged to protect themselves develop appropriate and effective communication strategies?

In 1987, Hazen and Shaver (cited in Derlega, Metts, Petronio, & Margulis, 1993, p. 70) reported that early *attachment* experiences affect later willingness to disclose. Adults classified as secure, avoidant, and anxious/ambivalent held different expectations for relationships. Secure individuals whose parents were sensitive to their needs perceived relationships as secure and safe, and reported that they found it easy to disclose and get close to others. Avoidant persons whose parents were insensitive to their needs characterized relationships as lacking trust and closeness, and reported discomfort in revealing themselves and being close to others. Anxious/ambivalent individuals whose parents were inconsistent in meeting their needs saw relationships as a source of anxiety—a struggle between intimacy and loss—and reported worry and fears about the effects of their disclosures: Partners would not return their love or wish to stay. Thus, the nature of early bonds affect the relationship model later in use, including the willingness to disclose to a partner.

In highly challenging circumstances, children must develop rules for disclosing potentially damaging information. Petronio, Reeder, Hecht, and Ros-Mendoza (1996) examined these "boundary access rules" that children and adolescents use to reveal information about sexual abuse and "boundary protection rules" to preserve privacy. *Access rules* permitting disclosure include obtaining "tacit permission" from a listener by responding to inquiries and reciprocating partner disclosures, "selecting the circumstances" by choosing safe havens for disclosing, and "incremental disclosure" by building sequences of increasingly disclosive messages. *Protection rules* limit disclosure by taking into account target characteristics such as trustworthiness, level of responsiveness, and capacity to understand, as well as considering the anticipated reactions of the target to the information revealed. Note that protection rules may very well be based on parents' early sensitivity and responsiveness, and the resulting attachment model constructed to assess relational trust and risk. Some children, then, will be better prepared than others to reveal distressing personal information.

The open-closed dialectic probably begins in preverbal attachment experiences but quickly informs the developing model of relationships with consequences for disclosure, dissembling, and deception. While the child is learning how to manage the boundaries of self-information, he or she is also learning how to influence others' boundaries.

Persuasion and Conflict

The sophistication of persuasive strategies, along with their effectiveness, increases with age (Haslett, 1983). Older children give more reasons for the failure of their persuasion attempts, thus showing that they are working on the problem of which appeals will work (or not) with various listeners. Finley and Humphreys (1974; cited in Haslett, 1983) observed that older children use more appeals than younger ones in trying to reach interpersonal goals with a parent or friend. Haslett also found changes in the use of particular types of strategies with age; younger children used more *reactive* strategies (e.g., denials that depend on prior messages), whereas older ones preferred *active* strategies (e.g., threats that may be inserted at any time). She also noted a developmental shift at age 3, when active and reactive strategies were used equally: "Threes were not merely reacting to prior actions, but their responses reflected their attempts to exert social control through assertions, counter-assertions and questions" (p. 94). However, 3-year-olds used single strategies and failed to sustain reasoning on an issue, whereas the 4-year-olds used more active strategies, and could employ several in support of a single position. As early as 4, children are personalizing their strategies to particular others; that is, they show signs of perspective taking.

Although it should not be all that surprising that practice with conflict interactions fosters the development of perspective-taking skills (Selman, 1980), Piagetian explanations have socialized thought beginning around age 7, at the beginning of concrete operations, However, clearly children are capable of figuring out others' needs before this point. Their first conflict interactions are undoubtedly with primary caregivers, and later with peers; each type of relationship offers different lessons.

Much early conflict research approached *parent–child conflict* as a unidirectional phenomenon; the parent was assumed to direct the child's compliance (Canary, Cupach, & Messman, 1995). However, it is more fruitful to examine the negotiation between parent and child to get at how conflict affects the relationship between them. Mother–child conflicts begin simply (often with the child's early negation, "No," at 18 months or so) but become increasingly complex. With language sophistication, toddlers use justifications (Dunn & Munn, 1987), and mothers in response use bargaining and reasoning (Kuczynski, Kochanska, Radke-Yarrow, & Girnius-Brown, 1987). By the age of 2, children know when they can "win" by nagging and threatening (Lyle, 1994). Patterson (1979) found that older children use coercion (e.g., ignoring or disapproving) with parents, and not only are they effective at least half of the time, but parental punishment of such coercion only increased the probability that the child would continue to use it.

In *conflict with peers,* children learn social perspective taking (Stocker, cited in Canary et al., 1995, p. 77) and problem solving (Bukowksi & Hoza, 1989), and develop ways of thinking about relationship (Corsaro, 1981). It should be no surprise that opposition in children's disputes assists them to figure out how social life works. It is the dialectic between agreement and disagreement that must be managed in order to maintain relationships, particularly friendships (Canary et al., 1995). Although children report that disagreements are reasons not to maintain friendships, Gottman (1983) observed that friends engage in more agreements *and* disagreements than do nonfriends.

Young friends' conflicts are brief and infrequent (e.g., Shantz, 1987), but important nonetheless. Parker and Gottman (1989) pointed out that play must be coordinated, and thus conflict between each person's desires must be negotiated. Typically, preschoolers' conflicts are about play objects, whereas grade school children report that they learn from their conflicts (Shantz, 1993) and engage in reciprocal behaviors about person control (e.g., teasing), physical harm, friendship rules, and opinions. While children are learning to negotiate the disagreement/agreement dialectic, they are also learning to be supportive of partners.

Supporting and Comforting

Supportive communication encompasses a complex of behaviors, and rests on complex social knowledge, most notably, empathy, morality, and perspective taking. Communication researchers have examined variables such as conversational sensitivity (Daly, Vangelisti, & Daughton, 1987) and confirmation (Cissna & Sieburg, 1981); however, how these variables function in early development remains unknown.

Conversational sensitivity, "the propensity of people to attend to and interpret what occurs during conversation" (p. 169), is related to interaction management and involvement, and rests on knowledge bases including self-monitoring and empathy. Daly and his colleagues (1987) tested the construct with college student populations and found that the sensitive conversationalist has a good memory for conversation, can detect meanings well, has an interest in listening and appreciating the nuances of interaction, and can generate a number of ways of saying something (p. 191). It is a sophisticated set of skills that has not been tested in children, but undoubtedly develops gradually and is honed throughout life.

The construct of *confirmation* and its dialectical complement, *disconfirmation,* arose from the study of humanistic psychology and pragmatics. To confirm is to recognize a partner's existence, acknowledge an affiliation with the partner, express awareness of the worth of the partner, or endorse the partner's self-experience, particularly emotional experience. Although studied extensively, confirmation has not been examined for developmental implications. However, it apparently shares ground with another construct, comforting, which has been studied with young populations.

Comforting acts are "messages having the goals of alleviating or lessening the emotional distresses experienced by others" (Burleson, 1994b, p. 136), and convey "care, commitment, and interest" (Burleson, 1994a, p. 5). Sophisticated comforting strategies are listener centered, evaluatively neutral, feeling centered, accepting of partner, and often include a cognitively oriented explanation of the partner's feelings (Burleson, 1994a). Note that there is some overlap between this construct and confirmation (express affiliation, endorse emotional experience). Burleson (1994b) assumed that the sophistication of the comforting strategy is related to developmental level; specifically, that developmental differences in cognitive complexity are associated with the levels of comforting strategies employed. Although most of this research also has employed college populations, a few have tested younger interactants.

Applegate, Burleson, and Delia (1992) found that the children of mothers who were able to use sophisticated comforting strategies were more advanced in social-cognitive development than were children whose mothers used less sophisticated strategies. Most recently, Burleson and Kunkel (2002) studied children in first and third grades, their peers, and their mothers. They found that the comforting skills of mothers and peers each contribute independently to the child's capacity to produce effective comforting messages. Most interesting is their finding that peers' comforting skills were associated with the child's perspective-taking ability. No direction of influence can be claimed, so it could be that the act of comforting peers stimulates the child to try to understand the perspective of others, *or* understanding the perspective of others moves peers to provide comforting behavior—perhaps by way of conversational sensitivity. Apparently, comforting parents have comforting children, and Burleson and Kunkel attributed this effect to learning by modeling. However, keep in mind that these relationships are dialogues and, as such, involve reciprocal influence, not one-way shaping. Once the model is structured between parent and child and practiced, then a system in which comforting is the norm is constituted and perpetuated.

CONTEXTS FOR DEVELOPING COMPETENCE

Communication competence is multifaceted, involving cognitive social knowledge, affective motivation, and behavioral performance. It is learned in relational dialogues, both verbal and nonverbal, in multiple relational contexts. For children, many of their peer relationships develop on the playground or in the classroom. Both familial and peer relationships are affected by media, in particular television and computer simulations. The case has been made that media characters not only provide additional models for communicative behavior, but indeed may substitute for real-time relationships. From a dialogic, relational perspective, the implications of "virtual relationships" for children's developing competence are worth considering, because the consequences of pseudo-interaction are unknown.

Play

Vygotsky (1966) noted in a 1933 lecture that "play is not the predominant form of activity, but is, in a certain sense, the leading source of development in preschool years" (p. 6). Young children need to gratify their needs immediately; however, when the needs are thwarted, children must begin to delay gratification. According to Vygotsky, it is play that teaches the child how to handle the conflicting tendencies between unmet desires that persist and the tendency toward immediate fulfillment. He interpreted play as "the imaginary, illusory realization of unrealizable desires. Imagination ... originally arises from action" (pp. 7–8). Peggy may want to get in the car with Dad in the morning but is not allowed. One way to handle the desire that is no longer fleeting (as it was before it could be kept symbolically in the forefront of consciousness) is to create an imaginary situation with her toys that enacts her wishes.

Furthermore, play involves the use of *rules* for social behavior. If Peggy is to act out the roles of Dad and Peggy with her dolls, she must know the rules for being Dad in relation to Peggy. For example, if the Peggy doll "says," "Can I go with you, Dad?" then, using her knowledge of Dad's resistance to including Peggy when he is working, the Dad doll "says," "Well, if you're quiet while I work." Vygotsky (1966) did not imply that all play is conducted according to rules set in advance (e.g., "hide-and-go-seek"), but rather that rules arise from the imaginary situation. However, the difference between rules imposed by adults (e.g., don't touch that vase) and rules for games (e.g., the vase holds forbidden treasure) is that the child makes up his or her own rules and they are the rules of self-determination.

Vygotsky (1966) pinpointed the child's release from the constraints of the immediate situation as occurring around the age of 3 and continuing in childhood. What becomes possible with this freedom is the creation of meaning that is disconnected from the real situation, and, by school age, the activity of play "is converted to internal processes ... [informing] internal speech, logical memory, and abstract thought" (p. 13). Note particularly the dialectic that emerges in play between impulsive pleasure and rule-governed self-restraint. Children in play do what they like for pleasure, but also use rules to renounce what they want; "play continually creates demands on the child to act against immediate impulse" (Vygotsky, 1966, p. 14). Why? Because "to observe the rules of the play structure promises much greater pleasure than the gratification of an immediate impulse" (p. 14). Thus, in the actions of role play and fantasy are found the means to develop self-control and disciplined will. In replacing action with action, object with object, the child transforms reality and his or her own capacities to deal with it. As Vygotsky (1966) noted, "Play ... creates the zone of proximal development" (p. 16) by setting up tasks and challenges the child has never before met, and motivating the child to find solutions.

Not only does play foster self-control, role-playing skills, and rule negotiation, but apparently play is related to conversation management and interaction skills as well. Olszewksi and Fuson (1986) found that children from 2 to 5 years increasingly are capable of talking about entities that are not perceptually present when they are playing in pairs. Two-year-olds can negotiate the use of objects in play, but do not typically talk about objects not present. By the age of 3, children still need a present stimulus to start their talk, but then may depart from physically present topics. By age 5, they easily pick up and continue conversational topics from their partners, and can converse about matters unrelated to whatever physical task involves them.

In same-age play triads, Black (1989) observed that younger children use more speech to plan their play, and depend more on props in the environment; whereas older children moved quickly to play enactment, displaying better skills at reading their partners' cues. Girls also used more describing and planning than did boys, and were more skilled in relating their turns both topically and interactionally. Girls apparently continue to have the edge for smooth conversational skills for some time. Boys turns were less cohesive, but they were more likely to generate play themes unrelated to the available props.

Children learn quickly to use symbols to remove themselves from the constraints and limitations of the physical present. Play informs skills for conversation, role play, influence, and humor. Early fantasy play, although it demands the construction of some rules for its conduct, quickly gives way to schoolchild games with formal, shared rules.

Education

Grade school teachers may choose to facilitate play among children (Irwin, 1975) in order to maintain the benefits of play for developing communicative competence. In studies of the effects of guided play on children with delayed communication competence, Irwin and McWilliams (1974) found that improvement in play ability brought improvement in verbalization. By the end of 5 months in a play program, children who were essentially nonverbal were relating their fantasies in speech that was more complex structurally and fluent linguistically than had previously been displayed.

Teachers, understandably, consider their primary role to be that of an instructor of cultural content, but they may not have the skill to convey that content. Contrary to the popular assumption that teachers typically know how to communicate effectively in the classroom, Hurt (1984) argued that there are indeed many bad teachers because they lack communication training. He pointed out that classrooms are dynamic systems in which instructional communication should find a ready environment. It is the teacher's role to provide the setting for instructional communication: "The process whereby participants create and share information with one another in order to reach mutual understanding for purposes of cognitive and psychomotor learning" (Hurt, 1984, p. 159). The relational implications are clear—learning occurs in an environment that nurtures interaction and participation. Early childhood educators often do rely on relational dynamics, but teachers at more advanced levels seem to forget the importance of interaction in favor of silent cerebration. However, children employ and practice both verbal and nonverbal skills in the process of learning facts as well as analytical and critical skills.

Anderson, Anderson, and Mayton (1985) assessed teachers' perceptions of student nonverbal skill across K through 12 levels. They found that teachers reported appropriate feedback and understanding of nonverbal signals across all levels, whereas pausing behavior for *turn taking* became more appropriate with advancing education. Teachers also reported that students become less effective across grade levels in signaling their emotions, with the fewest clear displays in Grades 7 through 9. Specifically, they learn to *suppress expressions* of anger gradually in grade school, and then to selectively express anger later in adolescence . These changes seem adaptive to classroom norms, but how do interaction skills shift with education?

Although one-on-one exchanges are not only more difficult to encourage given the time and task limitations of the classroom, but are also more difficult to capture within larger groupings, small group communication has always been possible and has become more popular with *team work* in classrooms. Socha and Socha (1994) found that 5- to 9-year-olds (K–3) belong to many groups and enjoyed that kind of interaction. They noted that first graders understood the concept of a group, although their "silly" relational behavior far surpassed their "serious" task-oriented behavior. From Socha and Socha's observations, they suggested that very young groups may be dominated by one powerful child, or may isolate the uncooperative child who chooses silence. Thus far, this is not so very different from some adult group dynamics. However, children's groups have more trouble with *turn taking* unless explicit rules (such as "no interruption") are put in place. In the absence of such rules, children may fall back on their intuitive strategies, such as "say it louder and more often," thus increasing the noise level greatly. Socha and Socha asserted that teachers not only set rules for teams, but refrain from directing group discussions. Children will be tempted to rely on adult directives to "fix" problems instead of learning the strategies necessary to resolve them.

But what of the silent cerebration that is encouraged in later grades? What has speech and interaction to do with that? If we assume Vygotsky's view of the link between spoken interaction and internal thought, quite a lot. Manning and White (1990) investigated the *private speech* of students in kindergarten through Grade 4 ("speech spoken aloud to self with no intention of communicating interpersonally to another individual," p. 365). They concluded that private speech becomes less intelligible to listeners, more covert or hidden from others, and more resistant to reexternalization upon demand (e.g., "Think aloud as you work independently," p. 371). That is, although the speech that children use to guide their own behavior becomes gradually less observable in grade school, it continues to be used to solve problems.

Bivens and Berk (1990) examined the relationship between private speech and school task performance across the first three grades. Their observations were that private speech was internalized over the early elementary years away from open comments about the activity and toward inaudible muttering or simply movement of the speech articulators without sound. Furthermore, they found that private speech in Grade 1 was associated with math achievement (the performance assessed across all grades) in Grade 2. They concluded that "attention comes increasingly under the control of private speech as children mature" (p. 459), and thus private speech takes time to have a cumulative effect on learning. That is, the process of solving tasks with words and symbols must be internalized gradually and become part of the analytic process.

Classroom discourse provides scaffolding in middle childhood, just as parents' discourse provides it for the toddler. Both peers and teachers can build the sort of scaffold necessary for learning in the zone of proximal development. However, Cazden (1988) looked at a specialized sort of classroom discourse as a *reconceptualization* that is stimulated by the IRE sequence typical of much classroom discourse (teacher *i*nitiation, student *r*esponse, teacher *e*valuation). Her view was that the learning process occurs in the third part, where the learner is exposed to "a new way of thinking about, categorizing, reconceptualizing, even recontextualizing whatever phenomena (referents) are under discussion" (p. 111). The more sophisticated communicator (teacher or peer) has the opportunity to enrich the meaning and move the pupil to the teacher's meanings. Peggy's teacher might ask, "What is photosynthesis?" to which Peggy could reply, "A plant uses light." The third part of this sequence could take many forms, depending on the goal, but suppose the teacher said, "Yes, the plant does use light—thus the *photo* part of the term. But *synthesis* refers to a trick it does in the presence of light—it combines water and carbon dioxide to make food." Thus, evaluation of student contributions—feedback—is where the teacher reinforces learning.

Wertsch proposed that the importance of guided learning as a critical aspect of development lies in the child accepting "a qualitatively different interpretation of the goal of joint activity" (Cazden, 1988, p. 114) that is now more intellectual than social. The child internalizes the discourse and transforms it for use in other contexts—a *recontextualization* or reconception. Of course, for this to work, the teacher must first understand the child's worldview; that is, take the child's perspective in order to frame material so that the child has some basis for understanding. For example, if Peggy replies to the teacher's evaluation with "I don't understand," the teacher might offer, "Think about how you absorb sunlight and use it to make vitamin D for healthy bones. You and the plant both use light for nutrition." In this way, the effective teacher is a model for competent communication as well as a framer of content knowledge.

As early as 1978, the Speech Communication Association (now the National Communication Association) established guidelines for speaking and listening skills for high school graduates, and more recently (NCA, 1988) published K–12 competency statements. There are 20 standards, expanded to numerous competencies for each standard. For example, Standard 2 reads: "Competent communicators demonstrate knowledge and understanding of the influence of the individual, relationship, and situation on communication" (p. 5). One behavioral indicator for this standard is "demonstrate ability to construct different messages that communicate the 'same' meaning to different people" (p. 5), or adapt messages in light of one's ability to take another's unique perspective. NCA articulated specific behaviors reflecting all the skill sets discussed in this chapter. Increasingly, educators are attending to the need for such assessments; similar standards have been set in various states.[48] If and when such standards are accepted in educational practice, teachers will have to be afforded training in modeling and assessing the skills, as well as in understanding their role in scaffolding these competencies. One set of those competencies we have not yet discussed has to do with the use of media.

Media

In the electronic age, we can expect media to affect our relationships. Much of the research on media effects has been on the influence of television on family interaction, although there is increasing interest (but little research) on the effects of computer use on communication. Given that "cyberspace is amoral and boundless" (Bennett, 1998, p. xi), children will need guidance with computer use or else their "relationship" with the computer can turn ugly and even dangerous. We do not know for sure what effects computer use will have on children's communication behavior, but we do know that kids are fond of splat-and-death games and of Internet chat rooms that can easily disguise predators' identities. We have all heard stories about child abductions connected to chat room use and deadly episodes among fans of violent games. In the absence of reliable data, what's a parent to do? At this uncertain time, Bennett (1998) suggested high parental involvement in children's computer use, from software selection to simultaneous web surfing. Indeed, these are the same sort of suggestions that media scholars make about TV use.

Television however has been a presence in American homes since the 1950s, so we do have more solid evidence about its effects. Some scholars think the effect on children has been largely negative, whereas others point to positive learning effects.

Young children (aged 4–5 years) can pay attention to television, but are less active, talk less, and make eye contact less often with people around them while they view. Older children, however, can anticipate program continuity while they engage in other activities (Wolf, Hexamer, & Meyer, 1982). Children do learn from television, and that learning may be facilitated by adult comments during and after viewing. In the absence of parental support and influence, children may compensate for that gap with media use, internalizing media messages that feature action, excitement, and instant gratification (Ashbach, 1994), to the detriment of developing interactive and critical thinking skills.

Media effects are not limited to the intellectual and social; *emotional effects* may be even more important. Television content can have long-term negative effects on a child's emotional well-being (Cantor & Mares, 2001). Even in seemingly benign programs, such as *Little House on the Prairie,* from the 1980s, children are exposed to frightening content. Cantor and Omdahl (1991) observed the results of exposure to media depictions of realistic threats on children's emotional responses. During exposure to scenes of a fatal house fire and a drowning, children were assessed for emotional responses (skin temperature and facial expressions, plus scales and questions). After the exposure, they were asked about their preferences for activities related to fire and water, the likelihood of threatening events in their lives, and their worry about such events. Cantor and Omdahl concluded that children exposed to such media depictions experienced more intensely negative emotions than did children exposed to neutral events. Moreover, children rated events similar to the ones they saw as more likely and the consequences as more severe, and reported greater worry about such occurrences. Clearly, children's expectations about threatening situations are affected by television, and those expectations apparently are mediated by their emotional responses to the depictions. What remains unclear is whether and how these effects may be alleviated by more direct interaction with significant others about the media event.

Kubey and Csikszentmihalyi (1990) suggested that television viewing is indeed a family pastime, and can be a context in which families grow closer. They discerned that people do other things while watching TV, and that talking is one of the most frequent of these activities. They concluded that "people who enjoy time with their families may be more inclined to watch TV together, and time spent watching together may reinforce and enhance family solidarity" (p. 115). They reminded readers of Plato's claim that "a sound education consists in training people to find pleasure and pain in the right objects" (p. 214), and suggested that parents and teachers are key to developing competency in media literacy.

Specifically, Kubey and Csikszentmihalyi (1990) offered offer ideas for parents to assist children in thinking critically about TV: Compare the current episode of a serial with previous ones, by focusing attention on plot, special effects, acting, and characterization; and turn off the sound and deduce what is happening, or listen only to the sound and guess the images. More formally, children should learn the "grammar and syntax of television" as well as plot construction and character development. For teachers, Kubey and Csikszentmihalyi suggested that students learn general aspects of television production and advertising, and that older pupils consider the economics and politics of media as well as the social and cultural effects. Their conclusion, that "the television experience cannot be improved significantly without improving the rest of life" (p. 216), is consonant with our perspective that relational dialogues are where development, growth, and change occur, and that this is not a weighty, onerous prospect—it is our nature and what we enjoy most.

SUMMARY

The question of competence is a difficult one to resolve, but is central to mapping the course of successful and normative communication development. In order to understand how skills develop (or do not), we must also examine the motives for acquiring skill, and the knowledge base necessary for adaptable skill use.

Motivational elements include temperament and emotion, and their relationships to identity and morality. Identity may be based on the reflections one receives from significant others, but quickly takes on value for children based on how they feel about the various characteristics they embrace. In much the same fashion, morality begins with the evaluations of important others and gradually becomes internalized, thus bearing the imprint of the individual's emotional states regarding moral decisions.

Knowledge is constructed in symbol systems, first in scripts for repeatedly useful communicative sequences, and then in generalized rules for appropriate and effective communication. Language rules develop in this way, as do less linguistic aspects of communication. Cognitive complexity—the extent to which the symbolic construct system allows for differentiation among people—may be related to capacities for taking the perspective of the other, and for monitoring one's own behavior in light of the other's perspective.

Skill is observable in behavior, and indeed is an accurate indicator of underlying components of competence in very young children before their knowledge structures are sufficiently sophisticated to dissemble and deceive. The rudiments of interaction management—including the effective use of turns and displays of involvement—are learned with language and gradually refined. Role play provides opportunities for learning the appropriate behavior for a variety of social positions. The child practices relational expressiveness as well as protectiveness in disclosure and deception, persuasion and compliance, and confirmation and disconfirmation.

We risk oversimplifying the process by implying that children simply add on skills and knowledge as they discover what works. Indeed, they discover what does work and does not by making choices with often unfortunate outcomes. These choice points make for dialectics of (in)competence (Spitzberg, 1993). The dilemmas inherent in learning and using competent/incompetent communication are of two types: when ability is in question, the actor must manage the "dialectics of motive"; when quality is judged, the partner uses the "dialectics of inference."

The "dialectics of motive" concern the decisions with which the learner is faced, given particular goals. For example, if Peggy would like to retrieve her "Chutes and Ladders" game and go home, but knows that the rest of the players will be upset if she does so, she is faced with a decision between effectiveness and appropriateness—or, to be more specific, between being assertive and being polite (Spitzberg, p. 141). The dialectics of motive influence the choice of performance with which an actor is constantly confronted.

On the other hand, the "dialectics of inference" concern the decisions that the interactional other faces when forming an impression of competence. In our example, if Peggy's behavior is very much different from what it usually is, Erin will be faced with deciding whether predictability ("Peggy never ends the game") or novelty ("Good for Peggy, she stood up for herself!") is more competent in this situation. Erin may know that Peggy's father was supposed to get out of the hospital this afternoon; therefore, the decision may rest on whether Peggy's behavior is viewed as context facilitated or context impaired (Spitzberg, 1993). The dialectics of inference affect the impression of competence created by the actor's performance. Because we make decisions about our behavior in recognition that it will be judged by another, and that judgment is mirrored back to us, competence is both an ability and a quality, and thus both sets of dialectics challenge the developing performer.

Infants are naturally competent—they behave relationally at the peak of their capacities. However, once the negative is available, the possibility of choice emerges. Dialectical choices include disclosure/deception, compliance/conflict, polite/assertive, and competence/incompetence. Choice is the gift and burden of symbol users. When children begin to use the negative, they have started the human journey. When they begin to play with communicative behavior, they are well on their way. And when they violate norms and break rules, they will be held accountable for their (in)competence.

NOTES

38. See chapter 1, particularly Assumptions 5, 6, and 7. Note in particular that #7.c. addresses the increasing sophistication that children develop in processing interactive experience by way of learning rules for differences. That is, children process interactive experience dualistically.

39. The interested reader is encouraged to refer to Spitzberg and Cupach's 1984 text, which cites the original sources for various parts of these definitions.
40. Dimensions of Duran and Kelly's (1988) Communication Adaptability Scale include five factors: social competence, wit, articulation, social confirmation, and appropriate disclosure. Articulation and disclosure accounted for little variance and were estimated at zero heritability.
41. The reader interested in rules theory may refer to Shimanoff (1980) regarding the necessary conditions for rule violation: that the communicator know the rule and be aware that the behavior does not comply (p. 134). Further material on children violating rules, especially in language pragmatics, includes Garvey (1977) on deliberate violations of speech act rules (p. 40).
42. Piaget (1932) suggested as much in his view that peer conflict allows children to negotiate as equals and to form rules for social conduct.
43. For an accessible resource regarding speech pathologies, see Retherford (1996).
44. The teacher's "Pygmalion effect" may be especially strong in the early years of school and for children who lack strong parental influence.
45. For a more complete review of the research into cognitive complexity, see Delia, O'Keefe, and O'Keefe (1982).
46. See Stiff, Dillard, Somera, Kim, and Sleight (1988) for a more complete discussion of empathic concern as well as an additional component labeled "fictional involvement."
47. For a more complete discussion of licenses and repairs, see Mura (1983).
48. The state of California recently completed a set of communication competencies for students; it is now under consideration for adoption as state education policy.

"What's up with Peggy's grades? She's always done so well in school." Roger was concerned. "She should go to a good college, but she'll need some scholarship money and I don't see that happening with a D in Algebra." Ellen looked up from the pot she was stirring. "She's been very negative about school lately, and she won't talk about it. I wonder if we should call the school office."

My parents have no idea, they really don't. And they don't want to know either. They're so lame about what's really going on at school. What I really want right now is for Josh to ask me to the concert next week, and they're worried about my grade in algebra. Algebra! I'd be glad to take it in summer school just to avoid the drug addict who sits in back of me and talks trash! My cousin, Janet, will get it. She had to deal with a pervert teacher in math last year. I'm glad she's coming up this weekend.

Roger:	"Peggy, we're thinking of calling school to find out what's going on, but we'd rather talk with you about why you don't like school anymore."
Peggy:	"I'll never forgive you if you call school. They don't know anything! I'm fine. I just hate algebra."
Roger:	"Why? Are you having trouble? We could get a tutor."
Peggy:	"No. I can get it. I'm just not interested."
Ellen:	"Is it something else bothering you? Something else happening at school?"
Peggy:	"There are some creeps. That's why I hang out with older kids."
Roger:	"Oh, by the way. I don't think it's a good idea for you to see Josh. He's too old for you."
Peggy:	"He is not. He's just a year and a half older. It's because he's in college, isn't it?"
Ellen:	"What creeps?"
Peggy:	"Oh, they're all creeps. But Josh isn't."
Roger:	"We'll see about Josh when your grades come up."
Peggy:	"You just don't get it."

Chapter 7

Adolescence: Flowers of Maturation, Seeds of Dialectics

The mother and father are your attachment
to beliefs and bloodties
and desires and comforting habits.
Don't listen to them!
They seem to protect,
But they imprison.

(Rumi, quoted in Barks, 1995, p. 25)

Once launched into the tumult of the teen years, there is no return to the comparative security and calm of childhood. The relatively ordered progression of skill and knowledge acquisition gives way to fits and starts, highs and lows, isolation and intimacy. Adolescence is often defined biologically as a period of sexual and physical transformation from child to adult; these are the universal changes of adolescence (Cobb, 2001). The remaining challenges—emotional, cognitive, and relational—may vary by individual and culture. Nevertheless, teenagers are probably the most homogeneous age-related demographic. No matter where you go in the world, teenagers face similar challenges as they move to adulthood.

In this chapter, we examine the range of such challenges, from physical to intellectual to social, as they relate to communication abilities. Once again, we'll organize the material by the components of (in)competence, with a special focus on the move toward dialectics.[49] Much of the literature on adolescence has been conducted in the context of Western, literate culture, and we note the special challenges of this ethos. Our goal is to understand the competency demands placed on the teenager and the process involved in striving toward adult values for communication knowledge, motivation, and skill.

THE PHYSIOLOGY OF PUBERTY

The most dramatic physical changes likely in a lifetime begin in late childhood, as the endocrine system releases hormones so powerful that they effect transformations in height, weight, and body contours (Cobb, 2001). From a very broad evolutionary perspective, these are changes that ensure the propagation of the species. From an individual perspective, they stimulate new sorts of relationships, new skills for dealing with them, and vast changes in the perception of self and one's place in the world.

The brief story of hormone shifts is that androgens increase in males and estrogens in females, thereby triggering changes in the reproductive organs. Although many factors influence the timing of their release, the hypothalamus is probably the most important center for biological rhythms, measuring out gonadotropin-releasing hormones to the pituitary, which manufactures gonadotrophic hormones for delivery to the gonads (ovaries and testes). Two of these—LH (luteinizing hormone) and FSH (follicle-stimulating hormone)—direct the gonads to produce their own sex hormones (estrogens and androgens). Both LH and FSH circulate during childhood but, by the beginning of puberty, the pulses regulating their production are more frequent during sleep than during waking hours. (Perhaps this accounts for the ability most teens have to sleep until noon.) By the end of puberty and through adulthood, hormone production evens out across sleep and wake cycles (Cobb, 2001).[50]

As the gonads release more of the sex hormones, they mature but also stimulate secondary sex characteristics in hair patterns and body contours. These latter changes are not immediate, and although they may occur in roughly the same sequence, the timing of onset can vary a great deal from teen to teen. Girls typically display secondary sex characteristics 2 years ahead of boys. For girls, breasts typically appear between the ages of 8 and 13, pubic hair between 8 and 14, menarche between 10 and 16½, and a height spurt between 9½ and 14½. For boys, testicle growth and pubic hair appear first between 10 and 15, body growth next from 10½ to 16, followed by penis growth and vocal changes from 11 to 14½ (Cobb, 2001).

Although 13-year-old Fred may well be physiologically capable of reproducing, his appearance remains that of a boy, whereas 13-year-old Peggy has attained her full height but is not producing viable eggs. Thus it was that Peggy towered over Fred, her first date, for the seventh-grade dance. This gender difference in the timing of growth spurts may serve human evolution, according to Bogin (1994): "Girls best learn their adult social roles while they are infertile but perceived by adults as mature, whereas boys best learn their adult social roles while they are sexually mature but not yet perceived as such by adults. Without the adolescent growth spurt, this unique style of social and cultural learning could not occur" (p. 33).

Sexual maturity not only is occurring much earlier than in the past, but also much more rapidly. Girls today reach adult height by 16 to 18 years; in the 19th century, females continued growth until age 21. Today, boys reach their full height by 20 or 21 years; 100 years ago, men continued to grow well into their mid-20s. Improved nutrition probably contributes a great deal to this trend; children get bigger sooner, thereby triggering hormone release. For example, Frisch (1983) argued that menarche is triggered in girls by achieving a critical weight, and that this weight is attained earlier with improved diet. This may be good news nutritionally, but to-day's teens are then plunged into additional emotional and relational stressors at an earlier age than their predecessors; perhaps before they are prepared to understand the consequences of their decisions.

THE MIND OF THE ADOLESCENT: PROCESSING EXPERIENCE

The Knowledge Base for Communication Competence

While dramatic biological shifts are taking place, the child continues to develop cognitively. Most importantly for our purposes are achievements in symbolic thinking, moral development, and identity formation. Because there is no universal path through adolescent development, save for the inevitabilities of physiological maturation, a rigid stage theory of adolescent development cannot hold up (Ianni, 1989). Nevertheless, Piaget is often cited regarding adolescence as the "final" stage of cognitive development.

Formal operations is the term Piaget coined to describe the last stage of cognitive development, characterized by "the ability to reason systematically and logically about abstract ideas" (Kamhi & Lee, 1988, p. 130). The mental operations of adolescents and adults, according to Piaget, is characterized by "hypothetico-deductive reasoning," or the ability to evaluate all the logical possibilities of a problem in a systematic fashion. To evaluate all possibilities, gradually discarding nonworkable solutions, requires competence with a sophisticated symbol system. Furthermore, a *written symbol system* may be required for formal operations (Neimark, 1975). This alone would be enough to conclude that not all adolescents (or adults) use formal operational thinking. Indeed, by some counts, only 30% to 40% of teens and adults demonstrate the ability to perform formal operations (Grinder, 1975; Neimark, 1975). In addition, Piagetian tests for formal operations are biased in favor of pupils who have taken mathematics, physics, and chemistry (Kamhi & Lee, 1988, p. 136); that is, toward those who have had the advantage of practice with specialized symbol systems in the context of formal education.

Elkind (1996) pointed out that the theory of youth expounded by Inhelder and Piaget (1955/1958) was influenced by the assumptions of early social science—that progress, universality, and regularity are necessary components of explanatory theories. Furthermore, the cultural bias of Piaget's Swiss education just before World War I led him to assume that all young men (young women were not mentioned) would create life plans based on their close-knit educational and social communities. The fact that many adolescents would not have the training or elaborated code system to perform formal operations may not have occurred to Inhelder and Piaget. Additionally, the idea that other forms of thinking are every bit as rich and enriching as hypothetico-deductive reasoning may have escaped them as well.[51] Elkind (1996) acknowledged the contribution that Inhelder and Piaget made to new thinking about development but reminded readers that even brilliant scientists "can never entirely transcend the social, cultural, and historical context in which they live and work" (p. 220).

One example of a different sort of complex thinking is *dialectical thought*: "reasoning that juxtaposes contradictory ideas and attempts to resolve their conflict" (Kamhi & Lee, 1988, p. 135). What we are calling dialectical thought may go a step further toward finding ease with dialectics rather than trying to resolve them, but that kind of maturity probably would not be found in adolescence. Although adolescents may begin to use formal operational thought, there is no guarantee that they will do so, and yet may proceed to construct other higher-order thought processes. Examples of these reviewed by Broughton (1984) include dialectical thinking, relativistic thinking, transcendental contemplation, as well as forms of consciousness that are highly contextualized and newly subjective or "recentrated" (p. 399). Because these forms are more likely to mature in adulthood, we pursue them further in the next few chapters. For now, let us assume that, under the right educational conditions, formal operations may come into use in adolescence. There is one specialized type of "recentration" that affects intellect in the teen years.

Adolescent Egocentrism

Although we have examined the role of egocentric speech in early development (chaps. 1 & 4), we have not looked specifically to its intellectual counterpart, egocentric thought. Egocentrism, for Piaget (1962), referred to a failure to differentiate some aspect of subject-object interaction. That failure is likely to recur at each stage of mental development but in a unique fashion each time. Elkind (1967) explained, "The mental structures which free the child from a lower form of egocentrism are the same structures which ensnare him in a higher form of egocentrism" (p. 1025). Thus, any new form of mental operations is accompanied by egocentrism of some sort. Elkind (1967) described the particular egocentrism that adolescents experience as an accompaniment of formal operational thought. Mentally, the teenager's task is to conquer thought—to discover all the possibilities in a system, to construct abstract propositions, to objectify mental constructions and reason about them, as well as to conceptualize the thought of other people. However, the adolescent fails to differentiate between the objects of his or her own thoughts, and the objects to which the partner's thoughts are directed.

As any seasoned parent will confirm, teens are primarily concerned with themselves and assume that everyone is as obsessed as they are with their own appearance and behavior (thus, the "bad hair day"). Elkind (1967) noted, "It is this belief that others are preoccupied with his appearance and behavior that constitutes the egocentrism of the adolescent" (p. 1029). Two concepts form the core of Elkind's explanation of adolescent egocentrism: the imaginary audience and the personal fable.

The *imaginary audience* refers to the construction of an anticipated audience and its reaction to the teen construer. Although adolescents are often self-critical, they are frequently self-admiring as well. Elkind attributed teens' self-consciousness, wish for privacy, and increasing concern with shame to the imaginary audience. On the other hand, it may also explain faddish dress, hair, and accessories (including body ornamentation) and the common pastime of imagining how others would react to the teen's demise. Come to think of it, these can be combined. If Peggy adopts a Goth look—wears black clothing, sports multiple and painful-looking piercings and tattoos, and applies black and purple cosmetics—she is making a statement about her acceptance of darkness and death, which she assumes will have an effect on others.

The *personal fable* occurs when the teen overdifferentiates his or her feelings. Peggy is special and unique and none have suffered so exquisitely as she. As contrary as it may seem, this can result in a conviction that she will not die, or what we used to call AIS: adolescent immortality syndrome. Thus, at the same time that Peggy dresses the part of the undead, she doesn't believe for a minute that she will die. Elkind (1967) suggested that the personal fable also explains the popularity of teen journals or diaries, the confidence in God as a personal confidant, and some aspects of middle-class delinquency. Teens who do not need the money may steal for the status it brings and/or their conviction that they will not be caught. In the same vein, Elkind posited that teenage girls become pregnant because they think it cannot happen to them.

One positive effect of adolescent egocentrism is a temporary increase in *self-monitoring*, particularly the ability to modify self-presentation (Allen, 1986). Given the teenaged flurry of identity testing with various roles, an increase in self-monitoring across adolescence would be communicatively adaptive (Pledger, 1992).

Adolescent egocentrism fades by the age of 15 or 16. The imaginary audience serves as a hypothesis to test reality, and the teen gradually differentiates others' actual reactions. According to Elkind (1967), the personal fable may never be "overcome" entirely, but the teen begins to view self more realistically in the context of intimacy with a partner who gives honest feedback. At this point, the adolescent can begin to "establish true rather than self-interested interpersonal relations" (p. 1033). This developmental step affects both intellectual and affective processes, and thus it interacts with both knowledge and motivational components of communication competence in the teen years. Before we consider the motivation to communicate competently and how it is affected by emotions, relationships, and culture, we take a brief look at new knowledge for language in adolescence.

Adolescent language takes on a different character with the increased repertoire of highly *abstract words, elaborate grammatical forms*, and *sarcastic humor* (Berk, 1998). The exception to the rule of increasing facility with language is second- language learning. As we know, there appears to be a critical period for language acquisition—a window of opportunity within which the child remains highly sensitive to language rules and structures. However, that window begins to close at puberty, when it becomes harder to pick up a second language. In a study of Asian immigrants, their knowledge of English grammar declined with increasing age. The youngest (3 to 7 years) mastered English as well as native speakers, but scores rapidly fell across adolescence (Johnson & Newport, 1989). The correct pronunciation of a second language also became more difficult with age (Flege & Fletcher, 1992). If Peggy takes French for the first time in high school, it is highly unlikely that she will ever be assumed a native speaker by Parisians (who will also give her a hard time for trying). Whether or not she is accepted by Parisians, 16-year-old Peggy undoubt-edly has her own specialized form of English that gives her entry to peer groups who use the same forms.

Adolescents have improved their perspective-taking capacities, and thus they may vary their language style according to situational demands. One specialized pragmatic form of language is *adolescent slang,* which teens use to signal that they are different from adults and similar to each other. One recent pervasive example of the specialized use of an English word is the new use of *all* in teenagers and young adults. Waksler (2001) distinguished this usage from its typical use as a qualifier, and analyzes the teen use of *all* as a "marker of a speaker's upcoming unique charac-terization of an individual in the discourse" (p. 128). In an array of samples from San Francisco teenagers, Waksler demonstrated the distinctive use of *all* and differ-entiated it from the formerly ubiquitous *like,* as in: "So she said she couldn't pick me up and I was *all like,* 'Whatever'" (p. 133). In her analysis, Waksler noted that *all* and *like* overlap in distribution: "Both are used to introduce reported or constructed di-alogue or nonverbal behavior" (p. 134). However, she further noted that they are not interchangeable (e.g., "Don't you have like a red one?" could not serve equally well as "Don't you have all a red one?"). *All* introduces a unique characterization of an entity or individual in the discourse, and often appears in emotionally charged stories "in which the speaker's particular interpretation of characters and events is crucial" (Waksler, 2001, p. 137).

The Motivation Base for Communication Competence

Emotions: Hormone Effects?

A common assumption is that the hormone shifts accompanying puberty are re-sponsible for the moodiness ascribed to adolescence. However, higher hormone levels are not strongly linked to greater moodiness, and thus they cannot be consid-ered as causes (Buchanan, Eccles, & Becker, 1992). By tracking mood fluctuations at random intervals, Larson and Lampman-Petraitis (1989) found that adolescents' moods were less stable than adults,' but that the shifts may have more to do with the rapid situational changes that teens experience. Larson and Lampman-Petraitis re-ported positive moods in leisure and hobby activities with friends, and negative moods in adult-structured situations such as school, church, or job settings. Ado-lescence is a time for finding one's identity, and that requires some separation from family members and closer relationships with nonfamily members. That sort of ex-ploration sets up conflicts, both internal and external, and conflict is often confus-ing and upsetting. Although adolescents typically wish to maintain family relationships, they are also challenged to explore external sources of identification to expand their sense of who they may become.

One example of the shifts that may be stimulated more by situation than by hor-mones is increased aggression noted in early adolescent boys. Pellegrini and Bartini (2001) followed boys in early adolescence as they made the transition from primary to middle school. Increased aggression has been observed before as boys enter adolescence, but these authors noted that after an initial increase, aggression declined at the end of the first year in middle school. They explained that the boys negotiate dominance as they move into a new school and establish new relationships, and that as relationships stabilize, the aggression is no longer needed. Boys use aggression to establish status, and then affiliation becomes more important. Pelligrini and Bartini further observed that teacher-rated dominance (both aggressive and affiliative dimensions) predicted dating behavior at the end of the first year of middle school. Rather than reacting to a biological/hormonal imperative, boys are displaying social competence to establish their status in the peer group. However, the sexual urges that lead them to dating the same playmates they avoided the year before surely are related to physiological changes.

Social and Cultural Hazards: Sex, Drugs, and Rock and Roll

Although we explore the nature of relational dynamics and relational models in the next section, it is worth noting some of the external influences on adolescent emotional and motivational states.

Sexual activity is something all teenagers have to consider soon after puberty. How they choose to act on their sexual urges is influenced by parental communication and modeling, by peer communication and modeling, by education, and by cultural mores often conveyed by mass media. Early sexual activity is linked to a range of factors, including parental separation and divorce, family size, sexually active friends, poor school performance, and low educational aspirations. Many of these factors are also associated with low-income families, so early sexual activity is common among teens from economically disadvantaged homes (Berk, 1998). However, adolescents from all economic strata are experiencing sex at earlier ages than did their parents, who were products of more conservative family beliefs about sex; the majority of adolescents have engaged in sexual activity before leaving high school. To put this into a current, global perspective, teenage sexual activity is about as frequent in the United States as it is in Western Europe (Creatsas et al., 1995).

The problems accompanying early sexual activity however are more serious in the United States than in equally prosperous countries. American teenagers have far higher rates for pregnancies, births, and abortions than do teens from any other Western industrialized countries (Warren, 1995). Furthermore, urban American teens display high levels of knowledge about AIDS transmission and prevention, but they lack awareness about the prevalence of common STDs, how they are transmitted, and the potentially serious consequences of exposure (Cohall et al., 2001). Why are American teens handling their sexual behavior less successfully than European teens?

Although the United States legalized the distribution of birth control information in 1965, *sex education* remains largely ineffective, and parent–child communication about sex probably does not fill in the gap. In 1986, 3 states required sex education in public schools; by 1994, 17 states did, and an additional 30 recommended public sex education (Sex Information and Education Council of the United States, 1993). The problem is that most states do not have credentialing requirements for sex education instructors; thus, the quantity has increased but not the quality.

Warren (1995) maintained that we know little about *parent–child communication about sex* and the role that parents play in influencing their children's sexual orientation. A few older studies (Fox, 1981; Philliber, 1980) noted that parent–child communication about sex has been generally indirect, infrequent, and uncomfortable, but nevertheless may influence children to delay sexual intercourse and to use contraception (Fox, 1981). We do not know what makes the difference in sexually responsible behavior among teenagers in other countries; however, high teenage fertility rates across all countries are linked to a high degree of professed religiosity, lack of societal openness about sex, and low distribution of gross national product to the poorest population quintile (Alan Guttmacher Institute, 1981; cited in Warren, 1995, p. 189). Developed cultures with lower rates of teen pregnancy and abortion are also more open and accepting of sexual behavior; Warren theorized that the average family in such a culture would display similar openness.

Although we need to better understand the effects of various forms of parent–child communication about sex, Warren (1995) made several suggestions based on current findings: parents should begin talking and listening in a supportive atmosphere, parents should be incorporated into sex education programs, and television networks (being the financial beneficiaries of gratuitous sexual displays in their media) should allot free time to disseminate information about responsible sexual practices.

Support for Warren's emphasis on parental influence comes from a study of *noncoital sexual activity* among adolescents (Woody, Russel, D'Souza, & Woody, 2000). First, Woody et al. noted that sexual activity does not always include intercourse, but the distinction can make a huge difference in risk factors. Noncoital sex is common among virgins and nonvirgins, and rates are similar for males and females. However, among teenagers who did include intercourse in their sexual activity, they report greater use of alcohol, fewer moral influences, fewer traditional messages about sex from parents, and lower evaluation of their first intercourse decision. Females reported a less positive emotional response to the decision and poorer outcomes than did males. Again, Woody et al. concluded that parents and sex educators should be involved in exploring with adolescents the full range of options regarding sexual activity. Clearly, communication scholars could contribute to the literature describing the content and context of effective parent–child communication about sex.

Drugs are often linked with sexual behavior in the perceptions of many, and in the messages conveyed in the media. Several studies report that the link has some basis in fact. Both males and females are more likely to engage in sexual activity early in the teen years if they use alcohol, marijuana, and other illicit drugs. The higher the drug involvement, the greater the probability of early sex (Rosenbaum & Kandel, 2001). Van den Akker and Lees (2001) found that leisure-time activities (and the companions for these activities) were linked to sexual behavior and drug involvement. Teenagers who spent leisure time with family or church members were less likely to engage in risky behaviors, although risk taking (e.g., drug use) and age were the major predictors of sexual activity.

Priester (2001) attempted to explain the process by which adolescents make *decisions about drugs and sex*. Attitudes often have both positive and negative components; these ambivalent attitudes are more likely when the teenager is bombarded by positive evaluations from media and peers, and negative evaluations from parents and other authorities. Such ambivalence creates tension between the contrasting evaluations, which leads teens to feel conflicted about decisions regarding the use of sex and drugs (including alcohol). Many teenagers will not be ready to integrate positive and negative extremes, nor be comfortable with them. Although they can reason about causes and consequences, in all likelihood they still think dualistically. Many teenagers who decide that alcohol is negative believe it to be entirely negative, as any parent who has been lectured about a glass of wine can tell you. Thus, the most important others in their lives will have a great effect on how they resolve this conflict.

Media and Emotions

Media use and effects have dominated the literature in adolescent communication (Manning, 1996), probably because we have fears about media's influence on values and subsequent behavior. One reasonable fear, borne out by research in the early 1950s, was that high TV viewing was related to low social interaction, thus precluding some opportunities for positive emotional growth and values for sexual responsibility. However, research on TV viewing in Sweden in the 1970s and 1980s demonstrated the opposite effect; it found that viewers were also interactive socially (Rosengren, 1991). In chapter 6, we reviewed research that suggested that TV viewing can have a positive and unifying effect on families. In part, this has to do with the vast increase in scheduling and viewing choices, but it may also be related to changes in media technology that brought about changes in use.

One innovation that has shifted viewing habits is the capacity to personalize viewing schedules that was made possible by VCRs and DVDs. Today, the average VCR household uses it for 6 hours a week, almost 2 hours in recording and another 4 or so in playing back tapes (Lin, 2001). The use of tapes to record programs for later use makes the users more active in determining not only when to view, but what they may skip rather than view, and what they would like to see again; thus, the viewer has more control of content (Lin, 2001). Moreover, the VCR may be used to create a social occasion—to plan a time when several people may view a TV event or movie, with the option of pausing or stopping for interaction. Thus, VCRs give parents more options in terms of regulating children's viewing and interacting with them about content. However, the same advantage does not hold for teenagers—parental mediation decreases with children's age. Nevertheless, family members who must share the VCR also must negotiate its use, thus encouraging communication as a means of coordinating schedules and viewing events (Lin, 2001). However, this communication is likely to involve conflict.

Although VCR use may intensify TV as a central focus of family interaction (Goodman, 1983), it can also modify the way family members relate (Morgan, Alexander, Shanahan, & Harris, 1990). Morgan and his colleagues found that teenagers from social-oriented families (stressing harmony and obedience) more frequently use the VCR for all uses from recording to renting, whereas those from more concept-oriented families (stressing self-reliance and negotiation) more often view rented tapes. Family conflicts about TV strongly predict family conflicts about the VCR, although the latter are less common. Adolescents who frequently argue with family members use the VCR more frequently. Hence, they are either using the VCR to avoid conflict, or VCR use generates conflict. Morgan et al. favored the first explanation based on their longitudinal data, but concluded that family tension may impel VCR use, *and* that VCR use may alleviate that tension. A clue to the explanation is in Morgan et al.'s finding that, in social-oriented families, the parents make frequent comments about TV and use TV for escapism and the teenagers are more likely to have arguments about TV and VCR with family members. Concept-oriented families emphasize negotiation and independent thinking; teens in such families are more likely to rent movies, and their parents are less likely to use TV for escapism. The fact that concept-oriented families have fewer conflicts may be because media usage among members is more complementary than competitive. When Peggy rents a movie she has been waiting to see, her parents are likely to accede use of the equipment to her unless one of their regular news shows is airing, in which case Peggy is well aware of their viewing preference.

Popular music has traditionally been used very differently from TV, but with recent music videos, it has become a growing component of TV viewing as well. Teenagers report that listening to music stimulates more emotional involvement, higher motivation, greater excitement, and more openness than other media (Larson & Kubey, 1983). Popular music, directed to a youth market, speaks to their concerns specifically, and therefore may affect emotional responses more intensely than the usual television fare. Adolescents report that a primary reason for liking a song is distraction from everyday worries and thus relaxation; in addition, songs adjust mood, can be danced to, and express how the teens feel (Rosenbaum & Prinsky, 1978). Wells and Hakanen (1991) found that adolescents increasingly used music for mood management, with ninth graders less likely than twelfth graders to choose this use. Nevertheless, most respondents used music for emotional management, either mood enhancing or tranquilizing, with women ranking items such as "lift my spirits" and "mellow me out" higher then men, and men choosing "get me pumped up" more often than women.

Media use is implicated in adolescents' emotional shifts and mood management, and we might expect media to affect identity development as well, particularly in how the adolescent feels about the sense of self.

Identity Challenges: Motivation and Knowledge at the Core

Adolescence, in Erikson's schema (1950, 1960), is a time of intense questioning of the stable dualisms depended on in childhood. The task in this stage of identity development is to integrate childhood identifications with biological drives, endowments, and social role opportunities. The danger is that identity diffusion, unavoidable in this period, may result in either a permanent inability to commit to identity or in a fixation on an early and negative identity founded in rebellion (1960). Erikson (1960) asserted, "Every adolescent is apt to go through some serious struggle at one time or another" (p. 47). The teenager experiments, reviving some childhood identifications and discarding others; going for "extremes—total commitments and total repudiations" (Erikson, 1960, p. 47). That is, adolescents find identity in dualistic fashion; it is all or nothing for them, and they will need a delay or "moratorium" in committing to adult values. It is in this moratorium that teens need a period of "relaxed expectations" and "guidance to the various possibilities for identification ... none of which can be replaced by either moralistic punishment or condescending forgiveness" (Erikson, 1960, p. 50). The tolerant parent can assist the teen through moratorium to stable identity.

Marcia (1966, 1967) expanded Erikson's identity theory and focused on the adolescent stage of identity versus identity confusion. Furthermore, Marcia dropped the "versus" from the stage labels and called for dialectical language that allows the reader to see the "both ... and" nature of the constructs rather than "either ... or" (Muuss, 1996). In this case, the teenager experiences *both* identity formation *and* role confusion in the course of this developmental period.

Marcia's four statuses for identity achievement were based on studies with college students and adults. Although teens probably experience only two or three of them, all four of these are useful to us in later chapters: the *identity-diffused self*, who has not explored or resolved identity issues, nor made any commitment to beliefs or vocation; the *foreclosed self*, who also has not explored identity issues but has made definite commitments to goals and beliefs, usually those of parents or authoritative others; the *moratorium self*, who is in acute crisis and exploration and is actively searching for personal values and experimenting with alternative roles; and the *identity-achieved self*, who has explored and resolved identity issues and has made a well-defined personal commitment to goals, values, and beliefs (Muuss, 1996). Although these might appear sequentially, Muuss (1996) noted that "only the moratorium appears to be a prerequisite for the achievement of an identity" (p. 263). Marcia found increasing numbers of identity-achieved students in college years; we would expect to find most adolescents in one of the other three statuses, which means that most teenagers should be starting to explore identity options.

How likely is it that high school students will begin to form a positive, healthy identity? They face challenges to cognition and motivation that past generations did not. Although education offers the opportunity for the achievement of formal operational thought, many people pass through formal education without acquiring either literacy or causal thought, leaving them without the raw materials for critical thinking. In the absence of critical thinking, immersion in media that reflect and magnify substance abuse, irresponsible sexual activity, and mindless pastimes may thwart the motivation necessary for identity construction. When it is easy to find distractions from everyday difficulties and interpersonal confrontations, then the lessons to be found in those challenges may be postponed, or never met and conquered.

Graafsma, Bosma, Grotevant, and de Levita (1994) commented, "Identity involves the balance between something that is core and something that serves as the context to that core" (p. 163). In terms of communication, *the core is the totality of symbolic self-constructs* created in interactions and internalized over time, and *the context is the interactional milieu*—the personal relationships and mediated experiences that self chooses. Over time, the core self builds in complexity as it reaches to the contextual boundary for information about who it should be. For the adolescent who reaches to the boundary for stimulation and avoids the sort of conscious internalizing that creates a mature identity, the process will be prolonged. It will be much easier to remain in the state of certainty found in the "foreclosure" stage of identity development than to move on to the confusion of "moratorium." As we see in the next chapter, the college years allow more opportunities to focus on the vacillations inherent in the dialectics they are discovering.

BUILDING RELATIONSHIP SKILLS
AND CREATING RELATIONAL MODELS

The contrasts made possible by core/context distinctions begin in simple dualisms such as pleasant/unpleasant, active/passive, up/down, and boy/girl, but fast become more dynamic as "new forms emerge out of the tension of opposites" (Haviland-Jones & Kahlbaugh, 2000, p. 301). In particular, oppositions such as masculine/feminine appear first in dualities (e.g., the child identifies particular forms of behavior that must be adhered to for each gender), but as oscillations between the poles of that construct increase, the tension created between them results in a new kind of dialectical awareness of their connection. Although only the briefest glimmer of such awareness may occur to the teenager, nevertheless the makings of dialectical thought are set up in the teen years. The battles of the "moratorium" phase of identity occur between dualisms on the field of adolescent egocentrism, but peace is made by bringing together those poles in the tension of dialectics. Discovering the dialectic is a gift of varied and frequent interaction, internalized by a thoughtful, conscious mind. Although the process may begin in late adolescence, it is likely that dialectical thought and communication take a lifetime to craft.

Kinships: Struggles With Autonomy

As children enter the early teen years, they are faced with many decisions, but they probably are still making sense of them in black-and-white terms. At the age of 12 or 13, teens still see social conventions as arbitrary but they defer to the rules for practical reasons, even while they question the justification of the rule (Turiel, 1975, 1977). Not only does Peggy begin to question the reason why she has to be home by 9:00 P.M., but she also begins to question the legitimacy of parental authority, as in "It's none of your business when I come in" (Montemayor, 1983, p. 108). These challenges are typical of early adolescence, and related to shifts in the child's reasoning about social rules and norms. It's no surprise that satisfaction with parenting is at a low point in the early teen years (Hoffman & Manis, 1978), when the teens are balancing their own sense of independent identity with parental rules that they view as arbitrary and oppressive.

On one hand, we have *parents* who are trying to impart knowledge of social conventions as well as guidelines for moral and ethical decision making (Hart, 2000) and who are optimistic about their children's futures. On the other, we have children who are experiencing biological changes with physical maturity, and cognitive shifts in their models for self and for relationships. Although their major sources for emotional support are still within their families, their conflicts are increasingly about freedom and personal responsibility (Ianni, 1989). Gradually, those issues move from the family context toward the external world of friends, romance, and education.

The inevitable *conflict* that accompanies the shift in power relations between parent and child at puberty has received the lion's share of attention, but is not the entire story of this relationship. Neither is the conflict always highly stressful. People experiencing a transition from one role to another will have more difficulty if they are unprepared for the new role (Burr, Leigh, Day, & Constantine, 1979). Parents who are prepared to adapt their skills to adolescents will be less likely to be dissatisfied with their children's pubertal transition. Not only are parents often in the dark about the changes they will encounter, but children are also unprepared to cope with physical maturity and the new roles that accompany it. In some cultures, rites of passage accompany sexual maturity, but similar formal rituals to welcome children to adulthood are uncommon in Western cultures. Teens are left to their own devices to sort out the multiple challenges they face. The lack of affirming social acknowledgment may be one reason that young teens still depend on family for emotional support, at the same time that they challenge parental constraints.

In a review of the literature regarding parent–child conflict, Montemayor (1983) noted that the issues that raise the most disagreements did not change between the 1920s and the 1980s. Most *arguments* are about everyday family matters and rules for conduct, most notably "the hours you get in at night" and "home duties." Parents and their teenaged children rarely engage in overt conflict about sex, drugs, or religion, even though these are undoubtedly large questions for the adolescent. Parents may not bring up these issues because they do not affect the day-to-day interactions of family members, and children are likely to avoid topics they suspect will lead to disapproval. However, the adolescent who does express disagreement with parents is likely to be the one who is actively exploring identity (Cooper, Grotevant, Moore, & Condon, cited in Montemayor, 1983, p. 98). Conflict is undoubtedly a necessary element of the "moratorium" phase of identity formation, and thus healthy unless taken to the extremes of verbal and/or physical abuse.

Teens who experience highly *stressful family relations* are more likely to run away, join cults, marry early, become pregnant, use drugs, drop out of school, and engage in criminal behaviors (Montemayor, 1983). Conflict is less a question of "how much" as "how." Family supportiveness in general, and parenting styles in particular, are likely to affect whether conflict is stressful or growthful.

Earlier in this chapter, we noted that hormone shifts may contribute to moodiness, but also that much of adolescent's storminess has to do with the contextual and relational shifts they are making. However, we cannot dismiss entirely the *effects of biological maturation on conflict* behavior, especially conflict with parents.

Steinberg and Hill (1978) separated the effect of age from physical (sexual) maturity and found male adolescents' maturity (and not age) related to their conflict interactions. Specifically, they interrupted parents more and explained themselves less as they developed physically. Steinberg (1981), who noted that parent–child conflict peaks at the height of male puberty, found that mothers defer to their sons in late puberty as the conflict is beginning to subside, but that fathers become more assertive and sons more deferential. Sons mirror their fathers' competitive behaviors as they mature, and become more influential than mothers in the family system; after the dust settles, father and son have reached some new balance of power.

Open communication between parent and child about the physical changes occurring apparently affects how the child feels about self as well as the parent–child relationship. Unfortunately, children rarely disclose such matters to parents, which can lead to greater distancing and conflict (Paikoff & Brooks-Gunn, 1991). Because children tend to withhold feelings about physical changes during puberty, it may be up to the parent to invite disclosure in a nonjudgmental atmosphere. Of course, this becomes less likely when the child is challenging parental authority.

Because one of the tasks of adolescence is the kind of reasoning (and questioning) regarding social conventions that leads to improved *perspective taking* (Paikoff & Brooks-Gunn, 1991), some tolerance of this process is required of the effective parent. Unless parents accept their children's needs for personal control and can allow them to experiment with the values underlying their behaviors, the development of personal identity with an accompanying system of morality is thwarted. Note the downward spiral that can occur: If parents lack the communication skills to tolerate open discussion, their children have fewer opportunities to practice perspective taking about social norms, and thus may comply with parental demands without internalizing the underlying values. Furthermore, the unpleasant verbal arguments that can ensue when both parties lack communication skills can result in reciprocity of negative emotions, and ultimately in a distressed family system (Canary et al., 1995).

What makes the difference for children who need to talk? How do they decide whether to speak to family members, to other adults, or to peers? *Disclosure* is a dialectical phenomenon in the sense that the discloser faces a decision to reveal or conceal (Dindia, 1998). That decision is likely to be mediated by "boundary access rules" and "boundary protection rules" in a dance between the need to protect and the need to express (Petronio et al., 1996). *Access rules* include gaining tacit permission to tell by responding to inquiries or responding reciprocally to a partner's disclosure, selecting the circumstances by choosing safe and secure situations for telling, and using incremental disclosure by disclosing small amounts and judging the partner's responses. *Protection rules* are based on target characteristics such as trustworthiness and responsiveness, and anticipated reactions of the partner that might affect the relationship or the discloser's control of the information. Although these findings were based on data collected regarding the disclosure of sexual abuse, we may extrapolate to other issues that teenagers consider very private or risky to reveal.

Unless parents give permission, tacitly or overtly, for their children to tell them about nonconforming behaviors, they are unlikely to meet the boundary access rule. Parents then might consider that providing safe settings and open communication (disclosing feelings of their own and asking nonthreatening questions that show concern) will increase the likelihood of their teenaged children revealing their concerns. Of course, the protection rules also require that the parents' responses to disclosure be trustworthy, attentive, and nonjudgmental. Easy? Of course not, but that is why teens often reveal their problems to peers, siblings, or other adults rather than to parents.

Peggy and her older sister, Nan, went to breakfast early on a Saturday morning, and each invited her best friend. Peggy and her friend, Linda, were 15; Nan and Jill were 19 and on spring break from their university. The four ordered, chatting about their plans for the day—Nan and Jill had some research to do at the library before heading out to shop; Peggy and Linda were going to a track meet. Nan and Jill were discussing their project for a psychology class and mentioned some of the figures on sexual abuse in families. To their surprise, Linda started to talk about her older brother Daniel's regular visits to her bedroom from her 10th year on. She continued, addressing most of her comments to Jill, until she seemed to run out of steam. Jill softly asked if she'd told anyone else about her brother's behavior. She had not, and expressed great reluctance to tell her parents. Linda felt, and reasonably so, that it would change their opinion of Daniel and thus shift the family dynamic. Knowing that Linda was receiving some counseling, Nan asked Linda if she could talk to her therapist, and Linda agreed to reveal it in that context. Peggy was shocked and silent until she was alone with Nan later that evening, and then shared her surprise that Linda would choose to reveal her secret to a relative stranger. But telling Peggy directly would have threatened Linda's positive image. And, given the nature of the secret and the reactions she feared, Linda found this a perfect context to indirectly reveal it to members of her network.

Another option that some adolescents choose is to speak to *siblings*. Warmth in the sibling relationship is associated with disclosure, and those daily sibling disclosures in early adolescence are likely to concern unhappy emotions (Howe, Aquan-Assee, Bukowski, Rinaldi, & Lehoux, 2000). In our last example, Peggy, upset and confused by her friend's disclosure, discussed these feelings with Nan and asked for advice about how to speak with Linda about the abuse she revealed and her feelings about it.

For all of the troubled families with adolescent children, there are many more who are making it through this challenging period in a positive fashion. Parents who are optimistic about teaching values to their adolescent children are also more likely to grant autonomy and less likely to be punitive (Pratt, Norris, van de Hoef, & Arnold, 2001). Teenagers who experience their everyday home life as happy are typically from "complex" families in which they feel support, ease, and togetherness (Rathunde & Csikszentmihalyi, 1991).

A *complex* family system is both highly integrated and differentiated, whereas a *simple* family system is low in both features. Rathunde and Csikszentmihalyi (1991) commented, "Integration allows family members to maintain relations with others through a shared investment" (p. 144) in common goals, such as traditions, values, and so on. Differentiation "allows an individual to construct a separate self through having the control to invest in personal goals" (p. 144). Thus, the complex family blends individual needs for identity formation and maintenance with group needs for support and the development of social values. Parents in complex homes

> can be less vigilant about pressing their children to achieve, and pay more attention to helping them discover the ongoing rewards of pursuing goals ... by noticing how a child is feeling ... when a child is feeling bored, anxious, or apathetic.... Homes that are integrated make family members' thoughts and feelings more transparent to one another ... Family differentiation provides each member some opportunities to select and involve themselves with interesting challenges. (Rathunde and Csikszentmihalyi, 1991, p. 158).

Thus, just as important as knowing when to ask, and when to reveal, is knowing when not to interfere and to allow the child his or her own pace.

Part of knowing when not to interfere is knowing when teenagers need the input of their peers rather than that of parents. Adolescents appear to use two dialectical principles in choosing conversational partners (Rawlins & Holl, 1988). The first is the dialectic of historical perspective and contemporary experience, in which time frame is the deciding factor. Parents are often chosen to give historical perspective on issues with which they have more experience; peers are often chosen because they share perspective on events that affect the adolescent in the present.

The second dialectic is that of judgment and acceptance, which implies evaluation; typically, parents are viewed as being more judgmental and peers as being more accepting. Nevertheless, the decisions are not that cut and dried. The teenager weighs contemporary and historical perspectives, the likely evaluative response, and the level of caring the target partner feels for the adolescent before he or she decides to talk or avoid an issue with parent or peer. Rawlins and Holl (1988) emphasized that these options are not mutually exclusive, nor do they pit parents and friends against each other. Clearly, however, parents can increase the chances of being a chosen conversational partner by displaying that they care, and by being less judgmental in their responses. The irony is that parents' historical perspective can lead them to judge adolescents as part of their display of caring. However, evaluations may be perceived by the child as evidence that the parent is out of touch and cannot accept them. As is true of many dialectical decisions, this one is paradoxical, because caring can send the child to peer interaction. As Rawlins and Holl suggested, we need to further examine the communicative practices that might lead teenagers to perceive evaluation as judicious rather than judgmental. For now, we turn to the increasing influence of peers in the teen years.

Friendships: New Expectations

In addition to articulating an identity, adolescence is a time for learning the communication skills necessary for intimate relationships. Such skills are learned first in close same-gender friendships, later in cross-gender friendships, and ultimately in romantic relationships. By puberty, the *internal model of friendship* has evolved to include sharing personal concerns, reciprocal support, and assistance, as well as loyalty and fair treatment (Rawlins, 1992). Sullivan (1953) defined preadolescence as a turning point in the "need for intimate exchange" (p. 291), in which same-gender friendships are characterized by collaboration, self-disclosure, and consensual validation (Buhrmester & Furman, 1986). By adolescence, an additional need for sexuality is added to intimacy and peers of the opposite gender become included in the relational network.

Adolescents *choose friends* according to their "reputational salience" or ability to contribute to one's social reputation (Hartup, 1996). Often, this means that friends will be similar to self, or at least similar to how one would like to be seen. Teenaged friends are most similar to one another in terms of school achievement and aspirations, as well as normative social behavior "such as smoking, drinking, drug use, antisocial behavior, and dating" (p. 149), including sexual activity. Hartup (1996) noted three sources of *similarities between friends*: sociodemographic conditions, or the schools and neighborhoods that teens inhabit; social selection, or the construction of friendships with those perceived as being similar; and mutual socialization, in which teens model behavior for friends and receive reinforcement from them. Thus, not only is the available pool of friends important, but the child's own changing sense of self will influence the choice of similar pals, and then those pals who are perceived as being similar to self will reinforce similarity in behavior. For example, antisocial friends apparently reinforce each others' undesirable behaviors (Dishion, Patterson, & Griesler, 1994); the teen who admires a rebel may become more rebellious. Although friends play a crucial role in development, and foster supportive and intimate relational models, they may reinforce deviant activities with long-term consequences.

Recall that adolescents are preoccupied with themselves and believe that they are always being observed. Thus, their *rhetorical self-presentation* becomes very important in these years for building identity, but the standards for behavior set by various of their "audiences" may be contradictory (Rawlins, 1992). Family members may reinforce roles such as part-time employee, "A" student, or 4-H president, whereas peer cliques applaud cheerleader, football hero, or stage actor, and intimate friends subtly honor the sexually active dater or the hip drug experimenter. To the extent to which their choices diverge from family or conventional mores, they "encourage idiosyncratic options for defining self yet heighten the potential for conflict with other social formations. To the extent they mirror conventional social practices, they limit self" (p. 65) and minimize the challenges of contradictory standards. The teenager often feels that they are "damned if they do and damned if they don't," and rightly so. One safe place to practice conflict is with friends.

In contrast to the incompatibility that young children perceive between conflict and support in friendship, adolescents grow to understand that friends can both support and disagree (Berndt & Perry, 1986). *Adolescent conflicts* are no longer over objects, but are conflicts of personality (Smollar & Youniss, 1982), which are typically concerned with friendship standards and heterosexual behavior (Laursen, 1993). Teenaged friends are hammering out what is required of them, and what they can expect of relational partners.

Rawlins (1992) identified a dialectical tension between private communication and public comportment. Talk with close friends in the private realm is expected to be uncritical, or at least sensitively handled; trust is critical to maintenance. However, the public demands of popularity, in the interests of trying on various roles, may run counter to the maintenance needs of the close friendship. The popularity performance effective in peer-group interactions requires "adeptness at coopera- tion, compromise, and competition" (p. 70), whereas the collaboration effective in close friendships fosters "perspective-taking skills ... empathic support, and altru- istic concern" (Buhrmester & Furman, 1986, p. 56).

Rather than try to balance the two sets of skills, some teenagers may choose in dualistic fashion to specialize in one extreme of the dialectic. *Excessive public com- portment* may lead to "rigid adherence to social conventions" (Rawlins, 1992, p. 70) and the extreme other-directedness often found in high self-monitors. Although these skills may serve adolescents in peer groupings and foster leadership skills (Button, 1979), their social images may keep them from examining deeper identity issues in the context of intimate friendship. *Excessive private conduct* can lead to ex- treme inner-directedness, idiosyncratic notions of appropriate behavior, and unre- alistic intimacy expectations. In this case, the high ideals formed in isolation can restrict opportunities for relationships and increase the likelihood of disappoint- ment (Naegele, 1958). These teens orient exclusively to either family, romantic partner, or a single friend, thus limiting the possibilities to learn an array of perspec- tives and to try out identity affiliations.

Adolescents are challenged by a variety of contradictory impulses and dialectical challenges. Of increasing importance are those involving sex and gender. First, there are differences between *same-sex friendship* pairs. Female friendships are more exclusive, involved, and intimate; their speech involves disclosure and per- sonal topics. The emphasis placed on loyalty and confidence can in turn engender jealousy and rejection of "outsiders" (Rawlins, 1992). Male friendships are more in- clusive and group related; their speech is about activity. Males do things together, valuing activity and achievement. The resulting competition can hamper intimacy between male friends.

Generally, girls have more harmonious interactions with their friends, whereas boys are more confrontational. The better the friendship is, the more responsive the girls are and the more critical the boys are (Brendgen, Markiewicz, Doyle, & Bukowski, 2001). Female adolescents are more likely to disclose both positive and negative emotions with same-sex friends, whereas males rarely disclose their feel- ings in either same- or cross-sex relationships (Kiraly, 2000). Adolescents willing to disclose their feelings reported more validation, intimacy, support, productive conflict, and less conflict overall. Kiraly suggested that self-disclosure skills are valuable in adolescent friendships and could be facilitated for boys who have been socialized away from "feminine" self-disclosure. Of course, the advantages of cross-sex friendships lie in the skills that can be learned there.

Although *cross-sex friendships* are possible in the context of early adolescent peer groups, they have been viewed as less of a valued social achievement than romantic relationships have, and as more difficult to understand (Schofield, 1981). Later in the teen years, opposite-sex friendships are pursued with more frequency, although they remain more rare than same-sex friendships (Rawlins, 1992). Girls report twice as many opposite sex friends as boys do, which suggests that girls and boys define friendship differently. Boys are not reporting the friendships that girls are, yet they value the female friends they do report as giving them more ego support than their male friends do (Wright & Keple, 1981). Furthermore, cross-sex friends discuss a wider range of intimate topics than do dating partners (Werebe, 1987); indeed, many teenagers do not view dating partners as friends (Button, 1979).

Despite the advantages of communication with a cross-sex friend, the social pressures make them more fragile than same-sex relationships. Girls report that their male friends try to change the friendship to a romantic relationship, thus often damaging the friendship (Rawlins, cited in Monsour, 1997, p. 395) and losing access to a source for understanding the male–female dialectic. Monsour (1997) asserted, "Insider perspectives are particularly valuable because they help individuals to establish gender identity and to recognize similarities and differences between themselves and their cross-sex friends" (p. 395). Emerging sexual and social needs campaign more strongly for the romantic dimension of cross-sex relationships.

Romantic Relationships and Intimacy

Erikson (1968) noted, "It is only when identity formation is well on its way that true intimacy—which is really a counterpointing as well as a fusing of identities—is possible" (p. 135). Although adolescence is the time to construct a personal identity, it is also the time to explore sexuality. In the process of understanding self and developing the capacity for deep relationships, teenagers are likely to have many romantic relationships before they know true intimacy. Levitz-Jones and Orlofsky (1985) identified several relational styles possible in late adolescence, from "mergers" (characterized by dependency and enmeshment), to "isolates" (formal relationships only), "stereotypic" (superficial relationships based on mutual need fulfillment), "pseudointimate" (sexually committed but superficial), "preintimate" (not in a committed sexual relationship but capable of intimate friendship), and finally "intimate" (a committed partnership involving mutuality, openness, caring, and sexual expression).

Apparently, *sex-role orientation* mediates the identity-intimacy link (Kroger, 2000, p. 101), at least for women. Men typically develop a sense of identity before they experience intimacy. But women oriented to feminine sex roles may fuse identity and intimacy in development, whereas those with a more masculine sex-role orientation develop identity before genuine intimacy, as men do. One reason for this distinction lies in the very different norms for sexual behavior set for males and females. Adolescent girls understand very well that their male counterparts' sexual behavior is an outcome of their sexual desire; in contrast, an appropriately gendered teenaged girl decenters sexual desire and experience from her own behavior (Senchea, 1998). Thus, boys can be appropriately identified as masculine and act on sexual desire in the absence of intimate relationship. The only way for girls to act on their desire and still be normatively feminine is to disguise their sexual behavior (perhaps even to themselves) as a required part of intimate relationship. Two identity patterns are open to women: one for those who focus on education and occupation, achieving identity before they leave the teen years; and the other for women who choose homemaking, putting off stable identity achievement until their late 20s or 30s (Schiedel & Marcia, 1985). No matter what track is chosen, all teens need a set of relationships to assist the transition to romantic partnership.

Peer friendships seem the natural precursor to romantic relationships in terms of practicing the skills for intimacy. Furman (1999) described the *peer group* as the context for romantic relationships, and cited (p. 146) Dunphy's model of peer groups to describe the process: unisexual cliques emerge; male cliques and female cliques merge to a crowd; popularity leaders of each clique begin to date, forming a dating clique; several dating cliques associate; and finally, couple relationships develop and the crowd begins to disintegrate. If you have some trouble dredging this phenomenon from memory, watch the process unfold in the movie *Grease*.

Romantic partners are not expected to be primary and committed until early adulthood, and indeed cannot appropriately be so until identity is well under way; thus, the peer group metamorphosis to dating service is highly functional. Indeed, early romantic partners are more similar to friends in terms of need fulfillment—both friends and dates provide companionship and intimacy, but parents remain the reliable source of affection and instrumental support (Furman, 1999).

Both Sullivan (1953) and Buhrmester and Furman (1986) proposed that only adolescents who have successful relationships with same-gender peers will develop positive romantic relationships. Testing this position revealed that acceptance in a same-gender peer group does moderate the links between romantic involvement and self-esteem (Brendgen, Vitaro, Doyle, Markiewicz, & Bukowski, 2002). Unpopular young teenagers who had romantic partners had lower self-esteem and higher levels of antisocial behavior. Popular young adolescents who were romantically involved did not differ from those without a partner on self-esteem or behavior. Brendgen et al. concluded that youngsters who are not successful with their peer group lack the necessary social skills and transfer their inappropriate strategies to the romantic partnership. Negativity with the romantic partner may then reinforce the strategies, leading to antisocial behavior. Aggravating this cycle is the fact that poorly adjusted teenagers tend to choose involvement with similarly deviant partners (Capaldi & Crosby, 1977). Of course, these teens may also have unrealistic expectations about romantic relationships and their promise for status, companionship, and intimacy. Unpopular children especially will be searching for need fulfillment that they cannot find in the absence of peer intimacy.

Research testing the *effect of peer group popularity on intimacy* outcomes was conducted with young adolescents. In a longitudinal study examining early peer and parental relationships and later romantic partnerships, Seiffge-Krenke, Shulman, and Klessinger (2001) found evidence to cast some doubt on the influence of early peer relationships on later love relationships. By the time these participants were 20 years old, the peer experiences at 14 and 15 apparently had much less influence than did past experiences with parents. Protective and trustworthy parents in mid-adolescence predict positive romantic relationships in early adulthood. Conversely, divorce evidently negatively affects attraction in the affected child's later romantic relations.

Apparently, *parental models for mature love and attachment influence their children's long-term mature love relationships.* Peer groups provide an early testing ground for practicing social skills as well as the field of available romantic prospects. Both function developmentally, but at different times and in different ways. But what of other adults?

Nonparental Adults

Although much as been written about education and intellectual effects, we have precious little information about the relationships between adolescents and *teachers.* Perhaps our public educational system is so overwhelmed that we cannot expect our teachers to attend to individuals or to perceive their students as relational partners in education. What we can assume is that adolescents vary in terms of how they handle their multiple stressors, and that they may benefit from nonparental adult relationships.

Using a "multiple worlds" typology, Phelan, Yu, and Davidson (1994) characterized teenagers by their success in handling their family, peer, and school "worlds." Type 1 teenagers, who have congruent worlds and experience smooth transitions among them, experience great pressure to achieve academically, often accompanied by a decrease in learning motivation and mental health problems, including depression. Most of these students do well in school and report that parents assist them with school matters. At the other end of the spectrum are Type 4 teenagers, who experience very different worlds and resist crossing the boundaries between them. They are often at risk of dropping out of school for academic reasons, they are discouraged about uncertain futures, and often blame themselves. However, these students report receiving little assistance from teachers, often feel "picked on," and rarely report that their parents are knowledgeable enough to assist them with schoolwork or future plans.

The family context affects adolescent achievement and behavior much more than do school and neighborhood factors, and thus parents are very powerful influences (Duncan, Boisjoly, & Harris, 2001). Nevertheless, adolescents may feel the need for additional assistance from adults at some time during the teen years. For Type 1 teenagers, the need might be for emotional support and relief from achievement pressure; for Type 4 teens, the need is more likely to be for an ally in the educational domain to counsel them academically. I would not conclude that parents don't want to fill their children's needs, but parents may not know what those needs are. Teens may be making decisions to avoid certain topics with parents that they feel are too risky to broach.

Adolescents make choices about what to disclose to parents, to peers, to siblings, and, as well, to nonrelated adults. Indeed, they may choose an adult specifically for his or her relative distance and lack of authority.

One type of adult who is technically related but often not considered an authority is the *stepparent.* Golish and Caughlin (2002) found that teenagers avoid talking about sex across all parental relationships, but typically avoid talking with stepparents about the "other" or true parent, deep conversational topics, and money issues. Golish and Caughlin concluded that talking with stepparents is risky and requires some self-protection. Reasons for avoidance include fear of being caught in the middle of conflicts between a parent and stepparent, reluctance to side with a stepparent, and failure to acknowledge the stepparent as an authority. Apparently, children tend to protect the parental relationship and to resist the stepparent.

Culture and Community

The rare teenager has relationships with caring and trusted adults other than parents. Given a state of identity confusion and lack of a safety net beyond the nuclear family, it is little wonder our culture faces a surfeit of troubled youth. Support systems are probably inadequate for American teenagers. Youth in other cultures find greater satisfaction in family and community support networks. For example, Indonesian teens rank family members higher than friends as support providers and companions (French, Rianasari, Pidada, Nelwan, & Buhrmester, 2001). In particular, Indonesian siblings are reciprocally responsible and supportive of each other, whereas U.S. teens turn to peers outside the family for support. Although teenagers in every culture vary a great deal depending on their closest interactional partners, cultural mores can certainly influence the degree to which adults feel responsible and adolescents feel supported.

Ianni (1989) maintained that the difference between troubled and well-adjusted youth in the United States lies in "youth charters." These are harmonious communities in which adults reinforce shared moral standards as the ideal for optimal development. Unfortunately, youth charters in which consistent expectations apply from all adults to all children are rare in the United States. Politicians continue to deplore the decline in "family values" without offering solutions, and parents are left to try to inculcate appropriate norms in isolation. If we accept that development is dialogical, then all the interactions we experience are influential in constructing identity and values. Even when parents do their best to provide consistent models for ethical behavior, if the larger community network fails to support those models, then the models may be gradually eroded by the influence of immature peers and by the neglect of well-meaning adults who fear "getting involved." Although representatives of the federal government speak in generalities about supporting families, it is more likely that local communities will have to salvage their own children with concerted adult involvement in reinforcing local ethical standards.

SUMMARY: DUALISMS TO DIALECTICS

With adolescence and the struggle to forge personal identity there also arises the possibility of discovering that what appeared to be dualistic choices may instead be dialectical challenges to relating, including to oneself. Young teens face torturous decisions about whether they will choose autonomy or dependence, whether they will rebel or conform. Although this may seem to be an *either/or* choice (e.g., "Shall I go to school as my parents wish or ditch to hang out with friends?"), older teens may recognize that they can choose *both* autonomy *and* dependency (e.g., "I will hang out with my friends in good time, but I agree that school is of value").

In terms of social thought, the early teen years are dominated by egocentric thinking that features self as the focus of attention. However, in the process of developing that "personal fable," the adolescent begins to supplant the "imaginary audience" with the real partners who have real characteristics and opinions. Thus, social sensitivity vies with egocentricity until there is a recognition that adjusting to others' needs does not preclude maintaining one's own sense of self.

At the same time, teens are faced with decisions about whom to tell their deepest secrets and feelings. The expressive-protective dialectic may at first be perceived as a choice between either keeping one's developing self intact (and thus making the personal fable immune to change) or expressing the dark secrets (and thus giving oneself over to another and losing self). In deciding whom to trust, adolescents are likely to make judgments about who cares and accepts them, and what perspective they wish to invite (present or past orientation). In weighing these choice points, they ultimately recognize that they can be both expressive and protective, maintaining the benefits of support and the integrity of self.

Finally, adolescents will be faced with decisions about what their relationships mean to their private life and how they contribute to public persona. As peers and autonomy become more important, the public persona will likely be very important to the developing personal fable. Then, the more private needs of the maturing self may choose the benefits of intimacy. But, finally, the necessity emerges to maintain *both* intimate idiosyncratic ties *and* social normative networks.

Not all adolescents will reach a balance point between these sets of apparently competing needs. Very few will find the tension between them a stimulus for play and enjoyment. In the college years, more opportunities for relating to very different others will be offered, many will be chosen, and the possibilities for maturation of identity and morality will burgeon.

NOTES

49. See assumption #7.d. in chapter 1: adolescents are increasing their sophistication by developing skills for synthesis—that is, they are beginning to perceive that the poles of dialectics are connected.
50. This means that teens need their sleep time for sexual maturation. Yet, they typically get less sleep than they did in grade school, because high schools often start earlier and jobs and social activities keep them awake later.
51. Buck-Morss (1975) provided insight into the cross-cultural implications of a bias for the structural form of abstract, logical thought without regard for the content of thought.

Peggy was in tears during registration day. They had lost her course requests and she was shut out of all her required classes. She was told to find the instructors and get signatures. She had no idea where to start and was tired, frustrated, and afraid of all these strangers.

Now, what am I going to do? Maybe I should just go home. The instructors won't just let me in now. Mom thought I'd like college. I don't. I hate it. I want to go home to my friends. Maybe I could get a job at Grossman's.

* * * * *

Beaming with achievement, but feeling slightly jaded in the aftermath of the wrangling she'd done in recent weeks on the board of the Environmental Coalition, Peg lined up with faculty and students to march into graduation. She saw Rob across the gym and waved, thinking of their move to the city and pushing doubts from her mind for the moment. Instead, she considered the people around her and marveled at how much she had changed from the frightened girl of 4 years ago. She didn't know who she was then.

I can't believe I was scared of these professors. They're just people, after all. I hated it when they challenged my ideas about relationships, and religion, and politics. But I figured out what I think is right. Mom and Dad hated it when I started to disagree with them, but they seem all right with it now. I think they disapprove of Rob and me living together, but they haven't said so. Today, they're just happy for me. And I feel sooo ... myself! Everything is ahead of me, and I can't wait!

Chapter 8

The College Years:
Rhetorical Challenge at the Boundaries

There are two kinds of intelligence: one acquired,
as a child in school memorizes facts and concepts
from books and from what the teacher says,
collecting information from the traditional sciences
as well as from the new sciences....
The second knowing is a fountainhead
from within you moving out.

(Rumi, quoted in Barks, 1995, p. 178)

Development continues after the teen years, whether the dialogues are encountered in adjusting to the workplace, in creating a family, or in the academy. Using the chapter title "the college years" implies that there are unique opportunities for development to be found in the transition from adolescence to adulthood, and particularly in the context of higher education. As Rumi pointed out, there are ways of knowing beyond the neat, concrete contrasts of childhood. Formal study seems to stimulate a few. As well, this sheltered time on one's own that college offers makes for explorations into self and values.

Competence, especially the knowledge component, is likely to develop differently for the college student than for the 18-year-old in the workforce. Nonetheless, the developmental challenges posed by higher education may be found in other experiences, and we explore some likely contexts in this chapter. The task of this transition is for the young adult to begin to perceive self and relationships more dialectically, and experience glimpses of dialogic awareness.[52] First, we will review the literature treating symbolic effects on cognition, morality, and identity in the college years. Next, we examine shifts in emotional regulation, coping strategies demanded in the transition from home to institution, and the challenges of finding and maintaining relational intimacy. Furthermore, we look at the relational skills that become increasingly useful in the rhetorical presentation of self. Finally, we project to worldly demands on the college graduate and suggest some qualities of the rhetorically effective and communicatively competent graduate on the verge of young adulthood.

Much of the research in social science is based on college populations. Thus, much of what we know about young adults—really, adults in general—has been extrapolated from 18- to 22-year-old students. Although this tells us quite a bit about the social and communicative skills of this cohort, we know little about whether generalization is warranted. We know even less about the nonstudent population of the same age group. Is their developmental process similar? If communicative development occurs in relational contexts, we would certainly expect nonstudents to continue developing, but perhaps in different ways. We propose some possibilities here, but keep in mind that we really do not know much about the variations of adult communication development.

KNOWING THE WORLD AND KNOWING SELF

Knowledge Appropriation and Commitment

Prevailing public opinion about higher education is that college attendance should guarantee not only sufficient technological skill to ensure better-than-average salaries, but also optimal adjustment to everyday social challenges. It is no wonder that demands for accountability have increased in recent years. Traditionally, higher education was undertaken for purposes of intellectual development rather than as a substitute for technical training or secure attachments. A college education cannot be all things to all people, but we take the view here that it certainly can and should stimulate human development (Kohlberg & Mayer, 1972), which optimally goes beyond formal reasoning to dialectical thinking.

Basseches (1984) commented, "Dialectical thinking is thinking which looks for and recognizes instances of dialectic—developmental transformation occurring via constitutive and interactive relationships" (p. 55). The difference between *developing* dialectically—"developmental transformation ... which occurs via constitutive and interactive relationships" (p. 22)—and *thinking* dialectically lies in the conscious awareness of how human changes and shifts occur. All of us do the former; some, the latter.

Abstract and Contextual Thinking

The possibility for *formal operational thought* arises in adolescence among formally educated individuals, but it is not the only possibility for cognitive development. Piaget emphasized the importance of developing a form of reasoning that may be, and often is, used entirely in abstraction from everyday events. Although abstracting is fundamental to symbolizing, the thinking known as "abstract formalism" specifically separates form from content (Buck-Morss, 1975), divorcing thought from experience in dualistic fashion. Since Piaget, others have argued that we need forms of thought beyond abstract formalism to inform further developments, such as constituting a mature identity, committing to personal values, and maintaining intimate relationships.[53] These challenges involve linking abstract ideas with concrete reality.

Two aspects of Piaget's work inform later revisions of his foundational work regarding intellectual development. The first is the assumption that mental structures become more complex through problem solving, and the second is that we grow by experiencing cycles of equilibrium and disequilibrium (1964). Disequilibrium is the discomfort we experience when our current mental structures fail to solve a problem; equilibrium is the preferred comfort we restore when we discover a sufficiently complex mental process to solve the problem. Thus, this is one of the ways we develop dialectically. Sanford (1962) added that through differentiation and integration we learn not only about things, but about self; we distinguish characteristics particular to self and integrate them to understand how they shape unique identity. Piaget's cycles of problem solving explain causal thought only. Perry observed later cognitive development for evidence of thought beyond the abstract formalism that serves individual problem solving to the kind of thought that may serve relational experience.

Perry (1968) interviewed Harvard students across the 4 years of their university experience to describe intellectual development that could not be encompassed by formal operational thought. His sequence of intellectual and ethical positions have been summarized in four clusters (King, 1978):

1. *Dualism:* Views knowledge and values through absolute categories; the "right answers" are determined by authorities. (The fact-finder: "Truth is absolute and I can know it by observing and studying facts.")

2. *Multiplicity:* Acknowledges multiple viewpoints, but feels that questions simply have multiple answers; all points of view are equally valid. (The debater: "There are a number of ways of looking at things and I can argue any of them.")

3. *Relativism:* Believes knowledge is contextual; multiple viewpoints fit together into a larger whole and may be evaluated; authorities are valued for their expertise rather than their infallibility. (The critical, systemic thinker: "The context of the problem is important and I can come up with a variety of solutions and evaluate them critically.")

4. *Commitment in relativism:* Believes knowledge is contextual *and* affirms own responsibilities in a pluralistic world. (The responsible, reflective evaluator: "Multiple views form reality and I must choose and be responsible for the viewpoint I construct.")

The *relativistic thinker* uses the dialectic to understand and integrate changing systems in a changing world. In terms of Piaget's cycle of equilibrium/disequilibrium, the postformal thinker uses a form of equilibrium that relies on understanding the inherent disequilibrium of open systems. Thus, mature cognition is all about the necessary tension created by a tendency to want equilibrium and an acceptance that neither the world nor our symbolic constructs of it are given to stable equilibrium. Another way of coming to terms with open systems lies in the perspective that "any change at all ... can be equilibrated if it can be conceptualized as a moment in a dialectical process of evolution (Basseches, 1984b, p. 230).

Kitchener (1986) expanded the final postformal cluster, "committed relativism," to a *reflective judgment* model of adult knowledge development. She started out in the same place as Perry, with the position that knowledge is a matter of absolute certainty based on observation; all problems are puzzles to be solved. However, once the realization hits that some problems are not so well structured so as to be solvable, then knowledge is "understood as a reasonable conjecture about the world or a reasonable solution to the problem at hand" (p. 77). Thus, solutions to some problems must be created in light of the context in which the problem is found—"a viewpoint may need to be constructed based on a higher order integration or synthesis of different perspectives" (p. 77).

Kitchener and colleagues tested her seven-stage scheme (from absolute certainty about facts to constructive knowledge claims) with various age cohorts and found that high school students' mean scores average between stages 2 and 3.5; college students' between 4 and 4.5; and advanced graduate students' between 4.5 and 6. Scores remain stable over short periods, but change of about one-half stage does occur over a 2- to 3-year period for most participants in the studies (Kitchener, 1986). In a nutshell, this means that students move from *dualistic* to *dialectical thinking*—"reflective judgments"—over a fairly long period from adolescence into early adulthood. Kitchener found that most graduate students have not reached the final stage, but do have "personal certainty about beliefs based on evaluations of evidence on different sides of the question" (p. 79). What does this reasoning progression mean in light of other developmental schemas?

Most people continue into adulthood to become better at solving puzzles, such as the well-structured problems on intelligence tests (Kitchener, 1986), but many successfully do so from a dualistic perspective. King (1978) found no relationship between reflective judgment and formal operations. However, verbal ability apparently is related to, but not the same as, reflective judgment. What is the connection? Kitchener and King (1981) suggested that experience with poorly structured, contextualized problems seems important to reflective judgment. It would seem that posing complex problems verbally and in context might make a difference to the development of reflective judgment. Although college students have many opportunities to deal with problems symbolically, verbally, and contextually, a college education is no guarantee of this kind of development. Conversely, a nonstudent could choose the kind of challenging work and social settings that stimulate the development of reflective judgment.

Following the lead of Labouvie-Vief (1982a) and Blanchard-Fields (1986), Sebby and Papini (1994) posed emotionally relevant problems to adolescents and young adults, assuming that the teenagers would have more trouble reasoning about the "real-life" problem than would young adults. The more relevant the problem posed to teenagers, the poorer their reasoning was about it; the less relevant the problem, the better their reasoning was. Conversely, problem relevancy facilitated reasoning among young adults. These findings confirm what the earlier studies found; that "adolescents ... have difficulty integrating relevant (emotionally salient) information with cognitive task demands" (Sebby & Papini, 1994, p. 398). That is, they cannot link abstract ideas to real issues. In light of adolescents' failures to think critically about highly involving and contextualized problems, they probably are unable to consider all the consequences of their behaviors, and thus their moral and ethical reasoning is immature as well.

Moral Reasoning and Argumentation

Kohlberg (1971) claimed that mature morality arises from logically derived absolute principles, based on the capacity for formal operational thought. Murphy and Gilligan (1980) challenged Kohlberg's concept of logical morality, using Perry's notion of adult *morality as a commitment to principles* chosen from a larger set of multiple valid principles. Their longitudinal data from adolescence into adulthood showed a regression on Kohlberg's scale, yet a progression on Perry's scoring system. Mature thinking and adult morality are not related directly to logical, formal thought processes. Is formal thought just a necessary step to more complex forms of thinking and evaluating?

Basseches (1984a) asserted that dialectical thought builds on formal operations. Sinott (1984) also posited a relativistic "stage" beyond formal operations. Kohlberg himself revised his original belief that moral development finalizes with formal thought and found evidence of further moral development in the 20s and 30s (Colby, Kohlberg, Gibbs, & Lieberman, 1983). On the other hand, Broughton (1984) argued that the inadequacies of a normative stage theory of adult thought call for a paradigm change rather than piecemeal revisions to stage theory. He pointed out that to compensate for a purely cognitive focus by adding affect is simply to reaffirm the dichotomy between them. The same is true for adding concrete particularity for problem solving to existing logical abstraction to come up with a new stage of problem finding. Broughton (1984) suggested that we need to seek "some deeper conceptualization of consciousness that would obviate the need for such oppositions" (p. 410). I would agree, but such an overarching theory has not been forthcoming from cognitive psychologists. The closest to such a goal would be those who have defined and tested dialectical thinking in adult development (Basseches, 1984a; Buck-Morss, 1975; Riegel, 1975), but have yet to expand dialectical ideas to a fully formed theory of human development. If we were to propose a dialectical view of moral development, what would it look like? Perhaps a communication perspective would bridge the gap between cognition and affect. Relational experience would then become the playing field for moral development.

Gilligan and Murphy (1979) observed that the transition to contextual relativity that influences moral judgment occurs during the 5 years *after* college. Although the groundwork may be laid during the college years, the move away from absolutes appears after the fact of recognizing shades of gray. Gilligan (1982) also observed gender differences in the shift in absolutes. For women, the absolute of care (for others) becomes tempered by the need for personal integrity. The balancing act necessitated in this dialectic manifests as a claim for equality that "changes the understanding of relationships and transforms the definition of care" (p. 166). For men, the absolutes of truth and fairness are challenged by experiences that demonstrate differences between self and other. Again, this crisis of self and other leads to "a relativizing of equality in the direction of equity" that gives rise to an "ethic of generosity and care" (p. 166). For both, judgment becomes contextually relative and leads to a new appreciation of choice and responsibility. With this new awareness comes the possibility for adult refinement of personal morality.

Peg, as she now calls herself, reveling in the competence she feels in her first professional job, goes home to her newly decorated apartment every night, and typically calls Rob to make plans for the evening. During their college years, she usually scheduled weekend plans, arranged to party with friends, brought food to Rob when he was studying, and generally showed that she cared for Rob in ways similar to what she observed her mother do for her father. Now, she is beginning to feel that Rob is taking advantage of her. She is putting in long hours to build her career as a graphic designer, whereas Rob is still job hunting. Nevertheless, he neither cooks, nor plan outings, nor seems concerned about her fatigue. She has asked Rob to bring food or massage her shoulders, and he rarely has complied. She decides she must move on without him. Rob is shocked and hurt. He thought everything was fine with Peg but he discovers, too late, that her experience differed from his. His thinking becomes more focused on relationship issues, whereas hers becomes more focused on personal competence and ensuring that her needs are met, both in work and relationship contexts. Thus, each is becoming more concerned with understanding both justice and care, but their judgments about what behavior constitutes equitable concern may not converge for some time—the 20s are fraught with these relational complexities. For adults, interaction provides the raw material for moral development.

The meeting place for the emerging identity and newly significant other is the boundary zone where morality gets hashed out in dialectics. Labouvie-Vief (1984) suggested a *dialectic of self-regulations* (based on personal goals) and *mutual regulations* (based on social goals) in the service of mature moral development. Once knowledge is seen as relativistic, logical certainty erodes and attention must move from abstract absolutes back to personal particulars. At this point, "the youth discontinues the search for logical certainty" (Labouvie-Vief, 1984, p. 176) and the comfort of absolutes, and turns to the search for personal commitment and specialization. The transition to autonomy may be marked by "destructuring and restructuring" (p. 177) or tearing down some of the learned dualistic knowledge systems in the interests of constructing one's own dialectic moral systems. Furthermore, the transition into autonomy occurs relatively late, between 35 and 55; may endure 5 to 20 years (Cytrynbaum et al., 1980); and is likely characterized by lagged internalization periods between destructuring crises and restructuring growth. If moral development is a lifelong process, and if it is particularized to individuals and their experiences, what kinds of communication experience foster it?

Most scholars of adult development believe that *perspective taking* and *empathy* are critical to the development of adult morality. Kohlberg (1969) proposed that moral development may be enhanced in individuals who have attained sufficient perspective-taking abilities by events that provoke disequilibrium. His implication was that formal operational thought is necessary for moral development.

In a test of the effects of interpersonal skills training on moral growth, Santilli and Hudson (1992) controlled for level of formal operational reasoning. Undergraduate students, aged 19 through 28 years, completed an 8-week interpersonal skills training course that included *role-playing* exercises. On the whole, class members showed gains in social perspective taking, but males accounted for much of the change. Females started out fairly high and raised their scores a bit, whereas males started out considerably lower and showed a greater gain, slightly surpassing the women's scores. The group did not demonstrate gains in moral reasoning until formal operations abilities were entered into the equation. The more advanced formal thinkers showed significant gains in moral reasoning, but those early basic formal reasoners showed losses. Although the sample size was small, in this sample, interpersonal skills training fostered perspective taking but contributed to moral development *only* for those students who had mastered all levels of formal operational thought. Kohlberg was evidently right about the need for abstract formalism.

Perhaps interpersonal relationships provide the context for developing moral concepts, but only if the experiencer has learned to consciously abstract principles from the relationships. This study is not the final word on the links among moral reasoning, abstract thinking, and communication, but it does provide some support for the notion that formal operations, or some form of abstracted conceptualizing, is necessary for the growth of moral reasoning and more complex forms of thinking. As reasoning becomes more complex, the sense of self shifts as well.

Identity Achievement and Commitment

Recall from the last chapter Marcia's (1966) four classifications of identity status, defined according to the presence or absence of crises and the firmness of commitments. *Achievers* have negotiated their self-exploratory crisis and are committed to a created, personal identity. *Moratoriums* are in the process of crisis but have not chosen to commit. *Foreclosures* have selected a system of beliefs and norms adopted from significant others. *Diffusions* have neither committed to any system nor have they explored any. Berzonsky (1989), who described identity as "a self-generated theory about the self" (p. 363), linked a set of qualities with each status.

The active self-explorers, Achievers and Moratoriums, are information oriented; they seek out and evaluate information and typically display greater *cognitive complexity* (Berzonsky, 1990, pp. 160–161). On the other hand, Foreclosures are passively norm oriented, and Diffusions avoid problems until the immediate context dictates their behavior. Statuses differentiate on a number of communication-related variables. Diffusions tend to be high *self-monitors*, perhaps as a response to the need to figure out what the current context requires. On the other hand, Diffusions are low in need for cognition, whereas Achievers and Moratoriums are high in information orientation.

Berzonsky concluded that information-oriented individuals may be characterized as "scientific" self-theorists who are responsive to feedback and willing to test self-constructs. Indeed, this sort may experience cycles of Moratorium-Achievement-Moratorium-Achievement across the lifespan (Berzonsky, 1989) which seems

very like "cycles of internalization."[54] The normative orientation of Foreclosures produces "dogmatic" self-theorists who are more likely to use self-serving biases and to
expend energy in defending existing beliefs (1990). Diffuse-oriented individuals operate as "ad hoc" self-theorists in their need to accommodate to situational influences. Their responsiveness to situations is likely ephemeral *compliance* rather than
stable restructuring.[55] Note that Berzonsky (1990) did not perceive these styles as necessarily indicative of progressive stages, but instead as relative differences in the process of constructing identity. By late adolescence, most people will have tried all of the
styles. The style assumed may be related to contextual demands or motivational factors. The shift from home to college is a huge contextual transition, with accompanying motivational shifts. We further examine the development and presentation of self
as we explore that transition and ensuing challenges.

Motivations to Communicate Appropriately and Effectively

To communicate consciously or not is a choice we constantly make, based on the
context, the available interactants, and our own emotional and cognitive states. The
transition from home and family to an educational institution brings change in
contexts and relationships with probable accompanying shifts in moods, emotional responses, and identity.

Transitions: Dependence/Autonomy Challenges

Whether high school graduates leave home for college, for marriage, or for the
workplace, they are leaving the family unit that has nurtured them and constituted their most significant relational context. High school seniors, flush with accomplishment or relief, feeling that they are finally adults, are cast into the role of
the beginner again. Now, however, they do not have the relative comfort and security of the family.

Although prospective college students are uncertain of their future, they do have
expectations for college and their place there. Students who are fearful about the
university experience prior to attending report over the next 4 years that they feel
more stress, depression, and poorer adjustment to university life than do those who
had optimistic expectations (Jackson, Pancer, Pratt, & Hunsberger, 2000). What
makes the difference between fearful and optimistic potential scholars? Those who
are underprepared for university probably are well aware of it and feel realistic apprehension. However, crippling or enduring fear is more likely in those who have
not tackled identity tasks.

Identity formation is still proceeding as the late adolescent prepares for college. Those who are proceeding toward secure identities are better able to adjust
to college demands, both social and intellectual. One of the tasks of late adolescence is to individuate from parents and form an independent identity. The
most frequently mentioned turning point in the parent–child relationship is
that involving physical distance, and the distancing event is often the move away
to college (Golish, 2000). Certainly, the relationship to parents will change with

distance, but the effects of change on the child are likely to vary with the quality of the relationship to that point.

Those graduating high school seniors who perceive secure attachment to their parents tend to make the later adjustment to college more easily than insecurely attached teenagers do (Larose & Boivin, 1998). The most important influence of this separation on college adjustment is *conflictual independence* (Lopez, Campell, & Watkins, 1988), which is defined as "freedom from excessive guilt, anxiety, mistrust, responsibility, inhibition, and anger in relation to mother and father" (Hoffman, 1984, pp. 171–172).

Orrego and Rodriguez (2001) considered it likely that the *family communication style* would have some relationship to the student's ability to separate, and thus to adjust well to college. Their strongest finding was that *protective families*—expecting strict obedience to family norms and characterized by rigid, militant, and *closed communication style*—produce students with less conflictual independence and poor college adjustment. These students come from families in which conformity to the rules is not a matter for discussion. They probably have been encouraged to adopt values and beliefs wholesale from their parents (Foreclosure), and thus are less likely to question moral and ethical issues or to make them uniquely their own. On the other hand, the *open communication style* found in *pluralistic families* has a positive effect on conflictual independence, although no significant effect on college adjustment. These students have less resentment of their parents, but may still experience some adjustment problems for other reasons.

The major shifts that students experience will happen in the first 2 years, and possibly in the first few months (Heath, 1968). Is all this change attributable to distance from parents? Undoubtedly not; the new context brings new relationships, new task demands, and accompanying shifts in self-perception, even if they are mediated by the quality of first attachments. Over the course of the college career, students develop more positive self-images and feelings of intellectual competence (Astin, 1977), become more introspective and independent (Corbin-Sicoli; cited in Loeb & Magee, 1992), and show greater autonomy and personal integration (Chickering, 1974). But are these changes simply progressively incremental?

Loeb and Magee (1992) tracked students' attitudes and *self-perceptions* from their first days in class, again 12 weeks later, and again near the end of their second year. The students' attitudes became more tolerant, and they experienced several shifts in self-perceptions. The first shift was negative; by the end of their first semester, the students described themselves as less friendly, less important, less trusting, and more average than when they first started classes. However, by the end of sophomore year, most ratings (except friendly and trusting) had moved back up. Part of this shift is probably contextual; the students had moved from high school, where they achieved success, to the unknowns of college where it is easy to lose bravado and experience doubt. But why the permanent decreases in self-perceptions of friendliness and trust, which are likely to affect the capacity for close relationships?

Possible answers include the distance from the social network of family members and long-term friends, a reordering of priorities toward academics (Loeb & Magee, 1992), or a wariness brought on by encountering a greater range of personalities and using new skills for critically analyzing those personalities. That is, students may be more particular about their choices. More complex causes for poor adjustment in college may have to do with the interrelationships among available relationship partners, shifts in self-perception, and comparisons to past close relationships. Thus, college students experience up-and-down cycles but overall become more independent and intellectually competent.

Loneliness and Depression

Loneliness often affects students in transition and the quality of *family relationships* is likely to influence how students cope with the transition. When students report that they experienced optimal parenting (high care and low control), they also report low levels of social anxiety and depression and high levels of self-worth (Massey, 2001). The same effects hold for students who report positive sibling relationships (high social support and low negativity). Students who recall conflictual relationships with siblings experience loneliness in college, whereas those who remember close sibling relationships are less likely to feel lonely (Ponzetti & James, 1997).

Loneliness may be a common transitional experience, but clinical depression, although less typical, may be life threatening. In a recent sample, 53% of the college students reported depression since beginning college, and 9% reported considering suicide (Furr, Westefeld, McConnell, & Jenkins, 2001). From twin studies we know that some people are genetically vulnerable to depression, but stressful life events such as separation from loved ones can trigger depression even in those not usually at risk (Goldberg, 2001). A predisposition for introversion (avoidance) and negative cognitive style may be risk factors for depression, but these are mediated by relationship experience. In particular, emotional maltreatment in childhood is related to suicide ideation in college students, and that relationship is mediated by cognitive style and feelings of hopelessness (Gibb et al., 2001).

Because many young adults will be meeting with diverse "others" for the first time in college, this is a good place to consider how students may cope differently, depending on their cultural backgrounds. *Cultural variation* in family communication and social network may influence coping skills. Although rates of depression are generally similar for African Americans and European Americans, there have typically been fewer African Americans among those treated for depression. One explanation lies in underrecognition or underdiagnosis among African Americans. Ilani (2001) compared student samples and found that African Americans scored higher on somatic symptoms of depression, whereas European Americans scored higher on affective symptoms. One cultural variation is apparently the degree to which one describes well-being as either an emotional or physical state (e.g., feeling sad or helpless vs. being chronically fatigued or achy). African American students from strongly supportive families generally experienced less depression; however, those with strong communal values experienced more depression (Harris & Molock, 2000). Emotional supportive families are likely to strengthen anyone's coping skills, but the larger cultural network of the community is more likely to be missed in the college environment by those who had relied on community for confirming their ethnic identity.

In a sample of Asian American college students, the quality of the parent–child relationship was the most critical predictor of psychosocial well-being, although differences in acculturation between parents and children apparently influences that relationship quality, and thus affects well-being (Dinh, 2000).

Gender differences in coping may also account for transition effects. Women tend to be more susceptible to depression than men (McGrath, Keita, Strickland, & Russo, 1990), and may cope with it differently. In one survey sample of college women, 35% had high depressive symptoms. In that group, negative thinking mediated between self-esteem and depressive symptoms (Peden, Hall, Rayens, & Beebe, 2000). Thus, low self-esteem leads to negative thinking or hopelessness, and thus to depression. Psychologists have suggested that problem solving—or reframing[56] an issue as a resolvable or controllable problem—is a more adaptive coping mechanism than depression. Over the course of her freshman year, Peggy feels lonely because her best friend and lover is 1,000 miles away. She might feel there is nothing to be done, that no one here likes her, and she will sit in her room crying; *or* she might make a decision that her problem—lack of companionship—is resolvable, and volunteer her time to an on-campus political action organization. Brack, LaClave, and Wyatt (1992) found that problem-solving confidence is an important moderator between long-term stressors and depression. They concluded that training women to develop confidence in their problem-solving abilities might be useful in preventing stressful experiences from turning into depressive responses.

Depressed men also experience negative thinking (failure, guilt, pessimism), but for men it is associated with restrictive emotionality (Shepard, 2002). The implication is that men may need more assistance with learning to express their emotional states. Dysfunction in emotion regulation is often at the root of depression in the college years. Min'-er and Dejun (2001) examined the relationship between emotion regulation and depression among college students in Beijing. Healthy students tended to avoid and suppress negative emotions, and to ruminate and reveal the positive ones. The reverse was true for depressive students, who tended to ruminate and reveal negative emotions but avoid and repress positive ones. Thus, the reverse of the healthy pattern occurs for depressives, but gender differences influence what is normative or healthy. Men generally expressed anger and suppressed positive emotions, such as joy and interest. Implied is that men typically may follow the depressive pattern for some aspects of emotion regulation.

From Ong's (1981) perspective on biologically based differences between the genders, women lack confidence (e.g., in solving problems) and men are insecure (e.g., in expressing emotion). Whether or not the emotional-motivational tendencies are biological predispositions or cultural norms, communication with significant others who model for us variations on our expressive habits can relieve some of our weaknesses in coping with emotion that result from embracing either gender role's standard.

Coping Behaviors

When self-regulation fails, maladaptive coping behaviors may take the place of emotion regulation, problem solving, and the like. Eating disorders and substance abuse are two risky responses to the stress typical of the college years.

Body image distortions are found in both genders and across cultures. Often, the blame for unrealistic body image perceptions is placed on media representations of young people, and there may be good reason for this attribution. Over a 25-year span of *Playgirl* magazine centerfolds, the male models have become more muscular. When two groups of college men viewed advertisements featuring muscular men or more neutral ads, the experimental group reported greater discrepancy between their current and ideal body shape than did the control group (Leit, 2001).

In a comparison of body image attitudes of Asian American and Caucasian American students, all groups showed similar dissatisfaction levels with body size: Women wished to be smaller and men to be larger. However, Asian American men placed the most importance on appearances and were the most negatively affected, in terms of depression and self-esteem, by body image dissatisfaction (Kawamura, 2001).

Although both men and women may experience body image distortions, more often women respond with *eating disorders*. In a depressed mood condition, women students wished to be lighter and men wanted to be heavier (Barber, 2001); thus, the gender stereotypes for attractiveness often lead women to unwise weight loss.

Strong support exists for the combined influences of perfectionism, perceived overweight status, and low self-esteem in predicting the development of eating disorders among women (Schwitzer, Rodriguez, Thomas, & Salimi, 2001; Vohs et al., 2001). Factors indirectly associated with eating disorders by way of the mediating variable of body image preoccupation include family conflict, family cohesion, childhood abuse, and struggles for independence (Mazzeo, 2001; Schwitzer et al., 2001). A typically "female" eating disorder—purging—may result from an interaction of anger and depression (Sharp, Terling-Watt, Atkins, Gilliam, & Sanders, 2001), thus reinforcing the view that failures in emotion regulation may turn maladaptive.

Risky behaviors such as drug and alcohol use are often considered rites of passage into adulthood, but they may be dangerously adaptive as well. Contrary to the belief that such experimentations constitute mindless sensation seeking, college women report justifications for risk taking that are goal oriented (a means to some end) or need oriented (to relieve loneliness or stress). Thus, risky behaviors may indeed be employed as coping mechanisms (Shapiro, Siegel, Scovill, & Hays, 1998) that diminish immediate discomfort in exchange for greater dangers.

Alcohol use is widespread among college students. Among young adults (18–29), 94% have used alcohol, and 87% reported use in the year just past (Johnston, O'Malley, & Bachman, 1994). Identified drinking motives include enhancement of recreational enjoyment, social aid, desire for conformity; and coping device. However, coping motives—drinking to relieve stress—predict problem consequences related to alcohol use (Cooper, 1994). Life stress and high emotional distress have been linked to alcohol use among adolescents and young adults (Colder & Chassin, 1993), and some scholars posit a self-medication model of alcohol use. However, the model holds only for some individuals in some contexts (Greeley & Oei, 1999). That sort of individual might be very sensitive to stress, and that sort of context might be an inherently stressful one, such as the transition to college.

Colder (2001) proposed that negative emotionality may moderate the effects of stress on drinking to cope. He found that among young college students who were easily aroused by aversive stimuli (constituting physiological stress), alcohol use is a functional coping behavior. He concluded that "individuals who allocate more attentional resources to process aversive stimuli are at increased risk for using alcohol to cope with distress" (p. 241). Hence, individuals who react negatively to stressful events, either by way of temperament or social adaptation, are more likely to use alcohol to dampen emotional distress. Does this explanation hold for the use of other risky coping strategies?

The higher the alcohol use by college freshman, the more likely the students are to engage in *other risky health behaviors*, including cigarette smoking, other drug use, and having multiple sex partners (Kim, Larimer, Walker, & Marlatt, 1997). The results of a large nationwide survey show an increase in the use of marijuana and other illicit drugs from 1993 to 1999, and 9 out of 10 responding students who used marijuana also used other illicit drugs, smoked cigarettes, and/or engaged in binge drinking (Gledhill-Hoyt, Hang, Strote, & Wechsler, 2000). One of four students report using marijuana within the past year; those students tend to be single, White partygoers (Bell & Wechsler, 1997). A syndrome of risky behaviors seems to appeal to college students experiencing stress and/or unmet social needs.

A common assumption is that *body modifications* such as tattoos and piercings are risky nonverbal expressions associated with other maladaptive behaviors. However, even though people without modifications perceive those with tattoos and piercings as being quite different from themselves, there are surprisingly few differences in personality, childhood experiences, or risky behaviors such as substance abuse (Forbes, 2001).

Communicative Coping.   If depression, loneliness, body image distortions, and substance abuse are to some degree maladaptations to the stresses of transiting to adulthood, what might be more *adaptive responses?* Beyond therapeutic counseling, suggestions include a variety of interactive skills, such as the social/cognitive release of *humor* and physical release of *exercise.* Lack of exercise was associated with loneliness among college students (Page & Hammermeister, 1995), although a direct effect is unlikely. If Peg feels lonely, she may have isolated herself by failing to engage in activities (such as exercise) that might lead to interaction and less loneliness. In the next section, we examine in some detail specific skills related to competent communication. We note here that socially anxious students tend toward loneliness, whereas humorous students enjoy more interaction. Specifically, those who are socially anxious report more feelings of loneliness and are rated by conversational partners as being low in social skills (Segren & Kinney, 1996). Students who report that they use humor to cope with stress also find pleasure in interaction, feel confident interacting, and spend more time with others (Nezlek & Derks, 2002). What comes first, confidence or social skill? That question is unresolved, but clearly self-perception is key.

Identity, Self-Esteem, and Motivation Factors

Recall from earlier in the chapter that college students are trying various processes to construct identities. Styles include scientific, dogmatic, and ad hoc. These identity processes may manifest in corresponding *communication styles*: rhetorical sensitive, noble self, and rhetorical reflector (Hart & Burks, 1972). It is the scientific or rhetorically sensitive style user who is either searching for commitment to a self-value (moratorium) or has clearly committed to such values or beliefs at some level (achievement). What is interesting to note is that female college students appear to use the scientific style more than males do and that their process of identity development is related to parental attachment, whereas male identity development is not (Samuolis, Layburn, & Schiaffino, 2001). If this is so, the average woman making the transition to college may have a more secure support foundation from which to explore her options than the average man has.

In general, college attenders are likely to be more advanced in identity development than are those of their cohort who work full time (Archer & Waterman, 1988). Employed late adolescents often achieve identity by foreclosure (Morash, 1980), possibly in response to the pressures to make rapid life-affecting decisions connected to the work environment, yet in the absence of time to consider the ramifications of those decisions for self and identity. Danielsen, Lorem, and Kroger (cited in Kroger, 2000, pp. 111–112) found that, among 18- to 24-year-olds, employed youths spent little time exploring life options before making commitments, whereas university students actively explored vocational, ideological, relationship, and lifestyle issues. The time to explore one's own beliefs is one of the greatest advantages that college experience bestows, in that the consequences for identity, work, and relationship satisfaction are long term.

Marcia (1966) identified, by way of Erikson, the dialectical challenges of adolescence as *identity and diffusion*, and the next challenge of young adulthood as *intimacy and isolation*. The college years allow the student to construct a personal identity through cycles of moratorium and achievement, and to begin to explore some of the tasks inherent in building and maintaining intimate relationships.

Relational Contexts and Skills

Intimacy and Identity

You have to love yourself before you can love somebody else. We've all heard it. Is it true? Beginning with Erikson, identity achievement has been linked conceptually with the capacity for intimate relationships. The results of a series of studies, summarized by Adams and Archer (1994), paint a picture of the passive identity (ad hoc and dogmatic) as mistrustful, low in self-esteem, domineering and demanding, and isolated with few relational commitments. The corresponding picture of the active identity (scientific) is one who is trusting, positive, supportive of others, and maintains close relationships.

One of the intriguing distinctions between the two types is that two dialectical dimensions of social living, *agency* and *communion*, are successfully integrated in the achieved identity and not before. *Agency* concerns separation, mastery, and differentiation, whereas *communion* has to do with belongingness, relatedness, and fusion (Adams & Archer, 1994). The individual who can commit to "a self-in-relation" (Josselyn, 1987, p. 22) is the individual who has come to balance the needs for agency and communion or, in familiar terms, individuation and integration.

Again starting with Erikson, the focus on one end or the other of the agency/communion dialectic has been attributed to male (agency) and female (communion) identity development. Gilligan (1982) argued that these are masculine- and feminine-gendered themes rather than dichotomous male and female sex traits. The male "voice" focuses on agency and individuation, whereas the female "voice" emphasizes communion and integration. Presumably, these themes arise from socialization for particular gender roles. When Dyk and Adams (1990) scrutinized this assumption, they found that identity predicts intimacy for *both* sexes when the gender socialization effects of sex-role identification are removed from analysis.

Adams and Archer (1994) concluded that if men are socialized to focus on individuation, then acquiring feminine gender-role characteristics will assist them toward integration and intimacy; likewise if women are led toward integration in their socialization, then acquiring masculine sex-role characteristics will facilitate their search for individuation and identity. How does one acquire characteristics so different from the ones that our early socialization experiences reinforce? Interaction with others unlike oneself seems the only method, and the search for those with a contrasting gender-role orientation may take the seeker to a variety of possible friends and lovers.

Friends satisfy our social needs more than any other relational source during single adulthood (Carbery & Buhrmester, 1998). However, the transition to college is likely to disrupt familiar high school friendships and lead to a series of quickly made and quickly broken affiliations. That explains the common experience of loneliness among college freshmen, 40% of whom report leaving friends and family as the reason (Cutrona, 1982) for their loneliness. Despite their relative freedom and opportunity to make friends, this age group expresses more loneliness than any other. Rawlins (1992) proposed a line of reasoning for the declining rates of loneliness across the lifespan: (a) unrealistic expectations and excessive demands of friends increase loneliness, (b) such unrealistic models are tempered by maturity and experience, and (c) young adults become more selective in choosing those who can meet their expectations.

Several studies support the high expectations and demands of friendships by students who complain of loneliness and depression. Between reported best friends, the partner who felt deprived and underbenefited also reported the most loneliness (Buunk & Prins, 1998). Those friends who subscribed to a social exchange model of friendship typically felt lonely whether they felt advantaged or deprived, whereas those who valued reciprocity of support in friendship were less likely to experience loneliness. That is, those who viewed friendship as a competition for scarce rewards felt a lack of intimacy whether they won or lost. Those who viewed friendship in terms of reciprocal support were better equipped to engage in intimacy.

Also noted among depressed college students is a tendency to seek reassurance. Davila (2001) proposed attachment security as an intervening variable between

depressive symptoms and excessive reassurance seeking, but I propose that identity style may also be a factor. Recall that passive identity types are likely to be isolates—indeed, 100% of the diffused/ad hoc subjects in the Fitch and Adams study
(1983) were isolates. Those who excessively seek reassurance may be uncertain of
themselves, either passively (ad hoc) or actively (scientific/moratorium), and
thus looking for confirmation. Of course, such constant questioning is likely to
wear thin for even the most giving of friends, hence contributing to isolation and
then depression.

Consistent with the male and female "voices" at work in constructing identity
and morality, males and females enact *interactional dialectics* differently as well
(Rawlins, 1992). Women report interdependence in their satisfying relationships,
whereas men do not (Wright, 1982). Male friendships are typified by their instrumental emphasis on "doing" things, and show less affection, whereas women's
friendships are characterized by affection and intimacy, but also by high expectations for assistance (Rawlins, 1992). Because of this, men specialize in the *instrumental* end and women in the *affection* end of this friendship dialectic, although
women seem to be able to combine the two to a greater extent than men can.

In terms of *acceptance and judgment,* women again apparently merge the two
in their involvements with friends. Indeed, men do not view intensely negative affect as an opportunity for intimacy, whereas women do (Ginsberg & Gottman,
1986). Regarding *expressiveness and protectiveness,* multiple reports converge on
the findings that women are more expressive in their friendships, and men are
more protective (Rawlins, 1992). Women are more likely to share concerns, to
support, and to express appreciation, whereas men express feelings indirectly and
limit their risk by revealing less.

Cross-sex friends pose special challenges in that each is likely to specialize very
differently in terms of how they approach friendship dialectics. Males see their
same-sex friendships quite differently from their cross-sex friendships. Their
same-sex friends are usually activity partners, whereas their cross-sex liaisons offer
the advantages of more emotional involvement and disclosure. However, men are
likely to interpret these as precursors to romance. Females do not make the same
distinction between same-sex and opposite-sex relationships; they can form close
involvements in either type. However, women do clearly distinguish men who are
friends from men who are romantic partners (Rawlins, 1992). Men and women also
find different benefits from cross-sex friends.

Men confide more in their best female friend than in their best male friend
(Komarovsky, 1974), and consult them more often about important decisions
(Olstad, 1975). Men also report giving less to, being known better by, and feeling
closer to female friends (Buhrke & Fuqua, 1987). Men are more dependent on their
women friends for emotional closeness than women are on men (Komarovsky,
1974). On the other hand, women report more companionship with male friends,
and more acceptance and intimacy with female friends (Rose, 1985).

Hence, even though men apparently receive more benefits than women from
cross-sex friendships, and those emotional benefits are unlikely to be met in their
same-sex friendship, men often undermine their friendships with women. They

perceive friendliness from women as seduction (Abbey, 1982), and many acknowledge sexual motivations for forming cross-sex friendships (Rose, 1985). However, as Rawlins (1992) pointed out, attracting a romantic partner is one of the tasks of young adulthood and males are expected to take the lead in initiating such partnerships, so we cannot blame men for considering romantic options. However, women seem better able to maintain platonic intent and are more deliberate about entering a romantic relationship (Rubin, Peplau, & Hill, 1980).

Certainly there are individual differences that influence cross-sex relational models. Bell (1981) found that nonconventional men and women had more positive attitudes about their cross-sex friends than did conventional ones. Some women flirt in intimate friendships, some do not; some men include physical contact as a component of cross-sex friendships, some do not (Monsour, 1992). As Monsour (1997) concluded in his summary of the topic, "sex role orientation has a pronounced effect on cross-sex interactions" (p. 399). That is, the degree to which one subscribes to normative masculine or feminine roles probably influences how one will behave in cross-sex friendships.

Conflict between adult friends, considered inevitable, nonetheless has not been researched extensively. In part, this gap in the literature may "reflect an ideology that romance and family are supposedly more important than are friends in adulthood" (Canary et al., 1995, p. 447). Dykstra (1990) found that conflict occurs as frequently in friendships as in other sorts of relationships, but that levels of enjoyment are higher than levels of conflict for friendships in contrast to other relational types.

As voluntary arrangements, in comparison to more obligatory kinships and committed romantic partnerships, friendships are relatively fragile. The more serious the conflict—when one friend did or said something that led to the other's dissatisfaction with the relationship—the more likely the response will be either to leave or neglect the relationship (Healey & Bell, 1990). Friends tend to avoid confrontation (Baxter, 1979), which may explain further why college students change allegiances so often. Not only are their expectations unrealistic, but when the expectations are unmet it is unlikely that students will directly discuss it with the friend who "failed" them.

One special type of friendship is a bit harder to leave behind, because it involves shared living arrangements. Most college students and many young adults will have *roommates*, and some of those roommates will be friends. These relationships are like friendships in that they are not obligatory kinships, but also something like siblings in terms of shared living arrangements (Canary et al., 1995). I consistently find that if I pose a problem to my students involving roommate conflict, they can easily relate to it. Typically, they have many complaints, and once those are aired, the students want to know what to do to resolve the issue. Clearly, they are motivated to maintain the arrangement as well as the relationship. Sillars (1980) examined both the conflict behaviors of roommates and their causal attributions. He found that if one person blamed the conflict on the roommate, said roommate was likely to reciprocate with negative, distributive messages and thus escalate the conflict.

Peggy's roommate, Diane, when entering their room, states, "What a dump!"[57] Peggy, perhaps relying on the relational model established with her older sister

Nan, perceives this is a complaint and reciprocates with a countercomplaint: "I haven't noticed you cleaning your stuff!" Now Diane is on the defensive, even if she originally was making an observation designed to call for a joint effort, and replies, "Well, it won't do much good if your underwear is still hanging from the lampshades!" And so on. On the other hand, it could go differently, and Sillars (1980) claimed the difference may again lie in the causal attribution.

If the roommate instead attributes the cause of the conflict to self, then cooperative, integrative behavior is more likely to ensue. Let's say this time that Peggy's relational model for sharing space is based on having her own room and dealing only with her mother about the use of that space. She came to view as reasonable her mother's request to keep it neat when she was expecting visitors who would share the room. Now, when Diane says, "This place is a dump!" Peggy laughs and agrees that indeed she had been ignoring it. Diane admits that she had too, and offers an evening time to clean her portion. Peggy has the time free as well, and they plan to get the cleaning done together. Obviously, such confrontations typically may not run that smoothly, but acceptance of responsibility and, I would add, a sense of humor go a long way to resolve the more concrete issues. One study by Weinstock and Bond (2000) examined conflict in close female friendships during the college years and found three models of conflict: avoidance, acceptance and appreciation, and engagement and development. Furthermore, there was an association between intellectual maturity ("epistemological understanding," or what we might call *reflective judgment*) and the habitual conflict model. The more complex the intellectual development was, the more adaptive the conflictual pattern was. Those who viewed knowledge as absolute tended to use *avoidance.* Those who viewed knowledge as something more subjective that they could figure out for themselves preferred the *acceptance and appreciation* pattern, in which they agreed to disagree. Finally, women who could apply procedures to analyze and critique knowledge and opinions more often chose *engagement and relational development,* which involved "discussing, exploring, backing up, evaluating, and entering into each other's perspectives" (Weinstock & Bond, 2000, p. 693). The more adaptive pattern, relying on complex cognition, appears to involve reasoned argument, perspective taking, and reflective judgment.

A final note on conflict among friends is that conflict entails oppositions of the sort set up in relational dialectics (Canary et al., 1995; Rawlins, 1994), such as expressive/protective (confront/avoid). To maintain balance between poles of a dialectic takes relational work; to accept that relational partners will be at odds dialectically takes maturity. It may be that we increasingly choose our friends for their characteristic tendency toward a dialectical pole complementary to ours, *and/or* for their capacity to tolerate the swings between oppositions.

Lovers

In Erikson's scheme, the next developmental challenge after identity construction is the formation of intimate relationship. In his view, in order to be truly intimate, one must have constructed an identity. In the college years, we are often trying to work on both at once. As any college professor can attest, that can make for student anxieties that have little to do with academic concerns. In one British survey of college lecturers, 97% had advised distressed students in the past year about problems including self-confidence issues, depression, health, and relationship problems (Easton & Van Laar, 1995).

Given the disruption of social networks in the transition to college, it would seem that identity construction would be stimulated (in the absence of parental influence and in the presence of challenging beliefs), and that relationship formation would be necessary and immediate (in the absence of prior alliances). In the position of searching for intimacy and working out identity, students are likely to experiment with a number of possible intimate relationships. In a series of three studies, Hendrick and Hendrick (1994) found that undergraduates typically identify their romantic love relationships in terms of "Storge" (Lee, 1973) or friendship love. That is, their relational ideal is a partner who can fill needs for friendship as well as passion. Does this mean they are forming intimate love relationships? Not necessarily. Are their romantic relationships contributing to their identity construction? Probably.

Those college students further along in their sexual development are more dependent on lovers; those less sexually mature depend on family and friends (Shimizu, 1979). One aspect of dependence has to do with who you choose to reflect who you are. High self-esteem is related to the *empathy, congruence,* and *unconditional acceptance* of romantic partners (Cramer, 1990); thus, whom you choose to love is key to what of the embryonic identity gets reinforced. The question, then, is how do we make these choices? Undoubtedly, many variables come into play, including physical attraction, availability and proximity, models of love based on family and prior relationships, affiliation and control needs, and more. No matter what the initial attraction factors, what keeps couples together apparently has much to do with their current social networks.

The difference between couples who stay together and those who break up begins with *dyadic* factors such as closeness and degree of conflict (Brines & Joyner, 1999). However, factors *external* to the couple also contribute to longevity. Romantically involved students will typically be more optimistic about their relationship's stability than will parents and roommates (MacDonald & Ross, 1999). But the opinions of others will affect the relationship: "The better friends know an individual's partner and the more they approve of the relationship, the lower the likelihood that the pair will break up" (Felmlee, 2001, p. 1276), but of interest is that the *perception* of approval from friends is a better predictor of stability than is *actual* approval. Although most lovers reported that friends rather than family influenced their relationship, some gave *anticipated* family disapproval as the reason for a breakup. Thus, a lover's perception of social network norms—the network model—influences the decision to continue or end a relationship. If the relationship can be incorporated into that model, then what? Many of the factors that apparently affect romantic relationships can be found under the rubrics of intimacy and control.

Intimacy in general is "a process by which a couple—in the expression of thought, emotion, and behavior—attempts to move toward more complete communication on all levels" (Hatfield, 1983, p. 48). That process can include experiences that are emotional, social, sexual, intellectual, and recreational (Schaefer & Olson, 1981), and communication variables such as *self-disclosure, empathy, perspective taking,* and *touch.* However, men and women tend to perceive intimate experiences differently. Many research findings converge on the distinction that "women link sex with emotional involvement whereas men associate sex with casual, physical involvement" (Canary & Emmers-Sommer, 1997, p. 67). Cultural stereotypes hold that men focus on sex and women focus on feelings. Regardless of the reasons for the difference—and there are many suggestions, including women's greater vulnerability and men's reproductive imperative—men and women do experience intimacy differently.[58] But how do they get to intimacy?

The literature on interpersonal *attraction* has stressed similarity as an important factor in decisions to approach. But what sort of similarity? Duck (1991) argued that personal qualities (e.g., physical appearance) don't make for similarity; similarities are discovered in the joint actions between people. That is, we don't know if we are similar until we start interacting, and then the similarities that count are those that allow us to express ourselves and know the other.

Cognitive complexity is one such point of similarity. Among dating partners, those with similar levels of cognitive complexity expressed greater intellectual attraction to one another. High-complexity perceivers are more attracted to high-complexity targets; however, so are low-complexity perceivers (Burleson, Kunkel, & Szolwinski, 1997). If you recall the zone of proximal development, the same is true for children; they are attracted to children slightly more sophisticated than themselves. Attraction to a more cognitively complex person may be socially adaptive in that it provides an opportunity to expand one's construct system. Of course, the fact that the highly complex party may not reciprocate could thwart this kind of growth. Despite the fact that cognitive complexity is related to perspective taking and persuasive skill, and thus is an important factor in sociality, it is not the only important variable in intimate relationships. Self-disclosure and nonverbal expressivity are also linked to intimacy.

Self-disclosure and emotional expressivity, although they may not occur routinely in daily interaction, are important to both men and women in close relationships, but college women seem to enjoy more intimate relationships than college men do (Reis, 1998). We typically like people who disclose to us, we disclose to those whom we like, and we like people to whom we disclose (see Dindia, 1994). Thus, to a point, disclosure is an effective social skill. But too much too soon can boomerang and lead to dislike.[59] Disclosure leads to reduced uncertainty about a new partner and contributes to the intimacy process; it is the behavior that allows us to negotiate the *expressive/protective* dialectic (Dindia, 1994). Dindia and Allen (1992) warned against drawing hasty conclusions about sex differences in disclosure. Sex effects are small and moderated by type of relationship. Having said that, there is some evidence that women disclose more in intimate relationships, and they may be more willing than men to disclose particular emotions—depression, anxiety, anger, and fear—to friends and lovers (Snell, Miller, & Belk, 1988).

In the context of intimate relationships, individuals make decisions about how much and what sort of disclosure is appropriate (Baxter, 1990). Clearly, disclosure for intimacy is not an all-or-nothing proposition, and requires careful deliberation about the effect of expression on the partner, on the relationship, and on self.

Nonverbal expressivity can include posture, facial expression, gesture, and the like; but in the process of intimacy, touch and in particular sex gain importance. A number of studies have confirmed an association between relational stage and touch both in public (Guerrero & Andersen, 1991) and in private (Emmers & Dindia, 1995). As intimacy increases, touch becomes more sexual, from hand holding through kissing and embracing, to petting and intercourse (Johnson & Edwards, 1991). Of course, sex also involves decisions about control.

Control is one aspect of the inevitable mutual influence we have on each other in personal relationships. Part and parcel of intimacy is interdependence. However, the dependence of each partner on the other is rarely perfectly balanced; thus, the dialectic of *autonomy/dependence* is featured in this aspect of intimacy. The cultural stereotype is that men hold the lion's share of power in romantic relationships, but this is too simplistic a statement to hold true. In relationships, power is potential influence negotiated between two people. Hence, who exerts control is more likely to be a function of expertise or interest than of sex. In one study of nonverbal cues, men demonstrated dominance when the topic was a masculine one, and women dominated when the topic was feminine (Dovido, Ellyson, Keating, Heltmand, & Brown, 1988). In a college sample, Trentham and Larwood (2001) manipulated power status in conflict situations and found that type of power status, but not gender, influenced deference to the relationship partner's wishes.

Dependence power—"the control that a partner who is less dependent on the relationship possesses in the eyes of the dependent party" (Lawler & Bacharach, cited in Samp & Solomon, 2001, p. 139), is a special sort of power that derives from the perceiver's commitment, perceptions of the partner's commitment, and judgments of the partner's alternatives to the relationship. Thus, to the committed partner, the relatively uncommitted partner with viable alternatives has more dependence power. This sort of power has a "chilling effect" on the committed party's willingness to discuss perceived problems. Interestingly, when the committed party considered how to respond to his or her partner's projected problematic behavior, the more alternative dating possibilities the partner had, the greater the chilling effect was. But when the committed party considered his or her own problematic behavior in retrospect, the fewer dating alternatives the partner had, the greater the chilling effect was (Samp & Solomon, 2001). When partners, on the other hand, were perceived as highly committed, there was an "enabling effect" on the decision to communicate about the problem. Hence, perceptions of the *autonomy/dependence* dialectic affect communication decisions in dating relationships in two ways: One's own dependence on the relationship "chills" the discussion of problems, particularly if the offending party appears autonomous; and the partner's perceived dependence stimulates the discussion of problematic behavior. Perceptions of extreme dependence might have negative effects on interaction in either case. What effect might equal levels of dependence have?

As *interdependence* increases with intimacy, partners can manage to get in each other's way, to "interfere" or interrupt each other's action sequences (Solomon & Knobloch, 2001). For example, if Peggy has a standing date with friends and Rob calls her requesting help with a paper, she is likely to allow him to "interfere" with her usual social routine. The process of reducing uncertainty, which appears to be a gradual one as intimacy increases (Solomon & Knobloch, 2001), apparently goes through a rocky period early in the relationship, when intimacy levels are relatively low and partners' influence and interference are high. The resolution of these disruptive patterns probably constitutes a turning point in the relationship. If the partners fail to weather this period, the relationship fails; if they succeed, the interference then decreases and intimacy increases. But what happens in extreme cases of interference?

The downside of dating, when intimacy and control merge in distorted fashion to negatively affect boundary maintenance, manifests as *victimization* or *violence*. Interference with another's activity can become intrusion, and when that intrusion becomes obsessive it may take the forms of stalking, abuse, or sexual coercion.

Obsessive relational intrusion is similar to stalking but occurs in the pursuit of a relationship (Spitzberg, Marshall, & Cupach, 2001). Unfortunately, this sort of unwanted attention is related to sexual coercion; the people who experience one often experience the other as well, and often from the same person. Perpetrators engaging in inappropriate "violation of another person's boundaries of self, space, time, place and property" (Spitzberg et al., p. 22) probably *lack interpersonal competence*. Stalkers generally have a history of failed attachments and tend to be narcissistic and egocentric, whereas sexually coercive men are likely to be hypercompetent in terms of effective manipulation skills and ability to read vulnerability cues (Spitzberg et al., 2001). In the first case, the lack of skills would lead to physical coercion; in the second, the specialization of skills leads to more subtle, psychological coercion. Although there are no easy answers for the victim, being able to recognize coercion early in a relationship and having the skills to resist intrusion can improve personal boundary maintenance.

Although sex is not always the issue in when the power balance goes awry, it becomes a negotiation challenge for dating couples who are still getting to know each other's communication patterns and needs. Given the nature of the typical heterosexual sex act, the female partner must be vulnerable to some extent and the male partner must be intrusive to some extent. Not surprisingly, males are typically initiators and females must choose to resist or comply; although the reverse pattern may occur, it is not the norm.

For example, Ron expresses, directly or indirectly, the desire to engage in sex with Peg. To respond, Peg must either acquiesce or resist his request. Resistance risks damage to the relationship and/or to Ron's "face" needs (the image he wishes to present). Thus, Peg's goals may be multiple and conflicting, particularly if one of them is to refrain from sexual behavior. According to Afifi and Lee (2000), Peg will probably choose a communication strategy to respond to a *direct advance* ("Let's make love") that attempts to preserve Ron's identity yet clarify her position, such as "We can do other things, but not that" (pp. 298–299). However, if the advance is *in-*

direct (wandering hands), college women will resist with less concern for the man's identity needs ("Hey, back off, perv"), presumably because the "sneakier" approach is less respectful of the woman's face needs. If the first resistance message is ignored or misinterpreted and another sexual advance ensues, the next resistance message is much more likely to be direct and face threatening. However, here's where things get dicey.

Once a requester gets a chance to make a second advance, perhaps after a face-saving and/or indirect resistance response, he (or she) may experience "consistency needs" to pursue the behavioral course to which he or she is now committed. Afifi and Lee thought it likely that Johnson's (1973) notion of behavioral commitment (consequences of pursuing a line of action that constrain the actor to continue) has important implications for sexual pursuit. I would tend to agree with a stimulus-response explanation of this sort only insofar as sexual behavior remains reactive and not highly conscious. However, I would add that once symbolic communication enters the sequence, it is possible to end the behavioral commitment, but it may take direct communication to do so. And, in a second resistance response, women's messages do become more urgent ("Stop it"). Although direct strategies are successful in ending sexual aggression (Motley & Reeder, 1995), women often start with less direct, face-saving responses and fall back on direct resistance after a failure. The wise woman might anticipate several advances in order to have a repertoire of responses suitable to her needs.

Trajectories of Romantic Relationships: Handling Dialectics

Once the couple has begun the relationship and negotiated some of the early discomforts of conflicting needs, desires, and behaviors, how does the relationship develop? This question has been answered in linear terms by describing the material and psychological resources partners that give and receive over time. However, more recent explanations use dialectical tensions to frame relationship changes (Werner & Baxter, 1994). Much of this research has been conducted with college students, although a few have used older populations.

In heterosexual college couples, the *turning points* that the partners most frequently recall include quality time, passion, get-to-know time, and exclusivity (Baxter & Pittman, 2001). Reminiscing as a couple about quality time usually is about special occasions when couples managed to suspend ordinary activities to be together. Telling stories to friends and kin is another way to retain these turning points in social memory and thus contribute to the relational model for that pairing. What makes them memorable? Possibly the dialectical contradictions negotiated at those points.

Baxter and Erbert (1999) examined the perceptions of both parties in 50 romantic couples attending college. Of greatest importance across turning points were the dialectical contradictions of *autonomy/connection* and *openness/closedness*. Again, quality time was the most frequently identified turning point, with external competition (rivals, competing demands) close behind. Another frequently chosen turning point featured different dialectics. Network interaction (social network effects on the relationship) involved external contradictions of *inclusion/seclusion* and *revelation/concealment*. As Baxter and Erbert suggested, network-related turning points may be peculiar to some relationships more than others; I suspect that college students place greater importance on friends' judgments of their romances than might older lovers. Several turning points had to do with shifts away from connectedness, including physical separation, negative psychic change, and disengagement. How do couples handle the communicative demands of distancing?

College students are often involved in long-distance relationships with partners from "back home," and many of them ultimately end those romances. Wilmot, Carbaugh, and Baxter (1985) asked students to report the *termination* strategies they and their partners used. Wilmot et al. found a preference for verbal indirectness (avoid asking for or giving information) and reported regrets from those who were direct (confrontation and reasons for ending). Verbal indirectness, or hinting, is in the interest of face saving for both parties, and allows the couple to move gradually to termination. Another advantage is that it allows the decision to be mutual rather than one-sided. According to Wilmot et al., mutual decisions produced fewer regrets and more positive emotional reactions. Interestingly, the majority of their respondents considered themselves "friends" after the relationship ended. How realistic that assessment is for a former relationship where the partners are separated by distance is another question.

Can former lovers *transform* their romance to friendship? Schneider and Kenny (2000) collected from each undergraduate in their sample reports of two types of cross-gender friendships: one a former romantic partner and one who was entirely platonic. Two striking findings are that perceptions of the platonic friend included more positive qualities than the former lover, and more romantic desires are associated with the latter. Specifically, students more clearly applied friendship rules to the platonic friend: loyalty, sharing, emotional support, trust, and so forth. They also reported greater benefits from the platonic friendship. So why hang onto the former lover? These friends reported greater romantic desire for the former lover and so the passion may persist. However, the friendship feelings they may have felt during the romantic liaison may also persist, thus predicting the transformation from lover to friend.

Relational Skills: Rhetorical Presentation in Intimate Relationships

Much of the literature reviewed in this chapter converges on the circular or perhaps spiral nature of the link between relational dialogue and communicative skill. Although most assume that relational satisfaction and success are linked to communication skills, few have addressed the origins of those skills. I profess that the interaction experiences found in a variety of relationships foster the development of such communication skills.

Nezlak (2001) tested the latter explanation over a 2-year period in college students. He found that "changes in the quality of day-to-day interaction led to changes in perceived social skills" (p. 386), but the reverse did not hold true. Neither did sheer quantity of interaction affect skill. Nezlak explained the results by way of the affective rewards resulting from quality interaction. These rewards affect psychological functioning in a positive fashion; social acceptance leads to improved self-esteem. More success leads to the perception of higher skill, which leads to rewarding interaction, and so on.

Thus, social life spirals out from early childhood: interaction to knowledge to skill to interaction to knowledge to skill ... across bumps and transitions and toward increasing competence, sophistication, and elegance. Well, that's the best-case scenario. But "virtually any behavior, when used in the extreme, is likely to be incompetent" (Cupach & Spitzberg, 1994, p. 38). Indeed, most of these skills have a curvilinear relationship to competence in that, as with our dialectical social life in general, the challenge is to find the optimal balance between too little and too much. Here, we summarize some of the skills that continue to challenge the balancing act.

Perspective Taking, Empathy, Persuasion, and Influence.   We know that perspective taking increases over time and opportunities to interact; we know that empathy is a feeling response related to perspective taking. We also know that perspective taking in particular is related to persuasion. However, being able to take another's perspective is no guarantee of good outcomes. There is such a thing as being too other-oriented in that one can lose sight of one's own view, thus crippling decision making, or use other-knowledge for exploitation, as in the case of relational intrusion or coercion (Cupach & Spitzberg, 1994).

Self-Monitoring: Sensitivity and Self-Presentation.   The ability to adapt one's presentation for the perceived demands of the situation apparently peaks in adolescence, as a response to the imaginary audience. But the other dimension of self-monitoring—sensitivity to others' expressive behavior—develops gradually but may not increase much after high school (Allen, 1986). What does this mean in terms of the relationship between skill and interaction experience? First, the self-monitoring scale is a self-report, so all we have are the perceptions of young people about their knowledge base for competence. As Allen pointed out, adolescents may see themselves as being more sensitive than they were only a few years before, thus inflating their report by contrast. Adults probably use a different and more dialectical comparison base: their *own* recent responsiveness as well as their relational *partners'*. Note that self-monitoring can reach "dark" coercion levels as well—in the capacity to change one's presentation to match what will move a partner to comply, and in the absence of concern for the partner's needs.

Self-Disclosure and Self-Protection.   As is true of self-monitoring and perspective taking, self-disclosure is a dialectical process (expressive/protective) that occurs within the individual and between relational partners (Dindia, 1994). Once speech is internalized, the speaker can begin to consider whether or not to reveal information and feelings by considering the consequences to personal boundaries. We find that revealing self-information gradually and appropriately can increase intimacy, but may also threaten relational and personal goals if used unwisely.

Seeking and Giving Social Support.   Given the stress inherent in the move to college and the accompanying changes that confront college students, they have high needs for social support but quickly develop expectations for where they will find it. Not surprisingly, friends are more likely to behave in supportive ways, although the type of behavior expected of men and women varies (Derlega, Barbee, & Winstead, 1994). Men who anticipate the discussion of a relationship problem with their male friends expect a dismiss response (minimize the problem). Women who face the same sort of discussion with a female friend expect solve (problem focused) and support (emotion focused) responses. From their male friends, women generally expect dismiss responses to any sort of problem, and escape (avoid and distract) responses to a relationship problem (Derlega et al., 1994). Thus, by the college years, we have developed expectations for interaction that distinguish between male and female communication patterns. Whether or not the expectations are fair appraisals, based on physiological sex or sociocultural gender, they influence our choices of partner and communication strategies. The gender/sex dialectic may be the most challenging we face as we confront the need to establish and maintain intimate relationships.

Masculine and Feminine.   To effectively handle dialectical challenges and move toward dialogic understanding, we must face the dualisms we've constructed and deconstruct them. Among these, especially as we attempt to build intimate relationships, we have to recognize the distinctions we perceive between men and women and come to view them less dichotomously. Far from being a matter confronted only in heterosexual relationships, this primary distinction among kinds of relational partners may be so ingrained in our social knowledge as to affect every aspect of social life and every relationship, regardless of the parties' gender or sexual orientation. Indeed, to move beyond simplistic, dualistic explanations, we may have to drop the idea of gender distinctions entirely.

To avoid the male/female dualism, Sonia Johnson (1991) renamed role styles as "woofer" and "tweeter" rather than masculine and feminine. Some of the woofer/tweeter distinctions that pertain to communication include: likes to do versus likes to talk; in an argument, withdraws versus rants; in initiation, asks directly versus behaves indirectly; when troubled, keeps to self versus seeks best friend's help (Tatnall & Balcerzak, cited in Johnson, 1991). If this all sounds familiar—good. We examine further the choices we make and the transformations we experience as we move into committed relationships and cross-gender career partnerships in young adulthood, addressed in the next chapter.

EFFECTS OF FORMAL EDUCATION ON COMMUNICATION

By way of summary, we end with a look at the demands of the "real world"[60] on college graduates, and the communication competencies we might expect of them. Employers expect college graduates to be able to find and analyze information, and to express themselves well in both the public arena and private conversation. The Public Forum Institute (2002) reported that "soft" skills are much more important in the workplace than are "hard" skills. In response to the question "Which job skills do you most look for in an applicant," employers placed *interpersonal relations* at the top rank (27%), followed by critical thinking (24%) and problem solving (22%), with computer literacy lagging far behind (3%). What employers do not expect is that graduates will know the specifics of the job, unless the college training was highly specialized, such as nursing or engineering. Although "hard" technical skills may be required for job performance, "hard skills can be taught if a person has the desired soft skills. In other words, it was important that applicants could demonstrate the ability to learn on the job" (Public Forum Institute, 2002, p. 6). Liberal arts graduates are valued for their superior abilities to think critically, listen carefully, analyze problems, find information, and communicate what they have found.

Universities are under fire for failing to produce "competent" graduates, and state systems have begun to demand assessment of such competencies. Whether or not assessment guarantees that every graduate will fulfill employer expectations, mandated assessment procedures have become a fact of academic life. Although we all hope that college students will develop—form a more coherent identity, increasingly think in more abstract and relativistic terms, communicate more effectively, and relate more dialogically—we also know that students reach thresholds at different rates.[61] Some juniors easily understand advanced theory and others consider the class an unfair barrier to graduation. Is it fair to expect every student to reach the same skill and knowledge levels? Probably not, but it is fast becoming a fact. And, although many instruments have been developed,[62] no single assessment procedure has become the standard.

Content coverage in communication programs includes broad categories such as communication codes (listening, language, nonverbal messages), oral message evaluation (distinguishing fact from opinion, identifying main ideas), communication skills (expressing clearly, defending a position, organizing messages, asking and answering questions, summarizing messages), and human relations (describing another's point of view, expressing feelings, performing social rituals; Rubin, 1982). Most communication departments expect these and often more. Recently designed instruments include not only scales for oral speaking skills, but also those for conversational skills, interaction involvement, self-disclosure, verbal aggressiveness, critical listening, speech anxiety, and affective and nonverbal communication, to mention a few.[63]

SUMMARY

For me, the question remains: *Will the competent performance of all these communication skills lead to true dialogue and dialogic awareness?* We don't know the answer. We might guess that this sort of development is more likely for the person who has mastered the basic knowledge and skills necessary for growthful relationships. However, what of the slick debater with excellent conversational skills who races to obtain an MBA? Well, it's possible we'll find a die-hard Machiavellian CEO a decade hence, but perhaps as likely that we'll find a human resources director for a nonprofit agency. Given sufficient skill and a secure identity, the grab for money may lose its glamour and the need for creative self-fulfillment will take its place. In that intervening decade, a lot can happen to polish those skills. Through cycles of internalizing external performance, as adapted to the relational needs of the moment, the young adult can hone raw skill into *rhetorical elegance.*

NOTES

52. See assumption #7.e in chapter 1. We employ this one throughout this and the following chapters concerning adulthood. The possibility for "playing the tensions" between dialectics in dialogic awareness is something that may be possible in the college years, but more likely to fully develop later in life.
53. Many of these views appear in Commons, Richards, and Armon (1984).
54. See Assumption #6 in chapter 1.
55. Note the similarity between Berzonsky's identity styles and the communication styles identified by Hart and Burks (1972): rhetorical reflector (ad hoc), noble self (dogmatic), and scientific (rhetorically sensitive).
56. See chapter 9 for an explanation of reframing as a highly adaptive strategy for coping with dialectical tensions in relationships.
57. Apologies to Bette Davis.
58. For a more complete discussion, see chapter 4 in Canary and Emmers-Sommer (1997).
59. See Dindia (1994) for a more complete summary of the literature.
60. Although, frankly, I find educational institutions about as "real" as anything else.
61. See Yingling (1994c) for an overview of the developments we might expect in college, and the difficulties of assessing them.
62. Rubin (1982) to Backlund (1989) developed earlier instruments, but communication departments are now developing unique procedures such as capstone courses, senior projects, and portfolios to meet the demand.
63. For a more complete overview of each instrument, see Morreale and Backlund (1966).

Men are babies. One minute he wants to be with me forever, and the next minute he's not sure he's had enough "freedom." He still wants to hang out with his friends a few nights a week, when I'd rather be with him, cook a nice meal, watch a movie on TV. I'm ready to marry now and settle into a family life. I know he's not and I don't know whether to confront him or move on.

After much internal deliberation and some discussion with friends, Peg did confront Rob, who admitted that he was not ready. Rob wanted to continue the relationship they had built in college, but Peg wanted more than sex and companionship; she wanted deep intimacy and the trust found in commitment to a shared future. Peg began to date, with long-term partnership in mind. Rob, bewildered and rejected, thought long and hard about what he wanted, spoke to a few close friends, and steered clear of marriage-minded women for awhile.

Young Adulthood:
Romancing Other and Self

The minute I heard my first love story
I started looking for you, not knowing
how blind that was.
Lovers don't finally meet somewhere.
They're in each other all along.

(Rumi, quoted in Barks, 1995, p. 106)

TOWARD DIALOGUE: DIFFERENTIATION FROM AND FUSION WITH

Identity Challenges of Early Adulthood

Thus far in our discussions, we have followed development from abilities to use contrast to dichotomous constructs to dialectical tensions. In preparing to examine adult development, we must return to the notion of dialogue. Rumi reminded us that our natural tendency is to find other in self and to find self in other, and he concluded that our connection to others is always there but we must come to realize it. What we must do first is to know the self; to fully realize identity. Next, we must recognize other as both same as and different from self. Only then may we begin to think and speak in true dialogue; to appreciate our dialogic nature—the pulsing push-pull energy within and between us.[64]

The challenge of adolescence lies in deconstructing and recreating self; the challenge of young adulthood is found in temporarily stabilizing the new identity and connecting intimately in relationship. Optimally, the young adult has just completed another individuation process. The first involved internalizing an image of the most significant other (caregiver) in infancy; the second involved relinquishing the power of this internalized other (Josselson, 1980) to allow the autonomous identity to rule. Thus, having a more or less stable sense of self rests, to some extent, on internalizing an earlier stable attachment (Kroger, 2000). If the foundation is se-

237

cure enough, the individual can replace the caregiver image with the newly consti-tuted image of self.

However, not all young adults have attained a fully dimensional sense of iden-tity. Those in their 30s are less diffused and more achieved in identity than are col-lege students, but only in ideological domains (values, beliefs, ethics); the same adults are more foreclosed than are college students in interpersonal domains. (Whitbourne & Van Mannen, 1996). Over half of the subjects in one study (Marcia, 1976) who had been rated as "achieved" identity in late adolescence were rated "foreclosed" by their mid-20s. A retreat to a more constricted view of life may re-flect limited opportunities for exploration (Kroger, 2000), and/or less willingness to remain open after career and relational choices have been made. Many older ad-olescents shift back to moratorium from achievement, suggesting that optimal identity development continues through repeated cycles of commitment and reas-sessment throughout the lifespan (Stephen, Fraser, & Marcia, 1992).

Young adults, faced with an array of choices about vocation and relationships, make decisions based on the current set of identity commitments and then are constrained by those decisions to a greater or lesser degree, varying the expecta-tions accompanying the choice. For example, if Peg and Ned marry and immedi-ately have a child, both may feel committed to role expectations internalized from the parental models that they had in their childhoods. Although they had plenty of opportunity to consider their ideological commitments in the college years, they may not have had similar chances to test interpersonal commitments, partic-ularly to unfamiliar roles of spouse, parent, or colleague. Thus, the domains of identity—ideological and interpersonal—develop at different rates dependent on available boundary experiences.

For Erikson, it is the interpersonal that is the most critical identity domain of early adulthood. Erikson defined intimacy in terms of mutual trust, sharing, and activity regulation between loving heterosexual partners. Those who developed a strong identity during college typically have more enduring marriages in mid-life (Kahn, Zimmerman, Csikszentmihalyi, & Getzels, 1985). However, men and women apparently follow different paths in terms of the relationship between iden-tity and intimacy. Men who failed to develop a strong identity in late adolescence tended to remain single into mid-life; women lacking strong identity did marry but their marriages tended to be unstable in later years (Kahn et al., 1985). The dialectic of intimacy/isolation affects later life relationships as well as identity.

Erikson's emphasis on normative sexual relationships as the key to intimacy has been questioned (Orlofsky, Marcia, & Lesser, 1973). Here we use the broader sense of intimacy, and assume that intimacy is a matter of degree. Young adults, particularly those with more mature identity status, develop increasingly intimate relationships of all kinds (Kroger, 2000) that continue to inform relational and individual develop-ment. Josselyn (1994) noted, "Identity emerges not from increasing separation and distinction from others but from the continually redefined capacity to make use of and to respond to others.... The crucial events that people recount in their odysseys of identity are usually fundamentally relational.... Identity is an integration of ways of being with others with ways of being with oneself" (p. 101).

Dialectics in Early Adulthood

Although we have looked at dialectical tensions in earlier chapters, we now turn to a more complete treatment of them as they affect adult relationships. One reason for putting it here is that much of the research has been with adult populations; the more important reason is that the more completely individuated adult is more likely to recognize and cope with dialectics than is the less fully realized younger identity.

Centrifugal/Centripetal Tensions

Relationship development occurs at the boundary between two malleable core identities. Of course, it isn't as simple as that; identity processes continue to be transformed at the boundary, and relationship processes also are informed by the core. Tensions created between boundary and core take many forms but, in essence, their oppositional nature is push/pull, movement either inward to self or outward to other.

Bakhtin viewed existence in terms of enormous energy—a force field created between centrifugal and centripetal forces. *Centrifugal forces* strive to keep things separate and different, whereas *centripetal forces* strive to keep things together and unified (Clark & Holquist, 1984). The former urge movement and *change*; the latter compel *stability* and stillness. Together, they make for dialogue in Bakhtin's very broad sense: communication between simultaneous differences. Although Bakhtin applied these concepts to every aspect of life, we examine this energy movement in human communication.

Montgomery and Baxter (1998) interpreted the effect of these two forces in terms of a "knot of oppositions" (p. 157) rather than a simple binary pair.[65] That is, they expected multiplicity of perspective, within and between partners. They expected partners to express both "prevailing centripetal themes and the implicated centrifugal themes" (p. 160). In their view, relationships are characterized by "dialogic complexity" rather than linear progress from unknown to known, from acquaintance to intimacy. Even in the most intimate relationships, then, centrifugal forces may serve the functional separateness of change (as a force pulling toward the core and reconstructing the boundary) rather than imply regression from intimacy (as a force pushing two cores apart).

Thus, these forces inherent to life will manifest in relationships; what varies is how each couple copes with them, and what matters to us is how couples cope communicatively. Montgomery and Baxter (1998) maintained, "If communication is the bridge between partners, then their relationship is at the gap" (p. 162). What is the nature of that gap? Again, Bakhtin assists: "I am conscious of myself and become myself only while revealing myself for another, through another, and with the help of another ... every internal experience ends up on the boundary.... To be means to communicate ... to be means to be for the other; and through him, for oneself. Man has no internal sovereign territory; he is all and always on the boundary" (as cited in Shotter, 1993b, pp. 109–110). Shotter added that our mental life is never entirely our own, because "dialogic inner speech is *joint action*, and joint action always creates that third entity—the context" (p. 110). What we do together is to shape a social reality; we make sense of communication not by recognizing a word's identity, but by understanding its novelty (Volosinov, 1973). We create in relationships a new kind of knowledge, which Shotter identified as a "moral kind" of knowing because it relies on the judgments of others for its ethical truth. Now you may think that we can access this kind of knowledge mentally, but it is from "within a process of 'inner speech,' from within an inner conversation, that such knowledge emerges" (Shotter, 1993b, p. 7); that is, from the words and phrases already given life at the boundary with another.

Hence, we stand at the gap between us in relationship, and then build the bridge with symbolic communication. Without a sense of self as separate, there is no gap. The developmental processes we covered in earlier chapters lead to the individuated self who stands in full recognition at the precipice between self and other. Without a sense of the other as well as self, there is no span to be bridged, and without our mutual orienting to words, we have no means for constituting self/other. Once identities are constituted, the gap between the two yawns; and once a symbolic bridge is built, the motivation increases to understand deeply and to be as deeply understood.

The Identity Dialectic: Intimacy and Isolation

Although human relatedness is our nature, happiness and satisfaction are elusive if we never experience isolation. The way that we incorporate meaning to social constructions (e.g., relational models, identity and esteem, memories, and plans) is by internalizing. Internalizing takes time—time to consider and reconsider the meanings created across the gap, and time to work them into our action routines. Isolation gives us downtime from the automatic everyday routines as well as the more conscious intimate dialogues. We can be concerned with both intimacy and isolation, but we can only actually *be* in one or the other. How do we balance these opposing needs, not only when we are beginning to recognize their importance in young adulthood, but throughout life?

The Relational Dialectic: Integration and Separation

Werner and Baxter (1994) posited that the most central of the three dialectical forces experienced prominently in relationships is integration/separation. This large cluster of oppositions is a broad one encompassing autonomy/connection, interdependence/independence, integration/differentiation, and intimacy/autonomy. It is the relational counterpart to the identity theme of intimacy/isolation, and as such the challenges of identity and relationship, I and Thou, are of a piece. Werner and Baxter noted, "Dialectical intimacy is predicated on the dynamic interdependence of autonomy and connection" (p. 357).

Further distinctions have been made between *internal* and *external contradictions* (Ball, 1979; Riegel, 1976). Internal contradictions occur within the unit of study (individual, dyad, group), and external contradictions take place between the

unit and the larger systems in which it is positioned (family, friends, coworkers, house of worship). The *internal integration/separation* dialectic is considered the primary contradiction for relationships, and as such is enmeshed with other relational dialectics (Werner & Baxter, 1994). Partner autonomy and dyad unity are at issue here. The *external integration/separation* dialectic has to do with how the couple manages time and space given the contradictory demands to both withdraw from social networks (to the relational pair) and to continue to interact with network members (from the relational pair). The composition and relative importance of these dialectics is likely to change across the span of a relationship, as well as across the lifespan.

For example, Peg and Ned at 25 have been dating for a year. At first, their decisions had to do with whether the promise of intimacy was great enough to risk a loss of autonomy. Both were feeling the confidence of identity commitments, but felt somewhat shaky when they did not agree on political issues. However, neither felt that their beliefs about partnership and family were in jeopardy, so they agreed to disagree about politics. External concerns became more important. Peg was starting a new job and felt she had to spend time with colleagues. Ned, not having found a career track yet, was in between jobs, and had more free time for friends. His needs for her time and her needs for her network were at odds.

Now, let's look at Peg and Ned 3 years later. They are married, have a 6-month-old child, and Peg has taken leave from work. Now that the reality of family has settled in, Peg is less sure that she wants to stay at home with Nell for the 5 years that she and Ned had discussed. Ned is confident that one parent should remain with the child until school starts, but it will not be him as his career is just taking off. In this case, internal and external needs overlap; Peg is feeling wobbly about her own identity as a professional and also misses the give and take of her job network. Ned's identity is solidifying around his roles as professional and breadwinner, although he occasionally misses pair-time with Peg. In terms of their relationship, both are feeling separation, although Ned's has to do with external demands and internal needs and Peg finds herself in the reverse situation. How do they cope?

Coping strategies for dealing with all sorts of dialectics are limited; there are only so many ways to manage contradictions. Baxter (1988, 1990) suggested four:

1. *Selection* occurs when both partners perceive both poles of the contradiction and "seek to transcend [it] by making one ... pole dominant to the exclusion of the other" (1990, p. 72). In this case, they may simply choose separation and live separate lives, either breaking up or sharing quarters as strangers.

2. *Separation* assumes the continued existence of both contradictory poles, but the partners deny the interdependence of these poles by separating them, "uncoupling" them by time or topic:

    a. Cyclic alternation is separation by choosing one pole at one time and switching to the other pole at another time. Some couples may choose to go their separate ways during the workweek, and get together for long weekends of intimate time. Distance relationships often work this way.

b. *Topical segmentation* is separation by parceling out particular activities for one pole and other activities for the opposing pole. Partners may decide that playing video games or watching soccer are autonomous activities and do not fall under the integration pole. Another couple may divide tasks by roles in this manner: Her specialty is to handle external integration tasks with the family network byplanning social occasions; his is to manage external separation by setting limits on network interaction in favor of couple intimacy.

3. *Neutralization* also acknowledges both poles, but involves diluting rather than intensifying the contrasting elements. Compromise is the goal, which may be accomplished by either:

a. *Moderation* or choosing the middle ground, such as each member of the couple gives up one night a week for friends, the couple devotes one night to a "date."

b. *Disqualification* or keeping the contradiction ambiguous, denying that there is a tension.

4. *Reframing* involves a "perceptual transformation" of the two poles "such that the two contrasts are no longer regarded as opposites" (Baxter, 1990, p. 73). In this case, partners may come to view autonomy as beneficial to their connection rather than in opposition to it.

What Baxter found was that certain strategies are chosen more than others for each dialectic. In particular, cyclic alternation is chosen more often when coping with the integration/separation contradiction; that is, partners take turns dealing with competing needs for closeness and autonomy. However, keep in mind that Baxter's data come from a sample of college students in relationships from 1 month to 16 years, but averaging 20 months. Older partners and more enduring relationships could choose different strategies.

Baxter also discovered that the choice of reframing, although infrequent, did increase with relationship duration; those partners who had been together longest were most likely to reframe dialectics. Reframing is the most complex of the strategies, requiring transformation of meaning with the result that the contrasting poles are not regarded as antithetical. For me, it comes closest to reflecting dialogic thinking about relationships—accepting the paradoxical nature of dialectics and appreciating the developmental effects of that movement between oppositions. Dialogic complexity in relational acting and thinking is undoubtedly the effect of many interactions at the boundary between two mature identities in an intimate relationship. Just as surely, in the course of partnering, couples face dialectical contradictions beyond integration/separation. Following are a few.

Expression and Nonexpression. Whether to reveal or conceal is a choice that comes up across all interactions but is a particularly critical decision in intimate relationship. The *internal expression/nonexpression dialectic* (Werner & Baxter, 1994) involves a choice between the open and honest disclosure on which intimate relationships are based, and the individual privacy of each complex identity. This dialectic subsumes the expressive/protective contradiction that Rawlins (1983) proposed; his version included the duty to protect an intimate partner from potential hurt that may accompany extreme honesty. Once again, how much expression each party desires will vary and must be negotiated in the relationship. In the college sample, partners chose segmentation to cope with the contradictory impulses to be open or closed (Baxter, 1990). In other words, it depended on the topic. If Peg and Ned know they disagree about politics, they implicitly negotiate a segmentation strategy to be closed about politics and open about work.

External expression/nonexpression has to do with whether or not partners reveal information about their relationship to third parties. Certainly, partners feel that some information should be confidential, and yet they also need the support of the external network to maintain the relationship. Peg may be concerned that Ned is working too hard. If he refuses to discuss it because it is in his work domain (which he has placed on the nonexpressive pole), she may look for advice, support, and relief from her worry by speaking to her mother. Of course, if she chooses to reveal her discussion to Ned, he can become even less expressive; thus, the internal and external dialectics influence each other.

Stability and Change.   We like to think that our relationships are fairly stable, that we can count on them to fill our needs in predictable fashion. On the other hand, we do get bored. Spontaneity and novelty are interesting and stimulating until they become chaotic, so we typically are happiest with some mix of the two. Dance and Larson (1976) commented, "It is communication that prevents change from being chaos" (p. 60). This capacity of symbolic communication to reduce uncertainty[66] led Berger and his colleagues (Berger & Bradac, 1982; Berger & Gudykunst, 1991) to formalize uncertainty reduction theory, which posits that uncertainty reduction facilitates intimacy—the more you know, the closer you become. Given what we know about the expression/nonexpression dialectic, there is clearly a limit to this claim. Yes, there is such a thing as "too much information."

The *internal stability/change dialectic* refers to the partners' simultaneous needs for certainty and novelty. We do want to know about our relational partner, and we like to anticipate satisfactory forms of interaction. However, boredom can lead to breakups (Baxter, 1986; Cody, 1982); but so can antagonistic selection by each partner, one waving the flag for change and the other for stability. For example, Ned prefers the stability of knowing exactly how he and Peg will interact, even if those interaction patterns have become rather negative. Peg has tired of the monotonous routines of nag-withdraw, insult-defend, and is ready to change the relationship. If Ned sees no reason for change, Peg may be headed to the therapist and divorce lawyer herself. Selection may not be highly functional for relationship maintenance, yet it is a common coping strategy (Baxter, 1990) that apparently damages relationship satisfaction. Most couples use a more functional means to cope.

Separation through topical segmentation was most often chosen by young adults for coping with stability/change in romantic relationships (Baxter, 1990). If our couple used this strategy, each would have preferred stability in some areas (e.g., everyday communication routines) and novelty in others (e.g., leisure time activities). For example, Ned might prefer to predict his and Peg's regular private times or a teasing pattern they've developed, yet enjoy the novelty of surprise visits from Peg at work or her questions about a favorite sport that she had previously ignored.

The *external stability/change dialectic* refers to the contradictory demands on the pair to construct a "unique pair identity" and to conform to the culture's relationship norms (Werner & Baxter, 1994, p. 360). Although there are good reasons for conventionalized expectations for romantic pairs—the protection of children, the perpetuation of cultural values, the maintenance of cultural institutions such as marriage—those expectations can crush the creativity possible in relational dialogue, and it can decrease the likelihood of exploring alternate ways of relating that could be of benefit to a pluralistic society (Montgomery, 1992).

One example concerns men as primary caregivers. Let's say Ned and Peg want to have more children, but Peg has returned to her job and is moving quickly ahead. Ned's company has been hit by the downturn in the dot.com industry and he is re-thinking his career. He offers to be a full-time father. Peg agrees wholeheartedly. However, their parents, pastor, and friends are concerned about Ned's fitness as a nurturer, his lack of ambition. Within a year, they tire of explaining their agreement; Peg takes extended leave and Ned returns to work. Their strategy was to *select novelty*, then they moved to *separation by cyclic alternation*. Is this the inevitable end to the scenario? No. They could try to *neutralize* the effects of the pressure for conformity by taking part-time jobs and sharing caregiving *(moderation)*, or by refusing to discuss the issue with network members or isolating themselves *(disqualification)*. Or finally, they could *reframe* the dialectic by viewing their situation as perfectly acceptable and socially competent. The only easy way to do this would be to shift their social network to one that is more accepting of alternative relational arrangements. They could move from Silicon Valley to Arcata, for example.[67]

Although these three dialectics seem the broadest and most typical of relationships, Werner and Baxter (1994) reminded readers that other contradictions are likely, including dominance/submission and love/hate. I would add that the cultural expectations for masculine/feminine gender role behavior constitutes a dialectic that influences how relationships function as well. In the later section on marriage relationships, we examine some of the variations on the cultural norm, but the important point is that there are cultural norms for gender roles, particularly in marriage. This is not to say that males always will select masculine styles and females feminine styles, but instead that the norm for separate roles is deeply ingrained.

The social norm for role differentiation in intimate romantic relationships is so strong that it pervades *all* relationships, even those not composed of a male and female. It is possible that some of the dialectics prevalent in our culture, especially dominance/submission, are governed by this very basic dialectic between male and female.[68] Johnson (1991) claimed that it is impossible to act as relational peers when we live in a culture that dichotomizes relationship by status; you are at any time either above or below your partner. In relationships that remain dichotomized, "our jockeying for the one/up position might be so delicate as to be nearly indiscernible and though the outcome might place us on only microscopically different levels, nevertheless such levels are invariably present" (Johnson, 1991, p. 200). Hence, Johnson was referring to what she called "stimulus/response" situations. These are the scripted situations we have learned to enact so we can get what we need. One of those needs is for sexual interaction and, for Johnson, that is the crux of the matter. We learn to trade power to get our needs met, and the extreme example is found in intimate relationships.

We know that children learn these gender-identified roles very early in life and proceed to develop their communication styles and scripts accordingly. They also become entrenched in our relationships. Scripts for relationships lend us ways to predict, to reduce uncertainty. Cognitive models for interaction bias our memories for conversations such that we are more likely to remember what fits with our expectations (Planalp, 1985). Now, although this helps us maintain the illusion of stability in relationships, it also helps maintain the status quo of relational roles. Hence, how can we break new ground and constitute unique forms of relationship? I would contend that the ability to deal with dialectics from a dialogic position is at the heart of that capacity.

DIALOGUE: BEYOND COMPETENCE TO RHETORICAL ELEGANCE

The New Dialogic Identity

Constituting and reconstituting identity across the spatiotemporal milieu of a life is an "improvisational art" of adjusting to changes in that milieu. The challenges to building identity have shifted as the cultural milieu changed from modern to postmodern. The "new self-conscious" of the postmodern individual is exposed to "technologies of social saturation" and thus to "the vertigo of unlimited multiplicity" (Gergen, 1991, p. 49).

Shotter (1993b) pointed out that "identity has become the watchword of the times" (p. 188) in its capacity to define our commitments. Although the generation just past defined itself in terms of authenticity and personhood, the current generation is all about identity and belonging. Apparently, the sort of shift to a "global village," which Marshall McLuhan predicted, is manifesting.[69] The voices that inform who we are, and the words they use, have greatly expanded sense of self in community and diminished the sense of self as individual entity. As Shotter (1993b) noted, "The ideology of individualism is now, it would seem, in trouble" (p. 190). With the expansion of communication media have come opportunities for previously silenced people to find "voice." Advocacy for the rights of women, ethnic groups, other species, and the environment has "arisen out of a complex interplay between identity and selfhood: between 'who' one is or can be, and one's feelings about one's 'position' in society" (Shotter, 1993b, p. 192). As the individual became invisible in the postmodern world, belonging as a unique person in a genuine community rose in importance.

For Shotter, this sort of identity-as-member, or identity-in-relation-to is less about who owns what and more about the access we have to "opportunities to give shape and form to one's own life" (1993b, p. 192). What are the implications for personal development? Growing up in a society is insufficient. Shotter (1993b) puts it this way:

> To be a person and to qualify for certain rights as a free, autonomous individual, one must also be able to show in one's actions certain social competencies, that is, to fulfill certain duties and to be *accountable* to others in the sense of being able to justify one's actions to them, when challenged.... Being someone in this sense is a rhetorical achievement. (p. 193)

Ah, this is the crux of the matter. To be a fully formed adult is to be able to participate in the discourse that constitutes community, whether that community is family, church, government, education, media, or all of the above. The problem is that we are asked to make sense of many voices that seem authoritative, but the really productive discourse for identity occurs between oneself and another. Shotter proposed that we need a way of talking about "the imaginary" that subsists only in the gaps or boundaries between people (1993b, p. 199). This 'imaginary' functions to "make a way of human being, a form of life possible" (1993b, p. 200). For Shotter, the fully formed human identity is a function of accountability between people. In the flow of the imaginary between people, we create ourselves.

If my identity, my mind, my morality is constituted in interactive discourse, then it can never be stable or static. Indeed, self-constructions only manifest in the rhetorical enactment at the boundary. Is it possible then to have "achieved" self or to even claim "your" self as your own? Probably not, although it is possible to work with a best approximation *at this time* and to be accountable for that *in the present* interaction. Is it possible to "know" another, or is it more a matter of "knowing" what we are creating in the process of working the boundaries? And how would dialogic thinking affect the process? My guess is that dialogic thinking allows reflective appraisal of the dialogic nature of relationships, and that is the hallmark of communicative flexibility. However, even if one reaches some level of dialogic facility, the manner in which it is manifested continues to change and mature in the course of the rich and challenged life.

Life crises are developmental opportunities (Basseches, 1984a). For children, many of the crises have to do with biological change or physiological maturation, as well as with external challenges to the mind constructed in interaction. Adult development has been shortchanged because the shifts are not as visibly apparent nor as dramatic. Nevertheless, adults do experience shifts in their thinking and relating. Some have viewed these shifts as cycles of change punctuated by critical events (Altman, Vinsel, & Brown,1981; Conville, 1991; Hudson, 1999). There is no fixed timetable for adult change as there is for, say, the acquisition of language. Basseches (1984a) maintained, "The most equilibrium one will find in adulthood will come from a way of thinking which recognizes all theories—all answers to life—as provisional, awaiting new data, new experiences, new relationships with other people, to be reconstructed in ways that incorporate more" (p. 337). This way of thinking, which Basseches termed dialectical, is a "developmental movement through forms" or a series of transformations "via constitutive and interactive relationships" (1984a, p. 22). I would add that this sort of developmental movement builds sets of contextualized logics that ultimately lead to the recognition of dialectics, as such. That is, the dialectical thinker sees that any apparent duality of dialectical polarities (e.g., stability/change) is just that, a duality set up in our mode of interacting. In that recognition emerges the possibility of true dialogue, dialogic action, in which the opposing tensions are ever present but playfully handled. This *"play within the tension"* is similar to Baxter's coping strategy of reframing a contradiction, which involves a "transformational change" in the way that relational partners define and treat the contradiction (Werner & Baxter, 1994, p. 362). Baxter (1990) found few cases of reframing, and only in the later stages of relationship development. Apparently, this strategy in particular is learned in the framework of complex intimate relationships, especially when they do *not* proceed according to expectations (Masheter, 1994). A communicatively competent adult, then, is coping with contradictions in relationships, and learning to do so in more complex ways by working the boundaries with intimates.

Distinctions Between Child and Adult Communication Competence

Before we consider the developmental challenges of adulthood, we might look back to see how we came to be known as "adult." Conceptualizing communicative competence in terms of knowledge, motivation, and skill serves well to explain the acquisition of effective and appropriate communication performance (Spitzberg & Cupach, 1984) and it continues to serve to identify by contrast the "dark side" of communication performance (Cupach & Spitzberg, 1994). These performances may be viewed as inappropriate, ineffective, or simply "edgy"—not entirely in the realm of the norm or what is comfortably sensible. They can typically be understood as glitches in either knowledge, motivation, or skill. Importantly, the reason we can label such performances as "dark side" is that we expect the maturing adult to have mastered the elements of competent communication so as to move toward and beyond refinement of skill in favor of creativity and transformation in the experience of relationship.

Children quickly learn the nature of the cooperative principle (Grice, 1975) in order to be viewed as competent communicators, and they typically perform to the fullest extent of their knowledge and skill. Healthy children with rich social environments are optimally motivated to perform with every tool they have. Children take the rules for language and interaction very seriously until school age, when they begin to realize that rules may be broken for fun and profit. Of course, there are rules even for breaking the rules; they should be explicitly flouted if they must be broken, or the violator may be called to account.[70] Children and others early in the process of learning social/communicative rules—those new to a culture or relearning after trauma—rigidly follow the rules as though they were laws. One reason we hold adults more accountable than we hold children is that we expect adults to have a grasp of the rules and to be able to use them flexibly and creatively. Flexibility in coping with relational dialectics and creativity in transforming them are key to the maintenance and growth of intimate relationships.

Cohort Effects in Early Adulthood Development: Crises We Share

When we speak of adult development, we are not speaking of growth across a life cycle so much as a situated life trajectory. Even Gail Sheehy, populizer of Levinson's data on male adult development, recalculated her view of life-span development. In the original *Passages* (1977), the life cycle proceeded in neat increments of invariant stages; in *New Passages* (1995), she not only added a second adulthood in mid-life, but proposed that we have the ability to customize our own life trajectory. Especially in early adulthood, we will be affected by our social and interactional context, by crises we share with peers.

Because different generations are likely to share particular sets of cultural events, they will develop their own ways of interacting about and within those events. In her more recent work, Sheehy sketched the distinctions among generations in the last 50 years, from the World War II cohort up to what she has labeled the "endangered generation." In the interests of comparing the shared critical events in life trajectories, here are summaries, adapted from Sheehy (1995), of the defining characteristics and challenges for the last three cohorts:[71]

- *The* "Vietnam generation" *(1946–55).* "I want to be different" was their theme, and they were. They were highly individualistic and as highly divided between cautious, controlling sorts and freewheeling liberals.[72] For the first time, adolescents dominated the music and movie industries, and teenaged self-indulgence became a taste for instant gratification. But this generation was also better educated than any previous generation, and have continued to value education throughout life. Many postponed marriage, and birthrates declined. They instead chose a long moratorium on commitments, exploring spiritual values in their twenties. After this long state of noncommitment, when they finally decided what they wanted to be when they "grew up," they worked hard in mid-life, working longer hours than their parents did. Their sense of personal power continues as they push mid-life further ahead of them and remain active and socially conscious.

- *The* "Me generation" *(1956–65).* "Everything here is mine, and why not!" is their theme. Scornful of the idealism of the Vietnam generation, they accepted and expanded their sense of entitlement. Prosperity was a given and the "Material Girl" an ideal. Although they shifted their values, putting ambition and leadership at the bottom of the priority list, and loving and parenting at the top, their search for balance was bound to be a challenge. At the same time that they were struggling with autonomy from parents with whom they did not share a culture, they expected those parents to continue to support them in the only (high) style they knew. Women continued to make gains in education and the workplace, but many would never marry or have children. Typically, they delayed commitments during their 20s because technological advances allowed them to put off the complications of intimacy. They could use devices like answering machines to avoid contact and birth control pills to avoid the consequences of intimacy.[73] They were the first generation really affected by the sexual revolution in their power to postpone adult values. As they began to hit 30, the median income dropped for those in the largest population cohort in the United States, but at the same time many were finally ready to commit to careers, marriage, and children. This was the beginning of the compulsory two-paycheck household in which members race from one task to the next.

- *The "Endangered generation" (1966–80).* "Whatever" is their motto. They act indifferent, skeptical, and without expectations. They long to believe and belong but they fear more disappointment. Most do not expect to be married until later in life, if at all. More of them than ever live at home, which also prolongs adolescence and delays learning about intimacy. They are pragmatic and realistic, but they miss fantasy—the creation of their own ideals and identity. Their fears keep them frozen; they are safety obsessed. They have no common external enemy as did the Vietnam cohort, but the internal enemies—drugs, guns, epidemics, poverty, job competition—are difficult to fight. Adolescent suicide has quadrupled, teenage pregnancy is higher in the United States than in any other Western nation, and AIDS continues to spread. Death could be noble for the heroes of World War II or for the civil rights activists of the 1960s, but death from a sexually transmitted disease or from a depressed and troubled teenaged gunman is all too meaningless. This generation is more racially diverse, and thus more accepting of multiculturalism. But even with their inclusiveness, no pivotal events bring them together. Many are inspired to advocate for human rights, the environment, or local community autonomy, but there is nothing to inspire them collectively.

Today's early adults, from 22 to 36, are "endangered." Worldwide, this cohort is at greater risk for depression (Sheehy, 1995), yet they are highly responsible. Over 50% have attended college by their 20s, partly in response to their resistance to structuring a life plan in the face of a sharp decline in spending power. Most will not be able to match their parents' lifestyles and are having trouble achieving financial independence. More young adults have to return home to live with their parents for financial reasons, and this not only disrupts their process of identity formation but also their opportunities for intimate relationship. Men will suffer intimacy shortages; unmarried men outnumber unmarried women in this cohort (Sheehy, 1995). The intimacy gap between the goals of "endangered" men and women may boil down to this: These educated women are in no hurry to marry, yet men are socialized to be taken care of by women. Is it any wonder they are returning home to mom?

Rather than leave our newest adults on this grim note, let's acknowledge that this recent cohort is smaller and thus will eventually face less competition. They can afford to take an extended time for education and try out aptitudes to prepare themselves for fairly flexible careers. One of the big advantages they have is their facility with computer technology; they are firmly entrenched in the electronic age. Competent communication of earlier generations was largely face to face and relied on excellent social skills. Computer geeks with poor social skills became they new ty-coons of the "Me" cohort. The "Endangered" cohort constitute the "global vil-lage"—they are multilingual, speak natural and electronic languages, and they are in the best position to be fluent in both. They are also likely to have a lower divorce rate than the previous generation (Sheehy, 1995); they are marrying later and more selectively. Thus, although they may have to put off career and relational commit-ments, they will be more likely to succeed when they do choose. Many will make a dramatic shift from continuing dependence on parents to confidence in their own values and goals at the end of their 20s. How will their relationships function in cre-ating this transition?

RELATIONSHIP MAINTENANCE AND CHANGE: NEGOTIATION AND REFINEMENT

In addition to constituting a unique identity among and with peers, young adults are challenged to create intimate relationships with unrelated others. Although some will have married earlier, as teens, the likelihood of forming truly intimate re-lationships increases after individuation challenges have been met. This is not to say that young adults cannot have intimate relationships with family members, but it is much more likely that they will be able to do so after they have forged new nonfamilial links from one mature identity to another. When you are 25, it is much easier to recognize the unique character of a complete stranger than that of your own father. To distinguish family members from the roles they served for you as a child takes a great deal longer.

Family Ties

Separation

Some distancing from parents and home is necessary for earning the "adult" la-bel. Establishing one's identity, distinct from parental identity values, is a process that may begin in late adolescence, but is not complete until "emotional emancipa-tion" is achieved (Nydegger, 1991, p. 102). This distance provides clarity about the self, but also allows a more objective view of the parent as a person rather than a role. Very strong emotions—positive or negative—apparently hinder this process. Thus, the 20-something who is angry about unresolved conflicts, or guilty about leaving, may still be enmeshed. As well, strong emotions may be related to whether the parents were overinvolved or underinvolved; whether the original attachment was secure or insecure.

Recall from earlier chapters that the *attachment* theorists claim that the type of attachment formed in infancy predicts the quality of later relationships. I believe we can safely say that early bonds may predict the quality of the early child–parent rela-tionship, but probably not all relationships. Rather than testing the commonly used general attachment style—unrelated to any particular relationship—Ross and

Spinner (2001) tested attachment in specific relationships. They found that most adults rate themselves quite differently on the dimensions of attachment across various intimate relationships. Among mother, father, sibling, spouse, romantic partner, and friend ratings, the family member ratings did *not* correlate with the general style measure, whereas the social network member ratings did. Ross and Spinner concluded that adults endorse more than one attachment style with their different types of relationships, and that the relationships from the family of origin were the *least* predictive of general attachment ratings. Thus, when young adults ($M = 24$ years) are asked to rate their "general" attachment, they are probably thinking of romantic partners and friends, which is appropriate given their need to distance, differentiate, and form intimate bonds.

Developing intimate, nonfamilial bonds—such as a romantic partner or spouse—can buffer the separation process (Nydegger, 1991) and thus strengthen identity. But the other effect of distancing—understanding the parent as not parent—is also critical to the adult self.

Personalizing the Parent

Although the young adult may leave with some self-confidence, it may take awhile to really comprehend the person who was parent. That comprehension lags way behind actual distancing; it takes a long time to internalize the person behind the parental role. Consider Vygotsky's notion of internalization and the oscillations between boundary and core that are the foundations of our kind of development. If we have just spent nearly 20 years interacting with our primary, powerful authority figures, it may take just as long to work out a new model for that relationship and a new understanding of those people. Furthermore, our interactions will be fewer, giving us less opportunity to work the boundaries and less material to internalize to the core.

Nydegger (1991) proposed that we ultimately need some understanding of the parents' social world (the critical events for their cohort) to understand them. Note that as the Vietnam generation reaches mid-life, there has been a resurgence of interest in World War II and the sociocultural context that the boomers' parents experienced.[74] Indeed, this perspective on the parent, especially the father, is not expected much before one's 40s.

Family Obligations

To distance is not necessarily to disengage. Parents and children do remain involved to some degree, particularly as children become parents. What seems to happen is that they become more objective and realistic about their relationship (Sarason, Sarason, & Pierce, 1994). They remain linked as family, and continue to feel obligations to provide support to each other in times of crisis and celebration. The kinds of responsibilities due to families vary somewhat, but most agree that primary obligations exist between parents and children, then among siblings, and then between grandparents and grandchildren (Rossi & Rossi, 1991). The agreed-on form of obligation among family members is financial (in crisis, e.g., losing a job, or in celebratory gift giving), whereas time and energy are more acceptable relational resources among nonkin relationships.

Rossi and Rossi (1994) also found that there is a steady decline over the lifespan in the assistance given by parents to adult children, which makes the current crop of returnees in their 20s and 30s particularly unusual and problematic. In the past, as children have moved into their 30s, their income typically rose as their parents' declined. As parents moved into retirement years, children began to provide more financial assistance. However, today's parents are increasingly providing monetary assistance to adult children. It will be interesting to see if the same reversal of assistance noted in the past occurs in 20 years.

Romantic Relationship: Dialectical Challenge

Integration/Separation: Variations on Intimacy

The ideal intimate relationship is characterized by depth, mutuality, caring, and commitment in the context of a sexual relationship (Kroger, 2000). However, many of the "practice relationships" constructed by young adults do not have all of these elements and yet serve the dabbler-in-intimacy to meet some integration needs. To assess the degree to which a particular identity functions in romantic relationships, Levitz-Jones and Orlofsky (1985) revised the original Intimacy Status Interview (Orlofsky et al., 1973) to describe seven relational styles, summarized by Kroger (2000):

Intimate:	In a committed romantic relationship featuring depth, mutuality, openness and caring, constructive conflict, and comfort in sexual expression.
Preintimate:	Not yet in a committed sexual partnership, but experiencing intimate friendships characterized by openness, mutuality, and equal decision making about shared activities.
Pseudointimate:	In a long-term, sexual commitment but lacking openness, emotional involvement, and mutuality; more of a superficial convenience.
Stereotypic:	Has friends and dates but no established commitment. Friendships are superficial and lack involvement, but fill needs.
Isolate:	Has no close relationships with peers, and other contacts are formal, scripted and stereotyped; withdrawn, lacks social skills.
Merger (committed):	In a long-term sexual relationship featuring enmeshment, dependency, and unrealistic perceptions. Tries to gain a sense of self through the relationships; does not pursue activities without the partner.
Merger (uncommitted):	Not in a long-term sexual relationship, but friendships feature dependency and enmeshment. Relationships are experienced as an extension of the self. (pp. 99–100)

Although all of these relational styles fill some social needs, they do so with varying degrees of success, and from a range of identity foundations. Those in the first two styles employ greater knowledge of their partners and are probably from the foundation of mature identity; those in the last three display little knowledge of others and have failed to individuate fully. In the middle we have identities who are using relationships to fill needs, but are unable to reveal themselves, or indeed know not who they are or what they have to reveal.

As more young adults put off marriage, they will give themselves opportunities to try different relationships. In the challenging interactions of those relationships, intimate or not, they may find sufficient opportunities for identity achievement as well. Indeed, some young adults, after many disappointing and dysfunctional relationships, are declaring themselves celibate, thereby taking a moratorium from the dangers of sexual enmeshment in which to explore the often conflicting demands of identity and intimacy development. For the rest, there is a morass of relationships, descriptions of which follow.

Dating and Mating

We discussed some of the dynamics of dating in the last few chapters, but it continues to be a viable practice field for intimacy into the 20s, 30s, and later for those who choose not to marry.[75] For singles, dating may become easier or harder with time, dependent on their own maturity and skill. Also, any particular individual is likely to swing between the poles of *integration/separation* at different times.

Those who are casual, uninterested, or skittish in their approach to romance tend not to use *affinity-seeking strategies* to initiate dating relationships, whereas other daters choose strategies such as eliciting and sharing disclosures (Bachman & Zakahi, 2000). The "passive" daters who wait for someone to choose them may be either stuck in foreclosed identity, confused, or in the uncommitted-but-considering state of moratorium. The "active" daters are either secure or clingy; the former have achieved identities searching for intimacy, and the latter are foreclosed and willing to merge into codependence.

A word here about the term *codependence*: It originates in the therapeutic community to describe a partner's enabling response to substance abuse; however, it has entered the parlance as a more general term describing a relational process that tends to perpetuate all sorts of patterns.[76] Note that interdependence is a natural feature of intimate relationships that allows us to create and grow together, and codependence is a form of interdependence that may become dysfunctional. A marriage counselor, Peter Moore (personal communication, April 24, 2002), helped me with the distinction: *Interdependence* is a compassionate recognition of what the other lacks; *codependence* is a compulsive recognition of what the other lacks. They are both intimate processes that vary in expectation, intention, and, undoubtedly, in communication patterns.

For example, Deb has been able to fill some social and sexual needs by becoming enmeshed with partners for limited time periods (likely foreclosed and merged). Her strategy for initiating contact is to be in the right place at the right time, looking fantastic and acting vivacious (Bachman & Zakahi, 2000). Don approaches an interesting partner by asking questions about her, listening carefully to the answers, showing understanding and acceptance, and sharing personal information of his own (likely achieved and preintimate). Let's project a little. Deb is clingy in her search to fill her identity gaps, and attracts partners who like her neediness and are only too willing to tell her what she lacks; she is likely to have a streak of codependent partners. Don has several long-term satisfying relationships before he marries at 31. Lynn, on the other hand, has just begun a highly involving career, is feeling very good about herself in that capacity, has good friends and colleagues, and is uninterested in dating (moratorium and preintimate). She does not approach men with dating in mind, but instead develops a close friendship with a colleague that turns romantic a few years down the road as she becomes comfortable with her career and personal commitments.

Those who choose not to or who cannot experience a long-term intimate relationship may fail to develop skills for intimate sharing, arguing, and coping with relational dialectics. For example, conflict is bound to occur if a dating relationship lasts long enough, but some will choose to end the partnership and others will negotiate through the conflict. Conflict, rather than causing breakups, tends to stabilize in growing relationships and increase in dissolving relationships (Canary et al., 1995). It is a reflection of the level of intimacy the partners can hold. But what of *destructive conflict*?

According to Olson (2002), as many as half of American couples experience some form of "common couple violence" that is "the result of a couple's inability to constructively resolve their conflict" (p. 104). However, the results are not uniform; they range from mild aggression to physical abuse including battering and murder. Much of the existing research is based on data from victim populations, so Olson collected a sample from community members to gain a broader view of conflict failures. Her interviewees experienced aggressive conflicts about twice a year that were initiated more or less equally by men and women. The communication patterns they described fell into three categories: aggressive, violent, and abusive. In *aggression*, both parties share power and use mild forms of verbal aggression and noncontact physical acts (e.g., name calling, hitting a table). *Violence* includes physical, forceful contact (e.g., pushing, grabbing). Both these types are symmetrical relationship patterns characterized by reciprocity, control, and aggression on both sides. Quite different is the *abusive* pattern, which is complementary, consisting of one-sided aggressive acts.

We do know what communication patterns work better than aggression and violence. Infante's research on argumentativeness suggested that skill in presenting and defending positions on conflict issues is frequently found in nonviolent marriages but much less so in violent ones. In violent relationships, Infante, Chandler, and Ruud (1989) found higher levels of verbal aggression, which involve attacks to the other's self-esteem rather than to the content issue. Thus, treatment for relational conflict dysfunction could include training in argumentative skill.

If we can consider most conflict as involving a dominance/submission dialectic, then the partners in the abusive pattern have chosen a segmentation coping strategy by selecting polarized conflict behaviors such that one is domineering and the other submissive. The violent pattern reflects the cyclic alternation form of segmentation, in which the parties vie for control and the power fluctuates back and forth between the two. The aggressive pattern seems to be a form of neutralization strategy that involved either moderation by metacommunication (e.g., about rules for conflict behavior) or disqualification by refusing to engage when the conflict starts to become aggressive (Olson, 2002). Because Olson's study was designed to elicit problematic conflict examples, there are no cases of reframing.

Is it possible to reframe the dominance/submission dialectic? Infante suggested *argumentativeness* as one way to reframe. Presenting and defending positions does not necessarily imply a win/lose solution, but rather a performance of each position; for example, reframing "fight" as "debate." A second alternative for reframing is the use of *humor*. Although humor can also be used to avoid, as a type of distraction from the conflict issue (Canary et al., 1995), I think it possible that humor can allow the parties to emerge from the dominance/submission opposition into a different and lighter perspective on the topic without dismissing their disagreement.

Still a third candidate for reframing would be the use of *equivocation*. Although ambiguous messages are rarely recommended by communication scholars, they can help avoid more dire fates than violating the conversational maxim for clarity.[77] Equivocation is "systematic ambiguity" (Chovil, 1994, p. 106) that may be used to evade the consequences of being explicitly truthful. For example, direct messages may be clear and truthful, but they may also be "relationship lies" in that they disregard the receiver's feelings (p. 117). Equivocation permits multiple interpretations, thus allowing partners to perceive similarity in their positions so they can continue to speak cooperatively. But how much information is too little, or too much?

Expression/Nonexpression: Revelations, Secrets, and Lies

In the context of close relationships, we balance vulnerability with expressivity. Some topics and situations call for discretion and thus we limit openness. Derlega and colleagues (1993) noted this as "a paradox of intimacy" (p. 85)—you must disclose to create intimacy, but it makes you vulnerable. In the context of romantic relationships, we expect our partners to know what information to protect. However, as Derlega et al. (1993) delineated, some information is too risky to reveal even to intimates. *Secrets* involve "content that we actively withhold and conceal from others" (p. 74), often because it is too threatening or shameful to divulge, or to reveal it would cause pain to either self or another. Typically, secrets are revealed on a "need to know" basis (p. 80), that is, the content is relevant to the relationship. This particular dialectical balancing act attempts to find the comfortable point between the extreme and disastrous "cult of honesty" popular in the 1960s and the equally damaging "cavalier deception" practiced by concealers who rationalize their lies as protection of the partner (p. 80). However, some discretion may be a good thing.

In close relationships, according to Derlega et al. (1993), some topics are *taboo* in that they either "give too much access to the partner or burden the partner with the responsibility of the information" (p. 74), as in "you don't want to know" (e.g., about my financial difficulties because you would either worry about me or try to fix it).

In a sample of opposite-sex relationships, some romantic and others not, participants identified taboo conversational topics (Baxter & Wilmot, 1985). The two most frequent taboos were *state of the relationship* talk and *extrarelationship activity* talk. In the first case, participants feared that such direct talk would undermine the relationship. If you consider that these were young adults, it might be sensible that their relationships were fairly fragile and explicit talk about unequal commitment might ruin them. In the second, the negative implications arose from talk about other relationships that could provoke jealousy or anger.

Avoiding some issues does seem to lead to relational satisfaction, but not when the issues are critical to the relationship. Satisfied marriage partners stay away from criticism, nagging, and conflict issues they can do nothing about; however, they also talk about important conflict (Finkenauer & Hazam, 2000). Indeed the quality of the sharing between partners was more important than the quantity. Interestingly, the individual predispositions of marriage partners to disclose or not has little to do with satisfaction, but the sharing that occurred between partners does. For example, Peg's tendency toward revelation does not necessarily mean she will be happy in relationship, particularly if her partner is not much interested in all that information. What Finkenauer and Hazam (2000) found is that the "relational match" between partners is critical (p. 257). Additionally, the partners who are matched well enough to create a context of comfortable sharing in which to talk about difficult relational issues will be satisfied. Partners constitute disclosure and secrets between them; they collude on the level of information their relationship needs. Undoubtedly, that process changes across the life of the relationship.

Stability/Change: Trajectories of Maintenance and Dissolution

Although we tend to think, in retrospect, that our relationships are built in orderly, linear, step-by-step processes,[78] the transformations in relationships are typically messier than that. In each relationship, partners create a trajectory of movement, sometimes forward toward togetherness, perhaps stabilizing for awhile, then swinging back in favor of separation. Relationships also experience periods of high and low disclosure, but once the partners "know" each other they are unlikely to "unknow" each other, and in that way relationships do not end but continue their existence in the relational effects they leave behind: predictions, attributions, relational models, and identity shifts. Peg believes, even after Rob has married and moved away, that he had an enormous influence on her life—her confidence in her abilities and the way she values relationships. Thus, although some life events (graduation, getting a job) may cause relational shifts in a linear fashion, others (features of talk like disclosure, or rituals like anniversaries) recur again and again, perhaps with a different quality, and so in a spiraling direction. Conville (1991) suggested a helical model in which relationships move from stable, secure periods to unstable periods prompted by dialectical tensions, and then on to a transformed, qualitatively different state of stability. Thus, relational crises stimulate change.

Disclosure is one of the features of interaction that has been tested extensively, particularly in terms of relational change. Hence, it will serve as our example of communication change in relationship, but keep in mind that other sorts of relational behaviors also need to be mapped developmentally.

Derlega and colleagues (1993) pointed to several "transformative agents" that influence the effects of disclosure including time, relational definition, liking, attributional processes, reciprocity, and goals (p. 15). Note that several of these agents are a function of how we think about self, other, and relationship, and how the relationship is internalized and transformed. We focus here on the effects of relational definition and time.

The definition of a relationship "represents the way partners individually and together think about the relationship and the behaviors that would be appropriate, given that definition" (Derlega et al., 1993, p. 17). When Peg and Ned first got together, they defined their relationship rather broadly and not too seriously (e.g., "playmates"). Later, as they became closer and redefined to "committed lovers," their expectations shifted again. When Peg left briefly for a job in another city, they loosely redefined and backed away from the expectation of commitment. However, when Peg returned to town, she expected Ned to fulfill leftover expectations from the older definition of lovers, whereas Ned set new expectations for unstructured friendship. Peg behaves affectionately and is open about her feelings; Ned withdraws from affection, avoids disclosure, and teases her. Both are unhappy with the behaviors that do not meet their expectations.

Disclosure also appears to change with the sheer march of time, although several trajectories are possible. Derlega et al. (1993) charted three: early decline, early "clicking," and long-term leveling or decline (p. 25). In the first, initial openness of revealing and reducing uncertainty is followed by a dramatic decline. For example, after 1 year of marriage, couples show less affection and are less disclosing than they were as newlyweds (Huston, McHale, & Crouter, 1986). In the context of relatively satisfying relationships, self-disclosure recedes, perhaps when other behaviors became more important.

Early "clicking" occurs when comfortable disclosure patterns are set immediately and maintained. Couples who stay together often "click" from the start, whereas this sort of fast-rise pattern is not found in relationships that discontinue.

Finally, the long-term leveling pattern involves a gradual increase in disclosure followed by a long and gradual decline. Long-term marriages often demonstrate leveling off in that disclosure becomes less important to a couple who are satisfied that they know each other well. Note that in the "early click," partners may enter the relationship with similar relational ideals or expectations, thus they recognize all the features of their prototype being fulfilled. In the leveling pattern, it is more likely that their expectations are not entirely the same at the start, but become more similar over time. As intimacy increases and uncertainty decreases, the young couples' fancy turns to shared living arrangements.

Committed Arrangements: Cohabitation and Marriage

Cohabitation.   By one estimate, about 50% of heterosexual couples living together are *nonmarried cohabitants* (Aiken, 1998), although formally declared cohabitants account for only 9% of unions (Schmitt, 2001). In response to rising divorce rates in the sixties, Margaret Mead (1966) advocated "marriage in two steps" and many apparently have agreed with her. In the 1970s, cohabitation with the future spouse rose from 13% to 53% (Gwartney-Gibbs, 1986). Currently, young adults are the most likely to cohabit, and those whose parents were either unhappy or divorced are particularly apt to be candidates (Cunningham & Antill, 1995). Although cohabitors score lower on love and romanticism than do married couples, cohabitors who subsequently marry are equally satisfied and as happy as marrieds who do not first cohabit. Most cohabitants ultimately marry. On average, cohabitations endure for 1.3 years, culminating in marriage for 59% of them (Bumpass & Sweet, 1989).

Although the vast majority of current or past cohabitors believe that the experience prepared them for marriage (Kotkin, 1985), there is a high divorce rate among marrieds who previously lived together. Cunningham and Antill (1995) forwarded some probable reasons for the higher divorce rate:

1. Without cohabitation and the subsequent dissolution of the relationship, the divorce rate could be even higher.
2. If the total duration of the union is calculated versus time since marriage, there is no divorce rate difference between cohabitors and noncohabitors.
3. If cohabitation is seen as more of an alternative than a prelude to marriage, it is less likely to succeed (the longer the cohabitation, the less successful the marriage).
4. Premarital cohabitors have higher divorce rates up to the fifth year, then the noncohabitors exceed them.
5. Serial cohabitors have higher marital instability than single-instance cohabitors.
6. In the most recent cohorts, the differential divorce rates between premarital cohabitors and noncohabitors has reversed.

Apparently, the nonconformist, somewhat cynical cohabitors of decades ago have given way to the pragmatic cohabitors who intend to marry and have children, but not quite yet. Cunningham and Antill (1995) concluded that marriage is not going out of style, "it is merely occupying less of the average adult's lifetime" (p. 167).

Thus, young adults are allowing themselves opportunities to practice intimacy. But how do these "practice" experiences affect *internal models* for self, other, and relationship? Sprecher and Metts (1999) followed dating couples over a period of 4 years, assessing their romantic beliefs and the state of the relationship (love, satisfaction, commitment) at five time points. By the fourth year, about a quarter had married and over half had ended their relationships. Romantic beliefs include convictions that love overcomes obstacles ("love finds a way"), the partner is perfect ("my ideal"), and there is only one true love ("one and one only"). At the start of the study, romanticism was highly correlated with love, satisfaction, and commitment. No surprise to anyone over 25, the subjects' romantic beliefs declined over the 4-year period whether they separated or married.

Romantic ideals were related to relational shifts, but the only link to the stability and endurance of the relationship was between women's belief in "one and one only" and a lower rate of breakup. An interesting gender difference emerged: men's early romanticism predicted later commitment, whereas women's early commitment predicted later romanticism. Sprecher and Metts (1999) suggested that commitment is the more cognitive process, requiring an assessment of future potential of the relationship. Women, in their continuing role of primary childcare providers, have to assess the practical matters of dependability and material support potential in a mate, whereas men assess personal and emotional qualities (Fengler, 1974) and can afford to be less pragmatic in dating. With time and experience, both genders temper their romantic ideal without any necessary decline in satisfaction.

Marriage.   For those who do marry as young adults, the *transition to spousal roles* is likely to take some negotiation. Pasley, Kerpelman, and Guilbert (2001) noted, "Underlying this construction is the degree to which spouses desire and/or expect a conventional or egalitarian marriage" (p. 17). The dialectics they will have to confront include the male/female and dominance/submission oppositions. Not surprisingly, when both partners agree that they want an egalitarian relationship, or they agree that they want a conventional marriage marked by gender role specialization, the marriages should be stable because their expectations are congruent. However, if they differ in their wishes, or in the way they define relational equity, they are likely to experience negativity and instability. In theory, a couple facing oppositional choices can reduce incongruity in expectations by using any of Baxter's coping strategies. However, women are typically more willing than men to accommodate to their spouses (Knudson-Martin & Mahoney, 1998). Thus, a woman may choose moderation (compromise: "OK, you do the bills for now and I'll stay informed") rather than selection (each choose what they want: "We'll have separate bank accounts"), especially if her spouse balks at reframing or cyclic alternation (switching poles temporally: "You do the bills this month, I do them next").

Marital conflict issues run the gamut, but the top themes are personal criticism, finances, and household chores (Erbert, 2000). Personal criticism conflicts, the most commonly reported by far, were triggered by complaints about bad habits (e.g., smoking) and personal attacks regarding undesirable behaviors (e.g., leaving the empty milk carton in the refrigerator). After those top three, issues include children, employment, time, and communication with in-laws, holidays, sex, and vacations trailing behind. Although the participants in this study ranged from 20 to 52, the top three issues accounted for 42.5% of all reported conflicts, and we might reasonably expect them in young marriages.

Conflict involving *personal criticism* was seen as a challenge in handling the openness/closedness dialectic (Erbert, 2000). A direct personal attack is likely to trigger a defensive reaction; thus although one party negatively expresses a dissatisfaction to which a response is expected ("You smoke too much. Don't you care about your health?"), thus choosing the open position, the other defends ("My health is fine") or retreats ("I don't want to discuss it") to the closed position.

Conflict about *finances* involves both the autonomy/connection and open/closed dialectics (Erbert, 2000). Participants reported the need to be in control of money—financial autonomy—which often seems to require control over financial information as well. Peg complains that Ned wants to control the finances and yet she earns at least half of it and would like more financial autonomy. When she attempts to talk with him about it and find out more about where their money is going, Ned refuses to discuss the subject.

Conflict about *household chores* challenges both predictability/novelty and openness/closedness dialectics (Erbert, 2000). The necessity of housework is nothing if not predictable to the point of boring, but there is usually one party who is more concerned about household stability. Then the other partner may try to draw that party toward novelty. Ned is a neat-freak who has to have the dishes done before the evening is over. Peg likes to enjoy the dinner party and worry about the mess in the morning. One Saturday night she finally says, "I feel guilty when you start doing the dishes at midnight; come to bed with me and I'll do them tomorrow." Ned admits it's habitual behavior and agrees to let them soak ... this time.

Note that the most common conflict is personal criticism, which typically involves expressing negative feelings about a partner's behavior. Do couples vary in their expression of emotions and thus their abilities to handle conflict?

Shimanoff (1985) studied the rules that married couples use for *expressing emotion verbally*. First, wives think they disclose more emotions overall as well as more negative and face-threatening emotions, but in recorded conversations, husbands and wives shared emotions equally. Second, two rules about expressing emotion to a spouse emerged from self-reports and conversations: (a) "One should disclose face-honoring (I'm crazy about you), face-compensating (I'm sorry I flew off the handle), and pleasant face-neutral emotions (I'm so irritated with my boss) more frequently than face-threatening emotions (you hurt my feelings)"; and (b) "one should disclose unpleasant face-neutral emotions (that sort of thing gets me riled) more often than hostile emotions (I'm mad at you)" or "regrets for transgressions against absent others (I regret yelling at Jim)" (pp. 159–160).

Part of what we have to learn to cope successfully in romantic partnerships is to choose calm description and positivity over hostile and face-threatening expressions, which is easier said than done. Compounding the difficulty is a tendency to buy into stereotypes regarding gender and emotional expression. However, there are fewer differences between men and women in everyday verbal expressions of emotion than we commonly believe. Husbands and wives engage in conflict in similar ways, express anger equally in personal relationships, and hold similar expectations for expressions of love (Canary & Emmers-Sommer, 1997). However, more traditional marrieds focus on the experience of love, whereas less traditional couples are more likely to communicate love directly. In the next chapter, we will further examine what keeps marriages together and what drives them apart. For now, we'll look at how young couples begin to create "family." Some are choosing to start traditional families by having children; others are constructing their own versions of family.

Creating Family

Nuclear Family.   The *nuclear family* is a fairly recent innovation in the long history of human social systems, probably reaching its peak incidence in the mid-20th century. Conventionally, the nuclear family "is composed of a married couple living with their biological children, with the husband working outside the home and the wife staying at home as mother and full-time homemaker" (Turner & West, 2002, p. 19). However, it has come to encompass both the reverse arrangement, with wife as breadwinner, and the shared arrangement of dual wage earners with children. The nuclear family is the social prototype for childrearing, but is no longer the norm. In 1960, 45% of U.S. families were of this sort; in 1990 the number had dropped to 25.6% (Schmitt, 2001). Despite pro-family polemic, the nuclear family no longer serves as it did. Nevertheless, many young adults begin their procreative years in the nuclear family model.

Young Parents.   With the arrival of the first baby, the relationship between husband and wife is subject to stress and adaptation. Ambert (2001) advised, "Even couples who were well aware of potential stressors ahead are caught unprepared." (p. 55). Communication between spouses declines with the necessary split in attention to the baby. In a comparison of parents and nonparents in the first 2 years of marriage, MacDermid, Huston, and McHale (1990) found that both groups experienced declines in marital satisfaction, shared activities, and positive interactions. However, parents' activities become more child oriented and the division of tasks become more traditional. This division of tasks constitutes a violation of expectations for many young mothers. Fathers typically are less involved in home responsibilities than expected, and this negatively effects the mother's view of the marriage (Belsky, Ward, & Rovine, 1986).

However, these shifts pale in comparison to the demands of infant caregiving; over half of new parents' problems concerned infant nutrition and illness, compared to about 10% involving marital and role conflicts (McKim, as cited in Mebert, 1991). Mebert suggested that parents who prepared well, planned the pregnancy, and created an internal model of the family beforehand are those who make the transition gradually and well.

In the next chapter, we explore extended family and stepfamilies as arrangements that often—not always—are formed later in the life span. Now we turn to a family format chosen by those who do not fit the assumed heterosexual norm.

Created Family: Voluntary Intimate Groupings

Although the decision to "come out" to one's family of origin is a difficult one and may be fraught with both anticipated and actual peril to identity (Troiden, 1989), once it is done the question of creating family may seem moot. In our culture, "gay" and "family" have been treated as mutual exclusive categories (Weston, 1991). However, *lesbians* and *gay men* have social needs too, and have claimed their own kinship format. Weston noted that gay families have been constituted by contrast with "straight" or biological families; more specifically, through a series of contrasts: straight/gay, family/no family, and straight family/gay family. "Families we choose" or created families are people who are "there for you," "people you can count on emotionally and materially (p. 113), from friends and lovers to community members: "Families we choose interpose face-to-face relationships between … identity and a more holistic … vision of a unified community" (p. 206). Thus, created families function to link the individual to the social network in addition to providing the basic unit of childcare provision.

Note that Turner and West (2002) defined gay and lesbian families as "two people of the same sex who maintain an intimate relationship and who serve as parents for at least one child" (p. 21), which is a much narrower concept than Weston's ethnographic portrait conveyed. However, according to Turner and West's broader definition of family, created families would also qualify: "a self-defined group of intimates who create and maintain themselves through their own interactions and their interactions with others; a family may include both voluntary and nonvoluntary relationships; it creates both literal and symbolic internal and external boundaries; and it evolves through time: It has a history, a present, and a future" (p.8). Interestingly, Turner and West described another category, "communal extended families" that consist of voluntary families of friends (p. 23), whereas Weston chose the broader created family concept for lesbian and gay families that subsumes families with children.

Academics say little about voluntary families, but they do function for those who choose not to create a nuclear family. These run the gamut, from the communes of the 1960s founded often on political principles, to the Israeli kibbutzim which combine blood ties with more voluntary affiliations, to collectives based on religion, age, or convenience. Maggie Kuhn, founding mother of the Grey Panthers, was committed to bridging the age gap among generations and opened her large home to welcome a voluntary, unrelated family of all ages. Thus, any collection of humans that fulfills needs for intimacy, support, enrichment, respect, and companionship functions as family. Note, however, that family may be friends, but all friends are not family.

Friendships: Old, New, Changing

Monsour (1997) asserted, "The most important developmental milestone occurring in young and middle adulthood is whether an individual gets married or remains single" p. 401) The effect of that decision on *friendships* is huge. Young adults may experience three different family roles, each with different demands and social needs: single adult, married without children, and parenthood (Carberry & Buhrmester, 1998). *Singles* prefer friends as companions and confidants, and parents for reliable sources of affection and alliance. *Spouses* place each other above all other network members to satisfy every social need. Friends and mothers fill similar needs as for singles, but always secondary to spouses. *Parents* expand beyond their spousal focus to include children as providers of "affection, security, companionship, opportunity to nurture and reassurance of worth" (Monsour, 1997, p. 404). Indeed, children rival or exceed spouses as need providers, although parents' mothers return to fill a key confidant role and provide emotional support, guidance, and reassurance.

Friendships function most importantly for single young adults as primary sources of social support (Carbery & Buhrmester, 1998). Involvement with friends decreases markedly as a young adult marries and the spouse replaces friends' contributions of intimacy, guidance, and support. Carbery and Buhrmester (1998) noted that this effect is particularly pronounced for men who prefer their wives to fill these needs, whereas wives continue to receive emotional support and disclosure from friends. These "relational effects" arise from role prescriptions; women are seen as more competent at providing social support. And, despite the norm to rely on one's spouse for support, both men and women attribute greater support capabilities to women. As a result, many male friends find that "those wedding bells are breaking up that old gang of mine."

Not only do same-sex pals often fall by the aisleside, but cross-sex friendships are pretty much doomed. Cross-gender friendships are rarely initiated by married individuals (Bell, 1981), the assumption being that spouses should no longer need to have friends of the opposite gender (Leefeldt & Callenbach, 1979). Certainly, marrieds often continue cross-sex friendships, but at a more superficial level. After all, one of the advantages of the cross-sex friend is the insight they can provide about the opposite sex, and the married person now has a live-in source. Some of these less intense cross-sex friendships may include work friends and couple friends.

Couple friends are friends (often paired, but sometimes single) who are socially shared by the married couple as "our friends" versus "my friends." They fill some of the friend void created in the transition from single life to marriage, without threatening the spousal relationship. When couples share friends with each other, it decreases the threat and increases support for couple identity rather than personal identities (Milardo, 1982). Couple friends also support the marriage institution, validate the choices they have made, and socialize the dyad into the network of marrieds (Bendtschneider, 1994). Because intimacy in cross-sex friendships is constrained by marriage taboos (Booth & Hess, 1974), and couple friends are going to be cross-sex for one of the marriage partners, in general couple friendships are likely to be somewhat casual friends gleaned from the available pool of neighbors, coworkers, and classmates.

Although couples socialize with members from both partners' social networks, their closest couple friends are likely to be from the husband's pool (Bendtschneider, 1994), despite the fact that women have larger networks (Wellman & Wellman, 1992). Frequent and regular shared activities, such as potluck suppers or movie dates, maintain these friendships, and proximity is the most important factor in determining the future of the relationship. If couple friends move out of easy reach, or if more effort is required to maintain the relationship, it is unlikely to survive (Bendtschneider, 1994). Before we examine the demise of adult friendships in general, we turn to another unique form of friendship central to many young adults: work friends.

Work friends. Because single young adults are typically trying to preserve their intimate, formative friendships, they have fewer friendships with coworkers than do marrieds (Verbrugge, 1979). Spouses, having to rearrange their networks anyway, are more likely to form friendships with colleagues. Some work settings apparently endorse friendships more than others; for example, service professionals were more likely than business executives to form close relationships (Parker, 1964). No matter the profession, challenging dialectical contradictions arise in work relationships. Rawlins (1992) identified several: private/public enactments of the relationship, affection/instrumentality, judgment/acceptance, and openness/closedness.

Let's say Bob works for human resources and knows that Peg has applied for a better position in the company. He knows the vice president's interviewing agenda and could help Peg prepare, but the vice president has made it clear that he wants to keep the schedule under wraps so that he can get spontaneous answers. By telling Peg, Bob bolsters his friendship with *open* disclosure and *instrumental* support but risks being seen as *judgmental* when he coaches her realistically, and risks shutting down his own *affection* if he assumes that Peg only likes him for the assistance he can give. Of course, he also risks his job if he and Peg are *publicly* seen as friends. On the other hand, if he maintains his lock on the information, he closes down to Peg, avoiding work topics, and fails to provide her instrumental support, risking the loss of her affection, acceptance, and support.

Rawlins (1992) additionally noted a difference in the way men and women construct work friendships. Men, more accustomed to friendships featuring instrumentality, independence, and measured expressiveness, find the "friendship ethic of the working world" (p. 119) easier to handle. To women, who value interdependent friendships characterized by judgment and acceptance, confidence and candor, the glib style of working relationships may feel alien. Ultimately, both men and women who remain in the work world adapt to the multiple demands of working relationships, making distinctions between relationships of convenience and those of commitment as their adult lives become more complex. Some of these relationships will continue, but many will end. However, associates don't always become friends.

Enemies produce different sorts of relationships than we have considered, but they are worth noting in terms of the contrast they provide. Wiseman and Duck (1995) commented that enemies don't simply provide superheroes something to do, but are experienced "as real people who interfere with the processes of social life" (p. 44). Furthermore, friendship and enemyship are not two polar ends of a continuum, but instead are qualitatively different sorts of relationships. However, they do provide a counterpoint. Enemies make us feel vigilant and uncomfortable, and may negatively affect self-image; friends offer companionship and trust, and contribute to positive self-image.

Wiseman (cited in Wiseman & Duck, 1995) clarified several features of how we perceive enemies: their unannounced nature, in that they are not openly acknowledged and thus cannot easily be confronted; their nebulous nature, in that it is not a role that carries clear expectations; and an implied power differential, of which enemies are conscious and use against one another. Whereas friends range from best friends to superficial friends, an enemy is all or nothing (Wiseman & Duck, 1995). But how do we know we have an enemy, if it is unannounced? According to Wiseman and Duck, people report that they sense or intuit the development of enemies, read nonverbal hostility cues, and note sarcasm and negative comments. However, the true litmus test is the overt act that hurts, scares, or angers the target who feels surprise and powerless in response. This helplessness and astonishment is intriguing. Respondents claimed to be surprised when learning of the perceived hostile or hurtful act. They perceived that they had nothing to do with the development; however, among all of the thoughtless remarks and mindless oversights possible for any one busy interactant, at least a few may be taken as slights by hearers and have an enemy-making impact that is unintended. Regardless of how it occurs, there appear to be three sources of enemies: a relatively unknown person takes an inexplicable dislike to one, situational factors lead to enmity (e.g., work competition or neighborly spite), and former lovers and friends turn against one another.

Can we overcome enemies, confront them, charm them? Perhaps, but most people don't. The most common practice is to avoid enemies. Although we may hate them, in their presence we feel threatened, frightened, and self-protective (Wiseman & Duck, 1995). Few tried to change the relationship, perhaps because they felt at the mercy of the enmity, both free of responsibility and powerless to affect it. It would be interesting to find a few people who succeeded in transforming enemies to a more neutral role in relation to self. I suspect that the most mature of dialogic communicators (oh, say, the Dalai Lama) might report no enemies at all.

Fading Relationships

Unlike the ambiguous nature of enemies, we do develop "unwritten contracts" (Wiseman, 1986) about what we expect friends to do for us and how they should act. We will rethink a friendship or reduce its importance if the friend changes in a way significant to those expectations, or fails to provide help when needed (Wiseman & Duck, 1995). Models of friendship include expectations about interpersonal rituals and symbolic acts (e.g., regular phone calls, shared activities, personal disclosures); in declining friendships, we use these rituals and symbols to either decrease or end closeness.

SUMMARY

Young adults, new to their constructed identities, are faced with the challenges of intimacy and isolation. To serve both needs, they will encounter centrifugal and centripetal tensions—energies that move them out to others and back to self. They will try out strategies for coping with relational dialectics to handle those tensions. In so doing, they will experience the "dark side" of communication performance as well as glimpses of rhetorical elegance. They may be frustrated with relational failures, but suspect that there is more to learn about their complexities. Through friendship, romance, marriage, and family creation, the motivation to relate draws them to dialogic awareness. Even as we turn in disgust from the difficulties and darknesses of relationships, we are drawn back by their beauty and irreplaceability. Like the family with the uncle who thought he was a chicken, we can't dismiss him to a home for the very silly—we need the eggs.[79]

ACHIEVING INTIMACY AND ISOLATION

By age 30 or so, if decisions about the direction of life have not been made, there may be a crisis involving changing or confirming life values. In particular, if solid identities and satisfying intimate relationships have not been formed, 30-somethings may begin to question the values (for career, sport, partying) that have left them feeling empty. Their task is to prepare for the productive/reproductive years of middle age. There may be a flurry of mate seeking, a change of profession, or a commitment to community that brings them into generativity.

NOTES

64. Refer to chapter 1, Assumption 7.e. For the next few chapters, we concern ourselves with how adults learn to "play the tensions" of dialectics in a dialogical fashion—how they come to recognize the relatedness of any set of apparently contrastive oppositions.
65. For example, the relational dialectic of openness/closedness may also include openness/deception, openness/discretion, and openness/silence, among others. Montgomery and Baxter's (1998) dialogic approach to relational dialectics focused on how partners "manage the simultaneous exigency for both disclosure and privacy ... how the 'both/and'ness of disclosure and privacy is patterned through their interplay across the temporal course of their relationship" (p. 160).
66. See Dance and Larson (1976, chap. 4) for an overview of the effect of communication on entropy.
67. For those unfamiliar with Arcata, CA, it is a small, liberal community with a large university. It is known not only for its water treatment marshlands and ecological awareness, but for its Green Party city officials and nearby marijuana fields.
68. Although there are many treatments of this notion, two of the most radical and most interesting come from Sonia Johnson (1991) and Shulamith Firestone (1970). Firestone took Marx and Engels' class analysis one step further and proposed that the division of the genders is at the root of class distinctions (and thus, of hierarchical organization).
69. McLuhan's student, Walter Ong (1982), wrote accessibly about the shifts from preliterate (primary orality) to print to electronic (secondary orality) cultures: "Secondary orality generates a sense for groups immeasurably larger than those of primary oral culture—McLuhan's 'global village.' Moreover, before writing, oral folk were group-minded because no feasible alternative had presented itself. In our age of secondary orality, we are group-minded self-consciously and programmatically. The individual feels that he or she, as an individual, must be socially sensitive. Unlike members of a primary oral culture, who are turned outward because they have had little occasion to turn inward, we are turned outward because we have turned inward" (p. 136).

70. Grice (1975) called these understandings about breaking conversational rules *conversa-tional implicatures*. They may be called into play when a speaker cannot avoid breaking one rule in the process of upholding another. For example, if my aim is to speak the truth (quality maxim) and I am asked to reveal how I met my best friend, I may have to tell a rather longish story, thus flouting the quantity maxim. I may call attention to the implicature by requesting a license to break the rule ("Well, that's a loooong story").

71. In chapter 11, we more closely examine early cohorts: World War II and the Silent Generation (Sheehy, 1995).

72. McLuhan and Ong might agree that this generation was a pivotal one making the transition between print and electronic media cultures (see note 71).

73. This generation was the first to embrace the electronic age.

74. For example, movies such as *Saving Private Ryan* and *Pearl Harbor* were recently released in the last decade, along with books like Tom Brokaw's *the Greatest Generation* (1998), which ranked first on the *New York Times* bestseller list.

75. For elders, dating serves different purposes; see chapter 11.

76. Note that I am referring to enmeshment of communication behaviors between two insufficiently differentiated identities, rather than the chemical dependency collusion implied in use by the therapeutic community (Wright & Wright, 1995). As Wright and Wright correctly pointed out, codependency is a relational process that may occur for numerous reasons that are not necessarily dysfunctional.

77. Grice (1975) labeled this category of the cooperative principle the "Manner maxim." It calls for interactants to avoid obscurity.

78. Knapp (1984) constructed an attractive staircase model of relational development in which partners move toward more certainty and intimacy in systematic stages of coming together, and as systematically away from intimacy in coming apart. Individuals, reporting in retrospect about their relationships, tend to agree that these stages occur.

79. Apologies to Woody Allen, who told it better in his film *Annie Hall.*

She'll be fine. Caroline seems like a nice girl and Nell will be busy and happy for awhile before she ever feels homesick. But I'm child-sick. It's selfish, but I miss her already. We had such a great time this summer, shopping for her computer, linens, clothes. Spending a week at the beach. I'm really going to miss her. Not to mention that I can't avoid Ned anymore. He's been withdrawn, and seems to withdraw even more if I ask him what's wrong. I don't know what it is and refuse to play that guessing game. I don't really want to, but if this distance continues, I'm going to insist on counseling. I can't go on like this.

The very act of dropping Nell at her college dorm and knowing she'll return home to an empty nest and a silent husband is a huge transition for Peg. She has been dreading it for some time, knowing that this feeling of loss and loneliness was inevitable. She wants this opportunity for Nell—for her to hone her intellect and find her best self. But Nell has been the only buffer between Peg and Ned. Peg still loves Ned—she thinks so, anyway—and wants the marriage to continue. But she is afraid of the distance they have created and the empty hours ahead of her.

Middle Adulthood:
Nurturing and Relinquishing Youth

A new moon teaches gradualness
and deliberation and how one gives birth
to oneself slowly. Patience with small details
makes perfect a large work, like the universe.

What nine months of attention does for an embryo
forty early mornings will do
for your gradually growing wholeness.

(Rumi, quoted in Barks, 1995, p. 151)

Although mid-life has been redefined since the Vietnam generation, no matter where you place the boundaries, it is a time of life when you release youth to the next generation, when you recognize your own limitations while encouraging the widest horizons for those whom you nurture. It is about continuing to create and accept your whole self; and more then ever, it is about generating your contribution to the world, be it product or progeny, profession or principle. In this chapter, we continue to follow the process of giving birth to oneself through the relational tasks of middle age.

Mid-life is not what it once was. Sheehy (1995) pointed out that our life passages have moved upward about 10 years since the 1950s, leaving us with a first adulthood (to about 45), and a second adulthood including an age of mastery (to 65) and an age of integrity (over 65). In this chapter, we look at life transitions from 35 to approximately 55, although the communication literature is fairly silent on the topic of mid-life development. We extrapolate from studies about communication in divorce, remarriage, stepparenting, and work relationships to gain some understanding of the dialectical tasks of mid-life interaction.

TENSIONS IN MIDDLE ADULTHOOD: AGING, IDENTITY, AND DIALECTICS

The Physiology of Mid-Life

Aging is a reality most will resist. Even if cultural expectations change, the aging of the body proceeds, like it or not. We often can ignore the natural aging process in its early stages, but by middle age, wrinkles deepen, joints creak, and hormone levels fall. As the current crop of middle lifers has discovered, we can lift the jowls, replace the joints, and supplement the hormones, but we will have to acknowledge sooner or later that the way we think, perceive, and relate also will have changed if we have been awake and interactive for 40 or so years.

Although general intelligence declines with age from 30-something into the 70s, the verbal portions of IQ show much less of a decline than do the performance (spatial) scales (Aiken, 1998). Horn's (1985) explanation for this difference was that "crystallized ability"—including vocabulary, knowledge, and arithmetic skill—is more resistant to decline because it is acquired through experience and education, and thus is responsive to practice. "Fluid ability"—such as problem solving and novel response—is more genetically determined and linked to the physiology of aging. These fluid abilities begin a precipitous decline in middle age.

What I find heartening is that the abilities linked to symbolic experience are those that serve interaction and are sensitive to active use. Until memory declines precipitously (more on that in chap. 11), there is no reason that self-directed developmental processes cannot continue, unless interaction opportunities are limited by choice or circumstance. This should give you a new choice for the stranded-on-a-desert-island game: If you can't pick a lively companion, take crossword puzzles and a good dictionary.

Culturally Shaped Thresholds

Many of our transformational experiences will have been shared in their broad outlines with our cohorts: marriage, children, and career are more or less institutionalized as expected milestones. By the 30s, many of these decisions have been made and the everyday routine of maintaining these commitments can leave the achiever goal rich but time poor (Hudson, 1999). At the brink of 40, disillusionment with the pace and purpose of adult life sets in, and the gap between reality and expectations can lead to a reassessment of life goals in light of the constraints that former choices imposed. The 40s may be seen as the last chance to author one's life.

Hudson (1999) observed that either *self-reliance* or the mastery of *interdependence* dominates the 40s. In his view, those who focus on interdependence have "unfinished business ... from their twenties and thirties" (p. 164), and so choose to hone their relational skills. Those who have already succeeded at parenting or career reach within toward personal development and transformation. I suspect that he was noting what we know as the personal dialectic (integration/individuation) that requires regular rebalancing across a life. According to Hudson, *developmental* commitments (integration) include renewing the self and/or the couple, parenting grown children, nurturing aging parents, training for new skills, and reevaluating options. *Transformational* goals (individuation) move beyond ego to the more spiritual self. Similar to Jung's concept of individuation, the goal is to complete self—to *be* self rather than *project* self. As Hudson noted, this spirituality generates integrity, depth, and compassion, and leads to the sort of generativity Erikson elaborated as the identity challenge of middle age.

However many are reaching for the sublime, there are as many slogging through the ridiculous. Hudson (1999) and Sheehy (1995) called them "middlescents" in their similarity to adolescents testing their limits—except that these "rebels" have too many "causes" in the commitments they have assumed. They may feel lopsided in having mastered a career and failed at home, or vice versa. It can be a time for sorting out life priorities, but the effort will be worth it. By the 50s, "self-reliance leads beyond itself, to interdependence with others" (Hudson, 1999, p. 172); that is, the dialectic again rebalances. Often, 50-somethings form new friendships, find ways to fill increased leisure time, deepen intimacies, and accept volunteer leadership roles. They can relax into Maslowe's "unconscious competence" (Hudson, 1999, p. 176) at work, allowing time and space for spirituality and a broadened connectedness to community. They may be attracted to travel as they "see their world as an extended family" (Hudson, 1999, p. 175). There are many examples; one is actor Richard Gere. After a youth spent playing complicated bad boys and sullenly avoiding publicity, he now is a practicing Buddhist, actively supports the liberation of Tibet, takes on lively roles (as in *Chicago*), and chats playfully with the press.

Identity Challenges: Generativity and Stagnation

Of those born at the turn of the century, less than 5% could expect to live to age 65 (U.S. Bureau of the Census, 1997). Thus, middle age as we know it was not a planned span of life. Life expectancy has increased greatly; most of us will live into our 70s. Now that we can expect to live a third of our lives past the age of 50, we must "compose" a satisfying life beyond the childrearing years (Bateson, 1989). In that challenge lies an opportunity for deepening and broadening identity.

Kroger (2000) summarized the identity issues of mid-life, referencing Erikson's (1950) consolidation of generativity drives, as well as Kotre and Hall's (1990) changes in time perspective and personal power, and reclamation of opposite-sex qualities. Kroger added that, in psychosocial terms, these issues involve vocation, personal values, and "important relationships with others" (p. 181).

The *shift in time perspective* arrives with the realization that more than half of life has past, and mortality becomes a fact rather than a far-distant myth. With the recognition that one's generative achievements will end, the mid-lifer often reassesses what has been accomplished and what has not. For those who feel that they have failed to achieve their goals, this can be a time of depression and/or "acting out" in an attempt to recapture youth and its seemingly endless horizons. For others, it is a time to examine the legacy they wish to leave for portions that remain incomplete.

Generativity, or "a sense of caring, both for the present as well as future generations" (Kroger, 2000, p. 184), is a concern expressed in mid-life by those who have resolved earlier identity issues; whereas *stagnation*, or self-absorption, reflects difficulties with earlier identity construction (Erikson, 1950). Erikson (1982) noted two forms of stagnation: rejectivity, or the exclusion of individuals or groups from caring attention, and authoritism, or the use of power to regiment work and family life (cited in Kroger, 2000, p. 184). Both forms reflect rigidity in relating, separating self from selected others, and dominating partners in their inclusive relationships. The balance between stagnation and generativity, suggested Erikson, must be found in order to focus attention on one's desired impact on future generations. There is another sense of stagnation that we explore later in this chapter as the counterpoint to generativity.

Kotre (1984) expanded Erikson's notion of generativity to biological, parental, work, and cultural arenas. At its simplest, generativity can mean simply producing offspring, but most also provide care and guidance for their offspring. Increasing numbers of mid-life adults have not chosen parenthood, but do fulfill generativity drives by mentoring newcomers to their profession, or by participating in the maintenance of community, the expansion of spirituality, or the conservation of culture. To care about others/self sufficiently to reach this level of involvement and inclusion requires a clear sense of self in relation.

Jung (1931/1969) viewed mid-life as a transition to greater individuation and integration. With children on their own paths, and careers established, mid-lifers have "more time and freedom to explore their own needs and reintegrate important identity elements that may have been left behind" (Kroger, 2000, p. 175) as they structured their lives. Greater *individuation* often arises from the freedom of final goodbyes to parents. With the death of a parent, people often experience a "freedom toward fulfilling their own wishes" (Kroger, 2000, p. 175).

Integration often increases between the masculine and feminine aspects of the mid-lifer. The femininity that had been denied to men as gender roles were learned and competitive careers built now resurfaces in nurturing and involvement. More than one middle-aged man has remarried in early retirement to start a second family, now as the stay-at-home nurturer. At the same time, women who have focused on family and connection are eager to try more autonomous roles that capitalize on masculine qualities. Women in mid-life often return to education and career once their children no longer need constant mothering. To simplify, men develop by being different, women develop by being similar (Hudson, 1999). It is in mid-life that they begin to integrate the force opposed to their earlier sexual identity. Kroger (2000) observed that many women whose identities were foreclosed in college ("the guardians of the culture") broke free in mid-life to construct their own paths, whereas those initial diffusions ("drifters") made more traditional commitments in mid-life (p. 181). What seems clear is that identity challenges are available to be undertaken throughout life. And although social pressures may influence large numbers of a cohort to face these tasks at a particular time, the tasks may be taken on in a variety of ways. One thing seems definite about the process: Individuation and integration, although they may develop together, are both necessary for a fully meaningful life. In codeveloping, we inform each other's sense of self as separate, and are part of each other's sense of self in relation.

Dialectical/Dialogical Challenges

Before we consider relational dialectics in mid-life, let's look at an intriguing (and rare) dialectical view of "postadult life" (Keen, 1984). Keen noted that, in our culture, many experience mid-life "moral suicide," that is, in the absence of models for a postadult life, many people lose their passion. In our process of creating an identity that "fits" and follows the rules, we create "a psyche that is divided between conscious values and an entirely unconscious or shadow side" (Keen, 1984, p. 95). The shadow part of self is projected onto "other," or opposite—the opposite sex, the enemy, "them." In young adulthood, to keep social mores and norms in place, we must ignore a part of self. Rediscovering that part (the "dark side," the "other") is the task of integrity in "postadulthood."

Keen professed that "you can't become a full human being without being an adult" (1984, p. 96). The process toward adult status moves from the "child" who internalizes parental values to the "rebel" who rejects them, and finally to the "adult" who rediscovers serviceable social norms. However, Keen added, the passionate "postadult" is both "outlaw" and "lover." The outlaw—not criminal—moves outside the law of culture to find out things about self that have been prohibited and devalued socially. The outlaw strips off myths about all the roles learned so well and the rules that came with them. For example, I might strip off the myth of being "Catholic," which is no mean feat. I may also drop the luggage of being an "academic," or the expectations for being a "woman." To Keen, this shift meant we move toward androgyny, which is to move toward *self-love;* in my case, toward love with my masculine, nonintellectual, metaphysical side. The end of outlaw life comes with the recognition of others *as* self. When I have experienced your side as well as mine, I can see: "Ah, I'm related to you," and thereby see through the autonomy I've constructed. And as I see the porousness between "me" and "you," I become the "lover."

Here's the crux of Keen's (1984) passion: The "outlaw" and the "lover" are really one stage of life, "with continuous movement back and forth making up the whole second stage of life" (p. 99). As the outlaw, I am autonomous and individuated; as the lover, I am integrated, a "part of the web that connects." This primary identity dialectic is what can move us to the dialogical perspective: "We go back and forth between standing alone and knowing that we are always involved with others" (Keen, 1984, p. 101). Of course, this is a process that may start in mid-life but continue into our later years. For now, we look to the earlier transition from adult to postadult.

Integration/separation has to do with the level of engagement one has with others and, in this way, it is a variation of individuation/integration. For many mid-lifers, family engagement will shift as children continue their own individuation and separate more from parents. Even those who do not choose marriage and children will experience the loosening of ties with college friends, shifting coworker alliances, and changes in parental bonds by illness or death.

Although we often think of separation in a negative sense—in its implications for the ends of relationships—it is also positive to have a life apart. Jung (1957) considered separation an activity of the soul, "a breaking into parts things that were too tightly packed, and that needed differentiation" (cited in Anderson & Hayes, 1996, p. 172). The downside of the physical and emotional meshing that is considered the standard in intimate relationships is identity diffusion. On the other hand, work relationships provide opportunities to individuate in the context of relationship—to separate without fear of intimacy losses. However, despite Freud's (1905/1961) attribution of psychological health to love *and* work, there has been little attention to the function of work in the equation of integration/separation (Anderson & Hayes, 1996).

Anderson and Hayes (1996) concluded from surveys and adult life stories that "the cornerstone for self-worth for both women and men is achievement/work-related activities" (p. 283). Intimate relationships may bring joy, but are not "a primary source of self-esteem and self-definition" (p. 283). However, mentorships and friendships do contribute importantly to self-worth, in their relative freedom from enmeshment and their capacity for reflection of one's achievements.

Expressive/nonexpressive oppositions concern the balancing act between emotional, creative expression and keeping one's council. One way of framing this dialectic relationally is in terms of the "communication ritual" as an interaction event between relationship parties in which the sacred object of "self" is reaffirmed, yet transformed (Katriel & Philipsen, 1981). The communication ritual, in which co-construction of meaning is expected, involves the initiator asking the partner to devote full attention to the initiator's expression. This sort of expression can increase intimacy, but also may relieve stress and clarify thought and feeling for the discloser.

Expression can be self-serving, particularly when it does not contribute to the relationship or assist the partner to create new meaning. Certainly, we can justify the expression of feelings raised by major life events such as loss of a loved one, chronic conditions such as work frustration, and daily hassles such as the car breaking down (Burleson, 1990), but we may overload intimates because they are so conveniently present (Planalp, 1999). Not only are our intimates readily available, but they also know our emotional issues and can empathize easily with us. The flipside of empathic response is lack of distance.

If a partner empathizes only two well, then both members of the couple now feel fear, or anger, or whatever the emotion, and this can block a productive coping response. If the partner's response is very similar to the discloser's, then a fresh approach to the problem may be needed, and this is where friends and relatives may be more helpful. Another downside to expression in intimate relationships is the tendency of partners to protect each other from stress. If my partner is part of the problem or may suffer from the knowledge I want to impart, it may be tempting for me to "save" him or her.

Let's say that Peg's boss has made some overtures to her that she considers sexual invitations. She is very uncomfortable about it, mildly attracted to him, and unsure of her next move. Her response could affect both her job and her marriage. At this point, she feels she cannot tell Ned about it, because his response is likely to be distress and advice to charge harassment. She suspects her mother would give the same advice, so she goes to her friend Amy. To her surprise, Amy tells her to stop living a fantasy and tell the guy to back off. Still not ready to act, Peg consults a professional counselor before making her decision. Peg faces the fact of her own conflicting feelings and her responsibility for their consequences. She confronts her boss and tells him she is not available. In this case, Peg needed the response of a relative stranger to clarify her dilemma. Her closest intimates might have forgiven youthful peccadillos, but were less likely to overlook "inappropriate" expressions by a middle-aged woman.

We expect "adults" to be relatively disciplined about their emotions. However, there are two schools of thought on whether or not we can manage emotional expression. One says that powerful emotions are out of our control and we cannot be held accountable for our responses to them; thus, we acknowledge "crimes of passion." The other states that emotions can be controlled and that adults should manage them well enough to avoid harm. The literature gives more evidence for the latter position (Planalp, 1999). Planalp (1999) noted, "To a large extent, emotions are as controllable as we believe and train them to be" (p. 187); thus, our cultural views about what emotional displays are appropriate and justified are critical to our judgments about expression/nonexpression. As we age, we are expected to control our emotional responses more effectively.

Stability/change may be the one dialectic that spans all the others to capture the nature of development and cyclic process (Brown, Werner, & Altman, 1998). Cyclic processes involve "patterns that are repeated but have different meanings at different times in our lives" (Hudson, 1999, p. 39). I recently reread Louisa May Alcott's *Little Women* and noted political overtones that I had not noted at my first reading at the age of 10. I appreciated the book as much as I had years ago, but in a different way. In the same manner, a married couple may experience the "communication ritual" as somewhat anxiety producing yet fulfilling in their 1st year ("I'd like you to sit down and talk with me about our money situation"), as downright painful in their 10th ("We need to talk about our commitment to this relationship"), and as comforting and loving in their 20th ("Nell leaves for school next week; let's talk about our plans").

Successful marriages apparently maintain internal stability *and at the same time* tolerate each partner's needs for novelty; they manage to demonstrate external consistency with cultural norms *and* adapt to changing role demands. For example, as children mature and demand more autonomy, parents are still parents but the role requirements must shift. Do they let go entirely (laissez-faire) or clamp down rigidly (authoritarian)? In the next section, we examine some of the stabilizers and adaptors in relationships.

MID-ADULT RELATIONSHIPPING

To construct and maintain relationships in mid-life *should* be easier, given the considerable practice opportunities we encounter with roles and rules over the years leading up to mid-life. But is it? The personal mastery we feel will depend on the kinds of experiences we have chosen. If much of my time is spent in the classroom, or giving presentations, I will undoubtedly feel competent in articulating my position relatively unopposed. On the other hand, if my ex-partner and I constructed unproductive conflict patterns, and I carry those patterns into other interpersonal conflicts, I may feel quite inadequate to engage in interpersonal argument. Although I have learned to *react* appropriately in highly structured situations, I have failed to work out how to *respond* to another unique individual in a conscious fashion. The knack of responding situationally probably relies heavily on motivation—a will to dialog—that is hard to feign. We look first to the highly motivating romantic relationships.

Romance and Disappointments: From Delight to Disillusion

Intimacy for One: Dates, Appointments, and "Doing Something"

Most Americans wed at some point in their lifetimes, but not all remain married. The percentage of married women peaks in the mid-40s, whereas the peak for men is in the mid-50s; divorces peak for both in the 40s (Aiken, 1998). Very little communication research concerns the single, middle-aged adult, but we can look at the demographics for clues.

The few never-marrieds in our culture have been stereotyped as deviant and probably maladjusted. However, most singles are happy, socially adjusted people enjoying frequent interaction with friends, family, and colleagues (Cargen & Melko, 1982).

One large subcategory of never-marrieds are homosexuals. Legal sanctions for homosexual marriages are few, so they must create their own commitments. These informal arrangements are less stable than are legal marriages, but can last for many years and go through phases similar to marriages (Kurdek & Schmitt, 1986). Gay men who live alone seem to fall into three relational categories: functional men who have active sex lives and are comfortable with their status, dysfunctional men who are sexually active but troubled about their status, and asexuals who have little sexual contact and lead quiet, untroubled lives (Bell & Weinberg, 1978).

Interestingly, never-married heterosexual men seem to fit three similar patterns: sophisticated active men with many friends, social isolates who reach out for company when they needed it, and outsiders who are truly isolated and alone (Rubinstein, 1987). There have been fewer studies of single women, gay or straight, and thus we are unsure of their profiles. Many professional women choose to focus on their careers, and value their independence over the securities of marriage, so we might expect them to be better educated than are wedded women. However, a substantial number of single women have less than average educations (U.S. Census Bureau, 1992), so the reasons for choosing to remain single probably vary a great deal.

Given the lack of information about singles' communication habits, we might extrapolate and guess that the highly functional of the singles have had to extend themselves more than the marrieds have to meet their intimacy and companionship needs. The less social of them may have started out with fewer skills, which could make them less desirable partners. Alternatively, some singles may simply have tired of the effort of making dates and appointments, of asking "Wanna do something?" Thus singles, who must work harder to have a rich and rewarding relational life, choose to become adept or to settle into less interactive lives.

Monogamous Relationships: Commitment and Change

Although the standard for monogamous relationships, in both social science and American culture, is marriage, not all long-term couples are wedded. However, we assume for now that all long-term couples in the same cultural setting face similar challenges, married or not.

That the most social of creatures would devise an institution that formalizes sexual, companionate, and reproductive relationships should be no surprise. People marry for these benefits and more. Married men tend to live longer than bachelors do, but this may be because healthy men are better candidates for marriage. Women may benefit less (Gove, 1973) from marriage in terms of personal health, and some may choose husbands for their assistance in raising children over their spousal qualities. Whatever the reasons for taking on the legal, religious, and social responsibilities of marriage, it takes some adjustment.

Kurdek and Schmitt (1986) identified three phases through which couples pass in coping with the changes that marriage brings to personal autonomy: The *blending phase* (Year 1) involves living together and learning to consider the partners as an interdependent unit. The *nesting phase* (Years 2 and 3) brings exploration of compatibility and shared time. The *maintaining phase* (Year 4 and beyond) sees the recognition of partner individuality and establishment of family traditions. Disillusionment and stress are common in the nesting phase, but decline in the maintaining years (as cited in Aiken, 1998). Marital satisfaction usually starts out high, declines during the childrearing years, and then rises again as the children leave home (Berry & Williams, 1987). What have these satisfied couples created between them, and how does their relationship change them in a satisfactory way?

Note that the following discussion about relationship maintenance *may* pertain as easily to young adult couples. I include it here because it is an issue that will be faced by just about *every* mid-lifer.

Maintaining the Ship. Sonia Johnson (1991) spelled "relation Ship" in this way to draw the analogy of the Ship "that sailed into the living room" and took up residence. When the relation Ship is first sighted, it is beautiful, stately, and a joy to behold. But pretty soon, it needs polishing, scraping, repairing, and constant admiration, and the "crew" can lose sight of each other in their bedazzlement with the Ship. Although Johnson chose mutiny against traditional mate relationships, many people prefer to keep the Ship afloat rather than sink or swim.

Weigel and Ballard-Reisch (1999) asked both husbands and wives what they did to maintain their relationships, and assessed relational qualities of love, commitment, and satisfaction. Wives' use of maintenance behaviors was strongly related to marital quality, but then, Weigel and Ballard-Reisch found that wives typically use more maintenance behaviors than do husbands. Even though wives may do more of the "work" of maintenance, husbands' perceptions contribute equally to the couples' relationship experience. Thus, couples cocreate relational identities that then influence the perceptions they each hold of love, commitment, and satisfaction. But what sort of maintenance "work" makes a difference?

According to Dainton and Aylor (2002), the use of *assurances* is the single best predictor of satisfaction and commitment, with the routine rather than strategic use of *positivity* coming in close behind. On the other hand, *openness* and *advice* seem to be negative predictors of relational quality. Note that, in this study, only one partner was polled; therefore, we only know how one partner's maintenance behaviors relate to his or her view of the relationship's quality. We could reasonably assume, however, that a sincere, sunny attitude and supportive reinforcement are related to feelings of satisfaction and commitment. However, openness (e.g., expressing fears, needs, feelings) and advice (e.g., sharing opinions about the spouse's life) may be destructive to quality. Advice is often seen as an attempt to assert control or dominate (Rogers & Farace, 1975). Also, as you may recall, discretion is often the better part of valor in close relationships. Married couples evidently learn this over time; the longer a relationship continued, the fewer openness strategies were used (Dainton & Aylor, 2002, p. 59). Instead, *shared maintenance tasks* became more important as relationships endured, including *conflict management* (e.g., cooperating in disagreements), *social network use* (e.g., spending time with friends in common), and *shared task work* (e.g., doing a "fair" share of our work). Maintaining becomes less about revealing one's opinions and more about cooperating and supporting each other emotionally and instrumentally.

Wise spouses, rather than reveal all of their own opinions, try to "read" their partners' desires and needs. Koerner and Fitzpatrick (2002) found that accuracy in *decoding a spouse's nonverbal affect* was linked to the spouse's marital satisfaction, but not necessarily to the decoder's satisfaction. The satisfaction of the "reader" was linked to his or her ability to decode the spouse's relational positive affect (e.g., affection displays) and nonrelational negative affect (e.g., frustration with a coworker). Positive affect, accurately read, leads to good feelings about the relationship. Negative affect about a third party, accurately read, allows the reader to understand and be supportive of the spouse without feeling responsible for the negativity (Koerner & Fitzpatrick, 2002). Evidently, this latter effect is particularly pronounced for a husband's decoding of his wife's nonrelational negative affect; marital success is more likely if a husband accurately reads his wife's distress and attributes it to a cause outside the relationship ("Honey, you seem upset. Is your boss still pressuring you about that project?"). A heartening endnote to this study is that both spouses were "far superior in decoding each other's nonverbal affect" than were the nonpartisan judges (Koerner & Fitzpatrick, 2002, p. 48). Thus, spouses support each other, in part, by accurately attributing positive and negative affect to relational or external causes.

Social Support, Gender, and Relational Identity.   Spouses expect social support in marriage, but whether they feel supported or not depends not only on the actual support partners try to give, but also on enduring perceptions of relationship quality. Apparently, men and women differ in this equation. Their varying needs for *autonomy and connection* may go back to the primary mother–child bond: Boys must emphatically differentiate from mother to be masculine, whereas girls learn femininity by integration with mother (Chodorow, 1978). Although the process is undoubtedly more complex,[80] it can lead women to expect more specific kinds of social support, and men to evaluate support more globally. When asked to rate the supportiveness of a particular interaction, men's ratings reflected their pre-interaction perceptions of spousal support and marital satisfaction; women's ratings reflected the support behaviors they actually received during the interaction (Cutrona & Suhr, 1994). Thus, if a husband is dissatisfied, his wife's supportive behaviors won't help much; but if he fails to perform supportive behaviors, his wife will not be happy. So, what counts as supportive behavior?

Part of the support equation is *emotional* and part is *instrumental.* Although emotional support is important, simply getting things done affects the relationship as well. Again, each partner's needs for autonomy and connection influence how much each identifies with the relationship. Relational identity is the degree to which one defines self in terms of one's close relationships. Women more than men typically identify relationally. For wives, social support is related to relational and life satisfaction (Garrido & Acitelli, 1999), and that support includes not only reading her joy and distress (emotional), but also sharing responsibility for household work (instrumental). However, her husband's masculinity may be threatened by sharing in household duties typically performed by women. Given their opposing roles, are couples sentenced to unsatisfactory marriages? Not necessarily; Garrido and Acitelli found that the more relational one's identity is, regardless of sex, the more likely he or she was to perform household tasks traditionally seen as women's work. To spouses who recognize the importance to marital success of carrying out household tasks, this sort of shared household labor contributes to strong attachments and cohesiveness. Furthermore, "those who shared the most [household labor] were also the most likely to talk about men and women as essentially similar" (Coltrane, as cited in Garrido & Acitelli, p. 632). In dual-career marriages, this balancing act of autonomy/connection, or personal/relational, is particularly critical to success. However, there are other workable marriage configurations.

Marriage Types: Communication and Expectations.   Fitzpatrick's (1988) marriage classification scheme is based on spouses' perceptions of their interdependence and communication (affect dimensions), and ideology (gender role expectations and beliefs about control issues in marriage). From large samples of married couples of all ages emerged three types: *Traditionals* are very interdependent, expressive, and hold conventional values about marriage and their roles as spouses; *independents* are moderately interdependent, communicate very expressively, and hold nonconventional values; and *separates* are not particularly interdependent or communicatively expressive, and are ambivalent about their views of marriage (Fitzpatrick & Badzinski, 1994). Some marriages mix types, the most common being the combination of a separate (husband, usually) and a traditional (wife). In a similar vein, Gottman (1993) described three types of stable marriages according to their emotional tone: volatile couples (most expressive, similar to independents); validating couples (moderately expressive, like traditionals); and conflict avoiding couples (least expressive, like separates).

Even though both Gottman and Fitzpatrick observed a degree of stability within marriage types, married couples can change their emotional tone and role-related beliefs. For example, Peg and Ned as young adults started out as independents who believed they were not bound by gender expectations and could forge their own relational path. Then they became parents and found it just easier to apportion tasks such as cooking to the primary caregiver and shopping to the salaried worker; without explicitly identifying a new definition, the marriage became more traditional. In mid-life, as Nell left for college and Peg embarked on a graduate degree, the "couple experienced a more separate feeling, during which they had doubts about their marriage. Valuing their shared history, they sought counseling and again redefined the relationship toward the independent type. Some couples may maintain the same tone throughout their marriage, whereas others redefine it as emotions and external demands shift.

The more or less enduring marriage types have different communication qualities as well. Honeycutt (1999) noted that happily married spouses report pleasant imagined interactions, and speak of their marriages in "we" terms rather than "I" or "you" terms. Traditionals and independents may mentally anticipate or replay positive qualities of spousal interaction, resulting in relative happiness. Separates are less fond of their spouses, use fewer "we" statements, and report less excitement in their marriages, possibly indicating stagnation of the relationship. Separates' imagined dialogues with partners were less pleasant, possibly replaying old conflicts "while rehearsing for the next encounter" (Honeycutt, 1999, p. 289). Gottman (1994) suggested that separates, as conflict avoiders, live with the discomfort of unsolved, solvable problems, and become mired in them. Fearful of negative emotions, and unable to manage unavoidable conflict, their expectations rigidify and positive change becomes less likely.

Marital Conflict: Attributions, Accounts, and Gender. Conflicts will arise between any two unique identities; between spouses these conflictual issues are often about personal criticism, finances, and household chores (Erbert, 2000). The majority of couples in one community sample reported one or two unpleasant arguments per month (McGonagle, Kessler, & Schilling, 1992). Less serious conflicts, such as complaints, can be a daily occurrence for some couples.

Alberts (1989) identified five *complaint types* that married couples reported: behavioral (e.g., "You never cook a meal"), personal characteristics (e.g., "You're sloppy"), performance (e.g., "You're going to break that if you don't slow down"), complaining (e.g., "You're whining again"), and personal appearance (e.g., "Those pants are too tight"). Note that these are personal criticisms—the most common conflict theme. Dissatisfied couples are more likely to use personal characteristic complaints (Alberts, 1988), which are face threatening and likely to create defensiveness. Unlike the other complaint types, these are attributions from the speaker ("You're a nag"), unsubstantiated by behavioral descriptions that might be refuted or countered ("You've asked me four times today"). Well-adjusted couples prefer more behavioral complaints, use positive affect, and respond to complaints with agreement. However, even in the best relationships, individuals will protect themselves when they are injured.

In reporting conflict episodes to a researcher, spouses tended to emphasize their own needs and feelings, and to excuse or justify their own behavior (Schutz, 1999). However much these self-serving biases enter into *accounts* to a third party, they may be mitigated in direct interaction with the spouse. Among long-term marital couples who generally perceived their relationship quality as positive, *attributions* of responsibility were much kinder, resulting in increased willingness to forgive (Fincham, Paleari, & Regalia, 2002). Forgiveness is influenced by both cognitive (attributions) and affective (empathy) variables, but the decision process toward forgiveness varies by gender. Wives use more attributional activity to forgive, whereas husbands engage in more empathy to forgive (Fincham et al., 2002). Thus, Peg might attribute Ned's failure to remember her birthday to overwork and consequently forgive him. Ned, regardless of the reasons Peg offers for bailing out on vacation plans, forgives her because he senses she feels bad about it.

One particular pattern seems to crop up again and again in marital conflict. The much discussed *demand-withdraw* pattern occurs when women try to discuss relational problems and men respond with avoidance (Canary & Emmers-Sommer, 1997). Oddly, no such gender difference emerged from observations of actual partner interactions. Yet, in a follow-up set of self-reports of the same interactions, men complained about confrontations from their partners, but the women did not complain about partners' withdrawal behaviors (Markman, Silvern, Clements, & Kraft-Hanak, 1993). That is, although men perceived their wives as being confrontational, their wives were not as sensitive to the husbands' lack of engagement.

Canary and Emmers-Sommer (1997) proposed several explanatory factors for women's greater confrontations in personal relationships: inequity in marriage, physiological causation,[81] developmental variation, gender role identification, and marital types. Although all may contribute to some extent, we focus here on the communication implications of the fifth factor.

Traditionals are generally positive, save their direct confrontation for significant disagreements, and typically validate each other. Independents actively engage in conflict, give reasons and information, are likely to compete even over trivial issues, and are dissatisfied with avoidance as a strategy. Both these types are emotionally involved, and indeed affection appears to mitigate the negative effects of the demand-withdraw pattern (Caughlin & Huston, 2002). If positive behaviors are employed between arguments, they may diminish otherwise destructive effects (Johnson & Roloff, 2000).

Recall that separates are more or less emotionally divorced and remain married to maintain a traditional ideology without interdependence. They may effectively reach a truce by withdrawing or acquiescing early in conflict. However, the mixed type of separate husband and traditional wife demonstrates the clearest gender differences. Here, the wife seeks connection and tries to maintain conventional gender roles in which the marriage is primary for her; the husband is autonomous, protecting his feelings and avoiding confrontation (Canary & Emmers-Sommer, 1997).

Here is the perfect playground for the demand-withdraw pattern in which a dissatisfied and probably underbenefited wife confronts a closed husband who just wants to be left alone. Avoiding conflict may become, over the long haul, a relational rule that they both respect. However, it could as easily lead to distancing, unhappiness, and dissatisfaction. Arguing is not the worst that can happen, and it may be the best for some contexts.

Although *avoiding* some conflicts may be functional for the relationship, failing to confront critical relational disagreements over the long term is often dysfunctional (Canary, Cupach et al., 1995). Expressions of anger may lead to dissatisfaction in the present moment, but ultimately ends in satisfaction years after the angry interaction (Gottman & Krokoff, 1989). Thus, avoiding important marital issues (finances, household chores, parenting, time demands, etc.) can hasten the decline of a marriage.

Divorce and Remarriage: Starting Over

Marriages end for adults of all ages, but 40-somethings experience divorce most frequently. Marriages can end for many reasons, but the number one reason given for divorcing is "communication problems," followed by unhappiness, incompatibility, and emotional abuse (Aiken, 1998), all of which are undoubtedly related to interaction patterns. The divorced person, however, is single again, if temporarily. Forty percent of marriages in the United States are remarriages for at least one of the parties, and they are less stable than first marriages, with one exception: remarriage after the death of a spouse. Shortly after the divorce is the most likely time for a remarriage—for men more than for women, and for young more than middle-aged or older adults (U.S. Census Bureau, 1992).

Wives are most likely to initiate divorce, and husbands are most likely to suffer immediately following divorce, perhaps explaining their rapid remarriage rate. They feel rejection and failure, and tend to see their children less often (Ahrons & Rogers, 1987). However, women take the brunt of divorce in the long run; they usually get custody of the children, typically experience reductions in income, and with increased practical responsibilities they have fewer opportunities to find new partners (Aiken, 1998).

Can we predict which couples will divorce? Some point to husbands with low impulse control paired with highly neurotic wives (Kelly & Conley, 1987). Others suggest that early divorce is likely for those with lower incomes, less education, more children, and shorter courtships (Kurdek, 1991). But what of the communication that couples reported as the primary cause of divorce? In unhappy marriages, one partner is typically more emotionally dominant (Levenson & Gottman, 1983), and both reciprocate negative communication behaviors (Gottman, Markman, & Notarius, 1977).

Gottman (cited in Fitzpatrick & Badzinski, 1994), introduced a "cascade" model of marital decay that describes a gradual process in which spouses are unhappy, consider dissolution, separate, and ultimately divorce. The key mechanism for Gottman is "flooding," described by spouses as an experience of their partner's negative behavior as unprovoked, overwhelming, intense and "so disorganizing that they want to run away" (p. 740). And, evidently, they do.

But no matter how difficult the communication may be, couples typically separate in cycles of repeated distancing, reconciliation, renewed withdrawal, and so forth until they reach equilibrium (Weiss, 1975). Weiss (1975) attributed this approach-avoidance dance to the strength of attachment bonds that keep spouses together even after love fades. Recall that attachment gives rise to comfort when the attachment figure is present and distress when he or she is not. The strength of these bonds goes a long way toward explaining why partners may continue an abusive or dysfunctional relationship beyond what an observer might consider reasonable.

When they do part, partners are likely to engage in "grave dressing" (Duck, 1982) that is, come up with a story of the relationship that tells its history and allocates blame. Women are more likely to relate the dissolution of their relationship to interpersonal problems (e.g., conflict, disclosure failures), whereas men refer to more external factors (e.g., too many work demands; Hill, Rubin, & Peplau, 1976).

Ex-Spousal Relationships: Shaky Shifts. Divorced couples, particularly those with children, continue their relationships (Fitzpatrick & Badzinski, 1994), but must reconfigure them. A part of that process is what Hagestad and Smyer (1982) called "decathecting" or withdrawing emotional energy from the partner while continuing emotional energy with children. Not only do ex-spouses have to transfer their attachment to more appropriate intimates, but negative feelings may keep them from shifting the relationship to a more functional status (Coleman & Ganong, 1995).

Reconfiguring a spouse relationship occurs in the context of other relationships, and is often assisted by network members including the ex-spouses' children, friends, kin, new partners and their networks, coworkers, professionals, and so forth (Coleman & Ganong, 1995). Part of the function of network members is to listen in the "grave dressing" phase to the story of the relationship, thus giving ex-spouses opportunities to express their feelings and create a new story for the relationship.

Using stories told by middle-aged ex-spouses, Masheter (1994) described the strategies they employed to cope with the oppositions involved in shifting to former-spouse status. She found that some pairs of ex-spouses chose similar strategies, whereas others' choices were more complementary. For example, many of the women in her study were "openers" of taboo topics while the men were "closers" thus engaging in complementary topic segmentation. In another twist, some ex-husbands used unilateral neutralization when confronted about extramarital affairs, changing the subject, or counteraccusing. Bilateral neutralization—mutual avoidance—was also used to keep couples vaguely floating between poles of openness/closedness and autonomy/connectedness.

In less functional couples, Masheter (1994) found evidence of over-connectedness, a version of the selection strategy in which partners may abuse and withdraw, submit and threaten, all in the name of staying together. Some partners recounted series of typical episodes (the same argument over and over) punctuated by an atypical episode now and again that introduced novelty by way of cyclic alternation. In one example, a woman reported an "I-have-decided pronouncement" from her ex-husband that he was taking a job in Saudi Arabia to earn a higher salary. She supported his decision when he expected an argument, and he was so moved that he wept in a rare emotional display. She described this episode as a "peak experience in communicating with another person" (p. 93).

Perhaps the most function strategy, reframing, occurs when the parties find a new synthesis of oppositions. In one case, an ex-wife reported a turning point when her ex-husband gave her a complex camera for her business trips. Although puzzled because he had never before given her a gift except through the children and because he had belittled her technical abilities, she accepted it but resisted his "bossiness" and did not use it until she was ready. She saw her ex-husband as being open to her in a new way (giving her a gift that spelled respect) and she felt connected to him in a very different sense (as a competent equal). Masheter noted that all of these strategies may be functional depending on the context. Neutralizing by evasion may seem to be dysfunctional, but in the case of extramarital affairs, both parties may collude to avoid immediate pain and separation. Redefining intimate relationships as close as these takes time and care. But what of those marrieds left without the opportunity to redefine?

Death of a Spouse: Permanent Loss

Some spouses will face the premature death of their life partner. The unexpected loss of such a close attachment is likely to provoke anxiety and "searching" behaviors for the lost spouse (Bowlby, 1980). According to attachment theory, the survivor's attachment style is associated with predictable responses to grief. The anxious attachment type, who was likely to be in a dependent relationship (Parkes & Weiss, 1983), experiences chronic grief characterized by prolonged helplessness and excessive care seeking. The avoidant attachment type, who probably had a conflictual relationship, experiences delayed or absent grief. Delayed grief is characterized by minimal immediate distress followed by intense grief sparked by a later reminder of the death. Absent grief is characterized by a lack of overt grief accompanied by active grief-suppressing behaviors (e.g., taking care of others, overwork, overmedication) that often lead to long-term maladjustment. Field and Sunden (2001) tested Bowlby's propositions among mid-life bereaved spouses, and found support for the connection between anxious attachment and coping difficulty. The compulsive care seeking of anxious survivors was associated with greater emotional distancing, positive feelings for the deceased, and long-term maladjustment. Contrary to Bowlby's position, Field and Sunden did not find a relationship between avoidant attachment and maladjustment. Either the avoidant is less emotionally invested, or a degree of avoidance may be functional in bereavement. In the next chapter, we look at the more expected loss of an older partner.

Family Bonds

Children: Bonding and Letting Go

Experienced parents know that they will ultimately release children from the safe nest of home—or at least they used to. Now, confused older parents are having to reline the empty nest as many of their offspring are winging back for another crack at safe dependency. Although there are many well-publicized cases of mid-lifers starting families, the peak childbearing years are in the late 20s (Saluter, 1996), leaving most parents in their early 50s with a child-free home, if briefly. However, when adult children experience economic misfortune or personal difficulties, they often come home, leaving "the sandwich generation" (Dobson & Dobson, 1985) to cope with their position as "responsible adults" between dependent adult children and dependent aging parents. To make things a bit more complex, many families now are blended, consisting of birth children and stepchildren, biological parents and stepparents. When parents feel that they have fulfilled their parenting duties, they are ready to "accept [the] grown child's separateness and individuality, while maintaining the connection ..." (Galinsky, 1981, p. 307). However, the "departure stage" of parenting may not be as clear as earlier parenting transitions are.

During the first pregnancy, prospective parents imagine what it will be like to experience parenthood. Galinsky's "image-making" stage involves preparing for shifts in roles, and for feelings toward an actual child to supercede those for the imaginary one (as cited in Wapner, 1993). Once the main task—to form an attachment with the child—is accomplished, "nurturing" begins in loving care and attentive interaction. When the child begins to assert his or her own will, the "authority" stage begins, with parents learning to set limits, wield power, and deal with the myriad tensions involved in conflict, discipline, and the oppositions of protection and independence, restriction and liberation. When children can begin to reason and understand causation, parents must interpret the world for their children, answering questions, giving them access to skills and knowledge, and assisting in the formation of values (Galinsky, cited in Wapner, 1993). The "interpretive" stage—the bulk of parenting until puberty—demands careful balancing of parental and child needs, of parental and child perspectives.

In the "interdependent" stage of parenting (Galinsky, 1981), parents have to shift their concept of authority, and negotiate a new relationship with the adolescent child, rebalancing the tension between autonomy and connection (Wapner, 1993). Parents who are optimistic about their teens' futures begin to release power and grant autonomy (Pratt, et al., 2001). As departure looms, parents deal with conflicting needs: to release control, welcome their own freedom, and mourn their loss. However, some parents will find that these transitions work very differently for them. The realities of divorce and remarriage often mean that one parent will have to relinquish the residential aspects of parenting; the parent–child separation will be premature.

Blending Families: Stepping In and Out of Family Configurations. The traditional term *stepfamily,* as "at least two adults who provide continued care for at
least one child who is not the biological offspring of both adults" (Turner & West,
2002, p. 25), has been supplanted in some quarters by the term *blended family.* The
proponents of the latter wish to avoid the negative connotations of *stepfamily* and
to promote the emphasis on integration of new members to the unit (Baxter,
Braithwaite, & Nicholson, 1999). Those who retain the older term are bothered by
the implication that children lose their connection to the "unblended" parent
(Turner & West, 2002). No matter what we call it, a reorganization of family members is inevitable once living arrangements change.

When divorced or widowed parents decide to remarry, they may assume that
stepparenting is like parenting in a biological family, but Juroe and Juroe (1983)
pointed out the key difference: The stepparent is literally "stepping in" to assume
responsibility for raising another person's child. Given what we know about the
importance of attachment—and the early internalization of parental values,
communication patterns, and emotional expression—literally "stepping" into
someone else's parental role is not likely. Additionally, the tension between the
freely chosen marriage relationship and the accompanying and more imposed
stepparent relationship describes a dialectic particular to the blended family
(Cissna, Cox, & Bochner, 1990).

According to remarried parents, the first step in managing this dialectical tension
is to establish the solidarity of the marriage, setting some general *rules for family organization* (Cissna et al., 1990). These rules amount to assumptions underlying the reorganization they face: "a credible marriage is the core of the family," "the natural
family is an 'idealized' model for the stepfamily," and the statement made by the act of
stepmarriage itself–"the symbolic declaration that it is possible for them to succeed in
reorganizing" (Cissna et al., 1990, p. 57). The remarried parents form their coalition
through direct communication between them that explicitly defines their relationships in the reorganizing process. Cissna and his colleagues (1990) proposed that very
high or very low levels of such metacommunication may be dysfunctional; however,
they also observed that some spouses used very high levels with each other, and very
low levels with children. What may be critical is how and when such couples choose
to metacommunicate and how it is interpreted by the others.

The second task is to use the marital solidity to *establish the credibility of the stepparent* as an authority (Cissna et al., 1990). Clearly, to be perceived by the children,
authority first must be communicated by the parents, so that the reorganization
may proceed. Not only must the natural parent trust the stepparent's abilities, but
the child must come to trust the stepparent as well. Often, the natural parent's attitude can negate a stepparent's authority, undermining the relationship between
child and stepparent. As Cissna et al. suggested, "The internal dialectic between love
and affection on the one hand and discipline and authority on the other is especially
problematic in the stepfamily" (1990, p. 56).

So, given these tasks for blended families, how might they move through this
process of reorganization? Baxter et al. (1999) identified turning points in *the process of becoming a blended family.* Turning points are "transformative events" that

change relationships in important ways; they are the "sites of developmental change in relationships" (p. 294). From parents, stepparents, children, and stepchildren, reports were gathered about the transitions experienced in the first 4 years of blended family history. Of 15 transitions identified, the most frequent turning point concerned changes in household composition. These structural changes included remarriage and/or cohabitation, children's visits from or to a nonresident parent, and various shifts in family membership. Next in frequency were conflict transitions, followed understandably by reconciliation points, and then by the positively valued holidays, and quality-time events. Families experienced these turning points at different speeds and with different consequences to describe five clusters or developmental trajectories.

Baxter et al. (1999) found that the first and second trajectories account for almost 60% of the case families. The *accelerated trajectory* (#1) is a pattern of rapid movement toward member agreement on "feeling like a family" (FLF), during which members experienced mostly positive turning points. *The prolonged trajectory* (#2) reflects a slower movement from lower-base levels of FLF to progressively higher levels, again with positive turning points.

The next most frequent trajectory (#3) was labeled *high-amplitude turbulent* for its "roller coaster effect" created by rapid, high-amplitude change points with accompanying rapid increases and decreases in FLF levels. These dramatic and unstable families experienced great highs and lows in rapid succession.

The final two clusters ended the 4-year period at fairly low FLF levels. The *stagnating trajectory* (#4) showed low FLF at the start, which remained low throughout the 48 months. The *declining trajectory* (#5) showed very high levels of FLF at the start, which gradually and progressively declined to extremely low levels, experiencing mostly negative turning points along the way.

Both turbulent and declining types started out with very high FLF, but the declining pattern was characterized by many more negative than positive events. Disappointment of expectations seems to capture this type, whereas turbulent families who ended higher may hang on despite instability because of the high points they anticipate after the lows. The accelerated families started out with moderate FLF but experienced mostly positive events and low conflict, ending the 4-year period with the highest levels of FLF. The prolonged types started out lower in FLF but gradually rose in familyness. Stagnating families simple never "caught fire" as a family and stayed low throughout.

The factors contributing to blended family success apparently include beginning the venture with at least moderate levels of family feeling, balancing conflict with reconciliation, and managing to experience some quality time and enjoyable holidays together. How the newly married parents handle the restructuring at the start is probably critical. Their degree of cohesiveness as a couple, as well as their expectations for children and stepchildren, will affect this mix. Confounding the process is the fact that parents do favor their own children (White, 1994). Even though they were less supportive of their own children following divorce, they were least supportive of stepchildren. This is not to imply that good steprelationships cannot be formed, but they are apparently easier when the stepparent has no biological children, and when the relationships are positive between parent and stepparent, and between biological parent and child. Although *The Brady Bunch* may not be a realistic model of mid-life blending, it is possible for conscious, motivated remarrieds to handle the turning points with grace, if not constant raucous optimism.

Aging Parents: Nurturing Shifts

Sometime in mid-life, we will all have to face the fact of our parents' mortality, even as we are beginning to consider our own. Given increased life expectancies and lowered birth rates, the frail elderly live longer but have fewer children on whom to depend. Today's married couples often have more parents than children, and family relationships cross generational lines more than ever (Halpern, 1994). Not only will mid-lifers be faced with the needs of dependent parents, but their adult children are often returning home. When roles among the generations shift, conflict and dissatisfaction arise. Elderly parents are no longer in the authority position, adult children are no longer identifying with parental rules, and the "sandwich" generation feels the squeeze on their resources—emotional and material.

Among middle-aged siblings, women report about 50% more calls, visits, and assistance to parents than do men. But as the number of siblings in a family increases, the numbers of calls and visits declines; that is, they spread out the responsibilities (Spitze & Logan, 1991). Contrary to a common belief that children do not take care of their elderly parents, the majority of older Americans have regular contact with their children (Cicirelli, 1981). Nonetheless, 60% of daughters who already provided care to a parent felt guilty about not doing enough (Brody, 1985).

Much of the pressure for parental care falls to women; they are the "kinkeepers" (Leach & Braithwaite, 1996). Just as middle-aged mothers are finishing their parenting duties and returning to work or school (Halpern, 1994), they find that their aging relations need them more then ever. Of children who were primary caregivers to elderly parents, 75% have been women, many of whom also worked full time (Halpern, 1994). Cantor (1983) explored the new relationship between aging parent and adult child, finding that the adult caregivers did not feel understood by the parent, and only about half felt they got along well with the parent. The longer that ill or incapacitated parents continued to be dependent, the more dissatisfied they felt with their caregivers (Johnson & Catalano, 1983). Likely responses to this sort of relational strain are distancing or intensifying the relationship. In particular, adult daughters try to maintain close contact while increasing psychological distance by including other family members in care. Other caregivers intensify their total commitment, withdrawing from other social relationships and risking burnout and isolation (Johnson & Catalano, 1983). How might communication temper this sort of dichotomous choice between intensifying and minimizing the care relationship?

Caught in the middle of conflicting impulses to respect their parents' autonomy and to respond to their parents' dependency needs, middle-aged caregiving children may try to approach communication with the parent in such a polite manner that they risk being ineffective. In dealing with elderly parents, women of all ages groups (22–29, 40–55, and over 65) considered both direct and indirect control strategies as more nurturing than no control at all (Morgan & Hummert, 2000).[82] However, middle-aged women considered the direct control message as less respectful than did younger and older women. When adult daughters perceive that their elderly parents are no longer performing daily tasks well, they are likely to suggest assistance indirectly, at least at first (e.g., "Dad, are you happy with the way the lawn looks?").

Perceived incompetence in the elderly contributes to a general assumption that adult children should take more control of their parents' affairs. However, among nursing home residents, communication that encourages dependence can lead to increased dependency, whereas communication that stimulates independence leads to autonomy (Baltes & Wahl, 1996). Therefore, supportive communication may lead to an unfortunate dependency pattern, as we discuss in the next chapter.

The stress of caring for an elderly parent affects not only the adult child's relationship with the parent, but also that with the spouse. Even among long-term couples, married 33 years on average, marital satisfaction decreased after a parent moved into the adult child's home (Bethea, 2002), but increased slightly among similar couples who did not have a parent in the home. Bethea suggested that communication patterns may be disrupted by the additional presence. Less time for private talk can affect couples' opportunities to discuss their own needs as individuals and as couples. Suitor and Pillemer's 1994 study (cited in Bethea, 2002, p. 120) found that wives' new caregiving roles and duties affected marital quality such that husbands withdrew emotional support and/or interfered with caregiving. Undoubtedly, more families will be facing the responsibility for parental care as the "boomers" enter their golden years, and parental care may become a normative expectation for middle-aged couples. Not only are there few role models, given that previous generations typically lost their parents earlier, but research into adaptive communication for spouses and their dependent parents is just beginning. The generation caught in the middle is now having to figure out how to cope with their extended nurturing roles.

Death of a Parent: Letting Go of Primary Attachment Figures

Middle-aged children are likely to have to make end-of-life decisions for parents. One of those is whether to prolong a difficult and painful life or to allow a dignified death. Leichtentritt and Rettig (1999) studied end-of-life decisions among Israelis in their 40s and 50s. Capable moral problem solvers, they considered the issue of passive euthanasia in four contexts: for a citizen, for self, for a partner, and for a parent. A parent's death elicited the strongest emotional reactions and most difficult struggles in reaching a decision. They clearly distinguished their own death from parent's death. As one put it, "We just die our own death, with the death of others we have to live" (Leichtentritt & Rettig, 1999, p. 401). The death of a parent provides another opportunity for individuation, as we detail in the next chapter, but it also is a poignant and difficult loss of a primary attachment figure.

Generative Relationships: Beyond Parenting

One of the challenges of our middle years is to achieve some sense of our contribution to future generations. Although parents can point to their children as concrete manifestations of their contribution, many will choose to contribute beyond the biological to those who seek the wisdom they earned in experience. Opportunities to share expertise and energy are particularly important for those who, by choice or circumstance, did not have children. Recall that self-esteem in maturity often rests more on our relationships with colleagues and friends than with kin. Fending off stagnation in the link between self and society (Keyes & Ryff, 1998), mid-lifers are finding opportunities to leave a legacy in mentoring and other forms of guidance to initiates.

Mentor/Mentee

Those who have been in the workforce for 20-plus years are often senior members or administrators who can affect decisions about the organization, and can manifest their vision of the organization they know so well. Furthermore, they can share that vision, as well as the process that formed it, with younger members. Anderson and Hayes (1996) commented, "A mentor is a guide or exemplar in dealing with the central concerns of an individual's life" (p.151). Given our assumptions about internalizing significant interactions, identification does not end in childhood but instead throughout life contributes to self-worth, mastery, and creativity. As we begin any new task—be it material, spiritual, or intellectual—we look to "masters" for cues. If we are fortunate, we find one willing to share the mysteries of his or her mastery.

Although much of the research on mentoring has focused on its importance to men, recent attention has turned to women's needs, particularly as they formulate or return to careers in mid-life. The advantages bestowed by a mentor are not limited to the young; anyone embarking on a new path needs a guide. Certainly, young adults need mentors as much as ever, but older adults continue to change throughout life in response to crises and personal renewal. Mentors can assist the integration of the old self with the new in shaping and reshaping identity.

In a sample survey concerning retirement and self-esteem, 75% of respondents reported having had a mentor, and 60% felt that the mentor had influenced their life's direction (Anderson & Hayes, 1996). But how did this influence occur? What communication patterns or events were internalized? Unfortunately, most of the research uses the term *mentoring* in reference to training programs or strategies for retention in educational or work settings. Although we know much about superior–subordinate communication in organizations, the subtleties of other sorts of interpersonal communication in work settings, including mentoring, remain unclear.

Close relationships seem more likely among senior members of an organization who share equal status, work experiences, and mastery (Wilensky, 1968); whereas among younger colleagues competition for upward movement may interfere with friendly relationships. Between those of unequal status, wherein mentor relationships can flourish, there are barriers. Subordinates have a lot to gain or lose by such a relationship, and superiors have few incentives unless the impulse to generativity exists. Levinson, Darrow, Klein, Levinson, and McKee (1979) noted that the mentor relationship openly acknowledges its inequality and its primary aim as the junior person's advancement. Furthermore, the mentor/protégé relationship cannot qualify as a friendship until the junior is able to successfully stand alone and the relationship can be renegotiated on more equal terms (Rawlins, 1992).

Those who achieve the highest levels of success in their careers have typically been mentored (Vaillant, 1977), and that trend continues in the academic profession. Assistant professors with multiple mentoring sources, both within and outside the workplace, achieved higher levels of both objective and subjective success than those with one or no mentor (Peluchette & Jeanquart, 2000). Although protégés are positive about the value of their mentoring relationship, they are relatively unaware that their mentors also may benefit (Campbell & Campbell, 2000). One former protégé, Eleanor Covan (2000), reflected on her relationship with her mentor, Anselm Strauss, when recalling her work on modeling processes between elder models and their apprentices. In revisiting Strauss' mentoring role, Covan found that when mentors *consciously* model their roles, they perform "interactional work that is essential for social reproduction" (p. S7). That is, they contribute to cultural maintenance in a future-oriented fashion.

The mentor who can function generatively in such a conscious fashion may well be using advanced perspective-taking abilities of the kind available to dialogical thinkers. Basseches (1984a) described "stage 5 reasoning" as the "ability to criticize existing systems and justify more ideal ones using ... arguments that claim to take all people's perspectives" (p. 273). In the workplace, the stage 5 thinker adopts an "ideal observer" stance to problems, going beyond "efforts to reconcile the needs of the existing systems with those of constituent groups and individuals" (p. 350). This is the person who can consciously bring about organizational transformations in light of community or cultural needs, and convey his or her vision and ideals to protégés.

Friendships

The great divide for adult friendships is marriage. Despite the appeal of viewing spouses as friends, the realities of marriage and parenthood mitigate against achieving this relatively modern ideal (Rawlins, 1992). *Close friendships* are voluntary, equal relationships, oriented to the "person-qua-person," characterized by equality, trust, support, help, discussion, nonsexual affection, and caring (Suttles, 1970). With good reason, marriages are legally binding, sexual, and often instrumental relationships. That is, what the person does is at least as important as who the person is, per se (person-qua-person). Friends affirm each other's individuality; spouses depend on each other to fulfill parenting and spousal roles. A further effect of marital interdependence is the promotion of couple friendships they can share, and the discouragement of the solitary pursuit of friendships (Rawlins, 1992). *Couple friendships* are often recruited by spouses through work, and maintained by wives, on whom fall the duties of organizing the couple's social life (Gerstel, 1988). Although they do the lion's share of social tasks, wives continue to value at least one close female friend and confidant, whereas husbands typically consider their wives as their best friends (Oliker, 1989). Thus, married couples typically include couple friends, kin, and neighbors in their support systems.

In mid-life, the friendship patterns become entrenched. The number of men who see best friends regularly drops from 73% of single, young men to 36% of middle-aged fathers (Stueve & Gerson, 1977). However, women's friendships increase after their childbearing years (Fischer & Oliker, 1983). Mid-life finds women expanding their friendship pool, and men contracting. Even though mid-life brings changes that could be supported by a close friend, men have had little practice with the sort of "talking" friendships that women have cultivated. Even though men find cross-sex friendships more nurturing than same-sex ones, married men are much less likely than unmarried men to have women friends (Rawlins, 1992).

Research about friendship in mid-life is hard to come by. However, we can surmise that married men expend a great deal of their relational energy on family demands and collegial contacts, and have limited cultural training or opportunity to manifest close friendships. Women, whose friendships are likely to be "talking friendships" (Gouldner & Strong, 1987), and who are expected to maintain the social system for the family, are more likely to maintain close friendships. What effects does this differential benefiting from friendships have? The plight of middle-aged men was well portrayed by Jack Nicholson in *About Schmidt*. Warren Schmidt felt more connected to an African child he'd never met than to the friends and relatives in his life. However, that was fiction.

The truth is, we really don't know all that much about how men meet their social needs beyond spousal interaction. We do know that most remarry after the end of a marriage, but not all. The predominantly male samples in the mentoring research give us a hint; mentoring may provide the sort of sharing and expressiveness that women find in close friendships. Many men identify deeply with their careers, which is one of the hallmarks of a mentor. We are less certain whether women who devote much of their adult lives to parenting feel the same kinds of generative needs. A reasonable guess would be that generativity can be achieved by way of a variety of relationships, and that stagnation is more likely when relationships are limited and relatively static.

CONCLUSION: GENERATIVITY AND STAGNATION

Stagnation Complexities: Rigidity and Spiritual Death

As middle-age progresses, physical deterioration can no longer be denied, and younger colleagues edge into the career niches that require stamina. In our mid-40s, we begin to suspect that we are careening downhill and wonder if there are any surprises left. We've had the kids and mastered the career; but the kids have moved on and the mentees are eager to take on challenges that are easy for us. What's next?

We can no longer be rescued by parents; they either need our help or have died. We can decide we are done and glide, ghostlike, toward death; or we can recognize that a transition is immanent and avoid it, thus stopping our development and dying in effect; or we can release the old life and embrace a new set of challenges, a new life.

Generativity Complexities: Keeping the Meaning

Having mastered the tasks of "first adulthood," said Sheehy (1995), we find now that there is plenty of time left after empty nest, after early retirement, after menopause, after widowhood. Indeed, time for another life. Sheehy (1995) noted, "We have broken the evolutionary code" (p. 137) by moving out of the "normal" life span that had been defined by reproduction and then decline. Beyond mere survival, we now have the time to master life rather than simply react to its events. In the transition from "the old age of youth" (Sheehy, 1995, p. 45) to the "youth of Second Adulthood" (p. 50), we mourn our physical losses before rebirth into a more spiritually focused life. This "search for meaning" (p.148) is the meditative stroll through the maze of the potential selves we denied when we climbed on the roller coaster ride of career and parenting. One important step toward integration and authenticity is accepting one's own mortality. In facing the limits of life, we can choose to stop and wait for time to catch up with us, or we can find new value in life. With the additional time bestowed by medical technology, improved nutrition, and healthy exercise habits, we can choose to pursue our passions without reproductive responsibilities or the constant pressure to amass wealth. We can continue to mentor, to deepen friendships, to explore spirituality, to expand creativity.

NOTES

80. See Dinnerstein's *The Mermaid and the Minotaur* (1977) for a deeper treatment of the complexities of feminine and masculine identification.
81. Gottman (1994) and his colleagues (and others cited in Canary & Emmers-Sommer, 1997, p. 88) found that men are more negatively aroused when participating in conflict than are women. Men's heart rates rise, among other symptoms, they take longer to recover from this "flooding," and they are more aware of it than are women. That is, such confrontations are physiologically unpleasant to the point of a "cascading" negative affect.
82. Morgan and Hummert (2000) used a scenario in which 52-year-old Brenda notices, after knocking a book to the floor, a stack of unpaid bills flutter from it. When 72-year-old Mary asks what she is doing, Brenda might reply in one of three ways: "Well, I accidentally knocked over this book, and these overdue bills and this eviction notice fell out ..."

Direct control:	"Now, now, don't you worry about a thing. I'll straighten all of this out in no time."
Indirect control:	"Let me know if there is anything I can do to help. I'd be glad to sit down and help you straighten this situation out. You know how good we are at solving problems when we put our heads together."
No control:	"Well, I'm sure you'll work things out."

Going to funerals seems to be my major social activity lately. But the crowd gets smaller and smaller every year. I will miss Amy terribly. Almost as much as I miss Ned. Was it really 7 years ago? It seems like yesterday. And now Amy's gone.

Well, I'm getting out of these fussy clothes and into my sweats. I want to finish planting those seedlings before Nell and Anna come for dinner. This little kitchen is just enough, usually. It'll be a little crowded with three of us in here creating our specialties, but worth the chaos. That Anna is a pistol. Only 7 and she loves to make her chocolate pudding almost as much as she loves to hear my stories of the "olden days." Olden days indeed. Fabulous times we had....

Peg has outlived her husband and many of her friends. Her apartment is in an assisted living facility, where she is active in art classes and occasional tours. Nell, Pablo, and Anna live nearby and she looks forward to their visits, although she only visits them if invited. She hasn't forgotten how important privacy is to a young family. As she tells her stories to Anna, she realizes that she can feel good about a life well lived. She wouldn't change a thing, even the shadowy patches.

Chapter 11

Older Adulthood: Power
in Drawing Together and Falling Apart

Inside this new love, die.
Your way begins on the other side ...
Slide out the side. Die,
and be quiet. Quietness is the surest sign
that you've died.
Your old life was a frantic running
from silence.

The speechless full moon
comes out now.

(Rumi, quoted in Barks, 1995, p. 22)

TIME AND TENSIONS IN THE LATER YEARS

Releasing old habits and beliefs in the transition to "the age of integrity" (Sheehy, 1995, p. 345) can leave the elder with the serenity of feeling whole at last. Not literally dead, not yet, but dead to the old life of "frantic running" and reborn to the fullness of life. Because life expectancy has lengthened so dramatically, we may reach retirement age waiting for decrepitude to descend, and if it doesn't, we awaken to a new and liberating portion of life.

Erikson's dialectic of the final stage of life is integrity/despair: acceptance of the authentic life well lived and/or surrender to the belief that it is too late to create another. Sheehy called it the "hunger for harmony" and identified resilience and self-mastery as critical characteristics for elders reaching for integrity (p. 356). Moore (1992) addressed the dialogic nature of integrity directly: "Care of the soul means not taking sides when there is a conflict at a deep level. It may be necessary to stretch the heart wide enough to embrace contradiction and paradox" (p. 14). When the constant "tasking" of middle age slows down, there enters the time and freedom to feel both

295

despair and integrity. Moore noted, "When we can let go of the need to be free of complexity and confusion" (p. 304) we embrace our dialectical natures and accept dialogically the range of experience from despair to integrity. We can rediscover how to play and love and live, but this time from a more conscious vantage point. Is this heightened appreciation universal? Probably not. For some, the disintegrative aspects of aging may overwhelm the integrative possibilities.

Falling Apart: Aging Realities

Aging is inevitable and progressive, but the effects on cognition and communication are neither inevitable nor entirely negative. Certainly we slow down, which means reaction times increase and thus motor tasks like driving can be affected. But what of interaction behaviors?

Speech Physiology and Age

Spoken communication can be affected by slowed motor function, as well as by less efficient laryngeal musculature (Kahane, 1981), changes in dentition such as tooth loss, and the side effects of commonly used drugs on the soft tissues of the mouth (Maxim & Bryan, 1994). Hearing problems increase with age as well. These cumulative effects on auditory function are known collectively as presbyacusis, and include less sensitive hearing, particularly to higher-pitched voices and whispering; and reduced understanding of rapid speech, speech in a noisy environment, or by telephone (Maxim & Bryan, 1994). These effects can mean difficulties with conversation, and can ultimately lead to social withdrawal (Falconer, 1986).

Cognitive Function and Age

Working memory declines; semantic memory persists (Salthouse, 1988). With age, the difficulty of processing complex communicative tasks increases and results in slower word retrieval, particularly with proper names (Cohen, 1994). However, elders often substitute pronouns for proper names, adapting to the retrieval problem (Ulatowska, Cannito, Hayashi, & Fleming, 1985), but giving the impression of vagueness and lack of precision (e.g., "Would you get that for me? That thing over there").

The good news is that the verbal skills associated with "crystallized" intelligence (learned, symbolic forms) do not change much with age (Cattell, 1963). Language-mediated tasks resist the effects of aging in general, although specific functions such as word fluency tasks and effortful attention do decline (Maxim & Bryan, 1994). Interestingly, episodic memory may be more sensitive to environmental context than to age, per se. Elders in residential care recalled more from their earlier lives, whereas those living independently recalled more recent events (Holland & Rabbitt, 1991).

Istomina (cited in Labouvie-Vief, 1982b, p. 169) proposed a qualitative change in the aging memory. Although memory for immediate detail declines markedly later in life, memory for logical relationships mediated by active abstraction improves. These higher-order abstractions may be more important for development in the later years, when verbatim recall of detail gives way for the retrieval of more general principles. When Peg and her niece, Emma, are in a car accident, Emma recalls the time of day; the other car's make, color, and year; and the cross-street. Peg remembers that the young man in the other car appeared to be impaired (based on his gait, gaze, and word choice) and that Emma was remarkably calm and efficient given the situation (the side impact was unanticipated, Peg was injured, and the other driver wandered in circles). Peg concluded that Emma was not at fault, and could probably back up the general principles she derived by tracking the connections between the behaviors she observed.

Along the lines of "use it or lose it," the "disuse" hypothesis predicts that intellectually engaging activities buffer the general cognitive decline expected in old age (Salthouse, 1991). Although cross-sectional studies support this theory, longitudinal designs more adequate to the question reveal that those with higher levels of intellectual ability, education, and socioeconomic status are more likely to develop an engaged lifestyle that, in turn, helps to maintain verbal intelligence (Gold et al., 1995). More support for the disuse hypothesis comes from Hultsch, Hertzog, Small, and Dixon (1999), who found no relationship between changes in active lifestyle (physical and social activities) and changes in general cognitive functioning; however, they did find a relationship between novel information processing (intellectual activity) and changes in working memory. They point out that an individual's selected activity patterns are shaped by educational background and economic resources; thus, high-ability adults lead intellectually active lives as long as they are able. Hence, it pays to be intellectually active early, often, and as long as possible. A friend of mine, a retired teacher, has the habit of starting his day with crossword puzzles until he is alert enough to read, and only after his "brain is awake" does he schedule physical exercise and social activity. Those who can continue to think effectively are more likely to be socially effective as well, insofar as social cognition informs competent interaction.

Making attributions is one form of social cognition we use to understand others; social perspective taking is another. Older adults make more trait-diagnostic inferences about people based on their behavior (Hess & Auman, 2001); that is, they attend to behaviors that reliably and logically predict a trait characteristic (e.g., a person who steals is dishonest, as opposed to concluding that a person who returns lost money is honest). They conclude that an age-related increase in social expertise about the motivations for others' behaviors results in the procedural knowledge that allows accurate attributions. Thus, the wisdom of age allows accurate judgments of others, although they may become more difficult to express.

Such procedural knowledge becomes more automatized after a lifetime of interaction experiences from which to build categories of people, whereas perspective taking is a capacity for understanding particular others and what makes them unique. A common complaint about older adults is that they are egocentric; they no longer socialize their perspectives. Looft and Charles (1971) proposed that older persons regress to egocentrism as their social interaction opportunities decrease. In comparing young (college age) and old (age 66–91) adults, they found the young adults more capable of decentering, and the older adults more egocentric. Subsequent studies tested the assumption that inter-personal losses contribute to declines in perspective taking, and found that training and feedback improved performance. Schultz and Hoyer (1975) discerned that feedback on a test of egocentrism increased elders' perspective-taking scores; Isquick (1981) provided empathy training to older adults (age 52–78) and increased not only their empathy scores, but also their self-exploration (willingness to talk about personal feelings) scores. Practice in listening and understanding another's views improved competence on both sides of expressivity—disclosure and empathic listening.

However, all elders will not value these social skills equally. Some will choose to practice them and some will not. The key to that motivation may lie in temperamental differences.

Temperament and Age

You might think that personality traits linked to biology would remain more or less stable throughout life; but McCrae and his colleagues (McCrae et al., 2000) noted some evidence for maturational trends in temperament. They found declines from age 18 to 30 in neuroticism, extraversion, and openness to experience, and increases in conscientiousness and agreeableness. After 30, the same trends continue, but the rate of change slows. McCrae et al. proposed that these maturational trends may be evolutionary in that the first three factors could be useful in finding a mate, and the last two more important in raising a family. In any case, these general trends, which stabilize after 30, are undoubtedly complemented or tempered by cultural settings and individual experience. Indeed, emotions and moods (states) are more changeable than are traits, and thus have more to do with current circumstance such as physical decline or relational loss.

Expressive Effects of Aging

Gradually, the grammatical complexity of speech declines, as does idea density per number of words produced (Kemper, Greiner, Marquie, Prenovost, & Mitzner, 2001)—the "blah blah blah" factor. These are largely physiological effects, because differences in education or experience did not mediate them, although intellectual activity (in this case, years spent teaching) did moderate the decline. The combined influences of slower speech production and information processing on language production effected increases in the number of filler phrases (Obler & Albert, 1981) and hesitant interjections (Gordon, Hutchinson & Allen, 1976, cited in Maxim & Bryan, 1994) used by the elderly. However, the elderly excelled in other areas. Older storytellers used more elaborated language than younger ones did (Obler, 1980), and their stories were perceived as being clearer and more interesting than those of younger tellers (Kemper, Kynette, Rash, O'Brien, & Sprott, 1989). In written communication, elders used more complex language constructions, including more embedded sentences, than did younger writers (Obler, Mildworf, & Albert, 1977).

Impressions of Age

Age is one of the attributes of a speaker that is identifiable in the absence of visual cues. Loss of elasticity and muscle power in the larynx and lungs result in decreased vital capacity and pitch changes (see discussion in Maxim & Bryan, 1994, p. 8). Listeners perceive these effects as lower volume or power, higher pitch, and slower speech production. Judgments of older voices as weak, slow, and frail are based on vocal changes, but judgments beyond those are based on stereotypes either formed from limited exposure to elders or perpetuated in media examples of seniors.

In one of Giles' series of studies on age and class effects (reported in Giles, Fox, Harwood, & Williams, 1994), an actor in his 30s produced several versions of the same message. In the "elderly" condition, he was judged by young adults to be 62. Part of the actor's message included the comment "I didn't know what to think." When the speaker sounded young, the young participants reported that he wished "to withhold judgment given the complexity of issues at hand." When he sounded old, they reported that he was "confused" and, furthermore, that he was "egocentric, living in the past, and talking of trivia" (p. 133). Note that these judgments were based on the very same message in both conditions.

Another perception of elders' communication skills is underaccommodation, or failure to sufficiently socialize one's contributions for a listener. Indeed, Coupland, Coupland, and Giles (cited in Nussbaum, Hummert, Williams, & Harwood, 1996, p. 21) found that, in intergenerational discourse, elderly women spent more of their talk time disclosing personally painful information than did their young conversational partner. Coupland et al. suggested that the older women did not use their full complement of topics; that, in the effort to reveal themselves, they "chained" negative exchanges, reinforcing negative stereotypes and triggering underaccommodating, overaccommodating, or patronizing responses.

Younger interactants may choose to respond to perceived elderly incompetence by overaccommodating; tilting their heads and nodding profusely (Giles et al, 1994). Another option is to patronize the older conversant by simplifying grammar, vocabulary, and articulation; trivializing the content; and employing a demeaning tone, either overly familiar or overbearing (Hummert, 1994). In the extreme, Hummert (1994) noted, this becomes the "secondary baby talk" often used to institutionalized elders that corresponds to the baby talk that adults use with infants: higher pitch and exaggerated intonation. However, these responses are apparently most likely with the oldest age range (over 80); Hummert found that young adults hold more positive stereotypes of those under 70.

Senior Moments: Culturally Constituted Thresholds

Impressions of older interactants are likely the result of both the physical changes visible and audible to younger listeners and the cultural expectations we adopt about aging. Those perceptions may have to be revised as the life cycle expands. Retirement is not what it once was; it may be postponed or used as a gateway to another career. Even for those who choose retirement from salaried work, an active, generative life often continues in volunteer work, absorbing hobbies, or family activity. In days gone by, passive grandparents sipped iced tea on the porch of the family farm while the next generation rode the tractor to the back 40. Now, the younger generation are plotting mergers in the city, and the snowbirds have traded in the farm for a Winnebago and are cruising the Southwest. Or, perhaps, they have moved to a condominium, started working out at the local gym, and are tutoring children at the grade school.

Stereotypes of Older Adults

Despite the shifts in health and well-being for the current aging cohort, stereotypes of older adults persist. They are more likely to be negative if the target is aged 80 or above, in poor health, and in an environment that reinforces the picture of dependence, such as a nursing home (Hummert, Shaner, & Garstka, 1995). Positive stereotyping is more likely to be applied to those aged 70 or younger, in good health, and in contexts that highlight independence and activity, such as a vacation cruise (Hummert et al., 1995).

Although most of the data on stereotyping is from young adults, Hummert, Garstka, Shaner, and Strahm (1994) involved mid-lifers and older adults as well as the young. In all three age groups, three positive and four negative types emerged. Positive types included golden ager, perfect grandparent, and John Wayne conservative.[83] The middle-aged and elderly respondents strongly associated golden ager with older adults. Negative types were severely impaired, despondent, recluse, and shrew/curmudgeon.[84] Even though the categories were more complex with age (elders sorted traits into more groups than did younger adults), all age groups apparently use more negative than positive cultural stereotypes. Certainly, stereotypes serve us in making sense of people who are unfamiliar to us, but they cannot reflect the range of possible character sets among elderly. Whether media reflect these stereotypes, reinforce them, or create them, media portrayals are an important source for setting expectations.

Older adults have been underrepresented in both magazines and television (Roy & Harwood, 1997). In the early 1970s, older television characters were overwhelmingly portrayed negatively (Aronoff, 1974) and similar trends continued into the late 1980s (Roy & Harwood, 1997, p. 41). Considering the more affluent consumer niche that elders are beginning to fill, you might think that advertisers would begin to target them. Well, they are, but the commercials that best represent a realistic number of older adults are advertising financial services and retail chains. Elders are most underrepresented in ads for cars and travel services. Although the elder actors play positive roles as happy, active, and strong "elders," they are also predominantly male, generally in their 50s, and they are few and far between. Whereas 16% of our U.S. population is aged 60 or above, elders (or some approximation) account for only 6.9% of actors in evening commercials (Roy & Harwood, 1997, p. 50). But what of those elders who do look over 60, who are not healthy or particularly strong? How do these media portrayals affect their sense of identity? Or, more to the point for advertisers, how do these portrayals affect their consumer habits? Perhaps marketers suspect that active elders are more likely to spend money, but most media images tend to perpetuate age prototypes and contribute to ageist practices (Coupland & Coupland, 1995).

Despite the persistence of cultural stereotypes of the elderly, some older people are choosing to fight back and defy those deeply ingrained impressions. One of the most powerful political lobbies today is the American Association of Retired People (AARP), which in 1984 explicitly criticized the use of derogatory terms for elders (cited in Harwood, Giles, & Ryan, p. 149). Another organization set up to defy ageism is the Gray Panthers. Maggie Kuhn started the group in the early 1970s in response to the loss of her job, and it has continued to give voice to the concerns of an aging population. Institutional supports have been increasing for elders who choose to present themselves rhetorically in ways that confront cultural expectations.

Retirement: Work or Play?

No matter what form retirement takes today, it is no longer about "retiring" from work or an active life. It is more likely to be about the freedom to choose activities as one likes. Retirement age has dropped from the standard 65, thanks to economic incentives offered by many organizations experiencing the strain of top-heaviness in a difficult economy, as well as to changing attitudes about retirement as a beginning rather than an ending. On the other hand, workers capable of continued service may choose to remain, thanks to the 1987 Age Discrimination in Employment Act that bans the mandatory retirement age (U.S. Senate Special Committee on Aging, 1991).

Vaillant (2002) studied factors that predict healthy and happy aging and reported four activities that make for a rewarding retirement: Make new relationships to replace ones lost to work or death, rediscover how to play, allow creativity to be a primary goal, and continue lifelong learning. Furthermore, he pointed out that these activities overlap. For example, play and creativity are similar in that both may produce satisfaction and joy without any necessary motivation or reward. However, a playful attitude to any activity is just that—a mindset—whereas creativity is more passionate, it comes "from the heart and the gut" (Vaillant, 2002, p. 235), it can be transformative and awe inspiring. Note, however, that a playful approach, to making friends, to learning a new skill, to creating a sculpture, is a nonsomber approach to activity. Play, for the retiree, is "learning how to maintain self-respect while letting go of self-importance" (Vaillant, 2002, p. 229). Preparedness for these new tasks involves planning.

When a worker decides to retire, he or she forms expectations about what life will be like. Those expectations may be negative, including fears about financial problems, lost relationships (Perry, 1980), and increased illness (Ekerdt & Bossé 1982); or they may be both optimistic *and* realistic about the changes to occur, which will more likely result in postretirement satisfaction. Gall and Evans (2000) compared men's preretirement health and retirement expectations to later quality of life, 6 or 7 years postretirement. They found that expectations about activity, finances, health, and relationships predicted later quality of life (assessed by relationships and personal growth). Interestingly, actual changes in physical and psychological health from pre- to postretirement did not significantly influence later quality of life, nor did expectations about postretirement income. Thus, setting one's sights for an interactive and stimulating retirement is apparently more important to later satisfaction than money worries or health changes.

Apparently, the issue of choice is a critical one in early retirement. Those who retire because their health is compromised experience more uncertainty about the future and experience more adjustment difficulties than do those who choose to retire because their financial plan allows it (summary in Bernard & Phillipson, 1995).

One of the difficulties in facing retirement is the opposition between work and play that is our cultural norm—perhaps the legacy of the Protestant work ethic. The concept of "deserving" a break from work, of having "earned" one's play, is fairly common. However, this may give the oppositional activity, play, a frantic flavor with strong notes of guilt. To see the two dialogically is to recognize the interconnection of work and play, and to skate that continuum with delight. To find the play in fulfilling work and to acknowledge the work in play is to find integrity in activity.

DIALOGIC CHALLENGES OF OLDER ADULTHOOD

Integrity/Despair

Recall that openness to experience decreases after adolescence, and conscientiousness increases. Well, that very conscientiousness that served the generative years so well may begin to feel a lot like stagnation as we approach the transition to integrity. If it continues, despair may ensue rather than the joys of integrity. A dialogic thinker/communicator is likely to realize that life is about change, and attempts to control and stabilize it are bound for frustration or ennui. Sheehy (1995) commented, "Paradoxically the problem of regaining playfulness and curiosity is exaggerated for those who have a history of success in the world" (p. 357). Not so surprisingly, those who have felt they had to carefully control careers, families, and relationships are precisely those who feel burdened by it all and are looking for a way to rediscover play.

To play with people, with ideas, with life, is to recognize the embedded nature of our seemingly oppositional experiences. We tend to perceive our physical experiences in terms of tensions between opposites, in large part because of the way we are set up to communicate and process information. However, that tendency does not doom us to dualistic thinking. With recognition of the superficiality of simple oppositions, we look for another way to understand the overarching truths about relatedness and our places in the bigger picture. Rather than "transcending" oppositions, we can acknowledge their facility but take them less seriously. The true sage has a sense of humor that allows him or her to see more than dualities, to see beyond loss to gain.

Loss/Gain

Inevitably, elders begin to outlive their cohorts. Some of these losses will be more affecting than others, but all serve to remind the elder that life is finite. Later in this chapter, we examine relational losses more closely, including losses of spouses and friends. Despair may overtake some, but personal coherence is an option for many. Especially during the eighth decade, people begin to replace relationships with memories (Novey, 1968). In attempting to maintain their sense of life's meaning, they will rework the personal narrative in the interests of integration (Marshall, 1986).

Despite the loss of long-held relationships, elders often find new connections in later years with younger people: their grandchildren, their pupils, their caregivers. One comfortable form of intergenerational communication we examine more closely later in the chapter is that between preadolescent children and elders; the ease they find may have to do with their similar experience of time (Cohler & Galatzer-Levy, 1990). Both have a fearlessness and freedom born of the sense that now is the only time there is. The difference between their abilities to appreciate the present is that the elder sees the present from a much wider—and wiser—lens.

Material/Spiritual

Hope, faith, and love are assumed to be necessary identity tasks for full maturity. Jung contrasted the tasks of youth—getting socialized to the culture—with those of old age—getting acquainted with yourself and "the collective unconscious" (in Tornstam, 1999/2000). Erikson spoke of "basic trust" as a requirement of successful aging, and if basic trust depends on faith in the future, "then mastering the task of Integrity depends upon faith in the past" (Vaillant, 2002, p. 257). In theory, trust and faith should be related to spirituality and should increase with age. But does it? Vaillant, although he reported that he had noticed it in himself at 68, did not find in the Harvard study of adult development that the happy-well elders were necessarily more spiritual (inclusivity of faith) or religious (exclusivity of faith). However, in a large study of Danes over 75 years of age, Tornstam (1994) *did* find an increase in spirituality. Perhaps the difference is cultural and/or semantic. Is our focus on material wealth and security so overwhelming? Is it easier to view the cosmos dialogically without as many consumer attractions?

Interestingly, Vaillant's distinction between religion and spirituality employs the contrast between dualities and dialectics. Religious beliefs involve dogmas, which are rigid and serious laws, whereas spiritual trust involves metaphors which are open ended and playful: "Metaphors conceptualize; dogma enshrines" (Vaillant, 2002, p. 261). In youth, we understand dogma; we develop our cognitive structures from egocentric rules to dualistic laws to more relativistic morality. Religious belief serves the adolescent well in clarifying distinctions between "us" and "them," but spiritual trust serves maturity by including all, including God, in the relational web.

The wise are empathic and appreciate context (Vaillant, 2002); they not only have matured, they have learned from experience. Vaillant (2002) asserted that the path to spirituality requires the same components as wisdom "*plus* dialogue with others.... Surely, spiritual maturity requires a dialectic of science, ethics, psychology, religion, and generations" (p. 262). The spiritually aware feel deeply their place in the larger web, and yet appreciate the view of that web from other perspectives. In this sense, very advanced perspective-taking abilities are required for spirituality. Thus, it would be more likely for the dialogic communicator to reach beyond wisdom to transcendence.

Tornstam (1999/2000) called it "gerotranscendence." He noted that, after a long period of antipathy toward disengagement theory, many scholars of gerontology started to return to it to discover why it seemed valuable. "Disengagement theory," which used to provide the conceptual foundation for the study of aging, assumed an intrinsic tendency among elders to withdraw from life. This was countered by the theory of activity, which proposed that those who remained engaged aged more successfully. Well, it turns out that some elders remain active and some wish to be left alone, but *not lonely.* In earlier studies comparing young and old, Tornstam found that loneliness was highest among the young and decreased with age, despite losses.

Hence, Tornstam (1999/2000) substituted *gerotranscendence* for *disengagement* and described it as "the final stage in a natural process of moving toward maturation and wisdom" in which the individual "experiences a new feeling of cosmic communion with the spirit of the universe, a redefinition of time, space, life, and death, and a redefinition of the self" (p. 12). Of particular interest to us are the changes in self-definition, and in relationships. The changes of ego integrity include decreased self-centeredness and increased altruism, rediscovery of the child within, and self-confrontation. Relationships become more selective, and perceptions of them more dialogic. For example, a new recognition of the difference between *self* and *role* results in an urge to abandon roles while still understanding their utility. A shift in perceiving the *right* and *wrong* moral dichotomy leads to a recognition of their dialectical relatedness, with the consequence of withholding advice or judgment. These are but two oppositional shifts affecting interaction in relationships. There are others, including the commonly examined interpersonal triad: integration/separation, expressive/nonexpressive, and stability/change.

Dialectics

If some ability to play the tensions of relational dialectics has not been mastered in the transition from mid-life, then the ultimate acceptance of contradictions and oppositions as part and parcel of human relationships is unlikely.

Integration/Separation: The Essentially Differentiated Self in Community

Cultural stereotyping of the elderly has reinforced the notion that older people are increasingly dependent on others. Indeed, older people themselves often subscribe to the gradual decline in autonomy. However, our communicative practices with older people are likely to influence their perception of an autonomous self. "Instant aging" (Giles, Coupland, Coupland, Williams, & Nussbaum, 1992) occurs when older persons adapt their communication to fit the stereotypes applied to them. The patronizing speech often used with the elderly functions to control the older interactant (Hummert & Ryan, 1996), limits their communicative choices, and leads to dependency (Baltes & Wahl, 1996).

In a 3-year ethnographic study, Aleman (2001) observed the communicative practices of residents in a retirement hotel. She found many instances of *complaining* and considered its function to express dialectical tensions. Rather than a simple binary construct of autonomy/dependence, she found three variants of dependency tensions: independence and social constraint, independence and dependence, and independence and interdependence.

By virtue of living according to hotel regulations, the residents found a contradiction between those constraints and their views of themselves as independent. They complained about the quality and timing of the food service, as well as the pointlessness of serving on hotel committees when they saw no effect from their efforts. Furthermore, they used complaints about less independent residents as social comparisons to clarify who they were and how autonomous they could be.

They also complained about loss of control—over food choices and even the selection of a dining partner. Additionally, they complained about their own frustrations with their changing physiology, often asserting dependence at the same time as independence (e.g., about the constraints on the social activities available for someone using a walker).

Finally, the tension of independence with interdependence was manifest in complaining to get attention. They wished to remain an interdependent part of a community, but had to identify themselves as residents of an independent living facility. Much of the communication with staff members involved complaints—often a series of complaints to gain the attention of an authority who could take away the elder's sense of purpose. Thus, complaints, although often seen even by these residents as ineffective, give them some sense of control over their situation, and serve as a coping mechanism for handling relational tensions. I suspect that those residents who can take lightly their place in the community, even as they voice complaints from their situated selves, will be the most satisfied.

Expressive/Nonexpressive: Generosity of Sharing and Wisdom of Discretion

Older adults are better liars than are younger college-aged adults; they did not "leak" deception as easily when asked to dissemble about a fairly trivial matter—the taste of two comparison drinks (Parham, Feldman, Oster, & Popoola, 1981). Part of this capacity to encode deception successfully is probably a matter of experience with presenting a socially appropriate face. Despite their superior social competence from extended experience, elders are often viewed as "living in the past" and "rambling on." (Recall the "blah blah blah" factor.)

Although the extremely verbose elderly are not in the majority, they leave such a negative and lasting impression that the stereotype persists. Gold, Arbuckle, and Andres (1994) defined off-target verbosity (OTV) as speech characterized by abundance and lack of focus. According to Gold et al. (1994), those high in OTV tend toward extraversion, higher stress levels, and lower levels of social support. Egocentricity is also associated with OTV, regardless of age. That is, a high OTV of any age is likely to be egocentric, but older adults who are highly verbose are also likely to be suffering stress (regarding mobility or finances) and lack of social support (fewer calls and visits from family). Gold et al. did not reveal what high OTVs are saying.

One likely topic, given the shift in time sense that accompanies aging, is reminiscence. Themes may include family life and work environment, but usually are about the distant past and arise spontaneously in context (Nussbaum, Pecchioni, Robinson, & Thompson, 2000). Nussbaum et al. (2000) suggested that reminiscing may serve as a life review that helps resolve old fears and conflicts, thus contributing to integrity, and in that sense, to identity. On the other hand, it may also contribute to the historical sense of younger generations. But what happens to relationships when expressivity gets out of hand?

In intergenerational conversations observed by Coupland, Coupland, and Giles (cited in Giles et al., 1994, p. 139), the older partner commonly engaged in "painful self-disclosure" (PSD), constituting almost 17% of the interaction, whereas the young spent less than 2% of their time disclosing in this fashion. PSDs initiated by older adults revealed the "backgrounds, consequences of, and emotional responses to the painful events detailed" (Giles et al., 1994, p. 139). These created discomfort in younger interactants who could choose to be dismissive and risk incompetence, or to express interest and risk escalation of the disclosure. Often, the response was minimal or expressed surprise or sympathy; in any case, responses were bland and nonreciprocal to the PSD offered. But is the point of the PSD interpersonal expression, or self-clarification? The oldest adults, in particular, may be reviewing the patchwork of their lives to acknowledge for themselves both the pain and the pleasure.

Stability/Change: Recognizing Continuity in the Context of Flux

As our bodies slow somewhat, it is easy to assume that we will stagnate, but we are not simply our bodies. We are so accustomed to a mind/body duality that many aging adults claim that their minds (selves) are unchanging and that only their disagreeable bodies have aged. Tornstam's (1999/2000) "gerotranscendent" elders have no need to separate mind and body. One of his subjects, Eva, is able to "watch herself from the outside" (p. 13); that is, she can simply exist and enjoy both being and being conscious of being. Her joys have changed; as she put it, "Well, earlier it would have been things like a visit to the theater, a dinner, a trip. I wanted certain things to happen that I was a little excited about. My best times [now are] when I sit on the kitchen porch and simply exist ..." (p. 13). The sense of novelty, then, changes from the stimulants commonly available and approved in our culture, to the more personal appreciations of being and wondering at one's own contribution to the larger web.

CONNECTIONS AND DISCONNECTIONS: RELATIONSHIPS IN LATER YEARS

One thing to keep in mind as we examine relational forms in older adults is that much of the research thus far pertains to two cohorts: the World War II generation and the Silent Generation (Sheehy, 1995). Thus, the results may and probably will

change with future generations, including the Vietnam generation who are just beginning to plan early retirements. Those born between 1914 and 1929 were young
in the Depression and World War II.[85] Young men, in particular, were taken with
the romance of flight and the adventure of military service. Young women were tar-
geted early as consumers and, although often married before 20, largely waited until
the end of the war to have children. They were optimistic about their future and
confident that it would be better than their parents' Depression experiences. Gender differentiation was high and strictly normed. Women, after a brief stint working as part of the war effort, stayed home and cared for families. Men took on the
"missions" of their lives, created organizations in the image of the military, and became the ideal for leadership. The men of this cohort controlled the U.S. presidency
for almost 40 years (Sheehy, 1995).

Members of the Silent Generation were born between 1930 and 1945; they were
the "duck and cover" generation, who lived with a mushroom cloud over their heads
after the nuclear bomb was first used in Hiroshima. Their early years did not include
television, credit cards, tape decks, or computers; they did include at-home mothers,
in-resident grandparents, and regular chores. This cohort raced cars, listened to R&B
music, and drank. However, their adolescent rebellion was mild; this group had the
lowest rates in the 20th century for crime, suicide, and illegitimate births. This was
also the earliest cohort in the century to marry and start families. Most women started
families before their mid-20s and stayed home to raise them. Jobs were plentiful, and
men were more than willing to go corporate. They preceded the sexual revolution, so
men often rebelled in middle age by ending their marriages, which left many dis-
placed mothers without the work skills to support their children. Many women of
this generation returned to school after 40, and were put in the position of rethinking
their assigned gender roles. They were the women who began the consciousness raising that boosted feminism and civil rights. This cohort developed a social conscience
that led them to mediate between disparate groups; they produced top presidential
aides, but no president of their own (Sheehy, 1995).

The following trends have been predicted for our future elders and were summarized by Mares and Fitzpatrick (1995). Although a majority will still marry, more
people than ever will not, leaving elders with fewer kin resources. Divorces are increasing; one estimate is that two thirds of current marriages will end (Heaton,
1991), and more recent predictions run higher. Remarriage is decreasing, and of
those who do remarry, more are redivorcing as well. We know much less about the
future of alternative arrangements; however, I would guess, given the predictions
and my own conversations with 50-somethings, that there will arise more variety in
postretirement households.[86] In whatever way the next seniors handle their elder
years, they can anticipate having to adapt to changes in relationships.

The forms, functions, and outcomes of relationships appear to change again for
older adults. New functions of interaction in later life include protection against
cognitive decline and low morale. In comparisons of "young-old" (60 to mid-70s)
and "old-old" (mid-70s and above) adults, Hansson (1986) found that relational
competence, social involvement, and satisfying social support relationships were
linked with self-esteem and morale, *but only for the young-old adults*. He proposed

that the influence of others on well-being may be mediated by the changing meaning of social roles. Fewer demands to conform to social expectations along with less social contact in general may lead to satisfactory disengagement from some socially sanctioned roles, perhaps in the interests of gerotranscendence.

Age may be one mediating factor in the link between well-being and interaction, but the form of relationship may also mediate. In a recent study (Nezlek, Richardson, Green, & Schatten-Jones, 2002), well-being was related to quantity of interaction among aging adults (average age = 71.2 years), but not necessarily to quality. Only married participants demonstrated a link between rewarding interactions (largely with spouses) and well-being. Satisfied unmarried participants had plenty of interactions, but no specific person was central to their well-being in the way that spouses apparently are. Thus, marital status, in addition to age, affects the link between interaction and psychological health. But what of the link to cognition?

In a longitudinal study, adults in their 70s took a battery of standardized cognitive tests, including scales for language, abstraction, memory, and spatial ability (Seeman, Lusignolo, Albert, & Berkman, 2001). Participants remaining after 7.5 years retook these tests, as well as measures of their social networks and quality of their social support. Better cognitive functioning was related to greater emotional support, greater conflict with network members, and unmarried status. Apparently, one factor in maintaining brain function is complex and demanding interaction. The link between cognitive functioning and single status took them by surprise, because marriage has been linked to better health among younger adults. Seeman et al. reasoned that single elders have to be more actively engaged and self-reliant, and thus they maintain cognitive function. Does this pertain for all single elders, or is there a difference between the never-marrieds and the widowed?

Especially among elders, there is a difference between isolation and desolation (Gubrium, 1976). Isolation is "a physical state of aloneness" but does not necessarily bring the "loneliness and negativity of desolation" (cited in Nussbaum et al., 2000, p. 174). Never-married elders do not think about isolation and loneliness as many older people do, because they own their independent status, including its relative isolation.

On the other end are the widowed, who must mourn their loss and cope with the relative isolation it brings. However, widowhood does not usually result in profound, long-term negative effects (Palmore, cited in Nussbaum et al., 2000, p. 176). For one thing, widowhood does bring assistance; 34% of widows/widowers receive some help (Litwak, 1985) from relatives (financial, emotional, and identity support) and from friends (social opportunities and mutual gratification; Heinemann, 1985).

The number of singles, never-married, widowed, and divorced has increased greatly in the past several decades (Adelman & Bankoff, 1990). Although many will remain single and adapt to their status, other elders will marry or remarry.

Romantic Relationships

Some elders will adapt well to the loss of spouses and others will remain happily single; yet others will choose to enter intimate relationships late in life. Genevay (1986) identified *messages* that can lead elders to intimacy: reminiscing about the past, revealing difficulties, and talking about death. OF course, *sex* is a form of intimacy that may change with aging but does not disappear, although Americans act as though they'd like it to. Dailey (1981, cited in Nussbaum et al., 2000) noted the lack of communication about older adults and sex unless it is to joke about it. This "laughter curtain" (p. 45) constrains open communication among the elderly, and can leave them feeling uninformed and inadequate.

The truth is that sexual activity frequently continues at least into the 70s, according to the very dated Masters and Johnson studies (1968). Certainly, physiological changes affecting sex accompany other slowing mechanisms; both sexes are slower to become aroused, and older men are slower to develop erections and to ejaculate (Masters & Johnson, 1968). All of this would seem fortuitous for more mindful and soulful sex. However, both physical and mental well-being enter the mix as well. Conditions such as hypertension and diabetes, prostate surgery, and spinal cord injury can effect erectile dysfunction. But even more commonly, according to Masters and Johnson, men suffer secondary impotence by way of their experience of stress (career, economic situation, marital difficulties), including fear of impotence itself.

There is no necessary loss of love and passion in later years. Indeed, the very same Dr. Masters who performed the sex studies 30-some years ago revealed to Sheehy (1995) that he experienced both at the age of 77. At the time of the interview, Masters and Johnson were divorcing and he had recently reconnected with the love of his life, who through misadventure was lost to him when he was in medical school. Fifty years later, he reported, "The chemistry was there instantly for me, and I think for her too" (p. 366). Six months after the interview, he married his rediscovered sweetheart.

However, there are obstacles to love in later life. One is the privacy that is so important to intimates. Often, privacy is denied older people who are living with children, or in assisted living or nursing homes (Pfeiffer, 1977). And then there are the cultural creations of *dating and courtship*, both of which carry expectations that negate the needs of older people. In 1982, Troll (cited in Nussbaum et al., 2000, p. 169) pointed out that Americans created "dating" as a phenomenon for young people to practice opposite sex relationships in preparation for courting. For older people, the goals for dating are different. Elders do not experience the same social pressure to marry as do young adults, and there may be many economic reasons not to legally bond (fixed incomes, tax laws, medical benefits). Still, one goal of dating may be mate selection, but others include meeting additional potential partners, exchanging intimacy, engaging in social activity, and enjoying the companionship of the opposite sex. Bulcroft and Bulcroft reported in 1985 that elders also choose a wider array of dating activities than do younger adults, and are likely to move the relationship to intimacy more quickly. That can lead to marriage.

Family Ties

Marriage in Later Life

The research on marriage among the elderly has involved two cohorts: the World War II generation, and the Silent Generation. Keep in mind that there will be shifts as cohorts with different life experiences age. Indeed, findings about marital satisfaction varied according to the period studied (Ade-Ridder & Brubaker, 1983). Reports from the 1950s and 1960s described a linear decline in *marital satisfaction* with age, whereas later studies report high satisfaction among elderly couples (see Mares & Fitzpatrick, 1995). Longitudinal and cross-sectional studies often describe a curvilinear trend in which satisfaction in early marriage comes from companionship and new romance, decreases with the birth of children and increased stressors, and increases again peaking in retirement (Schumm & Bugaighis, 1986). Sillars and Zietlow (1993) also found the highest marital satisfaction among retirees.

Communication patterns vary within cohorts as well as between generations. Because communication behaviors are normed by gender, some of the variety will be related to *gender roles*. Sillars and Zietlow (1993) noted a softening effect of traditional gender roles for older husbands, but not for wives, who apparently changed little in their gendered characteristics. Both husbands and wives reported that husbands' feminine characteristics decreased after the early family stage to a low with adolescent children, then rose sharply again in retirement. On the other hand, *disclosure,* often considered a more feminine communication behavior, decreased for women later in life—a drop from earlier high levels—but husbands' levels started low and remained stable.

Conflict behaviors fell into two patterns (Sillars & Zietlow, 1993). The most common "noncomittal" pattern consisted of calm and pleasant messages. The other "confrontive" pattern was evidenced in only a small number of dissatisfied couples and involved bickering about highly salient topics. Sillars and Zietlow's cross-generational study found younger couples better at engaging in flexible, constructive conflict. Middle-aged couples were often nonconflictive, but became analytic in style when topics were salient. Because this was not longitudinal, we do not know whether these styles were characteristic of each cohort or shifted with age. However, young spouses (married 6 years on average) reported more sharing than did their parents (married 32 years on average), and scored lower on traditionalism than their parents did (Van Lear, 1992). Thus, it may be that as cultural norms have changed, so too have the communication patterns of married couples.

Life continuity theory (Cole, 1984) posits that patterns of interaction during the earlier stages of marriage are the best predictors of marital satisfaction in the later stages; hence, the spouses who develop early patterns of constructive conflict and balanced expressivity may be more likely to continue to enjoy their relationship, even if their communication patterns shift over time. Dickson's (1995) study of couples whose marriages lasted over 50 years revealed three variations in the way long-term couples handle *connection/separateness.* "Connected couples" tell stories as if they are jointly owned—they overlap each other's talk, validate each other's statements, and repeat the last words of their partner's statements. They report that they can read each other's minds. "Functional Separate couples" tell stories separately, acknowledge different interests, but show respect, validation, and caring toward each other. "Dysfunctional Separate couples" punctuate each other's stories with contradiction or lack of listening. Like other unhappy couples, they complain and criticize. They do not support each others' interests, and their individual stories have elements of fantasy to them.

One of the surprises of Dickson's (1995) data is that men presented a wider range of *emotions* in telling their stories than did women. Recall that wives in Sillars' and Zietlow's (1993) study reported fewer disclosures. Put in another way, men become more affiliative as they age, whereas women become more individualistic (Tamir & Antonucci, 1981). Remember that many a young woman has found her identity in relationship; thus, older women whose nurturing of children is completed may find the time to individuate and achieve identity apart from their family ties. At the same time, individuated men may find it a relief to relinquish the strong father-figure role in favor of more expressive and less controlled communication.

Caretaking Spouses

Although role identities may gradually shift for aging couples, illness can spin a couple into abrupt changes. When one spouse falls ill, the other is likely to take over more of the infirm partner's tasks; for example, men spend more time in household chores and women take on more financial matters (Stone, Cafferata, & Sangl, 1987). In caring for a recuperating spouse after a hospital stay, wives report more stress than do husbands but both continue to report satisfaction with the relationship (Johnson, 1985). However, the nature of the incapacity is likely to make a difference as well. In the case of a spouse with dementia, caregiving wives report more depression and more deterioration of their relationship, whereas more of the caregiving husbands report that their relationships improved (Fitting, Rabins, Lucas, & Eastham, 1986). However, after several years, the gender disparities disappear; both husbands and wives report more tolerance for memory and behavioral problems (Zarit, Todd, & Zarit, 1986).

One reason for this adaptation process is that spouses continue to find their conversations meaningful, despite some of the frustrations they encounter. Although the majority of their interaction is free of communication breakdowns, their success in resolving the interaction problems decreases over time with further cognitive deterioration (Orange, Van Gennep, Miller, & Johnson, 1998).

Women, given their sensitivity to the burdens of caregiving, experience what has been called "married widowhood" when they are married to husbands with dementia who are living in nursing homes. These women are largely alone, and beginning to disengage in "pregrieving" the loss of their husbands (Baxter, Braithwaite, Golish, & Olson, 2002). Baxter and her colleagues interviewed wives (average age 77) to uncover some of the dialectics they faced in this process.

The primary contradiction was *presence/absence*. Their spouses were physically present but mentally and emotionally absent. Coping strategies included the use of nonverbal communication (kissing, touching, sharing activities), taking over the work of interpreting their husbands' meanings (taking their perspectives, reframing their behaviors to construct a presence), using information mediators (gaining information and stories from nursing home staff), and finally, limiting contact with the spouse (removing themselves emotionally and/or physically).

Other contradictions included *certainty/uncertainty* experienced in fleeting moments of lucidity in an average background of dementia, and *openness/closedness* experienced in the desire to disclose to their "real" husbands, but uncertain how much to reveal and how much to protect. Coping with these oppositions involved engaging in small talk to maintain some connection, and intentionally avoiding some topics to either protect the spouse from confusion or sadness, or to protect themselves from guilt. The last opposition is one of *past/present*, experienced as living in the present with a spouse whose "true" self in relation to them was lost in the past. It should be no surprise that such women feel torn by the various contradictions experienced in their positions and that they use their past history of interactions with their husbands to cope with those oppositions and maintain some shadow of relationship with them. The alternative is true and irrevocable grief.

Grieving the Loss of Spouses

Women's greater longevity means that they are likely to suffer the loss of a spouse, and often at a relatively young age; the average widow is 56 (Atchley, 1994). Just as "there ain't no cure for love,"[87] there's no cure for grief either (Silverman, 1986). Depression is experienced by about a third of grieving spouses, and about half of those are still depressed after a year has passed (Troll, 1982). Silverman (1986) argued that widowhood must be learned, and Heinemann identified the necessary lessons as "grief work"—mourning—and "reality testing"— functioning in the world alone (cited in Nussbaum et al., 2000, p. 176). The support system is particularly important in time of loss, and typically widows do receive help from both kin and friends (Nussbaum et al., 2000).

Siblings

Brothers and sisters are really the only people likely to accompany us throughout our lives. They know us, the family dynamic that wove around us, the identity changes we achieved, the life we made. Moreover, they made up part of our enduring relationship webs. Of those who live beyond the age of 65, 90% will have remaining at least one sibling (Cicirelli, 1982). That timing is apparently functional. Sibling closeness (integration) tends to be high in childhood, more distanced in early adulthood, and greater again in middle and later years (Bedford, 1994). As the nest empties and retirement looms, sibling ties become more important (Connidis & Davies, 1992). Why? Goetting (1986) suggested several late-life developmental tasks with which siblings can assist each other: providing companionship and emotional support, and resolving sibling rivalry.

Sibling rivalry, a common form of competition and conflict in youth (Sutton-Smith & Rosenberg, 1970) evidently does not continue in that form throughout life (Ross & Milgram, 1992), but lingering feelings of differential parental treatment may have to be resolved for siblings to feel close in later life.

Companionship is a vague concept, but we might assume that companions not only entertain but also mirror our identities to us, and perhaps witness our crises and transformations. Emotional support includes validation or confirmation of our responses to life events and relationships. More people are choosing either not to marry or to remain childless and, for many of them, siblings are a large part of their confidant network (Connidis & Davies, 1990). Even for those who have raised children, offspring may be part of the support system but not to the exclusion of other members.

Intergenerational Relationships: Children and Grandkin

One Generation Apart.   Two competing cultural myths about the elderly parent–adult child relationship are current. One is that elderly parents are likely to become dependent and expect their adult children to give up their lives to assist them; the other, conversely, is that adult children are likely to abandon their parents to nursing homes (Nussbaum et al., 2000). Neither reflects reality. Most elderly enjoy contact with their children regularly and have close relationships, and older parents wish to remain independent, maintaining their own households for the most part and respecting the lives of their children (see Nussbaum et al., 2000). Of those over 65, few live in nursing homes, although the majority receive some degree of care from their children (Belsky, 1990). These statements represent the norm, but there are less positive outcomes. Insecure attachments and incomplete identities may continue to negatively affect the parent–child relationship.

The *attachment* behaviors formed early in childhood are likely to reemerge symbolically in adulthood (Cicirelli, 1981). If the original attachment was insecure, and neither party engaged in later relationship "work," then their relationship may continue to be characterized by either distance or codependence. As the pair transition from care-to-child to care-to-parent, dysfunctions continue but shift direction.

In any parent–child relationship, the power structure will shift as the adolescent child fights for autonomy, and again as the aging parent must come to accept the assistance of the child. Elderly mothers view direct control from their daughters as appropriate (Morgan & Hummert, 2000) to their renegotiated relationship. Indeed, this shift is part of late-life development and has been described as the achievement of "generational maturity" (accepting care without giving up generativity) by the elderly parent and "filial maturity" (providing care without infantilizing) by the adult children (Silver, 1993, p. 226). Silver (1993) suggested that this "mutuality of caring" is the third developmental theme in late life, after integrity and mourning. However, finding the balance between caring and being cared for may be a struggle for both parties.

Some of the older women Silver (1993) spoke with in life review sessions viewed caring as their motherly role and derived self-esteem from their competence in nurturing. However, others developed empathic understanding of their adult child's needs and continued to care for themselves as much as possible. The women who viewed caring as their duty simply gave up generativity altogether and demanded care; indeed, they felt justified in doing so because of the deal they felt they made in filling the role of caring mother. Silver posited that they saw generativity as a bargain that had not been kept, and thus failed to master adult generativity issues and to develop mature identity. In other cases, women refused care entirely, putting their health at risk. These elders did not trust their children to care for them, and may have established problematic relationships out of their own insecurities.

A majority of the women in Silver's study received care from daughters, as is often the case. She pointed out that "good mother–daughter relationships tended to be passed down from generation to generation" but problematic relationships often arose from disruptions in the elder parent's own mothering (p. 238). The most difficult relationships, in which the daughter infantilized her mother, were the most enmeshed. This sort of "overinvolvement" is related to increased interpersonal conflict (Litvin, 1992).

Even in the best relationship, *conflict* will arise. Between the generations, conflict themes are likely to concern: what is important in life, the care receiver's welfare, feelings of stress, and the degree to which the caregiver is perceived as filling the care receiver's needs (Litvin, 1992). I would guess that the more emotionally distant and detached the relationship, the less constructive the conflict. However, even the less than perfect parent–child relationships are unlikely to result in domestic violence against parents. The rare adult child who verbally or physically abuses an elderly parent is not only heavily dependent on the victim, but likely to suffer from a range of mental and physical problems, and have a history of hospitalizations, arrest, and substance abuse (see Pillemer & Suitor, 1991). Most children are more than willing to find the balance in mutual parenting.

Two Generations Apart.   Although grandparenting has not yet gone the way of the dodo bird, factors such as mobility, independent households, rising divorce rates, and employed grandmothers conspire to separate the generations (Aiken, 1998). Of parents over 65, 94% are grandparents and nearly 50% are great-grandparents (Hooyman & Kiyak, 1991). Grandparenting styles vary in terms of their involvement with grandchildren (see chap. 5) and there are many ways to be a grandparent. Role prescriptions are less restrictive in grandparenting than parenting; neither societal expectations nor grandchildren's preferences seem to influence how it is done. Grandchildren react to each grandparent individually; that is, they attach to specific people rather than to "grandparent" in general (Matthews & Spray, 1985). Thus, it has been difficult to predict what "works" for grandparents and easier to simply describe what each party gains.

We do know that some external factors influence the grandparent–grandchild relationship: acceptance of the grandparenting role, the quality of the relationship between parent and grandparent, physical proximity, and parental divorce (see Nussbaum et al., 2000). Most of these factors would affect the sheer amount of time grandparents are likely to spend with grandchildren. The flipside has an effect as well: Grandparents who live in the same home, babysit for, or have custodial care of the grandchild will have more opportunities for relationship development. For the nearly 4 million children living in their grandparents' homes in 2002 (U.S. Census Bureau, 1998), 65% also had a parent in the home. Clearly, the other half are being cared for by grandparents alone. Although this might be a joyful experience for some, it can create stress and delay development into the age of integrity.

Often, custodial care of grandchildren falls to women. If they are raising grandchildren alone, their health will be the poorest of their cohort (Solomon & Marx, 1999). Probably related to this decline is the social isolation that results from both decreased time and opportunity to socialize, and from the community's relative neglect of older caregivers (see Harm, 2001). Educational systems and social services have been structured to assist parents, and grandparents are often left behind. Add to that the fact that many custodial grandmothers hold down jobs and often have problem children, and you have a recipe for caregiver burnout, even though the grandchildren typically do quite well (Ambert, 2001).

The nature of communication between grandparents and grandchildren has not been studied extensively, but the few studies we do have give us a fairly positive picture. In a study by Harwood (2000), the most consistent predictor of relational solidarity between college students and their grandparents was each partner's perceptions of the other's accommodation to them. In other words, those most involved and content with their relationship believed that their partners complimented them, showed affection, showed respect, shared personal thoughts and feelings, and were attentive and supportive. Now, that makes sense. What is a bit more intriguing is that the strongest negative predictor was grandparents' overaccommodation; that is, grandchildren who perceived that their grandparent talked down to them or negatively stereotyped young people did not like the grandparent. Interestingly, it did not work the other way; grandparents were not as sensitive to either overaccommodation or underaccommodation.

McKay (1993) proposed that the grandparent–grandchild relationship functions developmentally for the grandparent's sense of continuity, part and parcel of achieving integrity. Internally, the relationship offers the grandparent the chance to reconnect with the past, to reinterpret life experiences and build a coherent whole. Externally, it provides a way to "contemplate the present and, by bonding with the grandchildren, to the future" (McKay, 1993, p. 177). Telling the story of one's life to grandchildren assists developmentally by way of making decisions about the future, establishing integrity about the past, and accepting the role of guide in grandchildren's lives. The narrative form serves to communicate the grandparent's life story, thereby contributing to integrity and ensuring the continuity of the elder's identity in the memories of grandchildren.

Friendships

Close friendships become increasingly stable over a lifetime (Brown, 1981), and even if friends are separated by time and distance they continue to assume benevolence of each other and continuity of the relationship (Rawlins, 1992). That is, "the actual and the imaginary underwrite the continuation of friendships across the expanses of adulthood" (Rawlins, 1992, p. 217). Nonetheless, the concomitants of age can influence abilities to maintain old friends or make new ones.

Health is the primary factor in subjective ratings of well-being (Larson, 1978), and interaction with friends is more important to well-being than is interaction with any others, including family (Nussbaum, 1994). Indeed, the best predictor of psychosocial well-being in the elderly is having at least one confidant (Rawlins, 1995). However, health problems can interfere not only with general sense of well-being, but also with the capacity to interact. For example, the skills basic to interaction—speech, vision, and lucidity—are the primary determinants of friendship in nursing homes (Nussbaum et al., 2000).

Tried and true friendships gain in *stability* unless health intervenes, and the meaning of friendship deepens as well. Nussbaum (1994, pp. 218–221) reported that older friends perceive some of the same characteristics of friendship important to other age groups (e.g., devotion, common interests, reciprocity) with several additional definers. Older friends perceive a stratification of relationships arrayed on a continuum of closeness, and they do not consider talk a necessary component of friendship. Whereas younger adults distinguish best friends from all others, older adults identify several levels of friends (e.g., acquaintance, buddy, friend); and whereas younger adults link frequent interaction to close friendship, older adults maintain important relationships even in the absence of overt interaction (Nussbaum et al., 2000).

One of the unique factors influencing late-life friendships is the shared *history* that older friends claim. In Matthews' (1986) words, such friends share extended "populated biographies" in their wealth of relationship experiences and can fall back on that history to reclaim common experience. Related to this shared history is *age similarity* as a factor in friendship. In the case of older friends, they not only share cohort experiences but a unique position in society. Certainly, older adults make friends with the younger people around them, but these relationships never quite fill the gap left by those lost to illness and death. This brings us to the third of Matthews' factors: the reality of *physiological deterioration* that can affect friendships. It is not simply the physiology of communication that can negatively affect friendships, but the inevitability of decline and death can also alter the equal power status of friends toward creeping inequality and subsequent discomfort.

Rawlins (1992) pointed out that providing too much assistance or making undue demands can disturb the balance between the *freedom to be independent* and *the freedom to be dependent,* although most older friends in reasonably good health manage to cope with this opposition. Older friends also report a great tolerance for the opposition of *judgment and acceptance*; their appraisals ignore trivia but retain important evaluation. As one elder put it, "If it's ridiculous, I'd like to know it.... That's the kind of friend I like to have" (Rawlins, 1992, p. 249). Finally, the dialectic of *expressiveness/protectiveness* appears to be finely honed with age as well: "Openness ... includes ongoing and careful monitoring and rhetorically informed practices regarding matters that are closed to discussion" (p. 250). One aging friend put it this way: "I think you should always be alert that the other person has feelings as well as yourself, and you shouldn't always speak out what you feel and hurt their feelings" (p. 250).

The death of a dear friend can be every bit as difficult as losing a family member. Particularly among older women, who have a long history of close relationships with same-gender friends and who often outlive spouses, very close friends comfort and sustain them through other losses. Roberto and Stanis (1994) found that, among older women, the death of a dear friend "triggers feelings of grief equivalent to that experienced with any personal loss of this magnitude" (p. 24).

RELATIONAL VARIATIONS

Nursing Home Residency: Old and in the Way?

One in four of us will spend some time in a nursing home (Kastenbaum & Candy, 1973). However, the prevailing image of nursing homes as storage spaces for our older adults is not entirely accurate. Although staff are not likely to be interaction partners, family and friends do continue their relationships with nursing home residents. Indeed, families are likely to maintain the same frequency of contact with an older relative after he or she is admitted to a nursing home as before (York & Calsyn, 1977).

Staff, however, are unlikely to engage in conversation with residents, preferring to engage with each other (Grainger, 1995). Reasons offered by staff for their lack of interaction with residents include time constraints (Meikle & Holley, 1991) and low expectations for residents' abilities to communicate (Gravell, 1988). Gravell (1988) also noted several factors in the institutional setting that constrained communication: loud televisions, poor seating arrangements (against the walls), and lack of external stimulation. Grainger (1995) found that when staff do speak to residents, it is about some task they must perform, and the message is constructed similarly to those used with young children (like motherese). Although the goal of nursing homes is ostensibly to enable independent functioning, the "softer" features of nurse-talk to the elderly, although polite, can promote dependency and passivity. Residents must turn to each other for communication among equals. Unless residents suffer severe communication deficits, they will make friends in the nursing home, in much the same way they did before.

Residents of about the same age draw together, and those in close proximity (roommates, neighbors) are likely to form alliances as well (Nussbaum, 1990). Indeed, elders are less likely to report feeling lonely in nursing homes than they do otherwise (Downs, Javidi, & Nussbaum, 1988). However, their *topics of conversation* are more restricted. Nussbaum (1983) observed that residents did not talk about community, national, and global events as much as other older adults did. Residents report that positive relationships with the nursing staff are important to them and, indeed, residents live longer and report higher quality of life and improved well-being when their relationships with staff are satisfying and affirming (see Nussbaum, 1990). But most residents are 75 or older; what of those who can no longer communicate well?

Competence Losses: Despair and Disintegration

Among roommates in nursing homes, nearly half never spoke to each other for reasons involving physiological limitations—speech and hearing impairments (Kovach & Robinson, 1996). Of those who did speak, roommate rapport predicted life satisfaction. Thus, communication skill and knowledge remain very important to quality of life, if not to sheer survival. However, most elders do continue to communicate well into late life. Clearly, deficits in hearing and memory can affect competence, but compensations are possible and likely for the motivated conversant. Social interaction is critical to the continuing sense of self-in-the-world.

Peg's older friend Harold took pride in his old home in the woods, filled with antiques and surrounded by gardens. His son had long ago moved to the city and rarely visited, but Harold refused to leave his beloved old house. When he was 82, his hearing was poor yet the hearing aid served well enough when he cared to use it. However, the batteries kept running down. Then his glasses broke and fit so poorly with tape on the bridge that he quit wearing them. He started to fall more often and stopped gardening. Within 6 months, he went from a lively presence, always ready with a fascinating story from his war service or many business ventures, to a muttering, stooped old man. Ultimately, when he no longer cared for himself, his son moved him to a nursing home. This is a true story of a man I knew when I was much younger. I suspected then that if his son had been willing to immediately assist in replacing his glasses and hearing aid, his participation in life would have been extended. As it was, he could no longer read the newspapers, could not hear well enough to converse, and became frustrated and cranky with his loss of competence. He died within a year of his move.

Power in Dialogic Understanding: Integrity and Joy

Many seniors, as long as they are able, continue to form new relationships and to find joy in their capacities for handling the paradoxes and contradictions of life. Voluntary organizations depend to a great degree on the involvement of older adults, including some over 80 (Babchuk, Peters, Hoyt, & Kaiser, 1979). One community project involved seniors in telling some of their life stories to elementary school children (Powers & Love, 2000). Not only did the children enjoy the stories, but the seniors developed their narrative skills, sought feedback, and transformed some of their memories in the process. Service can prolong the usefulness of youth. I recall overhearing my mother, at the age of 78, describe her volunteer work with a local agency as "providing rides for old people." As long as she could be helpful, she was not yet "old."

Many more adults are continuing their intellectual development into old age as well. Recall that age brings losses in fluid intelligence, but not in crystallized intelligence. Glendenning (1995) identified the first as *wit* and the second as *wisdom*, and further noted that the research that found age-related decrements in wit were performed with elderly populations who had much less formal education than did the general population (Belsky, 1990). Indeed, the noted decline in fluid intelligence is related to amount of full-time schooling (Stuart-Hamilton, 1991). This is very interesting in light of the fact that fluid intelligence is the "ability to solve problems for which there are no solutions derivable from formal education or cultural practices" (Glendenning, 1995, p. 469). Nonetheless, formal education apparently contributes to the ability to think flexibly. The implication is that *wit* can be fostered with opportunities for challenging intellectual demands. Many older adults are accepting the challenge in community extended education programs, or at colleges and universities that offer tuition waivers for seniors or that participate in Elderhostel.[88]

Remember that crystallized intelligence, or *wisdom*, does not decrease and indeed may improve with age (Stuart-Hamilton, 1991). The amount of knowledge a person can access accumulates throughout life, and yet our culture not only fails to use this wisdom, but seems to have forgotten that it is a resource. Granted, a few programs access retired executives' accumulated wisdom, but what of retired nurses, teachers, social workers, or engineers? Furthermore, these are just the kinds of thinkers who are most likely to be processing information dialectically and understanding communication dialogically. The educated and active elderly are more likely to have realized the limitations of dualisms and have found some comfort with the necessary tensions of a life of seeking the balance point. Culturally, we are experiencing the profound problems that result from dichotomizing both groups (men and women, Blacks and Whites, poor and rich) and individuals of unequal status (teen and parent, teacher and student). Our elders could be the source of healing resolutions.

PREPARING FOR DEATH

As Loss: Fear and Despair

Confronting the deaths of loved ones may, to some extent, prepare one for one's own. Patterson (1981) suggested that those who have experienced loss become more accepting of mortality. Fear of death seems to peak between 40 and 55, and then decreases with the acceptance of death's inevitability. Then there are those who willingly embrace "the golden casket" of death.[89] However, responses to personal mortality are varied and individualized. The experience of the dying person is, as throughout life's experiences, affected by relational partners.

Even though knowledge of one's impending death may lead to depression, most people do want to know if they are facing death (Schulz & Aderman, 1980). However, dying individuals are relatively unsatisfied with the communication they receive (Servaty & Hayslip, 1997). Unfortunately, our cultural inclination is to avoid talking about or dealing with death. If anxiety about death is at its highest in middle age, then the dying person's adult children as well as seasoned health professionals providing care will be unlikely to welcome communication about death. This can lead to social distancing or Kalish's (1976) notion of *social death*. In these cases, loved ones treat the dying person as dead before the actual fact, including preparing the person's body (wrapping), filling out autopsy forms, and communicative withdrawal (Sudnow, 1967). The problem with such distancing, aside from the obvious cessation of care, is that it deprives the dying person of control over the dying experience.

As Gain: Transformation and Integrity

Even if they have experienced long-term dependency as a result of illness or incapacity, dying persons will probably wish to exert some independence by controlling to some extent their own withdrawal from life (Nussbaum et al., 2000). They may wish to withdraw from most social relationships, and yet to maintain the intimacy of their closest relationships to the end. An *appropriate death*, according to Kalish (1976), features caring relationships, open awareness of impending death, and a belief system that lends meaning to the death. The "good death" is one that allows the dying person to approach death with integrity—to talk about the final transformation of life, to feel closure, and to experience the love of their intimates.

Most people facing death will experience denial at some point (Kubler-Ross, 1969), which may be functional in terms of coping with the news and preventing early withdrawal from supportive relationships (Beilin, 1981–1982). Most older people will not continue to "rage against the dying of the light"[90] but instead will come to terms with death. It is often by talking that they reach acceptance.

The Communication of Dying: Relational and Dialogical

As a person nears death, life may take on an added vividness. Any remaining tasks must be completed or released, including social and relational ones. In a longitudinal study of older adults, relationships with family and close friends improved over time, and as participants felt near to death, their emotional closeness with all others diminished (Lang, 2000). The social network contracted to those most intimate; the dying person restructured the social world to maximize emotional closeness.

Dying patients who live longest tend to be more assertive and to maintain responsive relationships with others (Weisman & Warden, 1975). Topics of conversation often involve their families (Kastenbaum & Aisenberg, 1972). The open communication that dying persons prefer is facilitated by responsive partners' attentive listening to the "life review," which allows the dying individual to make sense of life and to feel closure and integrity about it (Simmons & Given, 1972). Although such talk has clear benefits for the dying person, it also assists the living to cope with their emotions (FitzSimmons, 1994). What the survivors must do is cope with the dialectic of *affiliation and separation* (Kramer, 1997) in full recognition that permanent physical separation is immanent. Although not easy, the opportunity to conclude a close relationship with comfort and affection is desired by most (Fieweger & Smilowitz, 1984).

SUMMARY

Age ultimately affects the body's decline. Ironically, the older mind may be just as witty and twice as wise as ever. If my premise is right, the older person who has remained socially and intellectually active is in the best position to understand and appreciate human dialectical perception and dialogical growth. Although Western cultural practices tend toward ageism, the elders are in the best position to provide the kinds of insights that an increasingly uncivil culture needs. Elders are left to choose their own paths: to enjoy their hard-earned integrity, or despair of their lost opportunities; to continue to gain from their wisdom, or become lost in mourning; to value an increased appreciation of spirituality, or bemoan their level of material riches.

Facing the ultimate challenge of completing a life in integrity may be approached with fear and resistance, or with dignity and joy. The task of integrating the differentiated self, of placing this self into the web of life even while leaving it, is one that requires self-acceptance as well as other-acceptance. The communication knowledge and skills developed over a lifetime in a splendidly complex array of relationships serve the mature self in gaining a dialogic acceptance of self/other, male/female, light/dark.

NOTES

83. Originally reported in 1994 by Hummer, Garstka, Shaner and Strahm, these results are summarized in Hummert, Shaner, and Garstka (1995, p. 116):
    Golden agers' traits: Lively, alert, active, sociable, independent, fun-loving, interesting.
    Perfect grandparents' traits: Kind, loving, family-oriented, supportive, wise.
    John Wayne conservatives' traits: Patriotic, religious, reminiscent, emotional, proud.
84. Originally reported in 1994 by Hummer, Garstka, Shaner and Strahm, these results are summarized in Hummert, Shaner, and Garstka (1995, p. 116):
    Severely impaireds' traits: Slow-thinking, incompetent, feeble, incoherent, senile.
    Despondents' traits: Depressed, sad, hopeless, afraid, neglected, lonely.
    Shrew/curmudgeons' traits: Complaining, ill-tempered, bitter, demanding, inflexible, nosy.
    Recluses' traits: Quiet, timid, naive.
85. All the information about generational cohorts is summarized from Sheehy (1995).
86. For example, I have spoken to many women who are considering pooling their resources with friends in their later years. (Plans proceed for the O.S.W.'s home.)
87. Apologies and salutations to Leonard Cohen.
88. See Glendenning (1995) for a critical perspective on education for older adults.
89. One of the choices that Portia's suitors were afforded was the gold casket with the inscription: "Who chooseth me, shall gain what many men desire" (Shakespeare's *The Merchant of Venice,* act II, sc. vii, 5). Within was the death mask.
90. Dylan Thomas lived only to the age of 39.

Chapter 12

Human Communication Futures: Beyond Dualities to Dialogic Consciousness

The physical world has no two things alike.
Every comparison is awkwardly rough ...

Say the body is like this lamp.
It has to have a wick and oil. Sleep and food.
If it doesn't get those, it will die,
and it's always burning those up, trying to die.

But where is the sun in this comparison?
It rises, and the lamp's light
mixes with the day.

         Oneness,
which is the reality, cannot be understood
with lamp and sun images. The blurring
of a plural into a unity is wrong.

                       (Rumi, quoted in Barks, 1995, p. 177)

Much in the same way that human maturation in utero is similar to the *biological* stages through which the species evolved, human dialogic awareness eventually may become an easy and natural development reflecting a turning point in our *cultural* evolution. But for now, understanding the personal overarching stability/change dialectic—that human social life is a matter of constantly balancing dialectical tensions for one's own comfort as well as growth—is a developmental process that requires conscious effort and ongoing refinement. Material life, by its nature, is about the perceived distinctions among physical entities that, at a subtler level, are all one. That last statement may be taken as either a simplified summary of

323

new physics,[91] or a metaphysical belief about our spiritual natures. Whatever the cosmology, the recognition that relational dialogues give us the means to transcend our limited perceptual equipment is not a new one,[92] but it *is* a hard-won awareness for each individual.

Unfortunately, in our current cultural environment, the pursuit of personal attention is endemic and epidemic, much to the detriment of truly developmental dialogue. In a culture that celebrates individualism, "competition for attention is one of the key contests of social life" (Derber, 2000, p. XII) resulting in the cult of the "perfect" body, public self-disclosure of personal intimacies (e.g., Jerry Springer's "confessions" and the Internet's "blogs"), and conversational narcissism. This last is of particular concern to us. The prevailing practices of active and passive conversational narcissism function to take the topic away from a conversational partner by overuse of topic shifts and underuse of topic support (Derber, 2000). The result, for a pair of such users, is dueling monologues rather than relational dialogue. Neither conversant affects the other and the talk serves merely pseudo-attention. This sort of "interaction" is not developmental. That anyone currently arrives at dialogic awareness through relationships is the wonder. Nevertheless, some do. Let's take another look at that process before we project to futures.

THE RELATIONAL-DIALOGICAL THEORY OF DEVELOPMENT

1. *Human communicative development, although it begins with and continues for some time to be influenced by physiological maturation, is characterized by a series of progressive internalizations of symbolic interactions, or "boundary experiences," that result in the unfolding of individuality.* Throughout this book, we have noted the pervasiveness of the integration/separation dialectic for human social life, and indeed for humanness itself. Our physiology endows us with the basics for perceiving distinctions among things, but the means to build on those distinctions arises in spoken symbolic communication. From external interactions we acquire the means to build internal sense making, and in expressing that sense-making we bring the core back out to the boundary. In a spiraling direction, we build not only a more distinct sense of own core, but a more refined perspective of the Other (see chaps. 2, 3, & 5).

2. *These boundary experiences, or dialogues between self and other, are internalized in a process that creates the mind.* Thinking occurs "from the outside in," as Vygotsky and others have explained. Thought processes are first built on external dialogues, and first demonstrated in external monologues (egocentric speech). The process of internalizing these dialogues sets up the semantic and syntactic structures for thought as we know it, which gradually becomes silent, condensed, and abstract (see chap. 4).

3. *Mind is a mediating process between a material brain, subject to physiological maturation, and an energetic consciousness that is active at the boundary between self and other. The active mind, then, is materially aware of itself in relationship to another mind.* Mind is not the same as brain. The brain develops cellularly and structurally, adds myelin to network nerves for speed of processing, specializes in function—

and all this growth is in service of the activities of a mind. Whether you consider this active process of mind to be simply the manifestation of brain function or part of the energy field encompassing each human (and each living organism)[93] or the stuff of soul or spirit, it is probably where consciousness arises. Material experience is transformed into energy, energy is transformed to experience, and so forth[94] (see chaps. 2, 3, & 4).

4. *Mind, mediating between internal perception and external activity, processes experience in terms of a symbolic self, or identity.* The distinction between self and Other may be one of the primary contrasts emerging early in life. Once the differentiation is made, the self and Other as symbolic constructs start to acquire meaning. Meaning and value continue to accumulate to these concepts throughout life, leading optimally to a fully differentiated self that is simultaneously fully integrated into human networks. The self/Other dialectic is related in this way to the separation/integration dialectic (see chaps. 4 & 5).

5. *Identity is the ongoing symbolic process of being objectively aware of self as part and parcel of the constructed mind. Identity arises from cumulative internalizations of external experiences at the boundary between self and other. The self is that for which one is accountable to others; self is presented rhetorically for the Other, and the cumulative result, mediated by memory, is identity.* The self is built at the boundaries in negotiating relationships with others. In presenting an image of self for Other, we test the concept of self that we are constructing against the responses we receive. As our relational partners change, so too may the responses we receive. Thus, the interactants we choose are critical to the choices we make in building an orientation to self. Early in life, we are more likely to choose one pole of a construct to describe self (e.g., smart), and to gradually differentiate finer distinctions (e.g., smart about school, dumb about people; see chaps. 4-11).

6. *The development of personal identity is described by a series of cycles wherein external social experience is internalized. Identity is processual and multiple, more or less fluctuating, in that it is reflective of current self in interaction as well as expressive of the cumulative, selective self-perceptions constructed rhetorically in a series of boundary experiences.* Because experience is internalized cyclically over time, identity becomes more stable as some experiences are repeated and reinforced and others are fleeting events that fade. Although some reflections of self will be fairly consistent, others will confront assumptions about self, leading to shifts in identity. Constructing a rhetorical self to hold a consistent identity and to present a coherent image is a lifelong process (see chaps. 4-11).

7. *The nature of human communication—spoken symbolic interaction between identities in various states of transformation—allows increasing sophistication in processing interactive experience.*

    a. Unity with other: A presumed starting point for development from undifferentiated being to differentiated self. Recent evidence demonstrates primary distinctions in neonates; thus, birth may be the endpoint of unity (see chap. 2).

    b. Contrast with other: The first sorts of important differentiations are between my movements and those external to me, between the speech I produce and the speech produced by others. Infants are pattern seekers; thus, they use and master contrast early in development (see chaps. 2–5).

c. Rules for difference: Standards negotiated in relationships for the purpose of attaining goals. Rules begin in the expectations formed in relationships (e.g., "Mom will play with you as long as you don't whine"), and generalize to standards for play (e.g., "Hide your eyes to the count of 10") and work (e.g., "Raise your hand if you wish to speak in class") (see chap. 6).

d. Skills for synthesis: The performance of effective and appropriate social behaviors founded in knowledge and motivation. These communication skills allow us to continue relational conversations that contribute to our development, both differentiating self as unique and integrating self with social networks (see chaps. 7 & 8).

e. Playing the tensions: The recognition that social life is inherently dialectical, and finding comfort in balancing the tension between dialectical oppositions rather than attempting to evade or resolve oppositions (see chaps. 8–11).

8. *Variations in the rate of physiological maturation, in the nature of interaction experienced with others, and in sociocultural habits affect the speed and regularity of these cycles of internalization. That is, it is possible to describe threshold points in the way individuals perceive self and other. Some are stably related to physiological change, but others such as the nature and timing of life "crises" vary from culture to culture, between genders, even among individuals.* Especially early in life, we can describe thresholds that are related to physiological maturation, such as the optimal period for language development in the first 5 years, and its endpoint at puberty. However, our relationships within social networks are more likely to provide the raw material for building a self and a perceptual framework. Intense dialectical oppositions lead to transitions or threshold points, and invite creative change. The more dialogically aware the communicator, the greater his or her growth is (see chaps. 2–11).

Turning points in dialectical forces are likely to create change and spur development. We have begun to track some of the most challenging dialectical oppositions that create intense conflict (intrapersonal as well as interpersonal). The "turning points" marking these conflicts promise to more accurately reflect the path of human development than have "stages" of skill acquisition. For example, Peg in young adulthood experienced an identity shift from a fairly passive, nurturing, feminine identity to a more aggressive, self-protective, masculine style. She had experienced the extremes in her relationship with Ned, and found that her feminine position had become uncomfortable. The awareness of her own ultrafeminine identification led her to shift to more masculine-identified behaviors. She found in later years that she may have overcorrected. A colleague told her that other coworkers considered her forbidding and controlling. Aware again that she was not happy with that image, nor with the tension that those behaviors created in her life, she once more adjusted to a softer style. Peg grew through two turning points featuring the masculine/feminine dialectic, but not to the exclusion of other oppositions. The first included integration/individuation; the second involved judgment/acceptance. Later in her life, Peg was described as strong and kind, productive and flexible, hardworking and fun. She found her own way of skating the dialectics and enjoying the glide between oppositions.

IMPLICATIONS OF DIALOGIC DEVELOPMENT

Personal Growth

The person who can successfully harmonize opposing tendencies has become dialogically aware of the inherent dialectic of human life. "The T-person," as Csikszentmihalyi labeled the transcendent self (1993), is one who is "joyfully invested in complex goals" (p. 208). The kind of spiraling growth we have been describing, between differentiation and integration, between "turning attention inward and then outward," results in a person whose self-concern becomes "qualified by less selfish goals, and concern for others becomes more individualistic and personally meaningful" (p. 235). Csikszentmihalyi attributed this sort of growth to "flow" experiences, or very involving complex tasks that require formulating intentions and assessing feedback. Examples include mastering a musical instrument, the game of chess, or the sport of fencing. These tasks involve differentiating a challenge and integrating the necessary skills to follow through. If this seems suspiciously familiar—mastery of the differentiation/integration dialectic, for example—then flow may be the consistent experience of the person who simultaneously honors opposing tendencies.

In terms of communication, the competent person can maintain focus on a goal while accessing the skills to reach that goal. What will often be required, particularly when setting a relational goal, are skills that reduce needs for ego attention and expand concerns for Other. A fairly stable sense of differentiated self, born of uncountable internalization cycles, is the primary requirement for this sort of external focus. Csikszentmihalyi (1993) proposed that just as self develops through the life span, the human self also evolves historically. In his view, survival and security needs were primary early in human evolution and the ideal self was specialized in fertility for women and bravery for men. Later, community values arose in religious belief systems and conformity to social norms characterized the ideal. Since then, in Western culture, the development of individual potential has become the ideal[95] and some of these individuals have managed to develop their uniqueness for the common good. Thus, each stage has built on the last, but the transcendent self is not yet the norm. Given the damage that self-involved humans can do to the environment and each other, is there a way to speed the process of cultural evolution?

Human Communication Evolution

Few people have considered how communication has changed over the course of human evolution. One notable exception is Walter Ong (1967) who, influenced by the likes of Marshall McLuhan and Teilhard de Chardin (see later discussion), examined the shifts that have occurred in human communication and their consequences for human consciousness. In a nutshell, he traced shifts in the "sensorium" through three stages: oral/aural culture, alphabetic/typographic culture, and electronic culture. Ong declared that the sensorium is "the entire sensory apparatus as an operational complex" (p. 6). Humans communicate with the whole body, and their way of making sense of the world is affected by the prevailing sensory mode for communication. In each stage, the sensorium has been organized differently by a dominating communication mode. Although Ong's explication is rich with detail and rife with implications, here we peruse just the outlines of each stage.

In the stage of *primary orality*, the spoken word prevailed and audition was the primary sense. The spoken word is at the same time ephemeral—here and gone—and powerful in its capacity to focus thought and link people. The oral/aural culture was tribal and local, present and spontaneous, social and normative.

The *print* stage began with the invention of the alphabet, came into its capacity for manipulating ideas in ancient Greece, and reached its pinnacle with the invention of the printing press and the ensuing democratization of thought. Literate humans feature vision in the sensorium, resulting in increased individuation and isolation.

The most recent shift to the stage of *secondary orality* began with the inventions of electronic communication media (radio, television, personal computers), which in effect have shifted the focus back to audition. Some have taken this cultural transformation to be the death knell for print (Birkerts, 1994), and that is a sobering thought. But might the shift also bring positive changes?

How you answer that question will depend largely on your view of human evolution. As more than one student has told me, evolution is "just a theory." Yes, it is, but a pretty well-documented one. The theory you espouse will determine what you make of the evidence. As my Catholic mother is happy to point out to religious fundamentalists, God could have created the world in 7 days, but God days are probably very different from human days. In a more detailed explanation, another Catholic, Teilhard de Chardin (1955/1959), agreed with both evolution and creation, and for his efforts was promptly excommunicated. His is an intriguing and enduring theory, in that he traced evolutionary trends and concluded that man is "evolution become conscious of itself" (citing Huxley, p. 221) and, furthermore, that the threshold for reflective thought had to have appeared *"between* two individuals" (p. 171). Here is an evolutionary threshold created in the primary dialectic.

Human evolution reached consciousness—in particular, self-consciousness, or awareness of awareness—in dialogue. The implication is that our evolution relies no longer on chance mutations, but now on our links with each other, on our recognition that we can be T-persons, or better humans, only through each other. After a long period of differentiation into a variety of primate types and human racial groups, Teilhard de Chardin (1955/1959) suggested that divergence forces are giving place to convergence forces, or gathering to "a single block of mankind" (p. 243).

What Teilhard de Chardin called the "cosmic law of complexity-consciousness" is essentially a movement of dialectical forces. "The universe is ... in process of spatial expansion (from the infinitesimal to the immense) in the same way ... as [it is] in process of organic involution upon itself (from the extremely simple to the extremely complex)" (1955/1959, p. 301). This latter movement to interiorization reached a threshold point with reflective thought, at which time humans ceased to evolve in response to the random forces of expansion and began to experience the force driving us together for the "global evolution of the entire group" (p. 304). Teilhard de Chardin concluded that dialectics such as differentiation and integration, good and evil, are inherently evolutionary. The arrangement of biological evolutionary processes is expansive toward variety and differentiation; the centration of human consciousness is interior toward increased unity. To him, *evil* resides in disorder and decomposition (lack of arrangement or entropy), solitude and anxiety (of the wakening consciousness), and even growth itself in terms of the effort and pain inherent in moving toward unity. *Good* is to be found in the opposing but orderly forces of expansive arrangement and contractive centration. Consider how similar this is to Csikszentmihalyi's flow—differentiating a direction and honing in on it by acquiring the necessary skill. This is not a procedure without effort and even pain (evil), but it does bring great well-being (good).

Our species, having differentiated to multiple types of unique reflective selves who project out into the world, now should (in theory) double back around to gather in a unified consciousness. Could the unifying force emerge in conscious dialogue?

Human Communication Futures

Dialogue in the broadest sense, as Bakhtin used it, is communication between simultaneous differences, but it is manifest in the action of discourse or "consciousnesses engaging in simultaneous understanding" (Clark & Holquist, 1984, p. 217). From that boundary phenomenon, dialogic experience grows. However, to attain dialogic awareness requires many cycles of internalizing the dialectics of social/personal life. What are the larger social effects of this personal awareness?

Belonging to a Social Network

One part of having an identity is developing a sense of one's position in the social web, "a sense of 'belonging,' [in that] one has an automatic right of initial access to the community simply by virtue of having contributed, in developing oneself, to the development of *its* way of making sense" (Shotter, 1993a, p. 163). That contribution is the other part of the equation. Being positioned in a socially shared awareness, one must not only respect the boundaries of appropriate and accountable actions, but reproduce them continually (Shotter, 1993a, p. 162). Thus, developing an effective self in a socially accountable manner is the task of identity, but it is not without its challenges.

Increasingly, as Derber has pointed out, the opportunities to participate in this "political economy" (Shotter, 1993a) are at a premium, and we must compete for the chance to contribute with others who have the same need. We all need listeners who treat our speech "as having important consequences for them" (Shotter,

1993a, p. 163) and in the pursuit of attention, listeners are rare. Some take on the position as a duty—parents, teachers, counselors—but many more forget that in routine conversations and everyday relationships, we all need Other to help sustain our identities and positions of belonging.

In a larger sense, these "countless individual transactions at [the] boundaries" (Shotter, 1993a, p. 165) of social life maintain the integrity of the larger social group as well. As Shotter pointed out, isolated systems tend toward increasing disorder (evil), whereas constant energy exchange at the boundaries between systems and their chaotic environments tends to create more order and stability (good)—creating a niche for the continuously interactive system. Now, whether this system is one identity who interacts with many disparate others or a local government that maintains interaction with community members, the outcome will be the same. In times of stress or crisis, the interaction at the boundaries pays off by maintaining some order by way of those energy exchanges. If the energy exchanges cease, the disorderly surroundings prevail, and chaos ensues. Thus, the dialectic of order/disorder characterizes the social world as "a continuous flux … of mental activity containing regions of self-reproducing order, reproduced at their boundaries, surrounded by 'chaos'" (Shotter, 1993a, p. 166).

Social Life and Shared Responsibility

A "politics of identity" (Shotter, 1993b) involves sets of identities collectively inventing a citizenship in which everyone can have a "voice," or shape and reshape their lives. What is required is shared responsibility to engage in argument and influence, to share the responsibility for both speaking from the core and listening at the boundary. If we are fortunate, we are moving toward a recognition of the power of dialogue as a unifying as well as individuating force, a recognition of reciprocal responsibility to be both resource and recipient. Culturally, we may be emerging from the limiting traditions of a reductionist and bipolar perspective to an acceptance of a more pluralistic and dialogic view. If so, the communication capacities and skills we have been studying are transitional behaviors. If development is progressive and evolutionary, we may need to look to our most successful elders and precocious children—those at the boundaries of the social system—to find clues to the competencies of tomorrow.

Wisdom, Spirituality, and Personal Responsibility

In a text like this it is uncommon to speak of spirituality, but given our human proclivities for moving energy and for metaphysical explanations, it must be addressed. Although motivations to communicate can arise from many different kinds of value systems, mature values have become personal, whether they are compatible with a religion, a philosophy, or cultural traditions. In the sense that a personal cosmology is not borrowed wholesale from an external source, but instead is a part of one's achieved identity—one's essence—and functions in a manner similar to all communication, it reduces chaos and increases complexity:

> What is common to all form of spirituality is the attempt to reduce entropy in consciousness. Spiritual activity aims at producing harmony among conflicting desires, it tries to find meaning among the chance events of life, and it tries to reconcile human goals with the natural forces that impinge on them from the environment. It increases complexity by clarifying the components of individual experience such as good and bad, love and hate, pleasure and pain. (Csikszentmihalyi, 1993, p. 239)

However, our traditions no longer serve. Eastern spiritual traditions focus on harmony of the mind but fail to address reduction of social entropy. Western religions focus on an external supreme being as a source for social harmony, but in their failure to adequately address inner inconsistencies have increasingly lost their power. Everywhere, social systems continue toward entropy; norms for self-restraint fade and yet "the necessity for self-restraint is as urgent as ever" (Csikszentmihalyi, 1993, p. 241). Csikszentmihalyi suggested wisdom as an antidote for social entropy. As his concept of "wisdom" is similar to our "dialogic awareness," we look next to summaries of his three components of wisdom: cognitive, spiritual, and emotional (p.241–244).

Wisdom as a cognitive skill recognizes a reality bigger than our partial perception of it, and appreciates our impact on that reality. This sort of wisdom rests on the recognition that we create our realities symbolically, but there may be much more to the cosmos than we can encompass with our constructions. Knowing that we influence our perceived reality, we not only know that there is more that we do not know, but we must ultimately take our own constructions with a large grain of salt. The person who recognizes that dialogic tensions are inevitable in our way of knowing comes to view them dispassionately and with levity.

Wisdom as a spiritual virtue stresses internal as well as interpersonal harmony (a dialogic view of the individuation/integration dialectic). Csikszentmihalyi (1993) noted, "A wise person not only thinks deeply but acts on knowledge" (p. 243). This is a fully individuated person who brings his or her broader understanding of self and human dynamics—the relatedness of multiple social issues—out to the world beyond his or her personal concerns, and does so in joy.

Wisdom as an emotional achievement means that "it feels good" (p. 243) to be wise. Consider the Dalai Lama's smile. If he isn't smiling, he's laughing, and it's infectious. He has reasons to be sad, including the loss of his country, yet he says he is happy, and that, indeed, happiness is the purpose of life (Dalai Lama & Cutler, 1998). He affirms that to reach happiness, one must set goals (for him, inner contentment and the practice of compassion) and use internal discipline to reach them (replacing destructive with constructive mental states). This sort of self has expanded beyond ego concerns and thus "is less vulnerable to the threats that make others unhappy" (Csikszentmihalyi, 1993, p. 244) in that most ego "needs" have to do with the limits of what we perceive ... money, status, security. The constructions we've built symbolically lead us to expectations that, when unmet, make us unhappy. The exception is the dialogic thinker who is not in thrall to oppositions such as poverty/wealth, or secure/anxious.

An Ethic of Personal Development

Can it be that *dialogue, in creating the dialectical maze, also offers us the view from above that maze?* Perhaps if we speak of—symbolically reconstruct—the dialectics we have created, we can sketch a map, back up, and appreciate some of the complexity. Well, there is no tidy formula, because it is a matter of development, of individuation and integration over many cycles of external discourse and internal contemplation. However, note that the three aspects of wisdom are all related to symbolic communication. Cognitively, it is the kind of thinking that is mediated by symbols and informs our discourse. Spiritually, it is the capacity to link the individual with the social, and that is realized in communication. Emotionally, it is the ability to maintain joy, a levity of spirit, which is the result of the focus and discipline possible only in future-thinking symbol users. What suggestions can we make about the optimal development of human communication?[96] Taken out of context, these will sound simplistic, but they are grounded in the book's content overall.

1. *Develop and maintain a mind with clean yet permeable boundaries.* The successfully individuated person has not only constructed a mind through the interaction processes reviewed in previous chapters, but has maintained it by seeking dialogues with individuals who are different as well as similar to self. Remaining open to minds different from one's own may be difficult, especially early in life, but this challenges the mind to grow and encompass a wide range of perspectives, offering a broader view of humanity. *Take on tasks that are challenging but fulfilling to you.*

2. *View relationships as challenges and goals as well as support and entertainment.* Seek out complexity. Development, or actualization, is a lifelong process. Contrary to what we may have been led to believe, we are not complete at 22. *In relationships, focus on being very present for your partner, not only for the sake of the relationship but for the sake of your own growth.* As you run into people you dislike, consider the attraction/repulsion dialectic as reflective of what you lack and fear in yourself.

3. *Develop and maintain a stable and fluid self.* Welcome input to your mind/self whether or not it agrees with your established beliefs and values. This is not easy, but it becomes easier with practice. Develop the internal discipline and sense of personal responsibility necessary to transcend the vagaries of appearance, genetics, and traditional expectations. *Play at the boundaries in everyday life, and cherish the quiet moments you reserve at the core in order to consider the bigger picture.*

4. *Be responsible for self, nurture others, and contribute to the future.* The self-centered individual wants to control others in order to meet personal needs. Of course, this rarely works, because you can only affect others if they welcome you past the boundaries in dialogue, and into their core by internalizing. You can manipulate others into serving your will, but you cannot make them care about you. You can steal what others have, but their goods will not bring lasting joy. The only behavior you can be responsible for is your own—others must be responsible for theirs. This is not to say that you should not be concerned with others' welfare. Give back; regenerate the cycles of energy that have been given to you. *Invest in a harmonious future. Consider your part in it; use the skills you have for the greater good.* If the focus is constantly on the present, on fleeting concerns, or on defending against imagined dangers, there is little trust in the future. Whereas, if the focus goes to the future collective well-being of life, your current concerns are not so overwhelming and your value in the bigger picture is affirmed. Self-centered persons influence the future

negatively by increasing entropy; T-persons influence the future positively by anticipating their role in social order (Csikszentmihalyi, 1993).

5. *Value the "lightness of being" as well as its darkness.* We all have dark moments, even eras, and they can be growth opportunities. However, darkness can be addictive.[97] Choose to enjoy life, appreciating both its joys and sorrows. Consider the possibility that if everyone were in a state of "flow," we'd all be happy, nonharmful people. *Enjoy relationships of all kinds with a mix of levity and gravity.* I found the levity/gravity dialectic in Tom Robbins' (2000) recent novel: "If people are nimble enough to move freely between different perceptions of reality and if they maintain a relaxed, playful attitude well-seasoned with laughter, then they would live in harmony with the universe" (p. 388). This is the mix of open sharing and loving nonattachment, joy and irreverent wit, that results in being both "enlightened and endarkened. The ultimate" (p. 387).

Implications for the Study of Communication

Having set out the assumptions of a dialogical-developmental perspective and supported them with existing literature from a variety of disciplines, I am left knowing that this view of development is incomplete. To organize these statements into a true theory would require sorting out the links among the assumptions and specifying the communication variables that clarify them, thereby setting testable propositions. In this book, I attempted to bring in only the developmental evidence that dealt with human symbolic activity or its physiological precursors. The theoretical constructs I considered primary to such a perspective included communication functions of linking, regulation, and mentation; identity as defined by symbolic interaction; emotion mediated by symbolic activity; relationships and relational effects; and communication skills and strategies.[98]

Despite the fact that a lifespan perspective of communication is acknowledged as a good idea (Nussbaum, Pecchioni, Baringer, & Kundrat, 2002), past practice in the communication discipline treated development as either something akin to relational progression, or children's skill growth, or the process of aging. Although relationships can be viewed developmentally and aging does have some bearing on skill development, these pieces do not comprise a truly developmental theory. Most children's communication behavior has been examined either in a vacuum—as if it were not a developmental issue—or from a psychological framework, such as constructivism. I have no argument with interdisciplinary borrowing (clearly), but I do think we have to place communication in the central position in our theories—as the primary phenomenon of interest.

We now have some research on *turning points* in various sorts of relationships, but we have yet to examine how dialectical crises change us at many of the culturally anticipated shifts in life, such as the first day of kindergarten as well as the move to college, the first date as well as the first marriage, the first rejection as well as the first divorce, the early loss of parental presence as well as the later loss of a life partner.[99] It is in charting these turning points and their relational oppositions that we will have begun to map specifically human developmental processes.

We also have some solid *communication variables* such as uncertainty, expectancy, and control. But where are their origins in development, and how do they shift with sophistication? When do we first experience uncertainty, and how do we manage it communicatively? How does that management change with different relationships, and changing conceptions of those relationships? How does communicative control relate to physical abuse and neglect? Are persuasion and argumentation developmental skills that can change destructive control patterns?[100]

As a practical matter, if we are to find a way out of the morass of social ills plaguing us, we must have some maps for understanding how we got here and how we can get out. If isolation breeds individualism, then will McLuhan's "global village" of electronic networks breed communality? Will electronic networks be sufficient if people continue to use them for the pursuit of attention rather than for social unification? What communication skills are necessary for developing wisdom of the sort needed to contribute to that unification? We cannot prescribe what will work until we know who we are, communicatively, and how we got that way. I hope this book brings us a page closer to that knowledge, and provokes a new generation of scholars to look deeper.

CONCLUSION

This book began with "Oh, grow up!" which could be a blessing or a curse, depending on your early experiences and what you then chose to do with them. Perhaps the more accurate mandate would be "Oh, grow out and in!" which is not a comment on weight fluctuation, but instead on the human experience of expanding out to the boundaries and contracting in to the core. Personally, I stopped growing up when I was 13, but I continue to grow out and in, thanks to the relatives, friends, lovers, colleagues, teachers, mentors, and students in my life. I like to think that there are multiple nodes in my social network that I may never have the time or opportunity to activate. The possible boundary conditions are nearly infinite. However, finite choices pave our developmental paths, and those paths overlap and crisscross as we create and recreate boundary conditions together. This puts me in mind of Arthur, a hitchhiker through the galaxy,[101] who was thrilled to learn from a dimension-bending, pole-sitting ascetic from a distant planet that:

> We all like to congregate at boundary conditions.... Where land meets water. Where earth meets air. Where body meets mind. Where space meets time. We like to be on one side, and look at the other. (Adams, 1992, p. 109)

Here's looking at you.

NOTES

91. Interpretations of recent findings in physics that point to a unified "consciousness" of sorts abound. One accessible source is Gary Zukav's (1979) *The Dancing Wu Li Masters.*

92. Socrates and Plato revolutionized Western thought, at least in part, by introducing the notion of the "dialectic," the original function of which was "simply to force the speaker to repeat a statement already made, with the underlying assumption that there was something unsatisfactory about the statement, and it had better be rephrased" (Havelock, 1963, p. 209). The device was a question designed to disrupt complacent thinking and substitute the "unpleasant effort of a calculative reflection" (Havelock, 1963, p. 209).

93. Western scientific traditions have not welcomed research into human energy fields, but such research has been published in the USSR (e.g, Inyushin, 1981), in the United States earlier in the century (e.g., Ravitz, 1951), and more recently by nontraditional researchers (e.g., Pierrakos, 1975).

94. See Ricillo (1994) and Pribram (1986) for more detailed explanations of the energy-matter transformations between material and phenomenal, concrete and experiential, brain and mind.

95. Walter Ong (1967) had much to add on this development. His explanation involved the shift in the human senses that accompanied literacy and print media. He also predicted some of the shifts likely with the current explosion of electronic media.

96. These suggestions grew out of Csikszentmihalyi's (1993, pp. 248–249) four proposals for a more complex self, but with some additions and variations to build in the communication component more specifically.

97. For example, violence and even murder can be powerful, especially if other flow sources are unavailable. Killing others proves that the killer exists, and thus it can become the only source of self-affirmation for those who have not developed other resources (Csikszentmihalyi, 1993, p. 247)

98. This list was developed in more detail in Socha and Yingling (2001).

99. Longitudinal research designs will best serve these sorts of questions. See Nussbaum, Pecchioni, Baringer, and Kundrat (2002) for rationale and resources.

100. Infante, Chandler, and Ruud (1989) suggested that argumentation is amenable to training. Then, is training simply a more formalized kind of a development that could occur in the course of interactions with the "right" people?

101. From the Douglas Adams "trilogy," *A Hitchhiker's Guide to the Galaxy,* of which there were at least five books, including the one delivering this quote, *Mostly Harmless* (1992). These books are not only intellectually flexible, but extremely playful. Adams had levity/gravity licked.

Glossary

Many of these concepts have been adapted from scientific parlance and defined in lay terms for ease of use. For more scientific definitions, see the citations regarding the terms' use.

ACL: Adult–child language, or "motherese"; speech adapted to the child's needs.

adualistic confusion: The absence of differentiation. The inability to distinguish elements of one's environment; James' "blooming buzzing confusion."

affect: A general term referencing feelings from simple arousal to symbolic emotion.

anthroposemiotic: "Those sign system aspects of humankind's total communicative repertoire that are exclusively human" (Sebeok, 1968, p. 8; adapted by Dance, 1982, p. 144).

arcuate fasciculus: "A band of subcortical fibers connecting Broca's area and Wernicke's area in the left hemisphere of the human brain" (Gleason, 1993, p. 452).

associative complex: A set of referents chosen for their bonds to a nucleus referent. For example, if the first nucleus referent is a yellow, triangular block, then reasonable choices for a category of blocks based on it would be yellow blocks as well as triangular blocks.

attachment: The bond constituted in interaction between the infant and primary caregiver(s). The nature of this bond, according to attachment theorists, influences later relationships.

babbling: "Prespeech consisting of relatively long strings of syllables that may be used communicatively or as solo sound-play" (Gleason, 1993, p. 452).

binary: Something composed of two elements, not necessarily perceived as related.

brain: The physical structures within the skull, and extending to the spinal cord and nervous system, that govern motor behavior, body sensation, emotional responses, and serve the process of constituting a mind.

Broca's area: "Area of the left hemisphere in the frontal region" (Gleason, 1993, p. 453). Damage to this area produces difficulty with syntax and results in nonsyntactic utterances.

categorization: The ability to group qualities into a cluster of meaning.

chain complex: A set of referents chosen by consecutive links between one referent and the next. The attribute keeps changing as the set is constructed.

cognitive complexity: The number and complexity of constructs available to an individual.

collection: A complex composed of a set of referents chosen to be grouped together on the basis of one trait "in which they differ and consequently complement one another." (Vygotsky, 1934/1986, p. 114)

communication: In a very general sense, acting on information (see Dance & Larson, 1976, appendix A). Acknowledging input to perception.

communion: The empathic recognition of feeling states.

conceptualization: a term encompassing the "higher mental processes" humans typically develop beyond perceptual thought—concrete thought tied to the perceptual present—including "memory, planning or foresight, intelligence or cognitive insight … [and] evaluative judgment" (Dance & Larson, 1976, pp. 93–98). See also Vocate (1994) for a detailed explanation of the link between inner speech and conceptualization.

congruence: A tendency to synchronize one's behavior with an interactional partner.

construct: A reference axis made up of two poles of meaning; used to establish a personal orientation to people (or things).

contingency: A "temporal pattern between two events that potentially reflects the causal dependency between them" (Watson, 1994, p. 13).

convergence: A tendency to distinguish one's behavior from the interactional partner's.

conversation: Spoken interaction "in which the roles of speaker and hearer are exchanged in a nonautomatic fashion under the collaborative management of all parties" (McLaughlin, 1984, p. 271).

conversational sensitivity: The tendency to attend to and interpret conversational behaviors.

coregulation: The dialogic process of mutually regulating the interactive behaviors between partners, thereby creating consensual frames for structuring interaction (see Fogel, 1993).

critical period: "A period in development during which certain events must take place if they are to take place at all" (Gleason, 1993, p. 455).

crystallized intelligence: Learned, symbolically mediated forms of thinking.

deixis: The communicative performance of pointing out things in the environment, either literally or in deictic words. The use of immediate context in joint referencing. Deictic words: "From the Greek 'deiktikos' (able to show), words that are used as linguistic pointers, e.g., 'here,' 'there'" (Gleason, 1993, p. 455).

dialectics: The tension between two opposing but related positions. Hegelian dialectics seeks to resolve the contradictions between positions. Our view is that dialectics are not resolvable.

dialogics: The oscillation, or vibration, set up *in* the contrast between the opposing poles of a dialectic. It is this movement that stimulates change.

dichotomy: A division into two contrasting elements.

differentiation: The developmental process whereby an individual comes to perceive each object as separate and distinct from others.

discourse: Conversation that is structured by linguistic and pragmatic rules.

dualism: The perception that phenomena are divisible into two classes.

egocentric speech: Speech produced for one's own purposes alone; not adapted for the listener.

emotion: Specific mental states referencing some affective experience, usually with symbols.

emotional contagion: The process of feeling what the other is feeling, without distinguishing between one's own feeling and the other's.

empathic concern: A general concern for the welfare of the interactional partner that does not parallel one's own affect.

empathy: The capacity to feel what the other is feeling, while recognizing that the other's feeling is separate from one's own.

episodic memory: Recall consisting of entire scenarios in their contexts.

EQ/encephalization quotient: The size of the brain in proportion to body surface (Jerison, 1976).

expansions: "Providing a more adult version of the child's utterance—both phonologic and syntactic—while preserving the original word order" (Lane & Molyneaux, 1992, p. 98).

extensions: Providing "additional information on the topic expressed by the child" (Lane & Molyneaux, 1992, p. 99).

generalization: "Production of a learned response in a new environment" (Gleason & Ratner, 1993, p. 422)

glottal sounds: Consonantlike sounds (e.g., /g/, /k/) produced at the back of the throat, where the right angle of the oral cavity and pharynx is formed.

heap: A cluster of referents constituted on chance impressions alone.

holophrase: "Single word utterance used by children at the earliest stages of language acquisition that appears to carry the meaning or intent of a longer utterance" (Gleason & Ratner, 1993, p. 423).

identity: A developmental process of constituting meaning for self, based on repeated internalizations of external interaction, and the communicative performances subsequent to those internalizations that express, reaffirm, or reject the self-meanings so constituted.

indicating: Communicative procedures designed to bring the partner's attention to something.

individuation: The developmental process whereby an individual gradually perceives self as more and more clearly separate from Other; ultimately involves setting and maintaining permeable boundaries.

inner speech: Speech for self that is silent, covert, and purposeful.

internalization: The process of bringing external experience into the individual's core (mind) where it may be stored in symbols and restructured.

LAD: Language acquisition device (Chomsky, 1995); a hypothesized innate brain structure that predisposes humans to acquire syntactic language.

LASS: Language acquisition support system (Bruner, 1983); the set of more sophisticated interactants who model or scaffold language and communication behavior for the learner.

maturation: The biological process of development; the growth of one's physical structures.

means-ends relations: The ability to understand that achieving a goal (end) is associated with the behavior that preceded the achievement (means).

metalinguistic awareness: "Knowledge about language, that is, an understanding of what a word is and a consciousness of the sounds of language. The ability to think about language" (Gleason, 1993, p. 460).

mind: The process of thinking, which is constructed from perceptual experience using the instrument of brain structures, including neocortex and neural pathways.

MLU: Mean length of utterance; the average length of an utterance for either a particular person or, statistically, for a specific age group.

mood: A nonspecific feeling state that endures over time and across situations.

myelin: A fatty sheath that develops around major nerve fibers and enhances conductivity.

nasal sounds: Consonantlike sounds produced by closing the soft palate so that air resonates in and escapes from the nasal cavity (e.g., /m/, /n/, /ng/).

neocortex: The newer portion of gray matter covering subcortical structures.

neonate: A newborn, immediately after birth.

object permanence: The ability to understand that an item has a existence independent of one's visual observation of it.

ontogeny: The developmental process of individuals.

Other: In its capitalized form, refers to the generalized other, or the sense we develop of the generic human interactant as social audience

perspective taking: The cognitive capacity to adopt another's viewpoint; symbolically mediated.

phonemes: The smallest distinctive speech sounds that humans use to signal meaning.

phylogeny: The developmental process of the species; evolution.

predication: Asserting something about the subject of a proposition (Wall, 1974); the comment about a topic.

presbyacusis: The condition of less acute hearing that occurs with age.

private speech: Speech used to solve problems that have not yet been internalized.

proprioception: Receptive information about one's own movements in space.

pseudoconcept: A bridge sort of meaning between complexes and true concepts. Still constructed on the basis of concrete similarities and distinctions rather than abstracted characteristics.

quantal sounds: Maximally distinct sounds made possible by the right-angle bend in the two-tube human vocal tract.

reciprocity: The act of responding in kind; mutual exchange.

recognition memory: Involuntary recall that occurs only when triggered by a stimulus.

reference: The process of alluding to an object or idea; a function of the mind that may be expressed communicatively.

relationship: A connection between two distinct selves, constructed by both symbolic and nonsymbolic interaction, and constituted dialogically.

role play: Practicing the set of behaviors one has associated with a particular social role.

scaffolding: The process of modeling a behavior or set of behaviors for a learner. The idea is to provide enough structure so that the learner can expand from that foundation.

script: A scaffold for social behavior; a set of standard routines for accomplishing social activity.

self-awareness: A dialectic of objective self-awareness (internal focus on self) and subjective self-awareness (external focus on environment).

self-monitoring: The tendency to monitor the social environment for cues to inform appropriate adaptation of one's social behavior to the context.

self-reflexiveness: The capacity to perceive self objectively, as another object of analysis.

semantic memory: Recall that may be voluntarily cued by the use of symbols.

sign: "A stimulus announcing that of which it is a part; concrete and fixed regardless of context" (Dance, 1982, p. 125).

signal: A subset of signs which acquires its "sign characteristics through the process of pair-wise conditioning" (Dance, 1982, p. 125).

significant symbol: A symbol that has at least some degree of shared meaning for interactants; that is, the meaning is significant for both in a similar way.

social cognition: "The process by which individuals develop the ability to monitor, control, and predict the behavior of others" (Rochat & Striano, 1999, p. 4).

social interaction: Communicative performances among identities.

socialized speech: Speech produced in recognition of, and adapted to, the interacting other.

spoken symbolic interaction: Communicative performances conducted with spoken symbols; peculiarly human communication.

subglottal pressure: The air pressure built up by closing the larynx over air held in the lungs.

symbol: "A stimulus whose relationship with that with which it is associated is a result of the decision or arbitrary agreement of human user(s)" (Dance, 1982, p. 126).

syntax: The structural properties of language; the rules that allow us to recognize parts of speech and their ordering to express complete ideas.

supralaryngeal vocal tract: All parts of the vocal tract above the larynx, including the pharynx and oral and nasal cavities.

temperament: "A slight initial bias that favors certain affects and actions" (Kagan, 1994, p. 35); a proposed genetic predisposition to either approach or avoid social interaction.

Wernicke's area: "Speech area in the posterior region of the left hemisphere" (Gleason, 1993, p. 467). Damage to this area results in problems with attaching meaning to sound—poor comprehension and meaningless, although syntactically correct, speech.

zone of proximal development: "In Vygotskyian theory, the range of behaviors available to a child in the helpful presence of a guiding adult" (Gleason, 1993, p. 467).

References

Abbey, A. (1982). Sex differences in attributions for friendly behavior: Do males misperceive females' friendliness? *Journal of Personality and Social Psychology, 42,* 830–838.

Abe, J. A., & Izard, C. E. (1999). Compliance, noncompliance strategies, and the correlates of compliance in 5-year-old Japanese and American children. *Social Development, 8*(1), 1–20.

Adams, D. (1992). *Mostly harmless.* New York: Ballantine.

Adams, G. R., & Archer, S. L. (1994). Identity: A precursor to intimacy. In S. L. Archer (Ed.), *Interventions for adolescent identity development* (pp. 193–213). Thousand Oaks, CA: Sage.

Adams-Webber, J. (1985). Construing self and others. In F. Epting & A. Landfield (Eds.), *Anticipating personal construct theory* (pp. 58–69). Lincoln, NB: UNebraska Press.

Adams-Webber, J. R. (1982). Assimilation and contrast in personal judgment: The dichotomy corollary. In J. Mancuso & J. R. Adams-Webber (Eds.), *The construing person* (pp. 96–112). New York: Praeger.

Adelman, M. B., & Bankoff, E. A. (1990). Life-span concerns: Implications for mid-life adult singles. In H. Giles & N. Coupland (Eds.), *Communication, health and the elderly* (Vol. 8, pp. 64–91). Manchester, UK: Manchester University Press.

Ade-Ridder, L., & Brubaker, T. H. (1983). The quality of long-term marriages. In T. H. Brubaker (Ed.), *Family relationships in later life* (pp. 21–30). Beverly Hills, CA: Sage.

Adler, M. J. (1967). *The difference of man and the difference it makes.* New York: Holt, Rinehart & Winston.

Afifi, W. A., & Lee, J. W. (2000). Balancing instrumental and identity goals in relationships: The role of request directness and request persistence in the selection of sexual resistance strategies. *Communication Monographs, 67*(3), 284–305.

Ahrons, C., & Rodgers, R. H. (1987). *Divorced families: A multidisciplinary view.* New York: Norton.

Aiken, L. R. (1998). *Human development in adulthood.* New York: Plenum Press.

Ainsworth, M. D. S., Blehar, M. C., Waters, E., & Wall, S. (1978). *Patterns of attachment: A psychological study of the strange situation.* Hillsdale, NJ: Lawrence Erlbaum Associates.

Ainsworth, M. D. S., & Wittig, B. A. (1969). Attachment and the exploratory behaviour of one-year-olds in a strange situation. In B. M. Foss (Ed.), *Determinants of infant behaviour* (Vol. 4, pp. 113–136). London: Methuen.

Alberts, J. K. (1988). An analysis of couples' conversational complaints. *Communication Monographs, 55,* 184–197.

Alberts, J. K. (1989). A descriptive taxonomy of couples' complaint interactions. *Southern Communication Journal, 54,* 125–143.

Aldous, J. (1975). The search for alternatives: Parental behaviors and children's original problem solutions. *Journal of Marriage and the Family, 37,* 711–722.

Aleman, M. W. (2001). Complaining among the elderly: Examining multiple dialectical oppositions to independence in a retirement community. *Western Journal of Communication, 65*(1), 89–112.

Allen, J. J. (1986). A developmental approach to self-monitoring behavior. *Communication Monographs, 53,* 277–288.

Allen, M., & Burrell, N. (1996). Comparing the impact of homosexual and heterosexual parents on children: Meta-analysis of existing research. *Journal of Homosexuality, 32*(2), 19–33.

Allen, R. R., & Brown, K. L. (1976). *Developing communication competence in children: A report of the Speech Communication Association's national project on speech communication competencies.* Skokie, IL: National Textbook Company.

Allen, V. L., & Atkinson, M. L. (1978). Encoding of nonverbal behavior by high-achieving and low-achieving children. *Journal of Educational Psychology, 70,* 298–305.

Allport, F. H. (1924). *Social psychology.* Boston: Houghton Mifflin.

Altman, I. (1990). Toward a transactional perspective: A personal journey. In I. Altman & K. Christensen (Eds.), *Environment and behavior studies: Emergence of intellectual traditions* (pp. 225–255). New York: Plenum.

Altman, I. (1993). Dialectics, physical environments, and personal relationships. *Communication Monographs, 60,* 26–34.

Altman, I., Vinsel, A., & Brown, B. (1981). Dialectic conceptions in social psychology: An application to social penetration and privacy regulation. In D. Stokols & I. Altman (Eds.), *Handbook of environmental psychology* (Vol. 1, pp. 7–40). New York: Wiley.

Ambert, A. (2001). *The effect of children on parents* (2nd ed.). Binghamton, NY: Haworth.

Anderson, D. Y., & Hayes, C. L. (1996). *Gender, identity, and self-esteem: A new look at adult development.* New York: Springer.

Anderson, P. A., Anderson, J. F., & Mayton, S. M. (1985). The development of nonverbal communication in the classroom: Teachers' perceptions of students in grades K–12. *Western Journal of Speech Communication, 49*(3), 188–203.

Anderson, P. A., & Guerrero, L. K. (1998). *Handbook of communication and emotion.* San Diego: Academic Press.

Applegate, J. L., Burleson, B. R., & Delia, J. G. (1992). Reflection-enhancing parenting as antecedent to children's social-cognitive and communicative development. In I. E. Sigel, A. V. McGillicuddy-Delisi, & J. J. Goodnow (Eds.), *Parental belief systems: The psychological consequences for children* (2nd ed., pp. 3–39). Hillsdale, NJ: Lawrence Erlbaum Associates.

Applegate, J. L., & Delia, J. G. (1980). Person-centered speech, psychological development, and the contexts of language usage. In R. St. Clair & H. Giles (Eds.), *The social and psychological contexts of language.* Hillsdale, NJ: Lawrence Erlbaum Associates.

Archer, S. L., & Waterman, A. S. (1988). Psychological individualism: Issues of process, domain, and timing. *Journal of Adolescence, 12,* 117–138.

Aronoff, C. (1974). Old age in prime time. *Journal of Communication, 24,* 86–87.

Aslin, R. N. (1987). Visual and auditory development in infancy. In J. D. Osofsky (Ed.), *Handbook of infant development* (2nd ed., pp. 5–97). New York: Wiley.

Astin, A. W. (1977). *Four critical years: Effects of college on beliefs, attitudes, and knowledge.* San Francisco: Jossey-Bass.

Atchley, R. C. (1994). *Social forces and aging* (7th ed.). Belmont, CA: Wadsworth.

Atkinson, L., Niccols, A., Paglia, A., Coolbear, J., Parker, K. C. H., Poulton, L., Guger, S., & Sitarenios, G. (2000). A meta-analysis of time between maternal sensitivity and attachment assessments: Implications for internal working models in infancy/toddlerhood. *Journal of Social and Personal Relationships, 17*(6), 791–810.

Babchuk, N., Peters, G. R., Hoyt, D. R., & Kaiser, M. A. (1979). The voluntary associations of the aged. *Journal of Gerontology, 34,* 579–587.

Bachman, G., & Zakahi, W. R. (2000). Adult attachment and strategic relational communication: Love schemas and affinity-seeking. *Communication Reports, 13*(1), 11–19.

Baldwin, J. M. (1896). A new factor in evolution. *American Naturalist, 30,* 441–451.

Baldwin, J. M. (1902). *Social and ethical interpretations in mental development.* New York: Macmillan.

Ball, R. (1979). The dialectical method: Its application to social theory. *Social Forces, 57,* 785–798.

Baltes, M. M., & Wahl, H. W. (1996). Patterns of communication in old age: The dependency-support and independency-ignore script. *Health Communication, 8,* 217–232.

Baranowski, M. D. (1982). Grandparent–adolescent relations: Beyond the nuclear family. *Adolescence, 17,* 375–384.

Barber, N. (2001). Gender differences in effects of mood on body image. *Sex Roles, 44*(1–2), 99–108.

Barks, C. (with Moyne, J.). (1995). *The essential Rumi.* New York: HarperCollins.

Barresi, J., & Moore, C. (1996). Intentional relations and social understanding. *Behavioral and Brain Sciences, 16,* 513–514.

Bartholomew, K., & Horowitz, L. (1991). Attachment styles among young adults: A test of a four-category model. *Journal of Personality and Social Psychology, 61,* 226–244.

Barton, M., & Tomasello, M. (1991). Joint attention and conversation in mother–infant–sibling triads. *Child Development, 62,* 517–529.

Basile, R. (1974). Lesbian mothers I. *Women's Rights Law Reporter, 2,* 3–18.

Baskett, L. M. (1984). Ordinal position differences in children's family interactions. *Developmental Psychology, 20,* 1026–1031.

Basseches, M. (1984a). *Dialectical thinking and adult development.* Norwood, NJ: Ablex.

Basseches, M. (1984b). Dialectical thinking as a metasystematic form of cognitive organization. In M. L. Commons, F. A. Richards, & C. Armon (Eds.), *Beyond formal operations: Late adolescent and adult cognitive development* (pp. 216–238). New York: Praeger.

Bateson, M. C. (1989). *Composing a life.* New York: Penguin.

Baumrind, D. (1966). The effects of authoritative parental control on child behavior. *Child Development, 37,* 887–907.

Baumrind, D. (1971). Current patterns of parental authority. *Developmental Psychology Monographs, 4,* 1–102.

Baumrind, D. (1989). Rearing competent children. In W. Damon (Ed.), *Child development today and tomorrow* (pp. 349–378). San Francisco: Jossey-Bass.

Baxter, L. A. (1979). Self-disclosure as a relationships disengagement strategy: An exploratory investigation. *Human Communication Research, 5,* 215–222.

Baxter, L. A. (1986). Gender differences in heterosexual relationship rules embedded in break-up accounts. *Journal of Social and Personal Relationships, 3,* 289–306.

Baxter, L. A. (1988). A dialectical perspective on communication strategies in relationship development. In S. W. Duck (Ed.), *Handbook of personal relationships* (pp. 257–273). London: Wiley.

Baxter, L. A. (1990). Dialectical contradictions in relationship development. *Journal of Social and Personal Relationships, 7,* 69–88.

Baxter, L. A., Braithwaite, D. O., Golish, T. D., & Olson, L. N. (2002). Contradictions of interaction for wives of elderly husbands with adult dementia. *Journal of Applied Communication Research, 30*(1), 1–26.

Baxter, L. A., Braithwaite, D. O., & Nicholson, J. H. (1999). Turning points in the development of blended families. *Journal of Social and Personal Relationships, 16*(3), 291–313.

Baxter, L. A., & Erbert, L. A. (1999). Perceptions of dialectical contradictions in turning points of development in heterosexual romantic relationships. *Journal of Social and Personal Relationships, 16*(5), 547–569.

Baxter, L. A., & Montgomery, B. M. (1996). *Relating: Dialogues & dialectics.* New York: Guilford.

Baxter, L. A., & Pittman, G. (2001). Communicatively remembering turning points of relational development in heterosexual romantic relationships. *Communication Reports, 14*(1), 1–17.

Baxter, L. A., & Wilmot, W. (1985). Taboo topics in romantic relationships. *Journal of Social and Personal Relationships, 2,* 253–269.

Bayer, C. L., & Cegala, D. J. (1992). Trait verbal aggressiveness and argumentativeness: Relations with parenting style. *Western Journal of Communication, 56,* 301–310.

Bearison, D. J. (1991). *"They never want to tell you": Children talk about cancer.* Cambridge, MA: Harvard University Press.

Beatty, M. J., Marshall, L. A., & Rudd, J. E. (2001). A twins study of communicative adaptability: Heritability of individual differences. *Quarterly Journal of Speech, 87*(4), 366–377.

Beatty, M. J., & McCroskey, J. C. (1998). Interpersonal communication as temperamental expression: A communibiological paradigm. In J. C. McCroskey, J. A. Daly, M. M. Martin, & M. J. Beatty (Eds.), *Communication and personality: Trait perspectives* (pp. 41–68). Cresskill, NJ: Hampton.

Beatty, M. J., McCroskey, J. C., & Valencic, K. M. (2001). *The biology of communication: A communibiological perspective.* Cresskill, NJ: Hampton.

Bedford, V. H. (1994). Sibling relationships in middle and old age. In R. Blieszner & V. H. Bedford (Eds.), *Aging and the family: Theory and research* (pp. 201–222). Westport, CT: Praeger.

Beilin, R. (1981–1982). Social functions of denial of death. *Omega, 12,* 25–35.

Bell, A. P., & Weinberg, M. S. (1978). *Homosexualities: A study of diversity among men and women.* New York: Simon & Schuster.

Bell, R. R. (1981). Friendships of women and men. *Psychology of Women Quarterly, 5,* 402–417.

Bell, R., & Wechsler, H. (1997). Correlates of college student marijuana use: Results of a U.S. national survey. *Addiction, 92*(5), 571–582.

Bellinger, D., & Gleason, J. (1982). Sex differences in parental directives to young children. *Sex Roles, 8,* 1123–1139.

Belsky, J. K. (1990). *The psychology of aging* (2nd ed.). Pacific Grove, CA: Brooks/Cole.

Belsky, J., Fish, M., & Isabella, R. (1991). Continuity and discontinuity in infant negative and positive emotionality: Family antecedents and attachment consequences. *Developmental Psychology, 27*(3), 421–431.

Belsky, J., Ward, M. J., & Rovine, M. (1986). Prenatal expectations, postnatal experiences, and the transition to parenthood. In R. Ashmore & D. Brodinsky (Eds.), *Thinking about the family: Views of parents and children* (pp. 119–145). Hillsdale, NJ: Lawrence Erlbaum Associates.

Bendtschneider, L. (1994). *"We all like to dance and play dominoes": The nature and maintenance of couple friends.* Unpublished doctoral dissertation, University of Iowa, Iowa City.

Bennell, C., Alison, L. J., Stein, K. L., Alison, E. K., & Canter, D. V. (2001). Sexual offenses against children as the abusive exploitation of conventional adult–child relationships. *Journal of Social and Personal Relationships, 18*(2), 155–171.

Bennett, S. (1998). *The plugged-in parent: What you should know about kids and computers.* New York: Random House.

Berger, C. R., & Bradac, J. J. (1982). *Language and social knowledge: Uncertainty in interpersonal relations.* London: Edward Arnold.

Berger, C. R., & Gudykunst, W. (1991). Uncertainty and communication. In B. Dervin & M. Voigt (Eds.), *Progress in communication sciences* (Vol. 10, pp. 21–66). Norwood, NJ: Ablex.

Berk, L. E. (1998). *Development through the lifespan.* Needham Heights, MA: Allyn & Bacon.

Bernard, M., & Phillipson, C. (1995). Retirement and leisure. In J. F. Nussbaum & J. Coupland (Eds.), *Handbook of communication and aging research* (pp. 285–315). Hillsdale, NJ: Lawrence Erlbaum Associates.

Berndt, T. J., & Perry, T. B. (1986). Children's perceptions of friendships as supportive relationships. *Developmental Psychology, 22,* 640–648.

Bernstein, B. (1971). *Class, codes and control* (Vol. 1). London: Routledge & Kegan Paul.

Bernstein, B. (1973). *Class, codes and control* (Vol. 2). London: Routledge & Kegan Paul.

Bernstein, B. (1977). *Class, codes and control* (Vol. 3, 2nd ed.). London: Routledge & Kegan Paul.

Berry, M. F. (1969). *Language disorders of children.* New York: Appleton-Century-Crofts.

Berry, R. E., & Williams, F. L. (1987). Assessing the relationship between quality of life and marital and income satisfaction: A path analytic approach. *Journal of Marriage and the Family, 49,* 107–116.

Berzonsky, M. D. (1989). The self as a theorist: Individual differences in identity formation. *Journal of Personal Construct Psychology, 2,* 363–376.

Berzonsky, M. D. (1990). Self-construction over the life span: A process perspective on identity formation. In G. J. Neimeyer & R. A. Neimeyer (Eds.), *Advances in personal construct theory,* (Vol. 1, pp. 155–186). Stamford, CT: JAI Press.

Bethea, L. S. (2002). The impact of an older adult parent on communicative satisfaction and dyadic adjustment in the long-term marital relationship: Adult-children and spouses' retrospective accounts. *Journal of Applied Communication Research, 30*(2), 107–125.

Bever, T. G. (1961). *Development from vocal to verbal behavior in children.* Unpublished master's thesis, Harvard University, Cambridge, MA.

Bever, T. G. (1982). Regression in the service of development. In T. G. Bever (Ed.), *Regressions in mental development: Basic phenomena and theories* (pp. 153–188). Hillsdale, NJ: Lawrence Erlbaum Associates.

Bidell, T. (1988). Vygotsky, Piaget and the dialectic of development. *Human Development, 31*(6), 329–345.

Bigelow, B. J. (1977). Children's friendship expectations: A cognitive-developmental study. *Child Development, 48,* 246–253.

Bigelow, B. J., Tesson, G., & Lewko, J. H. (1996). *Learning the rules: The anatomy of children's relationships.* New York: Guilford.

Biller, H. B. (1974). Paternal and sex-role factors in cognitive and academic functioning. In J. K. Cole & R. Dienstbier (Eds.), *Nebraska Symposium of Motivation* (pp. 83–123). Lincoln: University of Nebraska Press.

Birkerts, S. (1994). *The Gutenberg elegies.* New York: Ballantine Books.

Bivens, J. A., & Berk, L. E. (1990). A longitudinal study of the development of elementary school children's private speech. *Merrill-Palmer Quarterly, 36*(4), 443–463.

Black, B. (1989). Interactive pretense: Social and symbolic skills in preschool play groups. *Merrill-Palmer Quarterly, 35*(4), 379–397.

Blamey, P. J., Barry, J. G., & Jacq, P. (2001). Phonetic inventory development in young cochlear implant users 6 years postoperation. *Journal of Speech, Language & Hearing Research, 44*(1), 73–79.

Blanchard, R., & Biller, H. B. (1971). Father availability and academic performance among third-grade boys. *Developmental Psychology, 4*, 301–305.

Blanchard-Fields, F. (1986). Reasoning on social dilemmas varying in emotional saliency: An adult developmental perspective. *Psychology and Aging, 1*, 325–333.

Bloom, K. (1988). Quality of adult vocalizations affects the quality of infant vocalizations. *Journal of Child Language, 15*, 469–480.

Bloom, K., & Lo, E. (1990). Adult perceptions of vocalizing infants. *Infant Behavior and Development, 13*, 209–219.

Bloom, L., Lightbown, P., & Hood, L. (1975). Structure and variation in child language. *Monographs of the Society for Research in Child Development, 40*(2, Serial No. 160), 1–78.

Bly, R. (1979). A story in three stages. In S. Colegrave, *Uniting heaven and earth* (pp. iv–xiii). Los Angeles: Jeremy P. Tarcher.

Bochner, A., & Ellis, C. (1992). Personal narrative as a social approach to interpersonal communication. *Communication Theory, 2*, 65–72.

Bogin, B. (1994). Adolescence in evolutionary perspective. *Acta Paediatrica Supplement, 401*, 29–35.

Booth, A., & Hess, E. (1974). Cross-sex friendships. *Journal of Marriage and Family, 36*, 38–47.

Borke, H. (1971). Interpersonal perception of young children: Egocentrism or empathy? *Developmental Psychology, 5*, 263–269.

Bornstein, M. H., Tal, J., & Rahn, C. (1992). Functional analysis of the contents of maternal speech to infants of 5 to 13 months in four cultures: Argentina, France, Japan, and the United States. *Developmental Psychology, 28*(4), 593–603.

Boster, F. J., & Stiff, J. B. (1984). Compliance-gaining message selection behavior. *Human Communication Research, 10*(4), 539–556.

Bowlby, J. (1973). *Attachment and loss: Vol. 2. Separation.* New York: Basic Books.

Bowlby, J. (1980). *Attachment and loss: Vol. 3. Loss, sadness and depression.* New York: Basic Books.

Boyd, R. (1969). The valued grandparent: A changing social role. In D. W. Donahue, J. L. Kornbluh, & L. Powers (Eds.), *Living in a multigenerational family* (pp. 90–106). Ann Arbor: Institute of Gerontology, University of Michigan.

Bozett, F. (1987). Children of gay fathers. In F. Bozett (Ed.), *Gay and lesbian parents* (pp. 38–57). New York: Praeger.

Brack, G., LaClave, L., & Wyatt, A. S. (1992). The relationship of problem solving and reframing to stress and depression in female college students. *Journal of College Student Development, 33*, 124–131.

Brandstadter, J. (1999). The self in action and development: Cultural, biosocial, and ontogenetic bases of intentional self-development. In J. Brandstadter & R. Lerner (Eds.),

Action and self-development: Theory and research through the life span (pp. 37–66). Thousand Oaks, CA: Sage.

Brazelton, T. B. (1962). Crying in infancy. *Pediatrics, 29,* 579–588.

Brazelton, T. B. (1973). *Neonatal behavioral assessment scale.* Philadelphia: Lippencott.

Brazelton, T. B., Koslowski, B., & Main, M. (1974). The origins of reciprocity: The early mother-infant interaction. In M. Lewis & L. A. Rosenblum (Eds.), *The effect of the infant on its caregiver* (pp. 49–76). New York: Wiley.

Brendgen, M., Markiewicz, D., Doyle, A. B., & Bukowski, W. M. (2001). The relations between friendship quality, ranked-friendship preference, and adolescents' behavior with their friends. *Merrill-Palmer Quarterly, 47*(3), 395–415.

Brendgen, M., Vitaro, F., Doyle, A. B., Markiewicz, D., & Bukowski, W. M. (2002). Same-sex peer relations and romantic relationships during early adolescence: Interactive links to emotional, behavioral, and academic adjustment. *Merrill-Palmer Quarterly, 48*(1), 77–103.

Bretherton, I. (1987). New perspectives on attachment relations: Security, communication and internal working models. In J. D. Osofsky (Ed.), *Handbook of infant development* (2nd ed., pp. 1061–1100). New York: Wiley.

Bretherton, I., Fritz, J., Zahn-Waxler, C., & Ridgeway, D. (1986). Learning to talk about emotions: A functionalist perspective. *Child Development, 57,* 529–548.

Briere, J. (1989). *Therapy for adults molested as children.* New York: Springer.

Briere, J. (1992). *Child abuse trauma: Theory and treatment of the lasting effects.* Newbury Park, CA: Sage.

Brines, J., & Joyner, K. (1999). The ties that bind: Principles of cohesion in cohabitation and marriage. *American Sociological Review, 64,* 333–35.

Broberg, A., Lamb, M. E., & Hwang, P. (1990). Inhibition: Its stability and correlates in 16- to 40-month-old children. *Child Development, 61,* 1153–1163.

Brody, E. (1985). Parent care as a normative stress. *The Gerontologist, 5,* 19–29.

Brody, G. H., Stoneman, Z., & Burke, M. (1987). Child temperaments, maternal differential behavior, and sibling relationships. *Developmental Psychology, 23,* 354–362.

Brody, L. R., & Hall, J. A. (1993). Gender and emotion. In M. Lewis & J. M. Haviland (Eds.), *Handbook of emotions* (pp. 447–460). New York: Guilford.

Brokaw, T. (1998). *The greatest generation.* New York: Random House.

Broughton, J. M. (1984). Not beyond formal operations but beyond Piaget. In M. L. Commons, F. A. Richards, & C. Armon (Eds.), *Beyond formal operations: Late adolescent and adult cognitive development* (pp. 395–412). New York: Praeger.

Brown, B. B. (1981). A life-span approach to friendship: Age-related dimensions of an ageless relationship. In H. Z. Lopata & D. Maines (Eds.), *Research in the interweave of social roles: Friendship* (Vol. 2, pp. 23–50). Greenwich, CT: JAI Press.

Brown, B. B., Werner, C. M., & Altman, I. (1996). Choicepoints for dialecticians: A dialectical/transactional perspective on close relationships. In L. Baxter & B. Montgomery (Eds.), *Dialectical approaches to studying personal relationships* (pp. 000–000). Hillsdale, NJ: Lawrence Erlbaum Associates.

Brown, B. B., Werner, C. M., & Altman, I. (1998). Choice points for dialecticians: A dialectical-transactional perspective on close relationships. In B. M. Montgomery & L. A. Baxter (Eds.), *Dialectical approaches to studying personal relationships* (pp. 137–154). Mahwah, NJ: Lawrence Erlbaum Associates.

Brown, R. (1973). *A first language.* Cambridge, MA: Harvard University Press.

Bruner, J. (1975). From communication to language: A psychological perspective. *Cognition, 3,* 255–287.

Bruner, J. (1977). Early social interaction and language acquisition. In H. R. Schaffer (Ed.), *Studies in mother–infant interaction* (pp. 271–289). London: Academic Press.

Bruner, J. (1983). *Child's talk: Learning to use language.* New York: Norton.

Bruner, J. (1985). Vygotsky: A historical and conceptual perspective. In J. V. Wertsch (Ed.), *Culture, communication, cognition: Vygotskian perspectives* (pp. 21–34). Cambridge, UK: Cambridge University Press.

Bruner, J. (1986). *Actual minds, possible worlds.* Cambridge, MA: Harvard University Press.

Buchanan, C. M., Eccles, J. S., & Becker, J. B. (1992). Are adolescents the victims of raging hormones? Evidence for activational effects of hormones on moods and behavior at adolescence. *Psychological Bulletin, 111,* 62–107.

Buck, R. (1975). Nonverbal communication of affect in children. *Journal of Personality and Social Psychology, 31,* 644–653.

Buck-Morss, S. (1975). Socio-economic bias in Piaget's theory and its implications for cross-cultural studies. *Human Development, 18,* 35–49.

Buhrke, R. A., & Fuqua, D. R. (1987). Sex differences in same- and cross-sex supportive relationships. *Sex Roles, 17,* 339–352.

Buhrmester, D., & Furman, W. (1986). The changing functions of friends in childhood: A neo-Sullivanian perspective. In V. J. Derlega & B. A. Winstead (Eds.), *Friendship and social interaction* (pp. 41–62) New York: Springer-Verlag.

Buhrmester, D., & Furman, W. (1987). The development of companionship and intimacy. *Child Development, 58,* 1101–1113.

Bukowksi, W. M., & Hoza, B. (1989). Popularity and friendship: Issues in theory, measurement, and outcome. In T. J. Berndt & G. W. Ladd (Eds.), *Peer relationships in child development* (pp. 15–45). New York: Wiley.

Bulcroft, K., & Bulcroft, R. A. (1985). Dating and courtship in later life: An exploratory study. In W. A. Peterson & J. Quadagno (Eds.), *Social bonds in later life* (pp. 115–128). Beverly Hills, CA: Sage.

Bumpass, L. L., & Sweet, J. A. (1989). National estimates of cohabitation. *Demography, 26,* 615–625.

Burke, K. (1952). A dramatistic view of the origins of language. *The Quarterly Journal of Speech, 38,* 251–264, 446–460.

Burke, K. (1966). *Language as symbolic action.* Berkeley: University of California Press.

Burleson, B. R. (1986). Communication skills and childhood peer relationships: An overview. In M. L. McLaughlin (Ed.), *Communication Yearbook 9* (pp. 143–180). Beverly Hills, CA: Sage.

Burleson, B. R. (1990). Comforting as social support: Relational consequences of supportive behaviors. In S. Duck (Ed.), *Personal relationships and social support* (pp. 66–82). London: Sage.

Burleson, B. R. (1994a). Comforting messages: Significance, approaches, and effects. In B. R. Burleson, T. L. Albrecht, & I. G. Sarason (Eds.), *Communication of social support* (pp. 3–28). Thousand Oaks, CA: Sage.

Burleson, B. R. (1994b). Comforting messages: Features, functions, and outcomes. In J. A. Daly, & J. M. Wiemann (Eds.), *Strategic interpersonal communication* (pp. 135–162). Hillsdale, NJ: Lawrence Erlbaum Associates.

Burleson, B. R., & Kunkel, A. (2002). Parental and peer contributions to the emotional support skills of the child: From whom do children learn to express support? *The Journal of Family Communication, 2*(2), 79–97.

Burleson, B. R., Kunkel, A. W., & Szolwinski, J. B. (1997). Similarity in cognitive complexity and attraction to friends and lovers: Experimental and correlational studies. *Journal of Constructivist Psychology, 10*(3), 221–248.

Burr, W. R., Leigh, G. K., Day, R. D., & Constantine, J. (1979). Symbolic interaciton and the family. In W. R. Burr, R. Hill, F. I. Nye, & I. L. Reiss (Eds.), *Contemporary theories about the family* (Vol. 2, pp. 42–111). New York: Free Press.

Burton, L. M. (1992). Black grandparents rearing children of drug-addicted parents: Stressors, outcomes, and social service needs. *The Gerontologist, 32*(6), 744–751.

Butterworth, G. (1995). Self as an object of consciousness in infancy. In P. Rochat (Ed.), *The self in infancy: Theory and research* (pp. 35–51). Amsterdam: Elsevier Science.

Butterworth, G. E. (1992). Origins of self-perception in infancy. *Psychological Inquiry, 3*(2), 103–111.

Butterworth, G. E., & Cochran, E. (1980). Towards a mechanism of joint visual attention in human infancy. *International Journal of Behavioral Development, 3*, 253–272.

Button, L. (1979). Friendship patterns. *Journal of Adolescence, 2*, 187–199.

Buunk, B. P., & Prins, K. S. (1998). Loneliness, exchange orientation,and reciprocity in friendships. *Personal Relationships, 5*(1), 1–14.

Casaer, P. J. M. (1993). The human brain and longitudinal research in human development. In D. Magnusson & P. J. M. Casaer (Eds.), *Longitudinal research on individual development: Present status and future perspectives* (pp. 51–59). New York: Cambridge University Press.

Calkins, S. D., & Fox, N. A. (1992). The relations among infant temperament, attachment, and behavioral inhibition at 24 months. *Child Development, 63*, 1456–1472.

Calkins, S. D., & Fox, N. A. (1994). Individual differences in the biological aspects of temperament. In J. E. Bates & T. D. Wachs (Eds.), *Temperament: Individual differences at the interface of biology and behavior* (pp. 199–218).Washington, DC: American Psychological Association.

Campbell, D. E., & Campbell, T. (2000). The mentoring relationship: Differing perceptions of benefits. *College Student Journal, 34*(4), 516–524.

Camras, L. A., Malatesta, C., & Izard, C. (1991). The development of facial expression in infancy. In R. Feldman & B. Rime (Eds.), *Fundamentals of non-verbal behavior*. New York: Cambridge University Press.

Camras, L. A., Sullivan, J., & Michel, G. (1993). Do infants express discrete emotions? Adult judgments of facial, vocal and body actions. *Journal of Nonverbal Behavior, 17*(3), 171–186.

Canary, D. J., Cupach, W. R., & Messman, S. J. (1995). *Relationship conflict*. Thousand Oaks, CA: Sage.

Canary, D. J., & Emmers-Sommer, T. M. (1997). *Sex and gender differences in personal relationships*. New York: Guilford.

Canary, D. J., Stafford, L., Hause, K. S., & Wallace, L. A. (1993). An inductive analysis of relational maintenance strategies: Comparisons among lovers, relatives, friends, and others. *Communication Research Reports 10*(1), 5–14.

Cantor, J., & Mares, M. (2001). The effects of television on child and family emotional well-being. In J. Bryant & J. A. Bryant (Eds.), *Television and the American family* (2nd ed., pp. 317–332). Mahwah, NJ: Lawrence Erlbaum Associates.

Cantor, J., & Omdahl, B. L. (1991). Effects of fictional media depictions of realistic threats on children's emotional responses, expectations, worries, and liking for related activities. *Communication Monographs, 58*, 384–401.

Cantor, M. H. (1983). Strain among caregivers: A study of experiences in the United States. *The Gereontologist, 23*, 597–604.

Capaldi, D. M., & Crosby, L. (1977). Observed and reported psychological and physical aggression in young, at-risk couples. *Social Development, 6*, 184–206.

Cappella J. N., & Greene, J. O. (1982). A discrepancy-arousal explanation of mutual influence in expressive behavior for adult and infant-adult interaction. *Communication Monographs, 49,* 89–114.

Carbery, J., & Buhrmester, D. (1998). Friendship and need fulfillment during three phases of young adulthood. *Journal of Social and Personal Relationships, 15*(3), 393–410.

Cargen, L., & Melko, M. (1982). *Singles: Myths and realities.* Beverly Hills, CA: Sage.

Carstairs-McCarthy, A. (1999). *The origins of complex language: An inquiry into the evolutionary beginnings of sentences, syllables, and truth.* Oxford, UK: Oxford University Press.

Case, R. (1991). Stages in the development of the young child's first sense of self. *Developmental Review, 11,* 210–230

Cassidy, J., Parke, R. D., Butkovsky, L., & Braungart, J. (1992). Family-peer connections: The roles of emotional expressiveness within the family and children's understanding of emotions. *Child Development, 63,* 603–618.

Cattell, R. B. (1963). The theory of fluid and crystallized intelligence: A critical experiment. *Journal of Educational Psychology, 54,* 1–22.

Caughlin, J. P., & Huston, T. L. (2002). A contextual analysis of the association between demand/withdraw and marital satisfaction. *Personal Relationships, 9,* 95–119.

Cazden, C. B. (1972). *Child language and education.* New York: Holt, Rinehart & Winston.

Cazden, C. B. (1986). Classroom discourse. In M. E. Wittrock (Ed.), *Handbook of research on teaching* (3rd ed.). New York: Macmillan.

Cazden, C. B. (1988). *Classroom discourse: The language of teaching and learning.* Portsmouth, NH: Heineman.

Cherlin, A., & Furstenberg, F. F. (1986). Grandparents and family crisis. *Generations, 10,* 26–28.

Chickering, A. W. (1974). The impact of various college environments on personality development. *Journal of the American College Health Association, 23*(2), 82–83.

Chodorow, N. (1978). *The reproduction of mothering.* Berkeley: University of California Press.

Chomsky, N. (1957). *Syntactic structures.* The Hague: Mouton & Co.

Chomsky, N. (1965). *Aspects of the theory of syntax.* Cambridge, MA: MIT Press.

Chovil, N. (1994). Equivocation as an interactional event. In W. R. Cupach & B. H. Spitzberg (Eds.), *The dark side of interpersonal communication* (pp. 105–123). Hillsdale, NJ: Lawrence Erlbaum Associates.

Cicchetti, D. (1989). How research on child maltreatment has informed the study of child development: Perspectives from developmental psychology. In D. Cicchetti & V. Carlson (Eds.), *Child maltreatment: Theory and research on the causes and consequences of child abuse and neglect* (pp. 309–350). New York: Cambridge University Press.

Cicchetti, D., Beeghly, M., Carlson, V., & Toth, S. (1990). The emergence of the self in atypical populations. In D. Cicchetti & M. Beeghly (Eds.), *The self in transition: Infancy to childhood* (pp. 309–344). Chicago: University of Chicago Press.

Cicirelli, V. (1981). *Helping elderly parents: The role of adult children.* Boston: Auburn House.

Cicirelli, V. G. (1982). Sibling influence throughout the lifespan. In M. E. Lamb & B. Sutton-Smith (Eds.), *Sibling relationships: Their nature and significance across the lifespan* (pp. 267–284). Hillsdale, NJ: Lawrence Erlbaum Associates.

Cissna, K. N., Cox, D. E., & Bochner, A. P. (1990). The dialectic of marital and parental relationships within the stepfamily. *Communication Monographs, 57,* 44–61.

Cissna, K. N. L., & Sieburg, E. (1981). Patterns of interactional confirmation and disconfirmation. In C. Wilder-Mott & J. H. Weakland (Eds.), *Rigor and imagination: Essays from the legacy of Gregory Bateson* (pp. 253–282). New York: Praeger.

Clark, H. H., & Marshall, C. R. (1981). Definite reference and mutual knowledge. In A. K. Joshi, B. L. Webber, & I. A. Sag (Eds.), *Elements of discourse understanding* (pp. 10–63). Cambridge: Cambridge University Press.

Clark, K., & Holquist, M. (1984). *Mikhail Bakhtin.* Cambridge, MA: Belknap of Harvard University Press.

Clark, R. A. (1978). The transition from action to gesture. In A. Locke (Ed.), *Action, gesture and symbol: The emergence of language* (pp. 249–267). New York: Academic Press.

Clark, R., & Delia, J. (1976). The development of functional persuasive skills in childhood and early adolescence. *Child development, 47,* 1008–1014.

Clay, J. W. (1990). Respecting and supporting gay and lesbian parents. *Young Children, 45,* 31–35.

Cobb, N. J. (2001). *Adolescence: Continuity, change, and diversity* (4th ed.). Mountain View, CA: Mayfield.

Cody, M. (1982). A typology of disengagement strategies and an examination of the role intimacy, reactions to inequity and relational problems play in strategy selection. *Communication Monographs, 49,* 148–170.

Cody, M. J., & McLaughlin, M. L. (1980). Perceptions of compliance gaining situations: A dimensional analysis. *Communication Monographs, 47,* 132–148.

Cohall, A., Kassotis, J., Parks, R., Vaughan, R., Bannister, H., & Northridge, M. (2001). Adolescents in the age of AIDS: Myths, misconceptions, and misunderstandings regarding sexually transmitted diseases. *Journal of the National Medical Association, 93*(2), 64–69.

Cohen, G. (1994). Age-related problems in the use of proper names in communication. In M. L. Hummert, J. M. Wiemann, & J. F. Nussbaum (Eds.), *Interpersonal communication in older adulthood: Interdisciplinary theory and research* (pp. 40–57). Thousand Oaks, CA: Sage.

Cohler, B. J., & Galatzer-Levy, R. M. (1990). Self, meaning, and morale across the second half of life. In R. A Nemiroff & C. A. Colarusso (Eds.), *New dimensions in adult development* (pp. 214–263). New York: Basic Books.

Coie, J. D., & Kupersmidt, J. B. (1983). A behavioral analysis of emerging social status in boys' groups. *Child Development, 54,* 1400–1416.

Colby, A., Kohlberg, L., Gibbs, J., & Lieberman, M. (1983). Report on a 20-year longitudinal study of moral development. *Monograph of the Society for Research on Child Development, 48*(1–sup. 2), 124.

Colder, C. R. (2001). Life stress, physiological and subjective indexes of negative emotionality, and coping reasons for drinking: Is there evidence for a self-medication model of alcohol use? *Psychology of Addictive Behaviors, 15*(3), 237–245.

Colder, C. R., & Chassin, L. (1993). The stress and negative affect model of adolescent alcohol use and the moderating effects of behavioral undercontrol. *Journal of Studies on Alcohol, 54,* 326–333.

Cole, C. L. (1984). Marital quality in later life. In W. H. Quinn & G. H. Hughston (Eds.), *Independent aging: Family and social support perspectives* (pp. 72–90). Gaithersburg, MD: Aspen.

Cole, M., & Scribner, S. (1977). Cross-cultural studies in memory and cognition. In R. V. Kail, Jr. & J. W. Hagen (Eds.), *Perspectives on the development of memory and cognition* (pp. 239–271). Hillsdale, NJ: Lawrence Erlbaum Associates.

Colegrave, S. (1979). *Uniting heaven and earth.* Los Angeles, CA: Jeremy P. Tarcher.

Coleman, M., & Ganong, L. H. (1995). Family reconfiguring following divorce. In S. Duck & J. T. Wood (Eds.), *Confronting relationship challenges* (pp. 73–108). Thousand Oaks, CA: Sage.

Coley, R. L. (2001). (In)visible men: Emerging research on low-income, unmarried, and minority fathers. *American Psychologist, 56*(9), 743–753.

Collis, G. M., & Schaffer, H. R. (1975). Synchronization of visual attention in mother–infant pairs. *Journal of Child Psychology and Psychiatry, 16,* 315–320.

Commons, M. L., Richards, F. A., & Armon, C. (Eds.). (1984). *Beyond formal operations: Late adolescent and adult cognitive development.* New York: Praeger.

Condon, W. S., & Ogston, W. D. (1966). Soundfilm analysis of normal and pathological behavioral patterns. *Journal of Nervous and Mental Disease, 143,* 338–347.

Condon, W. S., & Sander, L. W. (1974). Neonate movement is synchronized with adult speech. *Science, 183,* 99–101.

Condry, J., & Condry, S. (1976). Sex differences: A study of the eye of the beholder. *Child Development, 47,* 812–819.

Connidis, I. A., & Davies, L. (1990). Confidants and companions in later life: The place of family and friends. *Journal of Gerontology, 45,* S141–S149.

Connidis, I. A., & Davies, L. (1992). Confidants and companions: Choices in later life. *Journal of Gerontology, 47,* S115–S122.

Conti-Ramsden, G. (1989). Proper name usage: Mother–child interactions with language-impaired and non-language-impaired children. *First Language, 9,* 271–284.

Conville, R. L. (1991). *Relational transitions: The evolution of personal relationships.* New York: Praeger.

Cook-Gumperz, J. (1973). *Social control and socialization.* London: Routledge & Kegan Paul.

Cooper, M. L. (1994). Motivations for alcohol use among adolescents: Development and validation of a four-factor model. *Psychological Assessment, 6,* 117–128.

Corsaro, W. (1981). Friendship in the nursery school: Social organization in a peer environment. In S. R. Asher & J. M. Gottman (Eds.), *The development of children's friendships* (pp. 207–241). London: Cambridge University Press.

Corsaro, W. (1985). *Friendship and peer culture in the early years.* Norwood, NJ: Ablex.

Coupland, N., & Coupland, J. (1995). Discourse, identity, and aging. In J. F. Nussbaum & J. Coupland (Eds.), *Handbook of communication and aging research* (pp. 79–104). Mahwah, NJ: Lawrence Erlbaum Associates.

Cousinet, R. (1938). On lying in children. *Journal de Psychologie Normale et Pathologique, 35,* 230–245. Abstract retrieved from PsycINFO database.

Covan, E. K. (2000). Revisiting the relationship between elder modelers and their proteges. *Sociological Perspectives, 43*(4), S7–S21.

Cramer, D. (1990). Disclosure of personal problems, self-esteem, and the facilitativeness of friends and lovers. *British Journal of Guidance and Counselling, 18*(2), 186–196.

Crawford, M. (1981). Not disengaged: Grandparents in literature and reality, an empirical study in role satisfaction. *Sociological Review, 29,* 499–519.

Creatsas, G. K., Vekemans, M., Horejsi, J., Uzel, R., Lauritzen, C., & Osler, M. (1995). Adolescent sexuality in Europe: A multicentric study. *Adolescent and Pediatric Gynecology, 8,* 59–63.

Crick, F. (1994). *The astonishing hypothesis: The scientific search for the soul.* New York: Scribner's.

Crockenberg, S. B. (1986). Are temperamental differences in babies associated with predictable differences in care-giving? In J. V. Lerner & R. M. Lerner (Eds.), *Temperament and social interaction in infants and children* (pp. 75–88). San Francisco: Jossey-Bass.

Cronkite, G. (1986). On the focus, scope, and coherence of the study of human symbolic activity. *Quarterly Journal of Speech, 72*(3), 231–246.

Csikszentmihalyi, M. (1990). *Flow: The psychology of optimal experience.* New York: Harper & Row.

Csikszentmihalyi, M. (1993). *The evolving self: A psychology for the third millennium.* New York: HarperCollins.

Cunningham, J. D., & Antill, J. K. (1995). Current trends in nonmarital cohabitation: In search of the POSSLQ. In J. T. Wood & S. Duck (Eds.), *Under-studied relationships: Off the beaten track* (pp. 148–172). Thousand Oaks, CA: Sage.

Cupach, W. R., & Spitzberg, B. H. (Eds.). (1994). *The dark side of interpersonal communication*. Hillsdale, NJ: Lawrence Erlbaum Associates.

Curtiss, S. (1977). *Genie: A psycholinguistic study of a modern-day "wild child."* New York: Academic Press.

Cutrona, C. E. (1982). Transition to college: Loneliness and the process of social adjustment. In L. A. Peplau & D. Perlman (Eds.), *Loneliness: A sourcebook of current theory, research and therapy* (pp. 291–309). New York: Wiley.

Cutrona, C. E., & Suhr, J. A. (1994). Social support communication in the context of marriage: An analysis of couples' supportive interactions. In B. R. Burleson, T. L. Albrecht, & I. G. Sarason (Eds.), *Communication of social support: Messages, interactions, and community* (pp. 113–135). Thousand Oaks, CA: Sage.

Cytrynbaum, S., Blum, L., Patrick, R., Stein, J., Wadner, D., & Wilk, C. (1980). Midlife development: Personality and social systems perspectives. In L. Poon (Ed.), *Aging in the 1980s* (pp. 463–474). Washington, DC: American Psychological Association.

Dainton, M., & Aylor, B. (2002). Routine and strategic maintenance efforts: Behavioral patterns, variations associated with relational length, and the prediction of relational characteristics. *Communication Monographs, 69*(1), 52–66.

Dalai Lama, H. H., & Cutler, H. C. (1998). *The art of happiness*. New York: Riverhead Books.

Daly, J. A., Vangelisti, A. L., & Daughton, S. M. (1987). The nature and correlates of conversational sensitivity. *Human Communication Research, 14*(2), 167–202.

Damon, W. (1977). *The social world of the child*. San Francisco: Jossey-Bass.

Damon, W. (1999, August). The moral development of children. *Scientific American*, pp. 73–78.

Dance, F. E. X. (1967). Speech communication theory and Pavlov's second signal system. *The Journal of Communication, 17*(1), 13–24.

Dance, F. E. X. (1979). Acoustic trigger to conceptualization: A hypothesis concerning the role of the spoken word in the development of higher mental processes. *Health Communication and Informatics, 5*, 203–213.

Dance, F. E. X. (1982). A speech theory of human communication. In F. E. X. Dance (Ed.), *Human communication theory* (pp. 120–146). New York: Harper & Row.

Dance, F. E. X., & Larson, C. E. (1972). *Speech communication: Concepts and behavior*. New York: Holt, Rinehart & Winston.

Dance, F. E. X., & Larson, C. E. (1976). *The functions of human communication: A theoretical approach*. New York: Holt, Rinehart & Winston.

Daniels, A. K. (1987). Invisible work. *Social Problems, 34*, 403–415.

Davila, J. (2001). Refining the association between excessive reassurance seeking and depressive symptoms: The role of related interpersonal constructs. *Journal of Social and Clinical Psychology, 20*(4), 538–559.

Dawkins, R. (1976). *The selfish gene*. Oxford, UK: Oxford University Press.

Delia, J. G., & Clark, R. A. (1977). Cognitive complexity, social perception and the development of listener-adapted communication in six-, eight-, ten-, and twelve-year-old boys. *Communication Monographs, 44*, 326–345.

Delia, J. G., Kline, S. L., & Burleson, B. R. (1979). The development of persuasive communication strategies in kindergarteners through twelfth-graders. *Communication Monographs, 46*, 241–256.

Delia, J. G., O'Keefe, B. J., & O'Keefe, D. J. (1982). The constructivist approach to communication. In F. E. X. Dance (Ed.), *Human communication theory* (pp. 147–191). New York: Harper & Row.

Dennett, D. C. (1994). The role of language in intelligence. In J. Khalfa (Ed.), *What is intelligence?* Cambridge, UK: Cambridge University Press. Retrieved 8/9/01 from http://ase.tufts.edu/cogstud/ papers/rolelang.html

Derber, C. (2000). *The pursuit of attention* (2nd ed.). New York: Oxford University Press.

Derlega, V. J., Barbee, A. P., & Winstead, B. A. (1994). Friendship, gender, and social support: Laboratory studies of supportive interactions. In B. R. Burleson, T. L. Albrecht, & I. G. Sarason (Eds.), *Communication of social support: Messages, interactions, relationships, and community* (pp. 136–151). Thousand Oaks, CA: Sage.

Derlega, V. J., Metts, S., Petronio, S., & Margulis, S. T. (1993). *Self-disclosure.* Newbury Park, CA: Sage.

deTurck, M. A., & Miller, G. R. (1983). Adolescent perceptions of parental persuasive message strategies. *Journal of Marriage and the Family, 45*(3), 543–552.

Devault, M. L. (1991). *Feeding the family: The social organization of caring as gendered work.* Chicago: University of Chicago Press.

Dickson, F. C. (1995). The best is yet to be: Research on long-lasting marriages. In J. T. Wood & S. Duck (Eds.), *Under-studied relationships: Off the beaten track* (pp. 22–50). Thousand Oaks, CA: Sage.

di Leonardo, M. (1987). The female world of cards and holidays: Women, families, and the work of kinship. *Signs, 12,* 440–453.

Dillard, J. P., & Burgoon, M. (1985). Situational influences on the selection of compliance-gaining messages: Two tests of the predictive utility of the Cody-McLaughlin typology. *Communication Monographs, 52*(4), 289–304.

Dindia, K. (1994). The intrapersonal-interpersonal dialectical process of self-disclosure. In S. Duck (Ed.), *Dynamics of relationships* (pp. 000–000). Thousand Oaks, CA: Sage.

Dindia, K. (1998). "Going into and coming out of the closet": The dialectics of stigma disclosure. In B. M. Montgomery & L. A. Baxter (Eds.), *Dialectical approaches to studying personal relationships* (pp. 83–108). Mahwah, NJ: Lawrence Erlbaum Associates.

Dindia, K., & Allen, M. (1992). Sex differences in self-disclosure: A meta-analysis. *Psychological Bulletin, 112,* 106–124.

Dinh, K. T. (2000). Predictors of psychosocial well-being in an Asian-American sample: Acculturation, intergenerational conflict, and parent–child relationships. *Dissertation Abstracts International, 60*(8-B), 4216.

Dinnerstein, D. (1977). *The mermaid and the minotaur: Sexual arrangements and human malaise.* New York: Harper Colophon Books.

Dishion, T. J., Patterson, G. R., & Griesler, P. C. (1994). Peer adaptations in the development of antisocial behavior: A confluence model. In L. R. Huesmann (Ed.), *Current perspectives on aggressive behavior* (pp. 61–95). New York: Plenum.

Dixson, M. D. (1995). Models and perspectives of parent–child communication. In T. J. Socha & G. Stamp (Eds.), *Parents, children and communication: Frontiers of theory and research* (pp. 43–62). Hillsdale, NJ: Lawrence Erlbaum Associates.

Dixson, M. D., & Stein, A. (1997, June). *Children's models of the parent–child relationship: What do young children expect?* Paper presented at the International Network of Personal Relationships, Oxford, Ohio.

Dobson, J. E., & Dobson, R. L. (1985). The sandwich generation: Dealing with aging parents. *Journal of Counseling and Development, 63,* 572–574.

Dodge, K. A. (1983). Behavioral antecedents of peer social status. *Child Development, 54,* 1386–1399.

Doherty, W. J., Kouneski, E. F., & Erickson, M. F. (1996). *Responsible fathering: An overview and conceptual framework.* Washington, DC: U.S. Department of Health and Human Services. Retrieved 11/19/03 from http://fatherhood.hhs.gov/concept.htm

Dore, J. (1974). A pragmatic description of early language development. *Journal of Psycholinguistic Research, 3,* 343–350.

Dovido, J. F., Ellyson, S. L., Keating, C. F., Heltmand, K., & Brown, C. E. (1988). The relationship of social power to visual displays of dominance between men and women. *Journal of Personality and Social Psychology, 54,* 233–242.

Downs, V., Javidi, M., & Nussbaum, J. (1988). A comparative analysis of the relationship between communication apprehension and loneliness for elderly nursing home residents. *Western Journal of Speech Communication, 52,* 308–320.

Downs, V. C. (1988). *The grandparent–grandchild relationship: Communication and continuity between generations.* Unpublished Doctoral dissertation, University of Oklahoma.

Downs, V. C. (1989). The grandparent–grandchild relationship. In J. F. Nussbaum (Ed.), *Life-span communication: Normative processes* (pp. 257–281). Hillsdale, NJ: Lawrence Erlbaum Associates.

Dressel, P. L., & Clark, A. (1990). A critical look at family care. *Journal of Marriage and the Family, 52,* 769–782.

Dubas, J. S. (2001). How gender moderates the grandparent–grandchild relationship: A comparison of kin-keeper and kin-selector theories. *Journal of Family Issues, 22*(4), 478–492.

Duck, S. W. (1982). A topography of relationship disengagement and dissolution. In S. Duck (Ed.), *Personal relationships: Vol. 4. Dissolving personal relationships* (pp. 1–30). New York: Academic Press.

Duck, S. W. (1986). *Human relationships: An introduction to social psychology.* London: Sage.

Duck, S. (1991). *Understanding relationships.* New York: Guilford.

Duck, S. (Ed.). (1993). *Learning about relationships* (Understanding relationship processes series, Vol. 2). Newbury Park, CA: Sage.

Duck, S. (1994). *Meaningful relationships: Talking, sense, and relating.* Newbury Park, CA: Sage.

Duncan, G. J., Boisjoly, J., & Harris, K. M. (2001). Sibling, peer, neighbor, and schoolmate correlations as indicators of the importance of context for adolescent development. *Demography, 38*(3), 437–447.

Dunn, J. (1988). Connections between relationships: Implications of research on mothers and siblings. In R. A. Hinde & J. Stevenson-Hinde (Eds.), *Relationships within families: Mutual influences* (pp. 168–180). Oxford, UK: Oxford University Press.

Dunn, J. (1991). The developmental importance of differences in siblings experiences within the family. In K. Pillemer & K. McCartney (Eds.), *Parent–child relations throughout life* (pp. 113–124).

Dunn, J. (1993). *Young children's close relationships: Beyond attachment* (Individual differences and development series, Vol. 4). Newbury Park, CA: Sage.

Dunn, J., Deater-Deckard, K., Pickering, K., & Golding, J. (1999). Siblings, parents, and partners: Family relationships within a longitudinal community study. *Journal of Child Psychology and Psychiatry, 40*(7), 1025–1037.

Dunn, J., & Munn, P. (1985). Becoming a family member: Family conflict and the development of social understanding in the second year. *Child Development, 56,* 480–492.

Dunn, J., & Munn, P. (1986). Siblings and prosocial development. *International Journal of Behavioral Development, 9,* 265–284.

Dunn, J., & Munn, P. (1987). The development of justification in disputes with another sibling. *Developmental Psychology, 23,* 791–798.

Duran, R. L., & Kelly, L. (1988). An investigation into the cognitive domain of competence II: The relationship between communicative competence and interaction involvement. *Communication Research Reports, 5,* 91–96.

Duvall, S., & Wicklund, R. A. (1972). *A theory of objective self-awareness.* New York: Academic Press.

Dyk, P. A., & Adams, G. R. (1990). Identity and intimacy: An initial investigation of three theoretical models using cross-lag panel correlations. *Journal of Youth and Adolescence, 19,* 91–110.

Dykstra, P. A. (1990). *Next of (non)kin.* The Netherlands: Swets & Zeitlinger.

Easton, S., & Van Laar, D. (1995). Experiences of lecturers in helping distressed students in higher education. *British Journal of Guidance and Counseling, 23*(2), 173–178.

Eccles, J. S. (1993). School and family effects on the ontogeny of children's interests, self-perceptions, and activity choice. In J. E. Jacobs (Ed.), *Nebraska symposium on motivation, 1992* (pp. 145–218). Lincoln: University of Nebraska Press.

Edelsky, C. (1977). Acquisition of an aspect of communicative competence: Learning what it means to talk like a lady. In S. Ervin-Tripp & C. Mitchell-Kernan (Eds.), *Child discourse* (pp. 225–243). New York: Academic Press.

Eder, R. A. (1994). Comments on children's self-narratives. In U. Neisser & R. Fivush (Eds.), *The remembering self: Construction and accuracy in the self-narrative* (pp. 180–190). New York: Cambridge University Press.

Edwards, A. D. (1980). Patterns of power and authority in classroom talk. In P. Woods (Ed.), *Teacher strategies: Explorations in the sociology of the school.* London: Croom Helm.

Eimas, P. D., Siqueland, E. R., Jusczyk, P., & Vigorito, J. (1971). Speech perception in infants. *Science, 171,* 303–306.

Eisenberg, A. (1985). Learning to describe past experiences in conversation. *Discourse Processes, 8,* 177–204.

Eisenberg, N., & Fabes, R. A. (1994). Emotion, regulation and the development of social competence. In M. Clark (Ed.), *Review of personality and social psychology, vol. 14: Emotion and social behavior* (pp. 119–150). Newbury Park, CA: Sage.

Ekerdt, D. J., & Bossé, R. (1982). Change in self-reported health with retirement. *International Journal of Aging and Human Development, 15,* 213–223.

Elbers, L. (1982). Operating principles in repetitive babbling: A cognitive continuity approach. *Cognition, 12,* 45–63.

Elkind, D. (1967). Egocentrism in adolescence. *Child Development, 38,* 1025–1034.

Elkind, D. (1996). Inhelder and Piaget on adolescence and adulthood: A postmodern appraisal. *Psychological Science, 7,* 216–220.

Emde, R. N. (1988). Development terminable and interminable: Innate and motivational factors from infancy. *International Journal of Psychoanalysis, 69,* 23–25.

Emmers, T. M., & Dindia, K. (1995). The effect of relational stage and intimacy on touch: An extension of Guerrero and Andersen. *Personal Relationships, 2,* 225–236.

Enright, R. D., & Sutterfield, S. J. (1980). An ecological validation of social cognitive development. *Child Development, 51,* 16–161.

Epstein, A. S., & Radin, N. (1975). Motivational components related to father behavior and cognitive functioning in preschoolers. *Child Development, 46,* 831–839.

Erbert, L. A. (2000). Conflict and dialectics: Perceptions of dialectical contradictions in marital conflict. *Journal of Social and Personal Relationships, 17,* 638–659.

Erel, O., Margolin, G., & John, R. S. (1998). Observed sibling interaction: Links with the marital and the mother–child relationship. *Developmental Psychology, 34,* 288–298.

Erikson, E. H. (1950). *Childhood and society.* New York: Norton.

Erikson, E. H. (1960). Youth and the life cycle. *Children, 7,* 43–49.

Erikson, E. H. (1968). *Identity: Youth and crisis.* New York: Norton.

Erikson, E. H. (1982). *The life cycle completed.* New York: Norton.

Ertmer, D. J., & Mellon, J. A. (2001). Beginning to talk at 20 months: Early vocal development in a young cochlear implant recipient. *Journal of Speech, Language and Hearing Research, 44*(1), 192–206.

Ervin-Tripp, S. (1979). Children's verbal turn-taking. In E. Ochs & B. B. Schieffelin (Eds.), *Developmental pragmatics* (pp. 381–414). New York: Academic Press.

Falconer, J. (1986). Aging and hearing. *Physical and Occupational Therapy in Geriatrics, 4,* 3–20.

Faude, J. A., Jones, C. W., & Robins, M. (1996). The affective life of infants: Empirical and theoretical foundations. In D. R. Nathanson (Ed.), *Knowing feeling* (pp. 219–256). New York: Norton.

Feldman, R. S., Devin-Sheehan, L., & Allen, V. L. (1978). Nonverbal cues as indicators of verbal dissembling. *American Educational Research Journal, 15*(2), 217–231.

Feldman, R. S., Jenkins, L., & Popoola, O. (1979). Detection of deception in adults and children via facial expressions. *Child Development, 50,* 350–355.

Felmlee, D. H. (2001). No couple is an island: A social network perspective on dyadic stability. *Social Forces, 79*(4), 1259–1287.

Fengler, A. P. (1974). Romantic love in courtship: Divergent paths of male and female students. *Journal of Comparative Family Studies, 5,* 134–139.

Ferguson, C. (1978). Learning to pronounce: The earliest stages phonological development in the child. In F. D. Minifie & L. L. Lloyd (Eds.), *Communicative and cognitive abilities—Early behavioral assessment* (pp. 273–297). Baltimore, MD: University Park Press.

Feshbach, N. D., & Roe, K. (1968). Empathy in six- and seven-year-olds. *Child Development, 39,* 133–145.

Field, N. P. (2001). Attachment style in adjustment to conjugal bereavement. *Journal of Social and Personal Relationships, 18*(3), 347–361.

Field, N. P., & Sundin, E. C. (2001). Attachment style in adjustment to conjugal bereavement. *Journal of Social and Personal Relationships, 18,* 347–361.

Fieweger, M., & Smilowitz, M. (1984). Relational conclusion through interaction with the dying. *Omega, 15,* 161–172.

Fincham, F. D., Paleari, F. G., & Regalia, C. (2002). Forgiveness in marriage: The role of relationship quality, attributions, and empathy. *Personal Relationships, 9,* 27–37.

Finkenauer, C., & Hazam, H. (2000). Disclosure and secrecy in marriage: Do both contribute to marital satisfaction? *Journal of Social and Personal Relationships, 17*(2), 245–263.

Firestone, S. (1970). *The dialectic of sex: The case for feminist revolution.* New York: Bantam.

Fischer, J. L., & Oliker, S. J. (1983). A research note on friendship, gender, and the life cycle. *Social Forces, 62,* 124–133.

Fischer, K. W., & Ayoub, C. (1994). Affective splitting and dissociation in normal and maltreated children: Developmental pathways for self in relationships. In D. Cicchetti & S. L. Toth (Eds.), *Disorders and dysfunctions of the self* (Vol. 5, pp. 149–222). Rochester, NY: University of Rochester Press.

Fischer, K. W., & Corrigan, R. (1981). A skill approach to language development. In R. Stark (Ed.), *Language behavior in infancy and early childhood* (pp. 245–273). Amsterdam: Elsevier.

Fitch, S. A., & Adams, G. R. (1983). Ego-identity and intimacy status: Replication and extension. *Developmental Psychology, 19,* 839–845.

Fitting, M., Rabins, P., Lucas, M. J., & Eastham, J. (1986). Caregivers for demented patients: A comparison of husbands and wives. *Gerontologist, 26,* 248–252.

Fitzpatrick, M. A. (1988). *Between husbands and wives: Communication in marriage.* Newbury Park, CA: Sage.

Fitzpatrick, M. A., & Badzinski, D. M. (1994). All in the family: Interpersonal communication in kin relationships. In M. L. Knapp & G. R. Miller (Eds.), *Handbook of interpersonal communication* (2nd ed., pp. 726–771). Thousand Oaks, CA: Sage.

FitzSimmons, E. (1994). One man's death: His family's ethnography. *Omega, 30,* 23–39.

Fivush, R., Gray, J. T., & Fromhoff, F. A. (1987). Two-year-olds talk about the past. *Cognitive Development, 2,* 393–409.

Flege, J. E., & Fletcher, K. L. (1992). Talker and listener effects on the perception of degree of foreign accent. *Journal of the Acoustical Society of American, 91,* 370–389.

Fodor, J. (1975). *The language of thought.* New York: T. Y. Crowell.

Fogel, A. (1982). Early adult–infant interaction: Expectable sequences of behavior. *Journal of Pediatric Psychology, 7*(1), 1–22.

Fogel, A. (1993). *Developing through relationships.* Chicago: University of Chicago Press.

Fogel, A. (1995). Relational narratives of the prelinguistic self. In P. Rochat (Ed.), *The self in infancy: Theory and research* (pp. 117–139). Amsterdam: Elsevier.

Fogel, A., & Thelen, E. (1987). Development of early expressive and communicative action: Reinterpreting the evidence from a dynamic systems perspective. *Developmental Psychology, 23,* 747–761.

Forbes, G. B. (2001). College students with tattoos and piercings: Motives, family experiences, personality factors, and perception by others. *Psychological Reports, 89*(3), 774–786.

Forman, E. A., & Cazden, C. B. (1985). Exploring Vygotskian perspectives in education: The cognitive value of peer interaction. In J. V. Wertsch (Ed.), *Culture, communication and cognition: Vygotskian perspectives* (pp. 323–347). Cambridge, UK: Cambridge University Press.

Fox, G. L. (1981). The family's role in adolescent sexual behavior. In T. Ooms (Ed.), *Teenage pregnancy in a family context* (pp. 73–130). Philadelphia: Temple University Press.

Fox, N. A., Rubin, K. H., Calkins, S. D., Marshall, T. R., Coplan, R. J., Porges, S. W., Long, J. M., & Stewart, S. (1995). Frontal activation asymmetry and social competence at four years of age. *Child Development, 66,* 1770–1784.

Freedman, D. G. (1974). *Human infancy: An evolutionary perspective.* Hillsdale, NJ: Lawrence Erlbaum Associates.

French, D., Rianasari, M., Pidada, S., Nelwan, P., & Buhrmester, D. (2001). Social support of Indonesian and U.S. children and adolescents by family members and friends. *Merrill-Palmer Quarterly, 47*(3), 377–394.

Freud, S. (1961). Some psychical consequences of the anatomical distinction between the sexes. In J. Strachek (Ed.), *The standard edition of the complete psychological works of Sigmund Freud* (Vol. 19, pp. 248–258). London: Hogarth Press. (Original work published 1905)

Freud, S. (1962). *Three contributions to the theory of sex* (A. A. Brill, Trans.). New York: Dutton. (Original work published 1905)

Frisch, R. E. (1983). Fatness, puberty, and fertility: The effects of nutrition and physical training on menarche and ovulation. In J. Brooks-Gunn & A. C. Petersen (Eds.), *Girls at puberty* (pp. 29–49). New York: Plenum.

Fuchs, D., & Thelen, M. (1988). Children's expected interpersonal consequences of communicating their affective state and reported likelihood of expression. *Child Development, 59,* 1314–1322.

Furman, W. (1999). Friends and lovers: The role of peer relationships in adolescent romantic relationships. In W. A. Collins & B. Laursen (Eds.), *Relationships as developmental contexts* (pp. 133–154). Mahwah, NJ: Lawrence Erlbaum Associates.

Furr, S. R., Westefeld, J. S., McConnell, G. N., & Jenkins, J. M. (2001). Suicide and depression among college students a decade later. *Professional Psychology: Research and Practice, 32*(1), 97–100.

Furstenberg, F. F., Jr., & Harris, K. M. (1993). When and why fathers matter: Impacts of father involvement on the children of adolescent mothers. In R. I. Lerman & T. J. Ooms (Eds.), *Young unwed fathers: Changing roles and emerging policies* (pp. 117–138). Philadelphia: Temple University Press.

Furth, H. G. (1973). *Deafness & learning: A psychosocial approach.* Belmont, CA: Wadsworth.

Galinsky, E. (1981). *Between generations: The six stages of parenthood.* New York: Berkeley.

Gall, T. L., & Evans, D. R. (2000). Preretirement expectations and the quality of life of male retirees in later retirement. *Canadian Journal of Behavioural Science, 32*(3), 187–197.

Gamer, E., Thomas, J., & Kendall, D. (1975). Determinants of friendship across the life span. In F. Rebelsky (Ed.), *Life: The continuous process* (pp. 336–345). New York: Knopf.

Gandhi, M. (1980). *All men are brothers: Autobiographical reflections* (K. Kripalani, Ed.). New York: Continuum.

Gardner, R. A., & Gardner, B. T. (1969). Teaching sign language to a chimpanzee. *Science, 165,* 664–672.

Garrido, E. F., & Acitelli, L. K. (1999). Relational identity and the division of household labor. *Journal of Social and Personal Relationships, 16*(5), 619–637.

Garvey, C. (1977). Play with language and speech. In S. Ervin-Tripp & C. Mitchell-Kernan (Eds.), *Child discourse* (pp. 27–48). New York: Academic Press.

Gelman, R., & Baillargeon, R. (1983). A review of some Piagetian concepts. In P. H. Mussen (Ed.), *Handbook of child psychology: Volume III. Cognitive development* (4th ed., pp. 167–230). New York: Wiley.

Genevay, B. (1986). Sexuality and older people. *Generations: Journal of the American Society on Aging, 10,* 58–59.

Gergely, G., & Watson, J. S. (1999). Early socio-emotional development: Contingency perception and the social-biofeedback model. In P. Rochat (Ed.), *Early social cognition: Understanding others in the first months of life* (pp. 101–137). Mahwah, NJ: Lawrence Erlbaum Associates.

Gergen, K. J. (1991). *The saturated self: Dilemmas of identity in contemporary life.* New York: Basic Books.

Gergen, K. J., & Gergen, M. M. (1983). Narrative of the self. In T. Sarbin & K. Schiebe (Eds.), *Studies in social identity* (pp. 254–273). New York: Praeger.

Gerstel, N. (1988). Divorce, gender, and social integration. *Gender and Society, 2,* 343–363.

Gewirtz, J., & Boyd, E. (1977). Experiments on mother–infant interaction underlying mutual attachment acquisition: The infant conditions the mother. In T. Alloway, P. Pliner, & L. Kramer (Eds.), *Attachment behavior* (pp. 109–143). New York: Plenum.

Gibb, B. E., Alloy, L. B., Abramson, L. Y., Rose, D. T., Whitehouse, W. G., & Hogan, M. E. (2001). Childhood maltreatment and college students' current suicidal ideation: A test of the hopelessness theory. *Suicide and Life Threatening Behavior, 31*(4), 405–415.

Gibson, E. (1995). Are we automata? In P. Rochat (Ed.), *The self in infancy: Theory and research* (pp. 3–15). Amsterdam: Elsevier.

Gibson, E. J., & Walker, A. S. (1984). Development of knowledge of visual-tactual affordances of substance. *Child Development, 55,* 453–460.

Giles, H. (1980). Accommodation theory: Some new directions. In M. W. S. Silva (Ed.), *Aspects of linguistic behavior: Festschrift Robert Le Page* (pp. 105–136). New York: Papers in Linguistics (No. 9).

Giles, H., Coupland, N., Coupland, J., Williams, A., & Nussbaum, J. (1992). Intergenerational talk and communication with older people. *International Journal of Aging and Human Development, 34,* 271–297.

Giles, H., Fox, S., Harwood, J., & Williams, A. (1994). Talking age and aging talk. In M. L. Hummert, J. M. Wiemann, & J. F. Nussbaum (Eds.), *Interpersonal communication in older adulthood* (pp. 130–161). Thousand Oaks, CA: Sage.

Gilligan, C. (1982). *In a different voice: Psychological theory and women's development* (3rd printing). Cambridge, MA: Harvard University Press.

Gilligan, C., & Murphy, J. M. (1979). Development from adolescence to adulthood: The philosopher and the 'dilemma of the fact.' In D. Kuhn (Ed.), *Intellectual develoment beyond childhood.* San Francisco: Jossey-Bass.

Ginsberg, D., & Gottman, J. (1986). Conversations of college roommates: Similarities and differences in male and female friendship. In J. M. Gottman & J. G. Parker (Eds.), *Conversations of friends* (pp. 241–291). Cambridge, UK: Cambridge University Press.

Ginsburg, D., & Gottman, J. M. (1986). Conversations of college roommates: Similarities and differences in male and female friendship. In J. M. Gottman & J. G. Parker (Eds.), *Conversations of friends: Speculations on affective development* (pp. 241–291). New York: Cambridge University Press.

Ginsburg, H., & Opper, S. (1988). *Piaget's theory of intellectual development.* Englewood Cliffs, NJ : Prentice-Hall.

Gleason, J. B. (Ed.). (1993). *The development of language* (3rd ed.). New York: Macmillan.

Gleason, J. B., & Ratner, N. B. (1993). *Psycholinguistics.* Fort Worth, TX: Harcourt Brace Jovanovich.

Gledhill-Hoyt, J., Hang, L., Strote, J., & Wechsler, H. (2000). Increased use of marijuana and other illicit drugs at U.S. colleges in the 1990s: Results of three national surveys. *Addiction, 95*(11), 1655–1668.

Glendenning, F. (1995). Education for older adults: Lifelong learning, empowerment, and social change. In J. F. Nussbaum & J. Coupland (Eds.), *Handbook of communication and aging research* (pp. 467–490). Mahwah, NJ: Lawrence Erlbaum Associates.

Goetting, A. (1986). The developmental tasks of siblingship over the life cycle. *Journal of Marriage and the Family, 48,* 703–714.

Goffman, E. (1974). *Frame analysis: An essay on the organization of experience.* Cambridge, MA: Harvard University Press.

Gold, D. P., Andres, D., Etezadi, J., Arbuckle, T. Y., Schwartzman, A. E., & Chaikelson, J. (1995). Structural equation model of intellectual change and continuity and predictors of intelligence in older men. *Psychology and Aging, 10,* 294–303.

Gold, D. P., Arbuckle, T. Y., & Andres, D. (1994). Verbosity in older adults. In M. L. Hummert, J. M. Wiemann, & J. F. Nussbaum (Eds.), *Interpersonal communication in older adulthood* (pp. 107–129). Thousand Oaks, CA: Sage.

Goldberg, D. (2001). Vulnerability factors for common mental illness. *British Journal of Psychiatry, 178,* s69–s71.

Golinkoff, R. M. (1983). Infant social cognition: Self, people, and objects. In L. Liben (Ed.), *Piaget and the foundations of knowledge*. Hillsdale, NJ: Lawrence Erlbaum Associates.

Golinkoff, R. M. (1986). I beg your pardon? The preverbal negotiation of failed messages. *Journal of Child Language, 13*, 455–476.

Golinkoff, R. M., & Gordon, L. (1988). What makes communication run? Characteristics of immediate successes. *First Language, 8*, 103–124.

Golish, T. D. (2000). Changes in closeness between adult children and their parents: A turning point analysis. *Communication Reports, 13*(2), 79–97.

Golish, T. D., & Caughlin, J. P. (2002). "I'd rather not talk about it": Adolescents' and young adults' use of topic avoidance in stepfamilies. *Journal of Applied Communication Resesarch, 30*(1), 78–106.

Goodlad, J. I. (1983). A study of schooling: Some findings and hypotheses. *Phi Delta Kappan, 64*, 465–470.

Goodman, C. C., & Silverstein, M. (2001). Grandmothers who parent their grandchildren: An exploratory study of close relations across three generations. *Journal of Family Issues, 22*(5), 557–578.

Goodman, I. I. (1983). Television's role in family interaction: A family systems perspective. *Journal of Family Issues, 4*, 405–424.

Gopnik, A., & Meltzoff, A. N. (1986). Relations between semantic and cognitive development in the one-word stage: The specificity hypothesis. *Child Development, 50*, 33–40.

Gopnik, A., & Meltzoff, A. N. (1988). From people, to plans, to objects: Changes in the meaning of early words and the relation to cognitive development. In M. B. Franklin & S. S. Barten (Eds.), *Child language: A reader* (pp. 60–69). New York: Oxford University Press.

Gordon, K., Hutchinson, J. M., & Allen, C. S. (1976). *An evaluation of selected discourse characteristics among the elderly*. Research Laboratory Report, Department of Speech Therapy and Audiology, Idaho State University, Pocatello.

Gottman, J. M. (1983). How children become friends. *Monographs of the Society for Research in Child Development, 48*(2, Serial No. 201).

Gottman, J. M. (1986). The world of coordinated play: Same- and cross-sex friendship in young children. In J. M. Gottman & J. G. Parker (Eds.), *Conversations of friends: Speculations on affective development* (pp. 139–191). Cambridge, UK: Cambridge University Press.

Gottman, J. M. (1990). Children of gay and lesbian parents. *Marriage and Family Review, 14*, 177–196.

Gottman, J. M. (1993). A theory of marital dissolution and stability. *Journal of Family Psychology, 7*, 57–75.

Gottman, J. M. (1994). *What predicts divorce?* Hillsdale, NJ: Lawrence Erlbaum Associates.

Gottman, J. M., Gonso, J., & Rasmussen, B. (1975). Social interaction, social competence, and friendship in children. *Child Development, 45*, 709–718.

Gottman, J. M., & Krokoff, L. J. (1989). Marital interaction and marital satisfaction: A longitudinal view. *Journal of Consulting and Clinical Psychology, 57*, 47–52.

Gottman, J. M., Markman, H., & Notarius, C. (1977). The topography of marital conflict: Sequential analysis of verbal and nonverbal behavior. *Jounral of Marriage and the Family, 39*, 461–477.

Gottman, J. M., & Parkhurst, J. T. (1980) A developmental theory of friendship and acquaintanceship processes. In W. A. Collins (Ed.), *Development of cognition, affect, and social relations* (Minnesota Symposia on Child Psychology, Vol. 13, pp. 197–253). Hillsdale, NJ: Lawrence Erlbaum Associates.

Gouldner, H., & Strong, M. S. (1987). *Speaking of friendships: Middle-class women and their friends*. New York: Greenwood.

Gove, W. (1973). Sex, marital status, and mortality. *American Journal of Sociology, 79*(1), 45–67.

Graafsma, T. L. G., Bosma, H. A., Grotevant, H. D., & de Levita, D. J. (1994). Identity and development: An interdisciplinary view. In H. A. Bosma, T. L. G. Graafsma, H. D. Grotevant, & D. J. de Levita (Eds.), *Identity and development: An interdisciplinary approach* (pp. 159–174). Thousand Oaks, CA: Sage.

Grainger, K. (1995). Communication and the institutionalized elderly. In J. F. Nussbaum & J. Coupland (Eds.), *Handbook of communication and aging research* (pp. 417–436). Mahwah, NJ: Lawrence Erlbaum Associates.

Grass, G. (1961). *The tin drum* (R. Manheim, Trans.). New York: Pantheon. (Originally published 1959)

Gravell, R. (1988). *Communication problems in elderly people: Practical approaches to management.* London: Croom Helm.

Greeley, J., & Oei, T. (1999). Alcohol and tension reduction. In K. E. Leonard & H. T. Blane (Eds.), *Psychological theories of drinking and alcoholism* (2nd ed., pp. 14–53). New York: Guilford.

Green, C. D., & Vervaeke, J. (1997). But what have you done for us lately? Some recent perspectives on linguistic nativism. In D. M. Johnson & C. E. Erneling (Eds.), *The future of the cognitive revolution* (pp. 149–163). Oxford, UK: Oxford University Press.

Green, R., Mandel, J. B., Hotvedt, M. E., Gray, J., & Smith, L. (1986). Lesbian mothers and their children: A comparison with solo parent heterosexual mothers and their children. *Archives of Sexual Behavior, 15,* 167–184.

Grice, H. P. (1975). Logic and conversation. In P. Cole & J. L. Morgan (Eds.), *Syntax and semantics, Vol. 3: Speech acts* (pp. 43–58). New York: Academic Press.

Grieser, D. L., & Kuhl, P. K. (1988). Maternal speech to infants in a tonal language: Support for universal prosodic features in motherese. *Developmental Psychology, 24*(1), 14–20.

Gubrium, J. F. (1976). Being single in old age. In J. F. Gubrium (Ed.), *Times, roles and self in old age* (pp. 179–197). New York: Human Sciences.

Guerrero, L. K., & Andersen, P. A. (1991). The waxing and waning of relational intimacy: Touch as a function of relational stage, gender, and touch avoidance. *Journal of Social and Personal Relationships, 8,* 147–165.

Gupta, S. (1998). Dynamic interplay between private and social speech: A microgenetic approach. In M. C. D. P. Lyra & J. Valsiner (Eds.), *Construction of psychological processes in interpersonal communication* (pp. 117–136). Stamford, CT: Ablex.

Gwartney-Gibbs, P. A. (1986). The institutionalization of premarital cohabitation: Estimates from marriage license applications, 1970 and 1980. *Journal of Marriage and the Family, 48,* 423–434.

Hagestad, G. O. (1985). Continuity and connectedness. In V. L. Bengtson & J. F. Robertson (Eds.), *Grandparenthood* (pp. 31–48). Beverly Hills, CA: Sage.

Hagestad, G. O., & Smyer, M. A. (1982). Dissolving long-term relationships: Patterns of divorcing in middle age. In S. W. Duck (Ed.), *Personal relationships 4: Dissolving personal relationships.* London: Academic Press.

Hall, S., Hecht, M., & Boster, F. (1985, November). *Artifacts in constructivist complexity research.* Paper presented at the Speech Communication Association, Denver, CO.

Halpern, J. (1994). The sandwich generation: Conflicts between adult children and their aging parents. In D. D. Cahn (Ed.), *Conflict in personal relationships* (pp. 143–160). Hillsdale, NJ: Lawrence Erlbaum Associates.

Hansson, R. O. (1986). Relational competence, relationships, and adjustments in old age. *Journal of Personality and Social Psychology, 50*(5), 1050–1058.

Harm, N. J. (2001). Grandmothers raising grandchildren: Parenting the second time around. In J. D. Garner & S. O. Mercer (Eds.), *Women as they age* (pp. 131–146). New York: Haworth.

Harre, R. (1988). *The social construction of emotions.* New York: Basil Blackwell.

Harris, J. R. (1998). *The nurture assumption: Why children turn out the way they do.* New York: Free Press.

Harris, S., Mussen, P., & Rutherford, E. (1976). Some cognitive, behavioral, and personality correlates of maturity in moral judgments. *Journal of Genetic Psychology, 128,* 123–135.

Harris, T. L., & Molock, S. D. (2000). Cultural orientation, family cohesion and family support in suicide ideation and depression among African American college students. *Suicide and Life Threatening Behavior, 30,* 341–353.

Hart, B., & Risley, T. R. (1995). *Meaningful differences in the everyday experience of young American children.* Baltimore: Paul H. Brookes.

Hart, C. H. (2000, August). Parents do matter: The myth that parents don't matter. *Marriage & Families,* pp. 2–8.

Hart, C. H., Olsen, S. F., Robinson, C. C., & Mandleco, B. L. (1997). The development of social and communicative competence in childhood: Review and a model of personal, familial, and extrafamilial processes. In B. R. Burleson (Ed.), *Communication yearbook 20* (pp. 305–373). Thousand Oaks, CA: Sage.

Hart, D., Kohlberg, L., & Wersch, J. V. (1987). The developmental social-self theories of James Mark Baldwin, George Herbert Mead, and Lev Semenovich Vygotsky. In L. Kohlberg (Ed.), *Child psychology and childhood education: A cognitive-developmental view.* New York: Longman.

Hart, R., & Burks, D. (1972). Rhetorical sensitivity and social interaction. *Speech Monographs, 39,* 75–91.

Harter, S. (1982). A cognitive-developmental approach to children's understanding of affect and trait labels. In F. C. Serafica (Ed.), *Social cognitive development in context* (pp. 27–61). New York: Guilford.

Harter, S. (1999). *The construction of the self: A developmental perspective.* New York: Guilford.

Harter, S., & Monsour, A. (1992). Developmental analysis of conflict caused by opposing attributes in the adolescent self-portrait. *Developmental Psychology, 28,* 251–260.

Harter, S., & Whitesell, N. R. (1989). Developmental changes in children's understanding of single, multiple, and blended emotion concepts. In C. Saarni & P. L. Harris (Eds.), *Children's understanding of emotion* (pp. 81–116). New York: Cambridge University Press.

Hartup, W. W. (1985). Relationships and their significance in cognitive development. In R. A. Hinde, A. Perret-Clermot, & J. Stevenson-Hinde (Eds.), *Social relationships and cognitive development* (pp. 66–82). New York: Oxford University Press.

Hartup, W. W. (1996). The company they keep: Friendships and their developmental significance. *Child Development, 67,* 1–13.

Hartup, W. W., Glazer, J. A., & Charlesworth, R. (1967). Peer reinforcement and sociometric status. *Child Development, 38,* 1017–1024.

Harwood, J. (2000). Communicative predictors of solidarity in the grandparent–grandchild relationship. *Journal of Social and Personal Relationships, 17*(6), 743–766.

Harwood, J., Giles, H., & Ryan, E. B. (1995). Aging, communication, and intergroup theory: Social identity and intergenerational communication. In J. F. Nussbaum & J. Coupland (Eds.), *Handbook of communication and aging research* (pp. 133–159). Mahwah, NJ: Lawrence Erlbaum Associates.

Haslett, B. (1983). Preschoolers' communicative strategies in gaining compliance from peers: A developmental study. *Quarterly Journal of Speech, 69,* 84–99.

Haslett, B. (1984). Communication development in children. In R. Bostrom (Ed.), *Communication yearbook 8* (pp. 198–266). Beverly Hills, CA: Sage.

Haslett, B. B., & Samter, W. (1997). *Children communicating: The first 5 years.* Mahwah, NJ: Lawrence Erlbaum Associates.

Hatfield, E. (1983). What do men and women want from love and sex? In E. R. Allgeier & N. B. McCormick (Eds.), *Changing boundaries: Gender roles and sexual behavior* (pp. 106–134). Palo Alto, CA: Mayfield.

Hatfield, S. R., & Abrams, L. J. (1995). Interaction between fathers and their children in traditional and single-father families: A multimethod exploration. In T. J. Socha & G. H. Stamp (Eds.), *Parents, children and communication: Frontiers of theory and research* (pp. 103–112). Mahwah, NJ: Lawrence Erlbaum Associates.

Hattie, J. (1992). *Self-concept.* Hillsdale, NJ: Lawrence Erlbaum Associates.

Havelock, E. A. (1963). *Preface to Plato.* Cambridge, MA: Harvard University Press.

Haviland-Jones, J. M., & Kahlbaugh, P. (2000). Emotion and identity. In M. Lewis & J. M. Haviland-Jones (Eds.), *Handbook of emotions* (pp. 293–305). New York: Guilford.

Hayden, B. (1982). Experience—a case for possible change. In J. C. Mancuso & J. Adams-Webber (Eds.), *The construing person* (pp. 170–197). New York: Praeger.

Hazen, C., & Shaver, P. (1987). Romantic love conceptualized as an attachment process. *Journal of Personality and Social Psychology, 52,* 511–524.

Healey, J. G., & Bell, R. A. (1990). Effects of social networks on individual's responses to conflicts in friendship. In D. D. Cahn (Ed.), *Intimates in conflict: A communication perspective* (pp. 121–152). Hillsdale, NJ: Lawrence Erlbaum Associates.

Heath, D. (1968). *Growing up in college.* San Francisco: Jossey-Bass.

Heaton, T. B. (1991). Time-related determinants of marital dissolution. *Journal of Marriage and the Family, 53,* 285–295.

Hecht, M. (1993). 2002—A research odyssey: Toward the development of a communication theory of identity. *Communication Monographs, 60,* 76–82.

Heckhausen, J. (1987). Balancing for weaknesses and challenging developmental potential: A longitudinal study of mother–infant dyads in apprenticeship interactions. *Developmental Psychology, 23,* 762–770.

Heinemann, G. D. (1985). Interdependence in informal support systems: The case of elderly, urban widows. In W. A. Peterson & J. Quadagno (Eds.), *Social bonds in later life* (pp. 165–186). Beverly Hills, CA: Sage.

Hendrick, S. S., & Hendrick, C. (1994). Lovers as friends. *Journal of Social and Personal Relationships, 10*(3), 459–466.

Henshall, C., & McGuire, J. (1986). Gender development. In M. Richards & P. Light (Eds.), *Children of social worlds.* Cambridge, MA: Harvard University Press.

Hermans, H. J. M., Kempen, H. J. G., & van Loon, R. J. P. (1992). The dialogical self: Beyond individualism and rationalism. *American Psychologist, 47*(1), 23–33.

Hess, R. D., Dickson, W. P., Price, G. G., & Leong, D. J. (1979). Some contrasts between mothers and preschool teachers in interaction with 4-year-old children. *American Educational Research Journal, 16,* 307–316.

Hess, T. M., & Auman, C. (2001). Aging and social expertise: The impact of trait-diagnostic information on impressions of others. *Psychology and Aging, 16*(3), 497–510.

Hetherington, E. M. (1988). Parents, children and siblings: Six years after divorce. In R. A. Hinde & J. Stevenson-Hinde (Eds.), *Relationships within families: Mutual influences* (pp. 311–331). Oxford, UK: Oxford University Press.

Hickey, T., Hickey, L., & Kalish, R. A. (1968). Children's perceptions of the elderly. *Journal of Genetic Psychology, 112,* 227–235.

Hill, C. T., Rubin, Z., & Peplau, L. A. (1976). Breakups before marriage: The end of 103 affairs. *Journal of Social Issues, 32,* 147–168.

Hinde, R. A. (1981). The bases of a science of interpersonal relationships. In S. W. Duck & R. Gilmour (Eds.), *Personal relationships 1: Studying personal relationships* (pp. 1–22). London: Academic Press.

Hoff-Ginsberg, E. (1991). Mother–child conversation in different social classes and communicative settings. *Child Development, 62,* 782–796.

Hoffman, J. A. (1984). Psychological separation of late adolescents from their parents. *Journal of Counseling Psychology, 31,* 170–178.

Hoffman, L. W., & Manis, J. D. (1978). Influences of children on marital interaction and parental satisfactions and dissatisfactions. In R. M. Lerner & G. B. Spanier (Eds.), *Child influences on marital and family interaction* (pp. 165–213). New York: Academic Press.

Hoffman, M. L. (1982). Development of prosocial motivation: Empathy and guilt. In N. Eisenberg (Ed.), *Development of prosocial behavior* (pp. 281–313). New York: Academic Press.

Holden, G. W., & Ritchie, K. L. (1988). Child rearing and the dialectics of parental intelligence. In J. Valsiner (Ed.), *Child development within culturally structured environments: Parental cognition and adult–child interaction* (Vol. 1, pp. 30–59). Norwood, NJ: Ablex.

Holland, C. A., & Rabbitt, P. M. (1991). Aging memory: Use versus impairment. *British Journal of Psychology, 82,* 29–38.

Holquist, M. (1983). Answering as authoring: Mikhail Bakhtin's trans-linguistics. *Critical Inquiry, 10,* 307–319.

Honeycutt, J. M. (1995). Imagined interactions, recurrent conflict and thought about personal relationships: A memory structure approach. In J. Aitken & L. J. Shedletsky (Eds.), *Intrapersonal communication processes* (pp. 138–150). Plymouth, MI: Midnight Oil & Speech Communication Association.

Honeycutt, J. M. (1999). Typological differences in predicting marital happiness from oral history behaviors and imagined interactions. *Communication Monographs, 66,* 276–291.

Hooyman, N., & Kiyak, H. A. (1991). *Social gerontology: A multidisciplinary perspective* (2nd ed.). Boston: Allyn & Bacon.

Horn, J. L. (1985). Remodeling old models of intelligence. In B. B. Wolman (Ed.), *Handbook of intelligence: Theories, measurements, and applications* (pp. 267–300). New York: Wiley.

Howe, N., Aquan-Assee, J., Bukowski, W. M., Rinaldi, C. M., & Lehoux, P. M. (2000). Sibling self-disclosure in early adolescence. *Merrill-Palmer Quarterly, 46*(4), 653–671.

Hubert, N. C., Wachs, T. D., Peters-Martin, P., & Gandour, M. J. (1982). The study of early temperament: Measurement and conceptual issues. *Child Development, 53,* 571–600.

Hudson, F. M. (1999). *The adult years: Mastering the art of self-renewal.* San Francisco: Jossey-Bass.

Hultsch, D. F., Hertzog, C., Small, B. J., & Dixon, R. A. (1999). Use it or lose it: Engaged lifestyle as a buffer of cognitive decline in aging? *Psychology and Aging, 14*(2), 245–263.

Hummert, M. L. (1994). Stereotypes of the elderly and patronizing speech. In M. L. Hummert, J. M. Wiemann, & J. F. Nussbaum (Eds.), *Interpersonal communication in older adulthood: Interdisciplinary research* (pp. 162–184). Newbury Park, CA: Sage.

Hummert, M. L., Garstka, T. A., Shaner, J. L., & Strahm, S. (1994). Stereotypes of the elderly held by young, middle-aged, and elderly adults. *Journals of Gerontology, 49,* 240–249.

Hummert, M. L., Nussbaum, J. F., & Wiemann, J. M. (1994). Interpersonal communication and older adulthood. In M. L. Hummert, J. M. Wiemann, & J. F. Nussbaum (Eds.), *Interpersonal communication in older adulthood* (pp. 1–14). Thousand Oaks, CA: Sage.

Hummert, M. L., & Ryan, E. (1996). Toward understanding variations in patronizing talk addressed to older adults: Psycholinguistic features of care and control. *International Journal of Psycholinguistics, 12,* 149–169.

Hummert, M. L., Shaner, J. L., & Garstka, T. A. (1995). Cognitive processes affecting communication with older adults: The case for stereotypes, attitudes, and beliefs about communication. In J. F. Nussbaum & J. Coupland (Eds.), *Handbook of communication and aging research* (pp. 105–131). Mahwah, NJ: Lawrence Erlbaum Associates.

Hundeide, K. (1985). The tacit background of children's judgments. In J. V. Wertsch (Ed.), Culture, communication, and cognition: Vygotskian perspectives (pp. 306–322). New York: Cambridge University Press.

Hurt, H. T. (1984). Communication competence for teachers: Avoiding aporia. In R. N. Bostrom (Ed.), *Competence in communication: A multidisciplinary approach* (pp. 151–173). Beverly Hills, CA: Sage.

Huston, T. L., McHale, S. M., & Crouter, A. C. (1986). When the honeymoon's over: Changes in the marriage relationship over the first year. In R. Gilmour & S. Duck (Eds.), *The emerging science of personal relationships* (pp. 109–132). Hillsdale, NJ: Lawrence Erlbaum Associates.

Huttenlocher, J., Haight, W., Bryk, A., Seltzer, J., & Lyons, T. (1991). Early vocabulary growth: Relation to language input and gender. *Developmental Psychology, 17*(2), 236–248.

Ianni, F. A. J. (1989). *The search for structure: A report on American youth today.* New York: Free Press.

Ignjatovic-Savic, N., Kovac-Cerovic, T., Plut, D., & Pesikan, A. (1988). Social interaction in early childhood and its developmental effects. In J. Valsiner (Ed.), *Child development within culturally structured environments* (Vol. 2, pp. 89–158). Norwood, NJ: Ablex.

Ilani, S. (2001). Acculturation and the self-report of depressive symptoms in African American and European American college students. *Dissertation Abstracts International, 61*(9-B), 4965.

Infante, D. A., Chandler, T. A., & Ruud, J. E. (1989). Test of an argumentative skill deficiency model of interspousal violence. *Communication Monographs, 56,* 163–177.

Infante, D. A., & Rancer, A. S. (1982). A conceptualization and measure of argumentativeness. *Journal of Personality Assessment, 46,* 72–80.

Infante, D. A., & Wigley, C. J., III. (1986). Verbal aggressiveness: An interpersonal model and measure. *Communication Monographs, 53,* 61–69.

Inhelder, B., & Piaget, J. (1955/1958). *The growth of logical thinking from childhood to adolescence* (A. Parsons & S. Milgram, Trans.). New York: Basic Books.

Irwin, E. C. (1975). Facilitating children's language development through play. *The Speech Teacher, 24,* 15–23.

Irwin, E. C., & McWilliams, B. J. (1974). Play therapy for children with cleft palates. *Children Today, 3,* 18–22.

Isabella, R. A., & Belsky, J. (1991). Interactional synchrony and the origins of infant–mother attachment: A replication study. *Child Development, 61,* 373–384.

Isquick, M. F. (1981). Training older people in empathy: Effects on empathy, attitudes, and self-exploration. *International Journal of Aging and Human Development, 13*(1), 1–14.

Izard, C. E. (1994). Innate and universal facial expressions: Evidence from developmental and cross-cultural research. *Psychological Bulletin, 115*(2), 288–299.

Izard, C. E., Lawler, T. B., Haynes, O. M., Simons, R. F., & Porges, S. W. (1999–2000). Emotionality in early infancy predicts temperament through the second year of life. *Imagination, Cognition and Personality, 19*(3), 213–227.

Izard, C., & Malatesta, C. (1987). Perspectives on emotional development I: Differential emotions theory of early emotional development. In J. D. Osofsky (Ed.), *Handbook of infant development* (2nd ed., pp. 494–554). New York: Wiley.

Jackson, L. M., Pancer, S. M., Pratt, M. W., & Hunsberger, B. (2000). Great expectations: The relation between expectancies and adjustment during the transition to university. *Journal of Applied Social Psychology, 30*(10), 2100–2125.

Jaffe, J., & Feldstein, S. (1970). *Rhythms of dialogue.* New York: Academic Press.

Jaffe, J., Stern, D. N., & Peery, J. C. (1973). "Conversational" coupling of gaze behavior in pre-linguistic human development. *Journal of Psycho-linguistic Research, 2*(2), 321–329.

James, W. (1890). *The principles of psychology.* New York: Henry Holt.

Jefferson, G. (1972). Side sequences. In D. Sudnow (Ed.), *Studies in social interaction* (pp. 294–338). New York: Free Press.

Jerison, H. J. (1976). Paleoneurology and the evolution of mind. *Scientific American, 234*(4), 90–101.

Johnson, C. L. (1985). The impact of illness on late-life marriages. *Journal of Marriage and the Family, 47,* 165–172.

Johnson, C. L., & Catalano, D. J. (1983). A longitudinal study of family supports to impaired elderly. *The Gerontologist, 23,* 612–618.

Johnson, J. R., Powell, R. G., & Arthur, R. H. (1980, November). *Communication and cognitive complexity: Issues and concerns for the 1980s.* Paper presented at the annual meeting of the Speech Communication Association, New York.

Johnson, J. S., & Newport, E. L. (1989). Critical period effects in second language learning: The influence of maturational state on the acquisition of English as a second language. *Cognitive Psychology, 21,* 60–99.

Johnson, K., & Edwards, R. (1991). The effects of gender and type of romantic touch on perceptions of relational commitment. *Journal of Nonverbal Behavior, 15,* 43–55.

Johnson, K. L., & Roloff, M. E. (2000). Correlates of the perceived resolvability and relational consequences of serial arguing in dating relationships: Argumentative features and the use of coping strategies. *Journal of Social and Personal Relationships, 17,* 676–686.

Johnson, M. P. (1973). Commitment: A conceptual structure and empirical application. *The Sociological Quarterly, 14,* 395–406.

Johnson, S. (1991). *The ship that sailed into the living room: Sex and intimacy reconsidered.* Estancia, NM: Wildfire Books.

Johnson, W. (2000). *Parenting and providing: The impact of Parents' Fair Share on paternal involvement.* New York: Manpower Demonstration Research Corporation.

Johnston, L. D., O'Malley, P. M., & Bachman, J. G. (1994). *National survey results on drug use from the Monitoring the Future study. 1975–1993, Vol. 2: College students and young adults* (NIH Publication No. 94-3810). Washington, DC: National Institute on Drug Abuse.

Jones, C., & Adamson, L. (1987). Language use in mother–child and mother–child–sibling interactions. *Child Development, 58,* 356–366.

Jones, R. A. (1977). *Self-fulfilling prophecies: Social, psychological and physiological effects of expectancies.* Hillsdale, NJ: Lawrence Erlbaum Associates.

Jones, W. H., Hobbs, S. A., & Hockenbury, D. (1982). Loneliness and social skill deficits. *Journal of Personality and social psychology, 42*, 682–689.

Josephs, I. E., Valsiner, J., & Surgan, S. E. (1999). The process of meaning construction. In J. Brandstadter & R. M. Lerner (Eds.), *Action & self-development: Theory and research through the life span.* Thousand Oaks, CA: Sage.

Josselson, R. (1980). Ego development in adolescence. In J. Adelson (Ed.), *Handbook of adolescent psychology* (pp. 188–210). New York: Wiley.

Josselyn, R. (1987). *Finding herself: Pathways to identity development in women.* San Francisco: Jossey-Bass.

Josselyn, R. (1994). Identity and relatedness in the life cycle. In H. A. Bosma, T. L. G. Graafsma, H. D. Grotevant, & D. J. de Levita (Eds.), *Identity and development: An interdisciplinary approach* (pp. 81–102). Thousand Oaks, CA: Sage.

Jung, C. G. (1957). *The undiscovered self.* New York: Mentor Books.

Jung, C. G. (1969). The structure of the psyche. In *The collected works of C. G. Jung* (Vol. 8, pp. 138–158). Princeton, NJ: Princeton University Press. (Original work published in 1931)

Juroe, D. J., & Juroe, B. B. (1983). *Successful stepparenting.* Old Tappan, NJ: F. H. Revell.

Jussim, L., & Eccles, J. (1995). Naturally occurring interpersonal expectancies. In N. Eisenberg (Ed.), *Social development* (pp. 74–108). Thousand Oaks, CA: Sage.

Kagan, J. (1987). Perspectives in infancy. In J. D. Osofsky (Ed.), *Handbook of infant development* (2nd ed., pp. 1150–1198). New York: Wiley.

Kagan, J. (1994). *Galen's prophecy: Temperament in human nature.* New York: Basic Books.

Kagan, J., Kearsley, R. B., & Zelazo, P. R. (1977). The effects of infant day care on psychological development. *Evaluation Quarterly, 1*, 109–142.

Kahane, J. C. (1981). Anatomical and physiological changes in the aging peripheral speech mechanism. In D. S. Beasley & G. A. Davis (Eds.), *Aging communication processes and disorders* (pp. 21–45). New York: Grune & Stratton.

Kahn, S., Zimmerman, G., Csikszentmihalyi, M., & Getzels, J. (1985). Relations between identity in young adulthood and intimacy at midlife. *Journal of Personality and Social Psychology, 49*, 1316–1322.

Kalish, R. A. (1976). Death and dying in a social context. In R. H. Binstock & E. Shanas (Eds.), *Handbook of aging and the social sciences* (pp. 483–507). New York: Van Nostrand.

Kamhi, A. G., & Lee, R. F. (1988). Cognition. In M. A. Nippold (Ed.), *Later language development: Ages 9 through 19* (pp. 127–158). Boston: Little, Brown.

Kastenbaum, R., & Aisenberg, R. (1972). *The psychology of death.* Oxford, UK: Springer.

Kastenbaum, R. J., & Candy, S. E. (1973). The 4% fallacy: A methodological and empirical critique of extended care facility population statistics. *International Journal of Aging and Human Development, 4*, 15–21.

Katriel, T., & Philipsen, G. (1981). "What we need is communication": "Communication" as a cultural category in some American speech. *Communication Monographs, 48*, 301–317.

Kawamura, K. Y. (2001). Body image attitudes of Asian American and Caucasian American women and men. *Dissertation Abstracts International, 62*(4-B), 2105.

Kaye, K. (1977). Toward the origin of dialogue. In H. R. Schaffer (Ed.), *Studies in mother–infant interaction* (pp. 89–118). London: Academic Press.

Keen, S. (1984). The passions of postadult life. In V. Rogers (Ed.), *Adult development through relationships* (pp. 88–102). New York: Praeger.

Keller, H., Scholmerich, A., & Eibl-Eibesfeldt, I. (1988). Communication patterns in adult–infant interactions in Western and non-Western cultures. *Journal of Cross-Cultural Psychology, 19*(4), 427–445.

Kelly, G. A. (1963). *A theory of personality: The psychology of personal constructs.* New York: Norton. (Original work published 1955)

Kelly, G. A. (1969). Ontological acceleration. In B. Maher (Ed.), *Clinical psychology and personality: The collected papers of George Kelly* (pp. 7–45). New York: Wiley.

Kelly, G. A. (1979). The autobiography of a theory. In B. Maher (Ed.), *Clinical psychology and personality: The collected papers of George Kelly* (pp. 46–65). New York: Wiley. (Original work published 1969)

Kelly, L. E., & Conley, J. J. (1987). Personality and compatibility: A prospective analysis of marital stability and marital satisfaction. *Journal of Personality and Social Psychology, 52,* 27–40.

Kemper, S., Greiner, L. H., Marquie, J. G., Prenovost, K., & Mitzner, T. L. (2001). Language decline across the lifespan: Findings from the nun study. *Psychology and Aging, 16,* 227–239.

Kemper, S., Kynette, D., Rash, D., O'Brien, K., & Sprott, R. (1989). Lifespan changes to adults' language: Effects of memory and genre. *Applied Psycholinguistics, 10,* 49–66.

Kessen, W., Haith, M. M., & Salapatek, P. H. (1970). Human infancy: A bibliography and guide. In P. H. Mussen (Ed.), *Carmichael's manual of child psychology, Volume I* (3rd ed., pp. 287–445). New York: Wiley.

Keyes, C. L. M., & Ryff, C. D. (1998). Generativity in adult lives: Social structural contours and quality of life consequences. In D. P. McAdams & E. de St. Aubin (Eds.), *Generativity and adult development: How and why we care for the next generation* (pp. 227–263). Washington, DC: American Psychological Association.

Kidwell, J. S. (1982). The neglected birth order: Middleborns. *Journal of Marriage and the Family, 44,* 225–235.

Kim, E. L., Larimer, M. E., Walker, D. D., & Marlatt, G. A. (1997). Relationship of alcohol use to other health behaviors among college students. *Psychology of Addictive Behaviors, 11*(3), 166–173.

Kimura, D. (1999). *Sex and cognition.* Cambridge, MA: MIT Press.

King, P. M. (1978). William Perry's theory of intellectual and ethical development. In L. Knefelkamp, C. Widick, & C. A. Parker (Eds.), *Applying new developmental findings* (pp. 35–51). San Francisco: Jossey-Bass.

Kiraly, Z. (2000). The relationship between emotional self-disclosure of male and female adolescents' friendship (Doctoral dissertation, Fordham University, 1999). *Dissertation Abstracts International, 60*(7-B), 3619.

Kitchener, K. S. (1986). The reflective judgment model: Characteristics, evidence, and measurement. In R. A. Mines & K. S. Kitchener (Eds.), *Adult cognitive development: Methods and models* (pp. 76–91). New York: Praeger.

Kitchener, K. S., and King, P. M. (1981). Reflective judgment: Concepts of Justification and their relationship to age and education. *Journal of Applied Developmental Psychology, 2*(2), 89–116.

Kleiner, K. (1987). Amplitude and phase spectra as indices of infants' pattern preferences. *Infant Behavior and Development, 10,* 49–59.

Klimes-Dougan, B., & Kistner, J. (1990). Physically abused preschoolers' responses to peers' distress. *Developmental Psychology, 26,* 599–602.

Knapp, M. (1984). *Interpersonal communication in human relationships.* Boston: Allyn & Bacon.

Knudson-Martin, C., & Mahoney, A. R. (1998). Language and processes in the construction of equality in new marriages. *Family Relations, 47,* 81–91.

Koch, H. L. (1960). The relation of certain formal attributes of siblings to their attitudes held towards each other and towards their parents. *Monographs of the Society for Research in Child Development, 24*(4), 134.

Koerner, A. F., & Fitzpatrick, M. A. (2002). Nonverbal communication and marital adjustment and satisfaction: The role of decoding relationship relevant and relationship irrelevant affect. *Communication Monographs, 69*(1), 33–51.

Kohlberg, L. (1969). Stage and sequence: The cognitive-developmental approach to socialization. In D. A. Goslin (Ed.), *Handbook of socialization theory and research* (pp. 347–480). Chicago: Rand-McNally.

Kohlberg, L. (1971). Stages and aging in moral development: Some speculations. *Gerontologist, 13*, 497–502.

Kohlberg, L., & Mayer, R. (1972). Development as the aim of education. *Harvard Educational Review, 42*(4), 449–496.

Komarovsky, M. (1974). Patterns of self-disclosure of male undergraduates. *Journal of Marriage and the Family, 36*, 677–686.

Kornhaber, A., & Woodward, K. L. (1981). *Grandparents/grandchildren: The vital connection.* Garden City, NY: Anchor Press/Doubleday.

Kotkin, M. (1985). To marry or live together? *Lifestyles, 7*, 156–170.

Kotre, J. (1984). *Outliving the self: Generativity and the interpretation of lives.* Baltimore, MD: John Hopkins University Press.

Kotre, J., & Hall, E. (1990). *Seasons of life.* Boston: Little, Brown.

Kovach, S. S., & Robinson, J. D. (1996). The roommate relationships for the elderly nursing home resident. *Journal of Social and Personal Relationships, 13*, 627–634.

Kramer, D. (1997). How women relate to terminally ill husbands and their subsequent adjustment to bereavement. *Omega: Journal of Death and Dying, 34*, 93–106.

Krashen, S. (1973). Lateralization, language learning, and the critical period: Some new evidence. *Language Learning, 23*, 63–74.

Krauss, R. M., Fussell, S. R., & Chen, Y. (1995). Coordination of perspective in dialogue: Intrapersonal and interpersonal processes. In I. Markova, C. F. Graumann, & K. Foppa (Eds.), *Mutualities in dialogue* (pp. 124–145). Cambridge, UK: Cambridge University Press.

Kroger, J. (2000). *Identity development: Adolescence through adulthood.* Thousand Oaks, CA: Sage.

Kubey, R., & Csikszentmihalyi, M. (1990). *Television and the quality of life: How viewing shapes everyday experience.* Hillsdale, NJ: Lawrence Erlbaum Associates.

Kubler-Ross, E. (1969). *On death and dying.* New York: Macmillan.

Kuczaj, S. A. II, & Bean, A. (1982). The development of noncommunicative speech systems. In S. A. Kuczaj II (Ed.), *Language development, Vol. 2: Language, thought and culture* (pp. 279–300). Hillsdale, NJ: Lawrence Erlbaum Associates.

Kuczynski, L., Kochanska, G., Radke-Yarrow, M., & Girnius-Brown, O. (1987). A developmental interpretation of young children's noncompliance. *Developmental Psychology, 23*, 799–806.

Kurdek, L. (1991). Marital stability and changes in marital quality in newly wed couples: A test of the contextual model. *Journal of Social and Personal Relationships, 8*, 27–48.

Kurdek, L. A., & Schmitt, J. P. (1986). Early development of relationship quality in heterosexual married, heterosexual cohabiting, gay, and lesbian couples. *Developmental Psychology, 22*, 305–309.

Kuterovac-Jagodic, G., & Kerestes, G. (1997). Perception of parental acceptance-rejection and some personality variables in young adults. *Drustvena Istrazivanja, 6*(4–5), 477–491.

Labouvie-Vief, G. (1982a). Dynamic development and mature autonomy. *Human Development, 25*, 161–191.

Labouvie-Vief, G. (1982b). Individual time, social time, and intellectual aging. In T. K. Hareven, & K. J. Adams (Eds.), *Aging and life course transitions: An interdisciplinary perspective* (pp. 151–182). New York: Guilford.

Labouvie-Vief, G. (1984). Logic and self-regulation from youth to maturity. In M. L. Commons, F. A. Richards, & C. Armon (Eds.), *Beyond formal operations: Late adolescent and adult cognitive development* (pp. 158–179). New York: Praeger.

Ladd, G. W. (1983). Social networks of popular, average, and rejected children in school settings. *Merrill-Palmer Quarterly, 29,* 283–307.

LaGaipa, J. J. (1987). Friendship expectations. In R. Burnett, P. McGhee, & D. Clarke (Eds.), *Accounting for relationships* (pp. 134–157). London: Metheun.

Lamb, M. E. (1976). Interactions between eight-month-old children and their fathers and mothers. In M. E. Lamb (Ed.), *The role of the father in child development* (pp. 307–327). New York: Wiley.

Lamb, M. E. (1977a). The development of parental preferences in the first two years of life. *Sex Roles, 3,* 495–497.

Lamb, M. E. (1977b). Father–infant and mother–infant interaction in the first year of life. *Child Development, 48,* 167–181.

Lamb, M. E. (1978). The father's role in the infant's social world. In J. H. Stevens, Jr., & M. Mathews (Eds.), *Mother/child father/child relationships* (pp. 87–108). Washington, DC: National Association for the Education of Young Children.

Lamb, M. E. (1987). *The father's role.* Hillsdale, NJ: Lawrence Erlbaum Associates.

Lane, V. W., & Molyneaux, D. (1992). *The dynamics of communication development.* Englewood Cliffs, NJ: Prentice-Hall.

Lang, F. R. (2000). Endings and continuity of social relationships: Maximizing intrinsic benefits within personal networks when feeling near to death. *Journal of Social and Personal Relationships, 17,* 155–182.

Langer, S. K. (1972). *Mind: An essay on human feeling* (Vol. II). Baltimore: Johns Hopkins University Press.

Langlois, A., Baken, R. J., & Wilder, C. N. (1980). Pre-speech respiratory behavior during the first year of life. In T. Murry & J. Murry (Eds.), *Infant communication: Cry and early speech* (pp. 56–84). Houston, TX: College-Hill Press.

Larose, S., & Boivin, M. (1998). Attachment to parents, social support expectations, and socioemotional adjustment during the high school-college transition. *Journal of Research on Adolescence, 8*(1), 1–27.

Larson, R. (1978). Thirty years of research on the subjective well-being of older Americans. *Journal of Gerontology, 33,* 109–125.

Larson, R., & Kubey, R. (1983, Spring). Television and music: Contrasting media in adolescent life. *Youth and Society,* pp. 13–33.

Larson, R., & Lampman-Petraitis, C. (1989). Daily emotional states as reported by children and adolescents. *Child Development, 60,* 1250–1260.

Lasky, R., Syrdal-Lasky, A., & Klein, R. (1975). VOT discrimination by four to six and a half month infants from Spanish environments. *Journal of Experimental Child Psychology, 20,* 215–225.

Laursen, B. (1993). The perceived impact of conflict on adolescent relationships. *Merrill-Palmer Quarterly, 39,* 535–550.

Lazarus, R. S. (1991). *Emotion and adaptation.* New York: Oxford University Press.

Leach, M. S., & Braithwaite, D. O. (1996). A binding tie: Supportive communication of family kinkeepers. *Journal of Applied Communication, 24,* 200–216.

Lecours, A. R. (1975). Myelogenetic correlates of the development of speech and language. In E. H. & E. Lenneberg (Eds.), *Foundations of language development: A multidisciplinary Approach* (Vol. I, pp. 121–135). New York: Academic Press.

Lee, C. L., & Bates, J. E. (1985). Mother–child interaction at age two years and perceived difficult temperament. *Child Development, 56,* 1314–1325.

Lee, J. A. (1973). *The colours of love: An exploration of the ways of loving.* Don Mills, Canada: New Press.

Leefeldt, C., & Callenbach, E. (1979). *The art of friendship.* New York: Berkeley.

Leichtentritt, R. D., & Rettig, K. D. (1999). My parent's dignified death is different from mine: Moral problem solving about euthanasia. *Journal of Social and Personal Relationships, 16,* 385–406.

Leit, R. A. (2001). The media's representation of the ideal male body: A cause for muscle dysmorphia? *Dissertation Abstracts International, 61*(8-B), 4413.

Lemerise, E. A., & Dodge, K. A. (1993). The development of anger and hostile interactions. In M. Lewis & J. M. Haviland (Eds.), *Handbook of emotions* (pp. 537–546). New York: Guilford.

Lenneberg, E. (1967). *Biological foundations of language.* New York: Wiley.

Leontiev, A. N. (1964). *Problems of mental development.* Washington, DC: Joint Publications Research Service. (Original work published 1959)

Leontiev, A. N., & Luria, A. R. (1968). The psychological ideas of L. S. Vygotsky. In B. B. Wolman (Ed.), *Historical roots of contemporary psychology* (pp. 338–367). New York: Harper & Row.

Lerman, R. I. (1993). A national profile of young unwed fathers. In R. I. Lerman & T. J. Ooms (Eds.), *Young unwed fathers: Changing roles and emerging policies* (pp. 27–51). Philadelphia: Temple University Press.

Lerner, R. M., & Walls, T. (1999). Revisiting individuals as producers of their own development. In J. Brandstadter & R. Lerner (Eds.), *Action and self-development: Theory and research through the life span* (pp. 3–36). Thousand Oaks, CA: Sage.

Levenson, R. W., & Gottman, J. M. (1983). Marital interaction: Physiological linkage and affective exchange. *Journal of Personality and Social Psychology, 45,* 587–597.

Lever, J. (1976). Sex differences in the games children play. *Social Problems, 23,* 478–487.

Levinson, D. J. (1978). *Seasons of a man's life.* (C. N. Dorrow, E. B. Klein, M. H. Levinson, & B. McKee, Eds.). New York: Knopf.

Levinson, D. J., Darrow, C. N., Klein, E. B., Levinson, M. H., & McKee, B. (1979). *The seasons of a man's life.* New York: Knopf.

Leviton, A., & Gilles, F. H. (1983). The epidemiology of delayed myelination. In F. H. Gilles, A. Leviton, & E. C. Dooling (Eds.), *The developing human brain* (pp. 185–203). Boston: John Wright.

Levitz-Jones, E. M., & Orlofsky, J. L. (1985). Separation-individuation and intimacy capacity in college women. *Journal of Personality and Social Psychology, 49,* 156–169.

Lewis, M. (1987). Social development in infancy and early childhood. In J. D. Osofsky (Ed.), *Handbook of infant development* (2nd ed., pp. 419–493). New York: Wiley.

Lewis, M. (1995). Aspects of self: From systems to ideas. In P. Rochat (Ed.), *The self in infancy: Theory and research* (pp. 95–115). Amsterdam: Elsevier Science.

Lewis, M. (1999). Social cognition and the self. In P. Rochat (Ed.), *Early social cognition: Understanding others in the first months of life* (pp. 82–98). Mahwah, NJ: Lawrence Erlbaum Associates.

Lewis, M., & Brooks-Gunn, J. (1981). Self, other, and fear: The reaction of infants to people. In E. M. Hetherington & R. D. Parke (Eds.), *Contemporary readings in child psychology* (2nd ed., pp. 87–95). New York: McGraw-Hill.

Lewis, M., & Michalson, L. (1983). *Children's emotions and moods: Developmental theory and measurement.* New York: Plenum.

Lewis, M., & Rosenblum, L. A. (Eds.). (1974). *The effect of the infant on its caregiver.* New York: Wiley.

Lieberman, P. (1973). On the evolution of human language: A unified view. *Cognition, 2,* 59–94.

Lieberman, P. (1977). *Speech physiology and acoustic phonetics.* New York: Macmillan.

Lieberman, P. (1991). *Uniquely human: The evolution of speech, thought, and selfless behavior.* Cambridge, MA: Harvard University Press.

Lin, C. A. (2001). The VCR, home video culture, and new video technologies. In J. Bryant & J. A. Bryant (Eds.), *Television and the American family* (2nd ed., pp. 91–107). Mahwah, NJ: Lawrence Erlbaum Associates.

Litvin, S. J. (1992). Status transitions and future outlook as determinants of conflict: The caregiver's and care receiver's perspective. *The Gerontologist, 32,* 68–76.

Litwak, A. (1985). *Helping the elderly: The complementary role of informal networks and formal systems.* New York: Guilford.

Livesley, W. J., & Bromley, D. B. (1973). *Person perception in childhood and adolescence.* Chichester, UK: Wiley.

Loeb, R. C., & Magee, P. M. (1992). Changes in attitudes and self-perceptions during the first two years of college. *Journal of College Student Development, 33,* 348–355.

Looft, W. R., & Charles, D. C. (1971). Egocentrism and social interaction in young and old adults. *Aging and Human Development, 2,* 21–28.

Lopez, F. G., Campell, V. L., & Watkins, C. E., Jr. (1988). Family structure, psychological separation, and college adjustment: A canonical analysis and cross-validation. *Journal of Counseling Psychology, 33,* 52–56.

Lovlie, A. (1982). *The self: Yours, mine or ours?* Oslo, Norway: Universitetsforlaet.

Luria, A. R. (1972). *The making of mind.* M. Cole & S. Cole (Eds.). Cambridge, MA: Harvard University Press.

Luria, A. R. (1982). *Language and cognition.* J. V. Wertsch (Ed.). New York: Wiley.Lyle, S. (1994). An investigation into the manipulative strategies of 10- and 11-year-olds in their relationships with their parents as reported by the children in an educational context. *Educational Studies, 20*(1), 19–31.

Lynn, D. B. (1974). *The father: His role in child development.* Monterey, CA: Brooks/Cole.

MacDermid, S. M., Huston, T. D., & McHale, S. M. (1990). Changes in marriage associated with the transition to parenthood: Individual differences as a function of sex-role attitudes and changes in the division of household labor. *Journal of Marriage and the Family, 52*(2), 475–486.

MacDonald, K. (1992). Warmth as a developmental construct: An evolutionary analysis. *Child Development, 63*(4), 753–773.

MacDonald, T. K., & Ross, M. (1999). Assessing the accuracy of predictions about dating relationships: How and why do lovers' predictions differ from those made by observers? *Personality and Social Psychology Bulletin, 25*(11), 1417–1429.

Mahler, M. S., Pine, F., & Bergman, A. (1975). *The psychological birth of the infant: Symbiosis and individuation.* New York: Basic Books.

Mannarino, A. P. (1980). The development of children's friendships. In H. C. Foot, A. J. Chapman, & J. R. Smith (Eds.), *Friendship and social relations in children* (pp. 45–63). New York: Wiley.

Manning, B. H., & White, C. S. (1990). Task-relevant private speech as a function of age and sociability. *Psychology in the Schools, 27,* 365–372.

Manning, L. M. (1996, February). *Research in adolescent communication: Review and recommendations.* Paper presented at the meeting of the Western States Communication Association, Pasadena, CA.

Mao Tse-Tung. (1965). On contradiction. *The selected works of Mao Tse-tung* (Vol. I, pp. 1–52). Peking: Foreign Language Press. (Original work published 1952)

Maratsos, M. P. (1973). Nonegocentric communication abilities in preschool children. *Child Development, 44,* 697–700.

Marcia, J. E. (1966). Development and validation of ego identity status. *Journal of Personality and Social Psychology, 3,* 551–558.

Marcia, J. E. (1976). Identity six years after: A follow-up study. *Journal of Youth and Adolescence, 5,* 145–150.

Mares, M., & Fitzpatrick, M. A. (1995). The aging couple. In J. F. Nussbaum & J. Coupland (Eds.), *Handbook of communication and aging research* (pp. 185–205). Mahwah, NJ: Lawrence Erlbaum Associates.

Markman, H. J., Silvern, L., Clements, M., & Kraft-Hanak, S. (1993). Men and women dealing with conflict in heterosexual relationships. *Journal of Social Issues, 49,* 107–125.

Marshall, V. (1986). A sociological perspective on aging and dying. In V. Marshall (Ed.), *Later life: The social psychology of aging* (pp. 125–146). Beverly Hills, CA: Sage.

Marwell, G., & Schmitt, D. R. (1967). Dimensions of compliance-gaining behavior: An empirical analysis. *Sociometry, 39,* 350–364.

Masataka, N. (1992). Motherese in a signed language. *Infant behavior and development, 15,* 453–460.

Mascolo, M. F., Fischer, K. W., & Neimeyer, R. A. (1999). The dynamic codevelopment of intentionality, self, and social relations. In J. Brandtstadter & R. M. Lerner (Eds.), *Action and self development* (pp. 133–166). Thousand Oaks, CA: Sage.

Masheter, C. (1994). Dialogues between ex-spouses: Evidence of dialetic relationship development. In R. Conville (Ed.), *Uses of "structure" in communication studies* (pp. 83–101). New York: Praeger.

Maslow, A. (1982). *Toward a psychology of being.* New York: Van Nostrand Reinhold. (Original work published 1968)

Massey, C. J. (2001). Parent and sibling relationship influences on late adolescent social anxiety and other adjustment outcomes. (Doctoral dissertation, West Virginia University, 2001.) *Dissertation Abstracts International, 62,* B1116.

Masters, W. H., & Johnson, V. E. (1968). Human sexual response: The aging female and the aging male. In B. L. Neugarten (Ed.), *Middle age and aging* (pp. 209–279). Chicago: University of Chicago Press.

Masur, E. (1982). Cognitive content of parents' speech to preschoolers. *Merrill-Palmer Quarterly, 28,* 471–484.

Matthews, S. H. (1986). Definitions of friendships and consequences in old age. *Aging and Society, 3,* 141–155.

Matthews, S. H., & Spray, J. (1985). Adolescents' relationships with grandparents: An empirical contribution to conceptual clarification. *Journal of Gerontology, 40,* 621–626.

Maurer, K., & Salapatek, P. (1976). Developmental change in the scanning of faces by young infants. *Child Development, 47,* 523–527.

Mavilya, M. P. (1969). Spontaneous vocalization and babbling in hearing impaired infants. *Dissertation Abstracts International, 3101A:* 0074.

Maxim, J., & Bryan, K. (1994). *Language of the elderly: A clinical perspective.* San Diego: Singular.

Mazzeo, S. E. (2001). Correlates of disordered eating behavior in female undergraduates: Development and validation of a structural model. *Dissertation Abstracts International, 61*(10-B), 5573.

McCartney, K., Robeson, W. W., Jordan, E., & Mouradian, V. (1991). Mothers' language with first- and second-born children: A within-family study. In K. Pillemer & K. McCartney (Eds.), *Parent–child relations throughout life* (pp. 125–142). Hillsdale, NJ: Lawrence Erlbaum Associates.

McCrae, R. R., Costa, P. T., Ostendorf, F., Angleitner, A., Hrebíčková, M., Avia, M. D., Sanz, J., Sánchez-Bernardos, M. L., Kusdil, M. E., Woodfield, R., Saunders, P. R., & Smith, P. B. (2000). Nature over nurture: Temperament, personality and lifespan development. *Journal of Personality and Social Psychology, 78*(1), 173–186.

McDermott, S. T. (1986, November). *Naturalistic observations of parental attempts at gaining compliance*. Paper presented at the Speech Communication Association convention, Chicago, IL.

McGonagle, K. A., Kessler, R. C., & Schilling, E. A. (1992). The frequency and determinants of marital disagreements in a community sample. *Journal of Social and Personal Relationships, 9*, 507–524.

McGrath, E., Keita, G., Strickland, B., & Russo, N. (1990). *Women and depression; risk factors and treatment issues: Final report of the American Psychological Association's National Task Force on Women and Depression*. Washington, DC: American Psychological Association.

McHale, S. M., & Gamble, W. C. (1987). Sibling relationships and adjustment of children with disabled brothers and sisters. *Journal of Children in Contemporary Society, 19*(3/4), 131–158.

McKay, V. C. (1993). Making connections: Narrative as the expression of continuity between generations of grandparents and grandchildren. In N. Coupland & J. F. Nussbaum (Eds.), *Discourse and lifespan identity* (pp. 173–185). Newbury Park, CA: Sage.

McLanahan, S., & Sandefur, G. (1994). *Growing up with a single parent: What hurts, what helps*. Cambridge, MA: Harvard University Press.

McLaughlin, M. L. (1984). *Conversation: How talk is organized*. Beverly Hills, CA: Sage.

Meacham, J. A. (1977). Soviet investigations of memory development. In R. V. Kail, Jr., & J. W. Hagen (Eds.), *Perspectives on the Development of memory and cognition* (pp. 273–295). Hillsdale, NJ: Lawrence Erlbaum Associates.

Mead, G. H. (1925). The genesis of the self and social control. *International Journal of Ethics, 35*, 251–273.

Mead, G. H. (1974). *Mind, self and society*. Chicago: University of Chicago Press. (Original work published 1934)

Mead, G. H. (1982). Consciousness, mind, the self and scientific objects. In D. L. Millea (Ed.), *The individual and the social self: Unpublished work of George Herbert Mead* (pp. 176–196). Chicago: University of Chicago Press.

Mead, M. (1966, July). Marriage in two steps. *Redbook*, pp. 48–52.

Mebert, C. J. (1991). Variability in the transition to parenthood experience. In K. Pillemer & K. McCartney (Eds.), *Parent–child relations throughout life* (pp. 43–57). Hillsdale, NJ: Lawrence Erlbaum Associates.

Mechling, J. (1975). Advice to historians on advice to mothers. *Journal of Social History, 9*, 44–63.

Meikle, M., & Holley, S. (1991). Communication with patients in residence. In M. Denham (Ed.), *Care of the long-stay elderly patient* (pp. 149–160). London: Chapman & Hall.

Meltzoff, A. N., & Moore, M. K. (1997). Explaining facial imitation: A theoretical model. *Early development and parenting, 6*, 179–192.

Meltzoff, A. N., & Moore, M. K. (1995). A theory of the role of imitation in the emergence of self. In P. Rochat (Ed.), *The self in infancy: Theory and research* (pp. 73–93). Amsterdam: Elsevier Science.

Messer, D. J. (1994). *The development of communication: From social interaction to language.* West Sussex, UK: Wiley.

Meyer v. State of Nebraska, 262 U.S. 392 (1925).

Milardo, R. M. (1982). Friendship networks in developing relationships: Converging and diverging social environments. *Social Psychology Quarterly, 45,* 162–172.

Miller, D. L. (Ed.). (1982). *The individual and the social self: The unpublished work of George Herbert Mead.* Chicago: University of Chicago Press.

Miller, E. M. (1994). Intelligence and brain myelination: A hypothesis. *Personality and Individual Differences, 17,* 80–832.

Miller, G. R., Boster, F., Roloff, M. E., & Seibold, D. R. (1977). Compliance-gaining message strategies: A typology and some findings concerning effects of situational differences. *Communication Monographs, 44,* 37–51.

Miller, J. B. (1993). Learning from early relationship experience. In S. Duck (Ed.), *Learning about relationships* (pp. 1–29). Newbury Park, CA: Sage.

Min'-er, H., & Dejun, G. (2001). Emotional regulation and depression of college students. *Chinese Mental Health Journal, 15*(6), 438–441.

Moerk, E. (1974). Changes in verbal child–mother interactions with increasing language skills of the child. *Journal of Psycholinguistic Research, 3,* 101–115.

Molfese, D. (1972). Cerebral asymmetry in infants, children and adults: Auditory evoked responses to speech and music stimuli. *Dissertation Abstracts International, 34,* 1298B.

Monsour, M. (1992). Meanings of intimacy in cross- and same-sex friendships. *Journal of Social and Personal Relationships, 9,* 277–295.

Monsour, M. (1997). Communication and cross-sex friendships across the life cycle: A review of the literature. In B. R. Burleson (Ed.), *Communication yearbook 20* (pp. 375–414). Thousand Oaks, CA: Sage.

Montemayor, R. (1983). Parents and adolescents in conflict. *Journal of Early Adolescence, 3,* 83–103.

Montgomery, B. M. (1992). Communication as the interface between couples and culture. *Communication Yearbook, 15,* 475–507.

Montgomery, B. M. (1993). Relationship maintenance versus relationship change: A dialectical dilemma. *Journal of Social and Personal Relationships, 10,* 205–223.

Montgomery, B. M., & Baxter, L. A. (1998). *Dialectical approaches to studying personal relationships.* Mahwah, NJ: Lawrence Erlbaum Associates.

Moon, C. M., & Fifer, W. P. (2000). Evidence of transnatal auditory learning. *Journal of Perinataology, 20,* S37–S44.

Moore, C., & Dunham, P. (1995). *Joint attention: Its origins and role in development.* Hillsdale, NJ: Lawrence Erlbaum Associates.

Moore, T. (1992). *Care of the soul.* New York: HarperCollins.

Morash, M. A. (1980). Working class membership and the adolescent identity crisis. *Adolescence, 15,* 313–320.

Morency, N. L., & Krauss, R. M. (1982). The nonverbal encoding and decoding of affect in first and fifth graders. In R. S. Feldman (Ed.), *Development of nonverbal behavioral skill* (pp. 181–199). New York: Springer-Verlag.

Morgan, M., Alexander, A., Shanahan, J., & Harris, C. (1990). Adolescents, VCRs, and the family environment. *Communication Research, 17*(1), 83–106.

Morgan, M., & Hummert, M. L. (2000). Perceptions of communicative control strategies in mother–daughter dyads across the life span. *Journal of Communication, 50*(3), 48–64.

Morreale, S. P., & Backlund, P. M. (Eds.). (1996). *Large scale assessment of oral communication: K–12 and higher education.* (2nd ed.). Annandale, VA: Speech Communication Association.

Motley, M. T., & Reeder, H. M. (1995). Unwanted escalation of sexual intimacy: Male and female perceptions of connotations and relational consequences of resistance messages. *Communication Monographs, 62,* 355–382.

Mura, S. S. (1983). Licensing violations: Legitimate violations of Grice's conversational principle. In R. T. Craig & K. Tracy (Eds.), *Conversational coherence: Form, structure, and strategy* (pp. 101–115). Beverly Hills, CA: Sage.

Murphy, C. M., & Messer, D. J. (1977). Mothers, infants, and pointing: A study of gesture. In H. R. Schaffer (Ed.), *Studies in mother-infant interaction* (pp. 325–354). London: Academic Press.

Murphy, J. M., & Gilligan, C. (1980). Moral development in late adolescence and adulthood: A critique and reconstruction of Kohlberg's theory. *Human Development, 23,* 77–104.

Murray, L., & Trevarthen, C. (1985). Emotional regulation of interactions between two-month-olds and their mothers. In T. M. Field & N. A. Fox (Eds.), *Social perception in infants* (pp. 177–197). Norwood, NJ: Ablex.

Muuss, R. E. (1996). *Theories of adolescence* (6th ed.). New York: McGraw-Hill.

Naegele, K. D. (1958). Friendship and acquaintances: An exploration of some social distinctions. *Harvard Educational Review, 28,* 232–252.

National Communication Association (1988). *Competent communicators: K–12 speaking, listening, and media literacy standards and competency statements.* Annandale, VA: Author.

National Institutes of Health. (1993). Early identification of hearing impairment in infants and young children. *NIH Consensus Statement Online, 11*(1), 1–24. Retrieved 11/19/03 from http://consensus.nih.gov/cons/092/092_intro.htm

Neimark, E. (1975). Longitudinal development of formal operations thought. *Genetic Psychology Monographs, 91,* 171–225.

Neisser, U. (1991). Two perceptually given aspects of the self and their development. *Developmental Review, 11,* 197–209.

Neisser, U. (1995). Criteria for an ecological self. In P. Rochat (Ed.), *The self in infancy: Theory and research* (pp. 17–34). Amsterdam: Elsevier Science.

Nelson, C. A. (1994). Neural bases of infant temperament. In J. E. Bates & T. D. Wachs (Eds.), *Temperament: Individual differences at the interface of biology and behavior* (pp. 47–82). Washington, DC: American Psychological Association.

Nelson, K. (1973). Structure and strategy in learning to talk. *Monographs of the Society for Research in Child Development, 38*(1/2), 1–135.

Nelson, K. (1986). *Event knowledge: Structure and function in development.* Hillsdale, NJ: Lawrence Erlbaum Associates.

Newson, J. (1977). An intersubjective approach to the systematic description of mother-infant interaction. In H. R. Schaffer (Ed.), *Studies in mother-infant interaction* (pp. 47–62). London: Academic Press.

Newson, J. (1978). Dialogue and development. In A. Lock (Ed.), *Action, gesture, and symbol* (pp. 31–42). London: Academic Press.

Nezlak, J. B. (2001). Causal relationships between perceived social skills and day-to-day social interaction: Extending the sociometer hypothesis. *Journal of Social and Personal Relationships, 18*(3), 386–403.

Nezlak, J. B., & Derks, P. (2002). Use of humor as a coping mechanism, psychological adjustment, and social interaction. *International Journal of Humor Research, 14*(4), 395–413.

Nezlak, J. B., Richardson, D. S., Green, L. R., & Schatten-Jones, E. C. (2002). Psychological well-being and day-to-day social interaction among older adults. *Personal Relationships, 9,* 57–71.

Nord, C. W., & Zill, N. (1996). *Non-custodial parents' participation in their children's lives: Evidence from the Survey of Income and Program Participation.* Washington, DC: U.S. Department of Health and Human Services.

Novey, S. (1968). *The second look: The reconstruction of personal history in psychiatry and psychoanalysis.* New York: International Universities Press.

Nudler, O. (1986). The development-adaptation dialectic. In C. A. Mallmann & O. Nudler (Eds.), *Human development in its social context: A collective exploration* (pp. 126–138). London, England: Hodder & Stoughton Educational.

Nussbaum, J. F. (1983). Relational closeness of elderly: Implications for life satisfaction. *Western Journal of Speech Communication, 47,* 229–243.

Nussbaum, J. F. (1990). Communication within the nursing home: Survivability as a function of resident-staff affinity. In H. Giles, N. Coupland, & J. M. Wiemann (Eds.), *Communication, health and the elderly* (pp. 155–171).

Nussbaum, J. F. (1994). Friendship in older adulthood. In M. L. Hummert, J. M. Wiemann, & J. F. Nussbaum (Eds.), *Interpersonal communication in older adulthood: Interdisciplinary theory and research* (pp. 209–225). Thousand Oaks, CA: Sage.

Nussbaum, J. F., Hummert, M. L., Williams, A., & Harwood, J. (1996). Communication and older adults. In B. R. Burleson (Ed.), *Communication yearbook 19* (pp. 1–47). Thousand Oaks, CA: Sage.

Nussbaum, J. F., Pecchioni, L. L., Baringer, D. K., & Kundrat, A. L. (2002). Lifespan communication. In W. B. Gudykunst (Ed.), *Communication yearbook 26* (pp. 366–389), Mahwah, NJ: Lawrence Erlbaum Associates.

Nussbaum, J. F., Pecchioni, L. L., Robinson, J. D., & Thompson, T. L. (2000). *Communication and aging* (2nd ed.). Mahwah, NJ: Lawrence Erlbaum Associates.

Nydegger, C. N. (1991). The development of paternal and filial maturity. In K. Pillemer & K. McCartney (Eds.), *Parent–child relations throughout life* (pp. 93–112). Hillsdale, NJ: Lawrence Erlbaum Associates.

Obler, L. K. (1980). Narrative discourse style in the elderly. In L. Obler & M. Albert (Eds.), *Language and communication in the elderly* (pp. 75–90). Lexington, MA: D. C. Health.

Obler, L., & Albert, M. (1981). Language and aging: A neurobehavioral analysis. In D. Beasley & G. A. Davis (Eds.), *Aging communication processes and disorders* (pp. 107–121). New York: Grune & Stratton.

Obler, L. K., Mildworf, B., & Albert, M. (1977). *Writing style in the elderly.* Montreal: Academy of Aphasia Abstracts.

Ogden, C. K., & Richards, I. A. (1953). *The meaning of meaning.* New York: Harcourt Brace.

O'Keefe, B. J., & Delia, J. G. (1982). Impression formation and message production. In M. E. Roloff & C. R. Berger (Eds.), *Social cognition and communication* (pp. 33–72). Beverly Hills, CA: Sage.

Oliker, S. J. (1989). *Best friends and marriage: Exchange among women.* Berkeley: University of California Press.

Oliveira, Z. M. R. (1998). Peer interactions and the appropriations of gender representations by young children. In M. C. D. P. Lyra & J. Valsiner (Eds.), *Construction of psychological processes in interpersonal communication* (pp. 103–114). Stamford, CT: Ablex.

Oller, D. K. (1980). The emergence of the sounds of speech in infancy. In G. H. Yeni-Komshian, J. F. Kavanagh, & C. A. Ferguson (Eds.), *Child phonology*, Vol. 1. New York: Academic Press.

Oller, D. K., & Eilers, R. E. (1988). The role of audition in infant babbling. *Child Development, 59*(2), 441–449.

Olson, L. N. (2002). Exploring "common couple violence" in heterosexual romantic relationships. *Western Journal of Communication, 66*(1), 104–128.

Olson, S., Bayles, K., & Bates, J. (1986). Mother–child interaction and children's speech progress: A longitudinal study of the first two years. *Merrill-Palmer Quarterly, 32*, 1–20.

Olstad, K. (1975). Brave new man: A basis for discussion. In J. Petras (Ed.), *Sex: male/gender: Masculine*. Port Washington, NY: Alfred.

Omdahl, B. L. (1995). *Cognitive appraisal, emotion, and empathy*. Mahwah, NJ: Lawrence Erlbaum Associates.

Ong, W. J. (1967). *The presence of the word: Some prolegomena for cultural and religious history*. Minneapolis: University of Minnesota Press.

Ong, W. J. (1981). *Fighting for life: Contest, sexuality and consciousness*. Ithaca: Cornell University Press.

Ong, W. J. (1982). *Orality and literacy: The technologizing of the word*. London: Routledge.

Orange, J. B., Van Gennep, K. M., Miller, L., & Johnson, A. M. (1998). Resolution of communication breakdown in dementia of the Alzheimer's type: A longitudinal study. *Journal of Applied Communication Research, 26*, 120–138.

Orlofsky, J. L., Marcia, J. E., & Lesser, I. M. (1973). Ego identity status and the intimacy versus isolation crisis of young adulthood. *Journal of Personality and Social Psychology, 27*, 211–219.

Orotny, A., Clore, G. L., & Foss, M. (1987). The referential structure of the affective lexicon. *Cognitive Science, 11*, 361–384.

Orrego, V. O., & Rodriguez, J. (2001). Family communication patterns and college adjustment: The effects of communication and conflictual independence on college students. *The Journal of Family Communication, 1*(3), 175–189.

Oshima-Takane, Y. (1988). Children learn from speech not addressed to them: The case of personal pronouns. *Journal of Child Language, 15*, 95–108.

Oshima-Takane, Y. Goodz, E., & Derevensky, J. L. (1996). Birth order effects on early language development: Do secondborn children learn from overheard speech? *Child Development, 67*, 621–634.

Oxford Dictionary of Quotations. (3rd ed.). (1980). Oxford, UK: Oxford University Press.

Page, E. B., & Grandon, G. (1979). Family configuration and mental ability: Two theories contrasted with U.S. data. *American Educational Research Journal, 16*, 257–272.

Page, R. M., & Hammermeister, J. (1995). Shyness and loneliness: Relationship to the exercise frequency of college students. *Psychological Reports, 76*(2), 395–398.

Paikoff, R. L., & Brooks-Gunn, J. (1991). Do parent–child relationships change during puberty? *Psychological Bulletin, 110*, 47–66.

Papousek, M., & Papousek, H. (1990). Excessive infant crying and intuitive parental care: Buffering support and its failures in parent-infant interaction. *Early Child Development and Care, 26*, 233–248.

Parham, I. A., Feldman, R. S., Oster, G. D., & Popoola, O. (1981). Intergenerational differences in nonverbal disclosure of deception. *The Journal of Social Psychology, 113*, 261–269.

Parke, R. D. (1996). *Fatherhood*. Cambridge, MA: Harvard University Press.

Parke, R. D., & O'Neil, R. (1999). Social relationships across contexts: Family peer linkages. In W. A. Collins & B. Laursen (Eds.), *Relationships as developmental contexts* (Vol. 30, pp. 211–239). Mahwah, NJ: Lawrence Erlbaum Associates.

Parke, R. D., & Sawain, D. B. (1981). Father–infant interaction in the newborn period: A re-evaluation of some current myths. In E. M. Hetherington & R. D. Parke (Eds.), *Contemporary readings in child psychology* (2nd ed., pp. 229–234). New York: McGraw-Hill.

Parker, J. G., & Gottman, J. M. (1989). Social and emotional development in a relational context: Friendship interaction from early childhood to adolescence. In T. J. Berndt & G. W. Ladd (Eds.), *Peer relationships in child development* (pp. 95–132). New York: Wiley.

Parker, S. R. (1964). Type of work, friendship patterns, and leisure. *Human Relations, 17,* 215–220.

Parkes, C. M., & Weiss, R. S. (1983). *Recovery from bereavement.* New York: Basic Books.

Parrott, T. M., & Bengtson, V. L. (1999). The effects of earlier intergenerational affection, normative expectations, and family conflict on contemporary exchanges of help and support. *Research on Aging, 21*(1), 73–105.

Pasley, K., Kerpelman, J., & Guilbert, D. E. (2001). Gendered conflict, identity disruption, and marital instability: Expanding Gottman's model. *Journal of Social and Personal Relationships, 18*(1), 5–27.

Patterson, G. R. (1979). A performance theory for coercive family interaction. In R. B. Cairns (Ed.), *The analysis of social interactions* (pp. 119–162). Hillsdale, NJ: Lawrence Erlbaum Associates.

Patterson, S. L. (1981). On death and dying. In F. J. Berghorn & D. E. Schafer (Eds.), *The dynamics of aging* (pp. 83–99). Boulder, CO: Westview.

Pavlov, I. P. (1928–1941). *Lectures on conditioned reflexes* (Vols. I & II, W. H. Gantt, Trans.). New York: International Publishers.

Peden, A. R., Hall, L. A., Rayens, M. K., & Beebe, L. (2000). Negative thinking mediates the effect of self-esteem in depressive symptoms in college women. *Nursing Research, 49*(4), 201–207.

Peisner, E. S. (1989). To spare or not to spare the rod: A cultural-historical view of child discipline. In. J. Valsiner (Ed.), *Child development in a cultural context* (pp. 111–141). Toronto: Hogrefe and Huber.

Pellegrini, A. D., & Bartini, M. (2001). Dominance in early adolescent boys: Affiliative and aggressive dimensions and possible functions. *Merrill-Palmer Quarterly, 47*(1), 142–163.

Peluchette, J. V. E., & Jeanquart, S. (2000). Professionals' use of different mentor sources at various career stages: Implications for career success. *Journal of Social Psychology, 140*(5), 549–565.

Pendell, S. D. (2002). Affection in interpersonal relationships: Not just "a fond and tender feeling." In W. B. Gudykunst (Ed.), *Communication yearbook 26* (pp. 70–115). Mahwah, NJ: Lawrence Erlbaum Associates.

Percy, W. (1954). *The message in the bottle.* New York: Farrar, Straus, & Giroux.

Perlin, M., & Grater, H. (1981). The relationship between birth order and reported interpersonal behavior. *Individual Psychology, 40*(1), 22–28.

Perry, G. (1980). The need for retirement planning and counselling. *Canadian Counsellor, 14,* 97–98.

Perry, W. B. (1968). *Forms of intellectual and ethical development in the college years: A scheme.* New York: Holt, Rinehart & Winston.

Petronio, S. (1991). Communication boundary management: A theoretical model of managing disclosure of private information between married couples. *Communication Theory, 1,* 311–335.

Petronio, S., Reeder, H. M., Hecht, M. L., & Ros-Mendoza, T. M. (1996). Disclosure of sexual abuse by children and adolescents. *Journal of Applied Communication Research, 24*(3), 181–199.

Pfeiffer, E. (1977). Sexual behavior in old age. In E. W. Busse & E. Pfeiffer (Eds.), *Behavior and adaptation in late life* (pp. 130–141). Boston: Little, Brown.

Pfouts, J. H. (1980). Birth order, age-spacing, IQ differences, and family relations. *Journal of Marriage and the Family, 42,* 517–531.

Phelan, P., Yu, H. C., & Davidson, A. L. (1994). Navigating the psychosocial pressures of adolescence: The voices and experiences of high school youth. *American Educational Research Journal, 31*(2), 415–447.

Philliber, S. (1980). Socialization for childbearing. *Journal of Social Issues, 36,* 30–44.

Phillips, A. S., Long, R. G., & Bedeian, A. G. (1990). Type A status: Birth order and gender effects. *Individual Psychology, 46,* 365–373.

Piaget, J. (1926). *The language and thought of the child.* New York: Harcourt Brace Jovanovich.

Piaget, J. (1932). *The moral judgment of the child.* New York: Harcourt, Brace.

Piaget, J. (1952). *The origins of intelligence in children.* New York: International Universities Press.

Piaget, J. (1954). *The construction of reality in the child.* New York: Basic Books. (Original work published 1926)

Piaget, J. (1962). *Comments on Vygotsky's critical remarks.* Cambridge, MA: MIT Press.

Piaget, J. (1964). *Judgment and reasoning in the child.* Paterson, NJ: Littlefield Adams.

Pierrakos, J. C. (1975). *The energy field in man and nature.* New York: Institute for the New Age.

Pillemer, D. B., & White, S. H. (1989). Childhood events recalled by children and adults. In H. W. Reese (Ed.), *Advances in child development and behavior* (Vol. 21, pp. 297–340). San Diego, CA: Academic Press.

Pillemer, K., & Suitor, J. J. (1991). Relationships with children and distress in the elderly. In K. Pillemer & K. McCartney (Eds.), *Parent–child relations throughout life.* (pp. 163–178). Hillsdale, NJ: Lawrence Erlbaum Associates.

Pinker, S. (1994). *The language instinct.* New York: Morrow.

Planalp, S. (1985). Relational schemata: A test of alternative forms of relational knowledge as guides to communication. *Human Communication Resesarch, 12,* 3–29.

Planalp, S. (1999). *Communicating emotion: Social, moral, and cultural processes.* Cambridge, UK: Cambridge University Press.

Pledger, L. M. (1992). Development of self-monitoring behavior from early to late adolescence. *Adolescence, 27*(106), 329–338.

Poizner, H., Klima, E. S., & Bellugi, V. (1987). *What the hands reveal about the brain.* Cambridge, MA: MIT Press.

Ponzetti, J. J., Jr., & James, C. (1997). Loneliness and sibling relationships. *Journal of Social Behavior and Personality, 12*(1), 103–112.

Powers, W. G., Jordan, W. J., & Street, R. L. (1979). Language indices in the measurement of cognitive complexity: Is complexity loquacity? *Human Communication Research, 6*(1), 69–73.

Powers, W. G., & Love, D. E. (2000). Exploring a consensual instructional communication strategy with elder adult development. *Communication Reports, 13,* 45–53.

Pratt, M. W., Norris, J. E., van de Hoef, S., & Arnold, M. L. (2001). Stories of hope: Parental optimism in narratives about adolescent children. *Journal of Social and Personal Relationships, 18*(5), 603–623.

Premack, D. (1971). Language in chimpanzee? *Science, 172,* 808–822.

Pribram, K. H. (1971). *Languages of the brain: Experimental paradoxes and principles in neurobiology.* Englewood Cliffs, NJ: Prentice-Hall.

Pribram, K. H. (1986). The cognitive revolution and brain/mind issues. *American Psychologist, 41,* 507–522.

Priester, J. R. (2001). Sex, drugs, and attitudinal ambivalence: How feelings of evaluative tension influence alcohol use and safe sex behaviors. In W. D. Crano & M. Burgoon (Eds.), *Mass media and drug prevention: Classic and contemporary theories and research* (pp. 145–162). Mahwah, NJ: Lawrence Erlbaum Associates.

Public Forum Institute. (2002). *Help wanted: Workforce development and the new economy.* Retrieved 11/19/03 from www.publicforuminstitute.org/publications/reports/workforce02.pdf

Putnam, F. W. (1993). Dissociation and disturbances of the self. In D. Cicchetti & S. Toth (Eds.), *Rochester Symposium on Developmental Psychopathology: Disorders and dysfunctions of the self* (Vol. 5, pp. 251–266). Rochester, NY: University of Rochester Press.

Rabain-Jamin, J. (1989). Culture and early social interactions: The example of mother–infant object play in African and native French families. *European Journal of Psychology and Education, IV*(2), 295–305.

Ramsberger, G. (1994). The human brain: Understanding the physical bases of intrapersonal communication. In D. Vocate (Ed.), *Intrapersonal communication: Different voices, different minds* (pp. 57–76). Hillsdale, NJ: Lawrence Erlbaum Associates.

Rank, O. (1952). *The trauma of birth.* London: Kegan Paul. (Original work published 1929)

Rathunde, K., & Csikszentmihalyi, M. (1991). Adolescent happiness and family interaction. In K. A. Pillemer & K. McCartney (Eds.), *Parent–child relationships throughout life* (pp. 143–161). Hillsdale, NJ: Lawrence Erlbaum Associates.

Ravitz, L. J. (1951). Daily variations of standing potential differences in human subjects. *Yale Journal of Biology and Medicine, 24,* 22–25.

Rawlins, W. K. (1983). Openness as problematic in ongoing friendships: Two conversational dilemmas. *Communication Monographs, 50,* 1–13.

Rawlins, W. K. (1992). *Friendship matters: Communication, dialectics, and the life course.* New York: Aldine de Gruyter.

Rawlins, W. K. (1994). Being there and growing apart: Sustaining friendships during adulthood. In D. J. Canary & L. Stafford (Eds.), *Communication and relational maintenance* (pp. 275–296). San Diego, CA: Academic Press.

Rawlins, W. K. (1995). Friendships in later life. In J. F. Nussbaum & J. Coupland (Eds.), *Handbook of communication and aging research* (pp. 227–257). Mahwah, NJ: Lawrence Erlbaum Associates.

Rawlins, W. K., & Holl, M. R. (1988). Adolescents' interaction with parents and friends: Dialectics of temporal perspective and evaluation. *Journal of Social and Personal Relationships, 5,* 27–46.

Reid, T. (1990). *An inquiry into the human mind: On the principles of common sense.* Bristol: Thames Antiquarian Books. (Original, 1764)

Reis, H. T. (1998). Gender differences in intimacy and related behaviors: Context and process. In D. J. Canary & K. Dindia (Eds.), *Sex differences and similarities in communication* (pp. 203–231). Mahwah, NJ: Lawrence Erlbaum Associates.

Retherford, K. S. (1996). *Normal communication acquisition: An animated database of behaviors* [CD-ROM]. Eau Claire, WI: Thinking Publications.

Richman, A. L., Miller, P. M., & LeVine, R. A. (1992). Cultural and educational variations in maternal responsiveness. *Developmental Psychology 28*(4), 614–621.

Ricillo, S. C. (1994). Phylogenesis: Understanding the biological origins of intrapersonal communication. In D. Vocate (Ed.), *Intrapersonal communication: Different voices, different minds* (pp. 33–56). Hillsdale, NJ: Lawrence Erlbaum Associates.

Ricillo, S. C., & Watterson, T. (1984). The suppression of crying in the human neonate: Response to the human vocal tract stimuli. *Brain and Language, 23,* 34–42.

Riegel, K. F. (1975). Toward a dialectical theory of development. *Human Development, 19,* 50–64.

Riegel, K. F. (1976). The dialectics of human development. *American Psychologist, 31,* 679–700.

Rizzo, T. A. (1989). *Friendship development among children in school.* Norwood, NJ: Ablex.

Rizzo, T. A., & Corsaro, W. A. (1988). Toward a better understanding of Vygotsky's process of internalization: Its role in the development of the concept of friendship. *Developmental Review, 8,* 219–237.

Robbins, T. (2000). *Fierce invalids home from hot climates.* New York: Bantam Books.

Roberto, K., & Stanis, P. (1994). Reactions of older women to the death of their close friends. *Omega, 29,* 17–27.

Roberts, R. E. L., & Bengtson, V. L. (1996). Affective ties to parents in early adulthood and self-esteem across 20 years. *Social Psychology Quarterly, 59*(1), 96–106.

Robertson, J. F. (1976). Significance of grandparents: Perceptions of young adult grandchildren. *The Gerontologist, 16,* 137–174.

Robertson, J. F. (1977). Grandmotherhood: A study of role conceptions. *Journal of Marriage and Familly, 39,* 165–174.

Rochat, P. (1995). Early objectification of the self. *The self in infancy: Theory and research* (pp. 53–71). Amsterdam: Elsevier Science.

Rochat, P., Neisser, U., & Marian, V. (1998). Are young infants sensitive to interpersonal contingency? *Infant Behavior and Development, 21*(2), 355–366.

Rochat, P., Querido, J. G., & Striano, T. (1999). Emerging sensitivity to the timing and structure of protoconversation in early infancy. *Developmental Psychology, 35*(4), 950–957.

Rochat, P., & Striano, T. (1999). Social cognitive development in the first year. In P. Rochat (Ed.), *Early social cognition: Understanding others in the first months of life* (pp. 3–34). Mahwah, NJ: Lawrence Erlbaum Associates.

Rodgers, J. L., Cleveland, H. H., van den Oord, E., & Rowe, D. C. (2000). Resolving the debate over birth order, family size, and intelligence. *American Psychologist, 55*(6), 599–612.

Rogers, L. E., & Farace, R. V. (1975). Relational communication analysis: New measurement procedures. *Human Communication Research, 1,* 222–239.

Rose, S. M. (1985). Same- and cross-sex friendships and the psychology of homosociality. *Sex Roles, 12,* 63–74.

Rosenbaum, E., & Kandel, D. B. (2001). Early onset of adolescent sexual behavior and drug involvement. *Journal of Marriage and the Family, 52*(3), 783–798.

Rosenbaum, J., & Prinsky, L. (1978). Sex, violence and rock 'n' roll: Youth's perceptions of popular music. *Popular Music and Society, 11*(2), 78–91.

Rosengren, K. E. (1991). Media use in childhood and adolescence: Invariant change? Some results from a Swedish research program. In J. A. Anderson (Ed.), *Communication yearbook 14* (pp. 48–90). Newbury Park, CA: Sage.

Ross, H. G., & Milgram, J. I. (1992). Important variables in adult sibling relationships: A qualitative study. In M. E. Lamb & B. Sutton-Smith (Eds.), *Sibling relationships: Their na-*

ture and significance across the lifespan (pp. 225–249). Hillsdale, NJ: Lawrence Erlbaum Associates.

Ross, L. R., & Spinner, B. (2001). General and specific attachment representations in adulthood: Is there a relationship? *Journal of Social and Personal Relationships, 18*(6), 747–766.

Rossi, A. S., & Rossi, P. H. (1991). Normative obligations and parent–child help exchange across the life course. In K. Pillemer & K. McCartney (Eds.), *Parent child relations throughout life* (pp. 201–224). Hillsdale, NJ: Lawrence Erlbaum Associates.

Roy, A., & Harwood, J. (1997). Underrepresented, positively portrayed: Older adults in television commercials. *Journal of Applied Communication Research, 25,* 39–56.

Rubin, R. B. (1982). Assessing speaking and listening competence at the college level: The communication competency assessment instrument. *Communication Education, 31,* 19–32.

Rubin, Z. (1980). *Children's friendships.* Cambridge, MA: Harvard University Press.

Rubin, Z., Peplau, L. A., & Hill, C. T. (1980). Loving and leaving: Sex differences in romantic attachments. *Sex Roles, 6,* 821–835.

Rubinstein, R. L. (1987). Never married elderly as a social type: Re-evaluating some images. *Gerontologist, 27,* 108–113.

Rymer, R. (1992, April 13, 20). A silent childhood. Parts I & II. *The New Yorker.*

Rymer, R. (1993). *Genie: An abused child's flight from silence.* New York: HarperCollins.

Saarni, C. (2000). The social context of emotional development. In M. Lewis & J. M. Haviland-Jones (Eds.), *Handbook of emotions* (2nd ed., pp. 306–322). New York: Guilford.

Saarni, C., & Crowley, M. (1990). The development of emotion regulation: Effects on emotional state and expression. In E. A. Blechman (Ed.), *Emotions and the family: For better or worse* (pp. 53–73). Hillsdale, NJ: Lawrence Erlbaum Associates.

Sacks, H., Schegloff, E., & Jefferson, G. (1974). A simplest systematics for the organization of turn-taking in conversation. *Language, 50*(4), 696–735.

Sacks, O. (1989). *Seeing voices.* Berkeley, CA: University of California Press.

Salthouse, T. A. (1988). Effects of aging on verbal abilities: Examination of the psychometric literature. In L. L. Light & D. Burke (Eds.), *Language, memory, and aging* (pp. 17–35). New York: Cambridge University Press.

Salthouse, T. A. (1991). *Theoretical perspectives on cognitive aging.* Hillsdale, NJ: Lawrence Erlbaum Associates.

Saluter, A. F. (1996). *Marital status and living arrangements: March 1994. U.S. Bureau of the Census, current population reports* (Series P20-484). Washington, DC: U.S. Government Printing Office.

Samp, J. A., & Solomon, D. H. (2001). Coping with problematic events in dating relationships: The influence of dependence power on severity appraisals and decisions to communicate. *Western Journal of Communication, 65*(2), 138–160.

Sampson, E. E. (1993). *Celebrating the other: A dialogic account of human nature.* Boulder, CO: Westview Press.

Samuolis, J., Layburn, K., & Schiaffino, K. M. (2001). Identity development and attachment to parents in college students. *Journal of Youth and Adolescence, 30*(3), 373–384.

Sander, L. W. (1977). The regulation of exchange in the infant–caregiver system and some aspects of the context-content relationship. In M. Lewis & L. Rosenblum (Eds.), *Interaction, conversation and the development of language* (pp. 133–156). New York: Wiley.

Sanders, R. E., & Freeman, K. E. (1998). Children's neo-rhetorical participation in peer interactions. In I. Hutchby & J. Moran-Ellis (Eds.), *Children and social competence: Arenas of Action* (pp. 87–114). London: Falmer.

Sanford, N. (Ed.). (1962). *The American college*. New York: Wiley.

Santilli, N. R., & Hudson, L. M. (1992). Enhancing moral growth: Is communication the key? *Adolescence, 27*(105), 145–160.

Sarason, I. G., Sarason, B. R., & Pierce, G. R. (1994). Relationship-specific social support: Toward a model for the analysis of supportive interactions. In B. R. Burleson, T. L. Albrecht, & I. G. Sarason (Eds.), *Communication of social support* (pp. 91–112). Thousand Oaks, CA: Sage.

Scaife, M., & Bruner, J. S. (1975). The capacity for joint visual attention in the infant. *Nature, 253*, 265–266.

Schaefer, E. S. (1959). A circumplex model for maternal behavior. *Journal of Abnormal and Social Psychology, 59*, 226–235.

Schaefer, E. S. (1997). Integration of configurational and factorial models for family relationships and child behavior. In R. Plutchik & H. R. Conte (Eds.), *Circumplex models of personality and emotions* (pp. 133–153). Washington, DC: American Psychological Association.

Schaefer, M., & Olson, D. (1981). Assessing intimacy: The PAIR inventory. *Journal of Marriage and Family Therapy, 7*, 47–60.

Schank, R. C. (1982). *Dynamic memory: A theory of reminding and learning in computers and people*. Cambridge,, UK: Cambridge University Press.

Scheflen, A. E. (1964). The significance of posture in communication systems. *Psychiatry, 27*, 316–321.

Schiedel, D. G., & Marcia, J. E. (1985). Ego identity, intimacy, sex role orientation, and gender. *Developmental Psychology, 21*, 149–160.

Schmitt, E. (2001, May 15). For the first time, nuclear families drop below 25% of households. *New York Times*, pp. A1, A18.

Schneider, C. S., & Kenny, D. A. (2000). Cross-sex friends who were once romantic partners: Are they platonic friends now? *Journal of Social and Personal Relationships, 17*(3), 451–466.

Schofield, J. W. (1981). Complementary and conflicting identities: Images and interaction in an interracial school. In S. R. Asher & J. M. Gottman (Eds.), *The development of children's friendships* (pp. 53–90). Cambridge, UK: Cambridge University Press.

Schultz, N. R., Jr., & Hoyer, W. J. (1975). Feedback effects on spatial egocentrism in old age. *Journal of Gerontology, 31*(1), 72–75.

Schulz, R., & Aderman, D. (1980). How the medical staff copes with dying patients: A critical review. *Perspectives on Death and Dying, 2*, 134–144.

Schumm, W. R., & Bugaighis, M. A. (1986). Marital quality over the marital career: Alternative explanations. *Journal of Marriage and the Family, 48*, 165–168.

Schutz, A. (1999). It was your fault! Self-serving biases in autobiographical accounts of conflicts in married couples. *Journal of Social and Personal Relationships, 16*(2), 193–208.

Schwitzer, A. M., Rodriguez, L. E., Thomas, C., & Salimi, L. (2001). The eating disorders NOS diagnostic profile among college women. *Journal of American College Health, 49*(4), 157–166.

Sebby, R. A., & Papini, D. R. (1994). Postformal reasoning during adolescence and young adulthood: The influence of problem relevancy. *Adolescence, 29*(114), 389–400.

Sebeok, T. A. (1968). Goals and limitations of the study of animal communication. In T. A. Sebeok (Ed.), *Animal communication* (pp. 3–14). Bloomington: Indiana University Press.

Seeman, T. E., Lusignolo, T. M., Albert, M., & Berkman, L. (2001). Social relationships, social support, and patterns of cognitive aging in healthy, high-functioning older adults: MacArthur studies of successful aging. *Health Psychology, 20*(4), 243–255.

Seery, B. L., & Crowley, M. S. (2000). Women's emotion work in the family. Relationship management and the process of building father–child relationships. *Journal of Family Issues, 21*(1), 100–127.

Segrin, C., & Kinney, T. (1996). Social skills deficits among the socially anxious: Rejection from others and loneliness. *Motivation and Emotion, 19*(1), 1–24.

Seiffge-Krenke, I., Shulman, S., & Klessinger, N. (2001). Adolescent precursors of romantic relationships in young adulthood. *Journal of Social and Personal Relationships, 18*(3), 327–346.

Selman, R. L. (1976). Toward a structural analysis of developing interpersonal relations concepts: Research with normal and disturbed preadolescent boys. In A. D. Pick (Ed.), *Minnesota symposia on child psychology* (Vol. 10, pp. 156–200). Minneapolis: University of Minnesota Press.

Selman, R. L. (1980). *The growth of interpersonal understanding: Developmental and clinical analyses.* New York: Academic Press.

Selman, R. L. (1981). The child as a friendship philosopher. In S. R. Asher & J. M. Gottman (Eds.), *The development of children's friendships* (pp. 242–272). Cambridge, UK: Cambridge University Press.

Senchea, J. A. (1998). Gendered constructions of sexuality in adolescent girls' talk. *Dissertation Abstracts International, 59*(05A), 1399.

Servaty, H. L., & Hayslip, B., Jr. (1997). Death education and communication apprehension regarding dying persons. *Omega, 34,* 139–148.

Sex Information and Education Council of the United States. (1993). *Unfinished business: A SIECUS assessment of state sexuality education programs.* New York: Author.

Shantz, C. U. (1975). The development of social cognition. In E. M. Hetherington (Ed.), *Review of child development research* (Vol. 5). Chicago: University of Chicago Press.

Shantz, C. U. (1987). Conflicts between children. *Child Development, 58,* 283–305.

Shantz, C. U. (1993). Children's conflicts: Representations and lessons learned. In R. R. Cocking & K. A. Renninger (Eds.), *The development and meaning of psychological distance* (pp. 185–202). Hilldale, NJ: Lawrence Erlbaum Associates.

Shatz, M. (1977). The relationship between cognitive processes and the development of communication skills. *Nebraska Symposium of Motivation* (Vol. 25, pp. 1–41). Lincoln: University of Nebraska Press.

Shapiro, R., Siegel, A.W., Scovill, L., & Hays, J. (1998). Risk-taking patterns of female adolescents: What they do and why. *Journal of Adolescence, 21*(2), 143–159.

Sharp, S. F., Terling-Watt, T. L., Atkins, L. A., Gilliam, J. T., & Sanders, A. (2001). Purging behavior in a sample of college females: A research note on General Strain Theory and female deviance. *Deviant Behavior, 22*(2), 171–188.

Sheehy, G. (1977). *Passages: Predictable crises of adult life.* New York: Bantam Books.

Sheehy, G. (1995). *New passages: Mapping your life across time.* New York: Ballantine Books.

Shepard, D. S. (2002). A negative state of mind: Patterns of depressive symptoms among men with high gender role conflict. *Psychology of Men and Masculinity, 3*(1), 3–8.

Shimanoff, S. B. (1980). *Communication rules: Theory and research.* Beverly Hills, CA: Sage.

Shimanoff, S. B. (1985) Rules governing the verbal expression of emotions between married couples. *Western Journal of Speech Communication, 49*(3), 147–165.

Shimizu, H. (1979). A study on the sexual development and targets of dependence in college students. *Japanese Journal of Psychology, 50*(5), 265–272.

Shore, C. M. (1995). *Individual differences in language development.* Thousand Oaks, CA: Sage.

Shore, R. J., & Hayslip, B., Jr. (1995). Custodial grandparenting: Implications for children's development. In A. E. Gottfried & A. W. Gottfried (Eds.), *Redefining families: Implications for children's development* (pp. 171–218). New York: Plenum.

Shotter, J. (1984). *Social accountability and selfhood*. Oxford, UK: Basil Blackwell.

Shotter, J. (1993a). *Conversational realities: Constructing life through language*. London: Sage.

Shotter, J. (1993b). *Cultural politics of everyday life*. Toronto: University of Toronto Press.

Siegel, D .J. (1999). *The developing mind: Toward a neurobiology of interpersonal experience*. New York: Guilford.

Sigel, I. (1987). Does hothousing rob children of their childhood? *Early Childhood Research Quarterly, 2*, 211–225.

Sillars, A. L. (1980). The sequential and distributional structure of conflict interactions as a function of attributions concerning the locus of responsibility and stability of conflicts. In D. Nimmo (Ed.), *Communication yearbook 4* (pp. 217–235). New Brunswick, NJ: Transaction.

Sillars, A. L., & Wilmot, W. W. (1989). Marital communication across the life-span. In J. Nussbaum (Ed.), *Life-span communication: Normative processes* (pp. 225–254). Hillsdale, NJ: Lawrence Erlbaum Associates.

Sillars, A. L., & Zietlow, P. H. (1993). Investigations of marital communication and lifespan development. In N. Coupland & J. F. Nussbaum (Eds.), *Discourse and lifespan identity* (pp. 237–261). Newbury Park, CA: Sage.

Silver, M. H. (1993). Balancing "caring and being cared for" in old age: The development of mutual parenting. In. J. Demick, K. Bursik, & R. DiBiase (Eds.), *Parental development* (pp. 225–239). Hillsdale, NJ: Lawrence Erlbaum Associates.

Silverman, P. R. (1986). *Widow to widow*. New York: Springer.

Simmons, S., & Given, B. (1972). Nursing care of the terminal patient. *Omega: Journal of Death and Dying, 3*, 217–225.

Simmons, S., & Given, B. (1980). Nursing care of the terminal patient. *Perspectives on Death and Dying, 2*, 115–123.

Sinott, J. D. (1984). Postformal reasoning: The relativistic stage. In M. L. Commons, F. A. Richards, & C. Armon (Eds.), *Beyond formal operations: Late adolescent and adult cognitive development* (pp. 298–325). New York: Praeger.

Skinner, B. F. (1957). *Verbal behavior*. Englewood, NJ: Prentice-Hall.

Smiley, P., & Huttenlocher, J. (1989). Young children's acquisition of emotion concepts. In C. Saarni, & P. L. Harris (Eds.), *Children's understanding of emotion* (pp. 27–49). New York: Cambridge University Press.

Smith, C. B., Adamson, L. G., & Bakeman, R. (1988). Interactional predictors of early language. *First Language, 8*, 143–156.

Smollar, J., & Youniss, J. (1982). Social development through friendship. In K. H. Rubin & H. S. Ross (Eds.), *Peer relationships and social skills in children* (pp. 270–298). New York: Springer-Verlag.

Snell, W. E., Miller, R. S., & Belk, S. S. (1988). Development of the emotional self-disclosure scale. *Sex Roles, 18*(1–2), 59–73.

Snow, C. (1973). Mothers' speech research: From input to interaction. In C. E. Snow & C. A. Ferguson (Eds.), *Talking to children* (pp. 31–49). Cambridge, UK: Cambridge University Press.

Snow, C. (1977). The development of conversation between mothers and babies. *Journal of Child Language 4*, 1–22.

Snow, M., Jacklin, C., & Maccoby, E. (1983). Sex-of-child differences in father–child interaction at one year of age. *Child Development, 54*, 227–232.

Snyder, L. (1975). *Pragmatics in language-deficient children: Prelinguistic and early verbal performatives and presuppositions*. Unpublished doctoral dissertation, University of Colorado.

Snyder, M. (1974). Self-monitoring of expressive behavior. *Journal of Personality and Social Psychology, 30,* 526–537.

Snyder, M. (1979). Self-monitoring processes. In L. Berkowitz (Ed.), *Advances in experimental social psychology* (Vol. 12, pp. 85–128). New York: Academic Press.

Socha, T. (1997). Group communication across the lifespan. In L. R. Frey & J. K. Barge (Eds.), *Managing group life: Communicating in decision-making groups* (pp. 4–28). Boston: Houghton Mifflin.

Socha, T. J., & Socha, D. M. (1994). Children's task group communication: Did we learn it all in kindergarten? In L. R. Frey (Ed.), *Group communication in context: Studies of natural groups* (pp. 227–246). Hillsdale, NJ: Lawrence Erlbaum Associates.

Socha, T. J., & Stamp, G. (Eds.). (1995). *Parents, children and communication: Frontiers of theory and research.* Mahwah, NJ: Lawrence Erlbaum Associates.

Socha, T. J., & Yingling, J. (2001, November). *Children are communicators too: Toward a developmental view of family communication.* Paper presented at the National Communication Association, Atlanta, GA.

Solomon, D. H., & Knobloch, L. K. (2001). Relationship uncertainty, partner interference, and intimacy within dating relationships. *Journal of Social and Personal Relationships, 18*(6), 804–820.

Solomon, J. C., & Marx, J. (1995). "To grandmother's house we go": Health and school adjustment of children raised solely by grandparents. *The Gerontologist, 35*(3), 386–394.

Solomon, J. C., & Marx, J. (1999). Who cares? Grandparent/grandchild households. *Journal of Women and Aging, 11,* 3–25.

Spitzberg, B. H. (1993). The dialectics of (in)competence. *Journal of Social and Personal Relationships, 10,* 137–158.

Spitzberg, B. H. (1994). The dark side of (in)competence. In W. R. Cupach, & B. H. Spitzberg (Eds.), *The dark side of interpersonal communication* (pp. 25–49). Hillsdale, NJ: Lawrence Erlbaum Associates.

Spitzberg, B. H., & Cupach, W. R. (1984). *Interpersonal communication competence.* Beverly Hills, CA: Sage.

Spitzberg, B. H., Marshall, L., & Cupach, W. R. (2001). Obsessive relational intrusion, coping, and sexual coercion victimization. *Communication Reports, 14*(1), 19–30

Spitze, G., & Logan, J. R. (1991). Sibling structure and intergenerational relations. *Journal of Marriage and the Family, 53*(4), 871–885.

Spock, B. (1977). *Baby and child care.* New York: Simon & Schuster.

Sprecher, S., & Metts, S. (1999). Romantic beliefs: Their influence on relationships and patterns of change over time. *Journal of Social and Personal Relationships, 16*(6), 834–851.

Sroufe, L. A. (1979a). Socioemotional development. In J. D. Osofsky (Ed.), *Handbook of infant development* (pp. 109–128). Hillsdale, NJ: Lawrence Erlbaum Associates.

Sroufe, L. A. (1979b). The coherence of individual development. *American Psychologist, 34,* 834–841.

Sroufe, L. A. (1988). The role of infant–caregiver attachment in development. In J. Belsky & T. Nezworski (Eds.), *Clinical implications of attachment* (pp. 18–38). Hillsdale, NJ: Lawrence Erlbaum Associates.

Sroufe, L. A. (1989). Relationships, self, and individual adaptation. In A. J. Sameroff & R. N. Emde (Eds.), *Relationship disturbances in early childhood: A developmental approach* (pp. 70–94). New York: Basic Books.

Sroufe, L. A., Egeland, B., & Kreutzer, T. (1990). The fate of early experience following developmental change: Longitudinal approaches to individual adaptation in childhood. *Child Development, 61,* 1363–1373.

Stansbury, V. K., & Coll, K. M. (1998). Myers-Briggs attitude typology: The influence of birth order with other family variables. *Family Journal, 6*(2), 116–122.

Stearns, P. N. (1989). *Jealousy: The evolution of an emotion in American history.* New York: New York University Press.

Steinberg, L. D. (1981). Transformations in family relations at puberty. *Developmental Psychology, 17,* 833–840.

Steinberg, L. D., & Hill, J. P. (1978). Patterns of family interaction as a function of age, the onset of puberty, and formal thinking. *Developmental Psychology, 14,* 683–684.

Stephen, J., Fraser, E., & Marcia, J. E. (1992). Moratorium-achievement (Mama) cycles in lifespan identity development: Value orientations and reasoning system correlates. *Journal of Adolescence, 15,* 283–300.

Stephens, W. N. (1963). *The family in cross-cultural perspective.* New York: Holt, Rinehart & Winston.

Stern, D. N. (1974). Mother and infant at play: The dyadic interaction involving facial, vocal and gaze behaviors. In M. Lewis & L. Rosenblum (Eds.), *The effect of the infant on its caregiver* (pp. 187–214). New York: Wiley.

Stern, D. N. (1977). *The first relationship.* Cambridge, UK: Cambridge University Press.

Stern, D. N. (1985). *The interpersonal world of the infant: A view from psychoanalysis and developmental psychology.* New York: Basic Books.

Stern, D. N., Jaffe, J., Beebe, B., & Bennett, S. L. (1975). Vocalizing in unison and in alternation: Two modes of communication within the mother–infant dyad. *Annals of the New York Academy of Sciences: Developmental Psycholinguistics and Communication Disorders, 263,* 89–100.

Sternberg, C. R., & Campos, J. J. (1990). The development of anger expressions in infancy. In N. L. Stein & B. Leventhal (Eds.), *Psychological and biological approaches to emotion* (pp. 247–282). Hillsdale, NJ: Lawrence Erlbaum Associates.

Stiff, J. B., Dillard, J. P., Somera, L., Kim, H., & Sleight, C. (1988). Empathy, communication, and prosocial behavior. *Communication Monographs, 55,* 198–213.

Stivers, T. (2001). Negotiating who presents the problem: Next speaker selection in pediatric encounters. *Journal of Communication, 51*(2), 252–282.

St. James-Robers, I., & Halil, T. (1991). Infant crying patterns in the first year: Normal community and clinical findings. *Journal of Child Psychology and Psychiatry, 32*(6), 951–968.

Stocker, C., Ahmed, K., & Stall, M. (1997). Marital satisfaction and maternal emotional responsiveness: Links with children's sibling relationships. *Social Development, 6,* 373–385.

Stone, R., Cafferata, G. L., & Sangl, J. (1987). Caregivers of frail elderly: A national profile. *Gerontologist, 27,* 616–626.

Streeter, L. (1976). Language perception of two month old infants shows effects of both innate mechanisms and experience. *Nature, 259,* 39–41.

Stuart-Hamilton, I. (1991). *The psychology of ageing.* London: Jessica Kingsley.

Stubbs, M. (1983). *Language, schools and classrooms.* London: Methuen.

Stubbs, M., & Delamont, S. (Eds.). (1976). *Explorations in classroom observation.* London: Wiley.

Studdert-Kennedy, M. (1979, April-June). Speech perception. *The Haskins Laboratory Status Reports* (SR-58), pp. 35–64.

Stueve, C. A., & Gerson, K. (1977). Personal relations across the life-cycle. In C. S. Fischer, R. M. Jackson, C. A. Stueve, K. Gerson, L. M. Jones, & M. Baldassare (Eds.), *Networks and places* (pp. 79–98). New York: Free Press.

Sudnow, D. (1967). *Passing on.* Englewood Cliffs, NJ: Prentice-Hall.

Sullivan, H. S. (1953). *The interpersonal theory of psychiatry.* New York: Norton.

Summer, L. (2003). *Learning joy from dogs without collars.* New York: Simon & Schuster.

Suttles, G. D. (1970). Friendship as a social institution. In G. J. McCall, M. McCall, N. K. Denzin, G. D. Suttles, & S. Kurth (Eds.), *Social relationships* (pp. 95–135). Chicago: Aldine.

Sutton-Smith, B., & Rosenberg, B. G. (1970). *The sibling.* New York: Holt, Rinehart & Winston.

Tamir, L., & Antonucci, T. (1981). Self-perception, motivation, and social support through the family life cycle. *Journal of Marriage and the Family, 43,* 483–497.

Teilhard de Chardin, P. (1959). *The phenomenon of man* (B. Wall, Trans.). New York: Harper & Row. (Original work published 1955)

Terrace, H. S. (1979) *Nim.* New York: Knopf.

Thomas, A., & Chess, S. (1977). *Temperament and development.* New York: Brunner/Mazel.

Thomas, E. A. C., & Martin, J. A. (1976). Analysis of parent–infant interaction. *Psychological Review, 83,* 141–156.

Thomas, R. (1979). *Comparing theories of child development.* Belmont, CA: Wadsworth.

Thompson, R. A. (1987). Empathy and emotional understanding: The early development of empathy. In N. Eisenberg & J. Strayer (Eds.), *Empathy and its development* (pp. 119–145). Cambridge, UK: Cambridge University Press.

Toda, S., Fogel, A., & Kawai, M. (1990). Maternal speech to three-month-old infants in the United States and Japan. *Journal of Child Language 17,* 270–294.

Tolman, C. (1983). Categories, logic, and the problem of necessity in theories of mental development. *Studia Psychologica, 25,* 179–190.

Tomasello, M. (1999). Social cognition before the revolution. In P. Rochat (Ed.), *Early social cognition: Understanding others in the first months of life* (pp. 301–314). Mahwah, NJ: Lawrence Erlbaum Associates.

Tornstam, L. (1994). Gero-transcendence: A theoretical and empirical exploration. In L. E. Thomas & S. A. Eisenhandler (Eds.), *Aging and the religious dimension* (pp. 178–202). Westport, CT: Auburn House.

Tornstam, L. (1999/2000). Transcendence in later life: A shift in how we reevaluate our world and our place in it. *Generations, 23*(4), 10–14.

Trentham, S., & Larwood, L. (2001). Power and gender influences on responsibility attributions: The case of disagreements in relationships. *Journal of Social Psychology, 141*(6), 730–751.

Trevarthen, C. (1977). Descriptive analyses of infant communicative behavior. In H. R. Shaffer (Ed.), *Studies in mother–infant interaction* (pp. 227–270). New York: Academic Press.

Trevarthen, C. (1979). Instincts for human understanding and for cultural cooperation: Their development in infancy. In M. von Cranach, K. Foppa, W. Lepenies, & D. Ploog (Eds.), *Human ethology: Claims and limits of a new discipline* (pp. 530–571). Cambridge, UK: Cambridge University Press.

Trevarthen, C. (1982). The primary motives for cooperative understanding. In G. Butterworth & P. Light (Eds.), *Social cognition* (pp. 77–109). Chicago: University of Chicago Press.

Troiden, R. R. (1989). The formation of homosexual identities. *Journal of Homosexuality, 17,* 43–73.

Troll, L. E. (1982). *Continuations: Adult development and aging.* Monterey, CA: Brooks/Cole.

Turiel, E. (1975). The development of social concepts. In D. DePalma & J. Foley (Eds.), *Moral development* (pp. 7–37). Hillsdale, NJ: Lawrence Erlbaum Associates.

Turiel, E. (1977). The development of concepts in social structure. In J. Glick & A. Clarke-Stewart (Eds.), *Personality and social development* (Vol. 1, pp. 25–107). New York: Gardner Press.

Turner, G. J. (1973). Social class and children's language of control at ages five and seven. In B. Bernstein (Ed.), *Class, codes and social control* (Vol. 2, pp. 135–201). London: Routledge & Kegan Paul.

Turner, L. H., & West, R. (2002). *Perspectives on family communication* (2nd ed.). Boston: McGraw-Hill.

Ulatowska, H. K., Cannito, M. P., Hayashi, M. M., & Fleming, S. G. (1985). Language abilities in the elderly. In H. K. Ulatowska (Ed.), *The aging brain: Communication in the elderly* (pp. 125–139). San Diego: College-Hill Press.

U.S. Census Bureau. (1992). *Marriage, divorce, and remarriage in the 1990's* (Current Population Reports, Series P23-180). Washington, DC: U.S. Government Printing Office.

U.S. Census Bureau. (1997). *Statistical abstract of the United States.* Washington, DC: U.S. Government Printing Office.

U.S. Census Bureau. (2002). *Household and family characteristics.* Retrieved 11/19/03 from www.census.gov/prod/2003pubs/p20-547.pdf

U.S. Senate Special Committee on Aging, American Association of Retired Persons, Federal Council on Aging, and U.S. Administration on Aging. (1991). *Aging America: Trends and projections* (DHHS Publication No.FCoA 91-28001). Washington, DC: U.S. Department of Health and Human Services.

Vaillant, G. (1977). *Adaptation to life.* Boston: Little, Brown.

Vaillant, G. E. (2002). *Aging well: Surprising guideposts to a happier life from the landmark Harvard study of adult development.* Boston: Little, Brown.

Valsiner, J. (1989). Organization of children's social development in polygamic families. In J. Valsiner (Ed.), *Child development in cultural context* (pp. 67–85). Toronto: Hogrefe and Huber.

Valsiner, J., & van der Veer, R. (2000). *The social mind : construction of the idea.* Cambridge, UK: Cambridge University Press.

Vandell, D., & Wilson, K. (1987). Infants' interactions with mother, sibling, and peer: Contrasts and relations between interaction systems. *Child Development, 58,* 176–186.

van der Veer, R., & van Ijzendoorn, M. H. (1988). Early childhood attachment and later problem solving: A Vygotskian perspective. In J. Valsiner (Ed.), *Developmental psychology in the Soviet Union* (pp. 215–246). Bloomington: Indiana University Press.

VanLear, C. A. (1992). Marital communication across the generations: Learning and rebellion, continuity and change. *Journal of Social and Personal Relationships, 9,* 103–123.

van Lieshout, C. F. M., Cillessen, A. H. N., & Haselager, G. J. T. (1999). Interpersonal support and individual development. In W. A. Collins & B. Laursen (Eds.), *Relationships as developmental contexts* (pp. 37–60). Mahwah, NJ: Lawrence Erlbaum Associates.

Verbrugge, L. M. (1979). Multiplexity in adult friendships. *Social Forces, 57,* 1286–1309.

Vico, G. (1968). *The new science of Giambattista Vico.* (T. G. Bergin & M. H. Fisch, Eds. and Trans.) Ithaca, NY: Cornell University Press.

Vocate, D. R. (1994). Self-talk and inner speech: Understanding the uniquely human aspects of intrapersonal communication. In D. R. Vocate (Ed.), *Intrapersonal communication: Different voices, different minds* (pp. 3–31). Hillsdale, NJ: Lawrence Erlbaum Associates.

Vohs, K. D., Voelz, Z. R., Pettit, J. W., Bardone, A. M., Katz, J., Abramson, L. Y., Heatherton, T. F., & Joiner, T. E., Jr. (2001). Perfectionism, body dissatisfaction, and self-esteem: An interactive model of bulimic symptom development. *Journal of Social and Clinical Psychology, 20*(4), 476–497.

Volosinov, V. N. (1973). *Marxism and the philosophy of language.* (L. Matejka & I. R. Titunik, Trans.). Cambridge, MA: Harvard University Press.

Volosinov, V. N. (1986). *Marxism and the philosophy of language.* Cambridge, MA: MIT Press. (Original work published 1929)

Vygotsky, L. S. (1962). *Thought and language* (A. Hanfmann & G. Vakar, Trans.). Cambridge, MA: MIT Press. (Original work published 1934)

Vygotsky, L. S. (1966). Play and its role in the mental development of the child. *Voprosy Psikhologii, 12*(6), 62–76.

Vygotsky, L. S. (1978). *Mind in society: The development of higher psychological processes.* Cambridge, MA: Harvard University Press.

Vygotsky, L. S. (1981). The genesis of higher mental functions. In J. V. Wertsch (Ed.), *The concept of activity in Soviet psychology* (pp. 144–188). Armonk, NY: M. E. Sharpe.

Vygotsky, L. S. (1986). *Thought and language* (A. Kozulin, Trans.). Cambridge, MA: MIT Press. (Original work published 1934)

Waksler, R. (2001). A new "all" in conversation. *American Speech, 76*(2), 128–138.

Wall, C. (1974). *Predication: A study of its development.* The Hague: Mouton.

Wallbott, H. G. (1995). Congruence, contagion, and motor mimicry: Mutualities in nonverbal exchange. In I. Markova, C. F. Graumann, & K. Foppa (Eds.), *Mutualities in dialogue* (pp. 82–98). Cambridge, UK: Cambridge University Press.

Walsh, D. (2002, April 14). Children learning game of friendship. *San Francisco Chronicle,* pp. A21, A23.

Wapner, S. (1993). Parental development: A holistic, developmental systems-oriented perspective. In J. Demick & K. Bursik (Eds.), *Parental development* (pp. 3–37). Hillsdale, NJ: Lawrence Erlbaum Associates.

Warren, C. (1995). Parent–child communication about sex. In T. J. Socha & G. H. Stamp (Eds.), *Parents, children, and communication: Frontiers of theory and research* (pp. 173–201). Mahwah, NJ: Lawrence Erlbaum Associates.

Watson, J. B. (1925). *Behaviorism.* New York: Norton.

Watson, J. S. (1994). Detection of self: The perfect algorithm. In S. T. Parker, R. W. Mitchell, & M. L. Boccia (Eds.), *Self-awareness in animals and humans: Developmental perspectives.*(pp. 131–148). Cambridge, UK: Cambridge University Press.

Watterson, T., & Ricillo, S. C. (1983). Vocal suppression as a neonatal response to auditory stimuli. *Journal of Auditory Research, 23,* 205–214.

Watterson, T., & Ricillo, S. C. (1985). Stimulus frequency and vocal suppression in neonates. *Journal of Auditory Research, 25,* 81–89.

Watts, A. (1951). *The wisdom of insecurity.* New York: Vintage Books

Weigel, D. J., & Ballard-Reisch, D. S. (1999). Using paired data to test models of relational maintenance and marital quality. *Journal of Social and Personal Relationships, 16*(2), 175–191.

Weinstock, J. S., & Bond, L. A. (2000). Conceptions of conflict in close friendships and ways of knowing among young college women: A developmental framework. *Journal of Social and Personal Relationships, 17*(4/5), 687–696.

Weisman, A. D., & Warden, J. W. (1975). Psychosocial analysis of cancer deaths. *Omega, 6,* 61–75.

Weiss, R. S. (1975). *Marital separation.* New York: Basic Books.

Wellen, C. J. (1985). Effects of older siblings on the language young children hear and produce. *Journal of Speech and Hearing Disorders, 50,* 84–99.

Wellman, B., & Wellman, B. (1992). Domestic affairs and network relations. *Journal of Social and Personal Relationships, 9,* 385–409.

Wells, A., & Hakanen, E. A. (1991). The emotional use of popular music by adolescents. *Journalism Quarterly, 68,* 445–454.

Werebe, M. J. G. (1987). Friendship and dating relationships among French adolescents. *Journal of Adolescence, 10,* 269–289.

Werner, C. M., & Baxter, L. A. (1994). Temporal qualities of relationships: Organismic, transactional, and dialectical views. In M. L. Knapp & G. R. Miller (Eds.), *Handbook of interpersonal communication* (2nd ed., pp. 323–379). Thousand Oaks, CA: Sage.

Wertsch, J. V. (1979a). From social interaction to higher psychological processes: A clarification and application of Vygotsky's theory. *Human Development, 22,* 1–22.

Wertsch, J. V. (1979b). The regulation of human action and the given-new organization of private speech. In G. Zivin (Ed.), *The development of self-regulation through private speech* (pp. 79–98). New York: Wiley.

Wertsch, J. V., & Stone, C. A. (1985). The concept of internalization in Vygotsky's account of the genesis of higher mental functions. In J. V. Wertsch (Ed.), *Culture, communication and cognition: Vygotskian perspectives* (pp. 162–179). Cambridge, UK: Cambridge University Press.

West, L. (1995, February). *The construction of self and identities: Examination of the shame construct.* Paper presented to the Western States Communication Association, Portland, OR.

West, R., & Turner, L. H. (1995). Communication in lesbian and gay families: Building a descriptive base. In T. J. Socha & G. H. Stamp (Eds.), *Parents, children, and communication: Frontiers of theory and research* (pp. 147–169). Mahwah, NJ: Lawrence Erlbaum Associates.

Weston, K. (1991). *Families we choose: Lesbians, gays, kinship.* New York: Columbia University Press.

Whaley, B. B. (2000). Explaining illness to children: Theory, strategies, and future inquiry. In B. B. Whaley (Ed.), *Explaining illness: Research, theories and strategies* (pp. 195–207). Mahwah, NJ: Lawrence Erlbaum Associates.

Whitbourne, S. K., & Van Mannen, K. W. (1996). Age differences in and correlates of identity status from college through middle adulthood. *Journal of Personality and Social Psychology, 63,* 260–271.

White, L. A. (1949). *The science of culture: A study of man and civilization.* New York: Farrar, Straus and Cudahy.

White, L. (1994). Stepfamilies over the life course: Social support. In A. Booth & J. Dunn (Eds.), *Stepfamilies: Who benefits? Who does not?* (pp. 109–137). Hillsdale, NJ: Lawrence Erlbaum Associates.

Wilensky, H. L. (1968). Orderly careers and social participation: The impact of work history on social integration in the middle mass. In B. L. Neugarten (Ed.), *Middle age and aging: A reader in social psychology* (pp. 321–340). Chicago: University of Chicago Press.

Wilmot, W. W., Carbaugh, D. A., & Baxter, L. A. (1985). Communicative strategies used to terminate romantic relationships. *The Western Journal of Speech Communication, 49,* 204–216.

Wilson, S. R., & Whipple, E. E. (1995). Communication, discipline, and physical abuse. In T. J. Socha & G. H. Stamp (Eds.), *Parents, children and communication: Frontiers of theory and research* (pp. 299–317). Mahwah, NJ: Lawrence Erlbaum Associates.

Wiseman, J. P. (1986). Friendship: Bonds and binds in a voluntary relationship. *Journal of Social and Personal Relationships, 3,* 191–211.

Wiseman, J. P., & Duck, S. (1995). Having and managing enemies: A very challenging relationship. In S. Duck & J. T. Wood (Eds.), *Confronting relationship challenges* (pp. 43–72). Thousand Oaks, CA: Sage.

Wolf, M. A., Hexamer, A., & Meyer, T. P. (1982). Research on children and television: A review of 1980. In M. Burgoon (Ed.), *Communication yearbook 5* (pp. 353–384). New Brunswick: Transaction Books International Communication Association.

Wolff, P. H. (1966). The natural history of crying and other vocalizations in early infancy. In B. M. Foss (Ed.), *Determinants of infant behavior* (Vol. 4, pp. 81–109). New York: Wiley.

Wolff, P. H. (1987). *The development of behavioral states and the expression of emotions in early infancy.* Chicago: University of Chicago Press.

Wood, D. (1980). Teaching the young child: Some relationships between social interaction, language, and thought. In D. R. Olson (Ed.), *The social foundations of language and thought* (pp. 280–296). New York: Norton.

Wood, D., Bruner, J. S., & Ross, G. (1976). The role of tutoring in problem solving. *Journal of Child Psychology and Psychiatry, 17,* 89–100.

Wood, D., Wood, H., & Middleton, D. (1978). An experimental evaluation of four face-to-face teaching strategies. *International Journal of Behavioral Development, 1,* 131–147.

Wood, V. (1982, Winter). Grandparenthood: An ambiguous role. *Generations: Journal of the Western Gerontological Society, 22,* 18–24.

Woody, J. D., Russel, R., D'Souza, H. J., & Woody, J. K. (2000). Adolescent non-coital sexual activity: Comparisons of virgins and non-virgins. *Journal of Sex Education and Therapy, 25*(4), 261–268.

Woollett, A. (1986). The influence of older siblings on the language environment of young children. *British Journal of Developmental Psychology, 4,* 234–245.

Wright, P. H. (1982). Men's friendships, women's friendships, and the alleged inferiority of the latter. *Sex Roles, 8,* 1–20.

Wright, P. H., & Keple, T. W. (1981). Friends and parents of a sample of high school juniors: An exploratory study of relationship intensity and interpersonal rewards. *Journal of Marriage and the Family, 43,* 559–570.

Wright, P. H., & Wright, K. D. (1995). Codependency: Personality syndrome or relational process? In S. Duck & J. T. Wood (Eds.), *Confronting relationship challenges* (pp. 109–128). Thousand Oaks, CA: Sage.

Yingling, J. M. (1981). *Temporal features of infant speech: A description of babbling patterns circumscribed by postural achievement.* Unpublished doctoral dissertation, University of Denver.

Yingling, J. (1984, May). *Infant speech timing: The development of individual control.* Paper presented at the International Communication Association convention, San Francisco.

Yingling, J. (1990/1991). "Does that mean 'no?'": Negotiating proto-conversation in infant–caregiver pairs. *Research on Language and Social Interaction, 24,* 71–108.

Yingling, J. (1994a). Childhood: Talking the mind into existence. In D. R. Vocate (Ed.), *Intrapersonal communication: Different voices, different minds* (pp. 121–143). Hillsdale, NJ: Lawrence Erlbaum Associates.

Yingling, J. (1994b). Constituting friendship in talk and metatalk. *Journal of Social and Personal Relationships, 11,* 411–426.

Yingling, J. (1994c). Development as the context of student assessment. In S. Morreale & M. Brooks (Eds.), *1994 SCA summer conference: Proceedings and prepared remarks* (pp. 167–178). Annandale, VA: Speech Communication Association.

Yingling, J. (1995a). *Control talk in five patterns of young friendships: Rules for friendly influence.* Unpublished manuscript.

Yingling, J. (1995b). The first relationship: Infant–parent communication. In T. J. Socha & G. Stamp (Eds.), *Parents, children, and communication: Frontiers of theory and research* (pp. 23–41). Hillsdale, NJ: Lawrence Erlbaum Associates.

Yingling, J. (2000). Verbal responses of children and their supportive providers in a pediatric oncology unit. *Journal of Health Communication, 5,* 371–377.

Yoder, P. J., & Kaiser, A. P. (1989). Alternative explanations for the relationship between maternal verbal interaction style and child language development. *Journal of Child Language, 16,* 141–160.

York, J. L., & Calsyn, R. J. (1977). Family involvement in nursing homes. *The Gerontologist, 17,* 500–505.

Youniss, J. (1978a). The nature of social development: A conceptual discussion of cognition. In H. McGurk (Ed.), *Issues in childhood social development* (pp. 203–227). London: Methuen.

Youniss, J. (1978b). Dialectical theory and Piaget on social knowledge. *Human Development, 21,* 234–247.

Youniss, J. (1980). *Parents and peers in social development: A Sullivan-Piaget perspective.* Chicago: University of Chicago Press.

Zahn-Waxler, C., Cole, P. M., Welsh, J. D., & Fox, N. A. (1995). Psychophysiological correlates of empathy and prosocial behaviors in preschool children with problem behaviors. *Development and Psychopathology, 7,* 27–48.

Zarit, S., Todd, P., & Zarit, J. (1986). Subjective burden of husbands and wives as caregivers: A longitudinal study. *Gerontologist, 26,* 260–266.

Zeman, J., & Garbor, J. (1996). Display rules for anger, sadness, and pain: It depends on who is watching. *Child Development, 67,* 957–973.

Zukov, G. (1979). *The dancing Wu Li masters: An overview of the new physics.* New York: William Morrow.

Zukow, P. G. (1989). Siblings as effective socializing agents: Evidence from Central Mexico. In P. G. Zukow (Ed.), *Sibling interaction across cultures: Theoretical and methodological issues* (pp. 79–105). New York: Springer-Verlag.

Author Index

Subject Index

415